THE CORRESPONDENCE OF ROGER SESSIONS

Music advisor to Northeastern University Press
GUNTHER SCHULLER

THE CORRESPONDENCE OF

ROGER SESSIONS

EDITED BY

ANDREA OLMSTEAD

NORTHEASTERN
UNIVERSITY PRESS

BOSTON

Northeastern University Press

Library of Congress Cataloging-in-Publication Data
Sessions, Roger, 1896–
[Correspondence. Selections]
The correspondence of Roger Sessions / edited by Andrea
Olmstead
p. cm.
Includes index.
ISBN 1-55553-122-9 (acid-free)
1. Sessions, Roger, 1896– —Correspondence. 2. Composers—
United States—Correspondence. I. Olmstead,
Andrea. II. Title.
ML410.S473A4 1992
780.92—dc20   91-39197
[B]

Designed by Diane Levy

Composed in Sabon by Coghill Composition Company,
Richmond, Virginia. Printed and bound by Edwards Brothers,
Inc., Ann Arbor, Michigan. The paper is Glatfelter Offset, an
acid-free sheet.

MANUFACTURED IN THE UNITED STATES OF AMERICA
97 96 95 94 93 92   5 4 3 2 1

Dedicated to the memory of

Gustave Reese
(1899–1977)
and
Vincent Persichetti
(1915–1987)

CONTENTS

ILLUSTRATIONS

ACKNOWLEDGMENTS

SINCE WORK BEGAN on this book in the fall of 1987 many friends, musicians, and librarians have contributed their time and help. First of all, I must thank Roger Sessions's daughter, Elizabeth Pease, for her cooperation, without which this book would not have been possible. David Diamond deserves the credit for having come up with the idea for the book: he wrote to me asking why no one had collected and published Sessions's letters and then followed through on this implied suggestion by allowing me access to his extensive collection of letters from his former teacher.

Thanks are also due to all of the people who sent me letters from their private collections. Sessions's niece, Sarah Chapin, prepared hundreds of family letters in her collection, which covers 1915 to 1925. Also generous was Aaron Copland: I received eighty-eight letters and photographs from Copland's collection (later given to the Library of Congress). Nica Borgese sent me two packages of letters to and from her father. Edward T. Cone, Mark DeVoto, Bernard Kalban, Miriam Gideon, Kenneth Frazelle, Janice Harsanyi, Peter Heyworth, Leon Kirchner, Madeleine Milhaud, Harold Schiffman, George Tsontakis, Paul Turok, and Beveridge Webster sent letters from their private collections. Elliott Carter, Louis Krasner, and Ernst Krenek directed me to their collections already in archives.

Sometimes extraordinary perseverance was required to obtain these letters, and it was then that others went out of their way to assist. For example, John Moore guaranteed that the Bibliothèque Nationale in Paris send me the letters to Boulanger; Paul Suits copied by hand fourteen letters in the Paul Sacher Stiftung in Basel; and Doris Freitag, a professional conservator, restored a water- and fire-damaged letter.

Music libraries also sent copies of their Sessions collections, and several librarians deserve special mention. John Shepard at the New York Public Library of the Performing Arts gave me good advice. Wayne Shirley, Wilda Heiss, and Kate Rivers at the Library of Congress Music Division were extremely helpful, as was Jane Gottlieb of The Juilliard School Library. Michael Ochs, Holly Mockovak, and Millard Irion made the Harvard University music library a welcome place to work. Barbara Humphreys at the Kent School should be thanked. The music reference librarians at the Boston Public Library, especially Diane Ota, Charlotte Kolcznski, and Elisa Birdseye-Clark, were helpful in myriad ways when I was annotating this work. The archives of the Boston Symphony Orchestra were useful. Libraries and collections that contributed letters include the University of California in San Diego, Yale University Library, the Library of Congress, Boston University Library, the Paul Sacher Stiftung, the Harvard University music library, the University of Florence Library, the Bibliothèque Nationale in Paris, the Archivio Contemporaneo "A. Bonsanti" in Florence, the Smith College Archives, the Arnold Schoenberg Institute, Houghton Library at Harvard University, and the Kent School Archives.

All of the translators for this volume were both patient and prompt and deserve many thanks. Pina Pasquantino translated Sessions's letters in Italian to Luigi Dallapiccola, and Valeria Short translated the letters from Dallapiccola; Theodore Levin translated Sessions's letters in Russian to Igor Stravinsky, Serge Koussevitzky, and Nicolas Slonimsky; Suzanne Bloch translated a letter in French from her father; Paul Suits translated two letters in French to Jean Binet; and Annette and Gerhard Koeppel tackled Thomas Mann's difficult German and translated two letters from Otto Klemperer. Juliane Brand helped to polish the Mann letter.

Thanks to all of those people, mentioned here and in the Sources section, who gave permission to publish their letters to Sessions.

Residencies in writing at the Virginia Center for the Creative Arts in 1988 and at the American Academy in Rome during the summers of 1988 and 1991 allowed me the time to transcribe the large number of letters collected and work on the manuscript. Both of those artists' colonies deserve my thanks for their support, which is measured in valuable time and a studio in which to work rather than in dollars. Financial aid came from a National Endowment for the Humanities grant to the Harvard Summer Institute on the Study of the Avant-

Garde in the summer of 1989. Vivian Perlis and David Diamond supported me by writing letters of recommendation to granting organizations.

I am grateful to all those who helped with the preparation of the manuscript. Wayne Shirley of the Library of Congress carefully read the entire manuscript and gave exceedingly helpful advice regarding both large-scale organization and editorial annotation. Robert Craft's advice and encouragement, given early and on the basis of one chapter, were very welcome. Larry Bell, my husband, read the complete manuscript and gave suggestions. He deserves credit for enduring a third book on Roger Sessions.

I would like specifically to acknowledge the following:

Letters of Arnold Schoenberg are used by permission of Belmont Music Publishers, Los Angeles, California 90049.

Letters of Ernst Krenek are used by permission of Ernst Krenek.

Letters of Ernest Bloch are used by permission of Suzanne Bloch.

Letters of Aaron Copland are © 1990 by Aaron Copland; reproduced by permission.

The photograph of Carter and Sessions is used by permission of the Eda Kuhn Loeb Music Library.

Letters of Thomas Mann are used by permission of S. Fischer Verlag GmbH, Frankfurt am Main.

Letters of Antonio Borgese are used by permission of Nica Borgese.

Letters of Luigi Dallapiccola are used by permission of Laura Dallapiccola.

Letters of Father Sill are used by permission of Ms. LaFontan, Kent School.

Letters of Otto Klemperer are © 1992 by Lotte Klemperer; reproduced by permission.

Letters of David Diamond are © 1990 by David Diamond; reproduced by permission.

Letters of Barbara Sessions are used by permission of Rosamond Sheldon.

Letters of Serge Koussevitzky are used by permission of Ellis Freedman.

Letters of Roger Sessions, Elizabeth Sessions, and Elizabeth Pease are © 1988 by Elizabeth Pease.

Letters of Henry Cowell are used by permission of Sidney Cowell.

Boston
June 1991

INTRODUCTION

ROGER SESSIONS'S stature among modernist American composers is rivaled only by Ives, Copland, and Carter, and his influence as a teacher compares favorably with that of Schoenberg, Hindemith, and Boulanger. The catalog of his forty-two compositions includes nine symphonies, three concertos, two operas, and works in other large formats, as well as chamber music. He won every major award, including two Pulitzer Prizes. Although he composed for three-quarters of a century (1910–85), his most creative period was from ages sixty to eighty-five.

During his tenure at Princeton University (1936–45, 1953–66), the University of California at Berkeley (1945–53), and The Juilliard School (1966–83), Sessions consistently attracted talented young composers, who themselves have taught many others. A partial list of Sessions's students gives a small indication of this influence: Peter Maxwell Davies, David Diamond, Edward T. Cone, Vivian Fine, Milton Babbitt, John Harbison, Andrew Imbrie, Miriam Gideon, Leon Kirchner, Donald Martino, Frederic Rzewski, and Ellen Taaffe Zwilich. Few other American teachers can boast such a distinguished musical progeny.

His two careers as composer and teacher are paralleled by a third career, that of a writer about music. A highly literate man, Sessions published four books and over forty articles in his lifetime. These books include his Norton lectures at Harvard University (*Questions about Music*), his harmony textbook *Harmonic Practice,* and his valuable *The Musical Experience as Composer, Performer, Listener.*

His essays, edited by Edward T. Cone, are published as *Roger Sessions on Music; Collected Essays.* To this list is now added the present collection of previously unpublished letters.

This volume of correspondence completes my trilogy of books on Roger Sessions. The first, *Roger Sessions and His Music,* was a biographical and analytical view of the composer and his works. *Conversations with Roger Sessions* consists of transcriptions of portions of our six and one-half years of weekly interviews at The Juilliard School.

Publication of composers' letters has historically lagged behind that of their literary contemporaries; American composers' letters in particular have rarely been represented in print. Although we now have collections in English of letters of earlier composers from Monteverdi to Busoni and Delius, with figures such as Mozart, Beethoven, and Wagner well treated, the twentieth century has been represented in print largely by the Second Viennese School and Stravinsky, whose three-volume collection was edited by Robert Craft. We have collections of both Berg's and Schoenberg's letters as well as one of the correspondence between the two. Correspondence between Richard Strauss and Gustav Mahler has also been published in English. The publication of Virgil Thomson's letters in 1988 inaugurated a time when American composers' letters will begin to enjoy intellectual and scholarly interest given American poets and authors.

It is fitting that Roger Sessions, along with Thomson, should be among the first American composers to receive such attention. Sessions corresponded with many of the twentieth century's most important composers and performers, with whom he had warm and friendly relations, including Ernest Bloch, Aaron Copland, Luigi Dallapiccola, Ernst Krenek, Igor Stravinsky, Arnold Schoenberg, Darius Milhaud, Serge Koussevitzky, David Diamond, and many others. The literary value of his letters and their revelations about the composer's life, as well as their historical interest, are considerable. Sessions's abilities as a writer are also evident, and one of these abilities—his use of foreign languages—is extraordinary.

Sessions's facility as a linguist is evident throughout this collection. Letters to college friends use the Greek he had learned in school. Love letters to his fiancée use French. Sessions also wrote at length in French to the Swiss composer Jean Binet, to Serge Koussevitzky, and to Darius Milhaud, but surprisingly he wrote to Nadia Boulanger in English. Although no letters from Sessions in German have been unearthed, he received letters from Otto Klemperer and Thomas

Mann in that language, which he had studied at Harvard. Later in life Sessions became self-conscious about his heavily accented German and, according to Milton Babbitt, avoided speaking in German. The early part of the correspondence with his librettist Borgese was written in Italian. His extensive correspondence with Luigi Dallapiccola was conducted entirely in Italian.

The most challenging language Sessions tackled was Russian, in which he wrote to Serge Koussevitzky, Nicolas Slonimsky, and Igor Stravinsky. In an unpublished 1932 article about Sessions (now at the Library of Congress), Slonimsky, himself an expert in many languages, addressed this ability in Sessions. "He studied languages with astonishing fervor for a non-professional philologist. Thus he acquired a perfect command of Italian, French, and German. As if this was not enough, he undertook the study of Russian. In this labor of love he achieved extraordinary progress. His letters, in Russian, to this writer are not only grammatical, but idiomatic as well—and occasional lapses in the field of Russian conjugations are the only signs of the correspondent's non-Russian birth."

Sessions's letter writing closely approximates his compositional style. The physical evidence of the letters helps testify to this fact. Almost all of the letters are handwritten in ink (a fountain pen and, in later years, a ballpoint), but few contain any corrections. Long sentences are begun, spun out with elaborate punctuation, and completed in virtuoso fashion without his crossing out a single word or phrase. Paragraphs are likewise highly organized in Sessions's mind and give the impression of being extemporized in his inimitable manner. Even Sessions's published prose, which one might surmise was rethought and edited, reads like his letters. Once he sat down to write letters, articles, or music, he gave the task his utmost concentration, and ideas flowed in *grandes lignes*. These long-breathed phrases of his music and his prose strikingly resemble each other. One must conclude that Sessions's thought processes for both music and words operated in long phrases.

Though the reader might surmise from Sessions's elegant prose that he wrote these letters with an eye to posterity, Sessions did not give much thought to preserving his work for future generations. He was notoriously careless about preserving his music; in the 1920s he regularly threw away sketches until a friend scolded him on the subject. Later, when he saved his sketches and music, he did so in a manner not meant to endear him to librarians and archivists: the music, like his letters received, was cast into boxes unfiled, and in one case left in a basement to suffer flooding. When I repeatedly offered to help him organize these boxes (a project he was continually planning to get around to), he put me off with the remark that we would need to find "some young man from Princeton" to help lift them. The boxes were never organized in his lifetime. Finally, a person as reserved as Sessions would be unlikely to write as revealingly about himself as he did to some intimates had he contemplated a wider audience for his private and self-critical musings. The inescapable conclusion is that each letter was meant solely for its recipient, with no eye cast in our direction.

Some composers, whether mindful of history or for their own reasons, kept copies of their letters, as did for example Giuseppe Verdi and Virgil Thomson. Verdi's correspondence was at first edited from his *copialettere;* the published collections of letters of Schoenberg and Thomson were both drawn from the composers' carbons, without the necessity of searching out original letters from their recipients. Unfortunately (but entirely characteristically), Sessions did not save copies of his own letters, thus making the musicologist's task more difficult. He would doubtless have been surprised that so many others saved his letters. Only in a few cases did his secretary, his former sister-in-law Rosamond Sayre, keep carbons of some business letters. Most published both-way correspondences—what the Germans call *Briefwechsel*—involve the exchange between two figures only (Brahms and Theodor Billroth, Schoenberg and Berg). The letters for such *Briefwechsel* need to be sought in only two places—the files of the two correspondents. Almost all of the letters I collected, in contrast, came from the recipients themselves rather than from the files of the sender. These letters were ferreted out of more than thirty locations, ranging from San Diego, California, to Basel, Switzerland.

Some of the letters found in Sessions's private collection meshed with those of his letters I had collected elsewhere, presenting a nearly complete correspondence (incompleteness usually was the result of Sessions's failure to save all of his correspondents' letters). Each of these exchanges, such as the ones between Krenek and Sessions, Copland and Sessions, and Dallapiccola and Sessions, is interesting enough to have produced a monograph. Although later in life Sessions cultivated a reputation for not answering letters, this reputation was undeserved until around 1940 and unwarranted when it came to his favorite correspondents.

I decided to concentrate on letters to other composers and musicians. (Since there were no other composers until Bloch—there appear to be no letters to Horatio Parker—chapter 1 deals mainly with letters to Sessions's best friend, his former headmaster, and his wife.) This decision was made partly because our main interest in Sessions is a musical one, and partly because one relative wished not to be mentioned, which restricted discussion of his family. But in fact Sessions's letters to composers reveal him as a man as well as a musician: they radiate personal concern and interest. A few letters from both of Sessions's wives are included to give the reader some glimpse into their complex personalities.

The letters of some correspondents, though polite and businesslike, such as Paul Fromm and Louis Krasner, are neither particularly revealing nor of much historical interest, and therefore are not included. On the other hand, almost all of the letters by Copland, Dallapiccola, and Diamond, along with all the surviving letters by Schoenberg and Bloch, are included. Sometimes letters do not reveal the closeness of the relationship; for example, Sessions's letters to Felix Greissle, which almost always deal with business, do not demonstrate their strong affection. And the absence of letters from Sessions to Milton Babbitt or Vincent Persichetti is not an indication of their lack of friendship. (Sessions saw both of them, and Diamond and Greissle, weekly for over a decade while in New York at The Juilliard School, and therefore had little need to write to them.) Editing my own letters to and from Sessions bordered on an out-of-body experience, and the sudden introduction in chapter 12 of the first person after eleven chapters of the third person is also likely to produce something of a jolt to readers.

There are many levels on which these letters may be read and interpreted. Various paths that might be traced through this collection would include the following, among others: the contrasting views of Sessions and Copland on "Americanism" in art; the shift in Sessions's attitudes toward Schoenberg; the continual indebtedness and struggle for money; and the changing political, sexual, and religious attitudes. The letters are also interesting for what they do *not* contain: for example, the lack of mention of the avant-garde (radical composers such as Cage never appear).

Sessions frequently failed to distinguish in his value judgments between the composer as a person and that composer's musical production. He often expressed his enthusiasm for the former as praise for the latter, with sometimes astonishing results: around 1920 the most significant living composer, he feels, is Ernest Bloch; around 1940 the foremost American composer is Walter Piston. Basing his opinion on his unpleasant impressions of unnamed Schoenberg "disciples" in Berlin in the early 1930s, Sessions consistently denigrates the twelve-tone method for over a decade; when he becomes close to the Viennese composer in California in the 1940s, he reverses his opinion. (The gradual development toward twelve-tone writing evident in Sessions's music is only once acknowledged in a letter, that to Beveridge Webster of 1952.) The effect of this fusing of personality and production on Sessions's teaching is hard to determine. The example of his many letters to David Diamond over the course of a long and often stormy friendship suggests that praise and criticism of a student's music was not always independent of personal relations.

Other personal shortcomings also surface in the correspondence. Sessions frequently sabotaged his own career. His early dealings with Henry D. Sleeper and Josef Stransky at Smith College, repeated later with Koussevitzky, Copland, and Elizabeth Sprague Coolidge, among others, expose habits of procrastination, excuse making, and deadline missing that undermined their faith in him and led to severe career and financial setbacks. In an arena where his immense familial, educational, and intellectual advantages were amplified by the sincere support of many of the century's most prominent musicians, Sessions seemed to be his own worst enemy. He enthusiastically embraced people only to fall out with them later. Examples are his relationships with George Bartlett (this was somewhat patched up), Ernest Bloch (whose personal problems caused him to fall from grace in Sessions's eyes), Nadia Boulanger (with whom he never reconciled), David Diamond (an uneasy truce was declared), and Barbara Sessions (they divorced).

Readers of these letters should remember that both the U.S. and European postal services used to be much more efficient than they are today. For most of Sessions's letter-writing career the U.S. Postal Service delivered mail on Sundays. Within New York City letters reached their recipients *on the day sent* or without fail on the next day, and they arrived at destinations across the Atlantic within a few days. Letters sent within Europe were received and answered in what today would be considered an astonishingly short time. The cost of long-distance calls, in contrast, seemed high to musicians of the 1920s and 1930s. People then wrote in many cases where they would now telephone.

This book is arranged chronologically in twelve chapters (after all, Sessions was a twelve-tone composer) of approximately equal length. It contains slightly over two hundred letters by Sessions, as well as about sixty by some of his correspondents. It will be helpful for the reader to keep in mind the parallels between the dates of the chapters and those of Sessions's six creative periods, which are treated in detail in *Roger Sessions and His Music*. The first period (1910–24) corresponds to chapter 1 of the letters and is clearly delineated by Sessions's last letters of that chapter. The second period (1924–35) corresponds to chapters 2 through 5. Chapters 6, 7, and 8 comprise Sessions's decade-long third period, 1936–47. His fourth period, in the 1950s, corresponds to chapter 9 and part of chapter 10. The period of the sixties (his fifth) relates to chapters 10 and 11. Both the fourth and fifth periods produced so much music and recognition that Sessions's letter writing declined; hence, there are more years represented in these chapters than in the earlier ones. Sessions's last period of creation (1970–81) corresponds to chapter 12.

Combined with his music, his books, and, for many, the memories of his teaching, *The Correspondence of Roger Sessions* helps to illuminate that most troublesome subject—the personality of an artist. In addition, it shows the relationships between artists, between the composer and the patron, and between the composer and the performer. Ultimately, however, the artist never gives up all his secrets. To document is not to explain. And to explain is not necessarily to understand.

NOTES ON THE EDITION

THIS VOLUME presents selected letters of Roger Sessions and some of his correspondents covering the period from 1909 to the mid-1980s. In addition to the approximately 400 letters in the Chapin collection (see the note on sources at the end of this volume), I have collected 440 letters, many of which were written in the late 1920s and 1930s.

Several criteria determined which of these letters appear in this volume. Longer letters with much philosophizing or description tended to win out over shorter letters, strictly business letters, or postcards. Letters that describe music, those that mesh well with letters received, and particularly revealing letters are included. A summary or brief excerpt in a footnote or one of the editorial interludes often presents the essence of a letter that, though valuable, could not be published in full.

The correspondence has been edited in accordance with the following guidelines:

1. *Dating and addresses.* When dates are missing but can be inferred from interior evidence, brackets surrounding them indicate my best reckoning. Dates have been found either on the letter or on the postmark, or have been completed by reference to a perpetual calendar. Sessions and his correspondents sometimes used the European format (5.IX.48 for September 5, 1948). For the convenience of the reader, all the dates have been standardized and moved to the top of each letter. The address of the sender is indicated beneath the date.

2. *Corrections.* Sessions's excellent spelling has required few cor-

rections. Trivial errors have been corrected tacitly. In the rare instance where an inadvertently omitted word has been added, it appears, as do other editorial additions, in brackets. When an abbreviation is thus expanded, the period is dropped unless it occurs at the end of a sentence. In one special case, a fire-damaged letter (August 10, 1937) to David Diamond, a great many words and syllables are added editorially.

3. *Translations*. Letters translated into English are indicated as such in a footnote, which also credits the translators. Numerous isolated foreign phrases, whether familiar or not, are glossed into English in brackets.

4. *Deletions*. Occasionally a portion of the original letter is either missing or its handwriting is illegible. A bracketted annotation informs the reader that the letter is at that point "[illegible]." In a few cases either the Sessions family or the recipient's estate demanded deletions. Such cases are so noted by italicized brackets and ellipses *[. . .]*. Although the general principle here has been to present each letter complete, in the interest of saving space, occasionally a redundant or superfluous paragraph is deleted and indicated simply in Roman brackets [. . .]. The Chapin collection, which covers letters from 1915 to 1925, is so extensive as to merit a separate publication as a book. As a result, the long letters from it in chapter 1 are more drastically cut than letters elsewhere.

5. *Annotations*. Abbreviations at the top center of the letter indicate whether the letter was typed or handwritten and the location of the original. All footnotes, which are numbered for each letter and for each introductory section, follow immediately. At the first mention of each person, especially those to whom Sessions wrote, I have tried to provide that person's dates of birth and death, as well as biographical information that amplifies Sessions's relationship with him or her. If someone mentioned in the letters is not annotated, it is because information was neither available in such standard sources as Slonimsky's *Baker's Biographical Dictionary of Musicians* (8th ed.) or *The New Grove Dictionary of American Music* nor excavated by more exhaustive research. Pieces of music are provided with their full titles and composition dates, and concerts are identified by date and performers. Books, articles, and newspaper columns are identified bibliographically. Again, if they are not identified, it was because I could not find them in major research libraries.

6. *Photographs and reproductions*. I have attempted to provide photographs of Sessions with some of his correspondents and of the

composer at various points in his life. I have tried to include photographs not published previously and to find ones that show both Sessions and the correspondent. The reader is sometimes directed to photographs published elsewhere. Like most people's handwriting over a long life, Sessions's script changed considerably. Reproductions of three of his letters are given both as examples of typical penmanship and to present letters not duplicated in the text.

ABBREVIATIONS

als	signed handwritten letter
acs	signed handwritten postcard
tls	signed typed letter
cc	carbon copy

Libraries and Private Collections

CH-Bsacher	Paul Sacher Stiftung, Basel, Switzerland
F-PBN	Bibliothèque Nationale, Paris
F-Pmilhaud	Madeleine Milhaud private collection, Paris
I-Fb	Archivio Contemporaneo "A. Bonsanti," Florence
I-Fborgese	Borgese private collection, Florence
UK-L	Peter Heyworth private collection, London
US-Bolmstead	Andrea Olmstead private collection, Boston, Mass.
US-Bu	Boston University Library
US-CAberger	Arthur Berger private collection, Cambridge, Mass.
US-CAhoughton	Houghton Library, Harvard University, Cambridge, Mass.
US-CAkirchner	Leon Kirchner private collection, Cambridge, Mass.
US-CAmus	Loeb Music Library, Harvard University, Cambridge, Mass.
US-COchapin	Sarah Chapin private collection, Concord, Mass.

US-DLC	Library of Congress
US-Kent	Kent School archives, Kent, Conn.
US-LA	Arnold Schoenberg Institute, Los Angeles, Calif.
US-MdeVoto	Mark DeVoto private collection, Medford, Mass.
US-NH	Yale University Library, New Haven, Conn.
US-NHwebster	Beveridge Webster private collection, New Hampshire
US-Nsmith	Smith College archives, Northampton, Mass.
US-Pcone	Edward T. Cone private collection, Princeton, N.J.
US-Rdiamond	David Diamond private collection, Rochester, N.Y.
US-SD	Library of the University of California, San Diego
US-NYgideon	Miriam Gideon private collection, New York
US-NYkalban	Bernard Kalban, E. B. Marks collection, New York
US-NYpease	Elizabeth Pease private collection, New York
US-NYtsontakis	George Tsontakis private collection, New York
US-Tschiffman	Harold Schiffman private collection, Tallahassee, Fla.

CHAPTER

1909-1924

ONE

$\int$ ESSIONS'S CORRESPONDENCE includes thirty letters to and from the headmaster at the newly founded Kent School, the Reverend Frederick Herbert Sill.[1] Father Sill was a member of the Episcopal Order of the Holy Cross, the order founded by Sessions's maternal uncle, James Huntington (1855–1935). Later Sessions addressed Sill, as did many others, as "Pater."

Roger's parents, Ruth Huntington Sessions[2] and Archibald Lowery Sessions,[3] hailed from the same old New England family, which could trace its ancestry directly to the 1630s. (Ruth's father was Archibald's grandmother's brother.) Married November 6, 1887,—their son Roger was born December 28, 1896—the couple separated at the turn of the century, when Roger was only four. Archie remained in New York, having given up a legal career for journalism: he edited the magazines *Ainslee's, People's,* and *Common Story* at the firm of Street and Smith on Seventh Avenue and Fifteenth Street and wanted to be a playwright. Ruth moved to Northampton, Massachusetts, near her ancestral home in Hadley, and ran Sessions House, an off-campus residence for students at Smith College, at that time exclusively for women. Even in Sessions's eighties he was at pains to explain his parents' relationship, especially because they lived separately for a quarter of a century but did not divorce. "Pater" may have replaced the absent Archie in Roger's mind. Certainly Sill was a father figure of some sort to all the boys at Kent.

One of Sessions's classmates, R. D. Perry, Kent class of 1910, recalled that Roger was "a peculiar little genius, but an expert piano player even at that young age."[4] Evidence of Sessions's ability was unmistakable: he began composing in the summer of 1909, and had already written an opera, *Lancelot and Elaine,* based on Tennyson's *Idylls of the King,* by the fall of 1910, when he announced to his parents that he wanted to be a composer. His father sought the opinions of several musicians about his thirteen-year-old son's musical prospects, including those of Engelbert Humperdinck and Giacomo Puccini, both of whom were in New York for the premieres of their works by the Metropolitan Opera. Years later, Luigi Dallapiccola, who had heard the story, told Sessions that Puccini had paced the floor all night over advice to some young composer and finally had decided he could not make a decision of that importance for someone else. That young composer may have been Sessions.[5] One disagreement between the two parents appears to have been their view of Roger's musical education. For example, Ruth Sessions, who had been Roger's first piano teacher, wrote Father Sill (March 11, 1910, US-Kent), "I have written [Roger] not to stick so closely to the piano this Spring." Archie, however, was concerned about sending Roger back to Kent for his last year, 1910–11, because of his "anxiety about instruction for him in his music." He hoped that more might be done to challenge Roger intellectually and to teach him "the value of sustained mental effort." Ruth's interest lay rather in Roger's religious education.

At the same time, Ruth had her doubts, which she confided to Father Sill in a letter of November 10, 1910 (US-Kent): "But he has promised me to try + do better, and from what Mr. Haley told me, I fancy the masters realize how much extra brain-matter is expended on his music these days. I do not feel sure that that is going to be his eventual choice by any means, for a life work; but it must be put to the test of hard labor, I think + then we shall know just how far it is likely to carry him."

Shortly after his fourteenth birthday (December 28, 1910) Sessions became ill with what his mother described as "a very large and virulent abcess in the ear," which prevented his returning to Kent for three weeks. The problem was caused by tonsillitis, which was operated on in late March. Ruth writes in the same letter: "He has promised me to be out of doors as much as possible, and is to *do no work on music* for the rest of the term. He is at a pretty nervous age, and we feel that he ought to spend what nerve-force he has into his school-work only" (US-Kent). Roger's illness seemed to provide her with an excuse to impose her own negative view of his study of music.

Presumably she was following medical advice when she wrote to another master at Kent (January 30, 1911, US-Kent) with the stark instructions: "If he should have any ear-ache, the orders are that the ear-drum should be pierced at once, without waiting for any further developments, and I would want to be sent for and to have the best specialist that could be found."

If Sessions was laconic in his letter writing in 1910, words poured forth when he wrote about music. He wrote two papers at Kent— "The Music of Wagner's *The Nibelung's Ring*" and "Wagner as a Composer"—totaling nine typewritten, single-spaced pages with narrow margins. Such an interest in opera was understandable in one who was already composing one himself.

Propelled through Kent at a faster-than-normal rate, Sessions entered Harvard University, where all of his male relatives had gone, in the fall of 1911. At fourteen, he was sensitive of his young age. His grades there, however, with the consistent exception of those in music, were only average, and occasionally he failed a course. All of his music teachers were heavily influenced by French music. They included Edward Burlingame Hill for orchestration, Archibald Davison for counterpoint and fugue, and Walter Spalding for a course in vocal and choral writing.[6] In June 1913, Sessions wrote Sill the following fall, he was "elected an editor of the *Musical Review,* and I have an article and an editorial in the November number, which I will send you" (US-Kent).[7]

Letters in the fall of 1914 and spring of 1915, both to Father Sill (US-Kent), show for the first time two traits that were to become a familiar complaint for many years. The first is a casting of the recent past as a failure to accomplish anything: "I feel that last year was a failure for me in every respect and am doing my best to atone for it." The second is his aversion to being classified by any terminology: "Needless to say, I have no more desire to be a 'conservative radical,' a 'radical conservative,' or a 'radical conservative radical,' etc. etc., than a plain ordinary radical or conservative" (US-Kent).

After having graduated from Harvard in the summer of 1915 (he had to make up a course and took military history that summer), Sessions entered Yale University to pursue a Bachelor of Music degree. New Haven's proximity to Kent allowed Sessions to travel there to teach; he was eighteen when he began his first job teaching music. His first letter from Yale to Father Sill was his only letter that school year to him, doubtless because he saw Sill every other week. At the end of the school year in 1916, however, Sessions stopped teaching at Kent.

Archibald Sessions in 1902. Courtesy of Sarah Chapin.

Ruth Huntington in 1885.

Sessions was homesick for Harvard and his friends there, to whom he wrote frequently during his first semester at Yale. These included Frederick van den Arend (known as Van) and George Hodges Bartlett, only two months younger than Sessions.[8] The three had frequently attended Boston Symphony Orchestra concerts together, events that Sessions sorely missed while in New Haven. Sessions read Romain Rolland's novel *Jean-Christophe*[9] in July 1915 and thereafter repeatedly insisted that his friends read the novel, one of whose themes was of "an international art [that was] to bring men of all nations together."[10]

In 1916, while at Yale, Sessions finished two compositions, a piano trio and a violin sonata (neither is among his currently acknowledged works), under the tutelage of the eminent American composer Horatio Parker (1863–1919). Parker had been chair of the department of music at Yale since 1894 partly as a result of the success of his oratorio *Hora novissima* (1893). He founded and conducted the New Haven Symphony Orchestra and had been the teacher of Charles Ives during his Yale years (1894–98). Sessions had not heard of Ives at this time, but was doubtless attracted to the idea of studying with Parker because of the latter's success as an opera composer: his opera *Mona* (1911) won a Metropolitan Opera prize and was produced there in 1912, and his opera *Fairyland* (1914) won a similar prize and was produced in Los Angeles. As Gilbert Chase has observed, Parker "personified the Anglo-American work ethic, which resulted in his demise at the age of fifty-six."[11] Parker died two and a half years after Sessions left Yale.

1. The Kent School was founded in 1906 in Kent, Conn. A description of Father Sill (1874–1952) can be found in Anson Gardner, "The Most Unforgettable Character I've Met," *Reader's Digest*, January 1961. A history of the early days of the school is given in William H. Armstrong, "The Miracle in Algo's Shadow," *Kent Quarterly* (Fall 1988): 26–33.

2. November 3, 1859–December 2, 1946.

3. Archibald Sessions (b. New York, January 12, 1860; d. Brooklyn, January 5, 1927) graduated from Harvard in 1883 and was admitted to the N.Y. bar in 1884.

4. Quoted in Judson Scruton, "Roger H. Sessions: 1896–1985," *Kent News* 71, no. 8 (April 20, 1985): 1.

5. Andrea Olmstead, *Roger Sessions and His Music* (Ann Arbor, Mich.: UMI Research Press, 1985), 11.

6. Hill (1872–1960) studied at Harvard with John Knowles Paine, graduating in 1894, and with George Chadwick and Charles-Marie Widor; he taught at Harvard 1908–40. Davison (1883–1961) also studied at Harvard (Ph.D., 1908) and in Paris with Widor; he taught organ at Harvard (1909–38) and conducted the Harvard Glee Club (1912–34); he retired in 1954. Spalding (1865–1962) graduated from Harvard in 1888, and also studied in Paris with Widor; he began teaching at Harvard in 1895.

7. Roger Sessions, "The Case against Professional Musical Criticism," *Harvard Musical Review* 2, no. 2 (November 1913): 3–6.

8. Van den Arend (1894–1979) was class president at Kent and attended Harvard. Sessions's and van den Arend's extensive correspondence is in the Sarah Chapin collection (US-COchapin). Bartlett (1897–1921) was extremely close to Sessions; he graduated from Harvard in February 1917 and taught music at Kent after Sessions left there.

9. *Jean-Christophe* appeared in France in ten volumes 1904–1912. Its English translation, by Gilbert Cannon, was published by Henry Holt and Co. 1910–13. Rolland was awarded the Nobel Prize for Literature 1915, which probably led Sessions to read this novel.

10. Van Wyck Brooks, *The Confident Years, 1885–1915* (New York: Dutton, 1952), 494. That Rolland (1866–1944) was a friend of Ernest Bloch's may have cemented Sessions's high opinion of Bloch. See Elaine Brody, "Romain Rolland and Ernest Bloch," *Musical Quarterly* 68 (1982): 60.

11. Gilbert Chase, *America's Music: From the Pilgrims to the Present*, 3d ed. (Champaign: University of Illinois Press, 1987), 380. For Sessions's later view of Parker, see Olmstead, *Roger Sessions*, 14.

▼

Roger Sessions to Ruth Sessions
als US-NYpease

[Fall 1909]

Dear Mother,—   Kent School, Kent, Connecticut

I have not got settled yet, and so have not begun my practice, but there is one thing that is against me—Fr. Officer is not here. He is the novice-master of the O[rder of the] H[oly] C[ross], so we will not have him here this year. There are 57 boys in the school at present, as hardly any of the boys who were here last year have left—only Sydney Allen,[1] another boy, and the alumni. I had quite a time coming down on the train, as you got an old time table, and found the 3:15 train instead of 3 o'clock. So I had to take the 4 o'clock express, which only would stop only for certain passengers—of which I was not one. But they stopped for me and I was greeted by all the younger boys! That is my adventure on the train. But a more severe calamity than that has happened. My new stockings were bought for school, not just to fill up the drawers at home, and Sister[2] has forgotten to pack them. So please send them as soon as you feel like it, as there is no hurry for them. I do not think there is anything else that I lack so you need not bother for anything else. You are probably too busy for anything else, and as I don't need anything else it is all right. I have already made some very good new friends, and am practising football.

My subjects are:—French, English, Algebra, Geometry, and Cicero, and Xenophon. Greek hurts my eyes so, I think I will take French as my favorite course. Tell John[3] I will send him a postal pretty soon. I am to have a room by next Saturday, as it is not quite finished yet. I hope you will like this letter, as I have taken special pains to write a good letter. I am getting hungry again, and have, as usual a large appetite. I will begin my piano next week. I could not take lessons yet anyway, as Mr. Whittingham[4] sprained his wrist.

Your loving son,
Roger

1. Sydney Allen graduated from Kent in 1911 and died in 1956.
2. Hannah (Nan) Sessions (February 16, 1889–March 17, 1961).
3. Sessions's brother (May 21, 1899–September 19, 1948).
4. William H. Whittingham, Sessions's first music teacher, after piano lessons with his mother. Before he began teaching English, history, and English literature at Kent in September 1907, he had been instructor of music at St. Stephen's College, Annandale, N.Y.; organist and choirmaster at St. Paul's Church, Baltimore; and organist at the Church of the Redeemer, Brooklyn, N.Y., St. Luke's, Baltimore, and Holy Trinity, Middletown, Conn.

▼

Roger Sessions to the Reverend Frederick Sill
als US-Kent

[December 1912]
Dear Father Sill,—   The Harvard Union

Thank you for the alumni letters and the *Quarterly,* which seems to be a great advance on the past numbers. The school seems to have developed greatly with the increase in size. I am very much interested in the musical club, and hope to hear it play when I go down to Kent next Spring. I am also interested in the political clubs. I am getting to be sort of half a Socialist, although I am more or less opposed to many of their ideas.

I have been busy this fall right straight along. I hope you did not think I was getting out of touch with the school. I am taking five courses this year,—Music 2a, 5, 6, Physiology I, History I, German F, and in the second half year, English D, and possibly German H. Music 2a, Music 5, German F, German H, and English D are half courses. My November marks were—Music 5 A, Music 2a A, Music 6 B +, Physiology I B, History I C, German F D—a much better

Letter from Roger Sessions to the Reverend Frederick Sill, April 6, 1910.
Courtesy of the Kent School.

showing, you see, than last year. I hope to pull up on everything at mid-years. In addition to my courses, I am playing the oboe in the College orchestra, trying for the new musical magazine—"The Harvard Musical Review,"[1] and trying for the Francis Boott Prize for a musical composition. I am a member of the Musical Club, and have been elected to the Pierian Sodality, the social organization which runs the orchestra. I have not been taken into the latter society yet, though.

I hope to get to Kent the same time as I did last year. I am looking forward to seeing everybody again. I hope you will be in Cambridge some time this winter, so we can talk things over.

I am glad we had such a successful football season. It is the first that has been really satisfactory. It is too bad we lost the second Berkshire game, but that was not the fault of the team.

Did I tell you that Cloyne had been after me to join the Alumni Association. Of course I would not think of such a thing. I think I shall write them pretty soon about it.

I am sending a money order for the alumni dues to Will Hall,[2] and am also renewing my subscription to the *Quarterly*.

Affectionately,
Roger H. Sessions

1. The monthly *Harvard Musical Review* (October 1912–March 1916) was edited by Sessions from April 1914 through January 1915; he contributed thirteen articles and several unsigned editorials.

2. William Hall graduated from Kent in 1909 and died in 1975.

▼

Roger Sessions to George H. Bartlett[1]
als US-COchapin

July 9, 1915
35 Concord Avenue
[Cambridge, Massachusetts]

Dear George,

[. . .]

I have finished the phenomenal task of reading *Jean-Christophe*— 1577 pages—in five days. Pardon me if I say it is by all odds the greatest novel I ever read. I could not put it down for a second, hardly. I spent all Sunday reading and eating, as I had no collars to wear to church. I wept over certain parts of it, as I wept over [Euripides'] *The Trojan Women*. As you know, it is in ten parts, each complete in itself. You will recognize the souls of all your friends that are worth writing about; for everybody that is living today is there in all essentials. There are some valuable musical ideas there, too. Above all, you will find a clear and keen analysis of the Germany and the France of today, and, if books mean anything to you, I think that you will find, as I did, that the book clarifies many of your ideas, and helps you and inspires you to live the kind of life and think the kind of ideas, and have the kind of opinions and emotions, that you want to have. *George, this is not a sermon!!*

[. . .]

Always your friend,
Roger

1. This portion of the letter was published in Sarah Chapin, "Sessions and *Jean-Christophe*," *The Roger Sessions Society, Inc., Newsletter* 3 (April 1990): 2.

▼

Roger Sessions to George H. Bartlett
als US-COchapin

[September 17, 1915]
Dear George,   Northampton, Massachusetts

[. . .]

Ludwig wrote 3 masses, I think, of which the Mass in C (Opus about 89)[1] and the "Missa Solemnis" in D (op. 123) are the only ones that count. The Mass in D and the 9th symphony are generally regarded as his greatest works, and the Mass seems to me, as to most of the bigger critics, far superior to the symphony. However, it is very difficult to understand, like most of Beethoven's later works. It is undoubtedly the one that Beethoven counted as his greatest work; and it is the one over which he wrote the celebrated inscription "Von Herzen—möge es [wieder] zu Herzen gehen." ["From the heart—may it penetrate to the heart again!"] The finest parts are, to me, the *Credo,* the *Agnus Dei,* and the short instrumental *Praeludium,* which comes between the *Sanctus* and the *Benedictus.* This latter suggests *Parsifal.* The only weak spot in the Mass is the fugue at the end of the *Gloria*—i.e. the words "in gloria Dei patris, amen." All the rest is greater than can be expressed except by the music itself. If you want a guide that will help you to understand it, the one in D'Indy's Beethoven[2] expresses in about 4 pages what many men would take up a whole book with. The organ part in the Mass is not very skillfully done.

To me, Wagner's greatest works are *Tristan, Die Meistersinger,* the *Ring* and *Parsifal.* I don't think *Parsifal* is so great all the way thru as some of the others—the first act, it seems to me, is a little barren at times, though the other two are marvellous. The same may be said of *Götterdämmerung.* I don't think, however, that there is a great, or even an important difference in value between those later works, though. They are all of them superhuman.

[. . .]

Yours very affectionately
R.

1. Beethoven's Mass in C Major, op. 86.
2. Vincent D'Indy, *Beethoven: A Critical Biography*, trans. Theodore Baker (Boston: Boston Music Co., 1913).

▼

George H. Bartlett to Roger Sessions
als US-COchapin

September 26, 1915
Cambridge

Dear Roger:

I have been meaning for some time to thank you most heartily for the volume of Strauss which you were kind enough to send me. I rank it with my most valued possessions. Your last letter was a dandy and it came to me at just the right time, because I was feeling quite low in my mind about several matters and I needed something to think about.

I realized when I was in Hadley that there was a struggle going on inside of you and of course I took what you said about your family with a grain of salt.

I shall always remember our walks with the greatest pleasure, especially that one to Amherst. Wasn't it a beautiful night? I shall never forget how solemn that cemetery looked in the pale glimmer and how startled we were by a pile of stones. I have started on "The Adventures of Harry Richmond"[1] and I find it very interesting but unlike any of the others. You may be pleased to know that John Burk[2] is reading *Jean-Christophe*. He has finished the first volume and doesn't say whether he likes it or not. I met Van and Hillyer[3] and Dillwyn Parrish in the [Harvard] Yard this morning and we all went up to John's room. Van says he has been to see you since I was there. I hope to see more of him later on. [. . .] I doubt very much if Miss R[ichmond][4] thinks you are too young for her. She was, in all probability, entirely sincere in what she said to you about your article in the *Monthly*. I often wonder what women think of us and how we appear to them. The poor things are so held in by convention that they must die of love before anyone knows what their feelings are.

Marjory left for [Nort]Hamp[ton] last Wednesday with two or three other girls. I have seen a good deal of her this summer but it has been in public usually so that we have not had a great many opportunities to learn to know one another better. I did have one good talk however, last Saturday. You know, I think that men, like women, have *monthlies*, but they are mental, not physical. It is an outward flow of something intangible and indescribable, and a sensitiveness to feminine impressions, especially those radiating from the personality of the one to whom you feel eternally bound. This, I know, is a crude explanation, but perhaps you can understand what I mean, and sympathize. I felt this way Saturday evening and as we both went to a dance I had the chance to relieve the pent up fires. Heaven knows what I would have done if I had had to stay at home. Bill Richmond and Paul Squibb[5] ran into me in Holt's today so we lunched together. Billy came to my room afterwards and spent some time writing letters. He sent his love to you and asked me to say that he would not be able to stop in Northampton on his way. On his way where, I don't know but perhaps you do. He told me something else that interested me and may interest you. He said he was reading the last letter you wrote him *to his sister* because it was so entertaining, and when he reached a place where you related how I tried my hand, or rather, my arse, at horse-back riding he didn't realize what he was coming to and so he read what you wrote about my *scraping the skin off my tail*. Isn't that delicious? He says his sister laughed as if she would split. Please don't tell him that I said anything about it but, wasn't it funny? [. . .] I went with my father last night to see *The Birth of a Nation*[6] and enjoyed it even more than the first time (that is, the performance, not the company).

A propos of writing for the Mus. Rev. what do you think of an article on some phase of Scandinavian music[?] I should like very much to have you suggest something. I am willing to write but my powers of expression are, I am afraid, far too inadequate. Billy R. has been wandering around all the evening looking for diversion. I took him to the Merle and treated him to an egg sandwich and a sundae. We both thought of all the food we have eaten there through your generosity.

You know, I have almost come to believe in contraception. Of late I have seen two or three families who would be far happier to-day if they had possessed the necessary knowledge. There is one which lives across the street from us and I suppose the poor Father can hardly be blamed for "playing the two backed beast," as Rabelais calls it, but he has worn his poor wife out and brought into the world eight or ten forlorn children whom he is utterly incapable of supporting. It is a sight like this which convinces me that possibly contraception would not be a bad thing after all. By the way, did you happen to read early in September of the Judge who was murdered in Scituate R.I. He was an upright man who had started an investigation concerning the numerous gambling dens, liquor houses and brothels which exist, unknown to the innocent public, in the *northwestern portion of Rhode Island*. A proof of the degeneracy which I have told you of.

And still, there is something romantic about these sequestered bawdy houses hidden in the scrubby woods, known to only a few patrons and protected from discovery by these same men. It is strange to think that such savages can really live in the midst of our civilization.

Don't forget to come and see me, Roger, when you are in Boston and please send me your Yale address. Have a good time with Miss R—— and remember that my heart is in Hamp as well as yours is.

Yours most affectionately
George

1. George Meredith, *The Adventures of Harry Richmond* (1871). Meredith (1828–1909) was a poet and a prolific novelist.

2. John Burk (1891–1967) received his B.A. from Harvard in 1916. He succeeded Philip Hale as program annotator for the Boston Symphony Orchestra in 1934.

3. Robert Hillyer (1895–1961) also graduated from Kent. His *Collected Verse* won a Pulitzer Prize in 1934.

4. Grace Angela Richmond (1895–1962) was the sister of Sessions's classmate William Richmond. A year older than Sessions, she graduated from Smith College with the class of 1916.

5. William Richmond, Jr. (1896–1967), had gone to Kent, served in the infantry in the war, and became a banker. Paul Squibb (1895–1984) also attended Kent and Harvard (class of 1918).

6. D. W. Griffith's 1915 Civil War epic, the most influential film of the silent era, was an unprecedented artistic and financial success whose racist portrait of the Old South coincided with the re-emergence in 1915 of the Ku Klux Klan after a forty-six-year somnolence.

▼

Roger Sessions to George H. Bartlett
als US-COchapin

September 28, 1915
[Northampton, Mass.]

Dear George,

I have just telephoned A[ngela Richmond] to make arrangements to see her tomorrow evening, and the sound of her voice has filled me full of creative energy, so I am writing to you to answer a letter that came this evening—one of the best that I ever got. Your little anecdote about A—— makes me love her more than ever, and confirms my estimate of her. I seem to need her like anything, for she has changed me and made a new person of me; so if I ever should approach my ideals and become a great composer, you had better write her a letter of congratulations. Gosh, I love her.

Remember, you are going to find out a certain gentleman's attitude

– 13 –

towards a certain gentleman's attitude towards a certain thing, and whether that gentleman is a good detective or not. I don't want to hurry you; but I am waiting in suspense till I hear.

Van and I had a *very* nice time together. We did not get into the old feeling, though till 12 o'clock the night before he left. We talked over all the old things, but until then we did not seem so congenial as before. Now that I have got out of college I have changed my mind considerably, and felt—unreasonably perhaps—a little older than he. My mother noticed it, too, and actually told me so. I shall be interested to see him when *he* graduates. That is the critical time.

I'm glad you liked the Strauss. Play *Zarathustra* over with lots of romanticism, and losing yourself completely in the music. If you don't get carried away by it, I don't know what you can do in the way of appreciating music.

I wouldn't begin an article just yet. Take your time. I will give you a list of books to read. The main thing, however, is to think. Whenever you read a criticism of a composition, compare it with your own impressions. Learn to think of works in a general way—as a whole. Guard against taking a critic too seriously, but listen to him. Don't let him convince you too easily. Above all, consider the spirit of the composer in a sympathetic way, and let that be the basis of your estimate of his work. Remember, it is a composer's faults, not his virtues, that are incidental. Finally, read:

Combarieu's *Music, Its Laws and Evolution*.[1] Read my article on "The Psychological Basis of Modern Dissonance" (Dec. 1914).[2] Then read less general, and more musical works such as:

> *Musicians of Today* (Rolland)
> *Wagner as Man and Artist* (Newman)
> Life of Beethoven (Rolland)
> "   "   "   (D'Indy)
> "   " Franck   (D'Indy)
> "   " Händel   (Streatfield)[3]

Don't read all of these if you haven't time. If I were you I wouldn't count on producing an article till Christmas time. When you do read a book, though, think about it. Remember that it is *music* you are writing about and *do not theorize on the subject, or let anyone else do your thinking for you. Use the musical library literally (not a pun).* Reading about music has its dangers; the chief of these is that one gets theorizing about music, and forgets the music; in other words, one's thoughts become mere literary exercises—as many thoughts are—and have no value. Please let me know whether you understand this or not, for, if you don't I will write you a letter on the subject; it is very important.

My list of books is very provisional—read all the bad critics—Dan Mason, L. Gilman, etc. Huneker is sometimes good, often rotten. I will not waste adjectives on Dan Mason, H. T. Parker, Olin Downes, etc.[4] If you want the *best* criticism, read my articles in the Mus. Rev., that is all *after* Oct., 1914., also the one in January, 1914; and my editorials in the last numbers.[5] Ponder carefully my communication in the same no. with Fritzy's article on the Hull's book[6]—Jan. 1915, it is—the communication signed Ragnan Brovik. I give you these, not to be funny or to be conceited, but because they are the best I know how to do. *Remember that all the great composers, even Brahms, were exceedingly great men, and that they have done a lot for the world. They are far greater than you or I. Remember also that great men have their faults and shortcomings—every one of them; but do not let their shortcomings blind you to their real greatness or their raison d'être.*

Remember that they must be human, and that without shortcomings they would not be human. And don't hesitate to point out these shortcomings, and even to dwell on them; but use your sense of proportion. Write me a short sample criticism of something you are interested in—a composer, or a long work. Take a Strauss tone-poem, for example. Try to get the spirit of it in words. If you do this I can give you much better advice. Take any Strauss tone-poem in your book, and write me all about it; how you like it, why you like it (or *vice versa*), where you think it fails, etc. Don't be discouraged at the size of what I have given you. After all, if you read *Jean-Christophe* thoroughly you will need to read very little else, if anything. So begin on that. Buy it.

I'm afraid I have bewildered you rather than helped you, but ponder my words of wisdom, then ask me questions. I am much interested. [Be] sure and write me soon, for I am crazy to hear from you again, also to learn the result of your investigation.

Very affectionately,
Roger H S

P.S. Remember me to your family when you write. R——

P.S. When you write, tell me a lot about college things, for I will hunger for them. Will write you about Yale when I get there—R——

1. Jules Combarieu, *Music Its Laws and Evolution* (London: K. Paul, Trench, Trubner, 1910).

-15-

2. "The Psychological Basis of Modern Dissonance," *Harvard Musical Review* 3, no. 3 (December 1914): 3–10.

3. Romain Rolland, *Musicians of Today,* trans. Mary Blaiklock, 6th ed. (London: 191?). Ernest Newman, *Wagner as Man and Artist* (New York: Dutton, 1914). Rolland, *Beethoven,* trans. Constance Hull, with a brief analysis of the sonatas and the symphonies by A. Eaglefield Hull (New York: H. Holt and Co., 1917). Vincent D'Indy, *César Franck,* trans. Rosa Newmarch (New York, 1901). Richard Alexander Streatfield, *Handel* (New York: John Lane Co., 1909).

4. Daniel Gregory Mason (1873–1953), a noted composer and influential teacher, was the grandson of Lowell Mason; he studied at Harvard with John Knowles Paine and in Paris with Vincent D'Indy. A professor of music at Columbia University 1905–42, he wrote numerous books on music and musicians. Lawrence Gilman (1878–1939), a critic for *Harper's Weekly* (1901–13) and program annotator for the New York Philharmonic and the Philadelphia Orchestra from 1921, wrote books on MacDowell and guides to *Salome* and *Pelléas et Mélisande.* James G. Huneker (1860–1921), the "Raconteur" columnist for the *Musical Courier* (1889–1902) and music, drama, and art critic for the *Sun* (1900–1912), wrote on Chopin and Liszt. American music critic Henry Taylor Parker (1867–1934) wrote for the Boston *Evening Transcript* 1905–34. Olin Downes (1886–1955), music critic of the *Boston Post* 1906–24 and of the *New York Times* 1924–55.

5. Roger Sessions, "Our Attitude toward Contemporary Music Tendencies," *Harvard Musical Review* 2, no. 4 (January 1914): 3–6, 23. By referring Bartlett to the articles after October 1914, Sessions meant to exclude the three articles he wrote in enthusiastic support of Richard Strauss. In the October, November, and December 1915 issues of the *Review* he was to reverse his position on Strauss. See Olmstead, *Roger Sessions,* 13–14.

6. Rolland, *Beethoven* (see note 3 above).

▼

Roger Sessions to George H. Bartlett
als US-COchapin

[late October 1915]
[New Haven, Connecticut]

Dear George,

[. . .]

I like Parker immensely. He scares most people; but I have decided not to be scared by him. I was terribly so at first; but now that I know more of him, I like him better. He certainly is magnetic, and I expect to be worshipping him later—as a teacher. He certainly is a wonderful teacher, and one who both inspires and stimulates. I have *determined* to win consistent praise from him the rest of the year. He hates to praise people, and has an awfully strong will; but I am going to be the stronger hereafter. It is wonderful, though, to be under such a man.

Yale is a funny place. All the men are alike; and there is so much "Yale spirit." You can spot them in the street, for they seem terribly affected, with their eternal "For-God-for-country-and-for-dear-old-Yale" look on their faces. I don't think I will make any very good friends here, though there are some very nice men, and able ones, too. But they don't appeal to me, somehow. Of course they are not *terribly* different from Harvard men; but the social system here compels them to toe the mark and lose their individuality and manhood and courage. I can't help comparing Parker with Spalding. The standards are so much higher here that one would not imagine the two to be both college music departments.

[. . .]

Very devotedly,
Roger

▼

Archibald Sessions to Roger Sessions
als US-COchapin

October 22, 1915
[New York]

My dear Roger,

Here are two checks for you which you'll know what to do with.

Your letter was extremely welcome not only because I'd begun to worry a little that I'd not heard from you but because it told me that you were so much interested and satisfied with the beginning of your work with Parker. It sounds as though you had got into just the right place for you and I'm glad. There isn't any wonder that you find that creative work comes hard. But I'll tell you—I hope for your encouragement—that it wouldn't be creative work unless it did. It's the hardest thing there is and nobody knows anything about it till he has tried it. And when one has found that out and thoroughly convinced himself that there aren't any short cuts to results in creative work he's won about three quarters of his battle, for he's established himself so that discouragement and disappointment don't weigh with him nearly so much.

So get all you can out of your music and don't bother about anything else. One's intellectual and spiritual life is of more importance than anything else. It's difficult to make most people understand it, but that don't make any difference.

Write me as much as you can and as you care to about yourself and your work and your affairs—no matter what they may be, there's no limitation on that—you know now, I guess, that there's nothing you need hold back from me if you want anybody to talk to.

Always your loving
Dad

▼

Roger Sessions to George H. Bartlett
als US-COchapin

October 29, 1915
New Haven

Dear George,

[. . .]

You are a little too hard on Brahms, I think. To me he is a man of great nobility and true genius—though no greater than some other men. As for his form, that is often calculated, and he is a slave to it; it is his chief limitation. He is too conscious of it, and it suffers for that. True mastery of form demands that there should be no hitches in the motion or awkward or manufactured bridge-passages in it. Brahms is full of these—you can easily find them; passages which remind us of our daily exercises in harmony and counterpoint.

Liszt was as great a man as Brahms, but in a different way. Englishmen and Americans do not care for him much—just as the French and Italians—who are incidentally *much* greater musical nations—detest Brahms. As a matter of fact, this age in the Northern nations could not for its life appreciate Liszt; for the latter's style is not in vogue at all. Above all, however, judge *for yourself;* and don't let the Harvard atmosphere stultify you. Remember that music is *music,* and does not necessarily have anything to do with literature on the subject, which is really very primitive so far. As a matter of fact, it is by far the most wonderful and the most universal of the arts; take my word for it. *Beethoven* was a far greater man than Homer, Shakespeare, Dante, or Euripides, or Goethe—much as I worship the last three. I think you will share my view in the course of time; for I intend that you shall hear a lot of it!

[. . .]

Roger

THE UNITED STATES entered World War I on April 6, 1917, and conscription for service began May 18. Sessions, along with another

Yale student, was arrested in July 1917 for distributing anticonscription literature. Sessions had considered himself a pacifist, but by April 1918 had changed his mind, saying later that "Wilson talked me around"; he tried to enlist, only to be disqualified for poor eyesight. The Armistice came on November 11, 1918.

As a student at Yale, a men's school, at a time when most of his able-bodied classmates were fighting in Europe, Sessions must have, despite his pacifism, felt pangs of conscience, possibly even guilt, for not fighting. He resolved his discouragement at not being accepted into the service with the view that "we, whose prospects of getting in are very small, have a very definite and great responsibility on our shoulders, and we can draft all our energies more and more exclusively for the disinterested service of mankind, and so I think it is now more than ever not only our privilege, but our duty in the strongest sense of the word to work and stand for the truth and the right as we are led to see it" (to Sill, August 4, 1918, US-Kent). Nonetheless, as he wrote Father Sill (September 1918), "it still is hard to see one's brothers and friends going out and sacrificing themselves and yet be unable to share their sacrifices with them, in the real sense." One of the friends he refers to is doubtlessly Frederick van den Arend, who had just returned from the front.

Much of Sessions's last year at Yale was devoted to the composition of his uncatalogued Symphony in D Major. The first movement won Sessions Yale's Steinert Prize; exhibiting the first signs of what was to become a lifelong pattern, however, Sessions could not finish the second movement in time for the performance. He conducted the first movement on May 24, 1917.[1] The symphony's dedicatee, George Bartlett, came to the event from Kent.

Upon his graduation from Yale in 1917 Sessions was hired by Smith College on the strength of his symphony. Returning to Northampton put Sessions in direct contact with his mother, still the matron of the Sessions House. Henry Dyke Sleeper,[2] who had hired Sessions, did so under the condition that Sessions finish the symphony. Further urgency was added by Josef Stransky (1872–1936), Mahler's successor as conductor of the New York Philharmonic, who, probably through Archibald's efforts, had promised to give Sessions a private reading of the symphony in October and perform the completed piece with that orchestra in January 1920.

Rather than working on the symphony, for reasons of internal politics and his own inability to work under pressure, Sessions campaigned to remove Sleeper as chairman of the music department.

Helpful in this goal, no doubt, was William Alan Neilson, president of Smith and a good friend of the family's, and Roy Dickinson Welch,[3] another member of the department and friend. Sessions succeeded in removing Sleeper, but not in finishing the symphony. Sleeper did manage to convince Sessions that it was not polite to keep Stransky dangling and to write him finally that the work would not be completed.

In an October 1918 article inspired by the appearance on Smith's faculty of the Russian choral conductor Ivan Gorokhoff, Sessions wrote:

> Russian music differs from that of other nations chiefly by virtue of the fact that it is the music, not preeminently of great individuals, but of a whole people. . . . The Russian ballet represents the upper class of Russia only, a class which fell with the Tsar. . . . In the liturgical music of the Russian orthodox church is embodied an art which has no parallels in the music of other countries. . . . The Russian service is even more largely musical than the Roman; and unlike the Roman service, its music is the work, not only of tradition, but of the finest Russian composers. . . . Profoundly emotional, yet at the same time dignified and intensely religious, it has neither the somewhat inconsequential solidity of most Protestant church music, nor the complex formal beauty of the Roman contrapuntal and Gregorian music.[4]

Sessions wrote to Bartlett about Gorokhoff (November 18, 1918),

> I have told you about Mr. Gorohkov, haven't I? In the spring of 1920, in honor of Beethoven's 150th anniversary we are going to give a big Beethoven festival here, the principal event of which will be a performance of the Missa Solemnis, which Gorohkov and I are going to work on together, i.e. he will train the chorus I the orchestra. Rehearsals will begin next February or March, in order that the performance may be as perfect as possible. But think of the opportunity for me, of starting my career as a conductor with the greatest of all works. And Gorohkov may be trusted to make the chorus a success. I sing in a chorus under him and he is the most powerful personality that can be imagined. He actually pulls the notes out of the most inert in an astounding manner. He is a man of the most elemental force and will force the chorus to bring out Beethoven's music in all its superhuman glory. I shall try to do the same with the orchestra.

However, there is no record that such a concert took place at Smith College in 1920.

In September 1918 Sessions met Barbara Foster,[5] a violinist and student at Smith who lived in an annex of Sessions House during her senior year. Sessions wrote first to George Bartlett (December 27, 1918, US-COchapin) and then to Father Sill (January 1919, US-Kent) of their engagement, maintaining at first that they would marry after she finished college. An air of unnecessary "utmost secrecy" pervades this letter, as it had those concerning the marriage in December 1916 of Sessions's sister, Hannah, to Paul Shipman Andrews (1887–1967). This kind of request for secrecy regarding marriage would reappear in future letters as well.

During the first six months of 1919 Sessions's relationship with Father Sill appears to have changed. His letters take on a somewhat adversarial tone, one that Sessions would never have used with Sill during the previous ten years. This was partly precipitated by his friend Frederick van den Arend's resignation from the faculty of Kent in a dispute over antiwar literature in which Sessions sided with him. A further bone of contention was Sill's opposition to Sessions's plans to marry during Lent.

Although the courtship was brief—September to December 1918— the engagement lasted longer than anticipated. Sessions wrote formally to Foster's father, Frank, requesting the hand of his daughter in marriage. Frank Foster responded not entirely enthusiastically (December 21, 1918, US-COchapin) that his acceptance of the marriage was conditional on Barbara's finishing college. The wedding was planned for Christmas vacation 1919, but postponed to March 18, 1920, because of Barbara's grandfather's illness. It was again delayed until slightly before Barbara's graduation, which she planned not to attend because it came during their honeymoon. Her teachers and parents, however, hearing of this and, unlike her, knowing that she would graduate summa cum laude, persuaded Roger to bring her to graduation to accept the surprise of her honors. The wedding finally took place on June 5, 1920, in Claremont, New Hampshire,[6] with only the two families present: Roger's parents, Ruth and Archibald; his brother, John; his sister, Hannah; Barbara's parents, Frank and Inez; and her sisters, Eleanor (1897–1986) and Rosamond (b. 1907). Rosamond Foster (later Sayre and Sheldon) remembers meeting for the first time the white-haired Archibald, whom she liked a great deal. Ruth she recalls as someone "I wouldn't have wanted to have had for a mother." George Bartlett, frequently asked in letters to play the organ at the ceremony, could not attend.

Roger Sessions in 1919 or 1920, during his engagement to Barbara Foster.
Courtesy of Sarah Chapin.

Barbara Foster in 1919 or 1920. Courtesy of Sarah Chapin.

1. The concert, "by students in the School of Music," included the awarding of the Lockwood Scholarships, the Steinert Prize, the Frances E. Osborne Prize, and other awards.

2. Sleeper (1866–1948), an organist, composer, and ordained minister, had studied at Harvard and taught at Smith 1899–1924.

3. Welch (1885–1951) taught in the music department of Smith College from 1914 to 1935, when he was appointed chairman of the music department of Princeton University, where he hired Sessions to teach.

4. Roger Huntington Sessions, "Russian Choral Music at Smith," *Smith College Monthly* 26, no. 1 (October 1918): 1–4. Ivan Timofeevich Gorokhoff (1879–1949) had been choirmaster at the cathedral in Kursk before coming to New York in 1912 to direct the choir in the Russian Cathedral. He taught at Smith College from 1918 to 1945.

5. B. Claremont, N.H., June 22, 1899; d. there July 4, 1980.

6. Not June 3 as in my *Roger Sessions*, 16.

▼

Roger Sessions to George H. Bartlett
als US-COchapin

September 29, 1917
Dear G,   Northampton, Massachusetts

If I haven't written before, it is because I have been experiencing new sensations, and even you have been a little hazy in my thoughts until now. My new situation [at Smith] seems so strange to me that I feel as if I were just beginning to get settled. I have two courses in Orchestration—Elementary and Advanced—also work in composition and appreciation—conference in the former, section meetings in the latter. My week's work finishes at 11 o'clock on Friday. This makes it very convenient for week-ends in Boston and Cambridge, as my 9 o'clock on Monday does not. I also have afternoons free so far—except for an occasional demonstration in one of Locke's courses.[1]

The first meetings of my courses were ordeals, but I found that my nervousness soon disappeared. In the Elementary Orchestration course I have two old friends, and was afraid they would presume on acquaintance and make things difficult; but I found them equally afraid I would do the same; so things are easier than they might be. The Advanced Course is learning at present to read score—a frightfully tedious though necessary performance for all concerned. Yesterday morning I could not help remarking about some of their transcriptions to the piano of Beethoven's 7th symphony, "This hurts me more than you." Which seemed to amuse them. I hope four weeks of it will not wear them out. I also tutor Miss Goode,[2] one of the piano teachers—in Orchestration.

My colleagues on the faculty are a queer lot. Six or seven of them I find more or less interesting and congenial—Locke, of course, Welch, who teaches Appreciation and History, Miss Holmes (violin)[3] and her assistant Miss Tanner[4]—the former a brilliant and open-minded, though conservative, old lady, an excellent musician of the Brahms-Joachim school, the latter a lively young creature with some intelligence; Miss Goode, a young (i.e. 28) piano teacher whom I find interesting and congenial as she like myself, is not entirely at home in an academic atmosphere; though she takes to it better than I do.

I must say that I usually find academic musicians uninteresting, that is, comparatively speaking. I don't hesitate to say that my interests are broader than theirs, as I think you will agree; at least my extra-musical interests—philosophical, scientific, and literary,—are more important to me than theirs are to them. It seems to me that their music is not really a part of their life, and that they are preoccupied with the side of music and art which is remotest from life. It seems to me that they regard music objectively and study it from that point of view. Their appreciation of music also lacks enthusiasm, and they seem to be quite ignorant of the genuine thrill that real beauty always gives. Their musical appreciation is just a little like their wives.

The faculty as a whole—and Northampton in general—has been almost aggressively cordial. I was welcomed vociferously at the faculty reception, and all the elderly people said they were so proud to see a Northampton boy grow right up into the faculty. So I am in good favor here, at least, with the exception of one or two influences which seem to be against me. To be the son of the foremost woman citizen is to be somewhat of a public character, and my pacifist opinions may cause me a good deal of discomfort. Though the war seems remote, Northampton is almost solid behind it; in fact, I don't believe there are any out-and-outers except my mother and I in the city. Luckily our general popularity saves us from things we would ordinarily encounter. Our sincerity is taken for granted and we are not assumed to be "slackers and cowards," except, perhaps, by our clergyman, whom I have told you about. But already I have received a note from one of the lady professors in the French department, enclosing a *Times* editorial which she asked me to "read carefully and meditate the lesson it conveys." The article in question was on the subject of "misguided zealots" duped by pro-German propaganda. I wrote the lady a letter which I consider about the best letter I ever wrote, and which I hope will disarm her. I had to explain that I was neither a propagandist, nor a pro-German; that I was not even an "American pacifist"; but that I was an internationalist, influenced almost wholly by Europeans—among whom was her own countryman Romain Rolland. I hope I will get an answer, but of course I may not. Of course I can understand her position. She has lost relatives—including a brother in the war, and naturally feels sore at people who seem unwilling to make sacrifices themselves.

I am, of course, perfectly willing to have people cut me on the street or denounce me from the pulpit if they want; but it is rather disagreeable at first, as I can't tell just who is friendly and who is hostile; though I have not encountered any really hostile people yet.

Later

Last week Saturday (or rather, a week ago yesterday) I received a most interesting letter from Van. He says the ambulance has been "taken over" (Aug. 27th) but intimates that he will go to Russia or join a French ambulance corps, but that he will see us in 1918 early. I am wondering if the American govt. has not drafted the men for ambulance service, though I trust not, though I shall be anxious till I find out. Have you heard from him since then? It was a most interesting letter—about the most interesting I ever received, I think. I am not too sanguine about his tales of French disaffection, because I have heard other reports from pacifistic people who have just returned. They report them very discouraged, but loyal.

I went to New York two weeks ago, and stopped in at the *Masses* office, among other things, and had a talk with Merrill Rogers.[5] He seemed sanguine about things in general, as I am inclined to be. It seems to me that the war henceforth is going to be a rather dull affair. I see signs that the President is waking up to some of the evils, and have no doubt that they will be efficiently remedied in time. That is, there will be reasonable freedom of speech (not *reasonable,* I don't mean, but sufficient to silence those who are on the fence) and sufficient consideration of conscientious objectors to silence the majority. Meanwhile I think peace will come within six months, as Germany seems to want it.

I haven't looked at Mr. Veblen's book[6] for some time, but will take it up again in a few days. I find it very hard to think clearly, but I cannot be satisfied with anything less than the truth. Mere moral objection to war does not satisfy me. If the war is the lesser of two evils really, I cannot see how I am possibly justified in not supporting it, even though I do so with tremendous qualifications—in fact, I could not support it otherwise. But I haven't yet been able to see things as most other people do; and that bewilders me either because I have perhaps too often been accustomed to look to the majority for support in crises like this, or because Mike Elliott and Fritz Anderson,[7] with whom I think so much in common, seem to be in favor of it. When I argued in favor of war in the now remote past (February and March 1916 and before) it was because, of course, I saw war as only the sentimental idealists saw it; for I still feel that the so-called "war-like virtues" are valuable. But even if modern warfare called them forth—and it does not—it would not be worth it.

[. . .]

It seems strange to be surrounded by women; I must confess that it is a little disturbing, because it is so easy to be attracted by them, and yet one cannot dream of a really lasting passion for any of them. Therefore I suppose I must expect to feel rather restless in that way, as long as I remain here. I am afraid I still cherish a secret hope that I may fall in love with a real woman some day; and if I do I will be, in the hackneyed phrase, the luckiest man in the world. But I won't find her in Northampton, or even, perhaps, in America.

I have a great scheme for an opera in my head, for future use—distantly future—perhaps. If I can work it out properly I think it will prove to be a great idea. The subject has been treated before, but not exactly in my way. Here again I am cryptic, however, and leave matters thus till I see you.

John [Sessions] reports that he is interested in Harvard. I hope you will see him, as I should like him to get to know some of my friends, as I think he rather needs intellectual stimulus. But, of course, I can't choose his friends for him. Nevertheless I should appreciate it if you would at least make him come to see you once. He lives at Standish A33.

Mother and I may be down for the day on Saturday. Why not come back with us—or if we do not go down, come sometime Friday and stay till Monday morning. You could come to my 9 o'clock in Elementary Orchestration, when we will probably have an illustration on the violoncello. Anyway, I am crazy to see you. I will let you know by Thursday if we are coming, and will you let me know by then whether you can come.

Ever yours
Roger

1. Arthur Ware Locke (1883–1969), professor of music at Smith College 1915–52.

2. Blanche Goode (1887–?), assistant professor of music 1913–22.

3. Rebecca Wilder Holmes (1871–1953), professor of music 1903–36.

4. Mary Creusa Tanner (1893–?), class of 1915 and assistant professor of music 1915–19.

5. *The Masses*, a socialist periodical published 1911–17 by Max Eastman, ceased publication when the Espionage Act of 1917 allowed the Postal Service to refuse to mail "seditious" literature. The magazine's editors, including Charles Merrill Rogers (1892–1964), were brought to trial for antiwar activities twice in 1918, with both trials resulting in hung juries. Rogers went on to work for *The Liberator* and *The Dial*.

6. The economist and social scientist Thorstein Veblen (1857–1929) is best known for his *Theory of the Leisure Class* (1899), but Sessions is more likely referring to his *Inquiry into the Nature of Peace and the Terms of Its Perpetuation* (1917).

7. Frederick Anderson received his Ph.D. from Yale in 1915. He was an instructor of Italian and Spanish there 1915–18.

▼

Roger Sessions to George H. Bartlett
als US-COchapin

September 24, 1918

Dear George,   Northampton

[. . .]

Naturally I feel a little shy in talking to you of the influence which touches me most deeply at the present time; for you will not believe me when I say that I am this time really moved by somebody real, whereas before it was only a painted goddess, which vanished at the slightest contact. Naturally you think I am again deceived until you have real proofs to the contrary, which will come to you in time. But I do wish you knew Miss F[oster]. Imagine the purest, humblest, and yet the strongest of spirits—strong enough to sustain and redeem a chaotic bundle of serpents like myself—which finds its expression in the most beautiful of all mediums—a wonderful speaking voice, which is commented upon by everyone and for which its possessor is famed everywhere; a spiritual beauty so overwhelming that one cannot wholly tell whether she has physical beauty or not—though to me she is most beautiful in every way. Well, I realize how futile this is—how silly and inadequate it sounds to me, how primly and Anglo-Saxonly proper (an admirer of Anglo-Saxonism would call it "bluff" or "manly"; Miss F—— would hate it as you and I do), how artificial-sounding it must seem to you; but you must try to see what I mean.

Some day, perhaps, I will be able to tell the world more adequately in music. So pardon me this; though I am making an ass of myself not through exaggeration but through a grotesque understatement. Moreover I have really scarcely the right to say such things, as I have no right to assume that she cares in the least for me—I merely have hopes.

Well, don't forget to write to me—all about yourself.

Affectionately
Roger

▼

Roger Sessions to the Reverend Frederick Sill
t/s US-Kent

[November 1918]
Dear Pater,—   Northampton

I wonder if you would let me come to Kent next Sunday for a very special purpose. For some time I have felt the need of a good talk with you, such as I have not had since I left school, on religious matters; as you know or may have guessed, I have had a great many difficulties of that sort during the last years, and I feel that the time has come when I can and must clear them up. I have some very fundamental things to learn, or relearn, and I need help which I feel that you could give me better than any one else. But I don't feel that I can afford to spend the money unless I can be pretty sure of being able to see you; so I hope you will tell me if you expect to be busy or away. This was a little in my mind when I was at Kent in September, but I was not ready to talk about it then, as I wasn't at all sure of myself, or rather of my feelings and the direction in which they were tending. I am afraid I don't express myself as I want to, but unless I hear from you I will arrive at Kent sometime Saturday—12 o'clock probably—and will stay until Sunday afternoon.[1]

I have spoken to Pres. Meiklejohn[2] again about the possibility of your preaching at Amherst, and he is enthusiastic about having you, and is going to give me a list of possible dates which I will bring to Kent on Saturday if possible.

Affectionately,
Roger

1. The two did meet and this meeting produced the touching exchange reproduced in the *Kent Quarterly* 5, no. 2 (Winter 1986): 4–5.

2. Alexander Meiklejohn (1872–1964), president of Amherst College (1912–24), helped found the American Civil Liberties Union (1920) and was awarded the Presidential Medal of Freedom (1963).

▼

Roger Sessions to George H. Bartlett
als US-COchapin

[December 27, 1918]
Northampton

Dear George,

I have hesitated long before writing you this letter, because in a way it is the most personal letter I ever wrote you, and I thought and wondered long before writing it whether you would understand its significance to me, and would be able to respond to it in a way which would show that you are entitled to the confidence which it presupposes on my part. I have come to the conclusion that you are, and so I ask you to share my joy with me. The news which I have for you will not be unexpected, perhaps; but I must ask you, for reasons which you will understand, to keep it in the utmost secrecy, except that I would like you to tell your mother and ask her to guard it very jealously also.

George, can you realize what it means when I tell you that I am engaged? I told you a little of how I felt, and I told you that it was the first time I had ever really been in love; and yet you had heard me say that very thing so often before that you chuckled inside—I felt you doing it—and set me down as having made an ass of myself once more. Perhaps you still think so; the consciousness that you felt that way prevented me from talking much about it, and you cannot have seen what was in my mind all the time. At any rate, no one was ever more in love, more profoundly moved by the greatest of experiences than I am, and it is because of this that I hesitated before telling you, lest you, who stand in the peculiar relationship to me of one who knows intimately one of my former selves, yet who seems to have lost touch with me since because of that very knowledge, should not understand what has come into my life. You see, we outgrow our old selves much faster than we realize it; and while I was at Yale and even later I had not learned to catch up with myself while I was with you. And you know very well that we have lost touch with each other since then. So I am telling you this because I want you again to be my friend, or rather our friend, for I have already ceased to think of myself as only one person.

I want you very much indeed to share and feel our joy with us, but unless you feel that you can, that I really mean something in your life, I shall merely trust you to keep our secret. If you really care about coming nearer to me and being a friend in the truest sense of understanding and loyalty, I hope you will write to her, not a letter of congratulation, but one of friendship. But before you write to either of us I hope you will think over very carefully our past friendship, and decide finally whether you think it is worth continuing. In case you do, you will find me ready to do my part and to help you always and in any way possible. I was wrong when I wrote you and told you that I was not willing to meet you half way. I am, and I hope you will forgive me for having said that, which may have been the whole cause of our misunderstanding. I can assure you, too, that there is not the slightest chance of anything sinister or ugly coming in to cast dark clouds over our friendship.

If you are my friend you are hers also, and just as dear to one as to the other, for we are one in spirit, and understand each other better than I ever imagined two people could. Unless you can realize this it would be far better for you not to write her; but if you can, she would appreciate hearing from you, the most friendly letter that you care to write her. I think she would appreciate your using first names. She is in New York during the holidays; Miss Barbara Foster, care of Dr. Francis C. Wood, 200 West 56th St. Or if you should write her after the holidays, 26 Green St. Northampton will reach her.

I will not tell you much about her except that she is the most wonderful person in the world, and that in her I have found the greatest love for which I have always longed. If you want a description of her which you may find more concrete, I can only tell you that she is about my sister's height, with light brown hair, blue eyes, very delicate skin, and the most beautiful speaking voice in the world. She comes from Claremont, N.H. and her family is composed of some of the most genuinely musical people that I ever met. Her father is a banker there, not very much interested in banking, a man who though largely self-taught, I understand, gives the impression of having a very unusual mind, and an outlook on life which is neither provincial nor superficial, but broad and profound in the most real sense. They do not own a Ford, but enjoy walking and driving and realize, and in fact live, in the pure joy of being close to nature in the best and most real sense. Barbara's sister [Eleanor] is a pupil of Gebhard,[1] and is one of the best pianists, if not the best, that I have heard off the concert stage. An older sister, of course, but at that only my age, or a little younger. She too is engaged, to a lieutenant.[2]

I am sure, George, that I am glad I told you; and let us forget the past and be natural, not self-conscious, with each other. I can't see how you can help but be moved by this news. Mrs. Meiklejohn has written me "It's truly what moves the stars and all the heavens—what you have found." She is right; and I hope you, too, will find it some day. But I do want to try to make you feel my joy now. It makes me very humble and will draw me nearer to my other friends whom I have told and shall tell.

As I said, I would like to have you tell your mother, and you can talk about it, if you like, with the Burks,[3] the Pater, Bruce Simonds,[4] Miss Holmes, the Meiklejohns, and the Neilsons, and Mr. Sleeper, as well as the members of our respective families, the Foster family and the Sessions family, I mean. With others—and most of those you don't know, I must ask you to keep it secret for the present, as it would be most disastrous to have it get around the college. It's going to be hard enough as it is. Later I may tell Van, and I certainly [will] tell Buzzy Cuyler when I see him again, unless I find that he is too indiscreet to be told.

Well, Happy New Year to you and the rest of the Bartletts. I hope, by the way, that you got the books I sent you. Did I include the Brahms Sonata? If not I will mail you a copy.

Good luck,
Roger

1. Pianist, teacher, and composer Heinrich Gebhard (1879–1963).
2. The flutist Merry Cohu.
3. John Burk had married Alberta Touchard in December 1916.
4. Bruce Tibbals Simonds (1895–1989) graduated from Yale College in 1917.

▼

The Reverend Frederick Sill to Roger Sessions
cc US-Kent

August 25, 1919
[Kent, Connecticut]

Dear Roger,

[. . .]

As to the fact that we have suppressed individuality here, I deny it absolutely. Pardon me for calling attention to your own case. At any other school you would have been started in those early days of your School life in a way that would have marred your character for life. As a matter of fact both before graduation and since you, with a very distinct individuality, have always been accorded every honor. Some day when you are here I should like to go over our list of Alumni and ask you whose individuality has been suppressed.

[. . .]

I am sorry you are obliged to set the date for your wedding in March for the simple reason that I am ever so anxious to show the generation ahead of me, of men like Father Huntington [Sessions's uncle], that we respect their feelings. But it has been a queer thing in your family that each generation seems to have done something, or adopted a point of view, which was hard for the generation ahead to swallow. Your grandfather [Frederic Dan Huntington (1819–1904)] was undoubtedly a source of grief to your great-grandfather Dan [Huntington (1774–1865)]. Father Huntington did many things which his father [Frederic Dan Huntington] had to put up with, and now the fourth generation is apt to do things which Father Huntington's generation, no doubt, finds hard to bear. You are a most interesting family. I only hope that if you ever send a son to me I shall be able to train him so that the thing above all else he will desire to do is to bring joy to the heart of his parents and older relatives.

God bless you my dear Roger.

Affectionately as ever,
[Pater]

BECAUSE OF Sessions's two years of difficulties in finishing the Symphony in D, he felt he needed to look in another direction for compositional guidance. In November of 1919 he traveled to New York to meet and play for the Swiss composer Ernest Bloch (1880–1959). Bloch had toured the United States in 1916 and in 1917 had begun teaching at the Mannes School of Music. In 1924 he became an American citizen. He married Margareth Schneider and had three children, Suzanne, Lucienne, and Ivan; Suzanne and Lucienne were lifelong friends of Sessions.

Sessions and Bloch hit it off immediately, and Sessions traveled to New York once a month for lessons. Bloch counseled Sessions to scrap the symphony and work on exercises and counterpoint to gain facility (advice Bloch was later to take himself).[1] Bloch's reputation as a teacher grew rapidly in the next few years. In 1920 he became the first director of the Cleveland Institute of Music, a position he held until 1925, when his radical teaching ideas—he proposed the abandonment of textbooks and exams, for example—led to his dismissal. Quincy Porter, Bernard Rogers, George Antheil (whom Bloch later disavowed as his student), and Herbert Elwell[2] quickly followed on Sessions's heels to study with Bloch in New York or Cleveland.

Carried away with enthusiasm, Sessions wrote Father Sill (April 18, 1921, US-Kent), "I hope you understand that it is the chance of a lifetime, since it means intimate association with a man whom I consider, and who is becoming more and more generally to be considered the greatest composer living today, and perhaps indeed the greatest that has lived for a good many years."

In addition to music, Sessions's literary and political interests figure prominently in the letters of these years. He wrote to George Bartlett (October 31, 1920, US-COchapin) that he would vote in the presidential election for Socialist candidate Eugene V. Debs, "but I would rather see [Democratic candidate James M.] Cox elected than Harding." The same letter mentions his reading *Satan's Diary* by the Russian novelist and playwright Leonid Andreyev (1871–1919), on whose work he would later base *The Black Maskers*. Letters between Roger and Barbara Sessions and George Bartlett continually discuss the many books they were reading. On January 10, 1921, Sessions wrote Bartlett, his closest friend, a long letter asking to borrow five hundred dollars, a sum representing a third of his annual salary at Smith. George sent most of the money, but was soon bedridden with an old ailment, a leaky heart valve. His mother wrote Barbara Sessions (March 14, 1921) that Bartlett was seriously ill. The Sessionses, and especially Barbara, continued to write and receive letters from him that spring. The twenty-four-year-old Bartlett died May 5, 1921. The chapel organ he had picked out for Kent was now dedicated to his memory.[3] Sessions had not repaid the money, nor had he finished his symphony dedicated to George. In fact, an association between his symphonies and the death of loved ones may have begun here.

In September 1921 Roger and Barbara Sessions moved to Cleveland, where Sessions taught at the Institute and Barbara taught school. Their letters to each other continued however, when Roger returned to the East in the summer of 1922 while Barbara remained in Cleveland, and again in the summer of 1923, when Roger stayed in

Cleveland and Barbara summered on Martha's Vineyard with Minna Curtiss.[4] While in Cleveland, Sessions, despite financial problems, bought a motorcycle, which he named Kundry, and drove it until he had an accident.

Sessions's relationship with Smith College was not severed. He had gotten some theatrical experience there in 1920; when students put on a production of *The Merchant of Venice*, Sessions supervised the composition of its music by members of the senior class.[5] The director, Samuel Eliot, Jr., suggested that the 1923 senior play be Leonid Andreyev's *The Black Maskers*. Sessions wrote the incidental music in Cleveland, dedicated it to Bloch, and conducted the performances in Northampton in June. Even though this completed work achieved some success, Sessions withdrew it. Sessions also wrote incidental music for performances of Carlo Gozzi's *Turandot* that took place May 8–10, 1925, in Cleveland. That music too was withdrawn. These works, combined with an aborted 1922 Nocturne for Orchestra, represent the sum of Sessions's output while in Cleveland.

In Cleveland—which Sessions called "Filth City"—he became friends with several of Bloch's students and colleagues: Theodore Chanler, Douglas Moore, and Jean Binet.[6] Binet and his wife, Denise, lived in Cleveland until 1923; during their stay a lifelong friendship with Sessions was cemented.

1. See Michael Nott, "Roger Sessions's Fugal Studies with Ernest Bloch: A Glimpse into the Workshop," *American Music* 7, no. 3 (Fall 1989): 245–59.

2. Porter (1897–1966) had also studied with Horatio Parker at Yale, graduating in 1921. After studying with Vincent D'Indy in Paris he returned to the U.S. in 1922 and studied with Bloch at the Cleveland Institute, where he later taught (1922–28, 1931–32). Rogers (1893–1968) had begun studies with Arthur Farwell; following a performance of his *To the Fallen* by the New York Philharmonic in 1919, he had spent a year in Europe on a Pulitzer traveling scholarship before coming to Cleveland for studies with Bloch. In 1927–29 he studied with Nadia Boulanger in Paris and in London with Frank Bridge, then joined the faculty of the Eastman School of Music (1929–67). Antheil (1900–1959), after studies with Bloch in New York, went on to Paris and studied with Boulanger, along the way developing a reputation as an enfant terrible of avant-garde music with his *Ballet mécanique* (1926). Elwell (1898–1974) studied with Bloch in New York and also with Boulanger in Paris; Sessions's predecessor at the American Academy in Rome, he returned to the U.S. in 1928 and taught at the Cleveland Institute, edited program notes for the Cleveland Orchestra, and reviewed music for the Cleveland *Plain Dealer*.

3. Sill's remarks about George Bartlett, as well as excerpts from some of his letters, are found in the *Kent Quarterly* 13, no. 3 (May 1921): 1, 60–65.

4. Mrs. Minna Kirstein Curtiss, who taught English at Smith, donated her holo-

graph score of *The Black Maskers* to the Library of Congress June 1, 1950. It is inscribed "For Minna with my love—Roger."

5. The music was published in Boston by C. W. Thompson, 1920.

6. Chanler (1902–1961) studied with Bloch in Cleveland and with Nadia Boulanger in Paris; he is known particularly for his songs. Moore (1893–1969), formerly a student of Parker at Yale and of D'Indy in Paris, studied with Bloch in Cleveland, where he served as director of music and organist at the Cleveland Museum of Art (1921–23). Binet (1893–1960) had moved from Switzerland to the U.S. in 1919 and studied with Bloch in New York, where he founded the Dalcroze Rhythmic School. He taught Dalcroze eurythmics in Brussels (1923–29) and spent the rest of his life in Switzerland promoting Swiss composers.

▼

Roger Sessions to George H. Bartlett
als US-COchapin

December 17, 1919

Dear George,   40 State Street [Northampton, Massachusetts]

I have just been going over some old letters, and the sight of yours has reminded me that you are still my creditor as far as correspondence goes—though I should appreciate more "dunning" than I ever get from you. Also, I must explain my mysterious telephone to you. And it is a very long story.

The symphony went so poorly that I got more than discouraged. I don't know whether I have told you or not; but for a long time I have felt that my technique was not large enough or well-developed enough to make me really satisfied with my work. You know what it has been—simply unconcentrated, unsustained patchwork. The week that I telephoned you I had decided to go to New York to see Ernest Bloch on the subject, not only of the symphony, but of my work in general. For the past year or more my one thought had been to finish the symphony as soon as possible and to then get to work on technical studies which would really enable me to do something. The week before I went down I got some "Psalms" of his for voice and orchestra, just published by Schirmer[1]—also a string quartet;[2] and was so carried away by Bloch's intellectual and emotional force that I kept the Psalms with me for two or three days, and did practically nothing but study them and play them over. They made a greater impression on me than anything else in modern music—by far. I should advise you at once to order Psalms 22, 114, and 137 in his settings as arranged for piano in vocal score, and published by

Schirmer—and share my enthusiasm, as you will when you know them.

If Bloch's music inspired me, Bloch himself did and does still more. Sometime I'll tell you about that and other interviews which belong to the future now. He suggested millions of things to me, and I have been a new man ever since. Indeed, his personality is such that one weighs his every word, to absorb it into one's mind and let it achieve a new and individual growth there. The result is that I have given up the symphony and have gone back to the roots of composition in my work with him. And I have cut down external activities so that I live almost wholly now in my music; but I will be able to do more fully when Barbara and I are married. Bloch is a very great man—I am convinced of his genius more truly than that of any recent composer except Debussy, of whom Bloch is in many ways the direct antithesis, his music being harsh, bold, dissonant, but teeming with life and vigor. The 22nd Psalm is a vast cry from the depths of his Jewish soul and from the soul of the world—strange, original, yet _great_ music, which _lives_. I wish I could begin to really describe to you his influence on me, but it's something that must be done by word of mouth. But he has effected a revolution in my life.

[. . .]

As ever,
Roger

1. Two Psalms (nos. 137 and 114) for soprano and orchestra (1912–14), dedicated to Edmond Fleg, and Psalm 22 for baritone and orchestra (1914), dedicated to Romain Rolland.

2. String Quartet no. 1 in B minor (1916) in four movements was published, like the Psalms, in 1919 by G. Schirmer.

▼

Roger Sessions to George H. Bartlett
als US-COchapin

April 29, 1921
Dear George,   Northampton

I can never forgive myself for putting off this letter for so long. When I make the familiar excuse, however, I feel that I am doing so with much more justice than ever before. Barbara has written you, no doubt, that plans for Cleveland have been concluded, and that we are actually going there. At present my mind is a little occupied with finding a place to live—a little. Then I have charge of the Senior Dramatics music this year, and have to rehearse the orchestra, correct the parts, etc.—a goodly amount of work. In addition, Roy Welch has suffered a breakdown, and I have been put in charge of two of his courses for the present—a course in analysis, and a course in Opera, to which I must lecture on *Pelléas and Mélisande,* and *Boris Godunoff.* However, I could not put off my letter a day longer, and here it is!

We have seen Fritz—we had a very nice visit from him Wednesday evening—and he brought us the joyful news that you are having a taste of spring from your porch. I hope that there are apple trees near by, so that you can get a taste of the delicious odor—which alas! reaches us only in combination with the odor—somewhat ubiquitous in Hadley, I'm sorry to say—of cow and pig manure. I think there must be great artistic possibilities in odor—I have a theory even of a scale of odors, resulting from my observation of the peculiarly contrapuntal way in which these smells reach us, a much more polyoderiferous effect than one would imagine from a knowledge of the possibilities of combined timbres. The apple blossoms are wafted deliciously (like the highest tones of the solo strings) over a deep bass accompaniment of pig-manure (weird arpeggio effects on the muted tuba) or the more spring-like and really fresh and animal cow-manure (contra-bassoon). You probably won't find my description in the least entertaining, but I assure you they describe my impressions with some accuracy. I really enjoy the fresh, spring-like cow-manure smell—there is a suggestion of eternal transmutation and fertility about it; but the feces of swine carry a somewhat less subtle and seductive appeal! I must say it is pretty awful in spots!

The last time I went to New York Bloch lent me the score of Israel,[1] and it has been a wonderful experience to get to know it. It is the crowning work of the Jewish period—a big symphony of Mahlerian emotional dimensions though not of Mahlerian length, with two movements and a Prelude. If I were not very much bored with criticism of the Paul Rosenfeld[2] type, I should try to describe the music with more vividness than I really can. Bloch told me when he lent it to me that he had recently played it over, and had had absolutely no sense of its being his own work; but that he felt then that it was one of the greatest and most moving things ever written. You can, of course, understand his spirit in saying that; so I feel that I am committing no indiscretion in telling you. To the violin sonata[3] it bears somewhat the same relation that the Eroica symphony bears to the C♯ minor quartet; the sonata is the more mature and subtle and intimate work, but the symphony is vaster and more majestic and impressive. The Prelude is only sixty-odd measures long—very serene and solemn. The first movement is complex—agonized at times, then mysterious, barbaric, gigantic, and resigned by turns. There is one passage in which old *Jahvé*'s voice can be heard in all its tremendous majesty and omnipotence. Finally the movement, which is intensely tragic in general character, rises to a stupendous climax, which I can only compare in its effect to some of Beethoven or Wagner's most thrilling climaxes; and the movement ends, with reminiscences of the Prelude, and premonitions of the slow movement, to which it is joined by a very beautiful and very long transition passage. The second movement is marvelously simple. Four sopranos and one bass sing, alternately, "Adonai, mon Elohim, entends ma prière—j'espère, j'ai confiance."[4] The music is quiet and serene, but profoundly sad and resigned. The final pages are of indescribable beauty. Since knowing Israel I am far more convinced of Bloch's greatness even than before.

He also lent me the Penitential Psalms of Orlando Lasso, which seem to me the finest music of the 16th century that I know, though I am not familiar, of course, with Palestrina's masses. The Psalms have a profound human quality which one does not wholly expect from 16th century composers, on account of our silly notions of what is "modern" and our tendency to exaggerate the sophistication of our race, nation, and generation. It is the independents, like Bloch, who must struggle for recognition today; it is they who refuse to make the sensation which would bring them recognition in the musical world today; for they must face a double enemy; those, on the one hand, who still are pious traditionalists and pedants (God knows why any of them ever compose at all, since what is good has apparently all been done generations ago, in their view); and those who make a fetish of new sensations and cultivate a manner, as is done in the little Mutual Admiration Society which is contemporary musical Europe. I have been undergoing a severe struggle this last year, without being conscious of the nature of the opposing forces; I am not sure that I recognize their proper alignment yet; but I have made my vow—just as Bloch made his thirty years ago; only mine is somewhat less the product of an impressionable child than was his made at the age of eleven. My vow is not simply to devote myself to composition; but also to keep myself pure and my individuality intact. God knows there was never a harder place to do this than contemporary America;

for our nouveaux intellectuals are, in the end, as deadening as our Puritans and Philistines, and the only thing a vigorous individual can do is to keep his mind grimly aloof, and to love the truth fanatically, and without respect to personalities or to the whirlpool, in the calm center of which the truth and reality lie.

I have not sent R. Bourne[5] yet; but will see that it gets wrapped up and mailed to you the next time one of us goes to Hamp. I'm sorry this isn't a more amusing letter; but I shall try to write you again next week; in the meantime I think of you a great deal. Please don't try to answer our letters; there will be plenty of time for that and for much more than that later on when you are stronger.

Affectionately as ever,
Roger

1. Bloch's *Israel*, a symphony with two sopranos, two contraltos, and bass (1912–16), first performed May 3, 1917, in New York with Bloch conducting.
2. Rosenfeld (1890–1946), an author and music critic, would champion *The Black Maskers* in *Port of New York* (New York: Harcourt & Brace, 1924), 145–52.
3. Bloch's First Violin Sonata (1920).
4. "O my Elohim, Thou art my refuge, Hear Thou my prayer, O hear my crying." Sung by two sopranos, two altos, and a bass, the language is similar to Psalm 143, verses 7–10.
5. No doubt a reference to *Untimely Papers* (1919), a posthumous collection of antiwar essays by the literary critic Randolph Bourne (1886–1918).

▼

Roger Sessions to Ernest Bloch
als US-DLC

June 25, 1921[1]
Hadley, Massachusetts

My dear Mr. Bloch,—

I agree with you that a 4 hand arrangement of Israel will be the most practical. I have avoided playing such arrangements generally when a 2 piano arrangement is available, as the players in 4 hand music are apt to crowd each other, and the arranger to upset most of the original chord groupings, etc., in the effort to attain greater sonority, + sometimes for perfectly senseless reasons, in order to bring out a subservient + purely decorative part with the solidity of harmony which is obtainable in the orchestra. With the exception of a few passages, such as the great *B minor* section in the first movement, I think my task will not be difficult. For that passage and certain others I shall have to find an effective way of transcribing the material for the 4 hands, and may have to take some slight liberties— at any rate, I shall try always to *realize* your ideas on the piano, rather than to give a slavish and pianistically clumsy, though literal, transcription.

Your account of the Cleveland boarding house situation is amusing! If you are inspired to give up your antisemitism, I shall have to become anti-American (which many people would consider me now!) or even bolshevik! I must say I am rather curious to see the middle west for the first time, and have suspected that it would produce just that effect on me.

The symphony[2] arrived this afternoon, and I have read it eagerly, though the sight of it terrifies me! It is certainly far more complex than any of your later works, and I have far more difficulty in reading it than I had with Israel. Your style has changed, as you say, and in more ways than one; but while with your later works I have been struck by the freshness and individuality of each one,—the way you have created a new style for each work—in this I am struck—on the most superficial perusal of the score—by the way certain traits in your later works—particularly the quartet—are foreshadowed here—especially in the scherzo. I am anticipating a very great treat. As I say, I have had only a very short time in which to look the symphony over, so far; but I have managed to get a good idea, I think of the general outlines. It will be a great inspiration to me, too, to study such an early work, and one that you set such great store by.

I am very happy, too, that you are having the proofs of the *Sonata*[3] sent to me; for that is the only one of your later works that I don't know *well*. By the end of the summer *Macbeth*[4] will be the only one of your works that I know about (except the very earliest) that I am not thoroughly familiar with.

We are at last settled in our cabin, after having dispossessed two families of squirrels, one family of field mice, and four large and aggressive families of wasps, from their winter homes, between the outside shutters and the windows. Tonight is our first night up here; it is very beautiful and peaceful here on the top of the hill, where we are entirely surrounded by trees, and where everything is so quiet that practically the only sounds we hear are the birds and the insects, with an occasional very distant railroad train. I anticipate a busy + fruitful summer. It is so wonderful at last to get out here by ourselves, where we can have two months of real living. I have a great deal to do this summer; but I feel at last that I will really be able to get something done.

I will bring all of your scores—including the Sonata—to Cleveland with me in the fall, so you can be quite free in your mind in regard to them.

I hope you all will have a good rest; it is certain that you deserve it, if ever anyone did! You are going to what must be a very beautiful place, and will undoubtedly be completely refreshed by two good months away from the dirt + smoke, not to mention the noise—to which Mr. Daniel G. Mason repaired after the *Viola Suite!*[5]

With kindest regards to all of you from Mrs. Sessions + myself,

Very sincerely yours,
Roger H. Sessions

1. All of Sessions's preserved letters to Bloch are dated 1921.
2. Bloch's Symphony in C♯ Minor, performed in part in Geneva, 1910; first American performance by the New York Philharmonic, May 8, 1918, Bloch conducting.
3. Bloch's First Violin Sonata (1920).
4. Bloch's opera *Macbeth* (1904–9) had been premiered by the Opéra-Comique, Paris, November 30, 1910, lifting the composer from relative obscurity to international fame.
5. Bloch's Suite for Viola and Piano, winner of the 1919 Coolidge Prize, had been performed in Pittsfield, Mass., in 1919; it was also arranged for orchestra. Mason would later attack Bloch on anti-Semitic grounds, denouncing his 1927 symphonic work *America*, with which Mason felt Bloch "capped his dealings with us by the grim jest of presenting to us a long, brilliant, megalomanic, and thoroughly Jewish symphony—entitled *America*" (Daniel Gregory Mason, *Tune In, America: A Study of Our Coming Musical Independence* [1931; reprint, Freeport, N.Y.: Books for Libraries Press, 1969], 160–62).

▼

Roger Sessions to Ernest Bloch
als US-DLC

August 27, 1921

My dear Mr. Bloch,—   Edgewood, Claremont, New Hampshire

I am glad my letter to Mrs. Sanders amused you.[1] I have since had a letter from her, slightly annoyed with me, I fear, but trying to smooth things over, and telling some rather clumsy and obvious lies. I am enclosing it; I shall answer her in my most oily manner! I really find these little feminine undercurrents rather amusing—except for the waste of time which they involve.

You must be having a glorious summer. I enjoyed your account of Mgr. Ganthier so much. More and more I see evidence of the illusory character of the barriers between man and man, set up by our little egotisms and our petty creeds and schools of thought. Yet it is a strange paradox to me that it should take the utmost self-discipline to transcend these things and to see things *as they are*. This I find terribly difficult especially in youth, yet I feel that, in the broadest sense of the word, it is the only thing in the world worth doing, whether in art, science, philosophy, or in any other activity.

This has been a very absorbing summer for me, from many points of view. I have done very little work, and a great deal of thinking. During the last few weeks I have come to a realization of my own incompetence, and have been seeking a way out. The truth is that I am utterly without self-discipline, in my whole life; and this has thwarted me and frustrated me at every turn. To give one instance: the work that I have done for you has been *false*, simply because I have put so little energy into it—through sheer lack of force of will. When I started out with you I wanted with the utmost sincerity to do my work justice; but my forces scattered themselves, and the work which I have always done for you is more than unworthy of what I could and should have done. This is humiliating and discouraging to me because of my failure to make the most of my association with you and the teaching you have given me—without which I would have become almost desperate in Northampton. But this is only one way in which I have failed; the disease affects everything I do.

Luckily, I know I have the strength to pull myself out; and, difficult and discouraging as it will be, I am determined to do so. The realization has been brought to me by my absolute failure to be able to put into notes the music which I have wanted to write this summer—a failure in technique, although I could almost hear some of it, and knew quite clearly what I wanted. Since it is something that stays with me, it may perhaps, when I have gained more real discipline, "compose itself," as you say. At any rate, I am doing nothing with it at all for the present, but am simply trying to work hard at my technique, and to put my own impulses into the work that I am able to do at this stage. Fortunately I never have lost beyond recovery my faith in myself; and I think I am speaking soberly in saying that I know that I shall cure myself. Fortunately, too, I have a wife who understands me perfectly, and yet believes in me.

So, you see, my summer has really done me a great deal of good. There is no happiness like coming face to face with the truth, even if it means changing one's whole way of life. I hope you will forgive me for writing all this; but since I am to be in Cleveland next year, you must know what kind of a person I am!

I think we will go out to Cleveland about the 15th, as Mrs. Sessions's work begins the 21st. Could you let me know what to do about getting rooms? and give me some advice on the subject? If you still approve of the plan of our all being together, I could be on the lookout for suitable places, and communicate with you. Mrs. Sessions is anxious to "get settled" as soon as possible, but we wouldn't want to miss the chance of being near you. If, however, you would rather, we can wait until you arrive. In that case, do you know of any place where we could live fairly reasonably, and get acclimatized, until finding a permanent place? I have heard very recently, by the way, that the situation there has improved, and that we will have comparatively little difficulty in finding a place to live.

It is splendid to think that we will be going out there so soon, for in spite of the sordid surroundings I am sure that, under your leadership, we will accomplish something. Perhaps I don't think enough of the obstacles that will be in our way; but, as you say, we know what we want, and that makes all the difference in the world. However, I can understand all too well your reluctance to go back among those people!

With kindest regards to all of you, from both of us

Yours most sincerely,
Roger H. Sessions

[P.S.] We will have returned to Hadley by the end of the week.

1. In response to the Cleveland Institute of Music's offer that he teach woodwinds there, Sessions had replied (letter to Mrs. Franklin B. Sanders, July 19, 1921, a copy of which was sent to Bloch) that his knowledge of those instruments was "almost entirely theoretical" and that the description of him as a teacher of woodwinds in the Smith College catalog was inaccurate and placed there against his will.

▼

Roger Sessions to Barbara Sessions
als US-COchapin

June 24 [1923]
Northampton, Massachusetts

Darling,

[. . .]

I suppose that a week from today will be your first day on Martha's Vineyard. I can't tell you how much I anticipate it for you, the four

Ernest Bloch (at the piano) and his class in composition at the Cleveland Institute of Music, 1922. From left to right: Jean Binet, Hubbard Hutchinson, Ruth William, Quincy Porter, Roger Sessions, Barbara Sessions, Aaron Bodenhorn, Isabel Swift, and Anita Frank.

weeks of real time for solitude and reflection will, I am absolutely sure, do you more good and give you more strength than anything—perhaps than everything combined—in the last four years. I, too will have the time to reflect and to grow; and our coming together after it will be like a new marriage, a new relationship. You may be sure that the faith Bloch has given me will stay with me, as it does still, in spite of the fact that I have opened myself to all possible doubts and reservations. It is, in other words, wholly possible that others may not find in my music what Bloch does or even that Bloch may cool to it later. I say this merely because my present attitude towards it is our total deficit. At the same time I am making myself a budget, and making myself live within that budget; and keeping careful accounts. I am asking you to do the same; it ought to be fairly easy for you to save most of the Martha's Vineyard money, since your expenses will be paid there; but I think that since we have not got unified control of cash, we have absolutely got to be responsible to each other, and to go ahead very carefully and with a sense of responsibility. The situation is very serious, and if we are to keep out of serious trouble in the future, I am *convinced* that we have got the guard every cent with the utmost jealousy. If we can do so, and deny ourselves, we will be the happiest people on earth, I'm sure; we then will be a position to go abroad, have children, and do a hundred other things that we haven't the slightest prospect of doing now. You see, having gained self-confidence as a composer, I feel that I have the possibility of getting a grip on life such as I never had before; I know you are with me on this, and always have been. But never again must either of us give a bad check. [. . .] I am terribly afraid this letter so far sounds like a sermon preached by the prince of hypocrites; but I assure you that it is in deadly earnest, that it contains a spirit of sackcloth and ashes, and that I love you to distraction. Well, hell, of course you will understand, *wonderfully*.

[. . .]

Your own
R

SESSIONS MET the young composer Aaron Copland (1900–1990) in Paris. For two men born in Brooklyn, their childhoods could not have been more dissimilar. Sessions, the scion of an old but financially strapped New England family, had been educated at a preparatory school, Harvard, and Yale; Copland, the son of Russian Jewish immigrants, had graduated from the Boys' High School in Brooklyn. Despite the contrast in their backgrounds, the two soon formed a close friendship that, though it would suffer from misunderstandings and differences of opinion, would remain warm sixty years later.

Copland was living in Paris, where he studied composition at the newly founded Conservatoire Américain with Nadia Boulanger (1887–1979), a brilliant teacher who had studied composition with Fauré and organ with Widor at the Paris Conservatoire, where her father had been a voice instructor. After the death of her sister Lili, a composer, in 1918, Nadia Boulanger had abandoned her own promising career as a composer to devote herself to teaching. Her influence on American musicians of Copland's and Sessions's generation is difficult to overstate. Copland was one of the first Americans to study with her; others included Arthur Berger, Marc Blitzstein, Elliott Carter, Theodore Chanler, David Diamond, Roy Harris, Walter Piston, and Virgil Thomson.

Influenced by Theodore Chanler's letter (January 23, 1924, US-

COchapin) describing his studies with her, Sessions, equipped with a letter of introduction from Bloch, arranged to meet her in Paris on his first arrival there. Still supported by his father, Sessions sailed on his first trip to Europe in June 1924 and returned in mid-September. He wrote long, detailed letters to his wife almost daily from London (where he saw Minna Curtiss), Paris (where he was shown around by Copland), Switzerland (where he stayed and spoke French with Jean and Denise Binet), and Florence (here he was on his own).[1] As the last letter in this chapter indicates, Sessions underwent a conscious change in the summer of 1924, one that corresponds to the end of his first period of creativity.[2]

1. These letters, in the Sarah Chapin collection, are represented here by a few significant examples. The letters to Barbara imply that Sessions had met Copland before Paris; if that were the case, they would have had to have met in New York before Copland's departure for Paris in 1921.
2. See Olmstead, *Roger Sessions*, 25.

▼

Roger Sessions to Barbara Sessions
als US-COchapin

Monday night, June 30 [1924]

Darling,—   Paris

[. . .]

Nadia was tremendously impressed with the B[lack] M[askers], which I played her through no. 5a, and which I am to finish tomorrow night. She was more enthusiastic about it than any one except Ernie, and saw what I consider its strong points immediately. That was a great encouragement to me, as you can imagine; for it gave me confidence in myself in relation to Europe such as I had not felt certain of before. Furthermore, as she is a person who adores Stravinsky and knows, for instance, every note of *Les Noces*, it gives me a little better sense of being understood by the people whom I want to have understand. I will write you more about her after tomorrow night; but we got along very well together, and she said she considered it not only a very fine work, but a very important work!

[. . .]

Your utterly devoted
Roger

▼

Roger Sessions to Barbara Sessions
als US-COchapin

Thursday, July 3 [1924]
London

Darling,

[. . .]

My last interview with Nadia was a complete success for my music and I think for me. I played her the "dirge" and the "fire music" [from *The Black Maskers*] and she said it was the most significant score she had heard for a long time. We went over it together after that, and she looked at some details. She evidently is a quite superb score reader and has a splendid eye for details, as she appreciated my intentions in a minute. I told her about Stokowski and she advised me to make an appointment if possible to play it for him next fall. She pointed out the fact that she had no idea what the play was about, but that the music seemed not only impressive, but absolutely clear, to her, logical not only in the separate parts but in the succession of the parts. She added that, of course, she had expected to be interested, from Bloch's letter, but that "of course one person's reaction is not the same as another's," and that she had been quite prepared for possible disappointment. Then we talked for about an hour, about Bloch, about Elwell, about the Six,[1] and their ideas. I told her what Dukelski[2] had said and she was rather amused—"in the first place, of course, it isn't true; in the second place, I have no patience with those who lay down rules for other people" etc. But she said that the present fashion of gaiety is undoubtedly a reaction from the horrible experience of Paris in war time and gave a very vivid description of the black nights, and the dread that hung over everything, in spite of the fact that life went on as usual. I could understand her very well, of course. I told her every thing about Bloch, while making it clear, of course, that I was his friend.[3] She was extremely sympathetic and just as nice as she could be. She is coming to Cleveland when she travels in America next winter.

Well—The next morning (yesterday, in other words) I took the train for London. The channel crossing was a little rougher than my trip on the Olympia; but I braved it with success, in spite of a hearty breakfast and a slightly upset stomach! But let me tell you about this and other things in my next letter, which will go on the Baltic tomorrow and should reach you a little later than usual, as this is a slow boat. You must have my first letter from Paris by this time, as well as the one written on the boat.

Dear darling, you know how much I love you! I can't possibly wait till September to be with you again—or at least I don't see how I can!

Your own devoted
Roger—

1. Les Six, influenced by the anti-Impressionist Erik Satie, consisted of six composers: Darius Milhaud, Arthur Honegger, Francis Poulenc, Georges Auric, Germaine Tailleferre, and Louis Durey. They espoused music that was direct in approach and free of pretentions.

2. The Russian composer Vladimir Dukelsky (1903–69) was in New York 1922–24 and in Paris and London 1924–29. Sergei Diaghilev commissioned a ballet, *Zéphyr et Flore*, in 1925; in the 1930s, back in the U.S., Dukelsky composed numerous popular songs, including "April in Paris" and "I Can't Get Started," under the pen name Vernon Duke.

3. By this summer, and after some emotional turmoil concerning Bloch and the Cleveland Institute, Sessions was growing away from his mentor. He wrote Barbara (July 31, 1924, US-COchapin), "we must not for a moment let ourselves become involved with the emotions of the Bloch family. [. . .] I have become convinced this summer more than ever that the Bloch point of view and all it represents is *not for me*, and I feel nothing but repugnance for all their 'alarms and excursions' [. . .] which lead nowhere. But you are *absolutely* right as *always* in giving Ernie the benefit of the doubt."

▼

Roger Sessions to Barbara Sessions
als US-COchapin

Thursday, August 21,
Friday, August 22 [1924]
Darling,—Dearest darling,   Florence

[. . .]

Did I tell you that I wrote some time ago to Mrs. Reis telling her that I had decided to give up the idea of writing the piece I had planned for the L[eague of] C[omposers]?[1] I know you will be disappointed, but I trust you to understand, much as you will be undoubtedly tempted not to! The point is that I have had so many new impressions here that I have found myself utterly unable to sit down and plan a work of any dimensions to order; I have had different thoughts, different preoccupations, and the one short thing which I have composed is—and was, quite without my asking it to be—along wholly different lines from what either Mrs. Reis or the League of

Composers or the composition which they wanted would require. The minute I had composed it (owing to the absence of a piano it is still a sketch which I may leave unfinished à la Leonardo) I realised that it opened up in a way a new path which henceforth I must follow and have already begun to. Though it is not much in itself I regard it as of the greatest importance for me and my development—a preparation for the Dante music[2] in the least obvious way. I will say no more of this now but will leave it among the thousands of things which there will be for us to talk about when we are together again. Dearest darling, the time is getting shorter!

I have had so many thoughts this summer—thoughts which have clarified my deepest impulses so much—and thrown light on so many things which precocity and other influences of my early life obscured. It is strange how one's intelligence can sometimes throw open doors which are so strangely liberating to instincts which have for years been groping for them and which have become partly atrophied from want of satisfaction.

All my questionings about the value of culture led me back—and continue to lead me back, every time I go out on the street—to the conclusion that whatever reality Michelangelo and Giotto and Leonardo and Dante and Botticelli and the rest (and Dante above all just now) have for the mass of people today, they have an intense reality for me.

I suppose it must seem strange to you that above all in Europe where the beautiful things of the past are almost a part of the landscape—where every tree has its association, I should have doubts like this. Yet of course it is just here that one has them; and I think that I have written you enough so that you are able to follow my thought and to see how inevitably it struck me.

Then I tried to think the thing out as clearly as possible—for I really found myself in a thoroughly perplexed state of mind, strange as that must seem to you—I tried first of all to find out what was at the root of my feeling; what its causes and its bases in reality were; and at the same time to discover how far I still believed in the past. The result was a complete readjustment of values for me—a readjustment which I feel is of the greatest importance for me, and which I would like to try to explain to you, as far as I can in a letter.

I came of course quickly to the conclusion that what is great in the past is not only valuable but necessary to us, to the development of a really strong and great personality; that the past is as much a part of reality as the present or the future; that, however, its supreme importance lies in those respects in which it is neither the past nor the present but in which it brings to us and holds before us the most eternal things. Naturally this is almost platitude, except for one thing perhaps. That is that we sometimes admire Euripides, for instance, because he expresses "modern" ideas. You will see that "modern" ideas of all kinds or any ideas which are the expression of a particular time or place have ceased to have any meaning for me, in this connection at least.

What I mean to say is that the past finally came to seem to me a part of life, which however must be interpreted in terms deeper than either the past or the present.

What is the present? I tried to think of many things which characterized it: I even made a list, one night at St. Cerque [Switzerland], of the various present day movements, personalities, events, psychological reactions, etc. which characterized it.—The war, the various things arising from the war and their manifestations—Psychoanalysis—The Einstein Theory—Picasso, Stravinsky, Proust, Joyce, etc.—Machinery—American business—Revolution—Reaction—the Orient, etc. etc. etc. These too one must understand, and I felt that I understood it very little, much less than I really wanted to. But as I thought it seemed not by any means the essential thing; nor the place that I wanted to live in principally. It seemed to me that this world of the present day is simply the stage, so to speak. One must know it and live in it; most of one's activities will take place with it as a background. But it is not the play itself.

What the play itself is was brought [home] to me very clearly. I think partly, it's true, by things which I have read and seen, but most of all by certain experiences which I have had this summer. First and greatest the marvelous afternoon and dawn at Gornergrat; the storm on the side of the Tour d'Aï (it wasn't a real storm, but simply a little rain, but it gave my imagination some idea of what a real storm would be like); the dawn on the Dôle; the sunsets on the ocean; the emotions of fatalism which made the implacability of the sea and of nature so very real to me; and a thousand *physical* sensations I have had—the glorious sensation of physical fatigue, of growing strength, for instance.

Aren't these the real things, after all?

What I crave *above all else* is a greater experience of the most elementary sensations; a closer touch with nature, with all the fundamental facts and conditions of our existence—the elementary sensations of the organism and the most intense and vivid experience of them. Do you see what I mean darling? This letter is terribly hard to write, because my thought is something so much more fundamental than a thought. But by what you have written I feel that you have felt exactly the same things, in a very different way, perhaps corresponding to *your* needs. I express it in such a horrible way, and give *no idea* of the intensity with which I feel it, of the overwhelming impulse which I have to pass my life in the future on the most direct contact with nature and to refer everything back to its simplest terms in organic sensations felt intensely and simply.

Have I made everything seem terribly complicated, darling? As I think it over, it seems almost absurd to write this way; for of course I have had enough vitality always to *live* much more this way than the average person, and certainly more than the average precocious person. But that is because my most vital impulses came out almost in spite of myself. Now I want to be *more conscious of them;* to base all my thinking and my activities on them.

Well—here is the central thing, after all, I have a gigantic task to fulfil in my life; I need all the resources possible to perform this task. The task is simply to be true to the promise which I feel so strongly in myself, and not to disappoint those many others who have felt it, too—in other words to *write great music.* But music, like everything which lives, is based on the most profound facts in the universe; as some one has said—the *movements* of the soul—it must be made first of all of those most elementary sensations of which I have spoken. Our knowledge of the past, our experience of the present, are the things which help us to give form and design to these elementary sensations; they are necessary parts of the whole. But they are not the *material* out of which life is made. And as for me personally I need all three of these things and want them all to a far greater degree than I have ever had them before; the *permanent* things. This summer I have gone a very long way towards getting them; although in a very fundamental way. I cannot get the third and most important really completely until I am with you; though I have had some wonderful and absolutely unforgettable experiences of that kind, such as the ones I have told you about.

I am afraid I have expressed things which are the most untheoretical and unintellectual in a wholly theoretical and intellectual way. Perhaps I should have waited until we were together before trying to say what I mean. But, dearest one, I so long to have you know all my thoughts and to enter into them with me, and to keep in as close touch with you as possible that I can't bear not to give you some indication of thoughts and experiences—experiences in this case much more than thoughts—which have been so vital to me as these, and so ever-present with me.

[. . .]

Your utterly and wholly devoted
Roger

1. Claire Reis (1888–1978), executive director of the League of Composers for twenty-five years, had on May 9 commissioned a work for vocal quartet or double quartet with accompaniment of string quartet and four woodwinds or string quartet alone. In August Sessions completed an Adagio for Organ, the first of his Three Chorale Preludes for Organ, dedicated to Douglas and Emily Moore. The other two preludes were completed in Paris in May 1926.

2. Unfinished, uncatalogued piece by Sessions.

▼

Roger Sessions to Barbara Sessions
als US-COchapin

Saturday, September 6 [1924]
Paris

Dearest one,

[. . .]

At this time I was in Florence, where indeed it was that the whole of my thoughts began to take real crystallization. My thoughts were full of the Dante music and what I wanted it to be—what it *must* be and what I could make it. I felt myself gripped by the personality of Dante and by the civilization, the period, the surroundings, and above all the emotions in which he lived; above all by the *eternal* aspect of his art and of that civilization and those spiritual surroundings. For the first time, I think, I began to realize what real immortality and permanence in art are. Certain passages of the Divine Comedy came to have an extraordinarily great personal and emotional significance for me, and the sound and the rhythm and the colossal and utterly harmonious structure of the whole began to enter my blood. I read the Vita Nuova, too; an extraordinary and really tremendously beautiful experience in Florence, although infinitely less so than the Divine Comedy, of course. Do you remember the passage in Thucydides where he speaks of his purpose in writing the history, and says among other things that he is writing for posterity? I don't know that I remember it particularly well, and perhaps all the thoughts which I have had since I read it, nine years ago, have altered it in my imagination. But it is a passage of which I think very often, and if I remember at all correctly, it expresses a little my feeling of what my music must be from henceforth. These thoughts came back to me with great force while I was in Florence; it is *eternity* that matters, in art as in every thing else, and only that. And from this point of view I tried to find a point of departure which would be a rough practical guide for me in my future work.

I couldn't possibly tell you, darling one, all of my thoughts on this subject. There are far too many of them, in the first place. And perhaps even here I tend to express them in a somewhat quaintly simple way. But they are really extremely simple thoughts; and if for the sake of brevity in a letter (which could not conceivably be a short one if it is to tell you anything at all) I strip them of many details, you will forgive me, dearest one, as you will forgive also the intense concentration necessary in order to give them a clear form, which I'm afraid may make them seem a little cold; but which isn't in the smallest degree an attempt at "good writing," which would be inconceivable—as I trust you know—in a letter from me to you.

Naturally, I thought a good deal about the Black Maskers, and in fact started out in what seemed to be the most logical way, by trying to estimate its ultimate worth, its weaknesses, its limitations, its shortcomings, as they appear to me. I realized that in spite of its beauties it represents in many ways a point beyond which I don't want to go any further, in the same direction. But I wanted to formulate absolutely clearly to myself the direction in which I do want to go.

In the first place, it is *psychological* music. That is certainly not in itself a weakness, and I believe, too, that in the Black Maskers it most of the time avoids becoming one. But I am here discussing a *positive* point of view, not a negative one; I say what I do not at all for the purpose of discussing the B.M. but to show you very clearly how my viewpoint has changed; hence perhaps you will understand if I simplify a good deal, and give me credit for nuances which I don't state.

What I feel is, to be brief, that the B.M. expresses a phase of my life which was entirely or almost entirely intellectual, which nourished itself on thoughts and images of a *purely* imaginative character, and that it gets its power from this source which is as far as possible removed from the sources of being. This makes it perhaps less universal, less truly vital, even though it certainly does not condemn it. The music that I dream of, and must create now, is music which is fundamentally of the *body;* that is based first of all on a direct appeal to the senses, the nerves, the muscles. The *Black Maskers* has of course this element, but I believe infinitely less than my music must have. I want to base my musical language on this absolutely elemental appeal.

What are the elements of music which carry this appeal the most? Rhythm, of course, and melody, first of all; harmony, color, polyphony too, but generally and with only a few exceptions through their accentuation of rhythm and melody first of all. And yet I feel that while I want to accentuate these two elements very strongly in my future work, it is really a matter of *emphasis!* For, as one thinks more and more of the problem, it seems more and more elusive—so absolutely subtle is the musical language and so inseparable are its elements. But I simply am indicating in a general and rough way what my tendency is; and content myself with generalities for that reason. It is almost necessary, too, to do that when one is speaking of any thing which is so completely a matter of intuition—a matter in the last analysis, of one's own personality and nothing more.

So I made up my mind to make an intense experimental study of *all* of these elements, to discover new relationships between them, and to establish a new, perhaps a shifting set of emphases, of relationships of this kind in my work.

I found other, less fundamental shortcomings, not so much in the Black Maskers, but in my style in general; parts which seem to me incompletely realized, forms which seem to me not absolutely suited to their substance, pages which were drawn quickly and in many cases extraordinarily well, but not given their final and complete form.

I repeat, and want to emphasize to you above all, that the purpose of these reflections was simply to *help* me to orient myself. I felt that in my musical activity of the future—immediate and perhaps distant, too—there must be always the element of study and experimentation, as well as that of creative work; that even if my work should prove to be small in quantity, it must be *first rate*, in the absolutely strict sense of the word:—*perfectly* realized, ultimately. That my personality and genius are sufficiently great so that I can aim with complete confidence at perfection, always. Perfection, that is, in the sense of *absolute* realization, as far as such a thing is humanly possible.

I don't tell you this last because it is so very different from what I have thought before. It is different in this, however; that self-confidence brings *energy* and in the past I have not felt it in every inch of my being as I do now, or so clearly. It seemed always nearly hopeless;

but now I am so full of new energy and new life that I know that nothing is impossible to me.

I have laid out for myself certain technical work, therefore, and have already begun it. Since there is only one composer—Bach—who *absolutely* satisfies me, who seems *absolutely* or practically great and perfect, I have taken this work once more as a basis for my study— the chorales, the fugues, the passacaglias, the inventions, to start with. My method will be partly that of the painter who learns by copying; and partly of course, that of applying the principles which I learn, in my own way. However, it would take too long to describe it here, or to go into any kind of detail. But I am sure it will interest you tremendously; and, if it will interest you at the time, this is a part of my work which I can share very much with you.

More important than this is the actual creative work I shall do. I have one work—of medium dimensions—planned to be completed before I begin work on the Dante music; as indeed my study of Bach must be, very largely. You see, the Dante music presents such a gigantic *musical* problem that I wouldn't dare begin it until I have a much greater mastery than I have now. It will make demands of the *most exacting* kind, which I am in no sense ready to meet now. But I am confident that with three or four months of intense application, with the time I will have, I can make myself ready to meet these, as they come.

This other work—as indeed, all my work from now on—will require above all *solitude* and *concentration*. Let me explain again what I mean; for this last is the most important part of my letter, in many ways—as far as *we* are concerned; and the most intimate. And I want you to remember all the time that I am speaking of *myself* alone here. It is not to involve you in any way; *however* I plan my life, you are to go ahead, with absolute confidence to plan yours absolutely according to your own desires. This will perhaps be a very hard thing to do at times—I can't say, as I cannot speak for you, my darling one. If you want to come with me, my way, I mean—it must be the result of your own absolutely free choice and, even more than that, your own profoundest impulse. I am quite prepared to have you feel that your way is a different one; and the most radical difference couldn't hurt or weaken my love for you in the slightest degree. You know that I am utterly and *passionately* devoted to you, and supremely eager to give you everything, and all that you want from me. And you know I hope, that if you ever have the smallest desire for proof of this, you only have to ask of me *whatever* you want.

Whatever road you go, we will always be near each other; the quality of your personality will always be leaving its mark on me, and presumably mine will be leaving its mark on you.

I ask of you only one thing: your confidence. I don't ask it on the basis of the past; I could not respect myself for a moment if I even suggested that. Perhaps confidence is not exactly the word. I mean simply this: I have gained this summer a sense which I have never had before, of the path which I must follow from henceforth; it is this which I am trying a little to describe to you here—and I have not finished yet. I must follow that path unquestioningly and uncompromisingly myself; I ask you to regard my decisions as to every detail of that path as considered and final, *as not involving you in any way* but to be unquestioned by you as far as *I* am concerned. I ask you also to feel yourself free, of any responsibility whatever for me, whether that of trying to modify impulses or emotions in me which you fear may be dangerous, or of shielding me from any influence whatever.

These two things I consider absolutely necessary for our happiness. If in addition to this you can have an *inner* confidence, joy, and pride, as well, you will give me *inconceivable* joy, vitality, and perfect ecstasy. This is what I shall strive always to deserve, with *all my soul!* But it is the last thing that either of us can demand, in the smallest sense.

And now, once more for what is concrete. I shall not say much now as to what I consider my ultimate goals, as they are as yet perhaps only dreams, and I don't wish them for the present to become more than that, or to have any place in my thoughts. Perhaps, after all, my ultimate goal may be summed up in the one conception of self culture.

At present, however, I want to feel even this as subordinate to my musical development, or rather as a part of it. The kind of music I want to write is above all the expression of the kind of person I want to be. If I seem to be putting the cart before the horse, however, you will understand that it is merely because, for the sake of order, discipline, clarity, I have put the musical aim first in my mind.

First, at the basis of everything is the body, as I realize more and more every day, even in my smallest daily sensations. At the beginning of the summer, when I was covered with hives, unhappy, and homesick here in Paris, I found that I *had* to take care of my body and keep it in some sort of health. Later I found that the changes which regular exercise made not only in my general state of being, but in my physique,—in my whole disposition and my personality,—I began to feel a strong impulse not only for keeping in good condition—keeping well—but in *building up* vitality and strength—a really vigorous and perhaps someday even a beautiful body, as I would so love to do, for you, my darling. I have gone so far; the results have been so obvious and so unexpected, that I think this thing alone has contributed quite inestimably to my summer; and it is something which I can never allow myself to lose hold of, even for a day, though it entails discipline which never ceases to seem difficult and severe. Naturally it is not only a matter of exercise, but one of food also.

Secondly—and this is perhaps the most difficult part of my letter, as it is a matter that depends so much on circumstances that have to be met as they come—there is the organization of my life with other people, the changes which I am determined to make in my relationships with them, and the organization of my life itself.

I feel in the first place that the tasks which I have before me are so great that I must make my life, in all its aspects, and above all the state of my mind and my attitude—as *simple* and as *clear* as possible. For this purpose I shall need a tremendous amount of self-discipline—to limit myself in a thousand ways; I may adopt some methods of procedure which will seem strange to you, and unduly strict; though I try very hard to keep everything of that kind absolutely within the bounds of practicality.

But that isn't important for this letter, as it is something which only circumstances can really determine, as they arise. I want to give you some idea of what my attitude towards other people will be, and towards the organization of my life in relation to the rest of the world of human beings.

First of all, my teaching. I haven't planned it out nearly so much in detail as I had wanted to—so full has my mind been of other things. I have, however, the intention of aiming always at being absolutely concrete—of proceeding from facts and not from generalities—but of deducing the generalities from the facts; of making my pupils depend—teaching them how to depend—on their own senses, and cultivate them.

It seems to me that the most fundamental thing in teaching is first of all cultivating in the students the *technique* of each of the processes through which they must go in order to learn. This is crudely put, perhaps. But first of all I shall try to show them how to observe, to simply use their senses. In musical history, for instance, I shall teach by means of illustrations, proceeding from these and commenting on them, rather than giving lectures and using the illustrations to supplement the lectures.

In my "theory" classes I shall go much more from the study of works than I did before, and deduce working principles always from *facts*—and from the most obvious facts possible—the works of the great composers, the exercises which the pupils themselves bring, and the corrections we make in them. I shall try above all to teach the pupils *how* to study and *how* to learn, and shall, as I began to do last year, leave as much as possible to them. In other words I shall eliminate as far as possible, *all theory,* and try to give my classes as much as possible the atmosphere of *practical* activity, using *theory* only as a sort of systematization, *ordering* of the knowledge gained through the solution of practical problems.—This is, I am convinced, the only way in which the courses can become profitable either for me or for the pupils—and in this way it ought to be intensely profitable for all of us. I have begun the planning of my courses from this point of view; but most of it will have to come, naturally, as the different problems arise—except in the *history.*

As regards the world in general, you will find that I am no longer, in any sense in *revolt* against it as I have been so often and in such a futile way, in the past. Self confidence has brought with it, I think I can honestly say, a much keener sense of reality, as has the mere experience of travelling. You will find some of my opinions changed by the contact that I have had with Europe, as well as by the shifting of values in my mind. Doubtless we will have arguments—but you will see that no one ever need fear an argument with me—that is another thing that self-confidence has done—and you, least of all, my blessed one. Over here things look very differently from what they do at home—there is absolutely no getting beyond that fact; and one is bound to change some of one's opinions, even if only to readjust them temporarily.

Finally, as to *personal* relationships. First I have spoken of my desire for *solitude.* This is only partly a matter of *physical* solitude; I must have *spiritual* solitude as well. The latter I feel and the former, too,—depends *entirely* upon myself. It is largely a question of attitude. I have already told you that I don't intend to get involved *in any degree whatsoever* in the spiritual crises or the personal situations of other people! In the first place this is a matter of self-preservation; but in the second place I believe that composure, self-command, is the only attitude that can be of use in any situation whatever. And I have determined to keep my mouth *tight shut* on all personal subjects, except with you; it is the only way, darling one, to keep from doing a good deal of harm and getting involved where one doesn't intend to.

This is to be practically an absolute rule with me, to be broken only in extremely rare cases where I see my way absolutely clear to be of use or of help in case of real need. When I have, moreover, such supremely important things to think about as Dante and all the other things connected with my music or with my experiences this summer, I don't expect to find such things of the slightest interest.

Furthermore, after being in touch, as I feel that I have been more closely at times this summer than ever before, with Dante, Leonardo, Bach, and many others of the really titanic and eternal spirits of the world, I will probably feel less eager than before to keep in very close touch with the spirits of Ruth Edwards, Betty Moore, or even Beryl Rubinstein[1]—and many other spirits of that general calibre! *Genuine friendship* always means a good deal to me—whether with equals (and beside you, darling, I consider only Bloch and Lucienne,[2] in Cleveland, as being in any sense my equals) or with fairly intelligent admirers, like Douglas. Other relationships—with the unintelligent, the simply more or less egotistical, or the not wholly sympathetic, require too much energy for their maintenance, and I shall not go any further than ordinary courtesy demands.

[. . .]

Your *madly, passionately, gloriously* devoted
Roger

1. Ruth Edwards (1895–1989) had joined the piano faculty of the Cleveland Institute in 1921 and taught there until 1972. Douglas Moore's wife's name was Emily, so he is probably not referring to her. Rubinstein (1898–1952) was a pianist and teacher at the Cleveland Institute of Music from 1921 and director from 1932.
2. One of Bloch's two daughters.

CHAPTER

1925-1928

TWO

SESSIONS RETURNED to the United States from Florence, via Paris and London, in mid-September 1924, and in the winter of 1924–25 was again in Cleveland. Copland published an article in *Modern Music* heralding Sessions and sixteen others as "America's Young Men of Promise."[1] Having struck up a friendship both in person and through their extended correspondence, Copland and Sessions conceived of presenting a series of concerts bearing their names in New York, London, and Paris. Since Sessions would remain in Europe until 1933, while Copland did the real work of organizing these concerts in New York, transatlantic letters were their means of communication.[2] Copland saved eighty-eight letters from Sessions and Barbara, and eighteen letters from Copland to Sessions survive (although there must have been many more).[3]

Three letters from Ernest Bloch to his most promising student are preserved, revealing the *Sturm und Drang* of Bloch's personality. He had become the director of the San Francisco Conservatory (1925–1930), where he wrote to Sessions (June 27, 1926). For most of the 1930s Bloch lived in his homeland of Switzerland, the fulfillment of his devout wish expressed in his letter of May 31, 1928.

Sessions's affection for Jean Binet was expressed in a collection of memoirs published after Binet's death in 1960.[4] "I owe to Jean more than perhaps to any other person—certainly more intimately than to any other—whatever knowledge I have of Europe itself. . . . No human being ever existed who was less capable of malice, and it was difficult if not impossible to sustain malice towards anyone whatever in Jean's presence. . . . Jean's music is above all else completely his own. Like Jean himself, it is first of all music of the country-side, of the land of Suisse Romande; music which one loves for its happy existence and its complete self-sufficiency." Sessions frequently expressed his fondness for Binet well into his seventies and eighties.

During the summer of 1926 Barbara Sessions underwent successful abdominal surgery in Paris, which, however, resulted in a lingering infection that was to plague her for the next several years. Barbara's sister, Rosamond, recalls her as a person of "delicate health." References to her ill health recur frequently in Sessions's correspondence with Copland and others.

Nadia Boulanger and her mother, Princess Raissa Mychetsky (1858–1935), continued to live in Paris; both Sessions's (fifteen) and Barbara's (nine) letters to Nadia frequently allude to Mme. Boulanger. The correspondence with Boulanger began with a letter dated August 30, 1926 (F-PBN), thanking Boulanger for her concern over Barbara and for another favor: "I hardly dare speak of the 1200fr— you were so good to lend them to me."

Serge Koussevitzky performed Sessions's Symphony in E Minor during the 1926–27 season with the Boston Symphony Orchestra. As was to become a pattern in Sessions's dealings with conductors and performers, Sessions delayed sending the score and parts, first, he writes, because of his wife's illness. The score was promised for the first week of January 1927, but by January 25 Sessions had completed only the first two movements. After complicated mailing arrangements were employed, the score and parts did arrive in Boston. However, Sessions was to change part of the symphony and revise the score after having heard it performed in Boston.

Sessions's first two letters to Koussevitzky are in French; later he would write three to him in Russian, and eventually both settled upon English for their correspondence. Koussevitzky was moved by the success of the symphony to write a laudatory letter of recommendation for Sessions to win the Rome Prize.

Russian-born Nicolas Slonimsky[5] described himself in relation to Serge Koussevitzky as a "surrogate orchestra." When Koussevitzky became conductor of the Boston Symphony Orchestra, Slonimsky played scores at the piano for Koussevitzky to rehearse conducting. Then he became de facto secretary and translator to and from French (he describes Koussevitzky's French as "lame.") At a crucial time in Sessions's relationship with Koussevitzky—the spring of 1927, when Koussevitzky conducted Sessions's First Symphony at the Boston

Symphony Orchestra—Slonimsky was fired from Koussevitzky's employ (by his wife, Natalie) and Slonimsky never saw him again.[6]

1. Aaron Copland, "America's Young Men of Promise," *Modern Music* 3, no. 3 (March–April 1926): 13–18.

2. For a discussion of the first season of the Copland-Sessions Concerts, with quotations from some of these letters, see Aaron Copland and Vivian Perlis, *Copland: 1900 through 1942* (New York: St. Martin's Press, 1984), 143–50.

3. For a discussion of their correspondence, see Andrea Olmstead, "The Copland-Sessions Correspondence," *Tempo*, no. 175 (December 1990): 2–5.

4. *Jean Binet—17 Octobre 1893–24 Février 1960* (Nyon, Switzerland: Courrier de la Côte, 1961) includes reminiscences of Binet by Jacques Chenevière, Ernest Ansermet, Frank Martin, Nadia Boulanger, Roger Sessions, Jean Cuttat, Luigi Dallapiccola, Franz Walter, and Adolf Streuli.

5. Nicolas Slonimsky (b. 1894) wrote his autobiography, entitled *Perfect Pitch: A Life Story* (London: Oxford University Press, 1988), and *Baker's Biographical Dictionary of Musicians* (8 editions), as well as *Music Since 1900*.

6. Slonimsky, *Perfect Pitch*, 105.

▼

Roger Sessions to Igor Stravinsky[1]
als CH-Bsacher

Sir,—   Sunday evening [February 15, 1925]

I wish to thank you for letting me speak with you yesterday evening, especially considering the pain that you were suffering.[2] You know well that it was a very great privilege for me, knowing of my admiration for you and for your masterpieces. It was also a privilege to be able to hear your magnificent Concerto, and it repaid me a thousand times for the trip from Cleveland.

Permit me the hope of seeing you again sometime, be it in America or be it in Europe; and please accept my best wishes for a good trip.

Very sincerely yours,
Roger H. Sessions

1. Translated from the French by Andrea Olmstead.

2. While on her first American concert tour, Boulanger was in Cleveland when Stravinsky conducted there (February 12 and 14, 1925). She introduced Sessions to the older composer, who invited Sessions to ride with him on the train from Cleveland to Philadelphia for a rehearsal and performance of the Piano Concerto, entertainingly described in Igor Stravinsky, *An Autobiography* (New York: Simon & Schuster, 1936; reprint, New York: Norton, 1962), 122. Although Stravinsky was friendly, Sessions's lifelong shyness got in the way of his talking further with him.

▼

Ernest Bloch to Roger Sessions[1]

als US-NYpease

June 27, 1926
San Francisco

My dear Roger:

As now you speak all languages and I speak none, you will not find it unseemly that I use my mother tongue . . . in this way, perhaps, the errors of grammar and style will be less obvious. Do not think that my long silence means anything at all—unless it be the harassed life of a 46-year-old man who, after ten years of exile and five of hell, had to start his life anew. But you know all this. My wife must have told you about my existence. The city is beautiful. I have good friends; nevertheless, I am not happy. My health is not good. One becomes old, the carcass creaks, one feels like an old rubber, wrinkled, broken, without elasticity. All is dulled in the end . . . even suffering.

Your letters, your beautiful letters—and cards—touched me and brought me great joy. And also the news that this [Guggenheim] Foundation has acted and done well. I had written them several times (for others had asked my support, G. Antheil, B. Rogers, and . . . de Leone!).[2] I had let them know that you were the one who had to come before the others, and for a reason.

So, here now, you are free, your own master . . . and deep in work, of which no one could rejoice more than I. Imagining what it means for you, and amicably, I envy you . . . I should have had this when I was your age. Now it is too late. I no longer belong to my time. I am a romantic fossil lost amidst this epoch that I do not understand, that I do not like, and . . . do not envy.

Your "explanations," dear friend, touched me also . . . But there was no need to explain . . . I have always understood—without even being Hans Sachs. It is normal, natural, and necessary that at a certain moment the seed has to detach itself from the plant and live its life. Do you remember a morning, in Cleveland, in the "Old Building," when you asked me what you should do with your students, and I sent you "packing"! I already felt then that it was necessary for you to bring out your own personality. I knew that it was there, latent in you, but a constraint, and "inhibition," as they say here, interposed itself between you and others. It is always a joy for me to see beings emancipate themselves, musically—for sentimentally, I would never permit myself to judge. To each his experience! For they also are necessary. It is almost indispensable in life to take sometimes the "wrong way" in order to appreciate the right, later.

You know, of course, that to my very great regret, I cannot think of going to Paris to see my family this year. I hope to make up for it next year and come in May to spend five months in Europe. I need to resume contact, be it for orienting myself a little, and perhaps tolerate more cheerfully my existence in America, though I have great fear of no longer belonging anywhere . . . except perhaps in some lost corner, cut off from the world, to live in peace what life is left for me.

Don't be put off, dear friend, by my silence, and continue to give me your news; you know that it is precious, and all that touches you, I take to heart.

I am certain that your actual work will come to a good end, and am impatient to know it. You know that I expect enormously from you, more than all the others.

My most affectionate thoughts to you and Barbara.

Your faithful,
Ernest Bloch

1. Translated from the French by Suzanne Bloch. Sessions was now living in Paris.
2. Possibly a reference to Bloch's student Robert Mills Delaney (1903–56).

▼

Roger Sessions to Jean and Denise Binet
als CH-Bsacher

Friday, July 30 [1926]
Dearest Binets,   14 via delle Campora [Florence]

Thank you for your letter, + for the photos. May I have some more copies of the latter? I know my family in America would like to see how we look now. The one of Barbara and that of both of us is adorable—the one of *Barbara sola* shows a little, I'm afraid, that she has not been well. But the first is one of the best she has ever had taken, + I [would] love to have it. No, Jean, it does not do you justice!

She is, alas, not here yet. Just as she had taken her trunk to the station + would have started the next morning early, there started a certain regular process which made it necessary for her to rest, for a few days; and as she was tired + excited, a little fever, also, came back. So she went right to the hospital—much the worst thing to do— and her doctor has advised an additional week's rest, to get completely rid of the little infection that is left. There is nothing dangerous whatever—only these things go slowly, as you may know. So I expect her quite confidently by the end of next week.

I am delighted that you are so happy at Pardigon. Your letter was so fresh + full of enthusiasm, and it did me good to get it, as indeed it always does me good to hear from you. I'm sure Pardigon must be a great deal like Italy, thought it's hard to believe it is quite so wonderful. But in coming along the Riviera except for the nightmares of Cannes, Nice, + Monaco, it looked quite Italian, even though when one crossed the Italian border one became aware of a real difference—more whiteness, more sunlight. But your little sketch of Gassin is *absolutely* Tuscany, provided the colors are the same.

All right, I won't speak more of the Villa delle Campora—if you persist in not coming to see for yourself! I understand—but *damn* understanding anyway!

How long will you be at Pardigon, anyway? Sh– sh– but how about some days together in September, along the Ligurian Coast—San Remo, Bordighera, Allasio, Santa Margherita? A visa costs less for you than it does for us, hence the suggestion of Italy instead of France. Don't breathe a word to Barbara but it might be possible.

Write us—and very much love to you all.

Roger

[P.S.] Love, greetings, compliments, whichever is most proper, to all Vernets.

▼

Roger Sessions to Aaron Copland
als US-DLC

August 24, 1926
Neuilly-s-Seine

Dear Aaron,—

This afternoon I heard Nadia play over your [organ] symphony,[1] and while I am not in the habit of writing this particular kind of letter, I can't refrain from giving you a piece of my mind on the subject. First of all the symphony is magnificent, and I was more impressed than I can tell you. While one does not, as you know perfectly well, get everything from a work on one hearing, I did carry away a big impression—a really big one. It was a revelation and a surprise to me—a revelation in an absolute sense, and a surprise,

– 65 –

because the other works of yours which I know did not lead me to expect nearly as much. It was also a very great pleasure, it made it possible for me to share to the full Nadia's opinion of you—an opinion of which I am sure you must be aware, + which I need not enlarge upon.

But all this is not the "piece of my mind" which I feel like giving you. *That* consists in an impulse to give you hell for two things. First of all, for allowing yourself when you can write music of your own like that, to take any interest whatever in other people's music, and especially in the music of other young Americans. Can't you see that any two pages of your symphony are worth all the collected works of the "jeune americains" that you so generously allow yourself to be interested in, and who have got to stand or fall on their own strength?—and that the really great contribution you can make with your own music is vastly more important than anything you can do by organizing performances for other people? Please take this from one who is quite aware of, and I hope not too ungrateful for, the effective efforts you have made for him. Seriously + quite impersonally, I would be thoroughly happy to see you push your own fortunes, without wasting precious energy on those of other people or on anything so vague and dubious as the "future of American music."

The second thing for which you deserve hell, and worse, is your assumption of the title and, let us say, the obligations of a "New York composer," or even a "young American composer." You are quite aware, I know, that I feel a certain irony in regard to schools and groups, and, in music at least, a respect for individuals who stand by themselves in the most profound sense. And if I find your symphony not only far bigger and more impressive, but in the real sense more *original* and more perfect than the Theatre-music, the nocturne, + the serenade,[2] I feel that it is because the others are the result, or perhaps the expression of a *parti pris* [fixed position], a deliberate attempt to mould your thought along lines which are not only *not* your own, but something far less that what you have in yourself. I mean that I find the music of Aaron Copland speaking for himself, incomparably finer than that of Aaron Copland the New York Composer, quite aside from the pleasure and amusement that the latter gives me. The former is far more interesting and far more original (in the real sense of the word) than the latter, whose language may be one that for the moment seems newer, but is certainly, as far as I can see, one which is not his own, and which is certainly an infinitely more limited one than that which he has shown he can speak, with assurance and authority.

Have I made myself clear? You know me well enough, I hope, to have confidence in my respect for you, + my sympathy with + interest in all that you do. I can't pretend that I think I have risked your friendship in speaking so frankly; but I do feel, in spite of my confidence in you, so strongly and so anxiously about this that I would take pretty big risks in order to express myself on the subject. And it would take a good deal less confidence than I have in you, to make me entertain any *serious* doubts about your future. I hope you know that.

You will be surprised, perhaps, to get this letter from France. As a matter of fact I did go on to Florence, as soon as it seemed sure that Barbara could follow me in a week's time; but she overdid after I left, + had to go back to the hospital for another + longer siege. So I waited three weeks instead of one, and finally, as the probable length of her stay was very uncertain I came on here three weeks ago. And finally the doctor says we can leave next Monday. Do write me again—14 Via delle Campora, Florence,—before you sail.

The summer has been pretty well upset, + I have been a good deal under a strain since the end of May with all this on my mind. But I plan to finish the [first] symphony in time to get it Koussevitzky early in January.[3]

The best wishes from both of us—+ do write to me. There aren't too many people with whom [I] can talk.

Always faithfully,
Roger

P.S. I speak rather unconcernedly, it seems! B—— has been at no time seriously ill—but it is first a long process of getting rid of infection— + one worries in spite of oneself. She is really in wonderful general condition now, but will have to go easy for several weeks more, + get good + strong. I would write more—if I were not very sleepy.

Good luck
R——

1. Copland's Symphony for Organ and Orchestra had been premiered January 11, 1925, by the New York Symphony Orchestra conducted by Walter Damrosch, who remarked to the audience, "If a young man can write a piece like this at the age of twenty-three, in five years he will be ready to commit murder." The symphony is dedicated to Nadia Boulanger, who played organ at the premiere.

2. *Music for the Theatre,* for chamber orchestra, had been premiered November 20,

1925, by Serge Koussevitzky, to whom it is dedicated, and the Boston Symphony Orchestra. Two Pieces for Violin and Piano (Nocturne and "Ukulele Serenade") had been premiered by Samuel Dushkin and Copland in Paris, May 5, 1926.

3. Copland had spoken to Koussevitzky on Sessions's behalf.

▼

Barbara Sessions to Nadia Boulanger
als F-PBN

August 29 [1926]

Dear Mlle. Boulanger—   Neuilly

Your kind messages of sympathy + encouragement have meant so much to me that I can't leave Paris without thanking you for them,— and also for other things of which it is more difficult to speak. Although I have seen you so rarely, the knowledge that I was near you was often a source of help and sustenance to me this winter, and whenever I did see you the experience was always an inspiration.

And most of all, of course, I am grateful to you for what you are to Roger: for the magnificent friendship and understanding which you give him, and for the encouragement which it is to him always to see you. He comes from you with his knowledge of his own powers strengthened, and happy because he can communicate with you so fully + freely.

I look forward to the time when I may myself see you more often, and perhaps more intimately. In a sense, my relation with you has thus far necessarily been rather an official one. It would be such a joy to welcome you in Florence, and we shall hope every day for news that you are coming.

In the meantime please accept again my thanks + my very best wishes for both you and your mother.

Most sincerely,
Barbara Foster Sessions

▼

Roger Sessions to Aaron Copland
als US-DLC

September 18, 1926

Dear Aaron,—   Florence

Thank you so much for your two letters. Note that I thank you for both of them, please! In other words hearing from you is a pleasure even when one of the letters contains a request for an article.[1] On one condition—that you never ask me for another! I have sketched out some notes on the concert and Barbara is at this moment in the act of trying to put them into intelligible shape. I trust that will do. I think you + Teddy [Chanler] are likely to still think of me in a friendly manner—I'm not so sure about G. Antheil + Virgil Thomson,[2] though. I have no illusions of a very extravagant nature as to what may be their present attitude. I hope you will see the article before it goes to press, + think in fact that I will send it to you in Paris. There will be one paragraph mentioning N.B., which I am a little in doubt about— + I shall leave you free to make any changes you see fit.[3]

As to your first letter, it flattered me, showed me that in some ways I had not made myself clear, and reassured me as to the immediate necessity of making myself clear, though I now proceed to do so. My letter was prompted not so much by a tremendous contrast between the symphony + the "Music for the Theatre" (though I do respond very much more to the former + feel that it is a more truly individual work) as by the memory of your having told me when we first met that the "Music for the Theatre" was your most characteristic work. It was that, + not any feeling of dissatisfaction with the "Music for the Theatre" itself, that led me to question whether you really valued the symphony highly enough. That, you see, combined with what you said about being a "N.Y. composer" etc. led me to wonder whether you were not—temporarily, no doubt—going off on a vein which was smaller than your truest one. For my own satisfaction let me tell you that of course I realized that you were not going to take me too seriously, since you alone know what you want, + that therefore I allowed myself the liberty of speaking as forcefully as I really felt. I would be the last to advise you *seriously* not to take an interest in other people's music; for I can see that it is so much a part of you. We are quite different in that way, to a certain extent at least, and I can see advantages in both attitudes, though of course I am highly prejudiced in favor of my own. As to jazz, here I must not have made myself clear; for I don't remember having for a moment any feeling that this influence was a bad one, musically; it was only what I had the impression *was* a "parti pris" in your present attitude towards your work which worried me.

Such a letter as I wrote is of course always written in order to provoke a reaction of some sort far rather than to *convince*. I hope you know that I have entirely too much respect for you + confidence in you as an artist—*especially* since I have heard the symphony—to want or expect anything more than a reaction. And nobody knows better than I that even a "parti pris" may be sometimes necessary + salutary as a phase of one's development. This has been more than once true in my case, I know, and it may be true in all cases provided one is independent enough to slide out of it at the right moment!

Well—to hell with words! Of course I am prejudiced against all aesthetic dogma—prejudiced against it in a sufficiently fundamental way to realize that it is necessary at certain moments and for certain individuals. But I am really happy that the "New York composer" idea has been given up, perhaps partly for the purely personal reason that it identified you in my mind with certain people whose work (in various fields of activity) is not for a moment to be compared with, or mentioned in the same breath with yours.

Here's hoping you will find a poem soon! And I hope the concerto is finished + above all it pleases you.[4]

Our villa is enchanting—perfect weather, tranquility. Barbara is gaining splendidly, + we both feel very happy to have passed through what, as we look back on it, seems a very dark time indeed. I hope that the next time I have a chance to see something of you, I will be more myself. I was not really myself at all, while I was in Paris this spring. But what we have now is really ample compensation. Florence is as gorgeous as ever. I have become a little reacquainted with the city after absence + concentration on my work. Lucienne Bloch is here, and I have had great fun showing her the places that I love the most. For some reason Florence + my home in Massachusetts are the two places in the world where I feel thoroughly free.

The symphony progresses. I am really enthusiastic about it.

I suppose you will be sailing before long. Do let me hear from you occasionally. And, by the way, however little credit you may assume, I shall always be grateful to you for speaking in my behalf to Koussie

+ also to Henry Allen Moe, Esq.[5] It helped—and even if it had not I would be as grateful.—Good luck to you.

As always
Roger

[P.S.] Give my best to Harold[6] please, when you see him. Address, after Oct. 1st, Villino Corbignano—Berenson, Ponte a Mensola, presso Settignano, Firenze. Till then, 14 Via delle Campora.

1. Roger Sessions, "An American Evening Abroad," *Modern Music* 4 (November 1926): 33–36, a review of the Société Musicale Indépendante's Paris concert in the spring of 1926, which had presented music of Boulanger's American students: Copland's Two Pieces for Violin and Piano and *As It Fell upon a Day* for soprano, flute, and clarinet; George Antheil's String Quartet No. 1; Theodore Chanler's Sonata for Violin and Piano; Virgil Thomson's *Sonata da chiesa* for clarinet, trumpet, viola, horn, and trombone; piano pieces by Herbert Elwell; and Walter Piston's Piano Sonata.
2. Virgil Thomson (1896–1989) studied with Boulanger 1921–22.
3. Evidently Copland cut the paragraph relating to Boulanger; she is not mentioned in the article.
4. Copland's Piano Concerto was premiered by Serge Koussevitzky and the Boston Symphony Orchestra January 28, 1927, with Copland as soloist.
5. The head of the Guggenheim Foundation.
6. The writer and director Harold Clurman (1901–80), later cofounder of the Group Theater, was Copland's Paris roommate and longtime friend.

▼

Roger Sessions to Nicolas Slonimsky
als US-DLC

January 25, 1927
Villino Corbignano
Settignano, Florence

My dear Mr. Slonimsky,—

I sent, this morning, the first two movements, and the first section of the finale, of the symphony, and am wiring you to that effect. The rest of the score I could not get copied quite in time, and will send it with the parts next week from Paris. It all ought to reach you not more than a week at the very most after this first package, as things go very much faster from Paris when directed especially to one of the big liners. This package goes in care of a friend, who sails this evening from Genoa, + reaches Boston on the 8th. I have arranged for a cousin of mine,[1] resident in Boston, to call at the boat for my package, and deliver it at Symphony Hall. In case she does not make the proper connections, the package will be mailed, either from Boston or New York, where the boat lands on the 10th, and where my friend will disembark.

I would be most grateful if you would cable me at my expense on receipt of the *second* package, so that I may be sure everything has gone through safely. SESSIONS, SETTIGNANO, is my cable address.

In regard to the score of the second movement: my original intention was to write the first section from [No.] 24 through 29 for solo violins and violas, and, at 27, solo 'celli; the same from 39 to the end. For three reasons I decided against this, and left the score as it now stands, violas and 'celli divided, half the first and half the second violins. The tone quality of the *solo* instruments would suit my ideas much better, however, and *if* (1) the solo instruments could play expressively without being swallowed by the brass, as seems quite possible, and (2) as seems less likely, the small body of tone resulting from this combination would not seem in too violent contrast with the sonority of the first movement, and (3) the opening notes of the viola can be brought out with the utmost clarity against the B (written D) of the trumpet; then I would rather keep to my original conception. I have purposely refrained from "bowing" most of the string passages in the *Largo* because it would make a difference whether solo strings or the entire body were used; and I thought that for that purpose either Mr. Koussevitzky, or one of the violinists of the orchestra, might be willing to go over this movement with me, when I get to Boston.

I hope the score is clear in other respects. I have not used many nuances, as it is my instinct, + has been pretty well confirmed by experience, that too many detailed indications of inflection are apt to supersede the natural musical instinct of the individual performer. So I have tried to make my indications as *general* as is compatible with accuracy. Perhaps I shall learn differently by experience, but it seems to me always that a performance according to the feelings of the performer is much more satisfactory even when it is not *completely* in accord with the composer's own ideas, as far as details are concerned.

I have chosen my tempi with care; and in general it seems to me that my music should be played without too much *rubato*. In the case of the first movement this seems to me absolutely essential. The tempo of the *finale* should be as fast as clarity permits.

But I have written too much already, + can only take refuge in

Rousseau's (or was it Emerson's?) excuse for writing a long letter because I had not the time to write a short one.

With best wishes to you + Mr. Koussevitzky.

Sincerely yours,
Roger H. Sessions

1. Catharine Huntington (b. December 29, 1889; d. February 27, 1987), Sessions's cousin, was an actress, director, and producer who managed the Provincetown Players. As such, she produced an O'Neill play every year for a decade: she owned the Provincetown Playhouse from 1940 to 1973 and acted until she was eighty-six. Sessions was devoted to her throughout his life.

▼

Roger Sessions to Aaron Copland
als US-DLC

February 25, 1927
Dear Aaron,—   Settignano

I hope we are still on speaking terms! and as a matter of fact I would have written you long ago if I hadn't been so busy that I put it off. I hope this was also the case with you, + that we *are* still on speaking terms—at least that. Barbara tells me always that, to people who don't know me very well, I misrepresent myself, + that what I intend as purely ironic and picturesque emphasis is taken seriously. If there was anything of that kind in the letters I wrote you last fall, I hope you will know how sincerely sorry I am. I really didn't mean to be either belligerent or, in any way, disrespectful, and I trust you to know it.

The immediate cause of this letter is twofold: first to tell you how much I liked your article on jazz in *Modern Music*.[1] It seems to me to be the final word in a tiresome and useless controversy; and you have said it so clearly that, if I had any faith in the ordinary run of human intelligence, I would believe that it would put an end to such controversy. While I am not sure that I entirely agree with you as to the possibilities of jazz, it is obvious to me that the discovery and exploitation of these possibilities is a matter of individual temperament and depends on what once was called "inner necessity"—an outworn phrase which, however, stands for something perfectly genuine, + which has never been satisfactorily replaced. What you say about the inevitable difference between European + American ideas of jazz is of course very true, and excellent.

The second reason why I am writing you is to tell you that I shall be in America from Mar. 15 to April 30th. I don't yet know what Koussie's exact plans in regard to the Symphony are. I had a letter from Slonimsky in January saying that he surely intended to play it, this spring, or, in case the music arrived too late, in the fall.[2] I sent the score in two installments, which arrived a week apart; both have gotten there all right, as a cable from Slonimsky last week told me. The parts will arrive within another week. I suppose that if Koussie had changed his plans, S—— would have told me so in the cable, especially as he knew I was planning to come—though, as I told him, I shall go anyway in order to be with my family. I will let you know how it comes out. But I do want to see you. If for any reason or excuse we could be in Boston together I would be more than delighted; but I shall in any case spend some time in N.Y. before sailing, + will see as much of you as I have time for.

I am most anxious, among other things, to hear your [Piano] Concerto.[3] A stupid female relative gave me a very bad morning by sending me the Boston reviews, with the implication that I would be happy at the supposed discomfiture of a rival! Needless to say the effect produced was a quite different one; it made me even more eager than I had been before to hear the Concerto; the critics were obviously challenged by it, and in spite of a real respect for Mr. Philip Hale, I seldom agree with him, especially in regard to contemporary music.[4] And the reviews gave a kind of what Bloch would call a "new Copland" which I am most eager to become acquainted with.

I shall not go into details about the symphony, as it always seems quite useless to try to write directly about music—especially one's own. But I do feel that I have left the [Organ] Chorales far behind, and the Black Maskers still further. The latter now seems very youthful + uncoordinated + over-intellectualized, the former very tentative and almost theoretical, though I was not aware of this at the time I composed them. [In the symphony] I think there is not a trace of Bloch; and while the influence of Stravinsky is obvious, I feel that it is a technical influence and not a spiritual one—if I may use a crude expression to indicate a very subtle thing. N.B., to whom I played it in Paris three weeks ago, had the same impression very strongly, and also felt that it was by far the best thing I had done. I have now started working regularly on *The Fall of the House of Usher,* of which I told you last summer, but have not fairly gotten into it yet.[5]

I hope you have had a good winter; I heard both from Eleanor Phillips[6] + Teddy Chanler that you have had at any rate a busy one.

Ours has been a peaceful and busy, and on the whole a very happy one, in spite of the fact that Barbara's complete recovery has been slow. I am going to leave her in excellent care at Bern, while I am in America, and we hope very much that she will be herself again, completely, by the time I return. The one really dark moment of the winter came with the death of my father early in January,[7] he was the member of my family whom I cared the most for, + with whom I had the most in common; and the loss is a very great one indeed— and for Barbara too, since she adored my father and he her. I am comforted in some measure by really wonderful memories, and the consciousness of his influence, which was of a kind that will be with me as long as I live—

This letter is already too long, + I bring it to a speedy conclusion; I must not however forget to thank you for playing the chorales and above all perhaps for your part in saving them from the harmonium— that would have been a disaster indeed, I must say! and I was horrified at the mere thought of it. If you get time do send a line to me at Hadley, Mass., where I shall go directly after landing on March 15. In any case I look forward very much to seeing you, + hope we can connect. Remember me, please to Harold Klurman + also to Eleanor Phillips, whom we enjoyed seeing very much.

As always
Roger H. S.

1. Aaron Copland, "Jazz Structure and Influence," *Modern Music* 4, no. 2 (January–February 1927): 9–14.

2. The Boston Symphony Orchestra did perform the symphony on April 22, 23, and 26, 1927, with Koussevitzky conducting.

3. Copland had performed his concerto with the Boston Symphony in Boston January 28 and 29, 1927, with Koussevitzky conducting and in New York February 3, 1927. This performance, and its favorable reception in New York, especially by Paul Rosenfeld, was to place Copland among important American composers.

4. Hale (1854–1934), music and drama critic for the Boston *Herald* (1903–33), also wrote program notes for the Boston Symphony Orchestra (1901–34). Hale wrote for the *Herald*, "Copland's Piano Concerto shows a shocking lack of taste, of proportion. . . . [T]he piano is struck by fingers apparently directed at random." H. T. Parker wrote in the *Evening Transcript* about "the ogre with that terrible Concerto" (quoted in Aaron Copland and Vivian Perlis, *Copland: 1900 through 1942* [New York: St. Martin's Press, 1984], 131).

5. Samuel Eliot, Jr., who had directed Smith College's performances of *The Black Maskers,* had proposed Sessions write an opera based on Poe's short story; it would be left incomplete.

6. Eleanor Phillips (1881–1975), a singer and Boston music patron.

7. Archibald Sessions died in Brooklyn, January 5, 1927. He is buried in the Old Hadley Cemetery.

▼

Aaron Copland to Roger Sessions
als US-NYpease

March 18 [1927]

Dear Roger,—   223 West 78th Street, New York

I was delighted with your letter, the idea of your being in America and the thought that we shall see each other soon (which, incidentally, will save me from writing at great length now.) And how delightfully silly of you to have imagined that there was a shadow of a misunderstanding between us when my not writing to you is quite simply explained by the concerto, that is finishing it and playing it. That was in February, and then of course I thought it was too late to write, since Teddy has been announcing your arrival for the past month and a half.

It goes without saying that I am very keen to see the Symphony. As far as I know Koussie expects to do it in April—he even told me he might do an All-American program, though he didn't say whether or not he thought of doing the Symphony then.[1] Anyway I know he is very favorably disposed towards you and that an eventual performance is certain. I would even say it was certain for April if one could say that any conductor's plans are certain. Let's hope that Fate wills me in Boston at that time; otherwise I will have to be satisfied with a muddled version over the radio.

You are apparently not aware of the fact that I am returning to Europe this spring due to the fact that they are doing the "Music for the Theatre" at the festival in Frankurt. Wouldn't it be nice if we could sail together? I am thinking of going on the Homeric, April 30th but have made no reservations yet. If you know the boat you are taking, do let me know it.[2] (I travel 2nd class as a rule, but am considering 3rd tourist—and you?) I shall be in Paris until the end of June—then to Frankfurt—and then somewhere for the summer in Germany or Italy.

I'm glad you like the Jazz article. It has helped considerably to get the whole business out of my system. You will find me a young man admirably stripped of all theories now. Let's hope it lasts.

Here's to seeing you soon.

Yours,
Aaron

P.S. My telephone no. is Susquehanna 0528

1. The program would not be all-American; other works besides Sessions's Symphony were Richard Strauss's *Tod und Verklärung* and the "Dance of the Seven Veils" from *Salome,* and George Whitefield Chadwick's 1915 symphonic ballad *Tam O'Shanter.* Chadwick (1854–1931), the director of the New England Conservatory and a noted composer in the Germanic tradition, was also present.

2. Copland and Sessions would travel together by boat to Europe in late April.

Paul Rosenfeld, who reviewed the premiere of Sessions's Symphony No. 1 for the Boston *Globe,* was predisposed to Sessions, having already written a laudatory essay on *The Black Maskers* incidental music three years earlier.[1] Calling Sessions "a notable talent," he wrote of the symphony: "In a program note Mr. Sessions says that he is 'aware of the strong influence . . . of Bloch and Stravinsky' upon his work. The Stravinsky influence is indeed obvious to any listener familiar with the rhythms of that composer's recent work. But one might have overlooked all traces of Bloch in Mr. Sessions' music had he not thus publicly confessed his obligation." Unfortunately, "several people were sufficiently annoyed by [the symphony] yesterday to hiss, nor was there general applause before the composer was led out by Mr. Koussevitzky."[2] Philip Hale reviewed the concert for the *New York Times.*[3] H. T. Parker wrote two lengthy and glowing reviews for the Boston *Evening Transcript.*[4] For him the sympony revealed "a mind and a hand move individual and fertile than the newest generation—so far as we in America know it—has yet upturned. Pray the gods that Mr. Sessions prove not a composer of a single piece." Sessions's sister-in-law Rosamond Foster attended the performance (Barbara Sessions was too ill to make the crossing with her husband, and doubtless they could not afford it); she remembers that Sessions was so nervous that he threw up, but regained his equanimity when he walked onstage with Koussevitzky. Parker states that Sessions was called onstage twice at the second performance.

Shortly afterward Sessions and Copland together made the crossing back to Europe, Sessions with the hope that Koussevitzky would program the work again. That hope was not to be fulfilled, even though Sessions would incorporate some of Koussevitzky's and Boulanger's suggestions for revision. In the meantime, Sessions was occupied with a ballet that was to illustrate scenes from Boccaccio's *Decameron* and had not yet abandoned his opera on Poe's *Fall of the House of Usher.*

1. Paul Rosenfeld, "Roger Sessions," in *Port of New York* (New York: Harcourt & Brace, 1924), 145–52.

2. Paul Rosenfeld, "New Symphony at Symphony Concert," Boston *Globe,* April 23, 1927.

3. Philip Hale, "First Performance of Roger Sessions's Symphony in E minor," *New York Times* (May 1, 1927), p. 8, 7: 2.

4. H. T. Parker, "Composer Revealed: The Mind and Hand of Roger Sessions," Boston *Evening Transcript,* April 23, 1927, 12, and "Weekend Concerts: Mr. Sessions Again," April 25, 1927, 9.

▼

Aaron Copland to Roger Sessions
als US-NYpease

May 26 [1927]

Dear Roger,   44 rue Jouffroy (17e), Paris

I'm settled at the above address—way over on the right bank for a change—and am looking forward to seeing you again. Israel,[1] unable to withstand the distractions of Paris, hastily withdrew to Gargenville where he now lies entrenched.

As a matter of fact, I've been meaning to write you for the past two weeks partly about my impressions of the trip and partly because of the [First] "Symphony," which N.B. lent me. Now that you are to be here so soon it's hardly necessary to do either. But I must say that only since that week on the boat do I really seem to know you. And the reflection of the real you I find completely expressed in the second movement (one part of "you" anyhow). I've played it over and over again and it seems to me more lovely and more profound each time. Forgive me if I say no more now.

Everything points to my being near you both this summer and if things turn out as I plan I should be in Florence by the 8th of July.

I'm so glad to hear about Barbara. Give her my love and tell her that if I get to Florence it will be at least fifty per cent on her account.

Till soon

Aaron

1. Israel Citkowitz (1909–74) studied with both Sessions and Copland in New York 1927–31. He also wrote for *Modern Music* and in 1933 was the first in the U.S. to write about the Austrian theorist Heinrich Schenker (1868–1935). In 1939 he taught at the Dalcroze School in New York.

▼

Aaron Copland to Barbara and Roger Sessions
als US-NYpease

August 18 [1927]
Hans Leopoldine, Am Hainerberg
Königstein in/T. [Germany]

Dear Barbara + Roger,—

I meant to write weeks ago to bless both of you for the leniency with which my deplorable conduct was overlooked. (Barbara's coals of fire particularly were a balm.) But, as you have probably discovered by now, I am a most efficient creature in everything except letter-writing. I remember your letters arrived just before I left for the festival at Baden-Baden—which, by the way was much more interesting than the one at Frankfurt.

The decision of the Sessions family to return to America has caused much excitement in France if I can judge by the letters coming from Juziers. Both Israel and Roy Harris[1] devoted a paragraph to the subject. I, for one, am DElighted, and shall do everything in my power to make America seem so nice that you'll want to stay for good. (The first thing being to start our Young Composer Society . . !)

My own days in Europe are numbered. I sail the 10th. Königstein has been very nice indeed, but the summer has seemed so frightfully short. I have been able to do little more than get a half dozen new things underway: a Trio on Jewish Themes,[2] a string quartet movement,[3] a new orchestral piece,[4] some E. E. Cummings songs,[5] some piano pieces.[6] And now, back to America, to fight for every half hour I can devote to composition—besides the enormous amount of time to be wasted on "lectures" on modern music. These are mere details—what I mustn't neglect to tell you is that Königstein hasn't been at all warm—nor so very lovely at that!

I am to hear *Electra* on Tuesday. Roger, mon cher, you had better be satisfied with your thrills of 10 years ago and not take a chance hearing a real performance in 1927 if I can judge by playing over the score. How naive and sympathetic the banality in Mahler is, compared to the empty, heartless banality of Strauss. Though I must admit Strauss's harmonic sense is extremely acute and he never fails one at the most dramatic moments. I have been spending much time over *Oedipe Rex*[7]—a very different story indeed and I look forward to the discussions we are to have concerning it.

I hope all has been going well with both of you—that Barbara is completely restored to health and Roger has his Violin Concerto almost finished.[8] Let me know when you expect to sail.

Faithfully, as ever,
Aaron

P.S. the Irony of Fate. Now that I am done with jazz an article by I. [sic] Goldberg is to appear in "the Sept. Mercury" on "A.C. and his Jazz!"[9]

1. Harris (1898–1979) had begun studies with Boulanger the year before; two Guggenheim fellowships in 1927 and 1928 allowed him to continue.

2. *Vitebsk, Study on a Jewish Theme* for piano trio, premiered by Walter Gieseking, Alphonse Onnou, and Robert Maas at a League of Composers concert, February 16, 1929, in New York. See letter dated November 8–9, 1928, note 4.

3. Two Pieces for String Quartet (Lento Molto [1928], Rondino [1923]) premiered by the Lenox Quartet May 6, 1928, in the Copland-Sessions Concerts. Copland's arrangement for string orchestra was played by Serge Koussevitzky and the Boston Symphony Orchestra on December 14, 1928.

4. Probably the *Symphonic Ode,* composed for the fiftieth anniversary of the Boston Symphony and premiered by that orchestra, Koussevitzky conducting, February 19, 1932.

5. "Poet's Song," on a text by e. e. cummings, premiered by Ethel Luening and Copland at the New School for Social Research in New York.

6. The one-minute "Sentimental Melody" is the only piano solo completed in these years.

7. Stravinsky's opera-oratorio *Oedipus Rex* had received its first (unstaged) performance in Paris on May 30, 1927.

8. Sessions's Violin Concerto would not be completed until eight years later, in 1935.

9. Albert Goldberg, "Aaron Copland and His Jazz," *The American Mercury* 12 (September 1927): 63–65.

▼

Ernest Bloch to Roger Sessions
als US-NYpease

August 30, 1927
Kurhaus Griesalp
Berner Oberlaur [Switzerland]

Dear Roger,

Coming back from a trip yesterday, I found your splendid letter and your splendid article.[1] I cannot *write* what both meant to me. If the unexpected visit of Riban and his wife had not interrupted my thoughts, I would have sent you a telegram to tell you at least that your going back to America, will *help me* to return there myself!

This case S[acco] et V[anzetti] has been a nightmare, for me too.[2] I could not sleep. I can[not] realize yet that such an abomination could be so coldbloodily perpetuated! That the *Boston Herald* could write that "it is better to execute two innocent men, than to have people doubt about the infallibility of American courts"—And the *apathy* of the people there! In a week, all will be forgotten! Not so important than the death of Rudolf Valentino! of the next Dempsey fight! I felt *ashamed* of being an American citizen—*afraid* to meet Romain Rolland! And I had to think of a few good and honest American people to be able to *bear* it. We all were upset by this terrible drama.

Then you may realize what your letter and your *decision* meant to me!

Yes, *we* have to go back! and *fight*—for the *honor* of *America,* for the conception of Right, Justice, Humanity. You are right. And I have told Mrs. Bloch the *same* thing. And *here* again, it is the same principle which helped me: a *real* doctor a *real* diagnosis—intelligence, and not "fad" or, if you will *spirit* and not *letter.* (The American doctors have perhaps, however, done irreparable *harm* to me, with their *easy,* and *criminal* mania of Xrays, ultra violet rays). Switzerland . . . my old mountains, the simple people, the silence, have helped me too. We stay here for 10 more days, probably. Then we will go to a general [illegible] in Evian-les-Bains (c/o Mrs. S. Hirsch, 56 Rue Natemale).

From there, I will visit friends in Leysin, Villeneuve, Genève, etc. Then about Sept. 16, to Paris, again, and I sail on the *de Grasse* Sept. 26. But you will hear from me before. I have found my old self again.

It will be hard to go back. But I repeat it, your letter helped me immensely. I knew it would come some day, as I know that you will find yourself completely too, and *freed* of all influences, and master of your own native mind. This too was a joy to me.

Affectionate regards, from all of us.

Your
Ernest Bloch

1. An advance copy of Sessions's "Ernest Bloch," *Modern Music* 5 (November 1927): 3–11.

2. Two Italian-American anarchists, Nicola Sacco and Bartolomeo Vanzetti, had been found guilty in 1921 of the murder of a paymaster and a guard during a robbery at a South Braintree, Mass., shoe factory a year earlier. When a convicted murderer, Celestino Madeiros, confessed to the crime in 1925, the trial judge, Webster Thayer, refused to reopen the trial, preventing the U.S. Supreme Court from overturning the verdict. In April 1927 the two men were sentenced to death. Despite international

protests that they had been convicted for their radical beliefs, Massachusetts governor Alvin T. Fuller refused to grant them clemency. On August 23, 1927, Sacco and Vanzetti were electrocuted.

▼

Roger Sessions to Jean Binet[1]
als CH-Bsacher

[1927]

Carissimo [dearest] Jean,   Roma (Avantino)

We heard your music in Settignano yesterday evening [on the radio] at the Berensons'![2] It went over very well until the last movement of the *Concertino*,[3] when the ethereal machine-guns began to make quite a fracas, that, unfortunately, made this movement and the Melodie a little difficult to hear; that is to say that I received an imperfect and very general impression. But I got a *very beautiful* impression from the Poèmes d'Apollinaire[4] and of the first two movements of the Concertino. You are one of the *very* few who write true music today, mon cher, and you must always be encouraged and write without ceasing. That would make me very happy.

It was very interesting for me to hear your music and to remember your personality, which is at the same time lively and delicate; this one feels very clearly in spite of the songs and the Concertino which are made on the exterior very differently. The Concert[in]o made a very beautiful impression on me—still more than I had expected. It seemed to me that the instrumentation was extremely brilliant, that which impressed me throughout was the slow movement, with the chorale and English horn, in the low register, and the chords in closed position—so simple, but very beautiful, and very personal. It seemed to me that they were played very well.

I was a little surprised at the *tempo* of the last movement; I had imagined it faster. But I am probably wrong, above all, as I have said, there was so much racket ("static" we say in English) that one could only hear fragments.

I also liked the Poèmes d'Apollinaire, that is to say, the songs of Binet; the first and the third perhaps more than the second, the three seemed to me to go together to make a perfect ensemble. Mlle. Anderossi, it seemed to me, sang them *very* well.

Pardon me if my writing in French is maladroit—execrable, to tell the truth—one cannot say that it does justice to your music; but you can have an idea of the joy there was for me—for us both—in hearing your music, and how I find that it is important to make music capable of being heard. I must also say that you must compose more—but it is not exactly I who should preach this observation!

We arrived in Rome in an hour and a half and are well installed at the Labrocas'[5]—after some marvelous days in Florence. Barbara will have told you all that I have written about the Congrés (musical!); with her I heard Rossini's *La Cenerentola,* a truly exquisite work, more beautiful and funnier than the *Barbiere di Siviglia,* and all made without a trace of garlic. This was given in one of the most beautiful theaters in Italy, where Casanova had gone in order to pursue one of his women, and the entire occasion (that is to say *La Cenerentola*) was charming—this opera is given very rarely because of the soprano role, with its range [♪] ! but truly it was a discovery.

Apart from this we have had a very pleasant journey, and we spoke much of you all, as you know, I hope. Now I am preparing myself to leave this enchanted country for some time and I must confess that the idea is not exactly agreeable: Dare I say that I hope to have some letters from you dear, a thousand times dear, friends of Trélex, and that I will respond faithfully? It is nevertheless necessary to have the courage to say that, [just as it is necessary] to risk seeming impertinent with the first phrase, and [illegible] with the second. You will be, unhappily for me, with Barbara, after I will be gone—and I must not forget to thank you for the stay at Trélex. Now, dear friends, you know always how much I love you. Let me have from time to time news of you, and don't forget.

Your
Roger

1. Translated from the French by Andrea Olmstead.

2. I Tatti, the villa of Bernard Berenson (1865–1959), the American authority on Italian Renaissance art.

3. Binet's Concertino for Small Orchestra (1927).

4. Binet's *Poèmes d'Apollinaire,* possibly revised as *Trois Mélodies* on Apollinaire for violin, piano, and orchestra, written in 1933.

5. The Italian film and theater composer, conductor, and critic Mario Labroca (1896–1973).

Roger Sessions to Nicolas Slonimsky
tls US-DLC

September 8, 1927

Dear Mr. Slonimsky,— Settignano, Florence

I can't tell you how grateful I am to you for writing to me again, and for giving me this very pleasant sense of gratitude to help overcome my confusion at having not yet answered your other letter— as well as letting you know that I did receive the New Yorker, and was much amused by it. The truth is that unless I answer letters very promptly I am apt to procrastinate hopelessly—and this summer has been a very busy one. We have had a series of friends and relatives here—the first demanding stimulating conversation, the second demanding filial and fraternal attention; and I simply put off writing!

Thank you for sending me [H. T.] Parker's article. He certainly never misses an opportunity to do his duty by Aaron and me—thus showing, I should say, an imagination and a sense of responsibility which is very rare in critics!

It also rather startled me that my cable to Fuller was printed in the Transcript;[1] if I had known that it would be, I should have used more picturesque language. As it was, I was constrained by the *mesquin* [petty] consideration of what would appeal most to Fuller, if by chance the wire should ever reach his eyes; and instead of telling him that his decision and his attitude smelled to Heaven (a literary allusion which the readers of the Transcript would have understood better, no doubt!)[2] I made my wire as matter-of-fact as I could. I can't tell you how this wretched business has affected me, and I can well understand your hesitation in becoming an American citizen—only too well. I must say I regard the whole affair as a decisive sign of what I have long realized, that America is no longer an Anglo-Saxon country, and that in fact these elements are simply in the way of her development. This summer I have been more than ever taking comfort in my French and Irish blood. As for "American institutions"—I imagine I feel more or less as you do. Perhaps even more so, since the charming institution known as Democracy seeks to make us all responsible for its vagaries. But unless we have a few intelligent people like yourself, I can see no hope that those institutions will ever change. So, for purely selfish and patriotic reasons I hope you will go ahead. I must confess, too, that I wouldn't object half so much to the institutions if

–84–

it were not for the people who run them; though there is a good deal to be said for the idea that such institutions inevitably produce and strengthen that kind of people—in fact that is what I myself believe.

The sad fact seems to be that even the kind of state which Sacco and Vanzetti would like to see established could not be so very much worse than that which, as Fuller has shown, actually exists in Massachusetts under his lead. For my part I must confess that I am old-fashioned enough to believe that such metaphysical concepts as justice and human dignity have a certain real meaning, and that without them anarchy is the result, whether this anarchy masquerades as "Democracy" or anything else.

Well—I am not as skillful, no doubt, in political theory as I am in music, and my only excuse for writing you all this is the illegitimate one that the most I can do under the circumstances is to let off steam.

I have had a fairly good summer; I have got started on a piano sonata and a violin concerto, in addition to my opera and my ballet, which are coming along rather more slowly than I had expected. We are going back to America in December, and will be there till June, in any case; and I look forward very much to seeing you, when we go to Boston. Alas! the *Weltstädte* [metropolises] are too expensive for us, and we will live in Northampton, in the western part of Massachusetts, where I lived for twenty years and where we have friends. But in the meantime please don't be discouraged by either the length or the infrequency of my letters, and do let me hear from you again.

And good luck to all your projects;[3] they interest me very much, and I shall certainly follow them with the greatest concern for their success.

Always most cordially,
Roger Sessions

[P.S.] I meant to write you, too, about Stravinsky's *Oedipus Rex,* which I heard in Paris in June. Of course you have seen the score; it seems to me a most remarkable work—one of the very finest that S—— has written.

---

1. After August 3, when Massachusetts governor A. T. Fuller announced his refusal to pardon Sacco and Vanzetti, letters and telegrams of both praise and protest flooded Fuller's office. The Boston *Evening Transcript* (August 8, 1927), reporting on the previous day's mail, stated: "The only cable from an American [abroad] was from Roger Sessions, Florence, Italy, which read: 'AS MASSACHUSETTS CITIZEN MUST PROTEST ENERGETICALLY SACCO-VANZETTI EXECUTION. ONLY CLEMENCY CAN REDEEM YOU AND MASSACHUSETTS IN EYES OF POSTERITY.'"

2. *Hamlet* 3.3.36: "O! my offense is rank, it smells to heaven."

3. Slonimsky had begun reviewing music for the Boston *Evening Transcript* and the *Christian Science Monitor* and conducting choruses in Boston and at Harvard. About this time he also organized the Chamber Orchestra of Boston, which gave first performances of music by Charles Ives, Edgard Varèse, and Henry Cowell (Slonimsky, *Perfect Pitch*, 105).

▼

Aaron Copland to Roger Sessions
als US-NYpease

October 17 [1927]
223 West 78th Street, New York

Dear Roger,—

I received your card a few days ago and am answering in haste since you aren't to be back till December. (Also the letter during my last week in Paris.)

The season has started off with something of a bang for me—I have three "first" performances in sight for the winter, with one already past. Besides, there are my lectures which attract hordes—literally— of people and make me feel terribly busy and important. All this, with an occasional article thrown in and the usual round of seeing people makes life interesting but exhausting. In reality I am very dissatisfied because no time remains for composition—and I am, after all, a composer. I see only one solution: some kind soul must be induced to give me a life-annuity. Otherwise . . .

You knew that Koussie was to do the "Three Dances" from my ballet [*Grohg*]?¹ Well, Reiner has accepted the "Scherzo" of my Symphony in its new dress for orchestra alone.² He is conducting the Philadelphia Orchestra the first part of the season and I already have my dates—Nov. 4th in Philie—Nov. 8th here. I rather look forward to this because I expect to get a really first class performance. Anyway, I need it, to console myself for the ruin which was made of my Cortège Macabre—also from the ballet—that a certain Russian up-start, by the name of Zaslawsky "conducted" with his newly created Beethoven Symphony Orchestra.³ No one warned me and when I discovered I was dealing with an amateur it was too late to wi[th]draw.

Teddy, in town for a day, came to see me and played me his new chorus.⁴ It is Teddy all over—delicate, poetic, impressionistic, and gives one a very lovely feeling—though I now think he agrees that it needs fixing as to harmonic relations, which at present lack variety.

Since coming home I have talked to no one about our "society." Everything waits on your return. . . .

Because of the necessity of studying him for my lectures I have an entirely new light on the later Stravinsky. My enthusiasm begins to rival your own. I now see the connection with the older works more clearly, and it all means so much more to me than it used to do—miraculously enough, since I knew all the notes formerly as now—but they seem to be transformed.

Teddy assures me your organ pieces are to be given with his chorus at the first League concert.[5] Congratulations. I hear the concert is not to take place until late in December and not on Thanksgiving Day as was formerly planned.

This is all—give my best to Barbara.

Yours

Aaron

P.S. If you pass through Paris and have time, get in touch with Israel—he'd love to see you, I'm sure.

1. The Three Dances became *A Dance Symphony*. The Boston Symphony Orchestra did not play the work.
2. In 1928 Copland completed his Symphony No. 1, a revision for orchestra alone of his Organ Symphony. Reiner conducted the Scherzo November 4 and 5, along with Handel's *Fireworks*, Haydn's Symphony No. 8, and Weber's *Euryanthe* Overture.
3. George Zaslawsky (1880–1953) had made his debut as a conductor at a special concert in Carnegie Hall April 12, 1926. In 1927 he founded and conducted a "Beethoven Symphony Orchestra" in New York, which was discontinued after a few concerts.
4. Theodore Chanler's *Ann Gregory* for chorus (1927).
5. Sessions's Two Chorale Preludes for Organ would be performed twice at League of Composers concerts: December 30, 1927, and December 10, 1930.

▼

Roger Sessions to Nadia Boulanger
als F-PBN

[November 1927?]

Florence

My dear friend,—

Your letter was more of a comfort than I can tell you. I knew that you were busy, and I trust that you always know that I understand. If I should say that "words are useless" I would be doing great injustice to my joy in receiving your letter yesterday. But to say that I am always conscious of your friendship, and understand all too well how busy you are—of this you can always be sure.

You are quite right in saying that the best way for me to help America is to be myself—I have been more and more conscious of this and what it means. I know too, that it is Europe—and Latin civilization—that have enabled me for the first time in my life to be myself, to know myself and to be at peace with myself—whether that is because of the French blood that is in my father's family or whether it is because of the Northerner in me longing for the South I do not know—but sometimes I feel as if in leaving Europe I would be leaving my home even more truly than in coming over here. But I feel I must go back, now that I have learned this, to see at least where I really stand in relation to my own country.

Thank you for your words of confidence—they mean more to me than I could possibly tell you, and you may be assured that I shall never forget them, and they will be always with me to help me when I am discouraged.

Of course we will be passing through Paris, in December—for a week perhaps; but I told you this in my other letter.

Forgive me if I write no more—I am terribly busy, + must send the new score + corrected parts of the Symphony to Koussevitzky within a few days. My changes in the first movement improve it enormously—I have re-touched certain parts of the instrumentation, + expanded the middle section, so that it has much more shape, and the recapitulation seems no more too long. The other movements I have not touched, except for a few nuances and instrumental details in the Finale.

With all good wishes to your mother—believe me always

Most affectionately
Roger—

[P.S.] Barbara, too, sends much love.

▼

Roger Sessions to Serge Koussevitzky[1]
als US-DLC

Thursday, November 10 [1927]
Dear Sir,—   Florence

I am finally sending Mr. Rogers[2] the score and the recopied and corrected parts to my *Symphony*.

I made my excuses for this delay; but the remainder that I did in the format of the first movement gave me more difficulties than I would have imagined—and then it was necessary to copy the parts! I have recopied the entire symphony, since the parts that were used last April were made very badly; and I believe that these will give the musicians and also the conductor less pain.

You will see what I did to the first movement. Indeed if that is not exactly what you had suggested or what I myself projected at first, it seems to me that it is right. The *Cadenza* remains; but, conforming more to my first conception, this is justified by the development that precedes it, a development that results in a true climax, and one that seems to me to render necessary this relaxation of the rhythm.

It seems to me that this also changes the proportions of the movement up to the point that the recapitulation no longer seems too long. At first I had the intention of abridging it, but with forty measures more in the central part that no longer was desirable.

This experience has been enormously valuable to me, and I am very grateful for your valuable and just criticisms.

Elsewhere I remade a transition episode (no. 17–19) making it more concentrated—and I retouched the instrumentation of the first and third movements.

I hope that you have still the intention of replaying it this season, since, after all, we have decided to spend the winter in America. We will arrive toward Christmas season, and without doubt Mr. [John] Burk will let me know what you intend to do with my score. In any case I will go to Boston at some time and I will hope to see you there.

On other things, I wish to finish my violin concerto this winter that you have suggested to me and that I have already begun.

Somebody asked me, for Mr. Reiner of the Philadelphia Orchestra, for information on my orchestral works that could be played this season. Since I still do not wish to have the Black Maskers suite that I showed you played, [and] since further it has been a year and a half that it has remained at the [Boston] symphony, I have responded that one must seek information from Mr. Burk, who will be able to speak with you. It was necessary for me to make some response; naturally the disposition of my score remains with you until that [time] you no longer wish it, and I am not pressed to have it played somewhere else.

Please accept my most cordial salutations to you and to Madame Koussevitzky, and my best wishes for a "successful season."[3]

Always sincerely,
Roger Sessions

1. Translated from the French by Andrea Olmstead.
2. Leslie J. Rogers, orchestral librarian for the Boston Symphony Orchestra from 1912 to 1956.
3. These two words in English.

Copland and sessions corresponded frequently in 1928 in order to solve the practical problems of presenting the first two Copland-Sessions Concerts that spring.[1] Sessions was temporarily—and unhappily—back teaching at Smith College in Northampton that semester. There he worked on his Piano Sonata for the first concert, leaving Copland in New York entirely responsible for raising funds, renting the hall, putting out publicity, and finding pieces and performers for the concerts. Even the two small assignments he gave Roger and Barbara Sessions—to come up with a title for the series and to write a prospectus for it—were in the first instance not completed and in the second unsatisfactorily so (Copland rewrote the draft).

The case of the First Piano Sonata was particularly trying for both composers. Sessions originally planned that twenty-one-year-old Rosamond Foster (to whom the work was dedicated) play the sonata, but when this seemed out of her technical reach, she suggested that her piano teacher at Smith, John Duke,[2] premiere it. Straining to complete a long piece at the last minute, Sessions found he could not finish it in time. Without her husband's knowledge, Barbara wrote Copland about the problems Roger was having and asked Copland to write him an encouraging note; Copland generously complied. The piece still was not ready in time for the second concert however, and was played incomplete then. Sessions said of this experience, much later, "I was being so hypercritical that until it moved naturally, it was torture. . . . The experience of writing this whole thing was much the toughest time I've ever had as a composer."[3]

Some of Sessions's most irritating features are revealed in this incident, which took place at a crucial point in his creative life: an underestimation of the difficulty of playing his music when it came to a member of his family (seen later, in the 1970s, when he wrote his Five Pieces for Piano for his eight-year-old granddaughter); an inability to finish works on time; and a tendency, already seen in the instance of the delivery of the parts of the First Symphony, to make numerous excuses for his delays.

Copland complained that "the moral responsibility of the occasion [of the first concert] was rather heavy on my slim shoulders." It must have been clear to Copland—and also frustrating to realize—that Sessions was going to be of no practical assistance whatever in organizing the concerts. In fact, he posed more obstacles than he offered solutions. This apparently did not detract from Copland's real affection for Sessions, while Sessions then seemed able to confide his true feelings in Copland alone. Indeed, when the sonata was finally completed, in 1930, Copland was so far to forgive Sessions for his role in this trying episode that he would glowingly praise the completed work: "To know the work well is to have the firm conviction that Sessions has presented us with a cornerstone upon which to base an American music."[4]

1. One letter of April 1928 from Sessions to Copland that is not included here is reproduced in Aaron Copland and Vivian Perlis, *Copland: 1900 through 1942* (New York: St. Martin's Press, 1984), 147.
2. John Duke (1899–1984), who taught at Smith College 1923–67 and later studied with Schnabel and Boulanger in Europe 1929–30, composed songs.
3. Taped interview with the author, November 20, 1974, at The Juilliard School. See Andrea Olmstead, *Roger Sessions and His Music* (Ann Arbor: UMI Research Press, 1985), 55.
4. Aaron Copland, "Contemporaries at Oxford, 1931," *Modern Music* 9 (November 1931): 23.

▼

Aaron Copland to Roger Sessions
als US-NYpease

Monday [March 1928]
Dear Roger,   [New York]

This is to satisfy whatever curiosity you may have about happenings after your departure.

I went immediately to see Moe. (If Mrs. R[eis] ever discovers this my "career" can be considered over!) To my astonishment he jumped at the idea of giving the concert without the L[eague] of C[omposers] so that we need merely await developments. The final decision of the Trustees is tomorrow and he agreed to break the horrible news to Mrs. R. Too bad you couldn't have seen the delight of the Ks at the recital of all this Friday night.

I went to see Human[1] to-day about the I[nternational] S[ociety for] C[ontemporary] M[usic] backing us. Out talk was anything but satisfactory. On the one hand, he agrees to our being czars and on the other he offers suggestions as to what we should play. He is afraid of our giving programs made up entirely of left-wingers in spite of all my reassurances. In a word, he's an ass and I have no desire to work with him. Besides he has no financial aid to offer and seems so busy that he'd have no time to run our very important affairs. I think we can just drop the idea and go ahead as before, alone. Tonight, I feel as if something would turn up for next year, if absolutely necessary.

I've talked to Minna L[ederman][2] about the wherewithal for photostating, etc. She was very nice about it and promised a definite answer in a day or two. I'll let you know as soon as I know what's what.

I sent the U.S.A. $1.20 income tax! Can you say as much?

Yours efficiently,
Aaron

1. Dr. Alfred E. Human (d. 1962).
2. Lederman (b. 1898) was sole editor of *Modern Music* 1924–46.

▼

Roger Sessions to Aaron Copland
als US-DLC

Thursday [March 15, 1928]
Dear Aaron,—   15 Adare Place [Northampton?]

Thank you so much for your two letters—and for the assurance of others to come. Is it OK for me to write + thank Minna Lederman + Mrs. Churchill.[1] If so, what is the latter's address? Also, you come in for a good share of gratitude in this case—by far the largest, in my opinion, since your time + energy are worth a thousand times more than their money!

Since your second letter arrived Barbara + I have subjected our brains to a gentle cudgelling for a name for our concerts. Thus far we have hit upon nothing very original. "The Enemies of Music"— suggested by a sort of converse of this old Puritan proverb that Hell is paved with good intentions seemed the best, but that would hardly do.—Please do not gather from this that I approach the problem in a flippant spirit!

How about the Porter works? Q. writes that he would rather have us play the quintet;[2] shall I write that we would gladly do so if he would furnish the performers? Of course, as you may remember, I was quite depressed by the works themselves, + I gather you were too. Perhaps I will write him anyway, committing us to nothing, but suggesting that in case we decide to give the work, his organization[3]— a more than fair one, by the way—might gain some useful publicity by a N.Y. appearance.

Bonime is in Europe, I believe, but R[uth] Warfield is, I am sure, willing to play.[4] I'll write her, however, + make sure.

The "long, sentimental letter" I had planned to write you must, I'm afraid, give way to matters of a more pressing nature, but it was not really essential, anyway. Nevertheless, you must know how much good it does me to see something of you, + to be in touch with you. It has been the chief compensation, + a rather "formidable" one, for a dull + disappointing winter in which my lingering illusions over my native country have disappeared, or at least fallen hopelessly ill! If I ever had any doubts about your future—and I never did have any serious ones—these would have been so more than effectually dispelled, that to even speak in this way seems thoroughly impertinent. Nothing seems surer to me now; and it is more than a comfort to me to feel that way, when my own future seems to me constantly to be hanging in the balance + or worse. *Yours* is something that I take absolutely for granted, and I have not—for all my doubting nature— had the suspicion of a feeling that I was deceiving myself.

Furthermore—you are the only person over here with whom I feel quite myself. If I rather hesitate to say this it is only because it savors a little of what Roy Welch calls "praising with faint Damns."—I am getting quite fed up with the absurd, pretentious, thoroughly second-rate people here, for instance. As far as I can see there are only three *men* in Northampton—complete human beings, I mean: one is [William] Neilson, who is rather inaccessible; another is [John] Duke, who is still rather immature + lacking in vitality, who needs to be pushed + awakened + bolstered up; + finally Gorokhoff, a real person, but unfortunately a rabid anti-Semite—a disadvantage when so many of my friends are Jews! Aside from these, Northampton is like nothing so much as a place where people come to take refuge from the consciousness of their own mediocrity. You can imagine how depressing it is—+ not the least depressing moments are those in which one is gently flattered + admired. Those are the moments when one begins to wonder about oneself! Of course I don't speak of the students—they are quite alive and undoubtedly aware of a great deal. But they have not really begun to live yet—and besides, I think the "present generation" has been made self-conscious by being so much in the limelight. They are amusing + sometimes beautiful to watch, but in a community like this quite hard to get at.

I'm glad Moe took the right attitude in the Reis affair. It has long been a theory that if women choose to take part in the "affairs of men" they should be treated on an equal, i.e. an impersonal basis. This, I am aware, has its difficulties; but Moe is in some position, as I thought he would be, to ignore them.

Please forgive my garrulity—+ let me know what I can do. We will send the suggested name and prospectus soon.

As always
Roger

P.S. As I write the *parts* of the Porter quintet have arrived. I'll hold them pending word from you.

1. Mary Senior Churchill, wife of the architect Henry Churchill and herself a wealthy patroness.
2. Quincy Porter's Quintet for Piano and Strings appeared on the second concert, May 6, 1928.
3. I.e., the Cleveland Institute of Music, where Porter was teaching.
4. Pianist Gertrude Bonime and violinist/composer Ruth White Warfield had played a sonata recital in Steinway Hall, January 8, 1928. They were managed by Arthur Judson. On October 7, 1929, Bonime would play a Town Hall recital including Warfield's Pavane.

▼

Roger and Barbara Sessions to Aaron Copland
als US-DLC

Dear Aaron,—   [March 21, 1928]

Thank you for your notes. I am enclosing the prospectus which B[arbara] has prepared; it seems to me quite good, + I hope you will like it. If not, you must, naturally change it as you see fit.

As for the name: "Laboratory concerts" would do, of course, but it goes a little against the grain. B—— says she too had thought of it, but that it smacks a little of progressive education, psychological research, + an atmosphere of earnest effort. Also I might add, young composers might be repelled by such a name, which sounds a little too much as if we were taking it for granted in advance that their work would be quite un-definitive. [I]f we could be sure of the Laboratory Theatre, that would change matters, as I see it. Of course the matter of a name is not of supreme importance, + it would no doubt be impossible to find one which would be perfectly satisfactory.

I didn't mean to give you the impression that my "discouragement" was a terribly essential thing in my life; indeed, it was rather merely a background before which to set forth your virtues! As a matter of fact I have recently—in the last week or two—begun to realize that we are leaving America before long, + almost unconsciously begun to take stock of my experiences, the essential ones, I mean. The net result is that I have decided quite definitely to establish myself permanently over here, when the time comes.

I won't go into my reasons in great detail; and I know I am not ready to do so yet—I mean, to establish myself, I need several more years of comparative solitude + contact with Europe, and have begun to make very definite plans as to how I shall spend those years. At the end I feel I will have enough self-assurance, musically, to come back, providing only that I can return to Europe every now + then, to keep in touch.

Furthermore, my head is full of certain projects which I want later on to discuss with you; projects which can + must wait until our concerts are pretty well established, + also until we are ready to start on them, which may mean several years hence; but things which will certainly, if they are at all possible, would [sic] mean incalculable things for music + for America. However, this must wait till I see you. Meanwhile I can assure you that I am farther than ever from the America-affirmers. The only thing is that here I have a sure + increasing feeling that anything is possible, the only problem being to make the best use of those possibilities. Excuse me for being vague, but I am in a hurry.

The sonata is taking excellent shape, I think.

I will write to M[inna] L[ederman] + M[ary] C[hurchill]. Also I should hear very soon from W[illiam] Q[uincy] P[orter].

How about spending a few days with us about the 6, 7, 8 of April? The fare is $5.43, + doubtless you could stay long enough to "make expenses!"

R——

P.S. Please send me as soon as you can a list of the lectures you expect to give next year, or could give. I have already spoken to Welch of the possibility of your speaking here, + hope something may be arranged. "Dr. Moog" also, I will approach in a good cause.

[P.P.S.] I have begun a po. arrangement of the *Largo* of my symphony, but its completion will have to wait on the sonata.[1]

[in Barbara Sessions's hand:]

Dear Aaron, March 21st

I apologize in advance for the many defects of my little production.
You, being on the spot, may find that it contains unfortunate nuances,
or mutes important points. Naturally, treat it as a preliminary sketch
+ transform it as much as you wish. We tried to keep it simple +
concise: as a result perhaps it sounds a little congested.

Best wishes, as always. Please come to see us.

Barbara

1. Copland was to play this arrangement as part of a lecture recital, "The Younger
Generation of American Composers," April 6, 1930, for the Arts Club of Chicago,
along with works by Harris, Antheil, Weiss, Thomson, and himself.

▼

Roger Sessions to Aaron Copland
als US-DLC

Dear Aaron— [March 26, 1928]

You have my O.K. on everything practical. The title seems very
good, + I would have suggested it myself if I hadn't thought you had
decided against it.

Modern Music arrived this A.M. + I like your article.[1] Yours and
mine,[2] in fact, seem the only decent ones in the number, but this
perhaps is praising with faint damns. Lourié and de Schloezer are
terrible; they say nothing at all.[3] I don't expect so much of de
Schloezer, but Lourié ought to do better.

I have forgotten to tell you that when my books arrived I went over
the piano pieces of Hindemith + am now crazy about the first two.
The 3rd is quite poor, in comparison at least; + the String Trio[4]
which I have [is] terribly tortured + teutonic. You must give me a list
of Hindemith that "every young man ought to know," so that I can
really become acquainted. The second of the piano pieces is really
marvelous, + I don't know, outside of Stravinsky, anything in contemporary music that appeals to me so much. I even fancy there are
certain analogies with my own developing style. However—

I shall regard the Sunday Times with close attention.

Affectionately

R——

P.S. No reply from Teddy to my cable.

1. Aaron Copland, "Music since 1920," *Modern Music* 5, no. 3 (March–April 1928): 16–20.

2. Roger Sessions, "On *Oedipus Rex*," ibid., 9–15.

3. "Neogothic and Neoclassic," by the Russian-American composer Arthur Lourié (1892–1966), is an important statement of Stravinsky's neoclassic aesthetic by a close associate of the composer's. Boris de Schloezer (1881–1969), a Russian-French author of monographs on Stravinsky and on de Schloezer's brother-in-law, Alexander Scriabin, offered "An Age of Plenty." The other articles are by Henrietta Straus, Domenico de Paoli, and Robert Simon.

4. Possibly the piano pieces are the *Übung in drei Stucken*, op. 37, no. 1 (1925). Hindemith's String Trio, No. 1, op. 34 (1924).

▼

Aaron Copland to Roger Sessions
als US-NYpease

Dear Roger,—   Monday [March 26, 1928]

The prospectus is off to the papers and should appear next Sunday. Mrs. Churchill "corrected" my arrangement so Barbara will probably recognize nothing of what she wrote. We decided to come out without a name now, but to add it in the next publicity containing composers, dates, etc. Therefore if you object to Copland-S—— Concerts of Contemporary Music say so now.

The second program was advanced to April 29 even tho that is the last day of Mrs. Coolidge's Festival;[1] and the first program is definitely April 22. We have the American Laboratory Theatre for April 22 and a promise for the 29th. The second program looks like this—vaguely, that is:

> Delaney—Violin Sonata
> Antheil—String Quartet
> Elwell—Nine piano pieces
> Copland—Two pieces for String Quartet
> Q. Porter—Quintet.[2]

(Elwell wrote that his Violin Sonata could be finished in time.)

(By the way, what piano does John Duke play—if any?)

I don't see how we can give the program if Antheil doesn't come across with the Quartet.[3]

It is still possible that we may change the theatre to one nearer the center of town.[4]

I tried to get in touch with Mrs. Warfield, but she is out of town until Friday. This worries me. Teddy's Sonata is not easy and if we wait for her return she'll have only three weeks to prepare it. If I knew where she went (they said Meriden [Conn.]) I'd write to make sure of her acceptance. Can you suggest anything?

I read the Oedipus article and like it very much—particularly the second part, i.e. everything from the discussion of the orchestral effects onward. And what's your verdict of my own piece in M.M.?[5]

I'm delighted to hear about the piano arrangement of the Largo.

As for my lectures they would have to take place in January. I have only planned single lectures. You probably know what I can speak on as well as I do.

The latest excitement is that I am engaged to play my Concerto at the Hollywood Bowl on July 19th? Charming, pas? They wanted Gershwin, but had to take me instead. This means I see New Mexico and America! *Now* will you be good. I'll probably return a rampant affirmer. My plans are to leave on May 15 for Santa Fe and remain there for two months, then to California and back to the MacDowell Colony for August and September. This all seems very far from you, worse luck.

I'll probably need to come to Northampton for a rest on April 6! But I fail to see at the present moment how I can get away. Anyhow thanks very much for the invitation and I'll let you know later whether I can manage it or not.

A

1. Elizabeth Sprague Coolidge (1864–1953) had founded the Berkshire Festival of Chamber Music in 1918 and moved the festival to Washington, D.C., before she founded the Elizabeth Sprague Coolidge Foundation at the Library of Congress in 1925. Her patronage of international composers and performers profoundly influenced American music in the second quarter of the century. The second Copland-Sessions Concert would eventually take place on May 6.

2. The Delaney, Copland, and Porter pieces were played on the second program, along with Two Preludes by Crawford, Three Preludes by Adolph Weiss, Three Paeans by Dane Rudhyar, and Sessions's incomplete Piano Sonata, but not the works by Antheil or Elwell. See Carol J. Oja, "The Copland-Sessions Concerts and Their Reception in the Contemporary Press," *Musical Quarterly* (April 1979): 220.

3. George Antheil's *Ballet mécanique,* first performed in Paris the previous year, received its American premiere April 10, 1927, at Carnegie Hall. Copland was one of the ten pianists in this performance, which created an uproar in the audience. Antheil's String Quartet No. 2 was not completed in time for the May 6th concert.

4. Both concerts took place at the Edyth Totten Theatre at 247 West Forty-eighth Street (later renamed the President Theatre).

5. See the preceding letter, notes 1 and 2.

▼

Aaron Copland to Roger Sessions
als US-NYpease

Dear Roger,—   Thursday [March 29?, 1928]

First, to practical matters. We are still haggling between the American Laboratory Theatre and the Edyth Totten Theatre and will decide definitely on Saturday. The material for the circulars for mailing purposes must be in by Tuesday so our programs must be complete by then,—works, names of separate movements, artists' names, etc. I feel very badly about the fact that I am forced to say to you, let's play this or that, without being able to show you the music first. I didn't realize how far in advance all these things must be decided and of course, now it is too late to dream of sending you the music to pass on. I console myself, by saying that of the two programs I sent, you are unfamiliar only with the Bob Delaney and Chávez.[1] I feel sure you'll like the latter and Delaney is the sort of person we want to encourage and shows "promise." I think we must also add to the first program some short songs by V. Thomson for voice and percussion.[2] He had never had a performance here and it's the only thing in the way of songs that I can find.

(I got in touch with Warfield and it's all arranged.)

I remember you were in favor of two programs. So is Mary Churchill. I think we'll announce both programs anyhow. In order to do so we must have a definite reply from Porter and the names of the people he is bringing with him to perform his work. (The second concert is definitely for April 29.) Write me how you want your Sonata programmed (with movements or what?)

For the circular we want a condensed and more personal announcement of our views to be signed by both of us. I am writing it and enclosing it to save time. Improve it however you like, but I must have it back by *Tuesday* A.M.

I am also enclosing a copy of the first announcement, revamped, as sent to 33 newspapers in N.Y. and Boston, musical journals, etc. No doubt, we'll be inundated with compositions from "promising composers!"

Your letter with the information about Porter changes matters considerably.[3] There is still time to change the date to May 6, but I must have a day in which to find out the how and the what. At any rate, even if we keep April 29 I think I can supply a Quintet so that it should go on the program in either case. I think it might be wise to write and ask him to send me the names of the people he would bring from Cleveland if we did do it on May 6. (This should reach me by Tuesday, also.)

This morning a letter came from Olin Downes saying "Your announcement is good news indeed. I shall be very glad to do everything I can to cooperate." This is an auspicious beginning!

Truth to tell, I'm all het up. *And* dying to get a glimpse of the Piano Sonata.

A

P.S. You might send us names of friends of yours who you think would like to know of the concerts.

1. Robert Mills Delaney (1903–56) studied in Italy and Paris with Boulanger and Arthur Honegger 1922–27. Carlos Chávez (1899–1978), the eminent Mexican composer and conductor, traveled to France in 1922 and lived in New York for several years. Neither Copland nor Chávez later seemed to remember when and where they met (see Copland and Perlis, *Copland: 1900 through 1942,* 380, note 2).

2. Thomson's *Five Phrases from the "Song of Solomon"* for voice and percussion. The other works on the April 22d program were Chanler's Sonata for Violin and Piano, Chávez's Three Sonatinas and Sonata for Piano (which replaced the Sessions sonata), and Three Pieces for Flute, Clarinet, and Bassoon by Walter Piston.

3. Sessions had written to Copland on March 28, 1928, "I haven't got a minute— but: Q. Porter must conduct here on Apr. 29th his famous "Ukranian Suite!" As he would have to play the viola in his Quintet that would be rather inconvenient, n'est-ce pas? I just talked over the telephone to see if the date here couldn't be changed, but it is impossible. Que faire? Can't we make it May 6th, again? i.e. if we *need* his work" (US-DLC).

▼

Aaron Copland to Roger Sessions
als US-NYpease

Dear Roger,   Sunday [early April 1928]

I am enclosing a letter just received from Antheil which I hope will amuse you.[1] Apparently, I frightened him off. We must find something to take the place of his quartet. Have you any suggestions? If so, let me have them by return mail. I have been only able to think of two possibilities, neither of which is very inspiring; a string quartet of Howard Hanson[2] or a ballad (do you know it?) of Douglas Moore.[3] I'm rather sorry about the Antheil being off as the program now seems to misfire—but I am more convinced than ever that a second program is necessary in order to impress the whole business on people's minds.

We came off fair to middlin' in the Sunday papers. Everyone cut the announcement except the Brooklyn Daily Eagle. Downes swore it was not on the main page thru an error and against his expressed wishes. Can one believe him? Anyway, people will have heard.

The second concert will be definitely May 6. We have signed a contract for April 22 with the Edyth Totten Theatre. It is a small, new theatre (313 seats) in the center of town—48th St. near 8th Ave. and ideally located. This is going to cost $125. but Mary Churchill felt it was worth the money, and after all, it *is* her money. Incidentally Mary has been very grand through this all—simple and efficient. There's an enormous amount of detail work to be done which I couldn't possibly handle alone (Minna of course aids her on the sly and as she is very experienced in all this, we profit by what the League has learned during the past years.)

After all that fuss about the statement for the circular, we will probably use a condensed version of the original announcement instead of what I wrote in haste I may add.

We are sending out the story of the first program for next week's papers.

Give my best to Barbara. Tell her to thank her lucky stars that she doesn't live in N.Y. these days or heaven knows what running from one end of town to the other she might have to endure.

Yours,
Aaron

P.S. Read your article in the Harvard Magazine.[4] Am I wrong or isn't it better even than the M.M. one?

1. Antheil's letter is not among Sessions's papers.
2. Hanson (1896–1981) had won the Prix de Rome (1921–24) and been appointed director of the Eastman School of Music (1924). His String Quartet (1923) was commissioned for the Coolidge Festival.
3. Moore had spent 1925–26 in Europe on a Pulitzer traveling scholarship. Neither Hanson's quartet nor Moore's *Ballad of William Sycamore* for baritone, flute, trombone, and piano (1926) was programmed.
4. Roger Sessions, "Notes on Music: Oedipus Rex," *The Hound & Horn: A Harvard Miscellany* 1, no. 3 (Spring 1928): 246–49.

Roger and Barbara Sessions to Aaron Copland
als US-DLC

Cher ami,— [April 12, 1928]

Excuse pencil + this paper.

I send string parts of Porter quintet.

Don't worry about the sonata. It isn't finished, but I *swear* to you it will be ready in time—you can count on it absolutely. Also, I like it—it is much better than the symphony.

Koussie was here yesterday + we had a grand time. Incidentally he gave a repeat concert[1]—I understood Tschaikowsky for the first time, as well as the Prelude to *Lohengrin*. The Bach-Schönberg chorales made the same impression as before—marvelous but, as far as I am concerned, false—I mean, I prefer Bach.

Don't worry or apologize about not including my sonata in the next announcement of the concert. As you know "modern music" in that sense bores me to tears, + I was very happy that I escaped. When we meet I may even take wild exception to that force of publicity which I don't feel advances our cause + might even do it harm. However, don't be alarmed, + I promise not to descend on you too hard!

So glad things are going so well. By the way K—— asked me pt. blank how things stood with the Guggenheim concert affair + I had to tell him. But you need fear nothing I'm sure, in approaching him. He said, "We must find the money somewhere else."

I too have much to talk about with you.

Barbara will write you our plans so you can arrange with Marg[aret] Naumburg.[2]

Affectionately,
Roger

[In Barbara Sessions's hand:]

Dear Aaron:

We plan to reach 1 Middagh St., Brooklyn (though Miss [Adeline] Sessions, 15 Clark St. would also reach us + is the better place to [leave] telephone messages) the 21st. We shall stay two or three days after the concert, though there is a possibility that we may have to leave Tuesday [April 24], on account of something here. Roger's mother, whom he has not seen at all, is coming down for the concert, and I'm terribly afraid we shall have to devote ourselves to her. We have disappointed her in all her places for meeting somewhere for a longer time. You understand what such situations are—*so* that I am afraid we can't do anything with Margaret Naumburg this trip, much as you know we would love to.

But—as I wired her, we are not sailing quite as soon as we at first planned. We'll go on the Rochambeau, May 4, D. V. [God willing] Roger is going to Washington with you (how nice of Fred!)[3] + will not come back here, before we sail but spend the intervening time in N.Y.—Perhaps that will give you a chance to arrange something with both M.N. (I'll arrive a day or two before we sail, too) + Alma Wertheim[4]—though if the latter is pressing you can of course go ahead with it for this first visit—but it couldn't be an evening on account of the aforesaid obligation.

Good luck with everything. The circular just arrived, + we think it splendid—very nicely done.

Sincerely as ever,
Barbara

[P.S.] Did Roger write you that we *finally* had a cable from Teddy saying "nothing available"?

1. Koussevitzky conducted the Boston Symphony Orchestra in Northampton on April 11, 1928. The program included Tchaikovsky's Symphony No. 6, Wagner's Prelude to *Lohengrin,* and Arnold Schoenberg's 1922 arrangement of two Bach chorale preludes: *Komm, Gott, Schöpfer, Heiliger Geist* and *Schmücke dich, O liebe Seele.*
2. Margaret Naumberg (d. 1981), the daughter of a nephew of Elkan Naumberg (1834–1934), the musical philanthropist. She co-founded the Walden School at Eighty-eighth Street and Central Park West and taught art therapy.
3. Frederick Jacobi (1891–1952), a member of the executive board of the League of Composers, had studied in Germany and in the U.S. with Bloch. Among other events, Stravinsky's *Apollon musagète* would receive its premiere at the Library of Congress Festival on April 27, 1928. It is likely that Sessions wanted to attend this premiere.
4. Alma Morgenthau Wertheim (d. 1953), Copland's patroness.

▼

Barbara Sessions to Aaron Copland
als US-DLC

Dear Aaron,   Friday [April 13, 1928]

I've just mailed you the official family bulletin. This is an unofficial appendix (+ must never be mentioned by you to anyone, please) the result of a sleepless night. I know how much you have on your mind,

+ don't want to add to your cares, but I must confess to you that I am just a little worried about the sonata. It's not done. Roger has been working devotedly, as hard as he can, and I am trying to do everything in my power to keep him calm + confident.

As a matter of fact, I think he is himself secretly in a state of panic which he can't admit to you because he has some kind of feeling that the more declarations he makes the more his will-power will be spurred by the feeling that he *has* to get it done at the risk of utter disaster. Naturally, this is none too good for the sonata. John Duke is being as patient as an angel. As fast as Roger finishes something consecutive he gives it to John to practice, but, at best, he will have very little time in which to get the whole thing together.

I dare say you may have already considered the danger of the situation and have some solution up your sleeve for an emergency. I don't mean to say that I think the emergency even *probable* to arise, but it is *possible,* Aaron.

Of course, if there were any chance of getting *your* things ready to substitute on the first program, or if Elwell's pieces could be hurried along, so that you could write Roger a benevolent letter telling him to get his sonata done for the second concert instead, it would be a wonderful relief.—But I realize that there may be unsurmountable difficulties. Failing this, my advice is—have something in reserve in case he simply can't finish in time—and, if you can possibly find it in you to be that generous and forgiving—write him as encouragingly as you can and don't hint at any alarm. I assure you it's not necessary. Aaron, you have no idea what *hell* he goes through—Well, you must forgive this incoherent letter, but "to whom can I tell the sad thoughts I think," etc. And above all, he mustn't know that I wrote this, or have ever felt any doubts and if you make any suggestions, they should come as if wholly from you.

Devotedly, As ever,
Barbara

▼

Aaron Copland to Roger Sessions
als US-NYpease

Dear Roger,—   Sunday [April 15, 1928]

Last week, when no letter came saying the "Sonata" was finished I naturally began to suspect trouble. Your letter therefore was reassuring. Don't worry, twice underlined, should satisfy anyone. However, you most certainly have my sympathy. I think writing a work to order for a set date excellent—when one has finished it. But, of course, the situation you are now in is horrible and my feelings as a fellow-composer and as a concert-manager are at war with one another. As the former, I should like to say, don't _you_ worry; after all it's the Sonata which is important and not its being ready by a set date. But, as co-director of the C——— S——— Concerts I should like to see the public get what it is promised. (As the other co-director, I know you feel the same.) O Hell;—I hope I don't sound as if I _were_ worried. I refuse to be like the famous cook who blew out his brains because the fish didn't arrive in time for the king's dinner.[1]

All things considered, it would seem highly desirable that the Sonata be finished. However, you have until five minutes before the concert—24 hours a day.

I was delighted to hear you are coming to Washington.

Thank heavens, you have at last found something of which you can disapprove. Naturally, I agree with you. Putting the importance on "modern" and "novel" is stupid—it simply happened because of a series of events which I can explain when I see you. I think, in general, tho, the publicity hasn't been bad. We already have about 30 subscribers for both concerts. Mary C[hurchill] calls me up in the greatest excitement every time a new subscription comes in. You're really missing half the fun.

There's been talk of a party after the concert. My idea was to ask people we like and the participants to go to some place after the concert. Mary C. was willing to stand the costs but I prefer it à la Boulanger, everyone paying for themselves. This will be a real innovation in modern music societies.

By the way, I hear thru dark channels that the L. of C. has decided to invite the two of us to join their board! Don't breathe a word of this, whatever you do.

There's nothing else.

Buhlig[2] is playing at our second concert nine pieces by Rudhyar[3] (Three Paeans), Adolf Weiss,[4] a pupil of Schoenberg's, and Ruth Crawford,[5] a girl who lives in Chicago. He refused to do the Elwell and I can't blame him (that I believe is my first real error as to music) so John Kirkpatrick[6] is doing them instead. (Keep this under your hat too.)

Affectionately

A

1. The famous anecdote about the reaction of the duke of Condé's chef, Vatel, to a mishap during Louis XIV's visit to Chantilly in 1671 appears in the *Lettres de Madame de Sévigné*.

2. Richard Buhlig (1880–1952) was a well-known pianist closely associated with West Coast composers. He performed the works by Ruth Crawford (Two Preludes), Adolph Weiss (Three Preludes), and Dane Rudhyar (Three Paeans), on the second Copland-Sessions concert.

3. The French-American composer and writer on astrology Dane Rudhyar (1895–1985) had come to America in 1916 after studies at the Paris Conservatoire. He was a founding member of the International Composers' Guild, organized in 1922 by Edgard Varèse and Carlos Salzedo.

4. Adolph Weiss (1891–1971), a twelve-tone composer and bassoonist who had played in the New York Philharmonic under Mahler, the New York Symphony under Walter Damrosch, and the Chicago Symphony, had studied with Arnold Schoenberg at the Prussian Academy of Arts in Berlin.

5. Crawford (1901–53) had studied composition at the New York Institute of Musical Art (later The Juilliard School) with Charles Seeger, whom she later married, eventually abandoning composition, in which she remarkably anticipated later avant-garde developments, to devote herself to her husband's political and ethnomusicological projects.

6. The pianist John Kirkpatrick (b. 1905) studied with Nadia Boulanger 1925–28. His premiere of Ives's *Concord Sonata* in 1939 was be a landmark in the history of that composer's public reception. Because the Elwell ultimately was not programmed, Kirkpatrick would not perform on this, or any, Copland-Sessions Concert.

▼

Aaron Copland to Barbara and Roger Sessions
als US-NYpease

Dear Barbara + Roger,—   Monday eve. [April 23, 1928]

I'm too tired and too sleepy to give you an adequate report of our debut but I'm rather happy about how it all panned out. I'm really sorry you weren't with us[1]—I should have liked you to have been there so that we could have discussed the music (particularly Chávez!), so that you could have passed on the spirit of the concert which I didn't think quite satisfactory, so that you could have helped out at the party, which was a dismal affair etc. etc. People asked for you both and the moral responsibility of the occasion was rather heavy on my slim shoulders. But I'm a man to accept the inevitable—and everything that happens in connection with the two of you I always place in that category! Margy Naumberg tells me you won't sail until after the 6th so you will be at one concert anyhow and that evens matters up considerably. As it happens, the Sonata will be an invaluable aid in bracing up the second program which had been weakish in its original form.

To me the most surprising thing that took place was the way the critics turned out. I think it's an indication of what the concerts mean to the musical life here generally. Mary C. is sending you all of the clippings. They all damned Chávez which I think is a sign of the real excellence of his music . . . Anyhow the critics were there and we seemed like a very important organization! (Mrs. Reis was astounded but very pleasant about it.) The audience seemed more literary and theatrical than musical. I don't quite understand why it was so. The enthusiasm, which was greater than at similar functions of the League, did not quite reach my expectations—does that surprise you?

Ruth Warfield, looking marvellously, played Teddy's Sonata rather badly which wasn't surprising considering her recent illness and the short time she had to prepare it. Piston was here for his final rehearsal and the concert and bowed in response to much applause—the audience liked the Three Pieces though they seemed to me to be little more than well written. I don't know what the Thomson sounded like because I played the percussion part to the astonishment of Henry Cowell.[2] I won't go into Chávez's stuff now. I have copies of his music to play for you as soon as I can get you near a piano and my article on him is appearing in the N.R. this Friday.[3]

Mary has been extremely efficient throughout, tho new problems have arisen which seem almost insoluble. The only wrong thing she did was to lose your telegram before I saw it, but I heard it from memory and if I hadn't been such an excited ass I would have sent one in return.

Yours, tired but happy,

A

1. There is no record of why Roger and Barbara Sessions did not attend the April 22d concert, though the failure to complete the sonata may have been a factor.

2. Henry Cowell (1897–1965), composer, pianist, and writer.

3. Aaron Copland, "Carlos Chávez: Mexican Composer," *The New Republic,* May 2, 1928, 322–23.

▼

Roger Sessions to Aaron Copland
als US-DLC

Dear Aaron,—   [late April 1928]

Just a line. The Sonata is going along splendidly, which I am sure will not be bad news to you! I'm desolate not to be with you + Fred [Jacobi] in Washington—but I am rather susceptible to the dangers of interruption.[1]

M[ary] C[hurchill] sent me the clippings—at least we received a good deal of attention. Downes[2] has risen 100 percent or more in my estimation—he alone seems to have realized that the event could be of any importance whatever, + his very timidity is a good sign, I think. It means, at least, that he is afraid to commit himself too soon. As for the others, Henderson[3] rather surprised me—he seemed next best, in spite of being an old war horse.

As for the others—they have quite revolutionized my ideas of what is old + what is new, + what provincialism can be. In spite of everything + all my prejudices against New York I would never have realized that Piston's or even Teddy's works were so revolutionary. As for Chávez you can't imagine what an alluringly confused idea I have of his style! The gentleman who pronounced Teddy's sonata "Gershwinized Prokofieff"—and Chávez "disjointed Bach, imitation Gounod with mock Hindemith accompaniment" seems particularly to have hit the nail on the head—whether the head of the nail, however, I'm not sure!

Well—have a good time in Washington. I shall expect all sorts of impressions.

Give my love to Fred and—à bientot.

Roger

1. Barbara Sessions, not her husband, answered Copland's April 23 letter in a letter of April 25, 1928 (US-DLC), in which she stated that he "has decided not to go to Washington [. . .] he didn't dare risk the sense of interruption it gave him, even were the actual time not so precious."

2. Olin Downes, "Music: Presenting American Composers," New York Times, April 23, 1928, 20. Downes "emphatically commend[ed] the plans of Mr. Copland and Mr. Sessions."

3. W. J. Henderson, "Present American Composers," New York Sun, April 23, 1928, 19.

T HE SECOND Copland-Sessions Concert was reviewed by Olin Downes ("Music: More New Music," *New York Times,* May 7, 1928, 29), who wrote that the "young composer of today is not at all badly off." And "The most significant of these compositions were the scores of Copland and Sessions," to whom he devoted two long and approving paragraphs. Samuel Chotzinoff, in "A Lot of New Music," *The World* (May 7, 1928, 11), ridiculed the idea of trying to "stimulate 'composers' to more prolific activity." Sessions's former teacher at Harvard, Edward Burlingame Hill ("The Young Composers' Movement," *Modern Music 5,* no. 4 [May–June 1928]: 32), pointed to the considerable influence of Stravinsky and Schoenberg on these composers, especially that of Stravinsky on Sessions's Sonata. However, there is no surviving correspondence by the two composers commenting on these reviews.

Copland's accounts of the expenses for these two concerts reveal costs almost outweighing income. For example, the first concert cost $497.56, the second $584.07, while the box office took in $67 for the first concert and $113 for the second and $265 in subscriptions. After adding $700 in unidentified deposits and donations, Copland figured that a total of $63.37 was "left over for next year."

Shortly afterward Copland and Sessions traveled in opposite directions: Copland to New Mexico and the West, and Sessions back to Italy to take up life at the American Academy in Rome. Sessions soon heard from Ernest Bloch again, who had rather unsettling news.

▼

Ernest Bloch to Roger Sessions
als US-NYpease

May 31, 1928
Dear Roger,   [San Francisco]

I am surprised not to have heard from you. Your last letter (Sept. 24) was announcing another one. It is true that it is *I* who owe you a letter. But besides many excuses, there was the queer feeling that I could not locate you. N. York, I know, but where? And I do not know who wrote vaguely that you had left again for Europe? Thus I am sending this letter to Northhampton [*sic*], "à la gràce de Dieu" ou plutôt des Postes des U.S. à qui est plus dangereux! ["By the grace of God" or, rather, the U.S. Post, which is more dangerous.] You may know more about me than I do about you, if you kept somewhat in touch with Lucienne [Bloch]. I broke down, in the Fall—and was very near losing my mind—when the head was settled again, the body broke, in turn. I had the worst relapses, not of my feet, but several parts of the body were attacked. For four months, it was a terrific struggle. Finally, I could master it, and since 2 months I enjoy a relative peace. I say relative, because I have to be always on the "qui vive" [lookout]—but acute sickness seems over. I have read so much now about it all, that I know more than all the American doctors I had consulted. I know that I cannot be cured, unless *perhaps* I get a radical change of life and go back to "normalcy," as our great late President Harding used to say. But what is normalcy, for an artist, at such a period we live in? I realize fully that the greatest cause of my actual troubles, and what prevents the organism to throw out all toxins elaborated since years (in fact, since my first attack in Cleveland 1921) is the constant conflict of my life. Conflict in my private life. A family . . . A family, for what? for my toiling, and my misfortune. Away from me, and with no real concern and affection for me. And conflict between myself and this world of business, superficiality, dishonesty, lack of conscience—especially professional conscience. Ich kann nicht "mitmachen" [I cannot adjust to it] and I do not want to, as I cannot prostitute myself. Thus I live outside of it all. But man is a social animal, after all, and I am not a man hater, at the bottom. As one cannot change the surroundings nor people, nor life itself, the only remedy is either to "conform" or if one cannot, to change one's reactions. This is what I have been trying to do, with great effort, and a little success. After all, what does it matter? We are of little pieces of dust, drops of water in the Ocean. And nowadays, more than ever, the individual does not count. See how Sacco and Vanzetti are forgotten. Not a thought of them! 25 years ago,—remember Drey-fus—the world would not be at peace. Nobody cares.

And in everything it is the same. But let us quit this sad subject. I would be interested to know what you are doing, and what you expect to do. If you are still in America, let me hear from you.

I have decided—but, in *great secret*—to sail for Europe, on June 20, via Panama—38 days of rest and relaxation. At Marseilles, Mrs. Bloch *may* expect me. We will go to the mountains, maybe Griesalp again, 6 weeks. And I sail back, by the same way, may be, with Mrs. Bloch, if she can decide to leave her girls alone. Six other weeks of peace.

I leave without a contract. Mine has expired. The committee will not sign another one before having raised the money. If, when I come, nothing has happened, I may then leave America altogether, and settle *for good,* away from all this nonsense, in some remote South Sea island, where life is cheap, quiet, and where "Progress and Prosperity" are unknown. That is really what I need. Since three months, my only escape, my only joy has been the discipline which I have imposed on myself. I study again. I started counterpoint—strict!—two parts, *very* thoroughly. Thus far, I have written more than 960 examples, in all the modes, some of them are good. I made immense discoveries, in that study—simple and deep—I got an *orientation,* amidst the fallacies and sophisms of our "modern aestheticism." I came back to life again, and an *Art* made, not for "machines" or superapes, but for "Man," within its *limitations.* More than ever the words of Goethe seemed deep to me and rich in teachings "Aeusserlich begrenzt, innerlich unbegrenzt." [Bounded on the exterior, unbounded inside.]

At the same time, I discovered (!) Josquin des Près, who is a *giant.* I hope that after 2 or 3 more months, I may start the [counterpoint in] three parts. Thus, in two or three years, I may know *something* of music,—real music—It has been an incredible refreshment. It has, in fact, saved my life. My pupils, humbled by my own example, and realizing that they did not know a thing, and were "killing the symptoms" all the time, on their own work, instead of facing courageously the *Truth,* imitated me, somewhat—came back, willingly to this start—even simple melody, and thus all my teaching was revolutionized! I really *begin* understanding what music is. No one, of course—save *one* exception, an accomplished composer here, a friend of mine, who wants to start again with me—shares my folly—but what does it matter? This isolates me still more but what I am losing (?) is amply repaid by the contact with the real great masters, who I appreciate more deeply every day.

Suzanne feels a little in conflict too with her actual surroundings—so does Lucienne. A good sign of growth. I advised them strongly to go to Germany for a year to see other people, its minds, its conceptions, to break with "cliques"—that death of independance—to become "free" which is so difficult. But they probably will not follow my advice.

You know probably that Suzanne is marrying Russell Collier, this coming summer. But she resolved herself to stay for another year abroad. Then, the poor girl will have to settle in Cleveland.

These are all the news "fit to print"—not very interesting, indeed. But out of dullness, one cannot create a world of great imagination.

S. Francisco is fine, and life agreeable here. As I say, to everyone, if I leave S.F., I leave America. This is the only place I have found, in the U.S. where Life is possible. And it really must be *marvelous,* when a man who has gone in tortures, mental and physical, since 2 years, can acknowledge that.

Well, dear Roger, let me hear from you. I hope Mrs. Sessions is well and that you feel more cheerful and happy than I do.

As always, affectionately yours,
Ernest Bloch

1928-1931

THREE

Within days of the second Copland-Sessions concert, Roger and Barbara Sessions were on their way back to Paris. The gloom of the failure to complete the Piano Sonata was lifted by the absence of a deadline, by the return to Europe, and by Sessions's attendance at several exciting concerts, about which he writes to the Sonata's performer, John Duke. Sessions was first to spend the summer of 1928 at Juziers, outside Paris, and ten days in the Swiss Alps with Jean and Denise Binet. In the autumn he would begin his fellowship at the American Academy in Rome. Even before the Sessionses reached Rome, in October, Sessions had begun his campaign to persuade Copland to apply for the Rome Prize, so that Copland would be in Rome during some of their stay. Copland had written to Sessions expressing his desire to stay in the U.S., especially in New York, rather than to apply for the Rome Prize. If Copland would not be moved to leave New York, Sessions advised him, "for Heaven's sake, go out to live in the country!!!!!!"

Roger Sessions to John Duke
als US-Nsmith

May 26 [1928]

Dear John,—   Paris-Brussels

We are en route for Brussels, + if my handwriting isn't all it might be, that is the reason! We have had a thoroughly absorbing week in Paris thus far. Saturday evening, after we had been in town for about six hours only, I heard a concert at which Stravinsky played his concerto; Sunday we spent the day at Versailles, where Nadia Boulanger drove us. Tuesday night we heard Stravinsky conduct the *Sacre du Printemps* + *Oedipus Rex;* Wednesday I saw a lot of old friends at the Boulanger's, including some of the most interesting people I know; Thursday was mainly devoted to Koussevitzky, with a rehearsal in the morning + a concert in the evening; and finally last night (Friday) we heard *Don Giovanni,* conducted by Bruno Walter—not bad for a beginning, you must admit!

I would like so much to write you in detail about all these things; but it would really take a small volume. Above all it is wonderful to be back here, more wonderful than we had in any way anticipated; even though it would be hard to say just why. When you have been here you will understand. First from a purely human point of view, one breathes freely again; there is an atmosphere of freedom, of individualism that, I am afraid, our country lacks. One feels that one can do as one likes, and not, certainly, merely because one is a foreigner. Everyone is alive, either enjoying or suffering intensely— while as you know, at home the majority of people are neither happy or unhappy.

Then, from a musical point of view, one feels still more contrast. Music is a real factor, here, in people's lives; even those people who don't love it—and France is not one of the most musical countries in Europe—find it important for the very reason that there are so many of those who do. And here one sees, constantly + in great numbers, really first class musicians. I have seen Milhaud, Prokofieff, d'Indy, Roussel, Stravinsky, of course, not to mention others whom you have probably not yet heard of. If the Salle Pleyel had been blown up on Thursday morning at Koussevitzky's rehearsal, Stravinsky would be about the only Russian composer left alive! I have met two very interesting young composers, one a German-Swiss, Conrad Beck,[1] and another a Russian, Lopatnikoff.[2] Both of them you will hear of in a few years, certainly. I have heard none of Beck's music, though it is spoken of very highly by some of my friends; but Lopatnikoff's *Scherzo* which Koussevitzky played was delightful—full of life + spontaneity, somewhat in the manner of Prokofieff, but charming + extremely promising.

However—I have had again, an enormous impression from Stravinsky—both his playing + his conducting have improved enormously since I heard it last. In his playing of the concerto one felt, above all, a simplicity + dignity so extreme that, while one felt that, all the time, he was merely *presenting* the music without interpreting or underlining a single note, the impression was enormously forceful—its extreme impersonality + objectivity were in themselves *forces*—they seemed the nth however of musical feeling, controlled and disciplined through its very strength. I assure you it was a surprise, for I have never considered Stravinsky a good performer; and it was, probably by reason of this surprise, a very significant experience for me. The same programme included an incredibly dull symphony of Mahler, which like all the works of Mahler contained both utterly magnificent + unbelievably trivial things, the whole being five times too long + far too richly scored. In spite of this he is a tremendously great musician—only one always has a very disagreeable impression, for the very reason that certain fleeting moments are so thoroughly remarkable. This particular symphony contains a slow movement that seemed like the cheapest gospel hymn swollen to elephantine proportions. That may sound extreme, but I assure you it is not. But, coming just after it, the *Concerto,* in its austerity, its incisiveness, its freshness, loomed very large indeed.

Stravinsky's concert of his own works was uneven, but on the whole extraordinary. One curious impression was that, after playing the *Sacre* all winter on the piano, I found the orchestral color disturbing; it seemed on that one hearing to reduce instead of magnifying the work. Then too the performance was ragged; and, having heard Str. conduct before,[3] I was a little uneasy about his getting through without mishaps. He did, perfectly well, however—and although I still think Monteux,[4] at least, does it far better, because of his greater technical equipment, still Stravinsky's performance was an extraordinary one. *Oedipus,* however, was the really great experience of that evening. I was surer than ever of the greatness of this music, hearing it done by Str. himself. The contrast with Koussevitzky was extraordinary, + really illuminating. I was quite aware that K—— is careless with his tempi; but at the same time I realized that he was trying tremendously hard to do it as he thought Str. would like it. The extraordinary thing was that under Str. it was far warmer + richer than under K——; obviously the man felt this music in every fibre of his being—felt it *as music* in all of its significance. Without losing any of its impressiveness it became lighter, more tense, and far more dramatic.

I'm tremendously pleased to hear about Rosamond's recital—+ that it went so well. It would not be at all a bad idea for her to go to Concord this summer; she would find it a little dull, I fear, but that would do no harm provided she doesn't get discouraged. Surette[5] himself is quite superficial, but he has "assistants" who are excellent musicians. Nadia B—— knows a good deal about the school + I shall ask her about it when I see her again. I still have hopes of hearing occasionally from Rosamond, though my hopes may be rather naive ones!

We have seen a good deal of Nadia B——; she is splendid, as always, + a marvelous friend. I have talked with her a little about R—— + she seemed much interested;—also about you. I told her, also, how much I liked Leedy's playing; she spoke very nicely of both him + his wife.[6]

I have, as you may imagine, not had much time for work as yet! But when we get back from these four days in Brussels I shall be tremendously glad to get at the sonata again. I am never quite happy unless I am working—+ working normally—and this week has been above all exciting + stimulating. There are plenty of events for some weeks ahead, but I shall have my own studio + shall be able to manage life better! In any case I am crazy to get back to the Sonata, which I feel I can finish in far better shape here than I could have at home!

Barbara + I both send our love. Forgive this formless letter, written on the train—+ do write me again soon. The same address will be good all summer, surely. And greetings to everyone—only very specially to Rosamond.

Always affectionately,
Roger

[P.S.] Good luck with your work! I am especially anxious to know how the *Suite* goes. Do tell me as much as you can about it.

1. Beck (b. 1901), a prolific Swiss composer, was affiliated with the ISCM.
2. The neoclassicist Nicolai Lopatnikoff (1903–76) was then living in Germany (1920–33); he moved to the U.S. in 1939 and taught at the Carnegie Institute of Technology (1945–69).

3. In Cleveland; see chapter 2, letter of February 15, 1925.

4. Pierre Monteux (1875–1964) had conducted the premiere of *Le sacre du printemps* and other works of Stravinsky, Debussy, and Ravel.

5. Thomas Whitney Surette (1861–1941), an educator and writer of popular articles on music, had founded in 1914 the Concord (Mass.) Summer School of Music, and in 1921 had become head of the music department at Bryn Mawr College. From 1937 to 1939 he taught at Black Mountain College.

6. Charles Leedy (1900–1964), professor of music at Mount Holyoke College.

▼

Roger Sessions to Aaron Copland
als US-DLC

June 26 [1928]

Dear Aaron,—   Paris (20 Rue de Berne)

I was delighted to get your letter, though it pricked my conscience about the "volume." To tell the truth I have a good deal to write! This is just the overture, however.

Business first: I felt as you did about the League, + had sent in my acceptance before your letter came. With somewhat different reasons I shall refuse to join the "Executive Board" or any other of the kind. I don't think it is good for composers.

Secondly, I have seen Beck, Lopatnikhoff, + Dukelsky (!!) + procured works from all of them for next year's concerts. More later about this; Lopatnikhoff a sonata, Beck a string quartet, Dukelsky three songs. All are published. Incidentally the Russians win, again; Beck's stuff I can see is promising but it seems to me intrinsically conventional. I suggest also Jean Binet; I find on hearing his work again that I have done him an injustice; but as I am so tremendously proud of the person I think you had better make the final decision, with myself simply strongly recommending. Lopatn. + Beck + Dukelsky I have promised. I have had a very curious time with the latter—we both chose to ignore completely that we met before, + got along splendidly—boon companions at the Kouss. rehearsals + receptions. His symphony I like, though more at the rehearsal than the performance.[1]

Prokofieff's stock has gone slightly down, as far as I am concerned (2d act of the opera "L'Ange de Feu";[2] Hindemith's *way* up (Viola Concerto).[3] There are certain things that still bother me considerably, though less in this work than in any other, but of the middle generation he seems by far the best. As for Honegger + Milhaud,—

−117−

and Poulenc; they have disappeared from my world. Roussel has gone up considerably—+ this was the greatest surprise, though I wish he had gone up still higher.

The "puissant + far-spreading Igor" (H. T. Parker) holds his own triumphantly with *Apollon* which I heard 4 times, besides getting to know the score quite thoroughly. I have again had the pleasure of shaking hands with him twice—the second time after the première of *Apollon*—which, judging from the faces + attitudes of others who followed us (N.B. + B.S. + I were the first, + found him after the performance alone with Ansermet[4] + Mme. Stravinsky), did not meet with whole general approval. S.K. however was enchanted + will play it at his second concert in Boston.

Of all the people I have met, or seen again I.S., Ansermet, + Hindemith define themselves clearly as *first-rate* personalities. I had only a few moments conversation with Hindemith, + the same with Igor; but Ansermet is a marvelous person—I look forward *very* much to seeing him in Switzerland in August. He is favorably inclined towards me + may play my symphony here next year, with his new Parisian orchestra. Of this *not a word,* however, as I must consult S.K. + as Ansermet himself must see my symphony at leisure, this summer, in Suisse, first.

Skyscrapers[5] was much better than I thought—jolly, well orchestrated, + at least superficially American—not a virtue in itself, but lending the music a certain character.

Messieurs Lazar + Tansman[6] were active as always in the court of the Rue Conseiller-Colognon, the former as picturesquely absurd as ever, the latter squirming in a slightly revolting way. Another one, quite revolting—his body much more revolting than Tansman, his mind idler + more stupid + therefore less keenly so than Tansman— P. O. Ferroud[7] appeared occasionally. Jesús Sanromá was always present, + we got to know him very well + to like him enormously. He played, truly magnificently, what seemed to me a very mediocre concerto of Ernst Toch.[8] Burgin[9] was here for a while, + Barbara + Jesús + he + I had good meals together on the Rue Darn + the Place des Tertres. The fat + jolly Hertz was also here.

Naturally we met Prokofieff + I like him personally very much— better than his music, on the whole, though the revised *Pas d'Acier*[10] isn't bad. I find in particular, + not only à propos of Prokofieff, that the orchestra has become unwieldy, + that in particular the huge mass of strings is unwieldy + indigestible. Was zu tun? [What to do?]

Igor played his Piano Concerto the evening of the day we arrived. His stock as interpreter of his own music rose very high, to sink again three nights later when I heard him conduct the *Sacre*. But this is unfair—I had gotten to know the *Sacre* so well on the piano that its orchestral color, a thousand times copied by his imitators, bothered me + seemed to lessen the power of the work. But his conducting of *Oedipus* was a *revelation*—or at least with the proper tempi (from the song of *Oed*. [at rehearsal no. 83] "Invidia fortunam odit" ["Envy hates the fortunate"] on) it became ten times as living, as dramatic, as emotional, as under S.K. Try this over on your piano. Alas—the nice G♭ in the piano part at "Trivium trivium" [at rehearsal no. 115] was a misprint, but the correct version is at least as effective.

I had sent to you the piano score of *Apollon*—if you will look at the title page you will find a tender message. I had in general the same reaction as to *Oedipus* at the first performance a very complete [illegible] in certain parts, but doubts of others. The doubts again vanished. I didn't play the work but once before I heard the first performance,[11] + again first before the last—I wanted to keep a fresh impression of its color. Judging from Fred [Jacobi]'s article[12] + your + his, as well as Kindler's (he too is here) accounts, I gather that the performance in Wash. must have been very much a misconception on both Kindler's + Bohm's parts.[13] Kindler is still unconvinced.— Ansermet says he considers *Apollon* one of Stravinsky's best works. In spite of some very ragged, typically *Ballet Russe* playing it sounded like a dream on the strings, + Little Igor was improved greatly as chef d'orchestre, though he still hears with his inner ear rather than his outer one.

I wish I could continue in this vein, but I have some slightly bad news for you. The Tiomkin concert[14] was a very poor show, + your piece ["Cortège macabre"] was presented under very unfavorable circumstances. *Euryanthe* overture, Liszt A major concerto, you + G[eorge] G[ershwin]. Golschmann[15] is a cheap exhibitionist + a very poor musician, Tiomkin an equally cheap + equally poor musician— Everyone except the silly Americans here were disgusted—even Gershwin himself, one says, though I can't verify this. Consequently your music suffered very much. I'm so sorry, + hope you will forgive me for having been partly an agent in having let it be played. N.B. felt as I did that it was unwise, but she also thought that since you had promised it, it was better in the end to go ahead. The result was a great disappointment to us both. I have no means of knowing whether it did you any real harm here, however, but on the whole gather not.

I do not feel that I can judge the work, except that it is obviously an earlier one of yours. But I do beg you to think again before you let it be played without the rest of the ballet. I may quite possibly be quite wrong, but it seemed to me not to stand well alone; and perhaps it is the other movements that it needs?

This letter is, obviously, more than the overture—rather it is the first act! Roy + Israel will have to wait, except that I have seen them both several times, + am going to spend the summer in *Juziers,* where among other things I shall work at the piano with N.B. as teacher! Teddy left for the USA two days before we arrived. His address is Geneseo N.Y.—I am writing him soon; but from both NB's + his own account he is very discouraged! His letter was really almost heart-rending.

This summer I shall finish the sonata + work principally on the Vl. concerto + another large symphonic work I have in mind.—Also the Nightingale + Usher! But this must wait for the second act, too!

Write me again. You sound quite blasé, by the way, about New Mexico. That's a very good thing, I should say. Incidentally I have felt anything but blasé about Europe!

All our love + good wishes—+ a thousand apologies for not having been a better correspondent.

R——

[P.S.] *Good luck at Hollywood!*

1. Dukelsky's Symphony No. 1 was first performed June 14, 1928, on Koussevitzky's Paris concert series.

2. Sergei Prokofiev's opera *The Flaming Angel,* after Valery Bryusov's story, was written in 1919–23 and revised 1926–27. A concert performance of act 2 was conducted by Koussevitzky in Paris June 14, 1928, the same concert mentioned in note 1.

3. Probably Hindemith's op. 36, no. 4, Kammermusik no. 5 for viola and large chamber orchestra (1927). He also wrote op. 46, no. 1, Kammermusik no. 6 for viola d'amore and chamber orchestra (1927), and he was to write a Konzertmusik for viola and large chamber orchestra in 1930.

4. Ernest Ansermet (1883–1969) conducted the premieres of Stravinsky's *L'histoire du soldat* and Capriccio for Piano and Orchestra.

5. John Alden Carpenter's *Skyscrapers: A Ballet of Modern American Life* (1926) received several European performances in 1928, where its American qualities elicited much critical comment.

6. The Romanian composer Filip Lazar (1894–1936), in Paris since 1915, founded Triton, a modern music society, in 1928. Alexandre Tansman (1897–1986), a Polish composer then living in Paris, had toured the U.S. in 1927–28.

7. Pierre-Octave Ferroud (1900–1936), a composer and music critic, had published a monograph on his teacher, Florent Schmitt, in 1927.

8. Jesús María Sanromá (1902–84), the Boston Symphony's pianist 1926–44, played the Piano Concerto by Austrian composer Ernst Toch (1887–1964) written in 1926 and premiered by Gieseking.

9. Richard Burgin (1892–1981), assistant conductor of the Boston Symphony Orchestra since 1927 and its concertmaster since 1920.

10. A revised version of *Le pas d'acier*, op. 41 (1924), appeared in 1928.

11. The European premiere June 12, 1928, in Paris with the Ballets Russes, conducted by Stravinsky and choreographed by George Balanchine.

12. "The New Apollo," *Modern Music 5*, no. 4 (May–June 1928): 11–15.

13. Hans Kindler (1892–1949) had conducted the premiere of *Apollon musagète* in Washington, D.C., April 27, 1928. Adolph Böhm danced the role of Apollo.

14. On May 29, 1928, at the Théâtre de l'Opéra. The Ukranian composer Dimitri Tiomkin (1894–1979) had emigrated to the U.S. in 1925, where he wrote over one hundred scores for films by Frank Capra, Alfred Hitchcock, and others, often incorporating American folk material, especially in westerns (his score for *High Noon* won an Academy Award in 1952). As a pianist, Tiomkin gave the European premiere of Gershwin's Concerto in F at this concert. In his autobiography, *Please Don't Hate Me* (New York: Doubleday, 1959), 130–40, he describes his and Gershwin's role in arranging this premiere, referring to Copland's piece only as a "short orchestral piece by the American modernist Aaron Copland" (140).

15. Vladimir Golschmann (1893–1972) promoted modern works in Paris as a conductor. He conducted the Saint Louis Symphony for more than a quarter century.

▼

Roger Sessions to Aaron Copland
als US-DLC

August 19 [1928]

Dear Aaron,—   Juziers

I was so happy to get your letter that, as you see, I am answering at once. Not that I have anything supremely important to say; but hearing from you is a pleasure that I am anxious to renew as soon as possible—+ as often!

Your account of "The Winning of the West" amused me enormously, + I can imagine nothing more diverting that an evening with you on this subject—your sensations while playing at the RR station, speaking over the Radio, etc., not to mention your impressions of Charlie Chaplin, + c. What a country we live in !?#*5()%"069§¶

However you seem to have come out alive, and for that I am grateful. And as for the "succès de scandale" you certainly don't seem depressed—it must have been amusing, at any rate.[1] Above all I'm glad things are so good at Peterboro.[2] You certainly deserve a good summer, now that the shouting is over.

I'm glad we agree about Israel. Since I wrote you we have become still better acquainted, + my impressions remain the same, or better. Incidentally, it may be useful for you to know that Mark Brunswick,[3] too, liked him enormously and, he gave me t[o] understand intends to do all he can to help him + interest other people in him. I shall also be writing shortly to Fred Jacobi, and will take pains to say something to him. Mark will probably get in touch with you sometime; but in any case you might as well have his address—853 7th Ave. He + his wife sailed yesterday. They are both very happy, + we have become very fond indeed of Ruth,[4] especially since the marriage, which solves many problems for them, and apparently in a really satisfactory way.

What you say about Roy, too, was welcome, especially as I had a slight qualm about writing so frankly when we—Roy + I, naturally!—were on such ostensibly, at least, good terms.[5] You are quite right, I'm sure,—and I have taken it more or less for granted from the start—that he is a different person with both of us. And I can see plenty of reasons—beginning with your unselfishness + generosity— why he should interest you more than me. And, after all, his type is one which is undoubtedly more familiar to me than to you—the Yankee farmer—so that I am less aware of differences than you.

We are really quite worried about N.B.[6] She had a bad liver attack, last week, + actually took a day off! But the real worry is a far more serious one than that. Ever since we came we noticed that she had something on her mind, and rather desperately so; and she apparently works herself to death in order to forget it. She has given us many signs that she is dissatisfied + discouraged with her life as it has turned out, + looks back with longing at what seems to her the abandoned possibilities of a normal woman's life, quite at the expense of her musical career. Beyond this we have no idea; whether something definite has happened, or whether she simply feels, as she has said, that she has gotten past the age where she can still regard such a change as possible, no one can tell. But she is obviously in a very critical state, both physically +, as the French would say, "morally"— she has promised us a visit to Italy next spring, + I hope she will really come; she needs every moment of rest that she can get, + there seems to be small likelihood of her taking it before that time. You can understand how distressed we are to see her in such a state.

The summer has been a fairly good one for me, thus far. We had a marvelous ten days in the Alps with the Binets; and when we got there I realized that I was dead tired + had been, in fact, all spring, not only as a result of my *surmenage* [breakdown] over the Sonata (!) but of various inner efforts I had made for over a year, in the effort to solve various problems for myself. Ten days of walking, getting sunburned, + taking a *real* vacation with such good friends (I have not idled so completely for years) persuaded me that the bad year was finished + made me quite myself again. So I am now working on the violin concerto in an effort to get some of it ready to show S.K. next month. The sonata is "on the shelf" for the moment, but when S.K. has gone back I shall work on it too, + finish it right up. I really feel very energetic, + am convinced that *this* year is to be an excellent one.

Since you have been confidential with me, I might as well be so with you too, + tell you that we *may* be rivals for the $25,000![7] I would say, we *will,* but I don't want to get into a tense state as I did with the sonata. In any case I am planning + to a certain extent working on a new symphony, + if it is ready I shall submit it. This too is a secret, at least I am going to follow your example + consider it so from now on, as I think you are very wise to do so.

I had an excellent interview with Lamond[8] the other day, + apparently he is making every effort to see that I will be happy + comfortable + free in Rome. Whatever misgivings I had about the Academy itself he dispelled rather completely, + I am sure now that I will have excellent working conditions. The only misgivings that remain are concerned with the people I shall have to talk to; Casella[9] + [Ottorino] Respighi certainly do not tempt me very much; and to judge from Steinert[10] I do not look forward to great edification from the other "fellows." After this, does it seem too much like "damning with faint praise" when I say that I don't see how I am going to stand more than a year of it, unless you come too—for the year after? You know, it would not require the least effort on your part—you would only have to submit already written, + already performed works, together with a letter from N.B. + one from Koussie, + there is certainly no chance of your failing to get it. The applications, etc. don't have to be in till the first of April, so as far as I can see you need not hurry!

I am still hoping to hear from Lopatnikhoff, but was assured at the Edition Russe the other day that his sonata would probably be out this month. I shall follow your advice about speaking to N.B. about Beck. The Quartet *is* no. 3, + though he spoke of it as his best work I am distinctly disappointed in it. It seems very academic to me; but I shall be glad to find something better. I shall also try to be on the lookout for other things, + will ask N.B. what she knows, if anything. Virgil Thomson suggested Naboukhoff,[11] Sauguet[12] + Maxime Pleyel, but I must confess I was unimpressed.—By the way I have talked to N.B. about Chávez; she is enthusiastic + would like to have his sonata played next year. So I'm letting her have my copy.

Do let me hear from you again soon—+ good luck with your work.

Affectionately,

R——

[P.S.] Barbara + Israel send their love.

1. Copland felt not enough rehearsal time had been scheduled for his Piano Concerto performance at the Hollywood Bowl July 20. He wrote to Chávez, "The *Concerto* caused almost a 'skandal'!" (Aaron Copland and Vivian Perlis, *Copland: 1900 through 1942* [New York: St. Martin's Press, 1984], 155).

2. The MacDowell Colony, in New Hampshire.

3. Mark Brunswick (1902–71) studied with Rubin Goldmark, Ernest Bloch, and Nadia Boulanger, and lived for several years in Vienna, where he studied with Anton von Webern. His second wife, Natascha, was to become a lifelong friend of Sessions's in Princeton.

4. Brunswick's first wife.

5. After discussing Harris's first symphony, sextet, and unfinished sonata, Sessions wrote, "As far as Roy himself is concerned, I must confess to a disappointment." The two had argued over Stravinsky's *Oedipus,* which they had heard performed. Also, "he bores me to tears, and embarrasses me whenever the conversation gets beyond a certain point of impersonality" (July 25, 1928, US-DLC).

6. Also in his letter of July 25 to Copland, Sessions had written: "N.B. is as busy as ever, + more [. . .] teaching from 7 A.M. till late in the evening without any let up, even for lunch" (US-DLC).

7. The *New York Times* (May 29, 1928) had announced RCA Victor company prizes in two categories, for native symphonic and jazz composition. Twenty-five thousand dollars would be awarded for a symphonic work "which would be truly American in conception." The judges were to be Mme. Olga Samaroff, Rudolph Ganz, Leopold Stokowski, Serge Koussevitzky, and Frederick Stock. The deadline for submission was May 27, 1929. Copland, unable to finish his Symphonic Ode in time, entered the Dance Symphony instead, which won five thousand dollars. Sessions began a second symphony, but abandoned it.

8. Felix Lamond (1864–1940) had been an organist and choir director at Trinity Church in New York City 1897–1918. He was director of music composition at the American Academy in Rome from 1918 until his death.

9. Alfredo Casella (1883–1947), Italian composer, pianist, and conductor, was a highly influential figure in Italian music in the twenties and thirties.

10. Alexander Lang Steinert (1900–1982) studied with Charles Martin Loeffler in Boston and with Vincent D'Indy and Charles Koechlin in Paris. He was a fellow of the American Academy in Rome 1927–30.

11. Nicolas Nabokov (1903–78), a composer and cousin of the writer Vladimir Nabokov. His first important work was a ballet-oratorio, *Ode,* first performed June 6, 1928.

12. A disciple of Satie, Henri Sauguet (b. 1901) had achieved some prominence when his ballet *La Chatte* was produced by Diaghilev in 1927.

▼

Roger Sessions to Aaron Copland
tls US-DLC

October 7 [1928]
Accademia Americana
Porta San Pancrazio, Roma 29

Dear Aaron,—

I am sending you the music I had planned to send, with the exception of the Lopatnikhov sonata, which I never received. In its place I am sending the Sonatina of Lopatnikhov, which is published, and has been since last spring. I daresay the Sonata is not ready yet.

Also, I spoke to N.B. about Beck. It was the quartet which she was so enthusiastic about—the Largo. But she admitted that it might be less good than she thought at first, as she only heard it once. I lent it to her, and we did not happen to speak of it again. In any case, she of course does not choose our programs for us. She spoke of a sonata for violin and flute which I am sending also. I think I prefer the quartet of the two; but I still have not been able to conjure up much enthusiasm for the latter. It reminds me too much of Bloch at his weakest, and the Largo, effective as it must be on the quartet, seems rather cheap. On the other hand, there is of course nothing whatever to say if we compare it with Porter, Rudhyar, or Delaney! I agree perfectly that we must have pretty high standards for the European works that we put on our programs; and it may well be that you will feel that nothing that I send measures up to the standard we ought to have. I do feel, however, that the Dukelsky and still more the Lopatnikhoff have a freshness and vigor or spirit that the Beck has not, in spite of Beck's superior musicianship and the greater pretentiousness of his quartet.

As for the Binet songs, I leave you entirely to judge. I like the first the best, in spite of one or two weak spots. But these also have a great freshness and charm, it seems to me. How far this is a result of my great affection for the person, I don't know, and it is impossible to tell.

Do let me know about the concerts—of course you will.

I will send you the piano arrangement of the slow movement of the symphony, and also a copy of the Piano Sonata when it is finished. The latter is coming along, and I hope it won't be long now. With various things I have been doing this summer, I believe my work will go much faster in the future. When we returned from our vacation in

Suisse I determined to face the problem of my limited output, and with the help of N.B. I devised for myself a course of sprouts which have already been an enormous help to me, in this way as in others. But I will say no more about this now; except that I am on top of the wave as far as my work is concerned.

[...]

Rome is marvelous; and even more marvelous is to get back to Italy. I have to realize that, much as I love certain things in France, it is fundamentally alien to me; there seems to me to be something *mesquin* [petty] even about the landscape. Bien entendu [Of course], I exaggerate. But here the sunlight, the warm and intense colors, the indescribable beauty of the landscape and of the people are all things which I need in order to be wholly myself, outside of a few acres in the Connecticut valley. This is so real that I must confess I myself was surprised at the intensity of my feeling when our train, the other day, came into Central Italy again. Then again—and this I feel more gradually, as is quite natural—Italy is far more alive, at this moment, than is France. This summer for the first time France itself depressed me—the "je m'en fou" ["I'm completely nuts"] attitude, so typically French, is so insidious and at the same time so all-pervading. Of course I don't speak of Rome itself; from my studio window and still more from the windows of the apartment we are probably going to take, the view of the city is superb—one of the choicest panoramas in the world, I am sure. Florence is much more perfect, and of course I shall always care the most for Florence; but here the color and the light is something that even Florence cannot touch.

As for the Academy, things have started out in the most propitious manner. Lamond, who is in charge of the music, seems to be laying himself out to make things just the way I want them. Working conditions should be ideal. As for the other "fellows," I have to take lunch with them; and I can tell you better about that later on—I go over for the first time tomorrow. I met Steinert in Paris and can't say I was deeply impressed; but he is very nice and a little tact will make everything easy I am sure. It won't do me any harm to learn tact, by the way!

Other news; the Black Maskers will be played in Cincinnati on November 23 and 24.[1] I didn't see S.K. in Paris last month, as that was just when my tooth was bothering me so much; but I am writing him, and I hope you will put in a good word for me when you see him. He was charming in June.

Write me soon—you owe me two letters, God Damn you. Barbara

sends her love. You might give mine to Minna L. and Mary C. and any one else you may come across, that I know. We had some very good times with Margaret Naumberg just before we left.

Affectionately as always

Roger

1. Sessions had been in communication with Fritz Reiner, then conductor of the Cincinnati Symphony Orchestra, since at least early 1928. On February 6 Reiner had written Sessions informing him that the *Black Maskers* orchestral suite was scheduled for April 13 and 14. After those performances had been postponed, Reiner wrote again on August 31 that the work was rescheduled for November 23 and 24 (US-NYpease). These performances also did not take place, though Sessions, in Rome, did not learn that fact for several months.

▼

Roger Sessions to Aaron Copland
tls US-DLC

November 8–9 [1928]

Dear Aaron,—   Villa Sforza, 31 Via Garibaldi, Roma 29

Thank you for your good letter. Your plans for the concerts sound very good. I am not too surprised that there is not more material, and wish only that I could make some further contributions from this end. My associates here (SSSSSSSSSSSSSSSSHHHHHHHHHHHHHH) are thus far doing nothing incredibly startling, and I am having a rather amusing time dodging various gentle hints regarding our concerts! As Hans Sachs would say, "the impresario's life is full of care." You should have seen how anxious to please were Messrs. Lazar, Tansman, et Cie., in Paris last spring. It is true that Steinert has not come back yet, and that I have never seen any of his music; but knowing both the man and what S.K. and N.B. among others have told me, I am not too hopeful in that direction, though for me, here, he will have his undeniable uses. There is a young boy here named Inch, from Rochester, who may be of some good;[1] if further investigation reveals anything I will let you know. As for Italians,—and don't forget that there is the French Academy, too—I have not met any except Respighi, as yet. But I may be able to give you some more definite information in the course of another month.

I of course, in accordance with my present policy do not want to promise anything. But I may quite probably, in the course of two or three months, have a set of Etudes, or Preludes, for the piano, which might fill up a gap on your last or even the second program.[2] In other words, I have one finished already—one, that is, which I consider good enough to play in public; and as that is the only one which I have composed I have hope for the rest. I have composed a lot of small things, but a good deal of it is worthless and some of the rest in rather sketchy form, though I believe that it contains some excellent material.

I am much interested that we are to have a try at resuscitating the fortunes of George Antheil. Paris seems to have forgotten him completely last spring—which is nothing against him, of course, and might possibly even be the making of him in the end.[3]

I have written Gieseking[4] and will send him the two movements as soon as I have heard from him definitely as to his present whereabouts; the finale to follow. Mrs. Reis urged me to urge you to write something, also, for Gieseking, which I hereby do; but I suppose that if you have already refused her, you had your reasons for doing so! I am sorry the poor dear lady feels slighted; you may assure her that I will come across, at any rate, to the best of my ability! Barbara suggests that Mrs. R—— would not like it if she knew I had used her name—+ in my case consider yourself urged; I would make it very strong if I had the least idea of what terms would seem convincing to you! I will also write Mary Churchill, as you suggest; and furthermore if you see Minna you may tell her, unofficially, that I am planning an article for her—a rather big article which will take me some time, as I have not too much time to work on it each day.[5] It is not, however, on Igor, with whom I am through for the time being; by which I mean to say that while I would be interested perhaps in writing on some single work, I don't feel like undertaking a general study of his work as a whole. What I have in hand—a definite study of contemporary musical problems and of the means, or rather the direction of the solution—seems to me much more important, for the moment at least.

My work continues to go well, and Rome grows on me increasingly. I have really nothing to add, in this respect, to what I wrote you before. The shades of Hanson and Sowerby still hang over the place to a certain extent;[6] but this has not seemed to affect either my status or my peace of mind! Good conversation, to be sure, is not abundant up here, but, I am forced to admit, neither is it anywhere else in the world. Furthermore, the least desirable characteristics of American Nordic Blonds (not to mention Blondes!) are reduced to impotence in the intensity of the Italian and Roman background;[7] so I have perfect solitude of the kind that one only attains in the society of those with whom one has exactly nothing in common. And I must admit that Lamond, the head of the Music Department here, has been more than kind. My private suspicion is that they are as much aware as I am that it would not be wholly to their advantage if I should not find the Academy wholly to my liking. Furthermore Lamond is a man of the world, which means a great deal; and I am all in all thoroughly satisfied with everything.

Of course I can understand your feeling about New York, even though I do not share it.[8] I do agree that in general it is theoretically best to be in one's own country; while on the other hand I find that for myself—on coming back here especially—that I am really more conscious of the America that I really believe in, America as she may become in the future, that is, over here than I am at home; and I feel too, that I can make my contribution very much more effective through being as thoroughly myself as possible; and this involves, for the present, my being here. Hoover's election and all that it means will not, I fear, lead me to believe that future any less distant! However you know very well what my point of view is, so I needn't waste time over it now. But for Heaven's sake, go out to live in the country!!!!!!!

Barbara will write you, or at least says she will! and will give you the impressions you ask for. I had a really remarkable letter from Israel a while ago, and am more hopeful about him than ever. Roy I am having to write to regarding an article that Irving Weil wrote in *Musical America* in Sept., on information which Roy gave him, and in which I am represented as a pupil of N.B. with no reference to Bloch whatever, and also as an earnest member of a little group of serious thinkers in Juziers, where "the new American idiom" is being "forged."[9] No doubt you have seen it—you too are in the article of course, but you belong there a little more than I do; even though it is no place for either of us, and in any case I have the rather unpleasant task of explaining to Bloch that I had nothing to do with the article or with the implied affront to him. I myself would never have seen the article if it had not been called to my attention by someone here: of course cheap publicity is inevitable and so long as I am not personally responsible for it I don't care, but I do, actually, owe everything to Bloch, while on the other hand neither I or, I am sure, Nadia, ever dreamed of my being her disciple. No doubt Roy had the best of intentions; but he really must learn to keep his mouth shut.

I really would like so much to talk with you about many things— things which I have not time nor inclination to write about—letters from Rome to New York are a rather unsatisfactory means of communication, unfortunately; though I must say that I am pleased and flattered to have received your, as you say, longest communication. Also, having written you two letters to your one makes me as proud as I feel when someone asks me to lend them money, and for somewhat similar reasons, if specious ones—i.e. that my laziness and inattention in these respects is not so absolute as I sometimes fear!

Let me hear from you again in any case!

Always affectionately
Roger

1. Herbert Reynolds Inch (b. 1904) had studied with Howard Hanson and later taught at the Eastman School and at Hunter College (1937–65).

2. These pieces were never performed and do not appear in Sessions's catalog of completed music. Sessions completed only one work—the Piano Sonata, two years after its promised date—during his three-year Rome Academy fellowship.

3. Antheil had left for the U.S. shortly after the premiere, in Paris, of his *Ballet mécanique* in June 1928.

4. Walter Gieseking (1895–1956) had given his American debut in New York on February 22, 1926. The League of Composers had announced a concert for February 16, 1929, at Town Hall at which Gieseking was to play "Music for Piano and Voice" by Hindemith, Sessions, and Szymanowsky. Schoenberg's Second Quartet was also scheduled.

5. Sessions did not publish anything in *Modern Music* until "Music in Crisis: Some Notes on Recent Musical History," *Modern Music* 10, no. 2 (1933): 63–78. This article discusses the Second Viennese School, among other things.

6. Leo Sowerby (1895–1968) and Hanson had been the first Rome Prize recipients, in 1921–24.

7. A reference to Hanson's Symphony No. 1, the "Nordic."

8. Copland had written to Sessions expressing his desire to stay in the U.S., especially New York, rather than apply for the Rome Prize.

9. Irving Weil, "American Group Evolves New Idiom at Juziers," *Musical America,* September 8, 1928, 7, 18. Sessions must also have seen two enormous articles about Bloch in *Musical America,* November 3 and 10, 1928, concerning that magazine's award to Bloch of three thousand dollars for his composition *America,* an "epic rhapsody" for orchestra with choral finale, chosen unanimously from ninety-two pieces submitted.

▼

Barbara Sessions to Aaron Copland
als US-DLC

December 16 [1928]
Rome

Dear Aaron,

It is very flattering to have a letter asked of me,—like being commissioned to write a symphony. I'm sorry I didn't get this one sent off to you a little sooner, so that it could at the same time give you our very best Christmas + New Year wishes. However,—perhaps you will accept them even though they come a few days late. We haven't forgotten our adventures of a year ago this end-December in New York—and we shall be recalling our January 1st tea party in Margaret Naumberg's apartment—and wishing you were here to observe the anniversary.

One of the rather amusing things about being poor is the way in which one's clothes accumulate associations. The other night I dressed for the evening in a dress which has become a veritable archaeological monument, and I began reflecting on all the occasions which it recalled to me: chiefly the League of Composer's "Old-New" concert of last year, Oedipus Rex, a dinner while you were at the Jacobis in Northampton,—later, Paris in May—the première of Apollon, S.K.'s concerts,—and, since you are not a woman, + I can be really frank, vistas reaching back even to Cleveland + the appearance of the Bloch Quintette. Trajan's Column itself is hardly a more complete or vivid document. One must take what comfort one can out of such inanimate witnesses, in a world where one's friends have a way of living thousands of miles away from one.

[. . .]

[Roy Harris] had written to ask for what help Roger can give him in his Prix de Rome candidacy. It is a subject we have thought about several times since coming here + seeing what the atmosphere actually is, + we have tried to keep our own feelings absolutely out of it (or rather *I* have tried to, for Roger is naturally far more generous than I!) There are many things here which if irritating to Roger would be almost fatally so to Roy, I fear—who (unless he marries or re-marries)[1] will have to live in the building with the other boys: a sort of belated collegiate enthusiasm, along with an intense + deep-rooted conventionality in ideas + behavior (in spite of frequent drinking parties, etc.) The music department is much more free than the others, because Lamond is infinitely superior to the directors of the other sections,—but you should hear how they all speak of Elwell, who kept very much by himself + whom they therefore considered absolutely unimportant. They are all a little afraid of Roger, and treat him at least politely: of course his living outside + having other associations in Rome are already a great defence. But back of all this is the most disheartening conception of art + its place in the world. They never seem to have heard of any definition of it except as a means like any other to a successful career, to good jobs, to a comfortable position in life.

I hope you will consider all this said in absolute confidence. These are things which Roger can put up with, as you could, because they do not touch him or his own life at all, and because they are only, in a crystallized and aggravated form, what we all live among wherever we are. We endure them, + ignore them, as partial payment for the chance to live in comparative comfort in this magnificent and *nourishing* place. While we are here, we simply have to have the decency to accept the conditions, and not to make it too apparent that our real interests are elsewhere. But I don't know at all that Roy could, or should, make these adjustments. They might be entirely too much for him. And sometime Roger will want to write you at greater length about the whole question as it may possibly affect your eventual plans for Israel.

Of course, Lamond is really capable of a great deal; and one hopes that something can be made of at least the music side of things. The material facilities—for performances, conditions of work, *tools* of all kinds—are most unusual, and Rome itself so marvelous, so stimulating, so *beautiful* that one could not have a better place in which to work + live. If we could, without arousing too much Academic suspicion (and here Lamond is of supreme skill) get the right sort of people to come for the next few years, I think the whole character of the place could be changed. The[y] can see really thrilling possibilities. Naturally, nothing could further these so well as your coming, I think. Roger's being here has already begun to make an impression + to create something new,—but one person alone is not enough—you have just what is needed to help the change enormously + to help it to become permanent. (I think myself it's rather clever of us to find such a powerful altruistic argument for your coming, since the more personal ones—both for your good + ours,—seem not to touch you!) We don't want to say too much when you have expressed yourself so soundly about your feeling that you need to be in New York or its vicinity. Of course you know what is best for you, and if the new orchestral thing is coming along so well, that is the best possible proof that you are right—but don't, *please,* put it entirely out of your mind. If you ever feel that you need to get away from the professional aspects of music, or to have just a change of some kind, even, you couldn't do better than to come here, I know. And for us, I don't need to say, there could be no greater pleasure.

Roger finds it a perfect place—for himself—in which to work, and is happier in his work than he has been for a long time, if not *ever.* The sonata is practically finished—and has continued to be what it promised to be last spring,—for me, that means a very great deal, and I think, for you, too.

We have had two incomparable concerts of the *Pro Arte:* Haydn, Debussy, Rieti (a little thing disappointingly like an echo of *Barabau*)[2], the 3rd Hindemith quintet (this brought about a temporary revival of Roger's enthusiasm), Stravinsky Concertino, Bloch quintet, with Casella—who, by the way, has been *very* nice. We have just been seeing [Alexander] Barjansky, Bloch's friend to whom *Schelomo* is dedicated. Roger played him the *Black Maskers* + has decided that he likes it again, even very much,—that he has been quite unfair to it. We wonder whether Reiner ever played it. I wish one could get some sort of an answer out of him.

This has been much too long a letter, and seems rather to have gone to pieces at the end. I am really frightfully embarrassed to have written you such a volume, and shall continue to be so until I hear something chivalrous from you to make me feel better about it. One more thing: we are both annoyed with ourselves for having neglected Mary Churchill so rudely. I do hope she is better. I have meant to write to her a dozen times, for I know so well what long illnesses are like. Please remember us to her, and assure her that she will hear from us soon.

I suppose your first concert is not far away—we shall be impatient for news of it. + wish you the best of success with it, as with everything you are doing: above all, write your own work. Forgive me for imposing such a letter on you, and answer it soon!

Yours, as ever,
Barbara F. S.

1. Roy Harris married four times, last in October 1936.
2. The ballet with chorus by Vittorio Rieti (b. 1898) premiered by the Ballets Russes in London, December 11, 1925.

THE THIRD Copland-Sessions Concert took place on December 30, 1928, in New York. The works performed were Nikolai Lopatnikoff's Sonatina for Piano (Colin McPhee, pianist), Henry Cowell's Paragraphs for Two Violins and Cello, Bernard Wagenaar's Sonata for Piano (John Duke, pianist), Marc Blitzstein's Four Songs for Baritone and Piano (Benjohn Ragsdale, baritone, and Marc Blitzstein, piano), and George Antheil's Second String Quartet. The works by

Blitzstein, Wagenaar, Cowell, and Lopatnikoff were dismissed by Olin Downes in the *New York Times*.[1] Arthur Mendel wrote in *Modern Music* that "Messrs. Copland and Sessions let us hear some works of young men who do not know that the musical Civil War is over." He accused George Antheil of returning in his quartet "not to Bach or Mozart or Gounod, but to Kreutzer and Popper."[2]

The fourth Copland-Sessions Concert, held on February 24, 1929, included Alexander Lipsky's Sonata for Violin and Piano, Vladimir Dukelsky's Three Poems of Hyppolite Bogdanovitch (with Copland at the piano), Roy Harris's Sonata for Piano, and the most controversial, Virgil Thomson's *Capital, Capitals* on a text by Gertrude Stein. The audience reaction to Thomson's piece was captured in the next day's headline: "Gertrude Stein's Words to Music Draw Laughter."[3] This critical reception was to inspire one of Sessions's lengthiest letters, that of March 22, 1929.

In the summer of 1929, which Sessions spent in Les Diablerets, Switzerland, Sessions wrote Copland four postcards and a letter containing a detailed rail and boat schedule to get there from Paris. One card accuses Copland of "stay[ing] in that little mud-hole [Paris] instead of coming to be near us." Such tactics worked and Copland did go to Switzerland, where Sessions was visiting his friend Jean Binet and seeing Frank Martin and Ansermet. The weather was cloudy for Copland's visit, Sessions wrote to Nadia Boulanger (September 8, 1929). This letter was primarily to introduce Rosamond Foster, whose family was visiting Barbara in Italy, to Mlle. Boulanger. However, Rosamond states that she never met Boulanger.

While living in Rome Sessions learned Russian partly by translating some of *War and Peace*. He wrote to Koussevitzky in Russian, and again projected a completion date—"this winter" (which was completely unrealistic)—for the Sonata, Violin Concerto, and Second Symphony. He did, in fact, finally finish the Sonata that winter, but abandoned the symphony, and did not complete the Violin Concerto for another five years.

1. Olin Downes, "Music: Younger Composers Heard," *New York Times*, December 31, 1928, 8.

2. Arthur Mendel, "Forecast and Review: First Fruits of the Season," *Modern Music* 6, no. 2 (January–February 1929): 30.

3. New York *Herald Tribune*, February 25, 1929, 15. See also W. J. Henderson, "Up-to-Date Music in Concert," New York *Sun*, February 25, 1929, 20; Irving Weil, "The Wizardry of Toscanini and the Latest from America," *Musical America*, March 10, 1929, 53; and Carol J. Oja, "The Copland-Sessions Concerts and their Reception

in the Contemporary Press," *Musical Quarterly* (April 1979): 220. Thomson's own reaction is chronicled in his *Virgil Thomson* (New York: Knopf, 1966), 136. Thomson revised *Capitals, Capitals,* and Boosey & Hawkes published it in 1968.

▼

Roger Sessions to Aaron Copland
als US-DLC

January 17, 1929
Firenze

Dear Aaron,—

I must answer your delightful letter, though the real answer will have to wait till later. So pardon, I beg you, a short and all too unexpansive document.

1. I confidently expected to send Gieseking the finished sonata to his boat. Unfortunately I got influenza + found it absolutely impossible. But I am moving Heaven + earth to send it off week after next—*Majestic,* Jan. 30. Hence my brevity now. I have been a *fool* over this whole business; luckily this year I seem to have, spiritually, a new lease o[n] life, + I can endure the spectacle of my own asininity without flinching! Of all this more later,—it is unimportant, especially as it is purely the result of a Sonata complex—dead wood fr. last Spring. I have wired Mrs. R[eis] + will wire again when the fucking thing is sent off. Its fate is in the hands of the gods—It is by no means bad music, I think, + don't mean to be too disrespectful.

2. Please keep me informed about the concerts + their success. I have already given the thing—the problem as you state it—a good deal of thought, + have reached certain conclusions—the chief one being that it would be a great mistake to give them up. My "moral support" as you so kindly put it has I fear not been a too tangible quantity; I hope to improve it. But I have no time to be too prodigal with it now—as far as words are concerned; + besides, I have reason to believe that press announcements + similar matters may have looked up since you wrote. Let me know about this. I think in any case I may have some ideas to contribute.

3. I shall send you in March some Preludes (or I shall probably call them Etudes or Sketches). You can depend upon them, I promise you. No more of this now—words are unnecessary.

4. I am writing Carlos [Chávez] to send you the photostat copy of the symphony. Perhaps you are right in regard to publication.[1] I myself thought it might be better to start with something more

−135−

accessible—the Sonata or the chorales—especially since, as you say, my music requires familiarity for its appreciation. However I leave all such matters to you + the committee; I am only too happy to do that. At least as far as *you* are concerned (+ I don't give a goddamn about the others). I always feel that you have my interest at heart at least as much as I have, + are a good deal more intelligent about them! I shall send the sonata, of course, + the chorales too. So, any decision you might make in regard to this, you may quote as being mine too.

5. I have decided to postpone the vl. concerto (it couldn't possibly be performed this year anyway) + concentrate on my IId Symphony, + try—for my own edification—to finish it in time for the prize contest [May 27, 1929].—Just enough "pressure," I think, to suit me. In spite of Serge's enthusiasm (he undoubtedly spoke to you just as he did to me about it) I am not too serious in my anticipation either for you or for me; I mean I find these contests absurd in principle—rather monstrous in fact, especially as my mother-in-law sent me the clippings of the Bloch affair. I must say that in the minds of the chorus of trimmers + sychophants + cowards + nonentities that the rest of the critics showed themselves once more to be, the lone sonorous voice of dear old Phillip Hale was quite admirable in its thoroughgoing contempt for the whole thing. That is not to say that I always agree with him, or even generally.

6. I am going to try to get the symphony away from Ansermet, unless he *promises* to play it this year, + send it to S.K. who I am quite sure *will*, this season. Alas, I shall not be there, but he gave very warm hints regarding Paris, last year.

7. Bless you for what you say about my slow movement; it does me no end of good. That isn't the only reason, however, for blessing you—

Forgive a letter in which none of the important things are said— + write again soon.

Always most affectionately,
R——

P.S. I am sending you the [Monteverdi] "Combattimento di Tancredi e Clorinda" for Christmas—it took a month to get it, otherwise it might have been on time, or nearly so![2]

1. The Cos Cob Press, founded by Copland and funded by Alma Wertheim, would publish Sessions's Symphony No. 1 later in 1929.
2. The work was to be performed on a League of Composers concert, April 25 and

28, conducted by Werner Josten (1885–1963), who conducted at Smith College 1923–49.

▼

Barbara Sessions to Nadia Boulanger
als F-PBN

January 23 [1929]

Dear Mademoiselle Boulanger, Florence

[. . .] Roger supposed that the piano sonata would be done before he came here. But it has been causing him again the very greatest difficulty. He has determined not to let it be played again until he knows that it is right, so I do not know whether he will be able to get it to Gieseking in time for the projected performance. It is more than worth the real agony which it has caused him, for it is becoming, it seems to me, a very fine thing,—the best thing which he has done. But it will be an enormous relief when it, and all its associations of strain, haste, and worry, are out of the way.

During his work on the sonata he has been having many ideas for his next symphony. It is curious to see this new work springing into life almost unconsciously, as a sort of by-product of the processes which are occupying the fore-ground of his attention. It seems to me tremendously instructive, both as a commentary on the nature of the creative function in general, and as evidence—as I like to point out to Roger when he [is] discouraged—of the real vitality of his inner impulses when they are not being hampered by the kind of exaggerated and desperate effort which sometimes paralyzes them while he is actually working out his ideas, and when there is some external reason for a sense of strain such as he has had with the sonata. I hope he will never promise a work again until it is done—and I am sure that this experience with the sonata has taught him a great deal about himself, so that it is not a bad thing in the end, in spite of all that it has cost him.

Rome has certainly had a wonderful influence, coming as it did after your splendid and stimulating talks with him. I am only sorry that the intensive work on the sonata, and the weeks here (he felt that he must stay on here until he had finished the sonata, but now we are going back, in any case, next week) had to interrupt the normal evolution of his mood as it had begun there. He was so much happier, and more at ease with himself and his surroundings, than he has been for a long time. But I feel that, once the sonata is out of the way, we can expect very great things of this relaxing and warming influence which Rome can certainly exert.

[...]

Very devotedly,
Barbara

▼

Roger Sessions to Aaron Copland
tls US-DLC

March 22 [1929]

Dear Aaron,—   [Rome]

I have your letters and clippings, and am glad that things are looking up—in comparison with your state of mind before the first concert, they seem very successful indeed! I must confess that as far as the reception of the concerts is concerned I expected little if anything more, and am sure that if the concerts are kept up there is a possibility of something very good coming out of them. The very violence of the reviews is of course a sign of life, and is in our favor; as long as this keeps up, things are prospering. And while being discussed in Greenwich Village is not exactly my idea of understanding, it is certainly true that those who are impressed by bad notices are no worse than those who are impressed by good ones, even if it is also true that they are no better! The fact that Downes or any other critic does not come is nothing; our original scheme, it seems to me, can be fulfilled as long as we have financial backing, whether or not we get any particular notice or not. For my part I would have been content with much less; as long as we can maintain a fairly high standard the notice is bound to come sooner or later.

In my last letter I promised you more moral support, and I mean to give it to you. In fact, I must give it to you, and we must devise some way whereby I can give it in the fullest measure, if I am to go on being a co-partner next year. I want to show you why I feel in a rather anomalous position regarding the concerts, so that we can remedy it if possible. Forgive me for being inconsistent in regard to a situation for which I alone am responsible.

In the first place, and most important, in regard to the programs. The point is simply that I have no means of knowing the situation in any real sense when I am absolutely ignorant of some of the music that is being played. I have as much confidence in you as I would have in anyone; and yet—*in spite of the fact that I myself am wholly responsible for this situation*—I am beginning to realize the very great inconveniences as well as the risks involved in my being a completely irresponsible partner. I have to all intents and purposes signed a blank page, and sponsored, as a musician and a composer, something for which I have no responsibility at all; and I have no sure means of knowing, as things are now, whether I would be willing to take that responsibility for the works that are played at the concerts.

To give you two examples: I know nothing of Henry Cowell's music, but I have instinctive doubts. These doubts come entirely from various articles which I have read, or rather tried to read, in M[odern] M[usic];[1] and these articles have seemed really unbelievable in their amateurishness. In the last one you must have noticed the quotation from *L'Histoire du Soldat,* in which the Clarinet and Cornet in A were transposed a tone instead of three half tones, with rather strange results. The other case is Blitzstein; I have not found him too interesting personally, and I don't know his music. But the flapdoodle about Whiteman, jazz, and the 'primeval sex-urge' or whatever it was, you must admit, has no possible interest with or without his music, entirely aside from the fact that that sort of thing is, to put it generously, fifth or sixth hand and at least fifteen years out of date; it dates from before the war—the old Masses, etc.—in fact. Nor does it give me a very good impression of Blitzstein's intelligence or his talent. He and Cowell may be both greater than Bach for all I know at first hand; but I feel that if I am to be the co-sponsor of the concerts I must be more responsible for what is played at them. That is difficult at a distance of 4000 miles, I'll admit. And I don't want to withdraw from them if I can avoid it. Well *was zu tun* [what to do]?

Secondly—and this matter is related to the first; are the concerts yet really worth so much publicity? I was surprised to see the full page articles in the commercial weeklies, with our pictures and biographies; I had understood, first of all, that we were to keep in the background and to make the thing as impersonal as possible, but secondly and more important it seems to me that what we have thus far had to offer is a little small compared to all the trumpet-blowing. Consider that among all the composers who have been played at our concerts by far the greater number are still far from mature, and that probably none of us has yet written a completely definitive work, I mean from the point of view of our development, and that even aside from that the very fact of our ages makes the future much more interesting than the past or the present. Please don't accuse me or suspect me of having a fit of modesty or anything of that kind; I know perfectly well that a lot of merde gets more publicity than our concerts do, and that the public doesn't deserve much respect. But it seems to me that just the people who are worth winning are the ones whom we will gradually lose by that sort of thing. Already—it seems to me as a direct result of that—we are being more or less put in the position of special pleaders for "a little group of serious thinkers" and while this is to a certain extent inevitable I think we would be building on a much more solid basis for the future if we worked more quietly. It is for this reason also that I think that you and I should be kept out of it as much as possible.

Have I made myself clear, and what are we going to do about it? I hope to see you in May or June; we must then have a good leisurely time in which to talk over the whole policy of the thing, and plan what we shall do in the future. I don't see any reason why, if we begin early enough, we couldn't plan the whole season pretty carefully and look over manuscripts during the summer. That would give me a chance to be a co-despot in more than name, and to keep in much better touch with things than I have been able to do. So many questions cannot be solved at all by correspondence; and as to publicity I feel honestly incompetent fully to judge without going over the whole situation with you, and pretty thoroughly. I am perfectly sure we agree in substance on all of these things; it has been my mistake in taking too much for granted and for having too little foresight.

One detail which has very little importance: I was surprised to read in the "biography" which appeared in *Musical America* et al, that I am living in Italy in order to get plenty of quiet! I thought that the reason was that I am paid $2000 a year, for the present, to live and work in Rome. And, aside from that, if I should decide to live in Europe it would be for exactly the opposite reason—that there is more going on in music over here, and that one has the stimulus far more than at home of meeting musical personalities of all types, and of closer contact—for good or ill—with "le mouvement" . . . Please do enlighten Mary Churchill or whoever needs to be enlightened on this subject—although it is not of very great importance it could easily be altered. And also I do think that the American Academy should be mentioned if my biography should be used again. But I would rather not have my biography brought in at all—it seems beside the point.

I hope we understand each other about this; for I am enough of an Anglo-Saxon not to like the role of carper and knocker and obstructionist. And for that reason I feel I must have some real responsibility, and must find some way of really cooperating.

Alas! here I go again . . . I must confess I have serious doubts about the Paris concert.[2] Don't you think it is a little premature; that our concerts have not really established themselves sufficiently in America; and that the whole thing would be received a good deal in the spirit of another piece of "arrivisme"—not very important but rather like the "Festivals Antheil" (or, if you like, Virgil Thomson, or Edmund Pendleton,[3] et al.)? For my part, as you know, I have always disliked this sort of thing to excess, and I seem to dislike it and feel less inclined for it every day. I mean I don't and cannot regard myself as a part of any "groupe" or "mouvement." All that I stand for is in a quite different direction, and nothing that I am in the least interested in achieving, for music or for America or for myself, has the least thing to do with this. I feel that I want my music absolutely to take its chances through normal channels, and am willing to stand or fall on that basis. So, as far as my name and my work can be of use to our concerts in New York, I am glad to furnish them; but in Paris or indeed anywhere in Europe the situation is quite different. Don't you, really, agree? After all, *you* have no need of such a concert; Roy's sextet is already known in Paris; and Nadia will take care of Carlos— at least she is very much interested in him.

Well—forgive me all this; it is really a sort of roundabout way of saying that I feel that we may have to curb Mary C[hurchill]'s ardor to some extent if the concerts are to become what we want them to be. I hate the written word—I loathe it; and I can never write of such things without feeling that I have made a damned mess of it. Forgive me if I have done this. The whole thing—in so far as there is a "whole thing!" is entirely my fault.

I have been having another mild attack of the flu, which has been raging wildly over Europe, and have been rather under the weather for that reason, for nearly a week. Aside from that we have been having a very good time. At last we have begun to find people who are possible, and more than possible—Germans and French and Italians and English and Russians, with an occasional American thrown in, though the Americans who live in Rome are as a rule not so hot. There is however a painter here named Maurice Sterne[4] who may be interesting, although I believe he has social ambitions and in this case would never do for us! Also I have met a very young composer named Rota,[5] a pupil of Casella whom they all—the Italian musicians—hope a great deal from in the future. I'll let you know about him later, and may possibly bring around something for our next year's concerts. He is certainly an intelligent and wide awake boy, and I have real hopes. As for the Amacadmy (cable address!) there is a lot to tell you; but here I *certainly* think the spoken word is best. It is certainly not an ideal place for me; but it is probably—the $2000, bien entendu, being taken well into account—as well as I could have done for the next three years. At least I am gradually learning the virtues of tact and discretion—by no means useless virtues in the present-day world, you will admit. And they let me severely alone, which reduces friction to the minimum demanded by the most casual contacts. That, I must admit, is quite enough; but at least the friction can remain in a not too warm undercurrent.

The winter has, as far as I myself am concerned, been thoroughly important; the most important year I have ever had, perhaps. Knowing that I had three years ahead of me has been an excellent thing, and I believe I have taken a big step ahead in many ways. My real music, I feel, I am only beginning to write; and in the same way I am tempted to feel that I am only beginning to lead my real life. Does this sound apocalyptic? Perhaps it is; and at all events my music alone will show you what I mean, if anything does. And when you see my music you might not agree; so I'd perhaps better say no more! What has happened, in so far as it can be described in a few words, is that for the first time in many years I have become fully aware of myself; and what was present, to be sure, in the Black Maskers and in the Symphony, but not wholly sure of itself, is coming out fully at last. It began to do so last spring in the Sonata, but that was only the beginning, and a more or less blind and unconscious one. But I believe you will see in the Sonata as a whole—in spite of all the trials it has given me—and above all in my new symphony, what I mean. The winter has not been without pain—au contraire, it has been chaotic and all too intense in all its varied emotions; but that after all is quite normal, for me at least, and not at all unsalutary . . .

It will be amusing to have P[aul] R[osenfeld] here, and I really look forward to it, for more than one reason. Quite aside from a purely personal pleasure in seeing him again I shall enjoy really knowing him better—also observing at first hand the behavior of a confirmed America-affirmer in Europe, and especially in Italy. He wrote in a rather depressed mood about the American musical season, with the single exception of your trio piece [*Vitebsk*], which I'm crazy to see and hear. And, by the way, how about the Music for the Theatre? Is it published yet? I want very much to get a copy when it is.

I can't say our season here has been thrilling, though I have had interesting impressions. First of all, Bloch's quintet really moved me in a way which was a real and great surprise, quite aside from the memories it aroused.[6] Secondly, *Tristan,* fairly well given at the Opera here, I found *great* and, in a curious way, disturbing, in spite of the fact that I have lived over many times since years every note in the score. Disturbing, I mean because: I am certainly no Wagnerian, but on the contrary aware of faults, weaknesses, etc., by the hundred or the thousand, if you like, and yet when all this is said over and over again, where is the single work written since his that can be compared for a moment with it, in real force, in essential significance, in necessity?—in importance, I mean, not to musicians, but to life as a whole? I have to admit that in spite of *Pelléas,* in spite of *Les Noces* and *Oedipus,* it makes la musique moderne seem like bien peu de chose [a mere trifle]; and that by no means by virtue of what it— Wagner's music—pretends to be, but by virtue of what it really is. Not that one should be depressed; for I cannot believe that this had anything to do with any movement or aesthetic theory—it seems rather that modern composers have simply not been big enough, not perhaps as musicians, but as human beings. And one cannot blame anyone for not having more personal force, more depth and strength and grandeur of vision, than God gives him. I come more and more to believe that this is the essential thing, though I have always believed it to a pretty thorough extent. Speaking of *Les Noces,* etc.—have you seen yet the score of "Le Baiser de la Fée"?[7] I haven't; young Rota spoke rather nicely of it the other day. I must confess that, the last pages excepted, *Apollon* has not lasted for me as well as I had hoped. This is, I suppose, a purely personal thing; for *Oedipus* still holds its own magnificently.

I liked your article on Milhaud[8]—far better than anything else in the number of MM that contained it. Almost, I might say, thou persuadest me to be a Christian; the only obstacle thus far is Christ himself, in this case. But it would be unfair to judge, especially in view of what you say about his being hard to grasp. I really know only the *Malheurs d'Orphée,*[9] which I find nice but not thrilling. But, I must add, I am not in a very French mood this winter; I tried too hard last summer, perhaps, and much as I love most French literature and also some French painting and sculpture, I'm afraid French music, with the exception of Rameau and Berlioz and Bizet and Debussy and an occasional page of Fauré, will always seem small and cold and dry to me. Why does M[inna] L[ederman] publish such inconsequentiality as the article of Malipiero or such flubdub as that of Sabaneyev or such drivel as the article on Jerome Kern?[10] and what has it got to do with music?

Our plans are not yet certain; we will both go to Geneva, of course, but come right back after the festival,[11] and then not leave again till late May or June. What are yours? for we must meet sometime, the sooner the better. Could I tempt you with Italy, or Switzerland in July and August? We will certainly go to stay near the Binets during the hot months, and it would be great fun if you could be around there too.[12] For May and June our plans are uncertain, though they will probably take in Paris. How about S.K.'s plans? Is the European tour really abandoned? But in any case let me know about yourself. It really would be splendid to have you within hailing distance this summer and surely must be arranged if possible.

Also I wish you could look up one Walter Helfer,[13] a young composer and former Prix de Rome, who might possibly have something to contribute for our concerts. All that I have heard about him personally I like; I have not seen any of his best works, but what I have seen has some possibilities, though in these works rather unrealized. In any case I think you would like him and you might find him interesting. I have not met him; but I am told that I resemble him. From that you could see either how little I show myself to these people here, or how little they understand me, or at any rate *something* very interesting! Anyway that is considered a great compliment around here . . . His address is in care of the New York office of the American Academy, I think at 101 Park Avenue.

I must stop this letter sometime, I suppose. Please forgive the typewriter and the prolixity it engenders; but I get really unpleasant cramps when I write in pencil or in ink. That is why my friends so seldom hear from me + why, when you do, my letters are so monstrous!

I wish, by the way, that I had known you were still looking for a place to live in the country; I would have told you to write to my brother—John Sessions, Phelps Farm, Hadley, Mass.—who is spending the spring and summer at the farm there, and who could almost certainly have let you have a room there. If it is not too late why not try it, in case you have not yet found anything.[14] You have met him and his wife in Brooklyn, and I'm sure they'd adore to have you if it is possible. Tell them I suggested it, of course . . . But I suppose you are already well established.

Forgive me again for the length of this letter as well as for the merde at the beginning of it, and in any case write me again!

Much love from us both. When does Barbara get *her* letter, by the way?!!!!!!!!!

Affectionately,
Roger

[in Copland's hand at top of letter:] Dear M[ary Churchill]—Please return, but I cannot answer this adequately.

1. Henry Colwell, "New Terms for New Music," *Modern Music* 5, no. 4 (May–June 1928): 21–27. The Stravinsky example appears on p. 25.

2. Copland was planning a Copland-Sessions concert; it would take place, with funding from Mary Churchill, at the Salle Chopin June 17, 1929. At Sessions's request (letter to Copland, April 12, 1929, US-DLC), the Copland-Sessions name was not to be used; Sessions did not attend. The works performed would be *Vitebsk* and Two Pieces for String Quartet by Copland, three songs by Israel Citkowitz, Chávez's Piano Sonata, songs by Virgil Thomson, and Roy Harris's Concerto for String Quartet, Clarinet, and Piano. In the same letter, Sessions suggested that for future concerts Copland take full responsibility for choosing works by composers in the U.S., and himself composers in Europe.

3. Edmund Pendleton (1901–87), organist at the American Church in Paris for forty years, had studied composition with Paul Dukas, organ with Marcel Dupré, and conducting with Charles Munch. For twenty years he was music critic for the New York *Herald Tribune*'s Paris edition and he taught music at the American College in Paris.

4. The Latvian-American artist Sterne (1878–1957) had just completed his *Monument to the Early Settlers* at Worcester, Mass. (1926–29); in 1935–40 he created the murals for the U.S. Justice Department building in Washington, D.C.

5. Nino Rota (1911–79) had already composed an opera, *Il principe porcaro* (1925), at the age of thirteen; he became best known for his scores to films by Federico Fellini, Franco Zeffirelli, and Francis Ford Coppola.

6. Sessions apparently had been present at the premiere of Bloch's Piano Quintet in New York on November 11, 1923. See Barbara Sessions's letter, December 16, 1928, above.

7. Stravinsky's ballet on themes of Tchaikovsky had received its first performance November 27, 1928.

8. Aaron Copland, "The Lyricism of Milhaud," *Modern Music* 6, no. 2 (January 1929): 14–19.

9. Milhaud's opera had premiered in Brussels May 7, 1926.

10. G. Francesco Malipiero, "A Plea for True Comedy," *Modern Music* 6, no. 2 (January 1929): 10–13; Leonid Sabaneyeff, "Russia's Strong Man" (a favorable look at Prokofiev), ibid., 3–7; Robert Simon, "Jerome Kern," ibid., 20–25.

11. The Seventh Festival of the ISCM, April 6–9, 1929, at which Ansermet conducted Sessions's Symphony No. 1.

12. Copland would join Sessions at the Binets' that summer.

13. Helfer (1896–1959) had studied at Harvard and the Paris Conservatoire, and in Rome with Respighi; he taught composition at Hunter College 1928–50.

14. Copland did not go to Hadley.

▼

Roger Sessions to Aaron Copland
als US-DLC

Thursday, July 12 [1929]

Les Diablerets [Switzerland]

Cher ami,—

At last I am writing to you. [. . .] I wonder therefore if you would care to meet me in some other place than that stuffy, bourgeois, + inartistic city [Paris], + perhaps we could take a trip together. Specifically, would you care to come here for a day or two, and then run around the north of Italy for a couple of weeks or so—or Switzerland, if you like? The main point is that if I can only see you in Paris I will go only on Sept. 8th, whereas if you would like to do the other I am at your disposal from Sept. 1st on. I thought too that if we went to Italy we could arrange to run into Barbara somewhere, + you could have a glimpse of her without our having to hook on to a caravan of belle-mères + belle-pères (or even belle-soeurs!)[1] Let me know then, + I will plan accordingly. I do agree, emphatically, that we haven't seen enough of each other, + hope very much that we can make at least a beginning, of some sort, in September.

Of course, you wouldn't mind Juziers as much as we did. For one thing, you are not at all an outsider there, in the sense that we are; you have really been Nadia's pupil, and can move freely, so to speak, in that group. I felt very much of an outsider—an intruder, in a sense. Then, you are a single masculine entity, and are not, presumably, the receptacle of various bi-lateral confidences of an extremely intimate nature, as B. + I were. [. . .] Finally, and I believe that is the most important thing—my relations with N.B. were very strange last summer. Not that I ever for a minute had any reason to doubt her affection or good will; but whether because of the state she was in, or from whatever cause, there was always a kind of wall—I had never felt it before—which I could not penetrate; + that was *agaçant* [bothersome]. I dare say it was in some way my fault; but never before, in my relations with anyone, have I reached just that kind of deadlock—where it was impossible either to make myself fully understood or to fully understand the other person, and yet where I could not seriously doubt that person's real affection + esteem. And since I went there entirely to be near Nadia you can see that Juziers was a disappointment; and neither the town itself nor the French life—flat, dull, self-satisfied—that one saw around one, offered any satisfaction whatever. The one *real* joy was Israel—a very real joy indeed; but I was not at all in good form last summer—I was in as *poor* form as I have ever been and I was unable to make the most of that relationship.

I'm sorry you didn't finish the orch. piece for the [RCA Victor] prize; but from all I know of prizes you are just as likely to get it with one work as another. In spite of S.K.'s enthusiasm I couldn't myself take the thing seriously enough to write something special for it, + anyway I think prizes are not in my line.[2]

What are your ideas about the concerts for next year? Do you want me to write to Fitelberg + to Ullman?[3] The latter was to have sent me a str. quartet, but hasn't done it; + I would like to be a little more certain of plans before I prod him. Not that it would bind us, of course; but I must know what the plans are, or can be.

I have heard nothing about the Paris concert except from Israel who was rather vague; but I'd like very much to know how that went, too. Minna L.[4] dropped in yesterday from Vevey [Switzerland] + we spoke of it but I would rather have your impression (!!). She was quite nice, though, + I think she improves away from N.Y. That is saying a great deal, I think—it is not true of most people. Did I tell you that we saw a good deal of P[aul] R[osenfeld] in Rome? What a strange creature! and how difficult—so utterly "feminine" without being in the least attractive. I am frightfully sorry for him—that is my net impression. We had a few good moments; but a person like that who is so incapable of reaching directly to anything—who must intellectualize, theorize, who one feels is in mortal dread of any simple + direct sensation or impression, is almost impossible to talk to. And yet I can't help liking him simply for his lovable qualities; + on the whole I was glad to have that time with him.

Have you the slightest idea what Reiner plans to do about the *Black Maskers?* I wrote him two letters last winter—or rather three! + have had no word from him at all. And if he doesn't intend to play it I want the score back, as there is an excellent chance for me to have it played in Rome; it would go better there than any later work, for the beginning; and I could conduct. Do let me know if you have any idea whether he plans to do it or not. I have written all this to him.—in

Feb. I think, and I registered the letter; but he has vouchsafed no reply.

Also, do you know anything of the whereabouts of John Duke? I wired him just before he left America + asked him to let me know his Paris address, so that I could put him in touch with N.B. He supposedly arrived on the 13th of July, but I have had no word, + have been wondering what has happened.

Barbara had a very good letter from you day before yesterday. *Please* don't feel that I didn't want to encourage you to come to Suisse for the summer. *Au contraire.* I assumed that both you + Israel were to be in Glion, + was rather shocked to learn that—partly through my delay in answering your letter—you were staying in Juziers. If I had been already to the Diablerets I should have urged you to come here; but you see Jean Binet's sister-in-law found the place for us + we had the idea that it was much nearer Glion than it actually is; and also I did not know at all what *Les Diablerets* was like. As a matter of fact at Glion you would have been nearly as inaccessible as at Juziers—1½ hours away on the train, with two changes. It is wonderful here *la haute montagne,* fresh air, bright sunlight, an *extraordinary* view, + very wild. I can't afford a piano, + it is quite good to be without one for a while—my imagination is freer in a way. And one leads an absolutely simple + really refreshing life. We have one floor in a peasant's chalet—+ Swiss peasants are wonderful—all the qualities of peasants everywhere, + *clean* into the bargain. So that *on est bien installé* [we are well settled]. I have had marvelous walks, + by the end of the summer will be as hard as nails. It's the real life for me, because unless I keep my body in condition I am only about half alive. But this summer is pretty nearly the high water mark of my life thus far, + when you see me again you will see an absolutely different R.S. from the half-baked, rather childish person I was a year + a half ago.

Excuse a rather superficial + dull letter—begun at 5 A.M. + finished just after breakfast. You know, we'd *love* to have you come *before* the 1st of Sept. if you care to. But I shall be busy till then, + B. will have to take care of my [in-laws], + anyway you said you wouldn't be free. After that you could come + stay in this house with me, + we could get out from here. I hope so much that that will appeal to you.

Give my *special* love to N.B. + her mother, and to Israel, and my love to Roy. I hope the latter is having a better summer than last.

Always affectionately,
Roger

1. Sessions refers to his in-laws.
2. See Sessions's letter of August 19, 1928, note 7.
3. In his letter of April 12, 1929, to Copland (US-DLC) Sessions had recommended for future Copland-Sessions concerts three composers whose music he had heard at the ISCM Festival in Geneva: Frank Martin (1890–1974); Viktor Ullmann (1898–1944), a student of Schoenberg; and "a young Pole named Jerzy Fitelberg." Fitelberg (1903–51) had studied in Berlin; he moved to Paris in 1933 and to the U.S. in 1940.
4. Minna Lederman had attended the Paris concert June 17, 1929.

▼

Roger Sessions to Serge Koussevitzky[1]
als US-DLC

Friday, October 18 [1929]

Dear Mr. Koussevitzky,— Roma

Please excuse me for not knowing your patronymic, and thus for not being able to address you according to true Russian custom, but in any case you'll be surprised, I think—and I hope that you'll also like the fact—that I'm writing you in your native language. We've already lived a year here in Rome at the house of some nice Russians and I thought it was a good opportunity to learn Russian. I've been studying it since April and I'm fascinated with your language, which is not only much more beautiful than I knew, but at the same time, much easier than I feared it would be!

I hope that you received a copy of my symphony, which I sent you some time ago. I was very happy to be able to send it to you, and I'm sure I don't have to tell you with what warm feelings and gratitude I did it.

I must apologize for not letting you know earlier about my work. To tell the truth, I felt that last year I had to work very slowly and at the same time, I had to get used to Rome, and to the American Academy in particular. Now I am working on a Sonata,[2] on a Violin Concerto, and on my Second Symphony. I really hope to finish all three pieces in the course of this winter. When I finish the concerto and the symphony, it would of course be a great pleasure for me to send them to you, even if it is too late for you to consider any of them for this season. I was very glad to learn that you are bringing your orchestra to Europe next spring,[3] and I'm looking forward to the pleasure of hearing you in one of several of the cities you'll visit. I was also very glad to know that my university did itself the honor of giving you an honorary degree. I want to congratulate you, but I think that it's Harvard University that I should congratulate!

Please give my warm regards to your wife from me and my wife, and accept our best wishes for a good winter and a successful season.

Sincerely yours,
Roger Sessions

1. Translated from the Russian by Theodore Levin.

2. Two days earlier Sessions had written Copland that the two finished movements of the sonata had been performed in Florence by Frank Mannheimer. He now felt that "John Duke was preeminently *not* the person to play it; first of all it needs a person with *guts* as well as sensibility." The same letter reveals that Barbara Sessions was to undergo another operation and a two-week hospital stay.

3. Sessions is not referring to the Boston Symphony Orchestra, which did not begin touring Europe until 1953, but to Koussevitzky's orchestra in Paris, which played each spring at the Théâtre des Champs Élysées.

▼

Roger Sessions to Aaron Copland
als US-DLC

Monday, November 25 [1929]
[Rome]

Dear Aaron,—

First of all let me thank you for the [Piano] Concerto[1] which arrived this noon, + for the very nice inscription. I am *delighted* to have both; I have already looked over the score and renewed the excellent impressions which I had in N.Y. two + a half years ago + whetted my appetite for further acquaintance.

[. . .]

As for concerts: I had already written to J[ean] B[inet] several days before your letter came + received word that he had written to Nabokoff again. Then four days ago I myself wrote to N. So I hope that I shall soon hear from that quarter. J.B.'s songs are not yet out, but they should be out very shortly as last proofs were sent in over a month ago. But I have seen Rota twice; + the second time he had already sent to Milan for his smaller things which he had left there; + as he asked for them to be sent *prestissimo* they should be here today or tomorrow. At all events the minute I have seen them I will send a package, either Fitelberg solo or Fitelberg plus Rota. Fitelberg I have played over again with somewhat better success than before—the slow movement in particular contains real music. Naturally Europeans in the U.S. are in your field—it would be too preposterous to have it otherwise. But after having concrete scores I am not so sure that you will not have the best things after all—+ that doesn't mean that I think that the best things you get will come from your Europeans in America, *au contraire!*

I had a long letter from Roy [Harris] today, + from it got my first glimpse of the person that you have always defended against the one I had hitherto seen. He speaks of going back to California in Jan., and all that he says about that + about his work is so genuine that I can't help feeling that he is really taking the right step + that it will be the making of him. His letter really made a splendid impression on me, + gave me much more faith in him as a person than I ever had before—and of course that means necessarily, as a musician too. Now if he only can sustain that mood—and it will be easier to sustain it in California than in Juziers, Heaven knows! I showed the letter to B[arbara] + she felt very much as I did; an excellent sign, I should say.

I agree that no more than one concert should be given unless the music warrants it; but your prospects look brighter on paper than they seem to in your mind.

I shall finish my sonata, I am quite sure, by the end of this year (not a word of this!); but it seems to me much better, don't you think? not to have it at our concerts again. I may possibly send you something else later on in the season; a "Serenade" I suppose I shall call it, for woodwind insts., but I am not sure.[2] I have written one short movement—a chorale—+ part of another; but the main thing for me, this winter, is to finish the Sonata + the Violin Concerto + to get well into the 2d Symphony, + whether I shall even go on with the other must settle itself. I am quite happy about the way both Sonata + Concerto are going. I have worked harder + much more lightheartedly than ever before—+ faster, too. Furthermore I have realized immediately that the reason I did not accomplish much of anything last year was at least in large part owing to the *one* of the "sterling Anglo Saxon qualities" I seem to possess—that is, of pretending that adverse conditions or surroundings in my life do not exist, instead of thoroughly facing them + accepting it, so to speak, as part of the inevitable conditions of life.

This year on the other hand conditions are better. There is one fairly intelligent boy here, a sculptor. He feels more or less as I do about the whole thing, + serves as an excellent safety-valve when I get too irritated, as of course I do every now + then. Josten[3] is here, too, for the winter; + although he has his limitations it is good to have a musician to whom one can talk, who is not mixed up too much with "movements," political + otherwise.

I am ashamed and sorry that you had my score[4] from Kalmus[5] + not from me—my infernal lack of ease about writing letters—particularly business ones. Do you know that since Sept. 20 I have had my score ready to send to Bloch, but that it has never been sent???—simply because I have not yet gotten up my courage to write the letter that must go with it?

There is plenty else to write, of course—but this letter must go. Fitelberg writes me that the Internationale Gesellschaft für [Neue] Musik [i.e., the ISCM] has looked with favor on my symphony + will probably perform it at an orchestral concert this winter—that in fact they intend to do so, if they give one. *Chi sa?* [Who knows?] Also there seems to be some prospect of a Brussels performance.

I do hope to write P[aul] R[osenfeld]—but he ought to know that I am to say the least a capricious correspondent (he is, himself, by the way!) and if he has got to have emotions about it all, to be annoyed or irritated rather than hurt. At all events, give him my love, + the same to all the others whom you hint at but don't specify. "Seid umschlungen, Millionen—etc. etc." ["Be embraced, millions."][6]

Always
R——

1. Dedicated to Alma Morgenthau Wertheim and published by Arrow Press.
2. This work does not appear in Sessions's catalog of completed music.
3. Werner Josten (1885–1963), a German-American composer and conductor, was a professor of counterpoint at Smith College 1923–49. In 1929 his *Ode for Saint Cecilia's Day* was played by the Boston Symphony Orchestra, Koussevitzky conducting.
4. The score of Sessions's Symphony in E Minor (no. 1).
5. Edwin F. Kalmus (b. 1893), then vice president of Copland's Cos Cob Press.
6. A quotation from Schiller's "Ode to Joy" and Beethoven's Ninth Symphony.

DURING THE WINTER of 1930 Copland produced three more Copland-Sessions Concerts in New York, February 9 and March 16 at Steinway Hall, and April 13 at the President Theatre. The February 9th concert comprised music by Jeffrey Mark, Robert Russell Bennett, Vladimir Dukelsky, Nino Rota, Henry Brant, and Robert Delaney. The March 16th concert included works of Chanler, Charles Griffes, Leo Ornstein, Chávez, and Copland (*Vitebsk*). Music by Roy Harris, Jerzy Fitelberg, Israel Citkowitz, Istvan Szelenyi, Pál Kadosa, and Imre

Weisshaus (pseudonym Paul Arma) appeared on the April 13th program. The inclusion of the Dukelsky, Rota, and Fitelberg were Sessions's contribution. The April 13th concert was reviewed in only three places; critics felt that in his String Quartet Harris had "not entirely succeeded in revealing his musical individuality."[1]

By August 17, 1930, when Sessions wrote to Copland again, he was in Hadley, Massachusetts. The two saw each other in America; Copland played the Symphonic *Ode* for Sessions. Sessions wrote to Copland November 26, the date he sailed back to Europe on the S.S. *Majestic* to continue his Rome Prize residency: "I have been inwardly cursing + almost weeping at the utter irrationality of my leaving the U.S. at this time. [. . .] I don't intend by any means to waste this next year; but neither can I see any reason for spending it in Europe, when I would rather be at home, especially as I have decided to pass the rest of my life in America" (US-DLC). He also observed, "Among the most important things for me was that I felt that the Copland-Sessions friendship prospered—I am very especially happy about that."

The only Copland-Sessions Concert of the 1930-31 season was an orchestral concert on March 15, 1931, at the Broadhurst Theatre in New York. Sessions sent his *Black Maskers Suite* from Rome, which was performed (Hugh Ross conducting) along with Copland's *Music for the Theatre* and music by Colin McPhee, Marc Blitzstein, and Darius Milhaud. The concert was devoted to music and film—the McPhee, Blitzstein, and Milhaud works were film scores. However, mechanical troubles plagued this concert when the film *Mechanical Principles,* which pictured moving machine parts at the Museum of Science and Industry, broke, necessitating earlier-than-scheduled performances of the Copland and Sessions.[2]

Sessions spent a month in Berlin in April 1931, having missed Copland, who had also been there. He returned to Rome in May and traveled to Oxford in July to hear his finished Piano Sonata given at the Ninth Festival of the ISCM, July 23. Although Copland did not have any music scheduled on the ISCM Festival, he too traveled to Oxford, where he heard the finished Sonata for the first time.

1. Francis D. Perkins, "Copland-Sessions Concert Offers All New Works," New York *Herald Tribune,* April 14, 1930, 17; the other reviews were Olin Downes, "Music: Copland-Sessions Concert," *New York Times,* April 14, 1930, 24; and Julian Seaman, "Music," *The World,* April 14, 1930, 11. See also Carol J. Oja, "The Copland-Sessions Concerts and Their Reception in the Contemporary Press," *Musical Quarterly* (April 1979): 223.

2. See M., "New York Concerts and Recitals: Copland-Sessions Concert," *Musical America* 51, no. 6 (March 25, 1931): 38.

▼

Roger Sessions to Aaron Copland
als US-DLC

Dear Aaron,—   Christmas Day [1930]

I am ashamed not to have written you before, especially after asking you to go to all the trouble + temporary expense of having more copies made of the Sonata. I hope the enclosed will cover the expense—+ if you have had to advance the money—as it occurred to me that you might have to do—I am covered with still more—+ more serious!—confusion. But both [Frank] Mannheimer + Dent,[1] whom I saw in London + Cambridge, urged me very strongly to submit the Sonata for the Oxford Festival,[2] + though I had not thought of the matter very much,—especially from all I had heard about the attitude of *Grünberg*[3] *et al.* at the time of the Geneva affair—I thought I might as well do it. Also I need that other copy here. You see I am beginning to feel that I had better begin to get a little busy in my own interests! I hope you won't disapprove—but it seems to me that I have been quite unnecessarily lazy + stupid in this respect, up to this time. Again, a thousand thanks, + as many apologies if I have put you to any inconvenience.

I am inclosing also a correction or rather a revision, of the first 3 lines on page 38 [of the Piano Sonata]—the result of a marvelous talk with N.B. in Paris. I feel that it really is finished now, + am especially pleased since it is one of two passages which I was not quite sure that I was satisfied with, but about which I was not entirely able to make up my mind, simply—you know the experience—from being in the work still too deeply. She put my mind entirely at rest about the other, but of course picked immediately on this one, + upon the thing which was wrong.—It was marvelous to see her again—after two years; she seemed in splendid form, + I felt that in a sense seeing her again—quite aside from the Sonata—brought the last two years + all the difficulties I had, to a complete + hence a satisfactory conclusion.—I feel as if all my friends had a lot to forgive me for, incidentally.

N.B. asked after you, of course, + I gave her your love. She spoke marvelously of you, as she always does. I often wonder if her warmth

+ capacity for friendship, or her musicianship, is the greater. They are of course both sides of the same thing; but it seems to me that the former is even more precious than the latter. Madame B—— was the same as ever, with her booming bass voice; like some huge Egyptian monument that never crumbles.

We had a good time in England, on the whole—though just as hectic a one as we had in New York. I spent a day in Cambridge where I found quite a colony of my friends—some of them *en passant.* I had a charming talk with Dent, *tête-à-tête,* largely about ISCM affairs. He has a delightful technique of being very discreet whenever his meaning is quite transparent in spite of discretion, + of being thoroughly indiscreet whenever discretion does not suffice! Let me add that the only American personality that came out whole was yourself. He spoke very nicely of seeing you in Frankfurt, + of your music there.

We went to Edinburgh with our friends to see a curious person named Donald Tovey[4]—a very interesting personality who attracted me much more than I expected—an Englishman with genuine temperament! though a thwarted one in very many respects. Another one of these people who don't really accept anything since Brahms— + yet who is obviously musical to the core. Quite unlike anything one ever sees in America, where that kind of conservatism invariably goes with hopeless pedantry + sentimentality + superficiality. With a man like Tovey there is very much to admire + really to profit by; and for me it was of extraordinary interest because one sees so clearly that his limitations come from a kind of hypersensitiveness—a need for self-protection of some kind—in a personality which still remains essentially a first-rate one. He is an admirable pianist, who really understands what he plays—it does make a difference! I got through a whole formidable program of Brahms, without drowsing for a minute.

I had a curious impression of the English, in spite of having had fairly intimate friends among them, + having once before spent a week in London. I never felt quite so un-Anglo-Saxon in my life, even though I found them much more friendly + *gemuthlich* [good-natured] than I expected. But even the young + "advanced" Cambridgians who are interested in "modern art" + "modern literature" bring a stodgy + pompous attitude into it, which makes them seem curiously out of the world. It isn't that they get everything out of books, the way so many Americans do; in their own way, they know how to live very well. But they have a way of dividing their lives into separate compartments which is very disconcerting—social theory goes into one compartment, sex into another, art into another, the British Empire into another, + so on. To be sure, this is not unknown elsewhere; but as far as my own experience goes it is infinitely more striking in England than anywhere else. It was an unexpected comfort to see some of my Italian friends there, + find them more sympathetic companions than ever before. But I suppose it is from that that the famous English "talent for compromise" comes—+ it is this that partly explains the really ghastly sordidness of the mining districts, which goes far beyond anything I have ever seen in Cleveland or Buffalo or the little industrial towns of Massachusetts. The uniformity and the filth—not earthy + robust filth, but artificial coal-filth—is something quite inconceivable.

I had a very nice visit with Israel [Citkowitz] in Paris—that is, it was very nice for us, though I was tired + coming down with an attack of grippe, + don't feel that I did justice to the occasion. He impressed me as having gained enormously in the last two years and I was quite delighted with the beginning of a new quartet he showed me. We discussed the school project with great enthusiasm—he seems to be as full of ideas as any of us; + I am sure we can all work out something excellent, provided we plan carefully + try to foresee all contingencies. I have somewhat enlarged my stack of notes on the subject + will soon begin to put them into presentable shape.

We stopped for six days chez the Binets in Trélex, near Lausanne. It was to have been only for a day, but influenza developed + I had to go to bed. We had a delightful time in spite of that. Jean has written a quartet which contains really beautiful things; I am delighted to *constater* [report] that he has really begun to "find himself." The Pro Arte is to do the quartet in Brussels + elsewhere;[5] otherwise I should have sent it on for our concerts. We spoke of you often, + I am sending him on your Concerto as he is thinking of writing an article on American music for the *Journal de Genève*.

We got back quite late to Rome + were received to my slight surprise, *aux bras ouverts* [with open arms]! It is going to be a very good year, I think; I feel in any case quite differently about the A[merican] A[cademy in] R[ome] this year—thoroughly independent, + able to use it for what it is worth. Lamond is, of course, thoroughly good hearted, even though he understands nothing. My influenza prevented me from being here for the Hanson concert—which must have been deadly from all accounts. Who knows, perhaps I would have taken better care of my cold if I had been going to hear Ansermet conduct the new Stravinsky work,[6] in Brussels that same day!

I spoke to Mario Labroca about giving me something for our concerts, + we are to go over his available work in a few days when the holidays are over. Also I am writing N.B. about sending me something of Markevich,[7] a young Russian pupil of hers about whom everyone is very enthusiastic. I didn't have time when I was with her— too much else to talk about in an hour and a half; + we were only in Paris for a day. I will also write at once to Ullmann; + I think those three contributions—if I can get the latter two—will really do a good deal to bolster up our programmes. I am also sending you the small orchestra version of the B—— M——. By the way, it actually came off in Cincinnati + apparently went well; I have a very enthusiastic letter from Reiner, with clippings from the three newspapers of Cincinnati.[8] The male critic was excellent; but the two ladies found it gruesome + repulsive. Apparently it sounded well on the orchestra, in any case; + that is all that matters to me, as far as that piece goes.

I am now busy with my *Strophes* (not *Elegy*) for orchestra, which I hope to send to Koussevitzky by about Feb. 1st.[9] It is surprising how easy everything seems after the Sonata.

I must end this long letter, now—you are first on a list of twenty-one—most of which, I hope, will be shorter!

Let me know when the *Ode* is to be played—+ best of luck + (all good wishes,[10] as the Russians say) from us both.

Always,
Roger

P.S. I am sending *two* enclosures; the second one—if you will be so kind—to go in the copy submitted for the festival competition.

1. The ISCM had come into being in 1922 largely through the effort of the English musicologist Edward Dent (1876–1957), who was its president until 1938.

2. The Oxford ISCM Festival was held July 23–28, 1931.

3. Louis Gruenberg (1884–1964) won the RCA Victor Prize with his opera *Jack and the Beanstalk* in 1931, and his jazz-influenced opera *The Emperor Jones* was produced at the Metropolitan Opera in 1933. Gruenberg evidently was upset that Sessions had submitted his sonata through the Italian, rather than the U.S., section of the ISCM for the Seventh Festival in Geneva, where it was performed.

4. Sir Donald Frances Tovey (1875–1940) was widely known as a writer and lecturer on music. He published in 1931 *A Companion to Beethoven's Pianoforte Sonatas* and *A Companion to Bach's "Art of the Fugue"* and, later, *Essays in Musical Analysis* in six volumes.

5. Binet had written his String Quartet in 1927 in Brussels, where he had taught the Dalcroze method 1923–29.

6. The *Symphony of Psalms,* performed December 13, 1931, by the Société Philharmonique de Bruxelles. Six days later it was given its Boston Symphony premiere.

7. Igor Markevich (1912–83), who had studied with Boulanger in 1925, had reworked material from a ballet commissioned by Diaghilev and left incomplete after the latter's death in 1929 into a cantata to a text by Jean Cocteau. The cantata's premiere in Paris June 4, 1930, generated much critical interest.

8. Reiner had performed the *Black Maskers Suite* with the Cincinnati Symphony December 5, 1930. A League of Composers concert five days later consisted of "Modern Choral and Instrumental Music" conducted by Lazar Saminsky. Sessions and eight other composers were played.

9. This work was not completed and is not part of the composer's catalog.

10. These words in Russian.

▼

Roger Sessions to Aaron Copland
als US-DLC

Thursday, February 26 [1931]

Dear Aaron,— [Rome]

Thank you for your nice note. I am glad you approve of what you call the *coup d'État,* though you credit me with both more guile + more political sense that I have! I'm so sorry your Concerto isn't being played—I didn't realize that you were submitting it.

It amuses me, the way I always fall foul of the American section [of the ISCM]—not that they can blame me for submitting the Sonata to the Italian section (in the most regular way) when they refused even to consider it. Well, *entre nous* [between us], I don't see that anyone will be greatly annoyed if they choose to disband. Who knows? It might even pave the way for a rejuvenation if the I.S.C.M. keeps on going!

I'm sorry the *Ode* has been postponed, not only for your sake but my own. We planned to go to Berlin for the first of March, to hear Klemperer[1] do the *Symphonie de Psaumes;* but at the last moment I have had to postpone going till March 17th. I suppose you will be leaving just after the *Ode* is played, but it would have been nice to feel that we would be arriving at more or less the same time. We will be in Berlin about a month—Klemperer, with whom we made great friends while he was here, has promised to see that we have access to everything we want there. So we are looking forward to it enormously. Kl.—— gave two concerts here, with the orchestra, + conducted Brahms's first in a way which I have not heard since Nikisch[2]—it gave me a new respect for old Johannes + made me feel that I had maligned him. No heaviness or self-importance, for a moment, but *music* in every bar!

Unfortunately I can't say the same for Mannheimer's performance of my Sonata which I heard over the radio, from London, Tuesday night! It was a great disappointment to me; too slow tempi, without exception even in the Andante; what seemed to me, even making due allowance for the radio, no sense of the line + shape; no fire whatever, and finally—last, but in view of the number, not least—so many false notes (*not* mistakes in the Mss.) as I could not have dreamed possible. He was obviously rattled—perhaps his first experience over the radio; but I felt sufficiently strongly about it to decide to postpone our trip to Berlin, to spend as much time as possible going over it with him here in Rome (he will be here from the 8th to the 17th) in the effort to pound it into his head + his nerves. Unfortunately the Italian section of the ISCM, at my instigation, has already more or less come to an understanding with him to play it at the Festival, + it is that which bothers me. It will be played here in May by someone else, whom I know will do it much better than that, at any rate. But Mannheimer is excellent, + careful,—provided he is made fully aware of what he is doing.

I have heard nothing from Gieseking, but since I have been too lazy to write him, it isn't surprising. I must say his N.Y. program of "Modern" "Music" didn't encourage me much![3]

I am most curious about the March 11 CS concert. Of course I understand fully about the Labroca work, + even proposed it with some hesitation, knowing how late it was, + realizing, too, that it might not be easy to find the voices. Perhaps however we could do it another year. I would like to do something for M[ario] L[abroca] principally because he never does anything for himself, + it is all one can do to even play his music for one. As for the B[lack] M[askers] I appreciate what you say about playing it—but I shall be so to speak relieved when it is over. I don't feel at all the same way about the big orchestral version, which is comparatively a very finished work—from the orchestral point of view, anyway. I shall look forward eagerly to your impressions, + I hope you will be quite ruthless.

Let me know when you will be in Berlin. We will be leaving here the 17th + no doubt will arrive the 19th. We plan to use the American Express Co., Charlottenstrasse.

And, good luck in everything—from us both!

As ever,
R——

1. The German conductor Otto Klemperer (1885–1973) had studied theory with Bloch's teacher, Ivan Knorr. In 1917 he had been appointed music director of the Cologne Opera. Ten years later he was made music director of the Kroll Opera in Berlin, where he had presented the first German performances of Stravinsky's *Oedipus Rex* and Schoenberg's *Erwartung*. He would be forced to leave Germany in 1933. Klemperer introduced Sessions to his concertmaster, Max Strub.

2. Arthur Nikisch (1855–1922), conductor of the Boston Symphony Orchestra 1889–93.

3. Perhaps Gieseking's Carnegie Hall appearance, October 12, 1930, at which he played, in addition to music by Bach, Schumann, and Debussy, Joseph Marx's *Praeludium* and Karol Szymanowski's *Calypso,* op. 29, no. 2, and *Tantris le Bouffon,* op. 34, no. 2.

▼

Roger Sessions to Aaron Copland
als US-DLC

Monday, May 11 [1931]
Rome

FORGIVE BLOTS! Please! I haven't the
least idea what happened, but haven't
the courage to begin again.

Dear Aaron,—

I was frightfully disappointed to hear that you had been in Berlin all those days, + that I missed you—especially since it was owing to a mere "fluke" that we missed each other. We *did* plan to leave the 26th + then just one little thing + then another made us put it off, literally from day to day. I wonder where you were staying all that time!—And of course by that time I had quite forgotten about having said we were leaving on the 26th, + had in fact rather given up hope of seeing you.

We had an exciting trip back to Rome, which I will tell you about when we see each other, if it seems interesting enough by that time! Dramatic, full of stormy + contrasting emotions—in Prague, of all places!

I'm so disappointed to hear about the *Ode;* it must have been extremely annoying to have to delay your plans so long. Berezowsky[1] told me about it, + I guess I already wrote you about it in my other note. But I am crazy to hear the Variations, + disappointed that there was an opportunity which I missed. Fred Jacobi wrote very enthusiastically about them.

Well—what would you suggest about our meeting before Oxford?

We plan to go up there about the 10th of July, + I am most anxious to stop in Paris on the way, for a few days (say the 11th to the 15th, or something like that?). This would seem the most practical thing for you, at the moment, unless you care to come to Italy, which of course would delight us. I imagine however that you don't want to move around too much; though you know, I am sure, that we would love to see you in Florence in June if you could manage it. Are you by any chance going to the Festival in Bad Hamburg?[2] All in all it sounds (*entre nous*) pretty deadly + I wouldn't go there for $1,000,000,000. But I have *very* much to talk over with you, + we must get together— quite aside I must say, from the pleasure of seeing you again!

I suppose Fred may have told you that my experiences in Berlin have "turned my head" or something of that kind—he seems to have taken very definitely that attitude; + I hope I needn't assure you that this is not the case. It is a pity that one cannot, with a certain type of person, show the least pleasure in one's experiences without being accused of giving them a quite false emphasis. F—— wrote the most inexplicable kind of letter to B[arbara] (*not* to me !?!), and if by chance he said anything to you about it,—well, I hardly think I need ask you to keep an open mind about it till we see each other; and I don't really think you consider me so weak in intelligence as Fred seems to do.

One thing more—there has been evidently some misunderstanding in the U.S. section about the circumstances of my submitting my Sonata to the Italian section; + I think Grünberg should at least know exactly what the circumstances were, whatever attitude he chooses ultimately to take in the matter. So I plan to write to him about it, + to state the facts as clearly as possible, so that he at least will have no grounds for any misunderstanding. But before I do so I think I should have a word from you. Do those people, or any of them, realize that I tried to submit the Sonata to them, through you? And have you any objection to my writing such a letter—any objection, I mean, on your own account? I wouldn't like to do anything that could possibly make trouble for you. And it is a quite small matter anyway; but as I am not guilty of any "lack of consideration" for the American section I would like at least to give them the chance to see that. But I shall do nothing till I have heard from you, + you may rely on my acting only according to your wishes, as far as your part in the matter is concerned.

After Fred's insinuations I hardly dare speak of such matters even to my best friends! but I think perhaps I can risk telling you that [the publisher] Schott has accepted my Sonata + hopes to have it ready by July. You will get a copy, of course!

Well—there is much more to say; but there is always plenty to say to you, + so I will not try to go on now. But *do* let me know the possibilities of getting together. If I had any money it would be easier but, as Goethe says, "Ach, wir armen!" ["We poor ones!"]

Barbara sends much love + asks me to tell you that not only is she jealous of me for having found two letters from you when we got here, but at the same time was quite struck down in her disappointment when she opened the envelope you addressed to her, + found only a postcard from someone else!

Always affectionately,
Roger—

P.S. Give our love to Strub;[3] I am writing him tonight.

1. As a violinist Nicholai Berezowsky (1900–1953) had played with the New York Philharmonic 1923–29 and was a member of the Coolidge Quartet 1935–40; as a composer and conductor he conducted the Boston Symphony Orchestra in his First Symphony in 1931. He committed suicide in 1953.

2. A Festival of American Music in Bad Hamburg July 6–8, 1931, billed as the first European festival devoted to American music, was to present pieces by Mann, Griffes, William Grant Still, Edward MacDowell, Howard Hanson, and Carl McKinley. Frank Mannheimer, whose chamber music was to be played, performed the concerto solo with an orchestra conducted by Oscar Holger.

3. Concertmaster of the Berlin Kroll Opera, Max Strub (1900–1966) formed a well-known trio with Elly Ney and Ludwig Hoelscher.

▼

Roger Sessions to Jean Binet[1]
als CH-Bsacher

Sunday, June 21 [1931]
Villino Corbignano [Florence]

Dear Jean,

I'm ashamed to have waited so long without writing you. Your letter was so nice and did me so much good that I feel like a monster of ingratitude not to have responded right away—but the last week at Rome wasn't just difficult and full of tension, it was also very disagreeable. We got a letter from Teddy [Chanler] that was disheartening—not because of money (everything's all right for the moment) but because of the accusations he made. When such a good friend makes accusations like that, one is forced to think about it, even if one can't find any reason for them—all this just by way of saying that I don't have any spirit at all these days.

So—where should I start? The news about Denise touched us more than I could ever tell you. You must know, dear, dear friends, how much we are thinking of you these days, and [illegible] best wishes for all of you—all *five,* we have to say now. And it makes us so happy, not just that a child is on the way, but above all that Denise is awaiting it with such joy—when is she expecting? Neither one of you said anything about it!

Anyway—here we are again at the villino—as you well know, it's paradise—the last time we were here in the summer, the Binets were here too—and should we be in danger of forgetting that, the smells, the walks in the twilight, the dinners on the terrace are all there to remind us. It is a nice good-bye to Italy and we can imagine that you are here with us, metaphysically at least. What a lovely souvenir!

We left Rome with very mixed feelings—too mixed to be exact. The feeling of being free from the American Academy was intoxicating for reasons which would be difficult to explain, especially since I'm convinced they have to do with my character—I'd like to say—and I'll tell you quite frankly—that I still haven't learned not to demand from life pleasures that aren't necessary and in the long run totally useless. But there also are places in which one doesn't believe; all my difficulties at the American Academy were only mental—nothing unpleasant, never, just continually *discontent,* and that's bad, isn't it?

Aside from the Academy, the last two years were *much* more pleasant than the first, above all this last one. We've seen a lot of the *Labrocas* and the *Casellas* and found them to be very good friends, from whom it was really sad to part. Casella is very charming in Italy, and I think he has changed a lot in these last few years, too. That isn't to say that I don't have reservations about his music! But as a *musician* (more so than as a composer) he is very interesting, and very simple and real as a person. Labroca is also very appealing, and many of Labroca's and Casella's friends are very nice. There was an environment there that became for us a sort of Roman "oasis."

Barbara wrote you about our experiences in Berlin. Those were six weeks of pure joy; very important for me. I think I fully digested (!) them (so to speak) and I can look back on them with a bit of distance and perspective. First of all, it made a big impression on me to see how rich and varied musical life there is—the same thing doesn't exist in any other country. Barbara wrote you that we stayed with Strub, Klemperer's concertmaster. We very quickly made friends with him;

we met all sort of musicians through him and Klemperer, and I found—(1) German musicians really *love* music, and with a passion. They never hate it. (2) The *professional life* of German musicians is a very special thing—the result partly of the fact that they *love* music (!) [and] partly of the fact that music in Germany is such a necessity, since one becomes a musician in the same way one becomes a doctor or lawyer, without needing a special aptitude for it—I mean that there is room for all sorts of musicians, provided they are well-prepared, even if they don't have much talent. A man who at home would remain the organist of the "First Congregational Church" in, let's say, Iowa City, could become in Germany the director and head conductor in a smaller city—that is to say, he would be a very good director, marvelously prepared, competent even if lacking much taste or fire, of course. In the theater he would give performances that would hold up to the opera in Rome or Paris—not at all bad performances of the German classics, of Verdi (including *Falstaff*), of Puccini and the newest German works (*Wozzeck,* [Hindemith's] *Neues vom Tage,* etc., etc.) (3) The general level of musicianship is extraordinarily high, thanks to the fact that there is a tradition and culture still very much alive, and because there is so much competition and opportunity.

On the other hand—the listening public is enormous, and therefore musical taste suffers, at least on the surface. I think it suffers above all on the surface, because I met many musicians who had about the same tastes as I do, and with whom I could speak freely and without explanations or reserves; that is to say they love Stravinsky and Hindemith above all among contemporary composers, they know the music of Debussy, Ravel, Milhaud *very* well—and Casella, Malipiero,—etc. This, of course, apart from certain *Echt deutscher* [genuinely German] localisms such as an admiration (a little inexplicable to a non-German) of Reger, for example. One could find parallels in any country, though—Nadia Boulanger's enthusiasm for Florent Schmitt or Roussel, for example. With those people I never had the sense of being a foreigner—aside from the language, which I found to be less difficult than I expected, however. I only want to say that I had the impression of a real fraternity of musicians—"Music unites all men in a common bond"—you remember the favorite saying of Emil.

Naturally I'm talking about performers and "musical people" and not about composers. That is another thing. I haven't met many of them—I've actually avoided the I.S.C.M. group (IGNM in Germany!) and in general I understand your reservations about this subject pretty well. There are thousands of composers in Germany—of all sorts—and that small group you hate (Rathaus, Fitelberg, Hauer,[2] etc. etc.) isn't after all only a German phenomenon, n'est-ce pas?—Those who frequent [music] festivals and the small music dealers—the German festivals must be *unbearable* affairs. After all, one could name other very un-German names. Judging from what I've seen, I'd say that those people don't have too much to do with the true musical life of Germany—or in any case perhaps, this winter there was a sort of reaction against "modern music"—a reaction which didn't have anything to do with Stravinsky or Hindemith, but was obviously against the *overproduction* of *useless music.*

Of course the listening public is enormous and diverse—there is a variety without equal in the other countries I know. There are snobs, of course; stupid people, devotees of Schönberg, devotees (horrible dictu) of [Hans] Pfitzner! I spoke with Hindemith about German publishers, and when I asked him what Breitkopf and Härtel are up to, he laughed and named some "official" composers whom I'd never heard of, "local" composers as he put it. I have the impression there are perhaps fewer snobs than in Paris, but to make up for it more old-fashioned and stubborn people than anywhere else.

Anyway—I can't say everything, not even all my impressions—and I did have others, some contradictory, which I absolutely have to tell you when we see each other next month!

I saw Hindemith several times, who was as nice as can be. You know him; sometimes he reminds me so strongly of my brother, that I had the feeling I know him very well. We spoke very little about music; but one day he showed me the conservatory, which he adores. He told me that the only thing he likes in Berlin is the conservatory—the Germany he loves with a passion is the Rhineland and Bavaria. I heard a very lovely *Concerto* (piano, brass, and 2 harps) of his,[3] with Gieseking and Klemperer. I played it, with [Artur] Schnabel, before, and then I heard the rehearsals and the concert. It seemed to me to be one of his best things, aside from the 2nd movement, which is a little bit conventional, "à la Hindemith." He has *a lot,* an enormous amount to give—I have the feeling he has hardly begun. And the only danger is that he remain too *facile*—a little bit superficial.

I also met other "personalities" I'd like to tell you about, but this letter is taking on slightly excessive proportions. My personal fortunes have all been very good. The people I played my music for—Klemperer, Toch, Schnabel, etc.—were very enthusiastic, with two nice results—1) Schott accepted the sonata and is trying to have it ready

for the Oxford festival—I sent back the corrected proofs yesterday—
2) Klemperer wants to perform a *Violin Concerto* (!) at one of his
concerts as soon as it is ready—and Strub, his concertmaster, is
excited about the idea, and wants to play it with other orchestras with
which he is engaged as soloist.

Several friends who know "musical Germany" very well assured
me that these things are very much out-of-the-ordinary, that I may
and should regard them as a real "success"—I know, as a matter of
fact, that Schott is hardly accepting anything new in this time of crisis,
and also that Klemperer, although he's been Berlin's apostle of
modern music, has been very discouraged the last two years and does
hardly anything new on his own initiative. But what makes me think
that it's very important for me to spend a lot of time in Berlin is
deeper than that; music is a serious thing there in the best sense of the
word—better—and only the best—that I can do, and that I would
always be around people who would accept me simply as a musician,
without being biased by race, nationality, or prevailing trends. It's
difficult to explain—of course I want to return to America, and until
six weeks ago I was intending to return next winter—but this experience was too important to leave hanging in midair, so to speak.

Well, I'm planning to stop at Trélex for at least one night when
Barbara arrives; and we'll have a lot to talk about! Also—I just have
to hear your Ode—I'm very [in English:] *excited* to hear about it. I
haven't forgotten the quartet—how's it going? Is it possible to have a
copy to show my friend Strub, who has just started a quartet in
Berlin?

I *really must stop,* though there are millions of things to tell you.
Forgive me for writing such a *one-sided* letter—+ not a really
satisfactory one at that.

But it brings very, very much love to you both—to the five of you—
it will be wonderful to see all of you, in such a short time now—Hugs
and kisses—

Yours,
Roger

1. Translated from the French by Paul Suits.
2. Karol Rathaus (1895–1954), a conservative Polish composer, left Berlin in 1932
and in 1938 settled in the U.S., joining the faculty of Queens College in 1940. The
twelve-tone experiments of the Viennese composer Josef Hauer (1883–1959) ante-
dated Schoenberg's.
3. The *Konzertmusik,* op. 49.

Picture postcard of Max Strub, Barbara Sessions, and Roger Sessions sent to Aaron Copland from Florence in July 1931. On the reverse, in Barbara's hand: "I sha'n't see you in Oxford, but here is a card to remind you at least how I look (approximately). All Good luck." In Strub's hand: "Herzlichste grüsse aus dem wunderbar schönen Florenz. Und eine gute Zeit in der Uhlandstrasse." ("Hearty regards from wonderful Florence and have a good time in the Uhlandstrasse.") In Sessions's hand: "Many greetings. I shall be seeing you very soon! You must come here sometime, really, you would love it, I assure you! —Roger. The Sonata is out, + I shall have a copy for you in Oxford." Courtesy of Aaron Copland.

CHAPTER

1931-1933

FOUR

Roger and Barbara Sessions lived in Berlin for a little over a year, until the rise of Hitler in early 1933. Sessions continued to work on the Violin Concerto with Max Strub, the intended soloist under Klemperer. The concert life was stimulating; the Berlin Philharmonic celebrated its fiftieth year in 1932. In the late 1970s Sessions would recall, "Berlin was by far the most exciting place then. Of course, the people I knew in France, Nadia Boulanger in particular, never forgave me for moving there. But as far as musical life goes, that was the high point of my whole life."[1]

Ernest Ansermet conducted Sessions's First Symphony in Berlin on December 9, 1931, as part of a Berlin Symphony Orchestra concert arranged by Copland and sponsored by the ISCM.[2] A week later, December 16, 1931, the last of the Copland-Sessions Concerts, called "A Concert of Contemporary American Music," took place in Aeolian Hall, London. On it Irene Jacobi performed Sessions's Piano Sonata, which had been heard at Oxford the previous summer at the Ninth ISCM Festival. The other works all received their British premieres: Chávez's Sonatina for Piano (Copland was the pianist); Paul F. Bowles's Sonata for Oboe and Clarinet;[3] Copland's Piano Variations (the composer performing); Citkowitz's Five Songs from "Chamber Music" by James Joyce; and Thomson's *Capital, Capitals* with the composer at the piano. Copland later recollected:

It is difficult enough to arrange concerts of contemporary American music under the best of conditions, but when the principal participants are scattered around the globe such an undertaking borders on the impossible. During the planning stages, Bowles was in Tangier and then Paris, Citkowitz in New York, Thomson in Paris, I in Berlin, [Sessions first in the U.S. and then Berlin,] and the concert in London! Various performers were in other locations. . . . I no longer recall the details of what went awry, but in a letter written to Virgil later (29 January 1932), I thanked him for being so nice "considering the concert was going about as bad as possible."[4]

Critics either disliked the music or said almost nothing about it.[5]

Barbara Sessions wrote to Boulanger on March 20, 1932, and she responded. Sessions then wrote back, for the only time, in French (F-PBN). His reason was that certain feelings can best be expressed in French. ("Je vous demande pardon, seulement, que je vous écris, si témérairement, en français; mais je trouve chaque jour de plus, qu'il y a des choses pour lesquelles il n'existe tout simplement pas de mots en anglais.") The content of this letter parallels one of May 2 to Copland (US-DLC): the violinist Strub has had a "breakdown" and will not play the Violin Concerto that spring. However, Sessions feels sure that it will be done on the next season.

That spring the First Festival of Contemporary American Music presented eighteen chamber works at the Yaddo estate, outside Saratoga Springs, New York, on April 30 and May 1, 1932. Sessions's Piano Sonata was again played and highly praised by critics, along with seven of Ives's songs and Copland's own performance of his Piano Variations.[6] Alfred H. Meyer wrote in *Modern Music,* "Roger Sessions's Sonata for Piano was one of the outstanding works of the festival. The long, expressive, almost Chopinesque melody of the two andantes shows him frankly unafraid of a tune. This type of fearlessness is not always to be found in a composer who writes meticulously polished Stravinskian fast movements. But cramping evidence of the care with which he writes is not absent from Sessions's finished product."[7]

Copland felt that Yaddo would take the place of the Copland-Sessions Concerts, and the two decided to give up the joint effort. The Yaddo concerts would not run annually after the second festival, in 1933. Sessions's Piano Sonata was repeated on the next Yaddo festival concert, in 1936.

1. Andrea Olmstead, *Conversations with Roger Sessions* (Boston: Northeastern University Press, 1987), 160.
2. The other works were Copland's First Symphony (the orchestral version of the Organ Symphony), Louis Gruenberg's *Jazz Suite,* and Carl Ruggles's *Portals.*

3. Paul Bowles (b. 1910) had been accepted as a student by Copland in Saratoga and by Nadia Boulanger in Paris, where he also took lessons from Virgil Thomson. Bowles's first novel, *The Sheltering Sky,* was very well received. In 1972 he wrote an autobiography, *Without Stopping.*

4. Aaron Copland and Vivian Perlis, *Copland: 1900 through 1942* (New York: St. Martin's Press, 1984), 191.

5. See "Modern American Music: Previous Impressions Confirmed," Manchester *Guardian,* December 17, 1931, 8, and "Modern American Music: Works Heard for the First Time in England," London *Morning Post,* December 17, 1931.

6. Reviews of the festival include Paul Rosenfeld, *Discoveries of a Music Critic* (New York: Harcourt, Brace, 1936), 352–60, and Arthur V. Berger, "Yaddo Music Festival," New York *Daily Mirror,* May 3, 1932 (final edition), 18. See also Rudy Shackelford, "The Yaddo Festivals of American Music, 1932–1952," *Perspectives of New Music* 17, no. 1 (Fall–Winter 1978): 82–125, and Marjorie Peabody Waite, *Yaddo Yesterday and Today* (Saratoga Springs, N.Y.: Argus Press, 1933).

7. Alfred H. Meyer, "Yaddo: A May Festival," *Modern Music* 9, no. 4 (May–June 1932): 174–75.

▼

Roger Sessions to Nadia Boulanger
als F-PBN

Sunday, December 20, 1931

My dear friend,—   Berlin

I wonder if you have any idea what a joy it was to see you; for me a very special and extraordinary joy. I can't believe that life holds anything more fundamentally satisfying or quickening than the sense of renewal that one feels in coming once more, and truly, into contact, after a long time of separation, with a friend who is truly and deeply a friend. I find more and more as I grow, how rare and how precious such friends are, and how grateful one must be to one's God or one's Destiny, that one is granted them. One feels that the measure of one's joy, one's gratitude, and the deep inner refreshment and renewal of faith that such moments bring one, is to a very real extent the measure of one's ultimate force, and even that at such moments, more than in all others, the true meaning and direction of one's life is revealed to one. I don't know whether what I write is clear or not; but I have had occasion more than once recently, not only in my own experience but in my observation of the experiences of others, to remember that marvelous passage in the *Purgatorio* of Dante, where Dante is left weeping by Virgil in the "Paradiso Terrestra," and Beatrice, finding him thus, rebukes him for his weeping, saying "Do you not know that here man is happy?"[1]

[. . .]

You asked me to write you my impressions of Israel and of his music. First of all as to the latter. On the positive side I felt, as I always have with him a very real and very precious (*cher* or *de valeur, not précieux!*) sensibility and feeling; a consciousness of musical aims, and, as far as *detail* went, ability to realize them. To be more specific; the tonal structure (f♯–e♯–g♯–b–f♯) [of Citkowitz's 1932 String Quartet] I found excellent and, in itself, irreproachably carried out; the voice leading excellent; and certain melodic details pleased me enormously.

On the negative side I was enormously aware—even more than I expected to be,—of what he has not yet learned; and of the *absolute necessity* for him of patience until he has thoroughly mastered the study of form in all its aspects. Principally I felt a great lack of plasticity and ease in the flow, both of the separate phrases and of the line as a whole. I felt a lack of *breathing* spaces which seemed to me to come from a lack of strong rhythmic profile in the inflections of the various phrases, so that the cadences never seemed inevitable or— for that reason—very definite. Then, the relation of the voices to each other did not seem clearly enough defined to me; this seems to me especially important in a string quartet, where the instruments are all of similar *timbre*. The three *subsidiary* voices are very often so written as to seem too complicated to be a mere accompaniment, and not sharply characterized enough to be something really more important. I felt the melodies themselves moved, sometimes rather stiffly—in the first phrase, for instance, where the repeatedly touched low C♯ seems to suggest a *harmonic* significance that is obviously not intended or made effective. I felt, finally, that after a kind of climax at the bottom of the first and top of the second page, there is far too much of a détente—so that the second climax, at the bottom of page 2, comes too quickly and without sufficient motivation, + produces the effect of a rather aimless rising and falling.

I talked with Israel to a certain extent about these things, and urged on him the necessity of going on with a great deal more technical study, of fugue and form, before he can stand on his own legs, as he (like all of us at his age, after all) would obviously like to do. I tried to impress on him that it is discipline and practice that count, even though one may take, eventually, a very different direction from the one which one has been taught. I don't know how far I succeeded, with him; he did not ask my advice, and gave no sign of welcoming it. But I feel very strongly about this; if music is ever to develop in America, we cannot afford to waste Israel!

I did feel one thing, and I hope you will understand my speaking of it. I have had the feeling, both last summer and this fall, that he has been living too long an absolutely solitary life, and has gotten, as we say, "bottled up" and tense. I don't know how you would feel about his taking, say, a month's vacation, perhaps travelling or perhaps staying on in Paris, but at all events getting away from the kind of concentration on himself and his own problems (musical and otherwise!) in which he has been living so concentratedly for the last four years. I feel certain that at the end of that time he would come back to you and to his work with fresh energy and enthusiasm. I had thought of suggesting his coming here, and of course we should be delighted—I could get him free tickets to very nearly everything in the way of concerts and opera, and we could see that he had a cheap and comfortable place to live.[2] But it might very well be that that would not be the best thing, so I certainly only mention it as a possibility. I am not at all sure, even, that he would want to do it. But I did have the very definite feeling that a "change of atmosphere" for a short time, would refresh him and give him both a better perspective on his problems, and a greater appreciation of what he has got still to do!

Well—I will not write more of this, though if I had the chance to *talk* with you about it there is much more, perhaps, that I would say. I do not forget that you are much more familiar with both his music and his problems than I and that I have perhaps written more than is necessary, and more than you asked me to write. If I can help in any way, I hope you will let me know. In some ways I believe I have a certain influence on Israel, and if I ever use it I should rather use it wisely!

So, please forgive me if I have written too long a letter. I hope so much to get to Paris before spring; it would be such a joy to see you again.

Please give devoted greetings from us both to your mother, and never forget our deep affection.

Yours,
Roger

P.S. If you should hear Klemperer's concert this week, and should care to speak to him afterwards, I know he would very much appreciate it.

1. The frequent and effusive letters to Boulanger from Sessions, otherwise not a punctual letter writer, might be explained by his perception of her need for such

treatment and a fear of losing her friendship. Robert Craft writes of her: "Nadia was quick to take offense at supposed slights and was notoriously vindictive, as in the case of Ravel, who failed to answer a letter, and in that of Bartók, who did answer but too tersely to satisfy her. Both composers were stricken from her orbit" (*Present Perspectives* [New York: Knopf, 1984], 63–64).

2. There is no evidence that Citkowitz ever visited Sessions in Berlin. Sessions's proposed solution to Citkowitz's musical problems sounds very much like self-analysis and self-prescription.

▼

Roger Sessions to Aaron Copland
als US-DLC

January 6 [1932]

Dear Aaron,—   Berlin

This is to introduce Normand Lockwood,[1] my successor in Rome (doesn't that sound Papal?) of whom I spoke to you in the fall. If you can help him in any way I shall be very glad.

Thanks for the nice letter from the boat. I had already heard from Irene [Jacobi] about the London concert[2]—also from Saerchinger[3] who has been here; but was glad to have your impressions too. Sorry things didn't go better; but I don't believe it matters in the long run. I still hear very nice things, + from quite unexpected sources, about the [December 9th] concert here, and have the impression that it was a really good thing for both you + me, in spite of some of the criticisms, which really have very little importance, as far as I can see.

Not much news to report. My concerto goes on steadily, + I am pleased with the way it is turning out. The second part + first, slow part of the third are nearly done. The whole must be ready by Mar. 1st at the latest + I have every hope that it will be. We spent three days in Weimar with the Strubs + family of Frau S.; charming, very cultivated people of the best German type—the father a retired actor who was quite famous in his day, up to just before the war. Weimar is a charming place—I felt as if I were really seeing Germany for the first time.

My money finally came, *Gott sei Dank* [God be thanked]—the day before Christmas. Shall send you a check in a day or two.[4]

I have seen Fitelberg + Lopatnikhoff once or twice, + spoken of you—they would send greetings if they knew I were writing. As for music, the only thing that I have heard worth mentioning is Klemperer's really beautiful performance of *Così fan Tutte,* which is a pure marvel of an opera—I never really appreciated it before, having seen only one poor performance some years ago.

I hope Kalmus got in touch with you in regard to the *Black Maskers* score.[5]

I won't write more now as I promised to send this to Lockwood to his boat.

As always,
Roger

1. Lockwood (b. 1906) had studied with Respighi in Rome (1924–25) and Boulanger in Paris (1925–28) and had held the Rome Prize fellowship (1929–32). In 1932 he joined the faculty at Oberlin Conservatory. He is now a professor emeritus at the University of Denver.

2. The final Copland-Sessions Concert, December 16, 1931. Pianist Irene Jacobi had performed on League of Composers concerts and was the wife of Frederick Jacobi.

3. César Saerchinger (1884–1971) was the foreign correspondent of the New York *Evening Post* and the *Musical Courier*. He lived in Berlin (1920–25) and London (1925–37) and wrote a book on Artur Schnabel.

4. To reimburse Copland's expenses in reproducing the First Piano Sonata. The check would not reach Copland until May 2. Sessions's money came from his Carnegie fellowship.

5. Cos Cob Press issued *The Black Maskers* later in 1932.

▼

Roger Sessions to Nicolas Slonimsky[1]
als US-DLC

[Spring 1932]
bei Casper, Lützowufer 10
Berlin

Dear Nicolai Leonidovich,—

I have no time to write you a long Russian letter, nor do I have any more [to write about] the beauty of Berlin (relatively speaking)—I'd rather say of her the naughty, the fleshy, the teasy.[2] And don't tell me that you don't have words like this. I made them up myself—so why tell me they do not exist? But—I forgot, when I wrote you the last letter, to enclose the piece about Lourié and Koussevitzky, so I'll do it now. I must confess that I'm amused by Lourié's book,[3] which must be very silly.

Cowell is here now and I see him often.[4] I also saw Adolph Weiss, who seemed very honest, though I must say openly that what I know of his music I find quite boring. I also wanted to write you about Fitelberg. He told me that you had told him that you could probably find people who would be able to help him a little. He doesn't want to write you about this, as he doesn't want to bother you if it would be an inconvenience for you. But maybe there is something that you can do. That's why I'm writing to you (and also to two or three others) to ask you if you can do anything. He's very ill and he can't see a doctor because he doesn't have money to buy medicine. Unfortunately, I also have very little money, but I want to help him. I will help him a little in May so that he can go to Vienna to a clinic (you can imagine what it's like when they tell you that he could have had this treatment for free, but he had no money to go there!) I'm only writing this to say that I would take him to the doctor if I had the money!

Excuse me for writing about this to you. I hope it's not too unpleasant for you and in any case, I'm the only one to blame! I'm writing completely independently. Naturally, I should say that I understand very well that perhaps it's impossible to do anything. In this case, you should write to me, not to Fitelberg. If it's possible to find money, I would prefer that you send it to Fitelberg himself, since I don't like to handle other people's money.

I don't think it's necessary to write any more about this. I would be very grateful to have a word from you concerning this, if possible.

In two weeks I'm going to Paris. There I hope to see Varèse and your mother and sister. Also if I have enough money I hope to find some writing paper which I really like. [. . .]

So, all the best. Please convey regards from both of us to your wife.

Sincerely,
R.H.S.

P.S. As to Fitelberg, I am sure even if there's very little money, just a little something, it will be a help. He's in great need. Excuse me for mentioning it again, but I only wanted to say that you shouldn't wait if you can't put together a large sum.

1. Translated from the Russian by Theodore Levin.
2. Slonimsky had been in Berlin earlier in 1932 while on a tour conducting a program of new American, Mexican, and Cuban music. He later wrote of this time: "In Berlin I was in daily communication with a kindred soul, Roger Sessions, who was there on a Carnegie fellowship. He was a person of inspiring intellect, a philosopher of life, a radical in politics, a linguist (he spoke fluent German, French and Italian, and even learned Russian). On a less lofty level, he was an amateur sexologist. We used to make regular visits to a sexualia shop in Alexanderplatz. Sessions bought stationery with naked women for a logo, and used it in our correspondence for several years" (*Perfect Pitch: A Life Story* [London: Oxford University Press, 1988], 132). None of the surviving correspondence is written on

such stationery, but its motif is carried through with a nude woman Sessions drew in a letter to Slonimsky, January 16, 1934 (US-DLC).

3. Arthur Lourié's worshipful *Serge Koussevitzky and His Epoch: A Biographical Chronicle*, trans. S. W. Pring (New York: Knopf, 1931).

4. Henry Cowell had received a Guggenheim fellowship the previous year to study comparative musicology with Erich von Hornbostel in Berlin.

▼

Roger Sessions to Aaron Copland
als US-DLC

Saturday May 28 [1932]

Dear Aaron,—   [Berlin]

Thanks for your letter—glad the check arrived safely + that there had been no pressing need for it sooner. I was really rather mortified.

I had already had some news of Yaddo through my mother's clippings—she sends them in profusion,— + am glad it went well. I did suspect however that the "Critic-Composer-Conference" was not quite as reported by the A.P.[1]—my suspicions were strong enough in fact to anticipate any feelings of relief which I might have [had] and from your account of it! I was really delighted when I heard that [Jesús] Sanromá was to play my Sonata—I heard it first from Toch, as a matter of fact.

Yes, we are staying on here another year, + I am glad of it. This winter did not really begin, for me till after Christmas, but it has been an intensely good one, full of musical experiences + new friendships and above all I believe I have gone very far ahead with my work + my general development. All kinds of problems in my life have seemed to iron themselves out + I feel ready for anything—at least, I shall feel so by the time we return to America next year.

I was surprised to have the U.S. [ISCM] section's suggestion that I act as delegate—"This is so sudden" as the saying goes—and shall certainly do so if they don't make conditions to which I could not agree. I feel that from the fact of having lived in Europe, + in various countries, I am in a more or less strategic position and think I might be able to be of help. However, I am waiting for the explanatory letter + am making no decision till it comes. I would have wired my good disposition if I had known whom to wire to, but the cable was unsigned.

Your plans for the next six months sound delightful. How I envy you the trip through the Southern States, where I have always longed to go.[2]

Our plans are quite simple—staying in Berlin through the summer, after Vienna, + making use of Wanusee as much as possible. I have loads of work on hand including the birthday quintet for Mrs. Reis + Co.,[3] which as far as I can see will not be at all a cheerful piece. Our new apartment is charming + quiet, over a delightful garden, + we don't dread the summer in the slightest.

I don't write long letters to anyone any more, so I shan't try to do so this time, especially as short letters are an excellent habit to have. So—*alles Gute* [all the best], + good luck in every way.

Roger

P.S. We see a lot of Stephen Spender,[4] + are very grateful to you for bequeathing him to us. I have an increasingly good opinion of his gifts.

1. On May 1, as part of the first Yaddo festival, a Conference for Critics and Composers drew only four critics—Alfred Meyer, Paul Rosenfeld, Arthur Berger, and Irving Kolodin. Angry and frustrated, Copland later wrote that "the time had arrived for critics to adopt new attitudes, and I accused the critics of neglect and lack of curiosity. 'Frankly,' I concluded, 'under such circumstances I consider daily newspaper criticism a menace, and we would be better off without it!' " (Copland and Perlis, *Copland: 1900 through 1942*, 191). An Associated Press reporter wrote for the *New York Times* (May 2, 1932): "The longstanding feud between composers and critics flared into the open at a conference in Yaddo, the Spencer Trask mansion."

2. Copland spent the spring at Yaddo working on the Short Symphony and the *Statements* for orchestra. On August 24 he left New York for Mexico to attend the first all-Copland concert, organized by Chávez.

3. The quintet, for the tenth anniversary of the League of Composers, would not be completed by its September 2, 1933, deadline and was abandoned, as had been a similar commission in 1924.

4. In 1933 the English poet and critic Sir Stephen Spender (b. 1909) published his first volume, *Poems*. His time in Germany with Christopher Isherwood during the early 1930s is described in *World Within: The Autobiography of Stephen Spender* (Berkeley and Los Angeles: University of California Press, 1951).

▼

Roger Sessions to Aaron Copland
als US-DLC

[Summer 1932]
Dear Aaron,—   Berlin

I have written Mrs. Reis a note with my "regrets + compliments" in regard to being the Berlin representative for Yaddo next year. I honestly don't think the "sämtliche werke" [complete works] of one

Remi Gassman [*sic*][1] would give me an exacting enough task to justify me in assuming an official position in connection with them, especially as I know in advance (having served for some time as his guide, philosopher + friend—partly in a musical + partly in a general spiritual sense—a sort of neben[second]-Hindemith or Ersatz-Nadia!) what the verdict would be. Since I strongly suspect you have been simply afraid my feelings would be hurt if I were not offered a finger in the pie, I am sure you will forgive me!

I have had various clippings + seen various *Äusserungen* [reports] on the subject of this year's [Yaddo] festival + though they none of them come from very brilliant sources they have at least roused my curiosity, or rather sharpened it. It will not be really satisfied, I fear, till I have been back + seen for myself.

What on earth are you up to with our "traditional enemies" the critics?![2] I wonder if I understand your point of view thoroughly. Naturally I sympathize with your point of view to a certain extent—theoretically, that is, but not practically. And if I understand you correctly, I don't sympathize entirely even from a theoretical point of view. It has always seemed to me that the very existence of the professional critic is a rather unhealthy symptom from the point of view of real artistic development; a really productive age does not produce them, + what criticism is needed by the artists comes from the ranks of producing artists themselves. The professional critic is a middleman, in so far as he is anything but a reporter; he is in his very essence unproductive, either because he has tried to produce and failed, or because from the first he has chosen an unproductive function; and he doesn't understand music in the least from the standpoint of the composer or even of the performer. His essential relationship is with the public, + here he fulfills an obvious and no doubt useful social function.

It seems to me that criticism is of four possible kinds, and that only the first is of any use to the composer as far as his artistic development is concerned. This is *technical criticism* in the broadest—style, etc.— as well as the narrowest sense. But it is exactly the kind that one cannot possibly get except from practicing musicians, + of which one can almost always get an excellent quality from them—from really good ones, I naturally mean. For that one needs *musicians* who have actual intimate + daily contact with musical material; the vague and platonic relationship to which even the best critic is limited does not suffice.

The second type is the more general kind which has to do with the essence of the composer's ideas + musical thought; and while that is what most critics try or aspire to give, I can't see that it is of any use to a composer. I mean simply that if a composer isn't sure of his own direction, it means that he has no inner compulsion, no inner certainty, and hence the case is really rather hopeless. At least, no external shoving can be of the slightest use to him. No doubt criticism of this kind can have an influence on anyone's temporary moods, but if they do more than this it seems to me a pretty sure sign that there is something fundamentally wrong with the composer. I can't see that this is less true today than it ever has been.

Thirdly, you say "American music needs nurturing"—and "like any new growth." Here again I disagree, and I hope you will understand what I mean. It has always seemed to me, + in this respect I have not changed my point of view since twenty years, that art and culture are far *too much* "nurtured" and "pursued" in America. These things grow of themselves when they are needed, and can only grow freely in the open air, this growth cannot be forced. Too much "nurturing" has placed American music in an entirely false, self-conscious category, just as it has too often placed "modern" music in a false category— + not only in America. Please don't think that I minimize the real problem that lies at the bottom of what you say. I certainly would be in favor of doing anything to put the composer— any + all composers—in a decent + independent *economic* position, which he certainly is not in now. Downes's attitude that the American composer has more than he deserves, in that respect, + his pretension that stipends, prizes, etc. have any *essential* bearing whatever on the situation are of course false and even a scandal. But—that seems to me only to illustrate the utter falseness of the values that have been created, and to be a product of those values created by just these ideas, that American music is a thing to be "nurtured." So, the American composer has been regarded too much as an object of charity, not as an individual who makes a positive contribution to American life—even American musical life, and it seems to me that this attitude has stood + will continue for some time to stand, more than anything else, in the way of real recognition of the American composer. And, though it is very good indeed of you to speak of my Symphony in this connection (this reads as if I thought *you* were proposing such a thing— + I hope you know I didn't mean to imply anything of that sort—but am speaking of the logical consequences only, of certain ideas) I certainly hope that no music of mine will ever be played or praised simply because anyone feels it his duty to encourage American music. I honestly think that this and similar movements and their attendant snobisms are one of the most depressing features and symptoms of modern musical life; an art that cannot stand on its own feet deserves to die.

An artist must learn to do without encouragement or recognition, it seems to me, for two reasons. The first is the obvious one, that he can't ever be sure of having it—it is the most uncertain thing in the world, and fortune is at any moment likely to change—not in the long run, of course, but certainly within the space of an artist's lifetime. Secondly because experience, both in the past and the present, offers proof sufficient for anyone that it is essentially irrelevant. Bizet died, after all, because of his disappointment at the failure of *Carmen,* which is not exactly an unpopular work now. Well, I don't need to tell you facts which you know perfectly well. I simply think it is unwise to raise false hopes or expectations in the young, or false standards; for a composer who goes in primarily for success generally gets it,—given a *reasonable* amount of talent—temporarily.

Well—the fourth type of "criticism" is propaganda + publicity, and no one would deny that that is useful. But that is hardly the plane on which you started the discussion, and after all it has nothing to do with artistic development. And the old saying goes, if one cares to apply it, "Every man has his price"—of one kind or another; though not *universally* true it is still true enough to be effective in certain obvious cases—and useful, too.

Of course, some day the critics in America will doubtless wake up to the fact that, without American composers, + conductors, too, they are more or less cultural parasites + entitled to no self-respect. But I can't see that anything but their own qualms of conscience can bring that day any nearer!

I suppose there is the danger that you will consider all this as a tirade! Really, it is not intended as such—it is if you like sheer *Geschwätzlust* [delight in gossip]—the Germans would certainly call it something like that, though as far as I know the word is my own!

Practically, of course, it seems to me that you are playing into the critics' hands. We don't want whatever music may arise in America encumbered by a mass of theory + dogma, do we? And until composers + musicians—individual or collective—are in full command of their own artistic situation—their inner situation—there is not, + never has been, any art. That is not idealism, but obvious sense, it seems to me.

Well, forgive me for writing at such length!

Not much space left (or time!) for other things! You have heard of course that I was elected to the [ISCM] Jury for next year—much to my surprise.[3] It was, quite aside from that, particularly nice in Vienna, though the Schönberg-Schuler fest—it amounted almost to that—was no more *ergebnisreich* [rich in results] than other festivals—a little less so, perhaps. At least there were more + longer dreary stretches than I remember either in Geneva or in England. I won't go into details, since you will doubtless have read various accounts, of various colors. I saw of course many friends—Ansermet, with a gorgeous Spanish lady whom he introduced to me as my—er—lady-friend, Mme so + so!; Casella, in a somewhat subdued mood, Dent, Fitelberg père,[4] not to mention Koussie, who left before the festival but with whom I had a few moments conversation, in three languages. Naturally the old guard—Hába, Steinhardt, Talich, Prunières, Glinski, Sanders, Slavenski,[5] Berg + Webern much in evidence; the latter is an *excellent* conductor + a charming person.[6] Wellesz—a charming man but, judging from the Bakchantinnen, a bad composer.[7] I enjoyed very much indeed Malipiero,[8] who is the best possible type of Italian. I hadn't known him before.

The Jury is sending around a letter (provided Pijper[9] will also sign it) to the various sections, recommending that they make a special effort in the preliminary selection of works to be sent; and it is possible that the Jury may meet twice, in order to prepare the program as carefully as possible. Also Fred [Jacobi] + I are preparing a report to the American section, with certain definite recommendations. I hope you will use whatever influence you have with the Am. Section to see that really good things are sent in—and it is very important that there should be a variety of different kinds (orchestral, chamber music, songs, etc.), and that they should later undertake to provide the best possible performers for it. Also, that they send in works that are really new. Why for instance did they send last year your Symphony, from 1924, when both the Ode + the Variations were available? The report we are going to send will, from my side at least, be a very carefully considered one,—and I think from Fred's side too; and I hope it will receive at least some attention at home. There is no reason why the American Section should not play much more of a part than it has thus far, if it wants to.

Well—I won't try to write more now. I'm busy on my "birthday quintet,["] as well as revising the Concerto, to show to Klemp. in the fall. He has not yet seen it, and I am not sure that that performance (by him) will come off, though I have no reason to think it won't, except the general political + economic situation, which seems to mean a general cultural *Abbau* [retrenchment], practically no modern music, relatively speaking. Klemperer did nothing new this year, except the Hindemith Oratorio,[10] if one calls that exactly a new work. Hindemith is a classic in Germany by this time.

Well—write to me some time. Barbara sends love.

As always,

R——

1. Chicago composer Remi Gassmann (1905–82) was to compose a cello sonata and a serenade (1956), both published by Associated Music Publishers. His later works would be co-written by German composer Oscar Sala. Gassmann's *Electronics* was the first electronic score to be choreographed by Balanchine.

2. Copland expanded on his remarks at the May 1st critics' conference in his article "The Composer and His Critics," *Modern Music* 9, no. 4 (May–June 1932): 143–47. He cited Sessions's Symphony as a "glaring example" of an overlooked work.

3. By an acrimonious vote at the Tenth ISCM Festival, in Vienna, June 20–21, 1932, Sessions had won out over Boulanger to be a member of the jury that would meet in Amsterdam in December 1932 to select the works for performance at the next year's festival, also in Amsterdam.

4. The Polish conductor and composer Gregor Fitelberg (1879–1953), the father of Jerzy Fitelberg.

5. The Czech composer Alois Hába (1893–1973), the Czech conductor Vàclev Talich (1883–1961), the French musicologist Henri Prunières (1886–1942), the Polish musicologist Mateusz Glinski (1892–1976), the American composer Robert L. Sanders (1906–74), and the Hungarian composer Josip Slavenski (1896–1955).

6. Anton von Webern had conducted the Workers' Orchestra of Vienna in a program containing works by Mahler, Schoenberg, and Berg on June 21, 1932, the Schönberg-Schuler fest Sessions refers to.

7. *Die Bakchantinnen,* an opera in two acts after Euripides by the Austrian composer and musicologist Egon Wellesz (1885–1974), premiered in Vienna June 20, 1932.

8. Gian Francesco Malipiero (1882–1973), the Italian composer and editor of Monteverdi and Vivaldi.

9. The Dutch composer Willem Pijper (1894–1947), director of the Rotterdam Conservatory.

10. *Das Unaufhörliche,* performed in Berlin November 21, 1931.

Берлинъ, 13го сентября

Дорогой Сергѣй Александровичъ, —
Я надѣюсь раньше при-
ѣхать въ Парижъ, но у меня
былъ немецкій ушибъ, и не
могу прибыть туда до субботы
утромъ, 17го этого мѣсяца.
Я очень бы хотѣлъ видѣть
Васъ, если это Вамъ удобно, чтобы
говорить съ Вами о нѣкоторыхъ
вещахъ. Между другими хотѣлъ
бы показать Вамъ первыя
двѣ части скрипичнаго концерта.
Послѣдняя часть еще не совсѣмъ
кончена, и еще не хочу показать

Letter from Roger Sessions to Serge Koussevitzky, September 13, 1932.
(The translation appears on page 184.) Courtesy of the Library of Congress.

▼

Roger Sessions to Serge Koussevitzky[1]
als US-DLC

September 13 [1932]

Dear Sergei Alexandrovich,—   Berlin

I hoped to come to Paris earlier, but I had a bit of flu and so I won't be there until Saturday morning, the 17th of this month.

I would very much like to meet with you, if you have the time, and to discuss certain matters.[2] Among other things I would like to show you the first two parts of the Violin Concerto. The last part is not quite finished and I don't want to show it yet, but if you don't mind, I would very much like to show you the first two finished ones.

Please, excuse me for such short notice but it was impossible to make a definite decision earlier. I would be very, very obliged to you if you could leave a word for me at Cook and Son, Place de Madeleine. Any time would suit me.

Please, give my best regards to your wife from both of us. I am very glad to think that I might see you soon.

Yours sincerely,
Roger Sessions

[P.S.] I must give you greetings from Schnabel and Hindemith.

1. Translated from the Russian by Theodore Levin.
2. The meeting did take place, but nothing came of it.

▼

Roger Sessions to Aaron Copland
als US-DLC

September 23 [1932]

Dear Aaron,—   Paris

I was really delighted with your letter which reached me here in Paris.[1] I want to answer it in detail, but am sure you will understand if I do not do so now; it deserves better treatment than I could give it while "on tour" so to speak!

The main reason for my writing you now is to ask you to be sure and send (or have Kalmus send) me a copy of your Variations. Naturally I have no right to commit myself in any way, as a member of the Jury; but I was considerably disturbed by the news that you were not to be in N.Y. when the works are selected to be sent for the Amsterdam Festival. I have of course the photostatic copy of the Variations but it would be better to have a printed one, I feel.

As you say, being a member of the Jury seems to be a very *anspruchsvoll* [demanding] task; I don't dread so much looking over the scores—in fact, I shall go into training for a couple of weeks beforehand + then expect to find it amusing. The choice of American works, however, will, I am afraid, be in some respects not so much a difficult as a thankless job. It has amused me very much (*strictly between ourselves*) how certain people have been sniffing around. I would honestly like to be *Kollegial*, as the Germans say, + think even that any other attitude in America is essentially absurd—but there are definite limits—!

I would of course be very glad to see Mexican scores, + if Chávez would care to send them to me in Berlin I would be delighted to look them over. Of course I have literally no idea how I will find things in Amsterdam—I have talked already with Malipiero + Talich (a *very* nice person) in Wien + with Butting[2] in Berlin, + gotten on very well with them. But whether things will go as smoothly in the meeting itself I have no means of knowing.

What you say about the question of the critics I found really very interesting—though it doesn't change my opinion, as I don't suppose you imagined it would.[3] I appreciate what you say of De Santis,[4] of course; I don't know Harold Clurman as a critic, but can understand what you mean in his case, too. But I do find that literary critics are in a special category, since they are *working with the same materials* as the objects of their criticism. To me this makes all the difference, + creates, conversely, what has always seemed to me an unbridgeable gulf between the critic of music and painting, and the musician or painter. I have always noticed, with [Bernard] Berenson, for instance, his tireless seeking to find some new light on the real nature of the painter's, or the musician's real activity, + have discussed the thing with him a hundred times, his attitude always being "You have nothing to learn from me, but I can learn always from you"—that, I mean, with every "creative" artist with whom I have ever seen him. And I do not mean to deny the value or the necessity of the critic. It is his relation *to the artist* that I meant to deal with.

Well—I am not going to yield to the temptation to go on with this now, as I know I can write much more clearly when I get back to Berlin.

I was delighted to hear from Koussie of your new orchestral Suite[5] being finished—also of your adventures in Mexico, of which you don't speak in your letter to me. I don't suppose you want to send the *Suite* to Amsterdam, do you?

I have spent also some delightful hours with N.B. + expect to see her again. If she knew I were writing she would undoubtedly send love.

Alors—everything good— + I will write again from Berlin.

As always,
Roger

P.S. I had a copy of the B[lack] M[askers] ready to send you—all inscribed! but found [at] the post office that it cost so hopelessly much to send, that I decided to ask Kalmus to let you have one from New York. It is beautifully printed, but literally *lousy* with mistakes—few serious ones, however.

Many greetings to Chávez.

1. Sessions was in Paris, where he saw Boulanger and Koussevitzky, from September 17 to October 7, 1932.
2. The German composer Max Butting (1888–1976).
3. A reference to Copland's article "The Composer and His Critics."
4. Renato De Santis (1901–74) directed the Italian music-publishing firm of De Santis.
5. Possibly an early title of the Short Symphony (1932–33).

▼

Roger Sessions to Nadia Boulanger
als F-PBN

Saturday, October 8 [1932]
Berlin

My dear friend,—

I was so sorry to leave Paris without seeing you again. First of all because I had such rich and truly wonderful hours with you, as it was—especially the evening I spent in Gargenville—that I would glady have had more! My whole visit to Paris was of the greatest possible importance, inwardly, to me, but it is of those times with you that I think with the deepest joy.[1]

But I should also have like to tell you of my visit to Solesmes—not so much because of the Gregorian chants, which you have heard, after all, as of the organ which Rudolf von Beckerath[2] is building there. I finally went there instead of to Poutigny, as I knew I should see my other friends at the end of the week, in Paris. I wish it were possible for me to give you an impression of that organ, from the standpoint of a specialist—which, alas, I am not!—for I feel sure you would be enormously interested.

In any case, I had a big surprise, even though I had already heard the organ which he built for himself in his family house in Hamburg, and was to a slight extent familiar with his ideas. My surprise came first of all from what seemed to me the very extraordinarily rich and characteristic *timbre* of the instrument in all the stops which I was able to hear at that time—that is, the diapason and flute stops of the first and third manuals, a part of the *Vox Humana* and of what he called the *Krummhorn* (practically no reeds are finished as yet)—you will know better than I what the last is called in French. It seemed to me to differ from other organ *timbres* which I have heard in being far more characteristic and sharply defined as a specifically *organ* timbre, with none of the flavor refined away as seems to me practically always the case, at least with American organs—the only ones I know at all well.

The second and more important surprise I had was the clarity with which I was able to hear every detail of the musical texture. I made repeated experiments of my own, after von Beckerath had shown me various combinations and possibilities; later I listened in the chapel while Père Letester improvised for my benefit, with the greatest possible number of combinations. From that distance the effect was of course even more striking. The adjustment of the instrument to the acoustic demands of the chapel seemed to me admirable, and I must say that I heard every note, of the inner voices as well as the outer ones, as cleanly as if they had been played by a well-balanced group of wood-wind instruments—something quite new, or almost, in my experience of the organ. To my disappointment Père Letester did not want to attempt a big fugue on the organ in its present far from complete state; but he played enough to con[vince me of the] impor-tance of what von Beckerath is doing—and what seemed to me even more indicative, to attract me to the organ as an instrument as I have never been attracted before.

So—I write you all this, with all reservations which are necessary in view of the fact that I am not an organist, and have never before had more than a passing interest in the organ as such. But I do feel that you would find it extraordinarily interesting, and well worth a trip to Solesmes, if you could possibly find the time to go there, after the organ is finished. Both Père Letester, whom I believe you know, and Beckerath himself, spoke of inviting you to the dedication—some six weeks hence, I believe—and both were regretting that it would be impossible on account of the *clôture*[3] to have you see the organ itself. I personally would be extremely interested to know what you think. I remember so well hearing you play the [Bach] E minor Prelude + Fugue in Cleveland, and from that as well as from everything else I know of you, my impression is that you would rejoice in such an instrument.

At any rate I hope I have not been indiscreet in talking a great deal about you to young von Beckerath and in urging him to get in touch with you again. He is an extremely shy young man, absolutely obsessed by his work, and does not find it easy to approach people; and of course he is tremendously excited by his first big independent piece of work. In any case I did so, in the same spirit in which I write this letter, with full consciousness of my responsibility to you, as a musician, as well as with enthusiasm for what seems to me a wholly admirable—and as far as I know, new at least for our time—principle in organ building, which obviously must have an enormous effect on organ music in general—composing and playing as well.

Of course the idea did not originate with Beckerath himself, but with Professor Jahn [*sic*][4] in Hamburg, with whom Beckerath studied and worked for some years. I believe however that some of Beckerath's ideas are entirely his own. In any case that is not so important; I only mention it because there has been some kind of personal situation which has placed him in a rather difficult position and made him if anything over-conscientious in not allowing himself to be given too much credit.

So—I have written already a long enough letter and taken an enormous amount of your time and will write no more now, much as I should like to do so. Please give many very warm greetings to your mother. It was a great joy to see her again; and I hope so much that the winter will be a good one for her.

I hope so much to be able to go again to Paris some time during the winter; in fact I need it. It was a tremendous refreshment to me to be there and though I am not conscious of having either rested or of having in other respects led a particularly valetudinarian life, both Barbara and most of our friends say I look a quite different person after coming back!

So—*au revoir*—in deepest affection and gratitude, in which Barbara joins me.

Ever your
Roger

1. Boulanger, upset over Sessions's selection to the ISCM jury over her, had given Sessions a "bad quarter of an hour" (*"mauvais quart d'heure"*) at their meeting.

2. Organ builder Beckerath (1907–76) had worked with Victor Gonzalez in Paris (1927–29) and for Theodore Frobenius in Lyngby, Denmark (1930). He studied extensively the pipe scales of Baroque organs, rediscovered by Hans Henry Jahnn, and introduced them into the work of Gonzalez's French firm. His hundred-plus organs gained a worldwide reputation due to their fine voicing.

3. Male-only rules of the monastery.

4. Hans Henry Jahnn (1894–1959) was a German authority on organ building who rebuilt the Schnitzer organ in the Jakobikirche, Hamburg. From 1931 to 1933 he was head of the experimental division of the German Council of Organists and Hamburg's official authority on all matters relating to organs.

▼

Roger Sessions to Serge Koussevitzky[1]
als US-DLC

[October 15, 1932]

Dear Sergei Alexandrovich,— Berlin

I am sending you the violin part and piano arrangement of the first and second movements of my violin concerto today. As I told you in Paris, I will send you the third (last) movement later; it is almost finished now.[2] I hope you can read the manuscript which I took care to review.

In my writing I used bars and some other subtleties which I owe to the help and advice of my friend, Max Strub, a concertmaster of the State Opera here, who frequently performs as a guest soloist with German orchestras. I think everything is correct—Strub has played these two movements a lot, and even when he at first found this or that bar strange, unusual, or exaggerated, in the end he was almost always in full agreement with it; in cases where I didn't manage to persuade him we worked together until we both reached an agreement.

I didn't mark his fingering because I thought [Richard] Burgin would probably want it different for himself. I am very glad Burgin will play the concerto for not only do I know he is a wonderful musician but I also have the impression that he's got a style which my music needs—a strong tone, a deep "breathing," *piena voce* [full voiced] expression.

It was a great pleasure for me to meet you in Paris and I'll be very glad to see and hear you next year—in America.

Please give my regards to your wife from both of us.

Sincerely yours,
Roger Sessions

1. Translated from the Russian by Theodore Levin.

2. The concerto now stands at four movements; this mention of only three indicates that the idea to add another movement came late in the day. The concerto would not be finished until 1935.

▼

Roger Sessions to Aaron Copland
als US-DLC

[November 17, 1932]

Dear Aaron,—   Kurfürstenstrasse, 126, Berlin W. 62

I was delighted to get the Variations and also your letter—both came yesterday. I hope soon to receive the Chávez + the Revueltas[1] works which I shall read + present to the Jury with much interest.

What you write about Mexico is most intriguing + *stimmt* [concurs] with what I had always imagined—especially since reading D.H. Lawrence's books which have Mexico for their background[2]—also his letters[3] which have just appeared in England + which Stephen Spender sent me recently. I certainly look forward to going there sometime. As you know I love the South above all else but know it only on this side of the water.

I must explain why you haven't had the *Black Maskers*. When I got back from Paris I discovered that I had quite misunderstood about the Cos Cob's policy regarding free copies that I was allowed. So I had already a considerable amount owing them for *faits* already *accomplis*—they haven't yet told me how much—and I returned all except one of the copies I hadn't already disposed of. They explained that copies were only sent out to conductors or other musicians *for examination,* which I didn't know at all. They were tremendously nice about it but at the moment I am simply not in a position to ask for any more since I can't possibly pay for them. I had intended to send you an inscribed copy from here but it is so *umständlich* [troublesome] to send such things out that I thought it would be better to do it from that end. I'm so sorry. But no doubt you could easily wangle a copy out of Kalmus. If you do be sure that a few essential errors, at least, are corrected. The score is [littered] with misprints, but most of them have no importance.

Just a couple of points in regard to your last letter. I think you have a little misunderstood me in regard to the matter of "nurturing." You must know that my objection has nothing to do with the ordering + performance of works which are really wanted, nor would I raise any objection to your activities, as you seem to think I would. My point is that it seems to me an entirely false + even perhaps to some slight extent dangerous point of departure when one "encourages" or "pursues" any form of culture out of a sense of duty, or for any reason except a real inner need. Both *a priori* and from what I have seen it seems to me so obvious that the culture thus attained is "traditional" or "modern," "classic" or "romantic" or "primitivist," "indigenous," or "foreign," or whatever you will—it is *indirect,* without roots, based on cerebral + theoretical + literary excitation + not on real + fresh experience + sensation. When the experience is direct all those other considerations take care of themselves, or at least they are only valid when they are part of a real + direct experience; any discussion of them is at all events is [*sic*] quite unreal unless this primary + all-essential impulse is taken for granted.

It seems to me that what you do you do with real conviction + not in any "buy home goods first" spirit—not, that is, out of conscience but out of real impulse + belief in the music. But when you tell others to take an interest in music composed in America because it is American it seems to me that you are rather excluding or pushing aside those other grounds, and even almost putting an obstacle in the way of real + genuine recognition of American music as something worth recognizing for its own sake. It is really not that I am "fatalistic" or "eternal" in my point of view but because I really believe that that is the only way that an *essential innerlich notwendig* [of inner necessity] musical impulse can ever develop in America. Otherwise there can only be a forced and essentially anemic Ersatz-Musik, a back-yard affair that has nothing to do with music itself, however pretentious it may look on the outside.

Of course I don't for a minute deny that there is a void in America, and a big one. But I can't see honestly how this can be filled artificially or by act of will. Only very gradually, by the accumulation of real and deep experience—and not only musical ones—of Americans. How can it possibly be otherwise? All these are no new feelings of mine, but have been *Selbstverständlichkeiten* [matters of course], instinctive feelings, as long as I can remember, which experience has only confirmed. The specific case of Ives, whose music I also know, I should diagnose somewhat differently from you, though I admit there is something there which is neither wholly without value nor unsympathetic. What seems to me to be lacking is rather fundamental—a really alert and active musical *instinct* which would have led him to what he really needed, even in America of that day. Don't misunderstand me; it is hard, as I gladly admit, always to draw the line in specific cases, as motives are so often mixed. I do not wish to condemn things *en bloc,* but it is a certain very clearly defined direction of the spirit that seems to me false.

I rather object to the word "eternal" in describing my attitude. It seems to me I dodge the issue + [it] certainly doesn't in the least describe my approach to the matter which is an instinctive and not a reasoned one; healthily disabused, I should say, rather than anything so high-sounding as "eternal."

Along with the tendency to base life on theory or conscious plan, worked out in advance—a kind of synthetic food-tablet conception of life (it doesn't matter whether the theory is "moral," "scientific," or "aesthetic,") rather than direct + profound experience it seems to me that the most discouraging thing in America is the way almost all people try actively to *escape* real experience, ignore fundamental though disturbing impulses + contrasts, + to live through compromise. That comes of course partly from the enormously varied + apparently irreconcilable elements present on our soil + partly also from the spirit of opportunism that was bred into nearly all Americans—irrespective of race or color—during the years of material + industrial expansion. It also, far more than Puritanism, has given the American people, along with a superficial + Ersatz emotionalism, their fear of *really* strong emotions and clear issues, as disruptive + dangerous. (Not only Americans, of course, but Americans more than other peoples have these characteristics.) It seems to me that the only way America can ever become a real community is by starting out on the basis of recognizing these basic impulses + contrasts,—especially the individual ones,—by facing them + their consequences + building on generous recognition of them + their consequences rather than an artificial + deadly ignoring them out of existence. Some individuals do this already.

But above all the kind of self confidence an artist needs is that which comes from within rather than the kind which comes from without—he must be absolutely sure of himself + his aims, + willing to accept whatever consequences this may bring him. This sureness no critic can possibly give or take away, it seems to me, or help him to have. Either one has instinctively this sureness—in which case the only thing that can more than superficially disturb one is being false to it—or one has not. If one hasn't it one must look into one's own soul till one finds it. It is the essence of an artist's *real* personality, the "inner necessity" without which no real art can exist; but there again how can seriously listening to others be of any help?

Or rather—one can of course not make rules, + every man will find what he needs if he really has the impulse to do so. You say criticism has been a help to you in knowing yourself + it would be absurd for me to contradict you or to deny for a moment the validity of your experiences. For my part I would say that one gains self-knowledge from a million different living contacts + since music is an integral part of life itself, by no means only musical ones—living contacts, of course, with things both inside + outside one's own personality—every *real* experience one ever has in fact. Musical criticism, of my own or other music, has never been a very real thing to me nor seemed to me to have much to do directly with music itself, except, in the case of a few great musicians—Mozart's letters, for instance, or some of Berlioz's writings. Which reminds me of Berenson's admitting to me once that the best critics in the world are the "creative" artists themselves, provided they take the trouble, as they of course mostly don't + provided of course that they are unprejudiced, as they often aren't.

So there you are. I do think there is a difference between us + I hesitated to write this much because I am always afraid you will get the impression that I think that difference is more important than I really do. And I've written in enormous haste. But after all I often feel that when I write such a letter I do it to clarify my own ideas, + so in this case you will take it for what it is, in any way you choose to do. But if it is a bore forgive me!

Barbara sends much love + so do I. Also, many greetings to Chávez!

Affectionately as always,
Roger—

[P.S.] The Mexican programs look *excellent* much better than what one generally gets here, especially since the wave of chauvinism has set in. But I still like it here.

1. In 1929 composer Silvestre Revueltas (1899–1940) had become assistant conductor to Carlos Chávez of the Orquesta Sinfónica de Mexico.

2. *Mornings in Mexico* (New York: Knopf, 1927) and *The Plumed Serpent* (1926).

3. *The Letters of D. H. Lawrence*, edited with an introduction by Aldous Huxley (New York: Viking Press, 1932).

▼

Roger Sessions to Jean Binet[1]
als CH-Bsacher

[November 1932]
My dear, dear friend—   Berlin

You can't imagine how many times (!?!) I've written you—not only in my thoughts, but in black and white too. I wanted to tell you a lot of things and ask you a lot of others. Finally I've decided to at least write you a few lines, pretty inadequate I'm afraid, but in any case from me to you! Forgive me—I don't have the courage to make any more excuses to you.

First of all, this year has in a sense been the most important one of my life, or at least seems to be. I've had a little bit the feeling of returning to the world, and of getting used to it again, of finding my bearings after years of sleep, I mean the years spent in Rome, and not the ones in Florence, of course. And then there was the necessity of getting to know this *strange land* of Germany—

So—should I confess that Germany deceived me? I don't have the *feeling* of having been deceived, but when I think of my state of mind the last time I was with you, I do have to admit it. Sometimes I think the only way, at least for me (perhaps it's the normal way) to understand things is to fall in love with them; and so last year I fell in love with Germany, and was doomed to disappointment. But I'm exaggerating, of course; above all it's my pigheadedness which has suffered from this gradual deception. I really needed this experience to understand Europe and above all to know myself.

This year, as you can easily imagine, was just right for such an experience; in Germany above all a year of crisis in which the German weaknesses of character have been revealed as clearly as possible, a fateful year also for the German culture. I've seen very strange things; for example, in September I spent two weeks in Paris, and when I returned I had to acknowledge some rather extraordinary about-faces on the part of some friends of mine—they were communists on September 15th, Nazis on October 1st! But it was above all striking because I'd been away. Here, even a little more than elsewhere, one sees the growing triumph of the stupidest, most cowardly elements, and in general of the blindest prejudices and the most petty resentments; and the increasing disruption of the strongest and best friendships. It's a little depressing, but quite interesting if one can manage to detach oneself from it. Above all an impression of a great *weakness,* perhaps fundamental.

It seems to me that, deep down, Germany hasn't really changed for at least one hundred fifty years—it remains a basically provincial country, one that could only retain its true character as long as it was a conglomeration of small states—and that everything that was best was the result of that and of an orientation toward southern and southwest Germany (including Austria of course). I've noticed the *tremendous* differences between European elements and, so to speak, Germanic elements—particularly the Prussians and the others. But at the same time I have a completely different conception of Prussia than I had before. This seems to me to be a neurotic folk—without any internal strength because of a lack of moral education, without confidence in themselves—with all the characteristics that go along with that; a distrustful bunch, uncertain, sometimes submissive and sometimes brutal, and above all putting their trust in dreams, in theories, in books rather than in realities and in experience. Now that they are missing *men* and real traditions of authority and discipline one has the impression of an *extremely* weak populace, and in spite of everything they say, it seems to me almost unbelievable that in case of a grave international crisis they would be able to stay afloat. The radical movements have no *positive* strength of conviction, instead they are outbursts of resentment, lacking inner discipline and missing any individuals of real ability.

This National Socialism seems to me to be a little ridiculous and confused. There is a side I'm capable of having a certain sympathy with—that is, one perceives a very evident reaction against *Berlin,* against big industry, in favor of rural Germany; the feeling that industry has become a monster and that the Germans have gone astray by losing contact with the earth—there are very interesting projects for disurbanization, with the goal of reducing unemployment and bringing a more normal and human, so to speak, sort of economic organization. That could have very important results and perhaps Germany could find its more or less definitive form in this way. People are entirely cognizant of the fact that the German character is totally opposed to urbanization, and upon my return from Paris I was able to express my opinion very frankly to them that Paris is *really* a big city where people are "to the manner born," in contrast to the men and women of Berlin who wear their silk stockings or their monocles! very awkwardly, almost uneasily, and who seem deep down to be only make-believe "Weltstadtmenschen" [men of the world] and really a bit ridiculous.

Everywhere one encounters a development even a little more monstrous than in England and America, of the intellect at the expense of the other faculties; that is, of course, in Berlin above all. One mustn't sleep with some him or her (the sex doesn't matter too much—ambidexterity is widespread) without looking in a book to make sure of *what one does,* and making sure one does it by the rules; there are all sorts of dietetic cults (no *gastronomic* ones, although one can also eat rather well here).

But it's impossible to relate everything, and I have to confess that I know very well that there is another Germany that one doesn't see in Berlin, and that I find that other Germany a lot nicer, and that *perhaps,* by virtue of the crisis everywhere, the other Germany will emerge victorious in the long run. There are a lot of people here who believe that. For myself I can only say that everything here seems problematic—if it came about I don't know what would happen to international relations, but I would think that the other European countries would be able to get along with such a Germany much easier than with the present one or before a war.

As for the musical life—that's a subject for you. You have no idea of the depth or the complexity—at least outwardly. Of all the persons I know here, I admire Schnabel the most—his is the greatest spirit and at the same time the most distinguished of all, I think. There are also Klemperer, Hindemith, whom I see occasionally, and others (Edwin Fischer[2] for example) in my opinion less important—I haven't met Schönberg, though I would be very curious to make his acquaintance. Hindemith is a sort of *Musikant,* very admirable, with the strength and weakness of the German *Musikant,* that is to say a phenomenal craft, an insatiable appetite for music, and an extraordinary facility; at the same time he has a real intelligence, which his colleagues are sometimes missing. What he is missing, it seems to me, is freshness; one hears it in his music, above all, when one knows the musical milieu here, it seems to me that the German musical tradition has become a tremendous burden, and that really new experiences are fatally missing. All the German past is in this music (including Reger and even Bruckner) but everything in it is a little worn and a little stale. Of all the German composers he is of course to me the most likeable, he is also fairly young, and in his oratorio, along with many things that I don't like at all there are things in which one can perhaps hear that he is finding ways that are new for him. Ansermet spoke to me of a *return to expression*—I know very well what he means by that, but just between us I find it a pretty stupid phrase, it is a question of the sort of expression. And whether one really has something important to say—the expression will come by itself in that case, and has never been abandoned. The prospect of a return to *expression German-style* doesn't seem to me very reassuring—and I think one will find there neither talent, nor music, nor Hindemith. He hasn't composed at all for several months—I've heard at least; I don't remember if he or someone else told me that. Perhaps it's a very good sign if it's true.

In general I've been surprised to find out to what extent musical life here is closed, with laws unto itself, untouched by the world beyond the German border. Debussy is a very modern composer for the majority of German musicians, and very "problematisch." Reger and Bruckner are universally loved and admired, and with passion. There is an *astounding* lack of taste, sometimes; sometimes one has the impression that no one can tell the difference between one kind of music and another, provided it falls into the framework of German convention. The only foreign composer fairly well known here is Stravinsky, and in my opinion he is rather poorly *understood,* and with the present nationalistic tendency, the school and sycophants of Schönberg are rabid against any opposing tendency—for the most part they are real idiots. After a short burst of enthusiasm in Vienna I find that whole school in the final analysis sterile [illegible] with Berg, Webern + Schönberg and from every point of view besides mathematics, pedantry, and the morbid *dissection* of the soul and feelings, completely petty.

But my friend, I'm writing you such stupidities! One can't *write* about these things and make much sense—what's needed are long conversations with you! And then I've lost a lot of ink and space which I could have used for more important things. I'm sure you can't imagine how much we think of you, nor how much you are truly at the center of our life, in our thoughts about everything that is dear to us. We think constantly of Denise these days and hope that she has reassuring news about Pierre. It is awful to think of everything you've had to go through this year, both of you; please *never* forget that we are *always* with you in our thoughts, just as much when I don't write as when I do.

And now I think I shouldn't write any more—because I'm going to Amsterdam in six days and have a million things to do before then—just a few words about some things you asked me.

1) The parts for Black Maskers are in America but I can always have them sent—Stokowski is doing it, I'm told; I don't know if it's true.[3] The *Finale* is the same music as before, only the orchestration is new. The only really new part is in the 2nd movement, that is, the viola solo and the trumpet music at the end of the movement—I wrote it in 1927 when I did the orchestra score.

2) Igor Stravinsky's visit to Berlin was a tremendous source of pleasure to me. It was in the most superficial sense very good and refreshing to hear a bit of *Non-German Music* in this atmosphere. And I liked the violin concerto *a lot* this time; last year I was very disappointed with it. In the Duo Concertante[4] I liked the first and last movements above all—the others seemed pretty but small and for S—— neither new nor unexpected—*wonderfully made,* that goes without saying. It seems to me nonetheless that this is perhaps a somewhat critical moment for Stravinsky. And I'm curious to see what these two movements of the Duo Concertante will mean for his coming work. When I say that, it seems to me that I've done an injustice to the music in seeming to consider it from a mistaken point of view, that is, indirectly. When *speaking* of I.S.'s work, one has a bit the habit of focusing too much on isolated spots, and sometimes forgets the music and the overall line—and that is unfair to the essence of the music, and to what is really important—as with all music, moreover.

So write me, about your work and about everything. In spite of its length what I've written is *quite* short and twisted, but at least it's a beginning—and for a long time now I've been writing letters more regularly than before. It's precisely because yours is the most important of all that it was *so* delayed.

And so hugs and kisses to all four of you! And with that I'm *forced* to stop for now! *Much* more than affectionately,

Yours,
Roger

1. Translated from the French by Paul Suits.
2. The Swiss pianist Edwin Fischer (1886–1960) taught at the Berlin Hochschule für Musik 1931–42.
3. Leopold Stokowski would conduct the *Black Maskers Suite* with the Philadelphia Orchestra October 20 and 21, 1933.
4. Stravinsky's Duo Concertante for violin and piano was first performed by Samuel Dushkin and Stravinsky at the Funkhaus, Berlin, October 28, 1932. The Berlin Funkorchester first performed the Violin Concerto in Berlin October 23, 1931, conducted by Stravinsky with Dushkin as the soloist.

▼

Roger Sessions to Nicolas Slonimsky
als US-DLC

November 26, 1932

Dear Nicolas, son of Leonides![1]   Berlin

[In Russian:][2] Don't be afraid, I beg you, that our friendship will be ruined only because I don't write letters. You know very well that I'm extremely lazy, particularly when I want to write a long or interesting letter—and when it has to be in Russian.

[In English:] I am still furiously busy as I am going to Amsterdam in a few days, so I send you a translation into English of the rest of my letter, as I must write as quickly as possible! By this time no doubt you have my postcard, + are reassured; but I will still postpone a really decent letter till I can call my soul my own again!

First of all let me tell you that you are very soon likely to hear, first of all, from my sister-in-law—my wife's younger sister [Rosamond]— Mrs. Daniel Sayre.[3] She is a *most* charming person—and also, my sonata is dedicated to her; she lives in Hingham, near Boston, her husband is a Professor (or some kind of teacher) in Boston Tech + also a well-known aviator, about whom you may have read recently in the papers—he is doing some kind of experimental work at very high altitudes and has recently been a good deal written up in Boston. She asked me if I could send her to some friend or friends in the Boston musical world who could perhaps advise her about getting a job. I don't know how well she plays now; she was really quite talented as a child + later in college was too attractive + popular to have much time for such frivolous amusements as piano playing. She was married a year + a half ago + has acquired a child (of whom I am a kind of ungodly godfather) but she still keeps up her music to a certain extent anyway—plays at people's houses + that sort of thing. She also taught in a children's school but gave up the job of her own accord when her own child came. You will like her I know; + anything you can do to help her will be a *great* personal favor to both me + Barbara. I wrote my sonata for her but it didn't turn out to be a woman's piece at all!

Secondly I hope very much you will at last hear from my cousin Catharine Huntington, of whom I spoke last spring. I must plead guilty to not having written her till the other day. She has been very ill—rather seriously I gather, + is now recovering from an operation.

She may not feel like meeting people for a while but I hope you may see her sooner or later.

Did I tell you that I think very seriously of settling in Boston when I come back to the U.S.? What is your advice in the matter? N.Y. seems to me hopeless—snobistic + half-baked + above all one has no time for anything, if one "leads the life"—if one doesn't "lead the life" what is the use of being there? (What is the use of "leading the life," anyway?) It is partly a question of where I can earn enough money to keep body + soul together so that I have time also to compose. My wife will also help out of course with that end of things if she can find something to do. Have you any suggestions? Can one get pupils in composition (harmony + counterpoint included?) in Boston? I had a pupil of Hindemith's for the summer, in Harmony, though it was only a short time, he got on so well that he would have stayed with me (partly because he studied *privately* with me, *in a class* with Hindemith, of course) had not the Hochschule offered all sorts of advantages which I could not provide; I mention this because I used to think I was a bad teacher, now I think I might be a good one. Can one earn money by writing for the papers, + could I get a job do you suppose? All advice, etc. received with extreme gratitude. In any case I must start making plans.

Thank you for your clippings. I am so glad all goes well with you. It would be splendid if you could do my symphony at San Francisco. Those asses I suppose think the *Black Maskers* is better because it has more dissonance (+ what in hell is dissonance, after all, nowadays?) or because it has a "subject" + hence is "related to life" in this sense of the word—or for some such reason. It *is* of course far easier to conduct than the Symphony, + in correcting the proofs I found it not so bad as I thought it was—quite different in fact from what I had thought. Also it will sound splendidly in the orchestra. But anyone with half a grain of musical sense or feeling ought to be able to see that the symphony is the far better work. Not that it means so terribly much to me one way or the other; the Symphony is six years old, the *Black Maskers* nine; I have left both behind. But there are *very* few people who can conduct the Symphony at all, + you are one of those. And I should like to have it played because I know you would give a *very brilliant* performance of it; + it needs to be played more. That looks like flattery but you know I don't flatter people—not even Koussevitzky! Well, no doubt in five or ten years' time the Symphony will be taken up + "discovered" as some people seem to be "discovering" the B.M. now. So, I should [not] worry. Anyway I am enormously grateful to you for wanting to do it now, + if it comes off I know I shall have an excellent performance to be grateful for.

I was sorry not to see your mother + sister in Paris. The first week I was there I was suffering from the effects of a change of diet—too good French food after the heavy + dull German diet!—and I postponed looking them up. The second week I had suddenly to go out of town to visit a friend[4] near Orleans or rather at Solesmes where he was building an organ— + when I got back I had only one very busy day left. I am so sorry—was disappointed not to see them: but I expect to return there in January + shan't fail then. I didn't look up [Boris de] Schloezer, for the same reason, + Varèse as Cowell had told me was out of town.

I won't write more now—forgive a rather dull letter. I have just been having a rather bad cold—rotten time of year in Berlin, one doesn't know how much the houses should be heated. The result is I have to work extra hard now. So, I will write a better letter next time.

[In Russian:] Cordial greetings to both of you from both of us, all the best, etc.

Yours sincerely,
P.A.C. [R.H.S.]

1. Slonimsky had remained in Boston. He taught at The Boston Conservatory of Music, where Sessions would later be a colleague of his.
2. Translated by Theodore Levin.
3. Daniel Sayre (1903–56), Rosamond's first husband.
4. Rudolf von Beckerath. See October 8, 1932, letter to Boulanger, note 2.

▼

Roger Sessions to Nadia Boulanger
als F-PBN

Monday [December 1932]
Berlin

My dear friend,—

I was so glad to have your letter and the list of works, for which I shall be on the lookout in Amsterdam.[1] I suppose you are sure they have all been sent, by their various sections.

What I can do I of course cannot really know till I get there Thursday morning. As I think you know the American section has been consistently suspicious and hostile to me ever since my works were chosen on purely European initiative for Geneva + Oxford and it has also complicated matters by sending a huge mass of works in to Amsterdam, and acting otherwise in a childish and arrogant way. That of course leaves me quite free from any slight feeling, which I might otherwise have had, of responsibility for their interests; though I certainly shall not on that account withhold my support from any composers (or works) whom I think deserve to be played. But this of course you know.

My concerto is out of the question, of course since works of Jury members can not be chosen.

Butting is ill, and may possibly not be able to come. It would be truly a joy if you should be there with me![2]

Please forgive this hasty note, and give many affectionate greetings to your mother, from us both.

Always most devotedly
Roger

P.S. I shouldn't think there would be any difference in difficulty between the Neugeboren[3] trio and sonatina—only if there is a question of *length*.

Thank you so much for sending us Boyden[4]—we found him very sympathetic indeed.

1. Sessions would later recall, "Two days before it came time to go to Amsterdam for the meeting, I got a letter in a familiar handwriting. It said, 'Dear Roger, I count on you for the following.' And she had a list of all the works submitted by her students there" (Andrea Olmstead, *Conversations with Roger Sessions* [Boston: Northeastern University Press, 1987], 220–21). The list comprised works by Copland, Marcelle de Manziarly, Jean Cartan, Lennox Berkeley, Igor Markevich, and Jean Françaix.

2. Max Butting did in fact attend. Boulanger apparently would have served as an alternate had he been absent.

3. H. Neugeboren published piano music in Paris in the 1930s.

4. Possibly musicologist David Boyden (b. 1910), who had recently graduated from Harvard University. He taught from 1938 to 1975 at the University of California at Berkeley, replacing Nin-Culmell as department chair in 1955.

▼

Roger Sessions to Nadia Boulanger
als F-PBN

Tuesday, December 27 [1932]
My dear friend,—   Berlin

I hope you will be fairly well pleased with the choice of French works—the *Concerto* of Manziarly[1] + the "Pater" of Cartan.[2] Of the other works about which you wrote me, Aaron's [*Piano*] *Variations*.

With the exception of the [Lennox] Berkeley *Sonata*[3] all the works about which you wrote were sent by the French section; + certain members of the Jury were definitely against the inclusion of more than two works from any one section.

I personally was surprised that neither Jean Françaix nor Markevich fared better. I spoke about both works with other members of the Jury but did not get the response I hoped for. However they both of them need performances, so to speak, far less than Mlle. de Manziarly + I can't say I am positively sorry that those two works were chosen.[4]

It was a curious Jury—Malipiero + I were in a very real sense allies, and Talich generally sat with us—we looked over the scores together very carefully. As a matter of fact we did not actually look at the French scores together; those I looked at first of all before we had that arrangement. But I discussed the French scores fairly carefully with Malipiero + we had very similar impressions.

Naturally one must expect, in such an affair, to be disappointed at certain things in the final choice. I am distinctly disappointed at the second American work,[5] + would have been glad if Aaron's Variations had been the only one chosen. It seems to me that the cause of American music (if one can speak of it as a "cause") can only be injured by the performance of such works, + it is hard for me to understand how any real musician can want them. However it doesn't really matter I suppose.

The Jury this year was distinctly tamer than last year's. No sharply defined conflicts of principle in which one could make a definite stand—only *undercurrent;* the only thing I really got excited about was the songs of Ruth Crawford—also to a lesser extent the Polish work that was chosen[6]—a *horrible* thing for string orchestra which got in more or less at the last moment—the same person was insistent on that as was insistent on Crawford.

I mustn't write any more. I still hope we will get to Paris before long: but we are having a rather bad time financially—I didn't get a renewal of my stipendium[7]—+ we are consequently, for the moment, up in the air as far as plans are concerned. This will bring you, however, our very best Christmas + New Year wishes, + I *hope* to see you soon— + will let you know beforehand. Meanwhile all good wishes to your mother, from us both.

Always most affectionately,
Roger

1. Marcelle de Manziarly's *Concertino* for piano and orchestra, to be performed June 13, 1933, with the composer as soloist.

2. Jean Cartan had died March 26, 1932, at age twenty-five; Roberto Gerhard conducted his *Pater Noster* for chorus a cappella June 10, 1933.

3. English composer Sir Lennox Berkeley (1903–89) lived in Paris 1927–33 as a pupil of Boulanger. The work may be his Sonata no. 2, op. 1, for violin and piano (ca. 1935).

4. In a later letter to Boulanger (January 9, 1933, F-PBN) Sessions would try to make up for the scant number of French works chosen by the jury with the uncharacteristic request that Jean Françaix send some chamber music to Dr. Hans Curjel, of the ISCM, for possible inclusion on "some concert," continuing, "let me add on my own account what you probably know, that the Germans swallow long and what they call 'serious' works more easily than short and amusing ones. You know what I mean, I am sure."

5. Ruth Crawford's *Three Songs*, to Carl Sandburg's "Rat Riddles," "Prayers of Steel," and "Tall Grass," to be performed June 15, 1933.

6. Jozef Koffler's *15 Variations* for strings, a twelve-tone work.

7. From the Carnegie Foundation.

▼

Roger Sessions to Aaron Copland
als US-DLC

January 13 [1933]

Dear Aaron,—   Berlin

Thank you for your note. I'd have written you before had I known where to reach you.

You know by this time your work was chosen.[1] I am very pleased about that; it is the one Am. work I felt like *insisting* upon. With R. Crawford I am not so satisfied; but I made it my job simply to see that the American works were carefully looked over, as everyone can be assured that they were. I sat between Talich + Malipiero + turned over the pages of every one of them—on the first afternoon of the sitting. Pijper[2] had looked them all over that morning, + Butting the next day. Ruth Crawford was his choice overwhelmingly to Pijper who no doubt has his own good reasons for urging its choice so strongly. I certainly made no *stand* against it, but wish America were represented by something better, for its second work; I don't find the Crawford songs good, or even particularly "interesting."

The final program is no better than other recent international programs—considerably less good, perhaps, than Oxford + just as bad as Geneva + Vienna, if not worse. One good thing is the Kadosa Concerto.[3] I should say the best. But the general level of works

– 204 –

submitted was very poor + apart from well-known names (which were finally eliminated, as the programs are short in any case—in reaction against the Vienna ones), there was *very* little. America made by no means the worst general showing, though the vast number of different styles is always confusing + will no doubt continue to be so till Europeans realize what is behind it, to make it inevitable, probably for many years to come. But the general result is that if one is to make programs at all one has got to be very lenient. If one runs across a work that is even *Konsequent,* as the Germans say, one is pleased. Even the technical level was sometimes *amazingly* low, though in general it was not that that was the matter.

I am convinced that all the members of the Jury were honest according to their various (or I should say *our* various, lights) + that allowing always for inevitable prejudices (for instance I do not consider that the French works were entirely understood by three of the members) the programs were absolutely fairly chosen. By far the most congenial person was Malipiero, as far as I am concerned. I got to know him very well + like him enormously—a splendid musician + a man who knows absolutely what he wants but has no illusions or axes to grind. The one Italian work was chosen spontaneously + unanimously, by no means a great work, I think but a good one.[4] Only in one case was there any suspicion of log rolling. The Jurors were constantly all together + in fact we hadn't a moment's leisure till it was all over—four days of good, solid work. The two works which got through on account of pressure exerted (I don't count the two Dutch symphonies, which are short + actually not the worst things on the program) did so simply because at the last minute things had to be found to fill the right places in the programs.

I had a letter from Miss Lawton,[5] very ingratiating, telling me how happy the Am. Section was about "all I was going to do for it." It surprised me a little, after the Oxford incident (about which I know *a good deal more* than certain people realize), that they should regard the matter in that light. I certainly did not, + if all the American works had been as bad as some of them were I should not have cared to take any responsibility for them at all. And had I wished to do so I could on the other hand have eliminated or pushed any works I saw fit. As things have turned out however I hope they will be satisfied, + even perhaps pleased.

I'm glad you had such a good time in Mexico.

Strub is well, + has just had a great success here,[6] which is a real joy to all of us. Fitelberg is not so well, + I hope very much he can go away soon for a real + fundamental cure which he needs. Lopatni-khoff I don't see very often, but he seems well + always amiable. Between ourselves he has really improved + become a better companion since the slight *Niederlage* [defeat] of his Concerto at Vienna![7] I see a great deal of Klemperer this year, also of Schnabel whom I enjoy really more than any one else; and we see also the Curjels[8] very often. There is of course a reaction here as there is everywhere else especially against foreign music + musicians; but I think the peak is already over. But I still find Berlin enormously stimulating + congenial, although I have gone through a period of decided disillusionment as far as the German people is concerned. One can't even like them, as a people, *completely,* or even be sure of continuing to like them—they are under a great strain, of course, and there is something that is not very solid or very sure at the bottom of their natures. Quite the reverse of the Italians + French, where the bottom is absolutely firm + the surface very flexible. But musically, in spite of everything, the Germans have something, something positive + necessary, which no other people has. I include of course the Austrians, with the Germans.

But I mustn't write more. Greetings to everyone. Barbara sends her love.

Affectionately,
R——

1. Copland's Piano Variations would be performed June 15, 1933.

2. Although Willem Pijper sat on the jury, his choral music would be performed on an ISCM all-Dutch program, and on June 13 his *Halewijn,* a symphonic drama in nine scenes, would receive its premiere.

3. Twenty-nine-year-old Hungarian composer Pál Kadosa played his Piano Concerto June 9, 1933.

4. Goffredo Petrassi's Partita for Orchestra would be performed June 13, 1933.

5. Dorothy Lawton, secretary of the U.S. section of the ISCM and music librarian of the Fifty-eighth Street branch of the New York Public Library.

6. The previous night Strub had played the Busoni Violin Concerto, with Klemperer conducting.

7. Lopatnikoff's Piano Concerto (no. 2, 1930) performed at the Vienna ISCM Festival in 1932.

8. Hans Curjel (1896–1974), art historian, theater director, and stage manager.

▼

Roger Sessions to Nicolas Slonimsky[1]
als US-DLC

Sunday, January 29 [1933][2]

Dear Nicolai Leonidovich,—   [Berlin]

Excuse me—I am not a good correspondent!—You know it.

I wrote the Guggenheim the following:

[In English:] "Mr. Slonimsky is without question one of the very finest American musicians, as well as one of the best informed. Though I do not in every respect agree with his general musical ideas I am very happy to express my admiration for his gifts and my interest in + respect for anything he has to say. I feel that the granting of any facilities whatever to him would, in principle, be eminently worthy of the traditions and the expressed purposes of the Foundation.

"His proposal seems to me of very great interest and has been so clearly put by him that further comment seems almost unnecessary. It is obviously very much worth doing, and in addition to his very great musical gifts he has marked ability as a writer. He seems, in brief, eminently fitted for what he proposes to do."

[In Russian:] I hope you liked it. I didn't want what I wrote for you to sound like a simple [in English:] "blurb" [in Russian:] as the effect in this case would be weaker. In any case, I am trying to help as much as I can. So—all the best.

My sister-in-law [Rosamond] wrote that she had the great pleasure of meeting you and your wife. I'm very grateful to you for everything you did for her.

At last, I'm almost ready to send the last movement of my violin concerto. I also had to compose a quintet for the League of Composers at the same time, and that was why I didn't work as quickly as I wanted. If I have enough money, I'd like to send you a copy of the score so that you can tell me how it plays and how it sounds.

I'd be very grateful if you speak (as you suggested) with Piston[3] about the job prospect for me at Harvard. I've thought a lot about it and though I'd prefer to be completely free, it seems to me that if there is such a possibility, it would be terrific—that is, if I always had time to compose.

I'm terribly busy and beg you to excuse me if I don't write any more today—and for this writing paper also—today is Sunday and I don't have anything else.

If you receive the Guggenheim thing[4] and won't be in Boston, I'll miss you *very* much next year! So it was *very* nice of me to write such a recommendation!!

So please give big, big greetings to your wife, and excuse me for this very bad letter!

Ever yours,
R.H.S.

1. Translated from the Russian by Theodore Levin.
2. Adolf Hitler would be sworn in as chancellor of Germany the next day.
3. The American composer and pedagogue Walter Piston (1894–1976), after studies with Boulanger in Paris (1924–26), had joined the faculty of Harvard University in 1926.
4. Slonimsky did not receive a Guggenheim fellowship.

CHAPTER

1933-1935

FIVE

Living in Berlin until the summer of 1933, Sessions witnessed Nazi anti-Semitism from a front-row seat. After the publication of the conductor Wilhelm Furtwängler's letter to Joseph Goebbels, Hitler's minister of propaganda, protesting the policy of discrimination against Jewish musicians, Sessions described in *Modern Music* the terms in which the policies of the government had been proclaimed: "In Berlin last spring one could often hear the opinion expressed by well-informed foreigners that a page from either one of the official Nazi organs, translated each day in the foreign newspapers, would prove a far more effective argument against the Nazis than any number of chronicles of terrorism." And,

> In practice, Germany has been deprived of such personalities as Walter, Klemperer, Schnabel, Busch, Schoenberg and dozens of others, whose offenses range from *Kulturbolschevismus* and "non-Aryan" descent to unorthodox opinions in regard to Wagner or Beethoven or merely to personal affiliations of an unorthodox nature. . . . Such a classic as Mendelssohn's Violin Concerto has been banned from certain concert programs, . . . while it is rumored that even Brahms's music has become suspect on account of a Jewish strain in his ancestry.[1]

On August 3, 1933, shortly after Sessions had returned to the U.S., he wrote to John Duke about the world situation: "But I do—though I think 'fear' is too strong a word—feel hostile above all to the economic + social forces in the world today which are promoting intolerance towards everything except easy solutions—call it pedantry or primitivism or complacency or obscurantism or whatever you like—in artistic fields as in all others" (US-Nsmith).

Sessions had accepted three teaching jobs in two cities, Boston and New York, and had rented a house in Hadley, Massachusetts, from which he commuted by car every week to those two places. In Boston, on Thursdays and Fridays, he taught at the Malkin Conservatory, an institution founded by three brothers that lasted from 1933 to 1943, and whose faculty Arnold Schoenberg also joined in 1933 after being forced to resign from the Prussian Academy of Arts in Berlin. Sessions wrote to Copland, September 23, "Boston promises to be interesting. What do you think of my having Schönberg for a colleague? I am quite excited about it" (US-DLC). The other Boston school was the Boston Conservatory of Music, founded in 1867. Both schools were located on Huntington Avenue near Symphony Hall. Sessions may have stayed Thursday nights with his cousin Catharine Huntington, who lived on Beacon Hill.

During the fall term of 1933–34 Sessions gave lectures at the New School for Social Research at 66 West Twelfth Street in New York. Copland had gotten him this position. The second semester brought him to the Dalcroze School, which in the fall of 1934 comprised the New Music School and the Dalcroze Institute at 9 East Fifty-ninth Street. The school's stationery listed only two names: Sessions and Paul Boepple. The Swiss Boepple (1896–1970) had been a student at the Dalcroze Institute in Geneva and taught there from 1918 to 1926, when he emigrated to the United States and directed the Dalcroze School in New York until 1932. He later taught at Bennington College in Vermont. In January 1934 Sessions joked in Russian to Slonimsky, who the year before had also begun teaching at the Boston Conservatory, and sent him a brochure for the Dalcroze School: "Unfortunately, it was necessary to omit in the announcement the motto of the N.M.S., i.e. No More Sodomy." Philosophical differences with the Dalcroze method contributed to Sessions's leaving the New Music School and the Dalcroze Institute.

Among those greeting Roger and Barbara Sessions's return from Europe was Douglas Moore, whose friendship with Sessions dated back to their days at Yale. Moore was teaching at Columbia University in New York. While arranging to meet Sessions he wrote on October 4, 1933, "I should always feel with you that no matter the time or behavior interval of our separation, we could walk into a room and meet with the same degree of intimacy and understanding that we have always had" (US-NYpease).

Besides renewing old friendships, Sessions also acted to maintain the newer friendships of his years in Europe. He responded to Anna Malipiero's plea (February 4, 1934, US-NYpease) to write something on the music of her husband, Gian Francesco Malipiero, that might placate his fascist enemies. Malipiero responded with gratitude in a letter March 22, 1934 (US-NYpease).

Also in March, Sessions contacted George Gershwin to arrange a meeting between the two. Gershwin wrote back on March 20, 1934, saying, "I should very much like to see you some time for a general chat" (US-NYpease). Whether the two met in New York is not known.

1. Roger Sessions, "Some Notes on Dr. Goebbels' Letter to Furtwaengler," *Modern Music* 11, no. 1 (November–December 1933): 3–12. Reprinted in *Roger Sessions on Music: Collected Essays,* ed. Edward T. Cone (Princeton: Princeton University Press, 1979), 271–81. Furtwängler's letter was published in the *New York Times,* April 16, 1933, sec. 4, 1–2.

▼

Roger Sessions to Aaron Copland
als US-DLC

August 11, 1933
Dear Aaron,—   Hadley

Excuse this delay in answering your letter. I had to take a flying trip to Boston in connection with one of my jobs for next year. I should be glad to speak at Yaddo,[1] if you want, on the relation between the composer + the interpreter; but feel that the subject could be stated better than in the question as it now stands, which seems to me rather to beg the real question. I mean, I cannot see that "obligation" enters into the matter at all. It seems to me that the discussion should be one about *facts + conditions* rather than "obligations" which are bound to remain theoretical. It seems to me however that it could be put in such a way as to admit of a serious inquiry into the realities of the present situation, + into how far that is abnormal, i.e. conditioned by factors into which artistic considerations do not enter,—and *how,* and *how far,* these difficulties can be alleviated. As a matter of fact I think you exaggerate in the belief that the situation is more unfavorable to the modern composer here than it is in Europe, as far as *performances,* publicity, etc., are concerned. The "American composer" it seems to me comes in for far more special treatment than native composers in other countries; but the difference is that here there is no well-developed and organic musical life, so that "American" + "modern" music are looked upon, so to speak, as "interesting" abnormalities, + tend therefore always to assume that character + to concentrate themselves into small groups apart from the main current of life, musical + otherwise.

One other thing: I don't believe much in a "composer's point of view" + therefore if I spoke at Yaddo would probably not be "representing the composers." Please don't think this is too carping of me; I only mean that it seems to me that in the deepest sense the *good* composer's deepest interests are inseparable from those of the musical development of the country as a whole, + can therefore best be approached from that point of view; the *bad* composers are opposed to it, + he instinctively realizes this.

I thought I read a twinkle of the eye between the lines of your letter + in any case I gather that our points of view are not so very far apart!

The Joyce song has thus far come out only in "The Joyce Book."[2] I have a copy here, but if you want it on the program wouldn't it be better for me to work on it here with Ada MacL?[3] Let me know.

I shall send in a day or two a sort of memorandum about the Reiner concerts, for your criticism, correction or approval. I shall send one also to Fritz + one to Piston + eventually one to Grünberg.

I enjoyed seeing [Paul] Bowles + felt that he had made great progress since three years ago, but that his harmonic + rhythmic resources were limited + his contrapuntal sense undeveloped as yet. I found him a very *sympathique* person + shall enjoy having him in my class next year.

The chief difficulty in regard to the class seems to be the problem of getting pupils who can afford to pay! Without two or three of these I don't see how I can give the class; not only I couldn't afford to come to N.Y. every week after the New School lectures are over, but it seems to me that it would be folly to *start* a class till I have a couple at least of paying pupils, to give the class a kind of standing, so to speak. If you can think of any helpful suggestions I would be most grateful for them. I can have plenty of pupils who are too poor to pay!

I shall spend the winter in this region, teach one or two days in two different conservatories in Boston, + come one day a week to give lectures at the New School in N.Y. The latter has offered me very good terms, + I am sure I can make it worth while. We have taken a house in Hadley, + I shall drive to N.Y. + Boston as often as I can; + I shall thus have four or five days a week for my own work.

Excuse this hasty letter. I hope you are having a good summer. I'm afraid there is nothing doing on my Quintet for Sept. 2 as I must work hard on the Concerto + the Summer has been already too much broke up. I'm sorry + it is very nice of you to want it that much!

Barbara joins me in *herzliche Grüsse* [hearty greetings]!

Always affectionately,
Roger

1. Such a talk would not take place.

2. Sessions's setting of James Joyce's "On the Beach at Fontana" from *Pomes Penyeach*, published in *The Joyce Book* (London, 1933).

3. Ada MacLeish, the wife of the poet Archibald MacLeish, had made her name as an interpreter of new music almost ten years previously. She had been associated with Copland and the Boulanger group in Paris.

▼

Roger Sessions to Carl Engel[1]
tls US-DLC

September 25, 1933
Dear Mr. Engel,   Hadley, Massachusetts

It has occurred to me to wonder whether, in planning her next festival of chamber music in Washington, Mrs. Coolidge might not care to consider including in the programs a concert of Schoenberg's piano and voice works by two younger German musicians, Frl. Else Kraus (pianist) and Frl. Alice Schuster (soprano), who have been giving such programs with great success in Europe during the past two years.[2] Frl. Kraus, who is a brilliant pupil of Schnabel, is widely known in Germany as an interpreter of modern piano music, and particularly of Schoenberg, all of whose piano works she plays from memory. She is in every way an "authorized interpreter," and I am sure that Schoenberg himself, as well as Schnabel, would give her the highest recommendations. Incidentally, she has appeared at at least one of the I.S.C.M. festivals, having played in Vienna last year a concerto by [Norbert] von Hannenheim,[3] perhaps the most interesting of the younger pupils of Schoenberg, whose reputation in Germany she has done much to further.

I myself heard Frl. Kraus and Frl. Schuster in Amsterdam at the time of the meeting of the I.S.C.M. jury there last December, in a program consisting of the entire piano works of Schoenberg, with the song cycle, *Der Haengende Garten*,[4] as a separate group in the middle. They have given this same program in London, where it met with particular success. I believe Frl. Schuster, who speaks English, also gave an explanatory talk on the works. They of course [could] arrange other programs if desired, but it is the Schoenberg for which they are particularly known, and which it seemed to me, especially in view of Schoenberg's promised presence in America, might have unusual interest if presented here, and so excellently, just at this time.[5]

I might add that political developments in Germany have deprived these two artists of any hearing there for the type of music in which they have specialized—an excellent example, by the way, of the way in which the effects of the anti-Semitic movement are spreading far beyond narrow racial boundaries. For this reason, too, I have felt that it would be helping a particularly good cause if these girls might be brought to America. There are a number of other possible engagements in view for them, but of course they could not undertake coming over unless there were some guarantee of their expenses, at least, being met. This can hardly be assured without some one engagement as considerable as an appearance at the Coolidge festival, for instance, would be. For obvious reasons, there would be no point in their applying to the commercial managers for a thing of this kind. If you feel that Mrs. Coolidge would be interested in the matter, or if you cared for any further information, I should be happy to assist you in any way, or to put you into touch directly with Frl. Kraus.

If I have not already presumed too much on your time, and since we are on the subject of "victims," in one sense or another, of the German overturn, I would like to ask you whether you would be interested in considering for publication in the *Musical Quarterly* a translation of the very brilliant address on the present situation of opera in Germany delivered by Dr. Alfred Einstein,[6] as a report at the International Music Congress in Florence in May. Dr. Einstein, who is now in England, is forced to depend for the time being on publication in foreign periodicals for a livelihood. I know that he would be delighted to submit anything for the *Quarterly* which you felt to be suitable, but I felt as I heard it that this report on German opera was of great interest and merited a larger public than the audience of specialists who heard it in Florence. Should you care to take the matter up with Dr. Einstein, I believe he is still to be addressed at his old Berlin residence, Nymphenburgerstrasse 10, Berlin-Schönberg. I expect to be hearing from him myself shortly, and if he gives me a new address, I would send it on to you immediately.

Dr. Einstein's report refers only incidentally to the effect of political action on the situation in opera, and is concerned rather with a more general analysis of recent tendencies, the attitude of the public, the significance of individual works, etc. Its interest is none the less great, it seems to me, and perhaps even more so, now that it has taken on the character of a memorial of things past!

Please forgive an already much too long letter, to which I will add only my most cordial greetings, in the hope that this winter, when I shall often be in New York, may bring me the opportunity of seeing you.

Most sincerely yours,
Roger Sessions

1. Engel (1883–1944) was chief of the Music Division of the Library of Congress and editor of the *Musical Quarterly*.

2. Else C. Krauss (1899–1979) twice recorded the complete Schoenberg piano works: in 1952 for the British label Esquire, and in 1961 for Barenreiter Musicaphon. Nothing can be learned of Alice Schuster.

3. Austrian twelve-tone composer Norbert von Hannenheim (1898–1943) studied in Leipzig and Berlin; he wrote seven symphonies, as well as chamber works, songs, works for chorus, and organ music.

4. Schoenberg's *Das Buch der hängenden Garten,* op. 15.

5. Schoenberg would arrive in the U.S. the following month.

6. Though he left Germany in 1933, the musicologist Alfred Einstein (1880–1952) did not settle in the U.S. until 1938, when he took a position at Smith College. While the article on opera did not appear in the *Musical Quarterly,* Einstein's article "Opus 1," on various composers' first publications, was included in *Musical Quarterly* 20 (1934).

▼

Roger Sessions to Aaron Copland
als US-DLC

September 26, 1933

Dear A—   Hadley

I have had no time whatever to practice my song; but if there *should* be time I might *possibly* do it, though it w'd probably be better if you did, even so.[1]

Ada sings it superbly. As regards interpretation—a dark + restless character, plenty of dynamic contrast + relief + as usual in my music, solidity of rhythm without the slightest *tenseness*. Plenty of pedal in the middle part, though without blurring—every note must be distinct. The tempo ♩. = 54 is exact; in the interlude (after the word "arm") there should be plenty of movement + of tone—on the word "ache" plenty of climax. Otherwise the words of the song are the best indication of how it should go.

Excuse all this writing which is really unnecessary as I am sure you will play it splendidly, + in any case better than I could.

We shall probably arrive Sat. A.M. just before the concert. Unfortunately I shall be working till late Friday in Boston.

Ciao.

Roger

1. Copland performed Sessions's "On the Beach at Fontana" with Ada MacLeish at the 1933 Yaddo Festival, September 30 and October 1. The performance was reviewed by Marc Blitzstein in *Modern Music* 11 (January 1934): 101.

▼

Roger Sessions to Otto Klemperer
als US-NYpease

Dear Herr Klemperer,—   [October 1933]

I was delighted to hear from you and to learn—as I knew, indeed, even before you wrote—of the success of your first concerts in Los Angeles.[1]

In regard to Harris's music—I find it hard to believe that you would really like it; but I could easily understand that—in case you felt obliged to play music by Americans you might find this music more sympathetic, *in intention,* than that of a great many others. Harris has undoubtedly serious aims; but he is musically quite uneducated, in the deeper as well as the more superficial sense. So, although there are moments in which one feels that he has talent of a quite genuine and sympathetic kind, the music as a whole is extremely fragmentary and uneven.

Such a case as Harris's is typically American, and to really do justice to it I should have to talk to you. If I may speak very personally—I must say that I find myself quite sincerely in a dilemma in regard, not to my opinion of the music, but in regard to my *attitude* towards it. I mean simply to oppose this as *bad music* (which it undoubtedly is) is not enough. It is above all *ungeschickt* [clumsy]

−216−

and *ungebildet* [uncultured] (perhaps a little *eingebildet* [conceited], too!) and like many uneducated people Harris has constructed elaborate theories on which he tries to base his music. But, if any musical life is going to develop in this country I would rather encourage a composer who has sincere but confused intentions, like Harris, than a more clever one whose intentions are the reverse of sincere. Unfortunately there is very little music by Americans that is even presentable; and I have certainly never urged, + never will urge, anything but the maintenance of high musical standards. But if I were *compelled* to choose, for instance, between Harris and Antheil, I should not for a moment hesitate in choosing the former.

I think you should know that Koussevitzky is playing a work of Harris this year on his program, and that the Pro Arte is performing a quartet of his.[2] Whether the latter will appear on their regular programs, or whether they accepted it on their own initiative, I don't know. Also I think it is quite certain that Harris will have a decided vogue for the next two or three years at least in New York;[3] and though you and I both know exactly how much that means, it seems to me that you must at least know it. Also, his home is in Los Angeles, even though he is living this year in New York.

If I may say so, I think it might cause you considerable trouble if you should refuse without qualification the League's request. But if you should tell them that you would be glad to see the work, but could promise to perform it only in case you liked it, they would certainly be satisfied; and that would leave you entirely free. I assume, of course, that you would make that a condition in any case.[4]

May I ask that what I have written you on this subject be kept quite confidential. I hope you know me well enough to know that I always am willing to tell my opinion when asked; but the relations between Harris and myself are, for reasons with which I will not bore you, slightly strained at present,[5] and if anything I have told you should be repeated, it could easily be misinterpreted by people who choose to be malicious.

We both send many greetings and wish you were nearer here, so that we could see you—and hear you—more often. As a matter of fact I have heard very little music, though we did go to Philadelphia where Stokowski gave an excellent performance of my *Black Maskers* Suite,[6] with great success. I miss you very much on my weekly trips to New York, though I have seen Schnabel each time except the last, when he was away. I have some good pupils there, and enjoy teaching them. Also I am working hard at my composing, which goes splendidly.

If you ever have time to write, it would mean a great deal to us to hear from you sometimes. And, if there is ever anything that I can do for you, please don't fail to let me know.

I must not forget to tell you that Schönberg arrived yesterday. I don't know when he will be in Boston. I haven't seen him yet, but undoubtedly shall soon.

Very affectionately,
Roger Sessions

P.S. Barbara was very much pleased that you used her first name! If you would care to use mine also, it would of course make me very happy.

And don't forget that I am still jealous of Labroca for the photograph you gave him!

1. Klemperer, who had just begun his tenure as conductor of the Los Angeles Philharmonic Orchestra (1933–39), had written to Sessions October 23, 1933, asking his opinion of Roy Harris's music.

2. Koussevitzky performed Harris's Symphony No. 1 on January 26 and 27, 1934, in Boston and on February 2 in New York. The Pro Arte played Quartet No. 2 (1933).

3. An encomium by Harris's former teacher Arthur Farwell in *Musical Quarterly* 18 (January 1932) had spurred a rising interest in Harris's music.

4. Klemperer conducted Harris's symphonic overture "When Johnny Comes Marching Home" with the New York Philharmonic October 31 and November 1 and 3, 1935. He did not program any of Sessions's music during his two-year tenure there.

5. One reason concerned the temporary mislaying of the parts for Sessions's *Black Maskers Suite;* see Sessions's letter to Copland (Spring 1934), below.

6. Stokowski's performances of the *Black Maskers Suite* with the Philadelphia Orchestra occurred on Friday and Saturday, October 20 and 21. The other works on the program were the Prelude to act 1 of Wagner's *Lohengrin,* Brahms's Symphony No. 2 in D Major, and Ravel's *Rapsodie espagnole.* Sessions provided extensive program notes for his own piece.

▼

Roger Sessions to Richard Donovan[1]
tls US-NH

January 31, 1934
New Music School, 9 East 59th Street
New York City

Dear Dick:

I was delighted to hear from you and wish we saw each other more often. As a matter of fact, on my way to New York I don't pass New Haven but take a back route.

In regard to operas, I should think that the smaller works of Kurt

Weill might be practicable, at least the most practicable of anything I know. They are easy and written for moderate orchestra and always had great success when performed in Europe. I should suggest either the *Dreigroschen Oper,* the *Jahsager* [*sic*] or *Mahagonny.*[2] If you should want a sort of curtain raiser, do you know Hindemith's *Hin und Zurück?*[3]

None of these works are tremendously serious, but they would be much more practical than the big works which require very elaborate preparation such as only a large organized opera house can generally furnish. The above works, however, are well worth giving in this country and if I understand you correctly, you are not planning to attempt anything on a very grand scale. *Mavra* of Stravinsky also occurs to me.[4] It has never been given in this country, but it has not achieved anything like the success of the works I have mentioned; however, my impression is that it is not really difficult either musically or scenically.

If I can help you further in any way, don't hesitate to write to me again, and if I ever do pass through New Haven, as I hope to sometime, I shall certainly let you know.

With cordial greetings both to you and Grace,

Very sincerely yours,
Roger S——

1. Donovan (1891–1970), an organist and composer, had taught at Smith College during Sessions's years there, was on the faculty of Yale University 1928–60, and conducted the New Haven Symphony Orchestra 1936–51. His music had been performed at the 1933 Yaddo Festival, and he and Quincy Porter organized the subsequent Yaddo festivals. Sessions's letter is a response to Donovan's inquiry about opera repertoire.

2. Kurt Weill (1900–1950) had left Germany in 1932 and, after time in Paris and London, settled in New York in 1935. The three works Sessions mentions are all to libretti by Bertolt Brecht: *Die Dreigroschenoper* (1928); *Der Jasager,* a two-act students' opera (1930); and the "songspiel" *Mahagonny* (1927), which Weill in 1930 had reworked as the three-act opera *Aufstieg und Fall der Stadt Mahagonny.*

3. This one-act palindrome, to a libretto by M. Schiffer, had premiered at the 1927 Baden-Baden Festival with *Mahagonny.*

4. *Mavra* was first performed at the Paris Opéra in 1922.

▼

Roger Sessions to Otto Klemperer
cc US-NYpease

February 17, 1934

Dear Herr Klemperer: [New York]

It was a great joy to get your letter which cheered me out of a kind of a mid-winter depression over the general condition of music in this country; a joy also to read again the really beautiful speeches of Schnabel. I sent it away at once and have since heard that it was very effective in your behalf. I hope very much that something may come of all this but it is still too early to know what the exact chances are.

I was much distressed to hear the news you wrote me about the orchestra in Los Angeles and hope with all my heart that you will be able to make satisfactory plans for next year. I had already planned, even before receiving your letter, to talk to Judson[1] and had a very satisfactory three-quarters of an hour with him on Wednesday morning. I am delighted to hear that he is definitely representing you as I know there is no one more capable of advancing your interests.

I told him what I had been doing, and he in his turn promised to let me know if I could be in use in any other way. I hope you also will count on me if there is anything I can do.

I gather from your letter that you did not receive the announcement of our new school[2] which I asked to have sent to but that Mrs. Brunswick sent you a copy [sic]. The school seems to have begun very well, so far, and I am really very much gratified by that. But there is an appalling amount of "up hill work" before the great majority of young composers here will begin to understand what composing really involves.

Barbara has had rather a miserable time since New Years; first an attack of influenza and then a very uncomfortable rash but she is practically cured by this time, as for me my work has been going very well.

I am nearly through with the concerto and have been looking on other things as well.

Sometime next month an evening of my work is to be given in New York and I wish you were to be there to hear it.

I should appreciate very much if you would let me know whatever plans you have for next year, and above all if there is anything possible which I can do to help you.

With affectionate greetings from both of us,

[Roger Sessions]

1. Arthur Judson (1881–1975), manager of the Philadelphia Orchestra (1915–35) and the New York Philharmonic Orchestra (1922–56); in 1930 he had become president of Columbia Concert Corporation as well. From this position of power he determined programs for both orchestras; orchestral members report his decisions brooked no appeal.
2. The New Music School (Dalcroze).

▼

Otto Klemperer to Roger Sessions[1]
als US-NYpease

March 12, 1934

Dear Roger,   The Town House, Los Angeles

Well, everything went very well.[2] The orchestra, after one reading and four rehearsals, played with great attention and great interest. The audience liked it. No criticism and warm applause. It would be a lie if I were to report to you of sensational success. But you cannot expect this from a music which does not look to easy success with audiences.

I don't read newspapers here. After they declared Schubert's C-major Symphony long-winded and weak, I have given up reading them. And so I cannot tell you anything about [reviews]. But several (more valuable) voices from the audience spoke with joy about the performance of your Suite. I find the music full of character and fresh. (Perhaps here and there with rather too rich a use of the ostinato.) I would like to get to know soon something *new* of yours. The

bassoonist had problems with I had the English horn play along with him. Since we have no D trumpet here, our (very good) trumpeter had to play everything on the B♭ trumpet, which is enormously difficult. Since he was rightly afraid of the D♯ (on the B♭ trumpet) which is held for two bars, I had three flutes play along for these bars and had the trumpet stop earlier. In this manner the ending was not endangered. I took the third movement slowly, in eight, and I also took the final movement slowly, perhaps even somewhat more slowly than the metronome indicates. The quiet beginning was very effective.

Yours and Barbara's letters gave me much pleasure. That Barbara thought, on December 5, of the Bach Mass from last year I found very touching. But that she was in so much pain disturbs me. Hopefully the spring will bring new juices and forces.

I was also bothered with pains in the past weeks because an inner injury (a fracture) remained from my Leipzig accident, which has to be treated. But it is (hopefully) not serious, only bothersome.

The future, dark, how dark. Here everything is uncertain. Friend Judson writes, "the conductorial situation is exceedingly complicated." That does not sound very hopeful. And Vienna? If this city, too, were to be lost, it would be devastating. I believe that one cannot write openly to Vienna anymore. (Avis au lecteur! [Let the reader beware!]) Brunswick is very pessimistic, which I do not take all too seriously, because Ruth really enjoys pessimism and it wears off on Mark. My wife writes *trustworthily*. We probably should believe her.

All the best for both of you.

As always in friendship.

Your

Klemperer

(P.S.) The parts will be returned via the office. Why don't you try to get the *New York Times* to publish a nice little note about the wonderful success of your music here[?][3]

1. Translated from the German by Gerhard Koeppel.
2. Klemperer had conducted *The Black Maskers* with the Los Angeles Philharmonic Orchestra March 8 and 9. The Sessions opened the program, which continued with the Benedictus from Bach's B-minor Mass; "Il mio tesoro" from Mozart's *Don Giovanni;* Mozart's Sinfonia Concertante for Oboe, Clarinet, Bassoon, Horn, and Orchestra; and Schumann's Symphony No. 4 in D Minor, op. 120. John H. Hamilton's brief program note stated, "The work of Mr. Sessions is very modern and courageous; his use of the ostinato is similar to Stravinsky's in Sacre du Printemps."
3. The previous day Sessions's article "Composition and Review" had appeared in the Sunday *New York Times,* March 11, 1934, p. 10, 6: 7. Later his letter praising Klemperer's performance of Beethoven's Fifth Symphony on a New York Philharmonic concert October 11–14, 1934, appeared in the *New York Times,* October 28, 1934, p. 9, 8: 3.

▼

Roger Sessions to Aaron Copland
als US-DLC

Thurs. [Spring 1934]
[Hadley, Massachusetts][1]

Dear A.—

I was delighted to have your letter + to hear of your plans for the Song + the chorales.[2] I'm delighted to hear that the cover of the latter will be gray, which I should think wd. be the best possible.

I sent A[lma] W[ertheim] a suggested version of the K[oussevitzky] testimonial; no doubt you have seen it. It was I who asked Israel [Citkowitz] to find out who wrote it; I assumed Alma W. was more or less behind the thing, since she mentioned no names in her letter. Needless to say I'd have written you if I had known, + not done it through Israel. No, I don't at all object to stressing "American music" except in the sense of taking it, so to speak, out of the world + placing it, psychologically, in a separate category. You are quite right about K—— + I think the gesture is a splendid + appropriate one to make at this time. I hope only that the list of signatures will be as varied + inclusive as possible, + I daresay it will.

I lent the Los Angeles B[*lack*] M[*askers*] notices to a friend but will let you see them as soon as I get them back. Prepare yourself for a good laugh! though I suppose for one to carp at them is a little like looking a gift horse in the mouth—when his teeth are protruding ones, though, what can one do? I'm sorry to hear about your fortunes with the journalism of the Middle West; I have the impression however that it is precisely there that conditions are worst.

In regard to the I.S.C.M.[3] we must simply make up our minds either to find new functions for it or to quietly let it die while the dying is good. I am going to see D. Lawton while I am in N.Y. + find out what she has to say. I wrote her a letter—the kind you'd call a tirade!—some weeks ago apropos of the impending meeting, + don't know whether she used it at the meeting or not. I want to make the thing as energetic as possible—since I'll be living in or near N.Y. next year I personally can give more time to it than I ever could from here.

Inzwischen [In the meantime]—anything you can write me about the situation + your views about it will be very welcome. I don't see why something should not be made of the thing—the framework + the skeleton are all there. Precisely what, + how, is of course the question. Anyway I am making notes of various points + want to go over the whole situation very thoroughly with you in N.Y.—In a way I have the feeling that the ISCM, being more amorphous than the League, is also—so to speak—in a more plastic state—am I right, or not?

I won't write more now. Our colds are both better: spring really seems to have come today, + it looks as if there would be no more bad weather. It's wonderful to be living in the country at this time of year.

With love from us both.

As always,
R——

1. Although this letter is written on New Music School stationery, the content clearly implies Sessions wrote it in Hadley, not New York.

2. Plans for the Cos Cob Press to publish the song "On the Beach at Fontana" and the Three Chorale Preludes for Organ were eventually dropped.

3. The U.S. section of the ISCM had its headquarters at 121 East 58th Street. Its president was Sessions, its vice president Carlos Salzedo, and its secretary Dorothy Lawton.

▼

Roger Sessions to Aaron Copland
als US-DLC

[Spring 1934]

Dear Aaron,—   [Hadley]

Thank you for your letter. I am better though I had a slight complication, nothing at all serious—which hasn't quite gone away. Barbara still has a bad sinus. But I shall be in N.Y. as usual Monday, though I am ordered by the Dr. to go by train.

All's well that ends well, of course, as far as Roy is concerned I am quite willing to drop the matter; especially as I am the gainer by having two sets of parts. I am delighted that V[ictor] K[raft][1] is apparently doing such a good job + am curious to know what he has found in the score, that escaped me.

As for my song; it is to be issued, shortly. I believe, by the Oxford Press, reportedly. In any case my contract stipulates that all the proceeds from the sale of the song are to go to Mr. Joyce. So—if you want to publish it I suggest simply that you write to The Sylvan Press or the Oxford Press + see what can be done about it. My "permission"—which I give for what it is worth—would be of no use to you, + I think as far as the English are concerned it depends absolutely on what they plan to do about issuing those songs separately.

As far as the Chorales are concerned, I am of two minds. First I am not at all sure whether I want them published at all until my work is better known. I have gotten so far away from them—they seem even further from my present feelings than the *Black Maskers*—that I may be inclined to judge them a little harshly. But they seem to me now rather crude + blind first attempts to find something that I really only understood later on. But I must look them over again before *deciding*.

Secondly, my whole experience— + forgive me for being frank with you about this, especially as it does not involve you, or, *I promise you,* my feelings about you, in any way—with the Cos Cob Press, has been an unhappy one, + I want to be a little surer about the attitude of certain people (I need mention no names) towards me before committing myself further to their care. You + I have discussed this affair of the Symphony as much as we need to, + I have gathered that you agree with me on that point; if it had been followed up as it *could* have been, *many* things would have been very different for me; for it is not as if my music had ever failed of public response *at the time of the performance.* Now—if it is true, what people have told me on both sides of the water, that the C.C. Press + other groups in N.Y. are interested in promoting certain works + certain people, + in sidetracking others, then obviously it is not to my interest to go on with the C.C.P.; if I started being really energetic on my own behalf I am quite sure I could scare up at least as many performances as the C.C.P. has done, + I would also have had the judgment not to give the parts to Roy H—— or anyone else for transportation to California until the contract for performance was signed.

You know, I hope, that I am not given to complaining, + as a matter of fact these things have been brought to my attention by others, in the first place—by various people who have no connection with each other. Also I am less interested than I ever was in going around + so to speak "drumming up" trade + publicity for myself. But I have determined, especially since coming back to the U.S., to cease allowing myself to be put in a perfectly false position, and—in connection with the Press,—what is fundamentally a very humiliating one. So I would far rather if necessary go on alone "with malice toward none + charity toward all" till I can make other connections which will be really solid ones.

Now—personally, *mon cher,* let me assure you once more that this has nothing at all to do with you. I have far more hope for the Press, since the thing is partly in your hands, than I had before, + if I could cooperate with it in any way—especially since you are on it, I would be delighted. But I must be sure, + have some definite reason to be sure, that my interests are going to be really looked after. And I have both seen + heard— + otherwise experienced—too much, not to be rather wary. Among other things I should like very much to know what happened a year ago, when I was approached by Mr. Kalmus on the subject of a contract for my work. When I answered explaining my willingness to consider the matter I simply received no answer— only six months later a peremptory note indicating that the Press would be pleased to "consider" my Chorales.

Alors—*assez de tout cela* [enough of all this]—and if this seems to you a "tirade" I do beg you, remember that it has to do only with a charming though (I am *told*) capricious lady, + with Kalmus himself,— + in no way with you. You see I have gotten very self-conscious about my letters to you.

I'm *very* anxious to see you soon + to hear your music. Let's arrange something for week after next perhaps; if the League isn't meeting, we could [meet] Tuesday at 4—. I really have missed seeing you very much.

My work is going splendidly by this time—the Concerto will mostly be ready, also a couple of other things I have up my sleeve.

Affectionately from us both
Roger—

1. Photographer Victor Kraft (ca. 1912–76). Copland had written to Chávez August 24, 1932, "I am bringing with me a young violinist who is a pupil, companion, secretary and friend. His name is Victor Kraftsov." Copland and Perlis, *Copland: 1900 through 1942* (New York: St. Martins Press, 1984), 213. At Copland's request, Sessions accepted Kraft as a nonpaying pupil under a condition of confidentiality (letter dated "Hadley, Saturday," US-DLC).

▼

Otto Klemperer to Roger Sessions[1]
als US-NYpease

August 12, 1934
Dr. Bircher-Benner's
Dear Sessions,   Sanatorium "Lebendige Kraft," Zürich 7

I am writing you today about an important matter and ask for your help with Judson.[2] You have perhaps heard about the many program calamities: namely that they took Mahler's *Lied von der Erde* from me and also refused me another program idea (for the third week, Debussy's *Three Nocturnes,* Stravinsky's *Psalms,* Mendelssohn's *whole Midsummernights Dream Music,* because the chorus for all three pieces would be too expensive. I have decided therefore to present Mahler's Second Symphony in C Minor for the third week.)[3] Perhaps you don't like this piece. It would be too much to write about it now. One thing is certain: for me as *Director* this piece presents possibilities for a big success. Much more than any other one. For me it's *very important* to do this piece. Think about my difficult program situation: I am not to do Brahms, I don't want to do Strauss, there are practically no new works. There nevertheless has to be success. You know how difficult it was for me to decide to accept New York (specifically because of these reasons of programming). So please help me with Judson (or with the board of directors) to do this symphony. It is *really enormously important* for me.

Recently I have been having trouble with my right arm. I am here for a cure and hope that it will help. But news from you will reach me in Vienna. How are Barbara and you? When are you moving? In Europe it was a hot summer (factually and politically). When will we have quiet?

To both of you all the best from my heart. Thank you for all you do for me. Hoping that you will have success in implementing my wishes

I am always,
Your
Klemperer

1. Translated from the German by Gerhard Koeppel.
2. Barbara Sessions had urged Klemperer (April 15, 1934, US-NYpease) to accept an offer to lead four sets of concerts in October 1934 as guest conductor of the New York Philharmonic Orchestra. Assuring him that his appearance first in the season would not make him a mere "curtain raiser," and acknowledging the difficulty of his getting away from his duties in Los Angeles at that time, she had hinted that his acceptance would place him in line as a possible successor to either Arturo Toscanini or Bruno Walter, at that time the Philharmonic's principal and associate conductors, respectively.
3. Of these works, only the *Symphony of Psalms* would be performed. The other pieces on the four programs would be Schoenberg's transcription of Bach's Prelude and Fugue in E♭; symphonies by Hindemith ("Mathis der Maler"), Sibelius, Bruckner, Beethoven, and Haydn; Schubert's Rondo in A for Violin and Strings, op. 107; Stravinsky's *Firebird Suite;* and Janáček's Sinfonietta.

▼

Roger Sessions to Otto Klemperer
draft of telegram US-NYpease

OTTO KLEMPERER, RUBRUNS, VIENNA   [August 1934]

RECEIVED LETTER ONLY TUESDAY NIGHT NEW YORK. JUDSON AWAY IN CANADA. UNFORTUNATELY NOTHING CAN BE DONE ABOUT MAHLER. SITUATION ENTIRELY IN CONTROL OF MANAGERS AND DIRECTORS. AM QUITE DISGUSTED BUT POWERLESS UNDER CIRCUMSTANCES. HOPE NEVERTHELESS YOU CAN ARRANGE SATISFACTORY PROGRAM AND WILL DO EVERYTHING POSSIBLE TO HELP. AFFECTIONATE GREETINGS.

SESSIONS[1]

1. Another telegram from Sessions, this one to an unnamed intimate of Klemper-er's, reads: "PLEASE EXPLAIN TO KLEMPERER UTTER IMPOSSIBILITY OF DOING ANY-THING ABOUT PROGRAMS IN NEW YORK. SITUATION CONTROLLED BY MUSICALLY IGNORANT MEN NOW INTRANSIGENT. FEEL SURE THAT WITH PATIENCE AND IRONY KLEMPERER CAN EVENTUALLY WIN EVERYTHING. PLEASE USE ALL INFLUENCE WITH HIM. MUCH LOVE. R." (US-NYpease).

▼

Roger Sessions to Aaron Copland
tls US-DLC

October 12, 1934
New York

Dear Aaron,

Thank you first of all for your letter and the news about the Yaddo decision. No reason to comment on it, you apparently know that [Nicholai] Berezowsky is teaching here. He has already spoken to me rather tentatively about it, and told me the circumstances that lead up to it.

I am writing primarily because Fabien Sevitzky[1] wants to play my first symphony this year and has in fact announced it for performance in December. He has asked me whether there would be any chance of his being loaned the parts free of charge. His orchestra is a cooperative organization owned and run by the musicians themselves. They consequently have no money to spend on royalties. This I have learned from Sevitzky himself and also from others. It seemed to me that since the symphony, on account of its difficulty, is bound to receive comparatively few performances, that you might be willing to make a special concession in this case. I would be grateful if you would let me and Kalmus know as soon as possible what your decision is, since Kalmus says it depends on you entirely.

Of course there is also the question as to whether Sevitzky is capable of conducting the work. I have been assured he is very conscientious as far as rehearsals go, and have also warned him of the tremendous difficulty of the score, although he apparently knew it well before he approached me on the subject. As I have never heard him conduct I cannot judge, and would appreciate your advice on the subject.

Do you mind being bored once more with a rehearsal of the still continuing vicissitudes of my relations with Kalmus[?] In June I received the proof of my song; I corrected it and sent it back a week later from New Preston Conn. where I was staying at the time. Shortly after the first of August I received a letter from Kalmus asking me to return the proof immediately. After considerable inconvenience on my part, the New Preston post office sent me a notice that Kalmus had acknowledged receipt of the package (registered) on June the twenty-third.

When I got back here last week I found still at the school the parts of the "Black Maskers" which should have been called for in May. I dropped in at Kalmus' office yesterday and called this to his attention, whereupon he assured me that a package had been called for in the spring and both sets of parts were at present reposing in the "archives" of the Cos Cob Press. When I got back in the evening I examined the package which was here at school, and found that the "Black Maskers" parts were there. The secretary of the school called him up today and he insisted a package had been fetched from school in May, but again seemed disinclined to investigate and demanded that we send him the parts over by mail. I must confess that I am beginning to be amused, although I find Kalmus himself slightly impertinent, and am therefore a little inclined to treat him like a worm. I don't suppose he likes that.

Please forgive me for always seeming to enjoy washing Mr. Kalmus' dirty linen before you. As a matter of fact now that I am in New York I don't suppose that such things need have any serious consequences whatever; but I suppose you as his boss want to know these things.

I have heard vague rumors that the Cos Cob Press is to be abandoned. Is there any truth in it?

It is fun to be living in New York and I look forward eagerly to your return [from Chicago]. We had a League meeting last night at which several things were actually accomplished. But after all the meeting lasted over three hours.

Always affectionately,
Roger

1. Fabien Sevitzky (1891–1967), nephew of Serge Koussevitzky, was a double-bass player and conductor like his uncle, who had suggested he truncate his name to prevent confusion. He conducted the People's Symphony Orchestra, founded in 1920, in Boston 1928–36, the Indianapolis Symphony Orchestra 1937–55, and the University of Miami Symphony Orchestra 1959–65. After Sevitzky resigned in 1936 the People's Orchestra was absorbed into the State Symphony.

▼

Roger Sessions to Serge Koussevitzky
tls US-DLC

November 12, 1934
New York

Dear Dr. Koussevitzky:

I am writing to tell you that Mr. Burgin has had, for some time, the violin part of my concerto and that I am orchestrating the last movement which I shall have ready very shortly.

I would be extremely grateful if you could let me know what are the chances for its performance this season. I am quite aware that I have not made it at all easy for you to plan for this work, and am, therefore, quite prepared for a negative answer. However, I am sure you understand better than anyone what are the problems involved in composing a work of this kind, and how impossible it is to finish a work before one is ready to do so.

I hope you will understand my attitude, when I tell you frankly, that a performance in Boston, and especially in New York, would be of great importance to me at this time, since I have recently returned to this country and begun my work here. It is a curious fact that while my music has been played widely in America, and Europe, I have not yet had a major performance in New York, and I believe that there is a real desire here to know my music better. So, I should naturally be not only pleased but very grateful if you could find it possible to put it on your programs this season.

Although I have had many inquiries about the concerto from both violinists and conductors, I have hesitated to take any steps in the matter, since I have considered from the first that the work was being written for you, and that you must be the one to decide regarding its first performance. But I hope you will understand if I ask you to let me feel free to show it to other conductors and violinists with a view to performance, in case you do not find it possible to perform it this season. Needless to say, I would much prefer to have it done by you and Mr. Burgin, but the work has been so long in preparation, that I am now anxious to dispose of it as quickly as possible.

I am looking forward with the greatest pleasure to your first New York concert,[1] and also to the great pleasure of seeing you again.

With warmest greetings to you and Mrs. Koussevitzky.

Most cordially yours,
Roger Sessions

1. The Boston Symphony Orchestra played two concerts in Carnegie Hall: on November 15, 1934, Mozart's Overture to *The Marriage of Figaro,* Beethoven's "Eroica" Symphony, and Moussorgsky's *Pictures at an Exhibition,* and on November 17, Mozart's Symphony No. 40, the New York premiere of Ravel's Concerto for the Left Hand with Paul Wittgenstein as soloist, and Franck's Symphony in D Minor.

▼

Serge Koussevitzky to Roger Sessions
cc US-DLC

November 19, 1934

Dear Mr. Sessions,   [Boston]

On my return to Boston I found your letter of the 12th which came while I was "on tour" with the Orchestra. I am very sorry I did not know of it when I saw you in New York.

To my great regret, I find no possibility to perform your Concerto this season. But I can say definitely, at this time, that I would be able to include it in our programmes during the first half of next season both in Boston and in New York. Now, if you cannot afford to wait, I will understand it, of course, and consider you perfectly free to offer your Concerto to a conductor and an artist of distinction, to whom you would entrust the premiere of your work.

I feel sure that you realize how difficult it is to insert a work of importance into programmes arranged some time before and completed, especially when the season is thus far advanced.

Find here my renewed regrets and kindest regards to Mrs. Sessions and yourself.

Most sincerely yours,
[Serge Koussevitzky]

▼

Roger Sessions to Serge Koussevitzky
tls US-DLC

November 21, 1934

Dear Dr. Koussevitzky: [New York]

Thank you for your extremely kind letter. I fully appreciate your point of view, and since you give me definite assurance of performances in Boston and New York during the early part of next season, I shall be happy to wait until then for the premiere.

Of course, from the artistic point of view, I should be very happy to have Mr. Burgin play the solo part. It occurs to me however, that it might be better for the work if this were entrusted to a violinist who could play it later with other organizations. With this in mind, I wonder if you'd object to my taking up the matter with Mr. Szigeti[1] and Mr. Spalding,[2] both of whom have expressed their interest in the work and desire to see it. Mr. Zimbalist[3] and Mr. Huberman[4] have also shown considerable interest in it, but I believe there is little or no chance of their actually wanting to play it.

I realize also that Mr. Burgin has seen the concerto and that in a sense, the first performance has been promised to him. Since I have the highest regard for Mr. Burgin, both as an artist and a man, I do not like to propose anything that would seem to show a lack of appreciation. I would be very grateful if you would take this also into account in advising me in this matter, as I would very much appreciate your doing.

Let me say once more what a rare pleasure it was to hear you and the orchestra again, and tell you how much I look forward to the other New York concerts.

With kindest regards to you and Mrs. Koussevitzky,

Most sincerely yours,
Roger Sessions

1. The Hungarian violinist Joseph Szigeti (1892–1973) was a champion of twentieth-century music, having played works by Stravinsky, Prokofiev, Bartók, and (in 1938) Bloch.
2. In his autobiography, *Rise to Follow* (New York: Holt, 1943), the American violinist Albert Spalding (1888–1953) leaves Sessions and the episode of the Violin Concerto entirely unmentioned.
3. The Russian-American violinist Efrem Zimbalist (1889–1985).
4. The Polish violinist Bronislaw Huberman (1882–1947).

▼

Serge Koussevitzky to Roger Sessions
cc US-DLC

November 26, 1934

Dear Mr. Sessions,   [Boston]

Thank you very much for your letter.

I appreciate your decision to wait until next season and leave to us the premiere of your Concerto for Violin.

I have spoken to Mr. Burgin and, after seeing your letter, he said he had no objection whatsoever to your taking up the matter with Mr. Szigeti, who will surely be interested in presenting the work and could play it later with other organizations.

With kindest regards and hoping to see you at my future New York concerts, I am

Sincerely yours,
[Serge Koussevitzky]

P.S. Incidentally, I just learn that the "People's Symphony"[1] are playing a work of yours at one of their concerts, in Boston, and must tell you that I avoid giving works of composers whose names have appeared on their programmes.

1. The People's Symphony Orchestra, or Koussevitzky's nephew, Fabien Sevitzky, was apparently a thorn in his side.

▼

Roger Sessions to Roy Harris
cc US-NYpease

December 11, 1934
[New York]

Dear Roy:

At the last meeting of the United States section of the I.S.C.M. we discussed your proposition regarding the preparation of records of American works.[1] The board felt, as I think Henry Cowell has already told you, that it would be unwise to plan to send such records to Europe for submission to the international jury; first of all because it would be unfair to those composers whose works were not recorded, and secondly because it would imply a reflection on the musical ability of the jury whose members are generally well trained musicians and can therefore read scores without difficulty.

However the section is very much interested in the proposition to issue records under its auspices, and would like to have further particulars in the matter. The question was raised as to whether the United States section or the international society would be given credit on the actual labels of the records. But otherwise there seemed to be a general disposition to accept in principle whatever definite offer the Columbia company will make.

So I shall hope to hear further from you on the subject, either directly or through Miss Lawton, so the matter can be brought up for definite action at the next meeting of the society, or if a quicker decision must be reached let me know and I will put it in the hands of a special committee.

I was sorry to miss the party at the Nortons, which I hear went off splendidly.

Most sincerely,
[Roger Sessions]

1. Harris, whose music was now being recorded by Columbia Records, was fast becoming a prominent figure in American music, thanks in part to commissions from the Boston Symphony Orchestra: Koussevitzky had conducted the First Symphony January 26, 1934 (Sessions had heard it on the radio), and called it "the first truly tragic symphony by an American." (Quoted in Hugo Leichtentritt, *Serge Koussevitzky: The Boston Symphony Orchestra and the New American Music* [Cambridge: Harvard University Press, 1946]: 130.) The orchestra premiered Harris's second and third symphonies in 1935 and 1937 respectively.

▼

Roger Sessions to Douglas Moore
cc US-NYpease

December 13, 1934
[New York]

Dear Douglas:

It was terribly nice to hear from you and I am almost ashamed to answer. You have probably been in New York long enough to have no idea how for a tenderfoot like myself the things under one's nose get such a disproportionate significance that one simply gets in the habit of postponing everything that lies outside one's immediate range of vision. Since I got here the first of October my furthest north has been 76th street, my furthest south 11th street!

I was very much interested to hear of the young man you write about,[1] and will be glad to help in any way I can. Naturally I don't like to judge too definitely until I have met him or talked further with you. I can see for instance that with such a boy New York might not be at all the best place, though quite aside from my own interest in having gifted pupils I am coming rapidly to feel that if an American composer can pursue his studies here and remain from the start face to face with American conditions he will be spared many problems later on. What you say about his social background is what makes me pause, though I have another pupil whom I should describe in very much the same way who is doing very good work for me.[2]

As for studying in Germany I am convinced that with conditions there as they are now it would be quite useless and possibly harmful for anyone to work in any of the big conservatories. If he wished to go on along those lines I should certainly recommend that he seek out Hindemith who of course will no longer be in Berlin, and presumably not in Germany. I could easily find out about this and if it should seem wise give him a letter of introduction.

In regard to Harvard I am sure that Piston is an excellent teacher. I am not so sure about the others, and you can judge as well as I whether in this particular case it would be better temporarily to relegate music to a more or less secondary place, as he would have to do if he took the regular B.A. degree. My own feeling is that while Harvard would be splendid as far as getting a wide background of musical and general culture is concerned, the training he would get there would be quite inadequate if he is to become a serious composer, and in fact that the curriculum is designed with quite other ends in view. Furthermore I am also more and more impressed with the fact that Boston has become, alas, a very small city indeed from a musical point of view.

However these are of course purely tentative suggestions, and I give them strictly for what they are worth. I should be very glad to meet him but first of all I hope to see you and Emily. I should have called you up if I had known where to reach you, but the telephone book says very sternly that you are unapproachable except between twelve and one on Tuesdays. But couldn't we get together sometime next week? I shall be here from Tuesday until Christmas and after Christmas until New Year's. You can always reach me at school or at my private (and very secret) number, Regent 4-4089.

Much love to you all.

Affectionately,
[Roger]

1. Although the young man was a student of Nadia Boulanger's, no one seems to fit Moore's description.
2. Possibly he means Edward T. Cone (b. 1917), who studied with Sessions privately and later at Princeton University.

▼

Roger Sessions to Serge Koussevitzky
tls US-DLC

December 18, 1934
New York

Dear Dr. Koussevitzky:

Thank you for your kind letter, and excuse my delay in answering. I have an appointment with Szigeti this Thursday and shall show him my concerto at that time. Meanwhile, I appreciate very much your attitude, and also Mr. Burgin's, in this matter.

The postscript of your letter disturbed me, I must confess, not a little. Obviously, you will understand that the very idea of making a choice between a performance by you and one by the People's Symphony is so ridiculous that I can hardly entertain it seriously. I may add, that I should not dream of giving a manuscript work to the latter organization or of taking any steps to bring a published work to their notice. I am simply not interested in the matter. The work in question however, has been published for several years, and has been performed several times here and abroad—it was originally performed by you—and I simply do not feel that I have the right to interfere in any way. First of all, it is no longer my property, and secondly, I feel that my work must take its normal course and follow its normal evolution without interference or even special interest on my part.

I may add that it has come to my notice that the conductor of the People's Symphony has serious doubts about the ability of his orchestra and possibly of his own ability to give an adequate performance of the work in question, and therefore it is more than doubtful whether the performance will ever take place. The matter however, is between him and my publisher, and I have nothing to do with it in any way.

I think I have shown you quite clearly how much it would mean to me to have you perform my violin concerto and how truly great a disappointment it would be if you should find it necessary to abandon the idea. I feel however, that the only thing I can do is abide by whatever decision you may make in this matter. After stating the situation frankly and openly to you as I have tried to do in this letter, in any case, I am sure that you, as the artist you are, will appreciate my point of view.

With affectionate greetings to you and Mrs. Koussevitzky, and the best of wishes for the holidays.

Most sincerely,
Roger Sessions

▼

Roger Sessions to Nicolas Slonimsky
cc US-DLC

February 28, 1935
Dorogoi Nicolai Leonidovich: New York

Thank you for sending me the tickets for your concert. I would be delighted to hear Kadosa and Stravinsky, but unfortunately, I'm in Boston only on Mondays. However, I shall try and put the tickets in the very best hands.

It was nice to see you recently in Boston, and I only wish my days there were not so hectic,[1] however I hope we'll see each other again soon.

Greetings to Dorothy and Electra[2]—aren't you really afraid to have a daughter with such a name?—also to Mme. Averino[3] if you see her.

Incidentally, I suppose you know Sevitsky played my "Black Maskers"[4] recently, which I suppose settles my hash, as they say, with S.K. I trust this will not interfere with our friendship!—yours and mine, I mean.

Kak vsegda,
[Roger]

1. In the fall of 1934, when Walter Piston had offered Sessions a temporary appointment as his replacement at Harvard University for the spring semester, Sessions had declined (November 13, 1934, cc US-NYpease), writing: "I have an extremely heavy schedule in Boston every Monday [at the Boston Conservatory and at the Boston University College of Music], and my classes in [the New Music] school here make it necessary for me to be in New York on Tuesday, Wednesday, Thursday, and often on Friday also. In addition to that, there is the fact that my life is already so complicated that I am afraid it would be folly to add any further obligations." Piston had then contacted Copland (November 15, 1934), who had accepted the job.
2. Sessions had written to Slonimsky August 26, 1933 (US-DLC), congratulating him on the birth of his daughter Electra.
3. Olga Averino (1896–1989), a lyric soprano and voice teacher, as well as wife of Boston Symphony Orchestra violinist Paul Fedorovsky.
4. Not the First Symphony, as had originally been planned.

IN THE SPRING of 1935 Sessions's hectic teaching schedule, involving a continual shuttling between New York and Boston, was beginning to take its toll. An ambivalence toward institutional education, one symptom of the physical and psychic strain that would erupt in the personal and professional upheavals of the latter part of the year, can be seen already surfacing in an exchange of ten letters between Sessions and the composer Randall Thompson dating from January to May 1935 (US-NYpease).

Like Sessions, Thompson (1899–1984) had studied with Bloch in New York and, also like Sessions, had been a Rome Prize recipient. Though he had then taught only briefly at Wellesley College and Harvard University (1927–30), Thompson was in 1935 preparing a report, *College Music: An Investigation for the Association of American Colleges* (New York: Macmillan, 1935). Asked by *Saturday Review* to review Thompson's report, Sessions commented (January 18, 1935), "I feel very strongly on this whole subject of education and feel that ultimately the trouble lies in many of the fundamental conceptions of education in general, rather than musical education in particular, the defects in the latter being only rather glaring symptoms of let us say, diseases which are at present in American culture as a whole" (US-NYpease).

Sessions already was considering giving up his teaching positions; he would, in fact, soon give up both Boston teaching positions. On March 14 he confided in Thompson his "decision to sever my connections with the American Dalcroze Institute. . . . The reasons for this have partly to do with the difficulty of maintaining an institution with two ostensible heads [himself and Paul Boepple], and two specific educational aims; partly also, with matters of finance which seem at this time almost insoluble." He wanted to stay in New York, but lamented "that the most talented pupils are very often unable to pay" and asked Thompson, in view of his association with the Carnegie Foundation, "to give me some idea of how to approach them in the most effective way" for a personal subsidy. His notion was

the establishment not specifically of a school, but of a kind of studio in which, with the help of one or two assistants, I would offer the most complete training possible in all the branches of music which are essential to the equipment of a composer.

The great problem of my life is, of course, finding time to compose, and

I feel that whatever I do, that is the thing which must take precedence over all other considerations. Alas, two winters have been very nearly fruitless in that respect, and this sort of thing can't possibly go on if life is to have any meaning for me at all—partly my own fault, of course. But also, to an overwhelming extent, a matter of sheer time and energy.

Thompson, sympathetic, told Sessions whom to contact at the Carnegie Corporation, but accurately predicted lack of success with them. He also wrote (April 18) enthusiastically about Sessions's First Piano Sonata and warmly invited Sessions to visit his home in Peace Dale, Rhode Island, which Sessions did the first weekend in May. Barbara Sessions, busy in Washington, D.C., was unable to go to Rhode Island.

CHAPTER

1935-1937

S I X

THE LETTERS in this chapter come from the unhappiest period of Sessions's life. His personal and professional problems erupted in two sequential episodes: The first was his decision to end his sixteen-year marriage to Barbara and to remarry. The second was his efforts to launch his largest work to date, the Violin Concerto. The first episode reached its culmination in late November 1936, a turning point in Sessions's life and career, just as the second entered its most heated phase. Overlapping the two was yet another instance of Sessions's failure to complete a commissioned work on time—in this case, the String Quartet No. 1 in E Minor.

Sessions spent the summer of 1935 teaching at the University of California at Berkeley. Finally, after eight years of work, he completed his Violin Concerto; the score is marked "San Francisco, Calif., August 1935" and is dedicated to Barbara Sessions. He stayed that summer, and the next, at the Cloyne Court Hotel, 2600 Ridge Road, in Berkeley. His marriage to Barbara was already at an end; she did not accompany him on either trip out West. It was during the summer of 1935 that Sessions fell in love with one of his Berkeley music students, Elizabeth Franck[1] from Spokane, Washington. Lisl, as she was called, was ten years younger than Sessions.

On September 22, 1936, Sessions's divorce became final; he and Lisl were married Thanksgiving Day, November 26, 1936. His relationship with Nadia Boulanger, already strained by the events surrounding the 1933 ISCM festival in Amsterdam, suffered a breach that was never reconciled. A devout Catholic, Boulanger had written to Sessions in September 1936 pleading with him not to divorce Barbara. Sessions had felt it was none of her business, never forgave her for the intrusion, and sent Boulanger's letter to his wife to answer (she didn't). One could speculate that Boulanger's disapproval of Sessions was broadcast to others, particularly those fond of Barbara Sessions, such as Copland. In fact, Copland's attitude toward Roger Sessions, which the letters of 1933–34 show to have become already more reserved, thereafter cooled considerably. Only more speculation could determine how this lack of support from Copland and Boulanger was to affect Sessions's career. In any case, this situation might help to explain the devotion the thirty-eight-year-old Sessions felt toward the nineteen-year-old composer David Diamond (b. 1915), whom the embattled couple may have seen as their only ally.

The first letter of this period is also the first in a long correspondence with Diamond, Sessions's best-known student in the 1930s. Diamond had begun study with Sessions at the New Music School and Dalcroze Institute in November 1934, supporting his lessons by working as a janitor in the building. A confidante of both Sessions and Lisl Franck during 1935–36, he sailed for Paris in June 1936 to study with Nadia Boulanger at Fontainebleau, setting the stage for a conflict between Sessions and Boulanger over the loyalty of a gifted student.

At the same time, Sessions was also in conflict with another influential woman in the musical world. He had met Mrs. Elizabeth Sprague Coolidge in California in the summer of 1935. The patroness conceived the idea of a concert to celebrate Harvard University's tercentenary in September 1936 and to commission from Sessions a work to be performed by the university's glee club. That request for a vocal work was met with Sessions's String Quartet in E Minor. Mrs. Coolidge was soon to experience the frustration with Sessions's tardiness that Copland, Koussevitzky, and others already knew. She, however, retaliated with the threat of nonpayment when it became clear that Sessions would miss the Harvard concert deadline of September 14.

In his letter to Elizabeth Coolidge of December 15, 1935, Sessions proposed a four- or possibly even a five-movement quartet, promising to have it done in June before he went back to California. The three-movement work was not done by July 19, when he promised, "I shall be all finished with the score, certainly, within the next two or three weeks." The last movement was still not complete by September 6, when Sessions wrote to Mrs. Coolidge:

I am so very sorry to have caused you the disappointment both of delay + of absence from Cambridge for the occasion, + hope that at least the quartet itself may not be a disappointment. As I have never written a quartet before I am not prepared to say that it is my best work but I believe I have put as much into it as I have into any other work I have written, + in any case I have done as well as I could. I believe it represents a definite state in the evolution of my work; but that is for critics(!) to determine + not for me.

In her letter to him—written the next day and therefore doubtlessly crossing his in the mail—Mrs. Coolidge renounced all "authority or rights of performance, as it really no longer belongs to me for the event for which I commissioned it." This was a serious financial blow: Sessions had counted on receiving the five hundred dollars in order to travel back east (see his letter of September 20, 1936, to Diamond).

Responding to Mrs. Coolidge's threat challenged Sessions's epistolary skills to the utmost. He rose to the occasion in his letter of September 12, 1936. Mrs. Coolidge soon relented and during his drive back east Sessions received a conciliatory note. (The five hundred dollars was not yet forthcoming, and Sessions was forced to borrow money from his aunt Adeline Sessions to make the trip.) Mrs. Coolidge shrewdly elicited more from Sessions than she gave: she now obtained the right to give the quartet to whomever she wanted to premiere it, while not yet paying for the work. But by Christmas time it was still not completed, and Sessions evidently missed yet another deadline—January 1.

Mrs. Coolidge did not know until the August 22d letter, as David Diamond surely did, that the reason Sessions could not be in Cambridge in September (even if his quartet were completed) was both personal and legal. In August Sessions took up a six-week residence at the TH Ranch at Pyramid Lake, Sutcliffe, Nevada, in order to obtain a divorce from Barbara. Sessions subsequently paid five hundred dollars a year in alimony until Barbara's death in 1982.

In a letter of October 26 to Diamond, which discusses Diamond's Violin Concerto at some length, Sessions ends with "Things go very well—Lisl comes the day before Thanksgiving + we'll be married Thanksgiving Day in Hadley— + we hope you can come for the occasion." Diamond would in fact attend the small wedding, held in Hadley. Ruth Huntington Sessions was there and presented Diamond with an inscribed copy of her recently published autobiography.[2]

In the midst of these negotiations Sessions also continued to pursue

Albert Spalding, whom he evidently thought was a bigger name than Burgin, as soloist for his Violin Concerto. He wrote to Spalding on September 20, 1936, that he was "very anxious to know how plans for the Concerto performance are progressing. I suppose the actual dates must have been set; and of course I am most eager to go over it with you, if you have the time to do so." Although Spalding had had the piano score of the first two movements since October of the previous year, at the last moment he would cancel the scheduled performance with the Boston Symphony Orchestra in early December 1936 on the grounds that the last movement was unplayable. Sessions's letters of December 1936 and February 20, 1937, to Spalding are polite, chalking it up to the "fortunes of war," even optimistic, but the composer must have had some notion of the serious consequences of this cancellation.

The two problems in Sessions's life (his divorce and his Violin Concerto) had been resolved the month before his fortieth birthday, one favorably, the other unfavorably. His personal life was finally in order; he had remarried, although by forfeiting Boulanger's (and possibly Copland's) support. His professional life suffered a blow from which it was almost impossible to recover; the canceled Violin Concerto (no matter for whose reasons) led Koussevitzky to banish Sessions's music from the subsequent twenty years of Boston Symphony Orchestra programs. (Spalding, however, was not banished; he continued to perform with the Boston Symphony for nine more years.) It would be twenty-four years before the concerto was heard in New York and even longer before it was heard in Boston.[3] It has never been played by the Boston Symphony Orchestra. Even long after the work was published, Sessions's reputation would suffer from rumors that the concerto was still not completed and was unperformable.

1. Born November 15, 1906, in Washington State, and died July 9, 1982, in Princeton, New Jersey.

2. Ruth Huntington Sessions, *Sixty-Odd: A Personal History* (Brattleboro, Vt.: Stephen Daye Press, 1936).

3. The premiere was January 9, 1940, in Chicago, Illinois, with Robert Gross, violinist. The New York premiere was February 15, 1959, with Tossy Spivakovsky and the New York Philharmonic conducted by Leonard Bernstein. On April 15, 1981, Eric Rosenblith gave the Boston premiere with the New England Conservatory Orchestra, Eiji Oue conducting.

▼

Roger Sessions to David Diamond
als US-Rdiamond

Dear David,—

June 25 [1935]
Berkeley, California

Just a word to tell you how truly happy I am for you.[1] It was nice of you to let me know.

I had a wonderful trip out here, through the southern states. I stopped in New Orleans, which is a wonderful place—and in San Antonio, which is also very beautiful + where I had to stay—as I did very gladly—because of the floods. One never can have any idea what this country really is till one crosses it, I believe. And it hasn't begun to find itself, or be really articulate yet. That's our job, partly. California is beautiful but I don't yet know how I really like it. The country is beautiful here though.

Good luck to you—+ I hope to see you in the fall. If you care to drop me a line occasionally I'll always be glad to hear, + will try to answer. Let me know if I can help in any way. I'd love to.

Yours sincerely
Roger Sessions

1. Diamond had won the Elfrida Whiteman Scholarship, allowing the nineteen-year-old composer to continue his studies with Sessions at the New Music School in the fall.

▼

Henry Cowell to Roger Sessions
tls US-NYpease

Dear Sessions:

July 6, 1935
Box 8, Menlo Park, California

I tried to get you yesterday both at the music dept. and at the hotel—I could not locate you, and did not know where to come. I do hope you will be free to have a visit with me on Monday afternoon. I teach until 4, then would come to wherever you wish. I will try to phone you Monday, but if you are out, could you please leave a message telling me if you will be free to see me, and where you wish me to come[?] There are so many things I wish to discuss with you!

Don't forget about Stanford on Thursday evening. Mr. Allen, the head of musical activities at Stanford, is having us to his home, where I wish to introduce you to my students in creative music, and also the others. Should you feel inclined to speak to them informally on how to begin the study of creative music, or any allied subject, I would be very grateful. This is no grim requirement, however!

Faithfully,
Henry Cowell

▼

Roger Sessions to Aaron Copland
als US-DLC

Saturday [September 7, 1935]
Dear Aaron,—   Hadley [Massachusetts]

Thank you for your note. I am sorry to say, though, that it's quite impossible to get ready for the concert by Oct. 11th.[1] In the first place I won't be in N.Y. till the 23rd of September + cannot make any final arrangements till then. Furthermore I shall want time to check up on L. Engel's arrangements.[2] Finally I have suffered so much from bad + hastily arranged performances that I would far rather give the whole thing up if it has to be done that way.

I am writing to Miss Eels + asking her if she will sing the songs but cannot ask her, + cannot myself consent, to take part if the concert is held before the 25th. I'm sorry to make difficulties for you but there is absolutely no other way. The songs will not be the two that Miss E—— did over the radio, but "On the Beach at Fontana" + two new ones.[3] If I get another work done by Oct. 1st I would also like to substitute that for the [Organ] Chorales.[4]

I don't know who will play the [First] Symphony with me, but I shall certainly be one of the performers.

If you had told me a month or so ago about this change in date I would have been glad to cooperate but at this time it is impossible. I'm sure you'll understand.

I'll see you soon.

As always,
Roger

1. Copland had arranged five concerts, each devoted to a single composer (himself, Sessions, Harris, Piston, and Thomson), at the New School for Social Research, where he taught in 1935. At one point the first concert, October 11, was to have been

Sessions's, but Copland would obligingly take that date for his own works to suit Sessions. Sessions's concert was reviewed by Lazare Saminsky, *Modern Music* 12, no. 2 (January–February 1936): 40–41. The pieces were two-piano versions of the Guisto and Largo from the Symphony No. 1, the song from the *Black Maskers Suite*, and the Concerto for Violin.

2. Lehman Engel (1910–82), a 1934 graduate of the Juilliard Graduate School, studied privately with Roger Sessions 1931–37. He later was involved for many years with musical theater as a composer and a conductor. His autobiography is *The Bright Day* (New York, 1956; rev. ed., 1974).

3. The new songs were "Nightpiece" and "The Last Invocation" to texts by James Joyce and Walt Whitman respectively, neither of which appears in Sessions's catalog.

4. The proposed work, a sonata for solo viola, was not completed as of Sessions's September 10th postcard to Copland (US-DLC), nor was it ever completed.

▼

Roger Sessions to Albert Spalding
tls US-Bu

October 15, 1935

Dear Mr. Spalding: 149 East 61st Street, New York[1]

I am sending the piano score of the first two movements of my concerto to Great Barrington from where I suppose it will be forwarded if you need it.

I just received your letter in regard to Koussevitzky and hope you won't mind if I write you very frankly about this matter. For several reasons I am inclined to think that we should not feel committed to him if there is an acceptable chance for performance elsewhere. First of all, it seems very strange to me that, after having announced the work, he should hedge in the matter. Secondly, he has on several occasions previously, made me unsolicited promises which he then failed to keep and I have no reason to think that he may not do so again.

Finally—and this would make no difference to me if I had not had the experiences of which I speak—a very eminent musician whom I do not of course care to quote, but of whose word there can be no question, told me last year that Koussevitzky had said to him in so many words: "My weakness is that I make so many promises; my strength is that I do not keep them."

I hope you understand the spirit in which I write this. Needless to say, I write it in confidence, but under the circumstances I am sure you will understand why I am not terribly eager to have us go out of our way to save this work for him.

Albert Spalding in the 1930s. Courtesy of Boston University Library.

I have had more than a nibble from Klemperer who, as you know, is a very good personal friend of mine and whom I should love to have give the first performance. I am to show him the score next week and think there is an excellent chance that he may want to do it. Also, I understand that Ormandy[2] has made inquiries.

The remaining pages of the piano part will be ready next week and I will send them to you immediately.

Most cordially yours,
Roger Sessions

[P.S.] Best wishes for your tour!

1. This was a studio apartment Sessions rented in order to live apart from his wife and to give private composition lessons in New York.
2. Eugene Ormandy (1899–1985) was then the music director of the Minneapolis

Symphony Orchestra. In 1936 he became the associate conductor, under Stokowski, of the Philadelphia Orchestra, and in 1938 permanent conductor.

▼

Roger Sessions to Elizabeth S. Coolidge
als US-DLC

Sunday, December 15 [1935]

My dear Mrs. Coolidge,—   New York

Again I must apologize for my tardiness in writing you; but this time my reason is that I have been thinking very seriously about the matter of the work for Harvard next fall and trying to visualize to myself what I want to do. It seems to me that if I wrote a work for solo voice, the voice would have to be a man's; a woman's voice would not be appropriate to the occasion, it seems to me, or even to the words I would choose.

The sad fact of it is that I have not been able to get up any enthusiasm for writing a long work for a man's voice alone. It is I suppose very largely a matter of the register + the color of a man's voice, also of a feeling which I have that a really good man's voice requires an orchestra to sustain it adequately, especially in a piece whose character would actually be festive and affirmative, rather than introspective.

I hope so much that you will understand my point of view + will not be disappointed if I propose, after all, to send you a quartet. The quartet I have in mind is one on which I began sketching some time ago, and it will be a work of decidedly large dimensions—four, + possibly even five, movements. If this is acceptable I would be very grateful if you would let me know, since I would want to deliver it by the middle of June at the latest.[1] I shall be going to California again and would want the quartet to be ready by the time I leave.

I hope you are still having a pleasant winter. And a Merry Christmas and Happy New Year to you all.

Most sincerely,
Roger Sessions

1. The String Quartet No. 1 in E Minor, in three movements, would not be completed until late 1936. The score is marked "New York, Pyramid Lake, Nevada, Princeton, 1936."

▼

Roger Sessions to Nadia Boulanger
als F-PBN

[Spring 1936]
New York

Dear Mademoiselle,—

I am sending this by my friend + pupil Mr. David Diamond; I know that when you meet him you will understand why I think so very much of him, + feel that he is one of the truly few.

This is not the place to write you a real letter—above all after so long. Very soon I shall write you one, however, + then I know you will understand why I have been silent—even though I cannot really excuse myself for having been so.[1] But it is, truly, a real joy to me to send you this friend, than whom I cannot imagine a more truly satisfying representation of myself.

Always affectionately
Roger

1. This is Sessions's last surviving letter to Boulanger. He had not sent her a condolence letter on the death of her mother, March 19, 1935.

▼

Roger Sessions and Elizabeth Franck to David Diamond
als US-Rdiamond

July 19, 1936
Berkeley, California

Dear David,—

Just a line in answer to your[s] wh. I was so glad to have. I am working furiously on the last stages of the quartet which, though it has gone much more easily than anything I have written since [illegible], is very taxing! I think it is turning out well, though in some respects it is a new departure in my work.

I'm delighted to hear that the ballet[1] is going so well + look forward to hearing more news of it, when you write a letter. I'm truly so happy for you that you have this opportunity to do it, + I hope so much that it is going to come out the way you would like to have it—

We had a splendid trip, though it was hellishly hot in New Orleans + in fact from there as far as Los Angeles, + I'm afraid Lisl was pretty uncomfortable a good deal of the time. But she says now that she only remembers how beautiful some of it was. The nicest part, aside from New Orleans + San Antonio, was the southeast, a leisurely drive through Alabama, [from] Tuskeegee to Mobile—wonderful, lush, southern vegetation; + then the next morning along the coast to N[ew] O[rleans]. The latter is absolutely unique; as I drove into it I felt almost as if I were entering some Chinese town. It's far more exotic than Europe—unless it be some places in Italy or, I imagine, Spain. Naturally I mean the French quarter; the rest is America with tropical vegetation.

I am living in the same [place] I had last summer. Lisl lives in San Francisco + I go over to dine and spend evenings with her. It seemed the most practical arrangement, finally—much cheaper for us to live here, + we would have had to be much more circumspect, if she lived here or in Oakland. As it is she is near her brother and sister in law, + near various friends. [illegible] we are tremendously happy together; we [have] decided to be married in Nov. + she will go to Spokane after I leave here, till she comes east.

I won't write more now—this isn't much of a letter but it must do for the present. And it brings much love from both of us.

Most affectionately
Roger

P.S. (1) The Pro Arte are to play my quartet all over the place next year.

(2) Did you hear that Henry Cowell is in San Quentin prison—sentenced from 1 to 15 years![2]

I think I'll ask Lisl to add a word to this tomorrow.

[In Elizabeth Franck's hand:]

Dear David—

I enjoyed reading your postal so much. I only hope the letter arrives before I leave here. I'm so curious to hear how you like Paris, and if the strikes there and general unrest[3] are noticeable to the innocent bystander. And be careful, David, and don't *you* embrace any cause and get shot for your principles.

Roger and I are having a beautiful time here and it is going all too quickly. I am going to be very forlorn and [illegible] when I am back in Spokane as I feel quite lost if a [illegible] passes here and we don't see each other. R. looks so well and [illegible] so much alone that I wish he could stay out here always. It's so unlike N.Y. and we have such a peaceful, quiet time here.

I think R. wrote about the trip—it was really beautiful almost the entire way—but hot—David 115° and 120°. I yelped a lot about the heat but R. cheered me up and spurred me on and didn't seem to mind it half as much as I did. It's funny, too—he's as cosy and warm as a Nuremberg stove in the winter and yet that intense heat didn't bother him so much.

Do write as often as you can as we are both so glad to hear from you, and have a marvelous summer.

Lisl

1. Diamond's unpublished ballet, *Tom*, set to a scenario by e. e. cummings, was written in Paris in association with Léonide Massine.

2. Cowell was convicted for performing a homosexual act with a minor. Under pressure from Copland and numerous others, the governor of California granted him a pardon five years later.

3. France experienced extreme political instability during the Great Depression. Riots in 1934 had brought the country to the brink of civil war. The Popular Front, formed in 1935 by French Communists and Socialists, saw the election in 1936 of its leader, Léon Blum.

▼

Roger Sessions to Elizabeth S. Coolidge
als US-DLC

August 22, 1936
TH Ranch at Pyramid Lake
Dear Mrs. Coolidge,—   Sutcliffe, Nevada

This is to tell you that the first two movements of my quartet are at last on their way, + will have reached Mr. Keller[1] by the time this reaches you. I truly thought I had them all ready when I saw you last; but a considerable section of slow movement failed at the last moment to satisfy me + I simply couldn't send it off in that shape. I ought to have let you know, + would have done so if I hadn't thought that it was simply a matter of a day or two. The result was, I felt hurried + got stuck. I am terribly sorry + ashamed; + though I know you will understand, I should not blame you in the slightest if you felt quite disgusted with me, + really annoyed.

As far as the last movement is concerned I am working well on it here where I have nothing to do but compose + can now devote all my time to finishing it up. I do not want to make rash promises but feel very sure that I can get it off by the first of September, or in two weeks at any rate. I am working extremely well here + the movement is far less exacting than the others, with far less difficult detail.

I see no reason why Mr. Keller could not—if he finds it possible to play one movement—do the slow movement by itself. It has occurred to me that the Finale is perhaps too much a Finale—+ in any case he would have far too little time in which to prepare it. Though the slow movement contains some difficult passages I believe it is musically easier than the first—+ I believe it stands alone better than the others.

You will see from my address the reason why I cannot come to Cambridge + why I did not give you a better reason for not doing so. It was hard for me, simply, to speak of my plans, especially under the circumstances in which we met each time in California. As you perhaps know, my wife + I have been living apart for two years + although the decision to make our separation permanent was not an easy one for either of us, it seemed to us both the wisest thing to do, + best also to do it in this way. Luckily the beauty of the country here + the joy of being able to compose uninterruptedly make up to some extent for what, under the very best of circumstances, could be in no way a happy experience.

But I am very sorry, however, not to be at Harvard, + appreciate so much your kindness in wanting to make this possible. I shall of course be thinking of all of you there at that time.

I shall let you know the moment the Finale of the quartet is on its way. Please once more accept my sincerest apologies for all this delay, + believe me, with all good wishes,

Most sincerely yours,
Roger Sessions

1. Harrison Keller (1885–1967), later president of the New England Conservatory 1952–58.

▼

Roger Sessions to Elizabeth S. Coolidge
als US-DLC

September 12, 1936
Dear Mrs. Coolidge,—   Sutcliffe, Nevada

I am of course very much disappointed that Mr. Keller had to decide as he did [against playing the quartet]. It surprises me, however, to hear that he did not receive my Ms. till Sept. 3rd. As the enclosed receipt will show you, it was signed for on Aug. 31st. Even that, however, was several days later than I was assured here that it would arrive. It is true that there was some delay in mailing it on account of the distance from the rather primitive desert post-office on which we depend for mail service. I don't know how much difference a few days more would have made, though since the quartet was disbanded till Sept. 1st they could not in any case have begun work on it before that day. But it does seem strange to me that the package should have apparently lain around for three days at the New England Conservatory, when Mr. Keller was presumably expecting it + when it was obviously sent by air mail. And while I understand very well that there may be circumstances of which I know nothing, a considerable experience makes it very difficult for me to believe that the slow movement could not have been adequately prepared in two weeks. From all of these circumstances I can only conclude that Mr. Keller had made up his mind in advance not to perform the work, or at least was unwilling to make any effort to do so.

Your decision with regard to the rights, coming as it has at this time, has been a serious blow, and I am trying very hard to understand your reasons for it. If you had reached this decision earlier in the summer, when the matter first came up, I should have understood without hesitation + could have made some provision for it. But since I had your assurance, both verbal + written that you wanted the work in any case, + would make other plans for its performance in case the Harvard performance fell through, I felt that my first responsibility was that of any artist worthy of the name—that of producing the best work of which I was capable. That I am sure you will be the first to understand. If I had done less I should have felt that I was giving you something second-rate, + that I had no right to accept either your money or your support.

On the other hand it is perfectly obvious that I failed in one particular to do as I had originally undertaken; and also as I have already written you I can easily understand your being annoyed at the delays. Please try to believe however that I did my best, as indeed anyone could abundantly testify who has [been] closely associated with me this summer, or so anyone whatever could see from the three hundred odd pages of sketches which I have made. It has been the cause of real distress to me, ever since I began to realize that if the work was to satisfy me I could not have it ready as soon as I had planned. Unfortunately I have always worked slowly—in this case faster and better than usual; and in the excitement of my work I have more than once underestimated the amount of time I needed for it. But far better men than I have also done this, and if I may say so it seems to me to be a very natural product of intense work under pressure.

However, for all the above reasons I am perfectly ready to abide by your decision if you still feel that you must hold to it, even though it means rather serious consequences for me. I have written you as I have done first of all because these consequences are serious, but also because I hope you will also feel that there is another side to the matter. In any case I believe I have the right to ask you not to doubt my good faith and my good will, which I shall continue to show in my attitude towards your decision, whatever it is.

I am certainly not asking you to change your mind if you are disinclined to do so; but I am taking no steps regarding the performance of the quartet till I have heard from you again. In any case I shall be here only about ten days longer and so would prefer not to entrust the two movements which you have in your possession to the mails just yet. If you wish me to do so I can send for them when I am in the East again.

I am a little embarrassed about the dedication, since you may not wish to have your name used at all in connection with this work. It is already on the cover, however, and since a dedication has always been for me much more than a formality I cannot think of the quartet as anything but yours. If you wish me to omit the dedication I shall of course understand perfectly; but I have tried to write a work that you would be glad to have dedicated to you + if you could still be willing to accept the dedication it would make me very happy.

I shall of course be thinking of you all in Cambridge during the next days and for more than one reason regretting that I cannot be there, as I certainly should be if quite exceptional and imperative circumstances did not make that impossible. I still look forward, however, to receiving the program, if you will have it sent to me.

Forgive me for troubling you with such a long letter, and believe me always,

Most sincerely yours,
Roger Sessions

▼

Roger Sessions to David Diamond
als US-Rdiamond

September 20, 1936
Dear David,—   Sutcliffe, Nevada

Your letter reached me here—but it was shortly before you sailed, + I was afraid I could not get a letter to you from the wilds of Nevada in time!—I haven't much time to write now—but let's hope we'll be seeing each other soon; my divorce trial "comes off" Tuesday (the 22nd) and I shall start driving east on Wednesday morning early!

But I have thought of you so much, + hope that the summer has been a good one. I had a letter the other day from Nadia B[oulanger] + she spoke so very nicely about you—only said you had not shown her you music—+ she was disappointed. How come?

But I'm afraid this letter must be chiefly about my own affairs—forgive me but I have so many things to do just in these days + have so little time to write.

First of all—Lisl + I will be married in the fall, but neither of us yet knows just when. I have had a rather severe blow, financially, about which I won't go into details just now; but this *may* force us to postpone our marriage till the Christmas vacation. In any case, we want you to be at the wedding,—as one of the witnesses if my brother should *not* be there, since of course I suppose he will have to act as witness if he is. But the two people we really want with us that day are you and my cousin Catharine Huntington. Also—I wish you wouldn't say anything much about the fact that I am to be married, just yet in any case;[1] I shall tell very few people, in any case, probably, as we want it quiet.

Secondly—are you planning to go on with me this year, on the same basis as last; + if so will you come to Princeton for your lessons, or will you want to have them in N.Y.? If the latter, we must arrange a time.

Finally; I wonder if you could possibly do me a great favor. The point is I shall not be able to get to N.Y. till later in the evening of the 29th, + I have to move the next day. I wonder if you could possibly go to my house + get the key, + meet me in N.Y. somewhere quite late that evening. I enclose a note to Mrs. Johnson, the caretaker, asking her to let you have my key. In case I should get in late I don't want to bother her, that's all. Could we plan to meet, say, at Child's on Lexington Ave. near 58th St. at 10:30 P.M. Tuesday the 29th?

Finally—+ I *hope* I'm not asking too much—could you find out a little about movers, + see what the possibilities are? I have to move out of my house on Wednesday + if I can possibly do so I want to leave everything unsettled till Wednesday itself. If it has to be done, however—could you *possibly* plan to be there on Wed. to see the movers for me?—Or, I suppose Mrs. Johnson would take care of that for me. I want my things moved out, of course, in any case, + it's just possible that I shall want them transported by truck to Princeton—some of them in any case. But that I can't decide till I have been to Princeton, Tuesday afternoon, you see.

The movers will perhaps be busy on Tuesday as it is the last day of the month—so the sooner you can see Mrs. Johnson + consult with her about this, the better. The problem is, of course, that big bed; the trunk, + the smaller things—even the books + music, I could probably arrange to carry to Princeton by car; but the bed, as far as I can see, will have to be carried downstairs at least by professional movers.

But if you could see Mrs. Johnson + consult her about this as soon as possible I would be very much obliged indeed.

There is of course another problem—I have to do this as cheaply as possible; it's simply that I have very little money, + have had this blow which makes the next few weeks an absolute nightmare from that point of view.—

I hope all this is [illegible] to you—I've had to write it in such a hurry that I could well believe it might not be! My final request is this; will you send me a line, c/o Mrs. Paul S. Andrews [Sessions's sister, Hannah], Wolf Hollow, Onondaga Rd., Onondaga, N.Y. mailed *not later than Saturday,* telling me how all this stands? The point is that I am going to be in New Brunswick + Princeton on Tuesday A.M. + that I may not be able to return till later that evening—If I don't hear from you there (I shall be there most of Monday + shall leave very early Tues. morning) I shall simply assume that you didn't get my letter in time or for some reason were unable to do this.

You see the trouble is that I can't possibly leave here till Wednesday morning + that will give me barely enough time to get to N.Y. before I have to move, + to Princeton in time for my classes! Otherwise I wouldn't dream of asking all this of you.—It is of course quite possible that you are still in Rochester. If you are, and would like to drive down to New Brunswick with me on the 29th—+ later, in to N.Y.—why not come to Syracuse on Monday—+ call me up some-

David Diamond in 1990. Photograph copyright by Phil Matt.
Courtesy of David Diamond.

time in the afternoon or eve. *chez* my sister, so that we could arrange to meet[?] You would save some money, + it would be fun. But nine chances out of ten this is just a wild idea of mine.

Anyway I'm crazy to see you.—

Affectionately as always
Roger—

1. This request for secrecy, reminiscent of Sessions's similar requests of Father Sill and George Bartlett at the time of his first engagement, was belated: Diamond had already told Boulanger about Sessions's divorce.

Roger Sessions to Albert Spalding
als US-Bu

[December 1936]
Dear Mr. Spalding,—   Pennington, New Jersey

Your very kind letter arrived on Wednesday and I should have answered it immediately had I not literally been occupied every moment since then.

I was of course quite prepared for your decision and you may be sure that I fully appreciate and respect your reasons for it. I hope that by this time you are convinced that nothing in your first letter offended me in any sense of the word. While I should have preferred it if the issue could have been raised earlier, I feel nevertheless that the whole matter is one of those possibly regrettable but thoroughly comprehensible things which may conceivably happen to any artist, and belongs, so to speak, to the "fortunes of war." I want you to know, too, how very much I appreciate your whole attitude in the matter, which has certainly, by way of courtesy and graciousness, exceeded what I should normally have had the right to expect. For this reason I would feel exceedingly sorry if you felt any misgivings or regrets on my account.

It is most kind and gracious of you to offer to help with possible expenses incurred in the projected performance—so much so in fact that I feel a little diffident in assuring you that I had none! The expenses for copying etc. were all borne by my publisher[1] who seems quite willing to regard the matter philosophically and to keep the material in readiness for possible future use. So please do not think me ungrateful if I have no occasion to accept your most generous offer.

It would be a real favor if you would send the Ms. of the violin part and the piano arrangement, at your convenience, to the Affiliated Music Corporation, 16th floor, Steinway Hall.

With cordial regards to you + Mrs. Spalding,

Most sincerely,
Roger Sessions

1. The Affiliated Music Corporation, headed by Vladimir Lakond, published the Violin Concerto in 1937.

▼

Roger Sessions to Albert Spalding
als US-Bu

February 20, 1937
Pennington, New Jersey

Dear Mr. Spalding,—

I owe you many apologies for delaying so long in answering your letter. I wanted to think over the whole matter of the Concerto + to give your suggestions the consideration they deserve as coming from an artist of your calibre. But there is no valid excuse for my not having acknowledged your personal message[1] + I only hope you + Mrs. Spalding will nevertheless accept a very belated apology + thanks. My wife and I both appreciated it so very much, and you would have heard from me long before this had I not waited for matters which I felt could not be rushed.

In regard to the Concerto you must be sure that I not only appreciate your frankness but that I should not have dreamed of expecting anything else. I think I realize at least to a very large extent the great demands that a contemporary composer makes on those who perform his work, and the very real problems with which the latter is faced. It is partly for this reason that I have never felt inclined to push performances of my works to any extent, since I believe in them sufficiently to be able to wait if necessary.

I hope that you will believe me when I tell you that I have taken your suggestions very seriously. You may be sure that I went over the work very thoroughly + seriously, and as open-mindedly as possible. Nevertheless, with regard to the last movement as well as to the rest, I could only come to the conclusion that I had written it exactly as I want it, and that to make changes which would under the circumstances amount to altering the whole conception of the work, would be out of the question for me.

If it were a matter of violin technique I should be more than glad to listen to your advice and to accept it. I have shown you, I think, how willing I am to do this, even though I had the collaboration of a first class violinist [Max Strub] in writing the first three movements and to a large extent the last also, and although I have heard the whole violin part played, to my satisfaction and that of other musicians who were present at the time.

When it comes to alterations in the music however, you yourself will surely understand that it is an entirely different matter. I have never written an unconsidered note, and, though I hope I have learned enough about music not to claim infallibility, I can take responsibility only for the music which I myself have written and to which I have given the best of which I am capable.

When you first told me that you found the last movement "unrelieved" I assumed that you were referring to the "emotional content" of the work and I tried to point out what, if properly understood and played according to my directions, should bring the necessary contrast. When you speak of "relentless staccato" (I should say rather *détaché*) I can only point to various more sustained passages which occur throughout the movement. This however seems to me not entirely relevant since, unless I quite misunderstand you, it is not this or that detail, but rather the music itself, its whole character and texture, that you find unsympathetic.

If this is the case please be sure that I should be the first to understand how such a thing can happen and that I want you to feel perfectly free with regard to the performance of the work. It goes without saying that I still hope you will feel like performing it next season. But while a further postponement would naturally be a disappointment to me, I would nevertheless be perfectly ready, in case you wish to withdraw, to accept the situation, since it would be wholly distasteful to me if you should feel any obligation to it on grounds not dictated by your own artist's conscience. Please forgive me if I seem to raise an issue which you yourself have not raised; but I am very keenly aware of your courtesy + your consideration of my interests in this matter, and appreciate it enough not to wish to incommode you in any way.

After having delayed so long in writing I can hardly ask for a prompt answer, but I am sure you understand that I would appreciate a word whenever it is convenient for you to write me about all this.

With kindest regards to you + Mrs. Spalding,

Most cordially,
Roger Sessions

1. Probably a congratulatory note on Sessions's marriage.

◥◣◢◤

SESSIONS'S STRING QUARTET NO. 1 in E Minor was performed by the Coolidge Quartet[1] at the Eighth Festival of Chamber

Music, April 10 and 11, 1937, in Washington, D.C. The *New York Times* critic Olin Downes reported:

> This quartet reflects the composer's care and scruple in his work. It is clean-cut writing, unified in conception and worked out with a musician's logic and modern feeling for rhythm. Whether the thematic material is slender or not, and the bloodstream of the music thin for the length of its course, are matters more intimate acquaintance with the work would clearly establish. Often what impresses as finical or cerebral at a first hearing becomes pertinent and salient at the second hearing or the tenth. The composition has an admirable clarity of line and directness of style. There is no thought of mere effect and there is the strictness, scruple and fastidiousness of method.[2]

Its subsequent New York premiere at a recital of the Chamber Music Society of America was reviewed by a young Elliott Carter: after the concert had "opened with a tiresome talk by Roy Harris, the new and important quartet of Roger Sessions was played. Though no single theme is outstanding (as is often the case with Beethoven) every detail, the cadences, the way the themes are brought in, the texture, the flexibility of the bass, were such as to give constant delight, and at times to be genuinely moving. His sense of a large line gave the music a certain roominess without ever being over expansive."[3]

Sessions wrote of the quartet's reception to his friend Antonio Borgese (April 27, 1937, I-Fborgese): "My string quartet was very successful both in Washington and in New York. The best reception I had after the First Symphony that had launched me in the world. It was very encouraging because it shows me that perhaps luck is turning towards me."[4] Borgese (1882–1952), formerly a professor of German literature at the University of Rome (1910–17), had come to the United States in 1917 as a visiting professor at the University of California. Sessions had met him in 1934, when Borgese taught at Smith College. In May and June 1937 Sessions wrote (again in Italian) to Borgese, who was then living in Chicago after a visit to Mexico, in response to Borgese's proposal to collaborate on an opera about the conquest of the Aztecs by Cortez.

Sessions had the opportunity in the summer of 1937 to travel to Mexico, where he, like Borgese, became inspired to write about its history. Thanks to the generosity of Elizabeth Sprague Coolidge, he was a participant in an event she sponsored, the first Pan-American Music Festival, held in Mexico City, July 13–24, with Carlos Chávez as artistic director. The Coolidge Quartet played on five of the six concerts, and the Ruvalcaba Quartet played works by Chávez; the festival's prizewinner, Jacobo Ficher; and the recipient of an honorable mention, Francisco Casabona. A concert by the Orquesta Mexicana, using both Indian and European instruments, must have struck Sessions deeply and influenced the percussion writing of *Montezuma.* The entire festival was written up in *Musical America.*[5]

1. The members at that time were William Kroll, first violin; Nicholai Berezowsky, second violin; Nicolas Moldavan, viola; and Victor Gottlieb, cello. The Sessions opened the long program, followed by the Brahms Quartet in B♭ and the winning quartet of the Coolidge Prize for 1936, Jerzy Fitelberg's Quartet.
2. Olin Downes, "Festival of Music Closes in Capital," *New York Times,* April 12, 1937, 14:3.
3. Elliott Carter, "Season's End in New York," *Modern Music* 14 (May 1937): 216.
4. Translated from the Italian by Valeria Secchi Short.
5. José Barros Sierra, "Pan-American Festival Held in Mexico," *Musical America* 57, no. 14 (September 1937): 8, 27.

▼

Roger Sessions to David Diamond
als US-Rdiamond

June 15, 1937
Dear David,—   Carter Road, Princeton

I'm sorry you had such an uncomfortable trip.[1] Also I'm glad to hear of the new orchestral piece.

We are in our new home and enjoying it tremendously, of course. It is a relief to have all this free time. [Illegible][2] frightfully busy. But I [illegible] a couple of hours out of [illegible] each day, + that has already me over. So the summer bids fair to be a good one. I shall be here all summer except for a couple of days in Chicago around July 1st. The symphony will be done, never fear.[3] No—don't say a word to Szigeti about the concerto; though I rather doubt if he is in Paris just now. I have written him that it is free + he knows all the rest. Much better if it remains quite between him + me.

Please be on the look out, at Fontainebleau, for a fifteen (16?) year old boy named Andrew Imbrie.[4] He is to be there for the summer— he is a Princeton boy who is to enter the university year after next. I think he has real talent—quite remarkable for his age, though undeveloped as yet + full of obvious influences— + I believe contact with you might do him good.

And don't *you* let *me* down! By which I don't mean, certainly any course of action which anyone—including myself—can [illegible] even in [illegible] most insidious guise of "opportunity" dull your sense of what you *have* to be + do. I daresay this seems like nonsense to you but you will understand some day. However it is one of those things which it does absolutely no good to say, since, if you really have in you what I have always believed, you need no advice— + if you shouldn't have the strength nobody's advice could save you. So—good luck + know you always have my best wishes, + more.

Give my love to N[adia] B[oulanger], + write again.

As always
Roger

1. Earlier in June Diamond had returned to Paris for further studies with Boulanger.
2. Some of Sessions's letters to Diamond were later damaged by fire, hence the large number of illegible words and tentative readings. Diamond saved all of the more than fifty letters he received from Sessions; of the eight letters from Diamond that Sessions saved, seven date from 1937.
3. Sessions later abandoned work on this second symphony.
4. Imbrie (b. 1921) grew up in Princeton, where he studied with Sessions at first privately, then at Princeton University. In 1945 he continued his studies with Sessions at the University of California at Berkeley (M.A., 1947), where he later taught (1960–91).

▼

David Diamond to Roger and Elizabeth Sessions
als US-NYpease

July 12, 1937
29 Rue de la Cloche

My very dear Roger + Lisl,   Fontainebleau

It's been so long since I've heard from you, and in all sincerity, I long for some word from you. Perhaps there will be mail in Paris at the American Express Co. I shall go into Paris tomorrow. As for my life and experience here,—all goes well, and Nadia treats me no differently than anyone else which leads me to think she has no intention of ever mentioning my staying on. She spends much time with me, going over my works I wrote in N.Y.,—the [First] Violin Concerto, the [String] Trio, the Psalm,[1] etc. also much counterpoint.

I thought it best to show her the counterpoint I did with you, as I am now working on 4 part counterpoint, 5th species, with two florid parts. I was amused with her corrections of my three part + four part ctpt. second species (which I finished with you) for she found many of the 3 part exercises good, but not in agreement with her idea of strict counterpoint. She said nothing about you but stated, "That everyone has a different preference when counterpoint exercises are concerned." I'm sure you'll be glad to know though that I am working hard at ctpt. and I'll be glad to get through the stuff next year for I'd much rather be doing analysis. I work now and then on the *Aria + Hymn*[2] with Nadia, and next week we shall play it for the composition class. I've begun the orchestration, and play it at two pianos with Nadia. Her general remarks on my work are that it is very serious, mature, and the work of a real creator. This is encouraging, and I know she'd not say it to me if she didn't mean it. *But* she thinks my style much *too* dissonant! Strange! I always thought it very lukewarm. My form she thinks excellent, and orchestration wonderful. All these are her own words. So I'm not exaggerating any, but giving a detailed report. She would like very much to have me watch out for *too many* notes in my music, and she may be right. All in all, her main intention is that I belong to you, and quite glad I am with her for the summer, and happy that she can see you, Aaron, and everyone else again in N.Y. in February. Now the surprise. Last Sunday, Stravinsky asked the advanced students of Nadia to his home with works. I was delighted that she asked me, and we played the *Psalm* for Stravinsky at one piano—4 hands from score. I was so nervous with Stravinsky behind me all the time I could hardly play but I think we both gave a good impression of the work. After I left, Nadia said he thought the work the most mature and provoking, the orchestration very original but *too dissonant!* And the use of syncopation in the allegro not varied enough. This alone made me happy. [illegible] are asked back again in two weeks and I shall bring either the Violin Concerto or the *Trio*. Nadia asked Andrew Imbrie to come, and Stravinsky was amused for he found the *Symphony* Imbrie is writing full of everything written in the past 35 years. Naturally he said he was very young. And one night, as I walked home with Nadia, her impression was that he is very young, but a *real* talent and she has her eye on keeping him *I'm sure.* Her whole attitude is *that* to him, while with me she feels it useless for "I have done so much already" (these are her words)—! So you see my dear Roger, as soon as the money is given me (from where I don't know) to come back, I shall do so with a great deal of joy and anticipation in seeing you again. How I'll live in N.Y., I don't know. I shall probably have to live in Rochester, and see you once a month, or work in New York. I must write for a Guggenheim application.[3]

I find Imbrie very sympathetic, very young, and eager to work. The Hofstaders are constantly with him, and I find them "bores," so I do not bother with anyone out here. As you can imagine, the general student average is dreadful as far as ability goes, and I have not met one who is sympathetic to my work. When I'm not writing the *Aria + Hymn* or the League commission[4] I usually go into the forest, or Paris. But Fontainebleau is so beautiful, and I have a fine room to work in. What more can I possibly want for 2 months? I attended the International Festival and saw Jerzy.[5] His new *Violin Concerto* is a really fine work, but the orchestration I find much too elaborate, and the length of great weakness. This seems to be his weakness. He asked of you, and no doubt will write. Roussel[6] said he is writing you. Has he? I saw him two weeks ago before he left for the country.

Met Mark Brunswick for a few moments at one of Nadia's concerts, and he seemed very kind. This is about all for news. You must write me about your summer, and what you work on. And one important thing. Do you feel, that if for some reason, Nadia can find a way to have me stay in Paris until she returns to America[7] because I am so unsettled about a way to live in New York this winter. Shall I stay on? I want *really* to come back in October, but what will I live on, where will I live, and how will I work? What did you pay for your room at E. 61st? Could you get a reduced rent rate for me? Can this be a possible solution? Or, do you think it would be indiscreet for me to write Aaron to let me live in his studio and work there if he lives at the [Empire] Hotel? You see how complicated it really is? Or would you feel Rochester (dreadful though the idea is to me) a better solution?

I can hardly rest at peace with myself feeling so unsure about my life this winter, and I want to do so much, and New York is where I belong to do it! Too, my sister[8] has been ailing with her pregnancy (she has lost one child, and is threatened with miscarriage again), so you realize how jittery I am, for my devotion to her is unbounded. If Nadia cannot tell me how my fare back will be taken care of by the next month, I shall have to ask Mrs. Reis to send me the $100 balance on the commission. Even this won't be enough for fare.

Do you hear from Nicky [Berezowsky] or Fred [Jacobi] at all? Haven't had word from either of them, but I imagine they are away for the summer. I look at your photo now, and am so thankful for all you've done [illegible] how much my [illegible] wonderful intuition and patience. Believe me with all my heart, I shall never let you down. I'd much rather die than ever do this. Truthfully. I hope you are happy for me, that my work goes well, and write. Please!

Always, my affection,
David

P.S. I shall send my ctpt exercises with Nadia to you at the end of this month.

1. The Violin Concerto was played in New York March 24; the trio is the unpublished 1937 String Trio; the Psalm for Orchestra received the Juilliard Publication Award in 1937.
2. Diamond's 1937 *Aria and Hymn* for full orchestra.
3. In September Diamond returned first to Rochester, N.Y., his hometown, then to New York City, where he took a three-day-a-week drugstore job as he had the previous winter.
4. Diamond's Quintet for Flute, Piano, and Strings.
5. Jerzy Fitelberg's Violin Concerto No. 2 was first performed at the Paris Festival of the ISCM, June 22, 1937.
6. French composer Albert Roussel (1869–1937) was influenced by Impressionism and exotic and mythological subjects.
7. Boulanger's U.S. tour of 1938–39, in which she conducted the Boston Symphony Orchestra and the New York Philharmonic.
8. Sabina Diamond Cohen (1901–91).

▼

Roger Sessions to Elizabeth S. Coolidge
als US-DLC

July 26, 1937
Dear Mrs. Coolidge,—   Hotel Reforma, Mexico City

I am leaving for Vera Cruz tomorrow,[1] and cannot go away from Mexico without writing you once more how tremendously grateful I feel for your kindness in sending me to the [Pan-American] Festival as your guest, and how much it has meant to me. From every point of view it was an extremely interesting and valuable experience for me, and I feel that I owe you a very great deal—not only the concerts but delightful and rich personal contacts which I found there, too—as well as the thrill of seeing Mexico for the first time.

I know you will want to hear all about the Festival, and I will try to write you my impressions as well as I can. First of all you will have heard already from others how completely the Coolidge quartet carried off the honors, as far as performance was concerned—at every concert except the first they received a veritable ovation, for the classic works which they played, and each time except the last they were obliged to repeat one of the movements of the quartet of the program. Their reception was utterly spontaneous and enthusiastic, and you would have been delighted at it. You will be delighted, too, I know, that Ernest Ansermet, who heard the Brahms and the Beethoven performed, expressed himself in superlative terms about the quartet. I need not tell you of course that you have every reason to be proud of them, but I know that it will please you to hear that they have been so sincerely and so spontaneously appreciated.

As far as the contemporary works are concerned, the public seemed, I should say, polite and occasionally interested rather than enthusiastic. I had the feeling that it was a public which is still very much in the process of education, and lacking in self-confidence and experience. I do not deduce this from the fact that its enthusiasm was not greater; simply its uniformly moderate response seemed to me that of an uncertain rather than hostile or even bored public. To some extent, perhaps, they responded more warmly to the compositions of a noticeably simpler style; but as far as I could judge this actually made little difference.

I myself was very much pleased to feel that the "North American" and to some extent the Mexican works[2] were the ones which really gave tone to the contemporary parts of the program; and since my attitude towards my colleagues has always been a very detached and often a decidedly critical one I feel that I am saying this quite impartially. If the performances from the Mexican side had been always up to the high standards set by the Coolidge quartet and by [Jesús] Sanromá, I could perhaps include the Mexican works unreservedly in the same category. I felt however that the Mexicans themselves did not show their works to the best advantage, and therefore I do not feel able entirely to judge them. The three Indian arrangements (I include the work of Chávez which was played on that occasion, though it is not entirely Indian)[3] on the second program, and the work of Revueltas on the fourth, however, were full of color + suggestiveness and seemed to me to go along with the works of Harris, Piston, and Copland as decidedly standing out among the modern works played. Of the three American works mentioned that of Harris,[4] in spite of considerable reservations, pleased me the most. I refer in particular to the slow movement which contains really beautiful things which I recalled with genuine pleasure, having heard the work in Pittsfield for the first time three years ago. The trio of

Piston,[5] and "Music for the Theatre" of Copland are works of more mature and complete musicians and if I like the Harris work better than them it is with due reservations.

As for the South American works on the programs it seemed to me that the prize quartet of Ficher[6] was by far the best; it was obviously a serious work, well written and especially in the second third and fourth movements, well worth hearing. The quartet played it, as far as I could judge, very well and I think all the musicians with whom I spoke felt that it was decidedly a stronger work than the work by Casabona which received honorable mention.

I felt that, all things considered, the Festival achieved its principal aims admirably by throwing into relief the characteristics of the different nations involved. As I said before, it was a real joy to see that the United States works were, by and large, the most serious, the most "evolved" and the most individual works played, while the Mexican works were the most highly colored and perhaps the most immediately striking. I do not mean to dwell on this point but it really seemed very clear, to the others in our party as well as to myself. In any case it was inestimably interesting to see what the achievement of this continent has been; and especially interesting to have this experience in Mexico, where—speaking at least for myself— one has such a sense of what autochthonous American civilization has been in the past and such a quickened hope for what it has the opportunity to become in the future. And while I still believe that music belongs to humanity as a whole and that it is in the very truest sense a universal—that is, a human rather than a parochial—language, it is of the first importance to us all to have had this opportunity to get a reasonably accurate picture of what the American (in the largest sense) achievement is as a whole.

After that, as I said to Mr. [Richard] Buhlig, American music has to stand or fall by comparison, first with the contemporary music of the world as a whole, and then, as a part of that contemporary music, with the masters of all time.

I hope I am not boring you too much with all this, and must tell you what a real pleasure it has been to see Sprague and Peggy.[7] It was very nice to find them in the train just out of St. Louis, and I very greatly enjoyed my trip down with them, as well as the many shorter visits I have had with them since. It has seemed to me a friendship so well worth renewing after a lapse of nearly twenty-five years. It was also a very great pleasure to see more of Buhlig, whom I liked quite extraordinarily much, and Miss Caldwell and Miss Gowdy. So you can see that also from the human side it was a very rich time for me, and for that too I am more grateful than I can say.

As for Mexico itself I have become a real enthusiast, as Miss Caldwell and Buhlig will tell you, no doubt, when you see them. I shall probably be boring all my friends with it for some time to come, so I will not begin by boring you with it now. But for this third reason, too, I am grateful to you. The only *real* sorrow—and a very considerable one—for all of us was that you could not be there. Literally we were speaking of you all the time and missed you not only for yourself but as part of the festival, so to speak. This letter is I am afraid a very unsuccessful effort to help make up for what you missed; but you may be sure it brings you all my affectionate thoughts and the feelings of really great disappointment which I shared with everyone else, that circumstances made it impossible for you to be there.

I hope so much that you have had a pleasant and successful summer. And let me express to you once more my truly deep gratitude.

With every good wish, and sincere affection

Yours
Roger Sessions

1. On July 29 Sessions wrote to Copland, who along with the pianist Richard Buhlig remained in Mexico City as a guest of Mrs. Coolidge's, expressing relief that Copland had escaped the earthquake. Copland was remaining in Mexico City for the premiere of *El Salón Mexico* on August 27, with Chávez conducting.

2. The U.S. was represented at the festival by music of Copland, Harris, Piston, Sessions, and Edward Burlingame Hill; Mexico by Carlos Chávez, Silvestre Revueltas, Manuel Ponce (1882–1948), Ayala, Sandi, and Huizar, as well as Indian melodies collected by Mendoza and arranged for chorus by Huizar.

3. Chávez's Sinfonía India for Orchestra (1935–36), unpublished.

4. Piano Trio, premiered September 20, 1934, at the Berkshire Festival.

5. Piston's Piano Trio no. 1 (1935).

6. The String Quartet No. 2 of the Russian-Argentine composer Jacobo Ficher (1896–1978). Argentina was also represented by music of José María Castro (1892–1964), Gallac, Luis Gianneo (1897–1968), and Espoile; Brazil by Heitor Villa-Lobos (1887–1959) and Francisco Casabona (b. 1894); Chile by followers of Schoenberg—Alfonso Leng (1884–1974), Isamitt, Negrete, and Carbajal—and by a pupil of Hindemith, Urrita Blondel; Peru by Indian melodies collected and arranged by Andrés Sás (1900–1967) and the French folklorist Marguerite d'Harcourt (1884–1964); and Cuba by Amadeo Roldán (1900–1939).

7. Mrs. Coolidge's son, Albert Sprague Coolidge (1894–1977), and his wife, Margaret Coit Coolidge (1895–1979). Sprague graduated from Harvard in 1915, went on to receive a doctorate, and then taught in the Chemistry department there. He was also a violist who performed occasionally at his mother's festivals.

Roger Sessions to David Diamond
als (damaged) US-Rdiamond

August 10, 1937
[My] dear David,—   Princeton

I didn't get your long letter till [a] couple of days ago. You see, Mrs. Coolidge [sent] me to Mexico, paying all my expenses, [and] your letter arrived here too late [to be] forwarded either to Mexico City or to [Vera Cruz] (where I stopped on the boat trip [a few] hours, + got mail) it was [some d]ays late in reaching me.

My time in Mexico was wonderful, [. . .][1] the really important + decisive experienc[e of] my life; but that isn't what I [want] to write about today, since you raise, [. . .] so many questions about you. [Most] of all I am so glad that your work [goes well,] as you obviously feel that it is.

This is the main thing; and about [the] actual work you are doing I can [really] not judge from the very general-[sounding] accounts you give me. As far as the [counterpoint] first goes N[adia] B[oulanger] is perfectly correct in [saying] that everyone's ideas differ—the main [thing is] to have a *consistent* discipline [and] to become able gradually to discover one's own values. As far as [con]cerns the "dissonant" character of your [music] I have felt, first, that your dissonance [was] not always well motivated (most of [the] reactions I have made in your music [have] been along those lines) + I have felt that, for instance, in a work like the Passacaglia [you] did for me last year, the specific diss[onant] character of the work was too [. . .] + rather cloying— that it showed [. . .] to speak preoccupation with [. . .] too little awareness of a who[le and] its need for contrast + relief. I should not be inclined to make [such] sweeping statements about your work— [you] know of course that it *was* so sweeping + [justi]fied, but just am going by what [you have] written. The main thing is to pre[serve a] real sense of proportion, + to let on[e's lines] speak for themselves, without overburde[ning] the texture + thus displacing [the atten]tion of the hearer from what is [essen]tial to something that is secondary [to] the whole. I have always felt tha[t] very general questions relating to the [. . .]ter of a style are beyond the logi[cal realm] of the teacher, + as you know [I have] always the tendency to be as [. . .] as specific as possible. I [. . .]ance as, in itself, either bad or good; it [is ne]ither right or wrong in a specific place, [I] would say that just as Stravinsky

-270-

[hims]elf has undergone very many changes + [. . .] evolution in this respect, so will you! [That] Nadia + Stravinsky think your work prom[isingly] talented doesn't either surprise or impress [me p]articularly, since I knew it already—[You] did too.

[With] regard to the various things about which [you seek] my advice, I will answer you as well [as I can]—+ you can always depend on me [for i]t—but I'm afraid you will be disa[ppointed] for you will see I have so little to add to [what I] have said to you already. It seems [to me] that you have two courses of action open [to you]. The first is to look around for someone [to su]pport you, either in Europe or America, or [. . .] + live off fellowships, +c. You might find such a person—+ then again you might not. If N.B. wants [she could] probably put this through for you, for a [time] while you study with her, + I shall as [a matter] of fact not be at all surprised if, [one of] these days, some such proposition is forthcom[ing fr]om her. Whether or not it happens from that source, [. . .] it is one of the possible alternatives [. . .], + I can sympathize to the full [know]ing how you must be tempted by it. [But I] find it quite wrong in principle + [the over]whelming probability very dangerous for you because I have seen enough act[. . .] go—actually been through it *to some extent* [—] to be able to see the consequences better [than] you can possibly see them. It is wrong [in prin]ciple fundamentally because it is [based] on something that in the world as it [is to]day, is quite unreal. First, because on[e is] "paid in advance" for achievement [that] cannot be fully realized [until the] quite distant future—you [would] be demanding + receiving support [on the] basis of mature achievement [as] a very promising young composer; [and that] support therefore would last as long as, in the eyes of the world, you do just that. That it would [disappear] would be, I should say, the most [natural] thing in the world, for nowadays it [is just] the artists who possess real glam[our for] the "patrons of music" are the very [same] ones—who are thrown quickly in [the] waste-basket as soon as they cease to [be] merely promising (look at Markevitch, [. . .] +c, +c)—and the really mature one[s whose] recognition is so unqualified that they [have] no need for patronage (Hindemith, [Stra]winsky, +c. +c). Between these two sta[ges] is a long painful, controversial [road, more] painful in the U.S. than anywhere [else] during which one's status in the [world] is neither that of a "young genius" [nor] of a fully arrived, mature artist; one is temporarily, as far as all but a *very few* admirers are concerned on the shelf, + the more [brillia]nt one's early career has been, the more likely [one] is to stay there. Simply for this reason; [that]

promise in itself is nothing—one has to [deliver] the goods, + this is the work of a [lifet]ime, of real struggle + patience. Furthermore [there] is the very real danger, for *everyone,* that the [early] success that one achieves very young will [go to o]ne's head; it is probably almost impos[sible to] achieve it, in fact, unless one really believes in [it, and if on]e really believes in it it seems to [me] two things are almost certain to [occur:] either one gets bored + cynical + [more] disillusioned about the whole thing, [or becomes] dried up inside so that one has no [more] inspiration left, or one is completely [bereft] when one is deprived of the ex[uberance] + stimulus + specious warmth [that] that kind of success has given one. [I'm] sure I don't need to supply you with [exam]ples—you can see them by the dozen [all] around you. The point is that one has [committed] oneself to living on a musical [level] pure + simple, + that none of the [. . .] with which this snobism answers itself [(and it] is absolutely nothing more than that) lasts [more] than two or three years at most. And [that] simply two facts of which you are undoubtedly [not en]tirely unaware at the moment—[that] the world, + America [by no] means least, is a very heartless place, + that people who have money [want] quick + "sound" returns on whatever [invest]ments they make.

That is one reason why I don't believe in that solution for you. There [are] other reasons too. First of all, if [you were] supported by an individual you wou[ld be] absolutely dependent on, + under [obligation] to, that individual, + though that [might once have been a] conceivable situation in a period [when] real classes + real standards exis[ted in] the XVIII century, it seems to [be a] dangerous one today. Simply [because] a relationship like that becomes far [too in]timate + too personal + is [subject to] the fluctuations + under-currents [that] any personal relationship is subject [to, all] the more so since money + its atten[dant] complications are involved. Unless [the person] who supported you were quite excepti[onally] wise + exceptionally understanding [you] would find yourself hideously in[volved] + situations would almost inevitabl[y arise] which could make you quite miser[able, complicate your problems immeasurably]. Then too—+ perhaps this above all—life would be on a basis which [would be eco]nomically unsound—there would be [a de]finite rela-tionship, economically, but [com]pensation, + goods actually deliv-ered [—although] this may seem quite unimportant [—would even]tually [become] far more important than you think, [and to] one's whole state of mind, + most im[portan]tly to one's work; simply because as long as the [source] of one's life is an equivocation of that[, then] one is simply not living in the real [world] at all. If we were talking this over [and] you cared to listen I could show you [exactly] what I mean by this; in a letter [it's] very hard to explain + perhaps even it is [ho]peless since one has to work these [things] out for oneself. And while I am [wholly] convinced that I am right about [th]ings, I sympathize with you more [fully] than you can possibly realize; for the [state] in which you + anyone else in [your po]sition, must find yourself, is a really almost a heart-breaking one.

The other alternative, of course, is to [come] back here, + find a job, + struggle [as] others have done on the spot where [ultim]ately you will be forced to do so, not because you are an American + can[not] escape that fact, but because Europe [is] getting every day more + more impossible [for] a European artist to live + grow in. I don't say this [on] my own authority at all but on that of [Euro]peans—+ first-rate ones—with whom [I']ve talked. If this were not the case, you would not see so many of [them] coming over here, not to gather dollars from an occasional tour, but actually [to seek] jobs, + establish themselves here. However [I] don't suppose I need to convince you [of] that. The point is that N.Y. is the [only] *place in the world* in which to really e[stablish] oneself, + the sooner you begin, the better[;] furthermore, though you yourself seem to [be] unaware of this fact, you have the [best] *possible* start here; you have good friends who have real influence [with] you + you are in a position [where] you have had performances, + in really an incredibly short time—[your music] has become known + really uns[. . .]. It seems to me—+ both Fr[ed Jacobi and Nicky Berezowsky] agree absolutely—that you really [need] to be aware of this, + that it is [a] possible basis for you here; *far more* [than] anyone else has yet had in Ame[rica] at your age or your stage of de[velop]ment. Everything here is in your [favor] + though *of course* you would have [your] struggles, like every other composer of [any] worth at all, there is no doubt that [when you] really set yourself to making a life [for yours]elf here, with a sense of reality + [a] real decision to do it, you could [progress] very quickly. Fred told me in J[uly] he had a job practically [in hand, if] you were only here to see about it you [could have had it] + you would see that there are other [oppor]tunities if you were willing to come [to] take hold of them. Don't for a minute [think] I am painting a "rosy" picture; I [am] not doing this, and in any case I [feel] that in your present state of mind [such a] picture which I might draw [might] seem quite drab. I have a long [talk] with Nicky—as I had talked with him already in Mexico—the day your letter came. [Fred and . . .] were here, in Pennsylvania, this [week] + he + Alice [Berezowsky] + I all agreed [that your] problem is a really hard one, for [you +] for any young composer. But we all felt, in the utmost friendship for you, [that] the solution is exactly as I have [outlined]—that here you have friends who [are] interested in you + will help you all they [can] + that the cards are stacked in your [favor] as they have been with no one else [we] know; and that the best we could wish [you] and your development [is for] you to come back this fall, and find [a] job, and work + create, on perhaps a [lower], but surer + above all more realistic [level]. So—if you want my advice, there, it's the best I can give, + it's given [with] my whole heart. I think you should [know] that I give it with a good deal of skepticism with regard to your attitude. When I [compared myself] to N[adia] + A[aron] I felt that nothing I [could] say at this time would carry any real [weight] with you + felt too that you had [made] up your mind. It was Alice who urg[ed me] to write you as clearly as possible what [we] all felt, as she felt that I had no [right] to withhold my really strong convi[ction as] to what would be really best [for you].

You see, my dear David, I [do] feel that in all of this business [you have not] really *faced* the problem yet. I [spoke] of this in the spring before you left that you were having quite unnecessary [com]punctions about the whole business [on my] account. I tried as hard as [I] could at that time, to remove these [com]punctions from your mind. Now in [turn] you must realize that it would [be fool]ish + irrelevant to let sentiment, especially sentiment which has [no] real relations to the facts of the case, [inter]fere with your decision regarding wh[at is] best for you. So please for heaven's [sake] be quite clear on the subject; whatever [de]cision you make will affect me very [much] one way or the other. Not at all th[at I] am not interested in you + your devel[opment,] you know that; but simply that I [feel, as] you too must do, that you [are] really in your hands alone + not in [those] of anyone with whom you might [stu]dy. You have simply got to learn to ["fo]llow your own star," regardless of others. [When] you learn to do this, believe me, it [wou]ld mean far more to me than any [act] of "loyalty" felt as an obligation.

You see, this *"vorrei e non vorrei"* ["I want to and I don't want to"][2] mind is excessively bad for you [when what] you have got to do above all is [make] a real choice,—one which will [accomplish] what you most deeply want, [one to] which you can be true without [any] compromise. When you have made this [choic]e all other problems will be sim[ple,] + though many things may seem [difficult] + even painful, you will not be [torm]ented or uncertain about them [wit]hin yourself, as you are now. What [ki]nd of a choice it will be, or what it [wi]ll involve for you I can't tell, except [tha]t it must be a choice of what *you* [wa]nt + not what you can get from here or [the]re with the help of other people. And [you] see, neither I nor anyone else [can] be expected to help unless we see [that] you *have* really made a choice, of your own will + not from mere oppor[tunity]. When we do see that you can be [sure of] all of us who are your friends, + [we] first of all will help all we ca[n]. And I think you will see in the [end] that that could mean a great deal.

However, I must tell you [one] thing very definitely; it isn't [easy to] tell you, but for your sake [as well] as my own it has to be [acknowledged] that [what] you have said about com[ing back] to me—both before you left [N.Y.] + since you have been in Paris [—you] have spoken as if your coming [de]pended on Nadia's decision + no[t on] yours—[and] on her intentions regarding [you, not] on yours regarding her. If I had chosen, I might have [drawn] very obvious conclusions from this—[and] the result would certainly not have [been] a favorable one as far as the [abi]lity of your continuing [to study] with me is concerned. I didn't [want] to draw this conclusion at all—[but] merely laid [the] thing [down] to uncer[tainty] + bewilderment in your own mind [and] that you didn't want to have [to make a] decision yourself. I understand the whole [thing,] mon cher, far too well to want at [this] time to confound you with alternatives [that] could only complicate the situation. I [don't] want to do that now either. But surely [you] must see that if you are to come back with me, it must be very clearly [understood] you want to do just that, + not be[cause for] any reason it is impractical [to] stay with N.B. Only if that [is clear] can working together be fruitful, for either of us; + while in ordinary cases my time + [my] energy are for sale, in your case the [situation is] a quite different one. I hope this [is] plain; if you come back to work [with] me it must be because I am your [first] not your second or third choice; + [while] I shall not ask to proclaim this [from] the housetops I shall expect it to [be per]fectly clear + unequivocal between you [and] me and anyone else whom it may [concern].—But remember above all that in your choice you are under no obliga[tion to] anyone but your own instinct as to [what is] best for you + your music—exactly [as I] told you in May.

I won't write more now, [Lisl] is here + sends you her love. And [be] sure you have, always, my affection [and the] very best of good wishes—

Roger

1. This is the most severely burned of Sessions's letters to Diamond. In this letter alone the brackets and ellipses indicate illegibility, rather than editorial deletions. The words and syllables in brackets are educated guesses.

2. A quotation from "Là ci darem la mano," from Mozart's *Don Giovanni*.

▼

David Diamond to Roger Sessions
als US-NYpease

August 22, 1937
Fontainebleau

My very dear Roger,

Your fine, long letter [of August 10] came today and believe me, it was wonderful to hear so much from you in regard to my state. I mailed you a note from one of the [illegible] here last week. Disregard that letter. [So] many questions are well taken care of in this letter, except that I would like to know about [the] room in 61st Street + how much I would [be] asked for rent if I could get it. Also, I've [been] thinking a great deal of my plans for next season. And though I've felt all along New York was where I belonged this fall, I could not state definitely anything for I believed I would be stranded in Fontainebleau until Mrs. Reis could send me the balance of $100 to use as fare to get back to America. Now I know definitely what I am to do! And am relieved a good deal. Firstly Roger you must never feel I am or ever did consider returning to you as a second choice after Nadia, for going on with Nadia is entirely out of the question and has always been so. As I told you in May, Nadia realizes quite well that I have made my studies with you, + before that in Rochester, and that her estimation of me is not that of a pupil coming to her for technical training, but that of any musician seeking her advice and getting a great deal of pleasure from being with her. Just as you do. Therefore, she thinks I am sure, that while staying in Paris would be good for me (and she has told me this plainly) the need for study with her would be only up to my will. She knows I cannot become one of her children, and I am happier that she considers me a friend rather than one of her Natellites. Too, I've felt that Nadia is a remarkable person to have as a critic for my works, but I know it's you I want for a long time to come and *only you,* and the sooner you realize this Roger the better. It has nothing to do with loyalty or the like. It means above all, that I know what you can offer me, and my music the last 3 years has not suffered by your guidance!!

But to tell you more of my plans! As I read Mrs. Reis is travelling in Europe, I hardly can tell when the $100 will be sent me, and this is the only way I can count on to get back, unless I accept the offer here of two friends to advance [me] the fare if I want to return at once. [I'll] look into Fred [Jacobi]'s offer which you wrote about [and] I shall certainly write Fred about [it] at [once]. I had written him before, but not a [word] has come yet so that your announcement [of] a possible job makes me breathe a bit easier. The real solution was for me to return to America and seek a cheap place somewhere along 3rd Ave. between 59 + 72 Streets. If this does not work out to return to Rochester until I can raise enough money through loans to keep me in New York through next spring. I understand so well the importance of my return to New York, but I don't ever want to go through the horrible conditions I faced in 1934 or last winter's jerking sodas from 9–3 for $12 a week on top of a stomach disorder. It was no joy, that I'm sure you know. And I certainly don't feel myself to be an opportunist! If I come back it's because I know definitely I must continue the good promises I've accomplished, and the loyal friends I have in New York are worth more to me than any kind of arrangement that could be made here by Nadia. Nadia had hoped to find a way for fare back, but she said the Polignac's[1] are away for the summer + she never [speaks of] my plans anymore for she has her own little complications now. As Nadia leaves here next week and if I receive Mrs. Reis's check I shall arrange passage back at once. If the check does not come, I'll accept the loan + return sometimes between late September and early October as I cannot stay on without a cent save $5 a week which I receive from my sister. I will not write more now as I have a great deal of work to finish up before I sail. The [flute] quintet is almost completed in ink + I shall send it to Barrère[2] very soon. Had a lesson on it with Nadia + she's quite happy over it, finds it fresh, very virile, + stimulating. The Romanza pleases her especially as does the Rondo. She thinks the first movement a bit too long, but I'm sure it's simply [that] she didn't read it through in the [quick]er tempo. She more or less analysed [one note] at a time. I'm pleased though that [she] likes the work, + know you will too. [It's] by far my best work, + I know the League will not repent having commissioned it. [Be] sure always dear Roger, though I'm not very good at handing bouquets, that being with you (aside from lessons) is one of the greatest joys I've felt. Often I think of the nights we've had boiled eggs + toast together + I'd give up a great deal to do it *this evening*. Please write soon, and if you see Nicky, ask him to write as I sent him my [String] *Trio* + am wondering whether he received it or not. As for Fred, no doubt I shall be hearing from him very soon. We'll go into Paris on Monday + shall see about boats sailing back then. I can stay with Winifred [Lansing],[3] if I can locate her. It seems she is away for the summer + I've not had a word from her since last July 12. If she has given up her apartment, there is Miss Wolberg's place. But definitely, I shall have to be in New York until I find an apartment as I have my furniture in storage. It's simply a question of finding a good place to work in. I shall send the *Aria* + *Hymn* in to the Philharmonic competition as I don't intend overlooking my chance of getting some money. If I've not cleared up anything, it's because I'm a dreadful letter writer. I have much to tell you of talks with Nadia—etc—

Do write soon—I shall be here until Sept. 20—that I'm sure of.

My love to Lisl—
David

1. Armande de Polignac (1876–?) studied with D'Indy and Fauré. She married the comte de Chabannes, and her Paris salon became a meeting place for artists.

2. Georges Barrère (1876–1944), the French-American flute virtuoso for whom Varèse had composed *Density 21.5* the previous years. Diamond's 1937 flute quintet is scored for flute and piano quartet.

3. Winifred Lansing (1912–86) and Diamond planned at one time to marry. See Diamond's letter below.

▼

Roger Sessions to David Diamond
als US-Rdiamond

August 20, 1937
Princeton

My dear David,—

Your second letter arrived two days ago + though I wrote you a long letter last week I am sending you just a few lines in answer to this one. First of all let me be specific in answering your questions about room, +c. I paid $52.50 for my apartment on 61st St. but I don't know whether it is free now or not. It seems to me you could get something much cheaper in another part of town, though; it seems to me that you could live still [more] cheaply if you could be outside of N.Y. + devote the year to work and study + nothing more. If you should be interested in coming to this neighborhood it might be possible to find something around here. But before I can do anything, you will have to decide definitely what you want.

Of course all this, I realize, depends on the sources of income which you have. If you *have* a source of income, well + good; otherwise the only thing for you to do is to find a job which will assure you a living— + give you as much free time as possible for your work + study. Please don't think I consider this an ideal solution; but it is life, + what hundreds of others—including the very greatest—have accepted as a matter of course. And all really first-class men (and a lot who are not first class) have managed to survive it + do their work just the same. Above all, it is life + reality—the only healthy basis for any life or career. Excuse me if this seems like preaching; but as I wrote you before it is the only advice I can give that seems worthy of you. Fred + Nicky are 100 percent with me in this, + some day if not now you will appreciate it.

I understand fully what you have meant by saying you are not ready to teach. Of course in a sense it is true—incidentally it is true of everyone in the world, + always has been. One can only give what one has— + you have a good deal more than most. It's necessary for you to remember that too, + to remember that your talent—like everyone else's—is a responsibility which means that you have got to develop *humanly* as well as otherwise; + no one can possibly develop humanly except through giving as well as accepting what is offered one.

Quite frankly, mon cher, I think you have got to take *your own* life in hand; + when you have done this you will find plenty of friends, + enthusiastic + true ones. But you see what I *don't* like is your writing me that, your decisions depend on my, or anyone else's, answers to your questions. I am not—as I told you in the spring—the least interested in bidding for you against N.B. or otherwise offering you inducements to come back to study with me. I told you months ago—before any of this arose—that I would teach you without charge if you wanted to go on. But it seems to me that you must realize that in this I am offering you something very real—my time + my energy—which is very tangible indeed in view of my schedule; + that it is up to you to see that it is sufficiently rewarding to make it worth my while. By this I don't mean anything personal at all; but simply that you come to my lessons with the real conviction that they are what you need + want, + that you support that conviction with hard work. You see, I have thought over the years you have worked with me, + seen very clearly that you made far more progress the first two years than you did this last year. There are no doubt good reasons for this—I can understand it very well. But if you come back + go on studying with me we have got to "pick up" on everything—that applies to me as well as to you, [illegible] you may be sure. I shall hold up my end. The only alternative would be for me to charge you for my time at my regular rate, + even if this were *possible* it would not work for either of us, after all that has happened. It's doubtful if it would work in any case.

So, mon cher, in the kindest + friendliest possible spirit—please try to grow up! It seems incredible to me that you should not have seen in advance that the money for your return was far from guaranteed—it all came from the fact that you were anxious to go to France + very anxious, too, not to antagonize N.B. You will certainly get the money from Mrs. Reis, + in any case I am showing your letter to Nicky this afternoon + if he thinks it's necessary or advisable we will speak to her too. But you must learn—for your own good + your own protection, to say nothing of your own development—to take care of these situations for yourself, + to solve your own problems; simply because in the long run no one else can solve them for you, + for that reason if for no other you have no right to ask them to try.

This is absolutely as much as I have time for today. You must know that you have, always, my friendship + very good wishes—+ that it is these which prompt me to write as I do. If that isn't clear to you, there is simply nothing I can do about it.

Lisl joins me in sending her love, as always

Roger

▼

David Diamond to Roger Sessions
als US-NYpease

August 29, 1937

Fontainebleau

My dear Roger,

Your second letter came this morning and truly after the perfect suggestions of the first one, I was a little aghast at what you bring up in this one. Honestly Roger have I been so much a deceiver that you cannot clearly see how deadening the whole business is? At once the 61st apartment is out for me, so how do I arrive in New York? Where do I go? a Hotel naturally, but one needs money for this until I eventually find a very cheap apartment. But out of a clear sky you say Princeton! After pages of your other letter in which you speak so strongly in favor of my finding a job! And I must tell you of this living situation more definitely. There have been many things that you've not known Roger concerning my own personal life, nor would I have expected you to probe it. But this you must know right off. That all last year there was a possibility Winifred [Lansing] and I might marry to facilitate matters [illegible] and general bucking up we gave each other after three years of this, we both came to one definite decision. We were so unlike and unsuited to live together that the possibility of doing this made it clear to us both that it was the wrong step and more an excuse to keep ourselves attached to each other than a good decision for a future life concerning us both. We separated last May with the understanding that we were still fond of each other, but that a compatability such as Winifred wanted was impossible. So any chance that Winifred may be some assistance to my living situation is finished though she holds a job on the W[orks] P[rogress] A[dministration], and I would not dare ask to share this with her for I would despise myself terribly, and on $24 a week she can hardly manage herself.

Then the second question, and one you also don't realize—my state of health! It seems silly that young as I am I should be threatened with illness. [illegible] a stomach condition [illegible] I see X-rays reveal very little, yet I am constantly tormented by pains and rashes until sleep has been impossible these last few weeks. Naturally, I realize a great deal is a nervous condition and this indecision is no asset to my recovery. But the life I had to lead in New York last winter made any kind of recovery impossible for me. Now to come back to New York to face the possibility of finding another horrible job like soda jerk is beyond my remotest wish. You speak about my growing up and facing reality. Very well Roger I'll face it clearly with your most honest answer. Can you say I have not had my share of reality (at its rawest state) from all I've had to do the last 3 years from the Dalcroze School to last winter's work? And still to have gone on writing which I felt I had to do? [illegible] since I was 13. And how you can expect me to settle down to hard work + study as you put it, I hardly know! I've got to find a way of living now and let study [slide] until I can settle myself comfortably enough to resume work with you. And this will mean and take a long time, until a job is found, and until an apartment is arranged to work in. But Princeton is out of the question. The atmosphere does not appeal to me and what I know of the social life doesn't exactly appeal to me. It's in New York I belong with a place to work in and a comfortable income to allow me complete time for study, otherwise I can only say I'll try my best to do as much as I can as I did last year a great deal of work on my own + let you see each new work as it comes out. I feel now I need your criticism of my new works more than a great deal of [illegible] counterpoint and analysis myself and [illegible] it is going well. So my dear Roger, if Mrs. Reis sends the $100 soon, I shall arrive in New York + go to a cheap hotel until I find a cheap place and a job of some kind. When these two things are secured then I can begin thinking of study again. Thank heavens I've finished the commission so this worry is off my mind. If Fred does not write soon about the job you mentioned he suggested for me if I were in New York to see in to it. I shall have to arrange my life to suit my immediate circumstances and the finances which govern them. Fred has two letters from me sent over 2 months ago + *not one word,* nor one word from Aaron as to whether I could share his studio since he lives at the Hotel, nor from Mrs. Reis about the $100, nor any answers to jobs I've applied for. One or two are filled already by older men. So I am being as patient [illegible] the New York office did not realize Mrs. Flagler's scholarship for me covered a full fare + she did not make proper arrangements now I learn. Mrs. Flagler[1] understood my board was being taken care of instead of passage which is silly. And about Nadia, I can only say she has been a grand friend, and our friendship has grown a great deal, but that she can take your place— No! No! No! Voilà you have it. Call me intolerant if you want, but I cannot bring work to you unless I do it well, + to do it well I must live well. I've had my fill of your *reality* and my life's been in my hands all my life long, but it's up to my neck. The fake + pretense which exists in America stifles me. You know well enough Roger, that if a few people were maneuvered correctly, a sum could be gotten for me to last through the spring—But enough of this, I must wait here until my fare back arrives. Can you not drop Mrs. Reis a line?

With affection,
David

[P.S. illegible] I remember your state last year concerning Princeton, how can I hope to find a job when all colleges, schools with music courses are full of sops who haven't seen the inside of a Palestrina madrigal or a Mozart + Beethoven Sonata? And this talk of Fred's concerning teaching is logical yes, but certainly not practical for me.

I've music to write + progress to make + I'll be damned if I'll be stopped by bad finances. I shall come to New York and barnstorm until I can raise some money for myself. Then we'll resume our work. How long it will take I don't know, but always keep faith in me.

I know you will like the *Quintet* + the *Aria* + *Hymn,* too. If no solution comes Rochester is left + there I shall go until a chance arrives to go on with you.

David

1. Anne Lamont Flagler (d. 1939), the wife of the patron Henry Harkness Flagler (1870–1952), president of the New York Philharmonic Society until 1934.

▼

Roger Sessions to Serge Koussevitzky
als US-DLC

September 1, 1937
Dear Mr. Koussevitzky,—   Carter Road, Princeton

I am writing to ask you whether you wish to make any plans regarding my Violin Concerto for this season. As you know, Mr. Spalding, after planning to perform the work last year, asked for a postponement at the very last possible moment. Later he asked me to make changes in the Finale which would have amounted virtually to a rewriting of the whole movement, and though I thought the matter over very carefully + seriously I found it impossible to do this; I found no reason, after a careful + conscientious reexamination of the score, to change any note that I had written, in accordance with my original conception of the work. I therefore offered to release Mr. Spalding—and he accepted my offer—from any obligation to perform it, since I felt it was unfair to all concerned + to the work itself, to hold him to an agreement to play it in spite of a disinclination on his part.

I feel I am not unfair to Mr. Spalding when I tell you, in justice to the work, that several violinists have played the part, with myself at the piano, to my satisfaction + that of other musicians who heard them. Mr. Serge Kotlarsky[1] of N.Y. learned the entire concerto in six weeks, in the midst of a busy season. I cannot feel therefore that the technical difficulties of which Mr. Spalding complained are insurmountable, and the fact that he had and studied the Concerto for nearly a year before deciding against the Finale convinces me simply that he found this movement uncongenial to him. Since you have the score you will of course judge this matter for yourself.

I still feel that not only are you the man whom I would most like to have perform the work, but that the rights to the first performance are still yours if you care to retain them for this next season. As for a violinist, may I mention three possibilities. Both Mr. Jacques Gordon[2] + Mr. Nicholai Berezowsky have assured me—the latter only a few days ago—that they would be happy to play the work at any time. Though Mr. Gordon spoke to me of his own accord last April after hearing both from Mr. Spalding + me about the situation of last winter + after studying the score, I am writing him now to confirm the assurances which he gave me at that time. The third possibility would be of course Mr. Burgin; he does not, so far as I am aware, know my score as do the others—but you might prefer him and I need hardly tell you that I would be happy + proud to have him play the concerto, + the same applies both to Mr. Gordon + Mr. Berezowsky. I lay all this before you in order that you may see what the possibilities are.

Naturally I am very eager to hear the concerto which has been ready for the past two seasons; naturally also I would be happy if you could see your way to performing it in New York as well as in Boston. There has been a good deal of stir about the work + I believe it would arouse very considerable interest in New York.

My publisher, Mr. [Vladimir] Lakond, is also writing you, + we would of course be more than grateful for a reply to one or the other of us very soon.[3]

With heartiest greetings to you + Mme. Koussevitzky, believe me always

Most sincerely yours,
Roger Sessions

1. Serge Kotlarsky (1893–1987), a violinist who toured the U.S. as a child prodigy with Enrico Caruso and who performed in the Soviet Union with David Oistrakh.

2. Jacques Gordon (1899–1948), a Russian-American violinist, concertmaster of the Chicago Symphony Orchestra.

3. Koussevitzky replied (September 24, 1937, US-NYpease): "Unfortunately, I regret very much to say that it will not be possible to include it in our programmes, for we already have two new concertos for violin in our repertoire this coming season. I am writing to let you know of it as I feel sure other organizations will be interested in the performance of your work." The concertos he mentions are those of Edward Burlingame Hill and John Alden Carpenter.

Roger Sessions to David Diamond
als US-Rdiamond

September 7, 1937
Dear David,—   Princeton

Your letter of Aug. 29 reached me this morning. I simply haven't the time to write you another long letter, + besides I feel that to discuss all these things further by mail can only lead to more misunderstandings. Naturally the letter I wrote you was intended to help you—I should not otherwise have taken the time or trouble to write you as I did. I am sorry if that was [not] clear.

When you arrive in N.Y. I advise you to get in touch, right away, with Nicky + with Fred. They are both real friends of yours—as good friends as I, + much better people; + I am sure they will do their best to help you where I seem to be unable to do so. If Fred hasn't written you it is undoubtedly in part because he has had really grave troubles of his own—both the children were seriously ill earlier in the summer + the Jacobis had a thoroughly bad time.

When you feel ready to start work let me know + we will discuss the whole situation in regard to your working with me. I will only say now that you misunderstand me utterly in thinking that it is a question of whether N.B. has taken or could "take my place" or that that could ever have other than a sentimental importance to either of us. If you can convince me that you were willing wholeheartedly to take *what I have to give,* you need have no fear.

As [always,]
Roger

Roger Sessions to Louis Krasner[1]
als US-CAhoughton

October 26, 1937
Dear Mr. Krasner: Princeton

After seeing you I wrote my publisher and asked him to send you my Concerto. He wrote me some days ago that it had been sent; and I should have written you before this if my days had not been so busy that I have had not a moment to call my own.

– 285 –

I am hoping very much that the work may interest you and that you may care to consider giving the first performance of it. Though I have unfortunately not yet had the pleasure of hearing you, the testimony which I have heard regarding your performance of the Berg Concerto has been so unqualified and so unanimous that there is no question in my mind that I should be happy to put the fate of this work in your hands and should consider myself very fortunate in being able to do so.

Please forgive me if I tell you a little more clearly than was possible the other night the facts of the Spalding episode; I feel simply that, since we talked of it, I do not want you to misunderstand in any way.

Just before I finished the work I had a letter from Mr. Spalding asking to see it. At that time I was in California; and shortly after my return to the East I visited him in Great Barrington—September, 1935—and showed him the Concerto. He expressed great interest in it at that time, and asked for the first performance, the rights to which I gave him. It was he who made connections with Koussevitzky; and plans were made for a premiere in the following season (1936–7). He had the music—i.e., the violin part and the piano arrangement—from Nov. 1935, and was, I suppose, studying it. He also spoke often of the Concerto and expressed himself with complete enthusiasm regarding it—over Bing Crosby's Radio Hour, even, and privately as late as Nov. 1936. I did not have the opportunity of going over the Concerto with him until the Fall of 1936; I waited until his return from a European tour, early November. At that time I spoke to him on the 'phone; he told me that he had gone to Europe confident of knowing the Concerto perfectly; but that on his return he had found that he did not remember it well, and that at the performance, set for one month later, he might have to use the notes. Since I had absolutely no objections to this, I was, of course, not disturbed.

Ten days later I went to an appointment which we had made—the performance was scheduled for two and a half weeks later. At that time Spalding told me that he had asked Koussevitzky to postpone the performance, simply because he did not know it sufficiently to play it. At the time, he was not sure whether the performance could take place in the following March or would have to be delayed until *this* season.

At the same interview Spalding complained about certain passages in the last movement; from the technical standpoint—especially—I remember the measures from Nos. 106–108, No. 131–132 and 153–154. I told him that the whole work had been played to my satisfaction, and even written in collaboration with good violinists, but that I was always willing and glad to accept suggestions of a violinistic nature, and that if he could show me better ways of achieving the results I wanted, I, as a non-violinist, would always be willing to listen.

He also told me he felt the last movement was "unrelieved" and asked me if I would be willing to make changes. I told him that a large part of the character, which I had in mind, lay in the very intensity of the movement, especially toward the end, but that I felt that this also was relieved most especially by the episodes, lighter in character, beginning at No. 112 and at No. 129. He did not pursue the matter further that evening and I felt then that he was willing to let matters rest there. He played the first three movements with me that evening, but was unwilling to play the *finale* for me.

About a month later I had a letter from him, in answer to one of mine in which I expressed again my willingness to cooperate with him in making whatever technical changes he thought necessary in the violin part. He reiterated his feeling that the finale was "unrelieved" and spoke this time of a "relentless staccato."

I considered the matter very carefully and went over my score,—as I felt quite able to do—in the most objective manner possible; for I wanted to give Mr. Spalding's criticism every benefit of the doubt. My only possible conclusion was the one I might have anticipated—I had written exactly what I had intended to write, and it would have been quite out of the question to make the kind of radical changes which Mr. Spalding demanded. I wrote him to this effect, saying that I felt the movement was fundamentally unsympathetic to him and that, therefore, I did not wish to hold him to any obligation to play it. He wrote me that he could not feel the conviction in regard to it that was necessary in order to do the work justice.

Please forgive me for going into these details. I think simply that it is only fair—both to you and to the work—that you should know the facts.

If there is a chance of your caring to undertake the premiere of the work—this season if possible, and early next season at the latest—I should appreciate your letting me know as soon as you can do so. Since the work is over two years old I am anxious to "launch" it as soon as possible; but I am also anxious to have you play it, and, should there be a chance of your doing so, would be willing to wait a little longer, if necessary.

In any case, I shall let you know before making any definite plans for a performance.

With every good wish,

Sincerely yours,
Roger Sessions

P.S. I shall come to Philadelphia on Nov. 27th for your performance, and hope to see you at that time.[2]

1. Krasner (b. 1903), later concertmaster of the Minneapolis Symphony Orchestra (1944–49), had commissioned and premiered Berg's Violin Concerto the previous year, and in 1940 gave the first performance of the Schoenberg Violin Concerto.

2. After receiving Krasner's enthusiastic response, Sessions wrote on November 11, 1937 (US-CAhoughton): "I do still feel that I would like to go ahead + plan with you for a really good first performance, perhaps in Boston next fall if Kouss. is still interested or if his interest can be revived"—a remarkable statement in light of Koussevitzky's unequivocal rejection of September 24. Sessions and Krasner met in Philadelphia after a Philadelphia Orchestra concert; though nothing immediate came of these efforts, Krasner performed the concerto ten years later.

▼

Roger Sessions to David Diamond
als US-Rdiamond

November 17, 1937

Dear David,—   Princeton

I have just written Mr. Moe on your behalf.[1] I think what I wrote him would please you, and feel sure that it will work in your favor, as far as any word from me could ever do so.

I hope that may in some measure make up for what will probably seem to you a piece of bad news. This is, that I feel, on the basis of your attitude since last summer and before, that we no longer agree on fundamentals sufficiently to make it fruitful for either of us to try to go on together.

You remember, I wrote you in August the conditions under which I felt that we could go on. I said that if you came back I expected it to be a real choice, made with *real conviction*. I put this as strongly, as definitely as I could. I meant not at all that I wished necessarily to be considered your best friend or your "master" or anything sentimental of that kind but simply that you come wholeheartedly + single-mindedly with a real decision to take what I had to give and to get down to work as you have not done, with me at least, for a year and a half. I meant, too, that you come with the idea of putting your life here in America on a solid basis of reality and stop living in the illusion that you must bend all your efforts towards finding some kind of fairy-godmother to support you + relieve you of all the problems which every composer has to face sooner or later. Had such an opportunity presented itself for you, I would have been glad, of course, for your sake; but it did not.

Meanwhile your whole attitude as I have observed it since your return—+ as you express it very clearly in your Guggenheim application—shows me that should your financial circumstances permit you would return to Europe at once without hesitation. I do not feel that you are nearly ready to be "on your own" to this extent nor am I willing to take the responsibility of letting you limit your work with me, at this point, to sporadic criticism such as you apparently wish. Furthermore it is quite impossible to reconcile this with your repeated statements to me, that it is I whom you really wish to have as your teacher. Above all I feel that you are seriously wasting your time and scattering your energies at a moment in your life when you can ill afford to do that.

I also feel that you are asking the world in general, and me in particular, to pay you in advance for what still is + must obviously remain for some time to come, merely a hope and a promise, and not yet a real and mature achievement. As long as I could feel that you were definitely moving in the direction of this achievement I was, as I always would be, very glad to do everything possible for you. You should know this better than any one. But as I have told you many times, mere talent and mere promise are nothing by themselves; they are not rare, and one gets quite cynical about them by the time one has seen as much as I have seen. And my time, too, is limited and valuable—I have to save it for my own obligations and for the people who really appreciate what I have to give them—+ show that appreciation not only by words but by loyal effort and work.

I am truly sorry that this has to happen; it is [illegible] more of a disappointment than you can know, to have been let down in this way by someone to whom I have given as much of myself as I have given to you. But as I wrote you last summer, I still believe in you to the extent of knowing that you can, if you wish, achieve very splendid things; and, in all sincerity, you can give me no greater happiness than by growing out of this phase of bewildered opportunism + becoming really positive and strong, and accomplishing what you have it in you to accomplish. This you can do if you really care enough to do it, and you do not need my help. Perhaps you can even do it better without me.

Until this phase, however, is definitely and palpably behind you, I don't want to discuss this matter further. We have talked and talked, and words have become quite meaningless between us. If you care to prove to me that I am wrong, you can do it very easily—by showing me through actual deeds that your attitude is not as I have interpreted it. Mine is, and will be, always, one of the sincerest good will and affection, even when I disagree as I do now.

Meanwhile I wish you, from the heart, everything good—and Lisl joins me in this.

As always
Roger

1. Henry Moe, head of the Guggenheim Foundation. In part because of Sessions's recommendation, Diamond was awarded the first of three Guggenheim Fellowships, which allowed him to return to Paris May–June 1938.

▼

Roger Sessions to David Diamond
als US-Rdiamond

November 29, 1937
Dear David—   Princeton

I shall send your Psalm again to the International jury for possible performance at the London Festival.[1] Naginski[2] is seeing to getting the package off—so you will probably hear from him. If not, please get it to Miss [Dorothy] Lawton by this Tuesday afternoon.

Your letter came; it made me feel very sorry for the conditions you are in now, and showed me too how really deep is my affection for you. I have never had the intention for a minute, of ceasing to be your friend or to take an interest in your affairs.

But your letter, too, made me feel that the step which I took was a quite necessary one—+ necessary above all for you. For obviously, in your present frame of mind nothing I can do for you will be of any use.

I am [sure] that you feel that I misunderstand you. But you must realize that it is consistent action and not words or letters or protestations, that really count. If I have told you often enough before, if one really wants to do things, one does them instead of using one's energy in thinking of excuses for not doing them—+ that is that.—

I know perfectly well that your financial situation is a bad one at present. It is however no worse than that of at least three of my other pupils; and together with the opportunities which you have—in *every* way—your position is a great deal better than theirs. Yet they don't complain; they are doing their best and showing that they have "what it takes"—And it is not because they have either essentially healthier or simpler natures than you—simply because they go at solving their problems with courage + realism. This you simply are not doing, at the moment. My hope is that soon you may rouse yourself + begin doing it.

You simply have no *right* to say that Nicky's plan for you is "vague" or to speak of it in the terms you do. It is entirely up to you to [make] it vague or not—if you work and really get your technique in shape, & go after it you can easily find out that it is not vague at all. But if, as seems to be the case, you have subconsciously decided to sit back + demand that everyone invest himself for you, this like everything else will turn out to be a failure. Especially if you go on blaming the world—as you are apparently doing—for misfortunes that are very largely your own making and that in any event are nothing more nor less that everyone, without exception, has to face.

It is above impertinence for you to write that the League has "folded up"—no such thing has happened; but in this as in everything else the only possible result of such an attitude as you are taking will be to alienate the people who would otherwise be inclined to meet you half way.

You speak of "trash" and "pretense"—it is perfectly true that there is trash and pretense everywhere—+ no more in N.Y. than anywhere else. You are not the first who has discovered this nor, by any means, the world's worst sufferer from it. Unfortunately self-pity can just as easily become entirely false, as anything else—it is about the most false attitude one can take. In every case if one lets oneself be defeated by these things, it is *entirely* one's own fault—+ no one else's! You have far less excuse for letting this happen than most people, and yet you go on stubbornly taking an attitude towards yourself + everyone else which, unless you change + brace yourself up, can lead nowhere except to defeat for you.

It is because I really care, David, that I write all this, + that I take the stand that I have. Perhaps a doctor could help you better. Anyone in the world who has any intelligence would say substantially the same thing, + few would have the patience which I have had. I am glad to have the patience as long as it is possible—but often in the last year—or almost a year—I have asked myself if that didn't do you more harm than good.

Don't forget the Psalm—and try to forgive me if you find all this unpalatable as I'm afraid you will find it.

Affectionately as always,

R—— S——

1. Diamond's Psalm would not be performed on the Sixteenth Festival of the ISCM in London.

2. Charles Naginski (1909–40) was a student of Sessions's who died by drowning in Lenox, Mass.

▼

Barbara Sessions to Roger Sessions
als US-NYpease

Dear Roger,   December 22 [1937]

I do hope this will reach you in time to wish you a very happy Christmas. I wanted to write much sooner, but my life is a rush of things determined by other people.

Your letter at Thanksgiving time took, of course, a little while to be assimilated, and I could not write at once.[1] I know you understood much of how it could not but make me feel. But in the most healing and happy way there has finally come for me a sense of deep satisfaction that for you this fulfilment is ahead. It is difficult for me to explain why this should be; it's an impersonal thing, in a way, outside ourselves. Yet I can think with real joy now of there being a child of yours, and I am profoundly happy that it is to happen. Please know this, my dear, and that I mean it with all my heart. I write stiffly because that is the only way these words will come. But I know you will forgive that and understand.

It was good of you to do so much [for] bringing the accounts into settlement.[2] Thank you, and know how much it helped.

Did you know that Dora Levi, B[ernard] B[erenson]'s great friend (I think it was after you left Italy in the summer of 1933 that I met him and his wife) had been in this country? He lectured at the Blisses on his Lietan excavations. Nicky [Mariano][3] sent a nice note by him, but I remembered him well. He is a charming person; unfortunately he seemed to think it incumbent on him to give me a whirlwind campaign of gallantry in the most stereotyped Italian manner. I found it curiously irritating, and humiliating, even!—which shows how thoroughly repatriated I have become. There's something so devastatingly impersonal about that kind of an approach—even though I knew quite well that it was being done half with tongue in cheek, in order if possible to have a good story to take back to Nicky and Alda! Also, Emilio Cecchi is in New York; possibly you've seen him.

This is all mere gossip. I must close, with all affectionate wishes and thoughts.

Barbara

1. Roger Sessions had written, around the time of the first anniversary of his second marriage, to inform Barbara Sessions that Lisl Sessions was pregnant. Barbara's long illness in Europe had foreclosed the possibility of her having children.
2. A reference to Sessions's alimony payments.
3. Berenson's secretary and mistress.

▼

Aaron Copland to Roger Sessions
acs US-NYpease

December 26, 1937
New York

Dear Roger,

We organized last Sun. as the American Composers Alliance![1] You were elected a member of the temporary Executive Comm. Said comm. is having a first meeting at my studio (115 W 63) on Sunday Jan 2 at 4:30. I hope you can come.

Yours,
Aaron

P.S. Let me know when the ISCM meeting is to be.

1. The original members were Marion Bauer, Evelyn Berckman, Abram Chasins, Arthur Cohn, Aaron Copland, Morton Gould, Ferde Grofé, Roy Harris, Harrison Kerr, Goddard Lieberson, Douglas Moore, Quincy Porter, Alex North, Wallingford Riegger, William Schuman, Roger Sessions, Elie Siegmeister, Virgil Thomson, and Bernard Wagenaar.

CHAPTER

1938-1942

S E V E N

$\int$ ESSIONS'S 1937 TRIP to Mexico, two years after Antonio Borgese's similar trip, led to the beginning of a long collaboration between the two friends, a collaboration that would culminate in the completion of the opera *Montezuma*. Steeped in William Hickling Prescott's three-volume *Conquest of Mexico* (1843) and Bernal Díaz del Castillo's 1632 eyewitness account of Cortés's exploits, Sessions enthusiastically set out on a project for which neither man was well prepared: Borgese had never written an opera libretto, and Sessions's previous vocal music consisted of only two published songs. Their greatest miscalculation, one not recognized until much later, was of the opera's length; Borgese's four acts of about forty thousand words would eventually be cut to three acts of some ten thousand words. This lack of experience and Sessions's slow pace of composition delayed the opera's completion twenty-six years.[1]

In the meantime, a sign of the two men's close friendship was the fifty-seven-year-old Borgese's wedding to the twenty-one-year-old Elisabeth Mann in Sessions's Princeton home on Thanksgiving Day, November 23, 1939—three years after Sessions's wedding on the same holiday. The bride's father, Thomas Mann, was at that time in residence at Princeton. Sessions was the best man, and the Austrian novelist Hermann Broch was the "bridesmaid."

Sessions wrote to Borgese six times during July and August of 1938. These letters were shorter and included arrangements for Borgese's trip to Princeton in mid-August. The title of the proposed opera was not settled by letter; they discussed several possibilities—

The Conquerors, The Conquistadors, Tenochtitlàn—and decided on *Malinche*.

Mann and Borgese were not the only refugees from Nazi persecution to enter Sessions's life at this time. Another was the Viennese composer Ernst Krenek (1900–1991), whose book *Über neue Musik* Sessions reviewed in *Modern Music,* commenting, "Many of his interpretations, both of phenomena and of values, and of the psychology of composition, are so much like the reviewer's own as to cause the latter genuine surprise and pleasure."[2] The two evidently met in January 1938 when Krenek played his Piano Variations at Sessions's Princeton home and for the League of Composers in New York. On his way back to Vienna, Krenek's plans were confounded by Hitler's annexation of Austria. Krenek's request for help from Amsterdam, written the day after the *Anschluss,* is one of his thirty-eight surviving letters to Sessions; twenty-one letters from Sessions to Krenek are extant.[3] Krenek always wrote with business in mind, whether it had to do with a performance of his music or, often, with seeking Sessions's aid in securing a teaching job. It appears that Sessions was only once successful: he helped Krenek get his first post in the United States, teaching at Vassar College from 1939 to 1942. Sessions himself continued to teach at Princeton University and also taught at New Jersey College for Women (now Douglass College) from 1935 to 1938.

Sessions's epistolary relationship with David Diamond continued, but their letters were much shorter and more businesslike, including one of April 4, 1938, congratulating Diamond on his receipt of a Guggenheim fellowship. Diamond briefly described his problems with Sessions in a letter February 14, 1938, to a fellow Sessions student, Charles Naginski: "R.'s word will count much [to the *Prix de Rome* jury], he is so highly respected. Don't be too unhappy about your work with him. He is very heavy, I know, but you come away with much after it is all over. Don't let his yawning upset you. It doesn't necessarily mean he is bored. Maybe there is something in the gland theory. Just don't feel you have to write music like his. He wouldn't expect you to. How I wish R. would not feel bitterly towards me. One day, perhaps, he'll see my decision to study with B[oulanger] was for the best."[4]

1. See Andrea Olmstead, "The Plum'd Serpent: Antonio Borgese and Roger Sessions's *Montezuma," Tempo* 152 (March 1985): 13–22, and *Roger Sessions and His Music* (Ann Arbor: UMI Research Press, 1985), 125–37.

2. Ernst Krenek, *Über neue Musik: Sechs Vorlesungen zur Einführung in die theoretischen Grundlagen* (Vienna: Verlag der Ringbuchhandlung, 1937), revised as *Music Here and Now,* trans. Barthold Fles (New York: Norton, 1939). Roger Sessions, "Exposition by Krenek," *Modern Music* 15, no. 2 (January 1938): 123–28; reprinted in *Roger Sessions on Music: Collected Essays,* ed. Edward T. Cone (Princeton: Princeton University Press, 1979), 249–55.

3. A photograph of Roger Sessions with Ernst Krenek appears in Mary Harris, *The Arts at Black Mountain College* (Cambridge: MIT Press, 1987), 95.

4. Gertrude Norman and Miriam Lubell Shrifte, eds., *Letters of Composers: An Anthology, 1603–1945* (New York: Knopf, 1946), 414.

▼

Roger Sessions to Antonio Borgese
als I-Fborgese

January 11, 1938

Dear Antonio,—   Princeton

I intended long ago to answer your good letter + the wire, which was quite the best birthday greeting I had—+ would have done so if the vacation had not been an unexpectedly busy + upset one. No need for details except that we were both ill—especially Lisl who had to go to bed suddenly Christmas Eve + stay there till a couple of days ago. It worried us considerably, though apparently without real cause.

I was disappointed not to see you at Christmas time, but of course quite understood. I am so happy to hear that *Goliath*[1] is on its feet; as a matter of fact I have had the impression that it is gathering momentum all the time. I hear of it from all sides + even had some difficulty, both in N.Y. + in Princeton, in getting two copies which I gave away for Christmas, as it was selling so rapidly that two stores were out of copies when I asked for it.

Some students here—the "Liberal Club"—have asked me if there is any chance of your being willing to speak before them at an "open meeting" sometime this year, on some phase of the Fascist problem. Naturally I told them I didn't know, but said I would ask you + would find out what your terms would be. I "pass this on" to you for what it is worth. Since you are to be in the East in March I assume the date could be set to suit you, + I know there would be tremendous interest in having you. Whether it would interest you is of course another matter! Furthermore I don't at all know what kind of fee they could offer you. However, I have asked you, as I said I would do, so my duty is done!—They have all read *Goliath,* I understand, + all but the Marxists are enthusiastic and *eingestanden* [in agreement].

Antonio Borgese.

Naturally, you must not feel that I am in any way *impatient* about the opera. Only very eager + still intending, positively, to get to work on it this summer. I am not yet able to get as much accomplished, during this time, as I hoped to do; but I am improving + learning to do so all the time.

Tante bellissime cose [all good things] for the New Year, + affectionate greetings from us both.

Yours
Roger S——

[P.S.] Just to add a line on receipt of your letter. I'm so sorry to have been so slow! Regarding Mexico, you may be sure my interest + eagerness is just as great as ever—we—you + I—are in quite the same position in regard to it, I think; that of cleaning up old "debts" to gain freedom for it.

Lisl is better—she has had a long siege, but the doctor is reassuring + says that the baby (or rather the prospective baby!) is getting along all right. But it has been a [wearing +] anxious time.

In any case—forgive my silence, *please*. Nothing but an inordinate mass of detail, combined with my disease of procrastination.

Wed. I go to be "inducted" into the "National Institute of Arts + Letters"!(??!??)

Many affectionate greetings from us both.

R——

1. *Goliath; the March of Fascism* (New York: Viking, 1937), Borgese's attempt to explain how Italy succumbed to Fascism.

▼

Ernst Krenek to Roger Sessions
als US-NYpease

March 14, 1938

Dear Mr. Sessions,   Amsterdam

now the worst become reality, it is for me of the greatest importance to settle my immigration to the United States during the summer. As I can never go back to Vienna I must try to get the Visa somewhere at an American Consulate. Of course, I have to expect a chain of difficulties because I do not yet know which passport I will have in future and if and where I can get the passport without going back to Vienna. Therefore I must try to have the most powerful support from the American side. I think the most efficient spell should be a call from some American Institution like an University or College or something like this. I am conscious that it will be extremely difficult to get such a thing, but nevertheless I dare to ask you if you could help me in this matter. It would be sufficient if the call were only a formal one, without special financial engagements of the institute, for instance it could be appointed privately that I must not work immediately for them; that I had "Urlaub" [leave of absence] or something like this, in order to avoid financial engagements which could be difficult to realize. The most important thing would be to have a convincing paper which proves that I have to go straight to America both for the question of the passport and for the Visa.

Please be so kind to help me in this extremely difficult and embarrassing situation, and write me as soon as possible to the address c/o

F. T. Gubler, Jakobstrasse 3, Winterthur, Switzerland. Many thanks, and all good wishes for you and Mrs. Sessions from us both very affectionately

yours
Ernst Krenek[1]

1. Sessions did not answer this letter until May 31. His letter did not reach Krenek until June 15, crossing Krenek's urgent telegram of June 14. Krenek wrote on June 15 that he had received his visa to the U.S. in Rotterdam a month earlier.

▼

Roger Sessions to Antonio Borgese
als I-Fborgese

April 7, 1938
[Princeton]

My dear Antonio,—

[. . .]

I should have written you days ago—I planned to do so just after I heard you speak at the F[oreign] P[ress] A[ssociation?] luncheon. Your speech was magnificent, especially coming after that *cretin* of an Englishman, + the somewhat negative + apologetic Sonia Tamar [?]. Others felt so too. I hope it will not seem like "damning with faint praise" if I tell you, too, that your words were the single refreshing feature of an [illegible] + rather depressing occasion. I must say that it seems to me a wholly perverted liberalism that invites, broadcasts, such statements such as that of Major Barnes, + also of Ciuscolo, + begs people to be courteous about them!—"die Diktatur des Lächelns," ["The Dictatorship of Smiles"[1]] as an Austrian friend of mine recently, + not without a good deal of justice, characterised the United States. If falsehood is to be listened to, and diffused, on exactly the same plane as truth, it seems to me that liberalism has become sick to death. And if certain sporadic and alarmingly consistent indications which I have recently had are as significant as I fear they are, Hitler's successes have already begun to poison influential opinion in this country, at least to the extent of lending aid + comfort to a very real + dangerous trend towards Fascism in the U.S. Luckily the "sense of the meeting" seemed entirely in your favor; + perhaps anyway I am impatient + even intolerant myself. But I know my compatriots quite well + am all too aware of what is at bottom nothing but indolence + passivity masquerading as good humour—a profound unwillingness to face unpleasant or even merely difficult or complicated facts.

I was of course tremendously excited by our short conversation regarding Mexico + have been quite naturally returning to the subject since you were here—both in my actual musical ideas + in my thoughts as to what I want to achieve. I have been making certain studies of English diction + also thrashing out in my mind quite concretely certain of the problems which the work may give me as a composer. The more I think of it, the more the element of *character*— in the broadest sense—seems to me absolutely to predominate, and that of landscape and folklore to recede into the background. I don't mean that they will be absent—but I feel that an atmosphere can be created with a very few slight touches, which could be far more powerful than some of the ideas with which I have been playing before. Your remarks apropos of [Verdi's] *Otello* have remained in my mind; + while I find it hard to agree that that work is "under-composed" (was that the word you used? at all events I understood what you meant) but do feel decidedly that a similar texture for our work would be quite inadequate.

Please think of me, as I think of you, as thinking constantly of this; you of course are in the midst of it now, as I am not as yet. But if ever, + whenever, you can let me have any definite clues in regard to it, please do so. I am more eager than I can tell you to begin giving my imagination more precise objects to work on than those which I have had thus far. You understand, I am sure, the sense in which I mean this— + will not interpret it as an attempt to hurry you in any way. Simply, if I can get a general idea of the architecture of the whole— + of the characters—I believe I could accomplish an immense amount of preliminary elaboration now. But—it must be entirely according to your wishes.

Lisl joins me in sending you our warmest + sincerest greetings.

Always your
Roger—

1. A play on the title of Franz Lehár's operetta *Das Land des Lächelns,* produced in Berlin in 1929.

▼

Roger Sessions to Antonio Borgese
als I-Fborgese

Dear Antonio,—   May 15–17, 1938

You may be sure that I was thrilled to get your letters—all three of them—regarding the opera. As a matter of fact when the second one came—the plan of the whole—I carried it around with me for days, + consulted it on all occasions—I made more sketches, under its spell. If I did not write immediately it is partly because I needed time to digest it— + later because I had a rush of work—two lectures + two long articles—to prepare in those two weeks. Now my work [teaching] at N[ew] J[ersey] C[ollege for Women] (New Brunswick) is finished for the year—Princeton will be finished in another week— + I, like you, have more leisure.

All of your notes have interested me enormously + I have given them a great deal of thought. First of all you have converted me entirely to the idea of an uninterrupted sequence of scenes without intermission. When I saw the plan in black + white, + had visualized, so to speak, the tempi, the contrasts between ensemble + solo parts + dumb show + interludes, it became clear to me that this was possible, besides being absolutely necessary.

Your observations regarding Marina's[1] character I appreciated very much. For obvious reasons she fascinates me more than the others—not only, of course, because she is a woman, + an extraordinary and beautiful one; but above all because, as you pointed out two years ago + as I have realized more + more, she is the crux of the deeper human + dramatic situation with which the drama deals.

In regard to the "Speaker" I am not yet clear, + in fact will have to wait for your text. I simply have not yet visualized his *rôle,* nor—as a natural consequence—have I any clear idea of what his musical language will be. The other characters have taken some musical shape—not only Cortez + Marina + Montezuma but also—should you use them—Alvarado, Padre Olmedo, Navaez, Diaz, and even Cuauhtemoc.[2] Is Diaz, perhaps the speaker: we spoke of this, of course; but in that case Diaz the octogenarian + Diaz the young warrior are still to be differentiated musically.

It is more exciting than I can tell you that some of the text is actually finished—and be sure that I would be the last to carp at the fact of its being only thus far, 300 lines! If you should feel at all that you can let me see some of it—at any time—be sure that I would be able to put it to good use in planning the work, + to get really started that much sooner. However, that is entirely "up to you."

I am pretty clear now regarding the general lines of what I have to do, + have avoided above all any very concrete preconceived ideas. What I need now is simply a clearer vision of the, so to speak, concrete object. When the play comes I shall of course devote some weeks simply to studying it—and getting its main outlines thoroughly assimilated, and setting in movement the process of unconscious elaboration. It is of course at that time that I would get a clearer idea of the work from the standpoint of musical structure.

For the present let me say only that it seems to me admirable, from every point of view of which I can be sure. There is only one—*very* substantive—problem that suggests itself to me; the answer will come only when I can see the whole + the way you have worked it out. This refers to the preponderance of mass action (in music, preponderance of the chorus + of dynamic intensity) in the early scenes as contrasted with Sc. 8, 10, and 11, which are clearly scenes in which the individual actors will bear the whole burden. Don't misunderstand me—I can visualize various solutions, especially as Scenes 9, 12, + 13 will undoubtedly surpass in intensity anything that has gone before. I am just [a]waiting your impressions, which will obviously be modified when I have the complete, visualizable text before me, and can see exactly what you have done with all of these scenes.

Scene 9 seems to me in many ways the climax of the work—I find it admirably placed. I had imagined it as coming earlier—but actually it seems incredible, now, to imagine it anywhere else than exactly where you have placed it. I am sure I need not elaborate—you will see what I mean in calling it the climax—in a sense quite other than the external + pictorial one, though in that too.

[. . .]

I think this is all for today. It certainly is enough.

Many affectionate wishes from us both.

Roger

[P.S.] Naginsky tells me you were going to hear his radio concert. I think you will be interested; he has made remarkable progress this year.

1. A major character in *Montezuma*, the captive Indian princess who served as Cortés's translator and mistress was called Doña Marina by the Spaniards and Malinche (Nahuatl for "tongue") by Cortés.
2. All characters in *Montezuma*.

▼

Roger Sessions to Antonio Borgese
als I-Fborgese

Dear Antonio,—   June 18–19, 1938

[. . .]

If I could have them [the completed scenes], it would establish a kind of contact without which my conceptions cannot really begin *definitely* to crystallize themselves + to begin to effectively germinate. My musical plans (+ by that I mean all of the conceptions necessary to the realization of the work) are like the tomato or cauliflower or sweet-potato plants that I buy for my garden; they will live in the moss which the store keeper wraps around the roots, for several days; but they cannot grow until they are transplanted into the soil. Even when that occurs they languish for a day or two till they have taken their root. I believe my musical ideas, especially in regard to this work, are good hardy plants! but they crave the sunlight + the nourishing soil of a definite text, even if it is only, so to speak, a little soil in a flower pot, while the garden itself is still being prepared.

You understand, of course, the weakness of such an analogy, but as I write I find the above a stronger one than most!

Secondly, I conceive of our collaboration as a kind of artistic marriage, entered into with the greatest possible enthusiasm and good will, +, at the same time I believe, a high degree of real sophistication. I think we are both quite aware of its dangers but I have never for a moment doubted that we will spare no pains whatever to make it a triumphantly successful one. For that reason I believe we have neither of us anything to fear if you should decide to send me these scenes. It seems to me rather that the process of active collaboration would start just so much sooner, + the inevitable adjustments be made so much more quickly + effectively.

[. . .]

Very much love to you from "tutta la famiglia."

Roger

Roger Sessions to Antonio Borgese
als I-Fborgese

Dear Antonio,—   Thursday–Sat. [June 23–25, 1938]

Well—I have "slept on" the two scenes; to tell the truth, I slept on them almost literally, since, while the baby's nurse *and* my mother-in-law are both here I spend my nights temporarily on a mattress on the floor of my study: I have been constantly with the Ms. ever since it arrived.[1]

I wired you my first + thus far quite unchanged impression. Though I expected a great deal, the result seems thus far even more beautiful; + as is to be expected, it grows with each new reading.

Where shall I begin?—First of all, old Bernal [Díaz] seems to me so beautifully conceived. In a sense he was the greatest surprise to me; I find him such a genuine + intensely vivid character. I have a curious feeling about him—he is the static element, so to speak, of the drama, and comes to us fully mature, completely equipped as a personality, and forms thus a very living + many sided framework against which the drama as a whole unfolds itself.

Technically, he thus far presents the greatest problems. First of all because from the very start he *is* so complete. As I predicted in my last letter, none of the means which I had conceived, of *locating* Bernal will be adequate, since they all of them subdued him too definitely, + gave him too remote and, I fear, conventionalized, (stylized?) a physiognomy. I begin to see him as a far more living figure—not only the *chorus* but (don't, please, misunderstand me!) in a certain sense the *gods* of certain Greek tragedies. The chorus, after all, does not view the drama in retrospect—at least to the extent that Bernal does.

Understand, too, what I mean when I speak of "problems." Thus far, at least, there is no doubt in my mind as to what these mean—i.e. such problems as there are, are now for *me* to solve; I am so delighted with your text + have so much a sense of your realization that it is for *me,* now, to find the solutions of them. My experience thus far has always been that for every technical problem there is a solution: it is only a matter of discovering it. In this case there is no question in my mind—I am so completely + enthusiastically in accord with your conception that I am confident of summoning the creative energy + insight which I need.

So—let me outline a couple of these problems, entirely in this spirit. As yet I do not know, entirely, what I shall do with the first three lines of Scene II, which I find extremely effective + beautiful in the text but for which, thus far, I have not been able to visualize a musical setting that doesn't seem rather *knapp* [meager] and casual. As I sit writing, however, with the text before me, a solution begins to suggest itself; one which may be of great importance for the shape of the work as a whole. I will not write further about this now—as it is only the suggestion of a suggestion, also, fundamentally, a detail.

The old Bernal, it seems to me, is a deep bass; the only slight misgiving I have in this regard is that the baritone is a voice capable of more varied shades of expression. On the other hand, the fact that he must be kept *very* clearly differentiated from the other characters seems to me to be very decisive here—as well as, of course, his age. In this case there would be no other bass—not even Olmedo, who in any case is a comparatively young man + above all far removed from the conventional operatic *basso profundo* priest (*Der Freischütz, Die Zauberflöte,* etc. etc. etc.); and I might even make use of a loud-speaker, at times, for Bernal.

Do I understand your conception correctly in feeling that the opening of Scene I, through the words "De la Santa Vera Cruz," the opening of Scene II through the words "with wail and weight," and of course the very end of Sc. I + the beginning of Sc. III are in a sense in old Bernal's world—i.e. that the real, *foreground* action of Sc. I begins with Cortez's speech + that of Sc. II with Alvarado's delivery of the prisoners on p. 3? Do I make myself clear—the contrast between *pantomine* + close-up, so to speak? The relative *tempi* suggest that to me.

I have already sketched a setting of the passage from "Tierra" ("Few voices") on page 1, through the "Adoramus te," and have made other, isolated sketches both of speeches and of orchestral *motifs*. The results have thus far confirmed my feeling that it is the right thing for me to have these scenes. *Bien entendu,* there are plenty of matters that cannot be settled till I have the complete text before me—others will need definite collaboration between the two of us. But when you come East I hope to have enough notes on paper— + "performable," for you—to provide a point of departure for us.

Cortèz and Olmedo are, certainly baritones; the young Bernal a rather light [tenor], Alvarado (it seems to me) a somewhat heavier tenor (Siegfried, so to speak!). Aguilar, I should say, baritone. Alonso and Andrès I have not decided upon. I shall have to wait + see whether you give them more pronounced individuality, later in the drama. Otherwise, like the Cacique (though I think of him, provisorily, as a tenor), their voices will be determined by the musical development.

Marina is a low soprano of big range. The way you have introduced her seems to me very beautiful indeed. I like tremendously her silence till the very end of the scene, + then only the three words "Mexico . . . Tenochtitlàn[2] . . . Montezuma."

In this passage between him + the Cacique (in answer to Aguilar) where these words are spoken, I conceive her as speaking, almost as in a dream, to herself. The Cacique speaks directly to the Spaniards + she echoes his words, almost "aside." Is this correct? I feel in her reechoing of these words a kind of premonition of all that is in store for her—bearing in mind also the quotation which you sent me, in April, from the book of J. E. Thompson.[3] Let me know whether this is correct. I trust I have made myself clear, + don't want you to think that I am not quite willing to stand on my own feet *vis-à-vis* your text; but I feel that this is a very crucial dramatic moment, + would not want to proceed too decidedly with my own inner elaboration till I were sure of your conception. I think you will agree that, while one must in general avoid a Wagnerian *over*-emphasis on such detail, this is one of the beginnings of the real drama + must above all not be *under*-stressed.

In my setting of the text I find myself not adhering to any fixed principle or stylistic prejudice, but using all the various resources of effect as the occasion (always very complex) seems best to warrant. It is here that, eventually, your impressions will be of quite overwhelming importance. Even at this early point I have been surprised at my own resources in this matter + hope to produce something really new in the way of expansive English musical prosody—which thus far, for the most part, has been either conventionalized, or quite slavish + without genuine musical expansiveness. I speak of course of the last 250 years, and of the great period of English music.

It seems to me that the lines ("Give them some beads, +c.") of which you speak definitely do not belong to Cortèz; but that because of what immediately precedes + follows, they also—still more definitely—do not belong to Alvarado. It seems to me this would make his role, at this point, much too heavy,— + more so even in the musical setting than in the text, since the music will inevitably intensify the latter, in its more formal as well as in its other aspects. I would suggest that it is a choice between Andrès, Alonzo, + the young Bernal, though perhaps in the end we might come back to Cortèz after all. I needn't write you in detail about this—your thoughts will certainly be the same as mine.

Finally—a few questions in minute detail. Would you object to "conquistador" instead of "conqueror" in the second line of Bernal's first speech? It seems to me that (musically speaking) "Conqueror" is rather weak in accent + rhythm for this point.

Such suggestions as these following I make with every reserve, since your text must not be sacrificed in a single point that seems to you essential to its beauty of expression. I have in mind, however, the musical shaping of such phrases in such a way that its meaning shall be as clear as possible. In each case it would be a matter of very slightly loosening the highly concentrated literary texture, with this end above in view. The one sentence that really bothers me in this respect is Alvarado's, p. 3 "Stab them if they harbingers weren't, of hidden treasuries." I have the feeling that here the contraction "weren't" is, again, perhaps rhythmically too weak—the word "treasuries" perhaps also; and the structure of the sentence, which I like tremendously apart from the musical problem, seems to me too recherché [studied] for my comfort as a composer! On page 4 Alvarado's line "isn't substantial" will not, I think, be clear when sung. Would you object to "Is not substantial"? On the other hand Bernal's "It wasn't since" seems to me very good, "was not" w[oul]d be too heavy. But the sounds "isn't sub . . ." seem to me too indistinct from the point of view of singing.

Also, in the following line I would like, with your permission, to add a conjunction. Perhaps "The wenches, though, are"?

You, of course, must be the one to decide these few details. I am sure you will understand me, + see how devotedly I am studying your text.

We will of course have to provide the Indian girls with Nahuatl words or syllables for the two passages on p. 5. That of course can wait.

I think that is all.

I find however on reading over these scattered notes that I have given you a very slight idea, only, of my enthusiasm, both for your text + for the way you have kept always in mind the *musical* form of the whole. It suggests so much to me—but obviously I can write you about this better after I have clarified my own plans for it. I shall study + absorb it—with only desultory sketching, for about two weeks more; then I shall begin real, connected [illegible] decided a couple of vital matters which I am still pondering, regarding the form of the whole.

Meanwhile—once more, my most heartfelt congratulations!

I forgot in my last letter not only to write you about "Le Roi David"[4] but to thank you for "The Wrath of David"—which I enjoyed tremendously + found suggestive in so many ways. Not only for the specifically Dantean amusements but for your general remarks and simplifications of course, regarding poetic genius + the workings of the creative mind, psyche, or impulse—and regarding history, also. It was a real delight, as has been, after all, everything that I have read.

As for "Le Roi David" I find it neither very good nor very bad. It lacks style, of course, + the inner intensity which alone, today at least, is capable of producing style, + I find it quite "external"— picturesque, if you like, a mixture of France, Russian pseudo-barbarism, baroque oratorio à la Handel, slightly sweetened Catholicism à la César Franck, + a few other elements, dished up in a by no means inept or ineffective manner. It is all "well-written," the work of a thoroughly competent, up-to-date composer. But not fundamentally "important" in my sense of the word.

[. . .]

That, + Mexico, are the only pieces of news we have, in fact.

Affectionate greetings from us all
Roger

1. Sessions had received the scenes on June 22 and wired Borgese the same day: "OVERWHELMED BY BEAUTY OF PAGES WHICH ARRIVED THIS MORNING ON TRULY IMPORTANT DAY. HAVE BEEN HARD AT WORK ON THEM THIS AFTERNOON AND MADE SEVERAL SKETCHES. WILL WRITE DETAILED COMMENTS SHORTLY WHEN I HAVE BETTER ASSIMILATED THEM. MEANWHILE HEARTIEST CONGRATULATIONS AND WARMEST THANKS. LOVE FROM ALL THREE OF US. ROGER."
2. The Aztec capital, near the site of present-day Mexico City.
3. John Eric Thompson, *Mexico before Cortez: An account of the daily life, religion, and ritual of the Aztecs and kindred peoples* (New York: Scribner's, 1933). Thompson (b. 1898) wrote numerous books on the Mayans.
4. Arthur Honegger's 1921 oratorio (or "dramatic psalm") *Le roi David* had been performed April 11, 1937, by the New York Philharmonic under Artur Rodzinski.

▼

Roger Sessions to Elizabeth S. Coolidge
als US-DLC

Saturday, June 25 [1938]

My dear Mrs. Coolidge,—   Princeton

Your extremely kind letter deserved a prompter answer + would have had one, had I not apparently strained my eyes somewhat badly on a long automobile trip at the beginning of this month. But I can't tell you how very proud I was made by what you wrote me in regard to my article on Vienna.[1] It is a truly great privilege to win the approval of one for whom I have such a cordial and unfailing esteem, and you made me more than happy by taking the trouble to write to me.

I now have heard that you are helping to make possible the publication of my [string] Quartet, and Mr. [Carl] Engel said I might write and thank you for that, too. Please know that I do so, most heartily.

In regard to Krenek I write with all sincerity that I believe him to be one of the truly gifted, + one of the most serious contemporary musicians. You will not, I know, mind my saying that I feel it is unjust to regard him as primarily a dramatic composer, in spite of the fact that his one spectacular success was made with "Jonny spielt Auf."[2] He wrote this work however fifteen years ago while he was still in his early twenties; it was a product of the *Zeitgeist* of that moment, and one which he has long since outgrown. It seems to me clear that one reason why his later work has not been more successful has been that it has been so much in contrast, through its much more serious aims, with that work.

In recent years he has become a convinced believer in the "twelve-tone system," though not, I believe, a strict disciple of Schönberg. As you presumably realize, I am not, personally, by any means of that persuasion; but I feel for that reason the more confident when I find myself able to respond to music written by those who are. Of Krenek's latest music I know only his *Variations* for piano which I have heard him play three times—twice in private here at my home, + once later in N.Y. at the League of Composers. It struck me each time as music of more than ordinary interest; it is not only music of great seriousness, distinction, and in the best sense of the word, aristocratic, but I found it often genuinely moving, and always authoritative in having "something to say" and saying it in clear and positive accents. In saying all this I feel that I am giving the work very high praise, and you may take my words as carefully "weighed" and considered. Adjectives, I know, cost nothing, but I assure you that in regard to contemporary music I use them with care and a decent economy! Above all, in speaking of Krenek I am dealing with music which (except for the cardinal fact of being genuine music!) is rather at the antipode of my own musical thought, and I try to express exactly what I feel, in as sincere and objective a spirit as possible.

As far as other names are concerned, I find myself unable to add substantially to what I said when you were in Princeton. Of my American colleagues the one for whom I have on the whole the greatest respect is Walter Piston. Copland and Harris, I feel, both have more talent, but I have thus far been able to enjoy their music only in spots. In any case I believe you told me you did not wish to commission someone who you already had commissioned. There are also Quincy Porter and Randall Thompson, both of whom are splendid musicians, but who have not, I believe, so much to say as the ones I have mentioned.

As far as younger Europeans are concerned, I have been disappointed in Markevich, who has seemed to me to go the way of so many young composers who achieve a too early + precocious success; in Shostakovich, whose first symphony seems a very promising work but whose later music, such as I have heard, seems without style or integrity. I do not believe much in Jean Françaix, whose music seems to me attractive but inconsequential. [. . .]

Please forgive me if I seem to send such a predominantly negative report! I would so gladly send you a better one; but I feel that the "composer" for whom music is something more than a *business* is an all too rare bird—as rare in Europe, latterly, as in the United States; and in fact I pin my hopes on a few quite young men in the U.S. who are still in the beginners state. Some day I hope I may be writing you about them!

Please forgive this long letter which I nevertheless hope may be of some use. I have had to write it rather in pieces as my eyes still get quite tired + bloodshot if I use them for too long at a time.

And—please be assured of my most sincere and, I hope I may say, affectionate good wishes.

Most cordially,
Roger Sessions

1. Roger Sessions, "Vienna: *Vale, Ave*," *Modern Music* 15 (May 1938): 203–8.
2. Krenek's *Jonny spielt auf*, op. 45, in two parts and with a libretto by Krenek, was written in 1925–26 and first performed in Leipzig, February 10, 1927.

▼

Roger Sessions to Antonio Borgese
als I-Fborgese

Dear Antonio,—   Friday, August 26, 1938

"The Conquerors" is certainly not bad, though I think I still prefer "Mexico." In a perhaps not entirely successful effort to formulate my thoughts I find that (a) the drama deals with an event that is far greater than any of the actors in it (b) the Conquered are at least as much the protagonists as the Conquerors.

How important are these considerations? I would say that even the idea of the "Conquest" is inadequate—even in a sense too small + too personal?

I'll think it over, in any case— + we have plenty of time. The above are "first reactions." —*Tenochtitlàn* is my really favorite title but perhaps it is for phonetic Titans!

I hope you may be free Monday. I'll have some time in the evening I think—though I'm not sure yet, quite.

Love from all three of us, + good luck.
Roger

▼

Ernst Krenek to Roger Sessions
als US-NYpease

March 7, 1939
Dear Mr. Sessions,   Hotel Whitcomb, San Francisco

thank you very much for your nice letter of congratulation and the sending of your quartet [in E minor].

I wanted to wait writing you until I had the opportunity to peruse the score at least superficially which I did several days ago. It interested me very much indeed, and I am glad you sent it to me. I like especially the originality of the harmonic features which give clear evidence of a very personal and deep expressiveness of your music. Furthermore, I was very much impressed by the long breath of some thematic developments, especially in the first movement. Of course, these remarks are only the result of a brief reading on the piano, and I wish sincerely I shall be able to hear a performance of the whole work.

-311-

As to Vassar College, I feel also very happy that this appointment will allow me to remain in closer connection with you and our mutual friends. You know that my personal inclination goes rather West and South. I think, however, that this engagement is very dignified and the best introduction to the academic life of this country I could possibly have obtained. I think also that a very important task awaits me there.

I heard from Mark [Brunswick] with great pleasure of the success of your first concert. I hope very much this organization will keep going on and may later be able to pay some attention also to what I tried in this field.

Thank you once more for the quartet and the most honorable dedication you put in the score. With very best wishes from us both to all of yours

most cordially yours
Ernst Krenek

▼

Roger Sessions to David Diamond
als US-Rdiamond

Tuesday [March 1939]
[Princeton]

Dear David,—

Your letter pleased me—of course.

But I do feel that there is one misunderstanding on your part, that I must clear up. My attitude towards you during the last two years was not due in the least to your having "hurt" me by going to study with N.B. I meant everything I said at that time, + continue to mean it. And at my age one is not "hurt."

What did cause my attitude was the feeling that you were "playing the game" with everyone else + therefore presumably with me too; + when that is the case, you will agree, there can be no real confidence as long as that attitude lasts. I felt also that you fell square into the trap which N.B. set for you, especially when she made you feel that your studies were really over + that you were not in a position to learn any more from counterpoint, or from a real study of technical problems— + since I had made myself responsible for your development I could only feel that that was a pity.

But it is not necessary to go into all that. The whole experience was valuable in that it showed me how little any teacher can assume of responsibility for his pupil's development + that it is both pedagogically unsound + unfair to the pupil for him to assume that responsibility. So I think that since that time I have been more effective as a teacher because I don't let my pupils depend on me so much, any more.

In regard to the first matter I can remember attitudes—quite unconscious + irresponsibly exaggerated—on my part which may have made it extremely difficult for you to be frank with me. I mean, not only that I spoke more freely + less seriously than I should have done, in regard to certain people; but I spoke about homosexuality, for instance in a way that must have seemed to you quite obtuse + insensitive; in a way that, certainly, misrepresents my real attitude *entirely*. It is just, you know, my habit of letting off steam + though you could not have been aware of that at the time, meant precisely nothing.

Don't doubt, *mon cher,* that all the affection of which you speak in your letter, is really there; + don't feel pained or embarrassed *in any way* that I should write like this. Truly, nothing more needs be said; if you can be always really simple + natural + *free* with me you may have no doubts whatever of my response.

Affectionately,
Roger—

▼

Roger Sessions to David Diamond
als US-Rdiamond

Dear David,—   March 19, 1939

I'm sorry I seemed "cold." I certainly did not, + have not, meant to be harsh with you, + do not mean to be now.

You ask me "surely our friendship is not through."— The truth of the matter is that it has seemed to me that, on your side, it has been through for some time.

Since you bring this subject up I assume that you want me to be frank. Let me say therefore that I feel that where there is to be friendship there must be a basis of real honesty + loyalty— + you know, at my age, if not before, one learns to judge people by their actions + by words spoken to others rather than simply by those spoken in one's presence. You surely are not so naive as to think that

I have been unaware, for the past two years at any rate, that these three things have frequently differed, sometimes quite considerably.

Please don't think I have been offended or even especially disillusioned by this. I have understood far more than you think + have, more often than not, given you the benefit of the doubt. But I can't seriously believe that you will misunderstand when I say that I came to the conclusion quite some time ago that my friendship means considerably less to you than you say it does.

On the other hand, if you wish assurance that my attitude is not antagonistic to you, you may have it, gladly. Only *friendship* is a different matter, + in this case depends on you much more than it does on me. I have many friends; I try to demand as little of them as possible, and, as you of all people should know, to give as generously as possible in return. If that is not enough I am sorry, but there is nothing I can do about it.

Alors—c'est ça! [Then—that's that!]

As for your violin,[1]—I didn't take it; but I spoke to the superintendent at 61st St. last spring + we thought we found it in the basement. I am pretty sure that I decided with him to wait till you returned so that you could identify it, before we removed it from the house. I would not have moved it on my own responsibility, since I could not identify it definitely as yours.—I shall ask Milton,[2] who went up there with me, if he remembers anything about it, + will then write the superintendent.

I'm glad you will come to at least one of our [ISCM] concerts. Everyone agrees that they are something quite new in the way of contemporary music programs in N.Y. + we plan, as a result of the success we have already had, to continue with the same sort of program next year.

As always,
Roger—[3]

1. Diamond had left a violin with Sessions for safekeeping while Diamond was in Paris. Sessions had left the instrument in the basement of the apartment building at Sixty-first Street in New York when he vacated his studio there in 1936.

2. Milton Babbitt (b. 1916) had studied privately with Sessions 1935–38. In 1938 he had begun teaching music and mathematics at Princeton University.

3. Diamond's answer apparently was immediate, for on March 22 Sessions wired him: "THANKS FOR REALLY SPLENDID LETTER. FEEL PERHAPS EACH OF US HAD MISUNDERSTOOD AND THAT WHAT WE NEED IS FRANK TALK. DO NOT WORRY AND ABOVE ALL PLAN IF POSSIBLE TO COME PRINCETON SUNDAY ELEVEN THIRTY TRAIN. LET ME KNOW. AFFECTIONATELY, ROGER."

▼

Roger Sessions to David Diamond
als US-Rdiamond

My dear David,— Friday, April 5, 1939

I found your letter when I got home yesterday, + and want to write you just a note to tell you what a good time I had with you yesterday morning.[1] It was for me a quite specially nice time, + you must know that I got the impression that a lot of my feelings + impressions of the last two years seemed very definitely out of date. Several things pleased me very much indeed; I shall not go into details, + in fact I don't see any sense in probing over things which are done + which need mean nothing, anymore, to either of us.

So I am not going to inflict any "frank talk" on you. I propose simply that we go ahead + start afresh. I have realized for some time that the old basis was not one which could last, + that you would under any circumstances whatever have felt very constrained by it sooner or later. For that reason + for others I don't think we sh[oul]d either of us have any regrets.

Well—no need to be self conscious, but please feel quite free in your mind + forget that there have been "problems."

No time, yet, to do more than glance at the 'cello concerto;[2] + I don't want to say too much. But the first impression was excellent. Please don't feel badly if I say that that of the *Heroic Piece*[3] was not so good. Was the performance a satisfactory one? I like some details, but the impression as a whole was scattered. The concerto seems to have much more continuity. But I hope I'll know *both* works better.

Affectionately as always.

Roger—

1. In New York City.
2. Diamond's Cello Concerto (1938) premiered in Rochester, N.Y., April 30, 1942.
3. *Heroic Piece* for orchestra was premiered in Zurich, July 29, 1938.

▼

Roger Sessions to Antonio Borgese
als I-Fborgese

July 3, 1939
Colorado Springs[1]

Dear Antonio,—

I was so glad to have your note + to learn where you are.[2] I had assumed that you had left Chicago already ten days ago. Needless to say, you have both been very much in my thoughts, which have been such happy + confident ones.

Colorado Springs is a very pleasant place + I believe I shall accomplish a great deal here. At first I had days of torpor + even of discomfort—my food disagreed with me + I felt constantly sleepy. I suppose that was the effect partly of great fatigue—reaction after the winter— + partly of the altitude. In any case it has worn off + I now feel splendidly.

My classes are small but I have eager + alert pupils + I am very much pleased with the way they are going. I always get new ideas during the summer, especially here in the West where the fresh air + the dry climate do me no end of good.

There are charming + even quite interesting people here—not, however, too many or too charming for my efficiency. In about three weeks there is to be a concert of my work. I shall play the accompaniment to my Violin Concerto at which I am practising quite hard.[3] We shall see whether or not Titans exist in Colorado Springs!

Above all I am composing, + for the first time in my life I seem to be establishing a real routine. The inner resistances which I have so often had to overcome at the beginning of a period of work seem to be very much lessened, + I have great hopes of what the summer will produce, both in the way of actual accomplishment + in the way of helping me to a more reasonable way of living. I am absorbing myself gradually in Mexico + believe I shall really have something to show you when we meet again.

[. . .]

I envy you Mexico, + believe that after all it is the best place for you this summer, from all points of view. Please do send me an occasional postcard, with a picture of a volcano or some other Mexican landmark or visage—besides writing when you have time.

Needless to say, I am more eager than I can tell you for the opera.

My love to both of you.
Roger

1. While teaching at Colorado College in the summer of 1939 Sessions completed the second and third movements of his *Pages from a Diary* for piano. Both the second movement, dedicated to Edward T. Cone, and the third, dedicated to Carter Harman, are dated "Colorado Springs, August 1939." Harman (b. 1918) studied with Sessions at Princeton University (B.A. 1940) and taught at Princeton 1940–42. He was a music critic for the New York *Times* (1947–52) and *Time* (1952–57). From 1976 to 1984 he was executive director for Composers Recordings Inc.

2. In Mexico.

3. The soloist for the July performance was Robert Gross. Gross (1914–1983), a violinist and composer, studied informally with Schoenberg and Sessions. He introduced the Hindemith Violin Concerto to New York in 1945, and gave first performances of the Imbrie Concerto (1958). He taught at Occidental College in Los Angeles 1949–79. Albert Spalding, incidentally, made a ghostlike reappearance in Sessions's life by giving a recital in Colorado Springs on August 8.

▼

Roger Sessions to Miriam Gideon[1]
als US-NYgideon

August 12, 1939
Colorado Springs

My dear Miriam,—

You see how bad I am when it comes to writing letters! I have thought of you so often + wondered about you, + how you were feeling, about Europe + everything. And then your letter came, just on the eve of my concert—of which more later! It has been so nice to think of you in Paris, + I can very well understand your falling in love with it. I don't remember what the particular association with a street corner was—perhaps Montparnasse + St. Michel—I don't remember exactly what the number on Montparnasse it was where I lived (was it 162?) + where so much happened in my life—but it is nearly opposite the "Closerie des Liles" which must still exist, + near that corner. In any case that was over 13 years ago, + I'm sure that Paris hasn't changed much; + it is just as good to think that you sometimes think of me in one place, as in another.

I am amused to hear of your possibly going to Fontainebleau and coming face to face with the famous "Nadia." If you do so you will feel her extraordinary charm + her vitality + enthusiasm as well. Naturally I hope you will not come away feeling that R.S. has perhaps behaved in a somewhat small way in feeling + sometimes talking about her as he does! Not that I really think you will—but I am perfectly aware of her qualities, + also of the fact that the kind of crisis that I passed through, in those years, makes one's feelings much more raw than they should be, even. In any case Fontainebleau is marvelous, + I know you will love it.

What you write of the refugees is distressing, to say the least, + I hope only that you feel that something satisfactory is being accomplished in the way of progress. It is strange to have to depend on Denver + Colorado Springs papers for one's news of the world. The press out here is disheartening not only because it is either hopelessly sensational or hopelessly provincial but because it embodies to the fullest extent the paradoxes + contradictions of the American viewpoint. On the Pacific Coast one is after all on the edge of the country, + aware of all kinds of world problems because of that fact; whereas here we are still 1200 miles from the nearest sea-coast (the farthest, by a long shot, that I have ever been for more than a couple of days). The result is that one comes up against the original western psychology of flight from civilization's complexities + wickednesses in a rather outspoken, but quite deep-seated form.

Colorado Springs is, however, not by any means a simple place. It is rather like Reno in various ways—chiefly by the mixture of the west + a large semipermanent increment of sick people from outside—the fact that they are emotionally sick in Reno + physically sick here only makes the resemblance more interesting + in fact quite enlightening. In addition to that the whole populations of Kansas + Oklahoma apparently move here for the month of August. I am decidedly anti both of those states but very pro-Colorado. With all its faults the West is *humanly* so far superior to the east, + it is really very healthy for me to live in a place like this for a while, especially after a hectic winter—it freshens me up tremendously + brings me closer to my essential self, if only because one has so much time to reflect + to come into real contact with oneself.

I have worked a good deal, especially on my Symphony[2] which I hope to be able to play to you this fall. I am very much hoping that this summer will give me the chance to make a regular routine (in the best sense) for myself + to accomplish far more than I have been able to do in the last three years at least. I won't write about the Symphony because I can't tell about it, being still so close to it, or rather in the midst of it. But I have great hopes for it, as a work in any case.

My concert was a genuine + very satisfying success;[3] still more satisfying was my study of the [Violin] Concerto which we played really quite well—*far* better, beyond all comparison, than the New York performance which you heard. It was very satisfying to find this work, which has in a sense been so unlucky, still better than I had realized + to again be excited + moved by it. I believe it is the best, or at least the most complete + characteristic work I have written— the best, that is, from the Sessions point of view!

This seems to be a rather long letter. I'm afraid you have done nothing to discourage a habit of loquacity in me! It will be nice to see you again. I am curious to see how everything will work out at the Chatham Square School; at all events it will simplify my life as far as getting around is concerned. I did feel quite sad, however, when I closed my studio; the year there was such a rich one + I feel that I must somehow achieve its equivalent this winter.

Thank you again for your letter— + the best possible wishes.

Roger

1. Gideon (b. 1906) studied privately with Sessions and with Lazare Saminsky, a cofounder of the League of Composers and music director of Temple Emanu-El in New York. She taught music at Brooklyn College, the Jewish Theological Seminary, The Manhattan School of Music, and the City University of New York, and in 1975 was elected to the National Institute of Arts and Letters.

2. Another reference to a second symphony, which was not completed and which does not appear on his list of works.

3. On August 9 Sessions had written to Krenek: "At a concert of my work which was given here at the Arts Center in July, Robert Gross and I gave what seemed to me quite an excellent reading of my Violin Concerto, and the work, which I have always been told was so difficult for the public as well as the violinist, was received with genuine enthusiasm. It was very pleasant, not only because this work has thus far been rather unlucky, but because in restudying the work for this performance, I came again to the realization that it is not only the largest, but in many ways the best, or at least the most characteristic, that I have written" (US-SD).

▼

Roger Sessions to David Diamond
als US-Rdiamond

Sunday, February 12, 1940
Dear David,—   [Princeton]

Naturally I am distressed over the loss of your violin. I am sure the people at 61st St. believe they are right, nevertheless they are mistaken, as I can prove, since one of my pupils was with me when I moved my things out. You will remember that there was a violin there at that time, + that I assumed it was yours but that you failed to identify it when you came later. The whole thing was a "misunderstanding," for which no one including yourself is wholly exempt from blame. If you had looked after the violin in October 1937 when you first returned from France, I'm sure we would have found it, since all the shunting [of] things around in the cellar at 61st St. was done after that.

En tout cas [In any case]—I too was partly responsible + have been looking around for a violin for you. Miriam Gideon says her husband has one wh. you can borrow[1]—please let me know if you can use that one—if not I will look elsewhere.

As to my "coldness," really, that is not the point. There is no personal issue between us as far as I am concerned.

But I am extremely busy, with far too much to do, + see much less of all of my friends that I w[oul]d like. So when three times last spring you broke appointments with me without letting me know, I simply felt I was wasting my time. On two occasions I went to the trouble of routing you out + found that there was really nothing the matter at all—I felt that in doing so I had met you half way, + that if it meant no more to you than that, I had a dozen ways of spending my time.

As for your music, I simply haven't had any luck with what I have seen lately. I feel that you are going through a phase wh. is no doubt necessary for you but wh., without wishing to cavil in any way, I don't find particularly sympathetic. Since I know you have fundamentally much more this does not worry me very much—I know it should some day come out. But it makes it difficult to write you since I hate to seem negative when in reality I am only waiting. In any case try to forgive me— + (I needn't say) go on composing! This is the best possible thing I could say to you, + should be the best possible sign of my real affection + good will. For [we] *will* get together some time, if you want to.

Always affectionately
Roger

1. A day earlier, Sessions had wired Diamond, "GET IN TOUCH WITH MIRIAM GIDEON REGARDING VIOLIN" (US-Rdiamond).

▼

Roger Sessions to Antonio Borgese
als I-Fborgese

February 27, 1940
Princeton

Dear Antonio,—

Excuse what I fear will be a very scrappy + inadequate return for the riches which the mail brought from you on Friday morning. I am on schedule now, + have not quite learned the routine; hence nearly everything I do bears some traces of haste.

The eighth scene is magnificent; as I told you before I feel that it is in a sense the turning point of the whole; this is obvious. As you have written it this seems still clearer—the whole seems to me magnificently realized + very beautiful. Don't misunderstand me—as a matter of fact, I am sure it is what you would most like to have me say—if I say above all I feel its immense musical potentialities. The beauty of your conceptions + your poetry I have learned to take for granted. But the further the play develops the more intimately it seems to me to be *opera*. The broad lyrical lines on which the scene is conceived, the lightning speed of the action when it comes are both such *necessities* and above all inspirations for me.

I am very curious to see what immediately follows—the tension of the scene is tremendous, of course, + I am eager to see what your resolution is. I can imagine it in several different ways; so I say nothing. The end of the scene is *immense,* especially (forgive me for the appearance but not for the real meaning of these words!) as I begin to visualize it.

Regarding the title *Malinche*— First reaction, one of elation + recognition that the title corresponds to my secret wishes + hopes for the final conception of both the character + the work.

Second reaction, a query, based I think upon the fact that I do not know yet the conclusion of the work + have, partly for purely physical reasons, not been able to keep entirely in touch with the evolution of your thought. You once wrote or said to me that Dona Marina was gradually to disappear from the scene, + wd. not appear at the end. I was mildly disappointed then, but gather that you have somewhat altered your plan. The above-mentioned query was the obvious one; does not that title shift the sense of the drama to a too personal emphasis?

Third reaction, also the obvious one— The query is answered by both your letter + the book of Harriet Long wh. you sent, + which I will return in a few days, when I have re-read it a couple of times + digested it a little more. I will not deny that my feeling is one of new energy + inspiration. Marina is so clearly for me, the *heart* (in the full + multiple sense of the word) of the whole thing, + I know from my own emotional response that the title is the right one. As regards the questions implicit in the above query, I trust your dramatic + poetic intuition completely. Let it be *Malinche,* then—with great joy.

We are visiting the Welches very shortly + I shall read the whole thing to them then. I had just put it off, as one so easily does in Princeton, especially with my schedule!

Regarding the Violin Concerto I believe I understand you completely.[1] The work is undeniably very difficult, + undeniably from my point of view at least, not definitive. I am quite sure that it is less "intransigent" than you find it—it is far less so, for instance, than the Piano Sonata, though the latter is intransigent perhaps in a different way from what you meant in using the term. This however is not really important; I appreciated + welcomed your remarks, + in a very curious + profound sense welcomed them. So rarely one hears something *real* said about one's work; + the *occasion* of a performance, whatever its "success," contains so much that is false, that one easily is disheartened—the work, + with it the best of oneself, seems so lonely, so naked, + so humiliated. One feels really comforted by such words as yours because, however qualified they may be regarding the work itself, they show such real + deep sympathy with all that the work aspires to be, + thus perhaps with its truest essence. For the rest, even the most deeply felt work is only one stage in its creator's life, so that in a sense he is of all people, once it is behind him, the least concerned in its fate. Needless to say, your words have the greatest possible value for me always—I need not tell you that.

So—send me more of the play when you can. I look forward to it more than I can tell you.

Love to you both. I think of you constantly. *[. . .]*

Roger[2]

1. Borgese had apparently heard the Chicago performance of the Violin Concerto, January 8, 1940, with Robert Gross, violin, and the Illinois Symphony, Izler Solomon conducting.

2. There are no extant letters from Sessions for the year separating this letter from the next. On September 5, 1940, Sessions, aged forty-three, again became a father— this time to a daughter, Elizabeth.

▼

Roger Sessions to David Diamond
tls US-Rdiamond

Dear David,—   Sunday, February 16 [1941]

I read your notes with real interest and am returning them to you.[1] I think the most helpful thing I can tell you is that you have *far* too much material there for the scope you propose. It isn't a matter of its being too weighty, but of there simply being too much. What you have outlined is not a series of four lectures, but a whole winter's course—even assuming that you plan the series carefully and make it as concentrated as possible; even, that is, if you should write the whole thing out and read it.

You will see what I mean if you will sit down with your notes and read them aloud to yourself, with moderate and clear enunciation. I would guess that this alone would take you at least an hour. Then, choose what would seem to you an adequate number of illustrations for such lectures and play them through. You will be amazed at the amount of time it will take, and I may assure you from long experience that if you were actually delivering the lectures it would take you longer still. Naturally you will need far more than six, or even sixteen, times as many words in order actually to deliver the lectures, than you have in these notes which after all are only a bare table of contents.

Secondly, you ought not to be offended if I say that Music History is no more your subject than it is mine. There are plenty of people around—and not by any means all stupid ones—who have devoted their lives to it, and I would be surprised if you, any more than I, could successfully compete with them in that particular field. Have you really any serious ambition to do so? What has musical history to do either with your work or mine, after all? I don't mean that you shouldn't speak of such things if you want to do so, but simply that I think you are on shaky ground in trying to make history relevant to aesthetic problems, which above all for a composer, are direct experiences and only to be approached directly. And I think too that in such a series of lectures you would be laying yourself open to competition from people whose whole experience and training would give them an incalculable advantage. Why should it be otherwise, after all, since this is not your job?

Of course, I disagree with a great many of your judgments and your conclusions, as far as I can see these in your notes. This isn't important in the least, and I would not let it interfere with any feeling I might have regarding the feasibility or even the value of such lectures. I simply think you will not find a "market" for this particular plan.

My advice, therefore, would be for you to consider very carefully the main points that you would like to make, and to build your lectures around these, in the simplest and most direct and clear manner. I think you would find very quickly that you could leave out by far the greater amount of the material you have gathered here, since what is effective as illustration in such cases is not quantity but relevance and clarity. What you have prepared is simply a syllabus of the most easily available material, and what is really necessary is a choice of a very few features on which you can comment at leisure.

Remember that I am saying this from experience. Whenever I plan a formal lecture I find that I have run way over the time allotted; and my lectures are always extremely concentrated and on the difficult side. So you can see that I know what I am talking about. I can't see why Douglas [Moore], at least, didn't tell you the same thing.

Please forgive me for being what I know seems to you like a very unsatisfactory friend. You are certainly in that respect one of my failures, by which I mean to imply that the failure is on my side and not on yours. It may be on yours too, but it is certainly on mine. I have, frankly, never had an experience quite like this, and I don't really know what to do about it.

It is perhaps that I once may have led you to expect too much of me, and certainly that I once expected of you more than one has a right to expect of any human being, especially a young one who is developing and who certainly cannot be expected to develop in any but his own way. All I can see now is that we have travelled along very different roads which—forgive me—seem to get wider and wider apart. This has nothing to do with my fundamental affection and abundant good wishes for you and it is certainly nothing that either one of us should deplore aside from the inevitable regrets that life often brings. The only trouble is that, since we once did expect a good deal more of each other in a purely personal way, misunderstanding and even wounded feelings can so easily arise between us. So that if I seem unresponsive it is only because I am a little at a loss to see just what there is to be done about it all; it is, I am quite willing to admit, a confession of inadequacy on my part. For one ought to be able to differ quite profoundly with some one and yet be able to give and take what is there.

I should, truly, like nothing better than to feel that we could both, without embarrassment and without false pride, lay all the cards on the table. Two years ago I felt that we were making a good start at doing just this. Perhaps some day we will achieve it yet. There is really nothing in my feeling for you that should make it impossible. Only, you see, I am not sure of you, and I have too much the feeling, you see, that you are in the last analysis not wholly sure of yourself, where I am concerned . . .

Well, in any case, thank you for sending me the notes, and don't misunderstand what I have said about them.

As always,
Roger

P.S. I just read your letter in the *Times*,[2] wh. I liked.

1. Diamond had requested Sessions's reactions to his outline for a proposed set of lectures he was to give at Smith College. Lisl Sessions attended the lectures, at which Diamond played parts of the *Pages from a Diary,* but her husband was not present.
2. Diamond had written the *New York Times* (Sunday, February 16, 1941, p. 6 of the drama and music section), responding to a letter in the previous Sunday's paper by a Mr. Strassburg, a student of Hindemith's: "There is a very dangerous and non-creative tendency on the part of young Americans studying with European musicians to swallow, hook, line, and sinker, all the philosophical and theoretical dogma with a kind of stoic insensibility. A genuine creative talent does not have to be warned of mannerisms."

▼

Roger Sessions to David Diamond
tls US-Rdiamond

Dear David,—   Tuesday, February 25, 1941

I'm sorry I haven't answered your letter sooner. The last week has been a hectic one, and I of course wanted to write you a real answer.

You see, my dear David, you wholly misinterpreted my letter. If I had it here I could probably see why. But I think the point is this; my feeling of real affection for you, of interest in your work, and of concern for everything that happens to you, are so self-evident to me that it is hard to weigh my words when I write, to the extent that the situation apparently demands. So it turns out that what I intended not as the shutting of a door but rather as a first gesture towards opening it—to open the way for both to "put the cards on the table" and really come into contact again—apparently seemed to you like the opposite of this.

You see, when I wrote that we seemed to have travelled along very different roads, etc., I had no idea that I was saying something that would hurt you, or that you would especially question. Certainly I did not mean that we had become hostile to each other or that we had reached any kind of impasse; I meant simply that, as you yourself write in so many words, you have had to travel "in my own direction." What perhaps you do not entirely understand is that I have never questioned this or regarded it as anything but normal; and though at one time it did cause me a good deal of unhappiness, I have never regarded this unhappiness as anyone's affair but my own—something which I had foreseen as inevitable and against which I perhaps, as a not entirely unreasonable human being, should have been better prepared than I actually was. And while it is true that I did not always agree—and that too is an inevitable part of such a situation, and a bitter one—I certainly didn't blame you for that either.

Also—as I read your notes, it seemed to me clear that each of us had in these intervening years shifted our positions vis-à-vis many matters to such an extent that, should we talk together now, there would be adjustments to make. No more than that. And is it such a serious matter, as far as our relationship is concerned? You may be sure it doesn't matter to me that your estimate of Hindemith and Bartók and Strawinsky, still less Copland and Harris, is a quite different one from mine—these would be things to talk about but certainly not worth quarreling over, above all in the present state of things, when we all of us should be down at the bedrock of essential human attitudes, and not making issues of the trivialities of aestheticism. I would not even mention them if I were not anxious to make clear what I had in mind—it really does not matter at all.

For every one in your generation, my dear David, and for you among the[m] most of all, I feel a sympathy that literally has no limits. Ultimately we will all understand each other better than can be possible with those *between* our respective ages. You are facing very much what I had to face twenty-three years ago, with certain differences, some of them favorable to one, some to the other of us; I know fully well both how hard that is, and am fully acquainted with the various forms of torture that one goes through. But you really ought to know, and I am sure you really do know, that *security* nowadays simply does not exist—it is nowhere to be found, in my life any more than in yours. The best we can hope for is that by a gigantic and multiple effort we can somehow help to restore it to the world.

Of course I am very, very sorry that as a "hero" I have "never quite measured up," as you say. But does it seem entirely sophistical when I ask you whether any one ever can, conceivably, measure up to some one else's demands? One is obliged first of all to measure up as far as possible to one's own, and I doubt if any one ever succeeds at that, even. Isn't it, after all, much better for any friendship to think of one's friend, whatever the difference in ages, as a human and fallible but essentially well-intentioned being? That is certainly what I have always been in your case, David, and I have never laid eyes on a human being, or heard of one, who would seem anything but incredibly pompous and presumptuous in attempting to be more than that.

If that is the case it ought to throw some light on what seems to you to be "confusion" and "egocentric doubt" on my part. Unless one is a little drunk with complacency I don't see how one can ever regard oneself as entirely blameless if a misunderstanding arises; and if you care to do so you will, I should think, not find it hard to see in my readiness to speak of *my* failure rather than yours, exactly that willingness to "give you the benefit of the doubt" which you complain is lacking. At least that was, purely and simply, what I meant.

Finally I have rather the impression that you didn't like what I said about the notes and their historical slant. Anyone who sees anything of me these days could tell you that in saying this I did not mean to imply that David Diamond was incompetent as a music historian, but rather that his musical and aesthetic judgments have primarily a value of their own and that to try to give them a historical basis or justification is both unnecessary and irrelevant, and that therefore that aspect of your lectures could easily be curtailed with only benefit to the main points which you apparently had in mind.

I'm not writing more now because I feel quite sure that to do so would be either at best unnecessary or at worst futile. I have just reread a letter which I had once from one of the people whom I have loved most. She found herself confronted by a terrible crisis which had only very indirectly to do with us but which, through no one's fault, threatened, and finally destroyed, our relationship. She sent her best friend to tell me what had happened, and at the same time wrote me that note in which she said "One can't *really* tell people things. They have to understand." To understand, in that case, was about the hardest effort I had ever had to make, and I had ultimately no consolation except a rather bitter pride at having succeeded. But what she said was of course utterly true. For this reason, in the spirit of the truest friendship in the world, I feel that if you want to understand, you will. I certainly hope you will want to—for this kind of hide-and-seek which we seem to have been playing seems to me as senseless and unnecessary as it is distressing.

>With all the affection which I have never ceased having,
>Roger

⌄⌄

$\int$OON THE BREACH between Sessions and Diamond was again temporarily repaired. Sessions wrote back to Diamond asking him to come to Princeton to talk. In early April Diamond traveled to Princeton and succeeded in patching up the friendship. Sessions wrote back (April 8, 1941), "It was *very* good, I thought, Sunday, + I hope you feel reassured about everything. Believe me, you have every reason to do so" (US-Rdiamond).

By May, however, trouble again arose. As president of the American section of the ISCM Sessions had secured a performance of Diamond's *Music for Double String Orchestra, Brass and Timpani* at the eighteenth Festival of the ISCM held in New York May 7–27, 1941. Sessions wired Diamond:

DOING EVERYTHING POSSIBLE TO BRING ABOUT PERFORMANCE OF YOUR WORK. WILL OF COURSE SUPPORT YOU COMPLETELY IN YOUR REQUEST FOR ADMISSION TO REHEARSALS BUT CAN ACCOMPLISH NOTHING WHATEVER IF YOU INSIST ON ROYALTY. THIS IS NOT THE OCCASION FOR SUCH A DEMAND WHICH WOULD BE JUSTIFIED UNDER ORDINARY CIRCUMSTANCES. BUT SUCCESSFUL FESTIVAL DEMANDS REAL COOPERATION IN ARTISTS CAUSE TOWARDS WHICH MANY FIRST CLASS MUSICIANS AND EVEN BUSINESS MEN ARE GIVING SERVICE ABSOLUTELY GRATIS. PLEASE THEREFORE PHONE [Henry] GERSTLÉ AT ONCE WITHDRAWING THIS DEMAND AND WE WILL DO OUR BEST TO PUT PERFORMANCE THROUGH ON BASIS OF YOUR OTHER CONDITIONS. WE HAVE LEANED OVER BACKWARDS IN TRYING TO SECURE PERFORMANCE OF YOUR WORK. THEREFORE I BEG AND EXPECT YOU TO HELP OUT. (US-Rdiamond)

Diamond "begged Roger to have it removed because [he] was not allowed to attend a rehearsal"; the work was not performed.[1]

Problems concerning the next year's ISCM festival led Sessions to send carboned letters on December 3, 1941, to committee members Copland, Belgian conductor Désiré Defauw (d. 1960), Joaquín Nin-Culmell, and Carleton Sprague Smith, who had been sidestepped in Sessions's decision to locate the 1942 ISCM festival in San Francisco, rather than in Latin America, as some of the members wished. While in San Francisco, Sessions explained, he had lobbied various musicians for the idea of the festival's being held there: these included the composer Darius Milhaud and Alfred Frankenstein, whom Sessions described in the letters as "the music critic of the *San Francisco Chronicle,* whose interest in Contemporary Music is very genuine, very broad-minded, and very conscientious." He ended by asking whether the committee members favored holding the festival in San Francisco and whether they wished "to repudiate or censure my actions as I have outlined them." The nineteenth festival of the ISCM took place in Berkeley, California, August 1–9 and consisted of eight concerts. (Twenty-seven-year-old Diamond's Concerto for Chamber Orchestra was played on the August 9 concert.)

We have none of Sessions's letters from the period between December 1941 and his first letter to Darius Milhaud, December 5, 1942. His friendship with the French composer probably began in California in 1942. In this letter Sessions informed Milhaud that plans to have him lecture in Princeton had fallen through because of timing; however, the two hoped to meet in New York or Princeton.

By 1941 Sessions had moved to 100 Bayard Lane, but by October 1943 he had moved to his third Princeton residence, 172 Prospect Avenue. It is from here that he wrote Miriam Gideon December 16, 1942.[2] The Arthur Berger article discussed in this letter was his review of the publication in French of Stravinsky's Norton Lectures at Harvard.[3] Berger wrote:

When [Stravinsky] wrote his autobiography he enraged critics by declaring music "powerless of expressing anything whatever." That is, the composer's aim is to *make* an auditory object, not to express a concept or feeling. These lectures will cause less indignation, since they are concerned not so much with what Stravinsky feels music cannot do as with what all will agree it can do: namely, embody a form. . . . Stravinsky's attitude toward content, even as reflected in his most extreme pronouncements, seems more justifiable if viewed as a working principle of this first musician of our time, rather than as a philosopher's carefully balanced theory. He may consciously deny the emotional aspect of his work. But, though he himself rejects Freud, as he indicates in several gratuitous asides, modern exploration of the unconscious offers proof that we express feelings without being immediately aware of them.

Sessions followed the letter to Gideon with a four-page letter to Berger, three of whose pages were devoted to discussing the review.

This letter led to the first meeting of the two in Princeton and to a long friendship between them. In Berger's "Roger Sessions: A Reminiscence" he quotes from the letter:

> Now I try as much as possible to avoid such words as "form" + "organization" which I think cause a certain amount of confusion. One knows of course what they mean in regard to music but they have a tendency to detach themselves from this specific sense + become abstract. Perhaps the essence of my thinking in these matters is that music + in fact each of the arts must be considered entirely in + for itself—first of all, at any rate. I can see that in literature + in painting + sculpture "form" + "content" may be considered separately, though this presumably would be only so far. In music I simply do not see how it is to be done. At least my conception of form = movement = gesture = expression leads me to the conclusion that though one may begin at either end (this is perhaps what you mean by isolating the two conceptions) one must cover the entire ground if one wishes to arrive at a satisfactory conclusion.[4]

1. David Diamond, letter to the author, September 10, 1988.

2. This letter was prepared for publication in Norman and Shrifte, eds., *Letters of Composers: An Anthology 1603–1945* (New York: Knopf, 1946), but does not appear in that collection.

3. Arthur Berger, "Stravinsky at Harvard," *The New Republic*, December 14, 1942, no. 1463, 800–801. This review is of Igor Stravinsky's *Poétique Musicale: Sous Forme de Six Leçons* (Cambridge, Mass.: Harvard University Press, 1942).

4. Arthur Berger, "Roger Sessions: A Reminiscence," *Perspectives of New Music* (Spring–Summer 1985): 117–18.

▼

Roger Sessions to Miriam Gideon
als US-NYgideon

December 16, 1942
Princeton

Dear Miriam,

[. . .]

I read Arthur Berger's review of the Stravinsky book last night—I suppose the book is in a sense important—I would have thought so about fifteen years ago; and Stravinsky's a name at the very least, and certainly an intelligent, cultivated, and highly gifted man. Certainly that book had to be reviewed and A.B. can do it better than most.

However, as far as *my* reactions are concerned, Stravinsky, rather than Berger, sounds to me curiously dated—his ideas, I mean. That kind of aesthetic quibbling seems to me a picturesque survival today, about as relevant as, say, Oscar Wilde. When I say "relevant" I do not of course refer to current fashions in music which are, alas, not very relevant either, as far as the general situation is concerned. I have the impression that in a sense—among the *avant-garde* (no disrespect intended) as represented in Mr. Berger and others—Stravinsky is just "coming into his own." What amuses me first a little and depresses me (a little) in one sense and encourages me a little in another is that I passed through that particular railroad station from ten to fifteen years ago, and it is now very, very far behind me. I am fourteen years younger, of course, than Stravinsky himself. It isn't a matter of undergoing influences, though, but of discovering oneself—very, very difficult for an artist nowadays; it takes very long—the longer the more there is to discover.

I have, however, had that sensation of *déja-vu* before. If the reactionary coalition in the U.S. doesn't destroy civilization in the meantime (and I am beginning to think perhaps they are too stupid to succeed in that, though we are going to have, probably, some very trying moments in the next two years and perhaps longer), R.S. will probably be around 1955–60, quite a "success"—if he does his work properly during the next five years. Not that it matters particularly, but it is inevitably clear to me, and I certainly have no inhibitions about telling you—you at least know that that is not my primary goal.

All the talk about "form" and "content" occurring in music is just so much baloney. I don't blame A.B. in the least for taking these questions seriously even though I don't think he has yet hit the point. The truth is so simple for us over-miseducated, hyper-intellectual audiences—all of us—to grasp. If one remembers only that music is basically song and gesture; that one can really respond to it only through song and gesture (inner or outer) not by *listening* in the narrower sense of the word, the whole thing becomes very simple. One should also remember that we cry and breathe (the first forms of song and gesture) even before we hear; these things are the absolutely primary experiences of human life and should have no purely inhibiting intellectualizations. They are *sensation*—very significant sensation. Music first develops, then organizes and refines these. They are so fundamental that one can either say that they are *action* rather than expression (i.e. more fundamental than expression) or the very essence of expression itself, according to definition.

Footnote to the above: song is, of course, a form of gesture, and the noise one makes is at first a by-product. Later it becomes—

through a very basic physiological principle, a means by which the original gesture is re-experienced or produced (in miniature of course) in others, by direct action of course—and that is music.

One might recall, too, that one considers one's experience of a poem adequate if one merely listens to a few readings of it—how can one grasp the still more complex language of music, then, by simply listening to performances of it. In this connection, which takes longer to memorize, a poem or a piece of music—in all details I mean (and in one's ear, I mean of course, not the printed text but the sound). As a matter of fact, I am not so sure, speaking for myself—perhaps the poem. But that is not perhaps the point, since I have both much greater gifts and much greater experience in music. The fact remains that the music is far denser than the poem. It contains more material in the same duration.

If you think A.B. would be interested, and you see him, you might read him the above. It needs considerable further elucidation, of course, and I could give it if necessary. If you do read it to him please make it quite clear that it is not at all a criticism of him and that I feel thoroughly friendly and in no way critical or condescending. I mention this only because I sometimes am misunderstood in such a way simply because I express my ideas with a certain gusto.

Forgive this long letter and greetings to you both.

Roger

CHAPTER

1944-1948

E I G H T

WE HAVE NO LETTERS of Sessions from 1943 to July 1944.
This chapter begins with a letter to a longtime friend, pianist John
Duke. The letter reveals Sessions's view of contemporary artistic and
social life and serves almost as a rough draft for Sessions's 1944
article on Arnold Schoenberg.

Sessions's article "Schoenberg in the United States," which first
appeared in *Tempo* 9 (old series) in December 1944, commemorated,
belatedly, Schoenberg's seventieth birthday, September 13, 1944. The
article states that Schoenberg's "main influence . . . has been exerted
through his teaching, the musicians with whom he has come in
contact, and finally the series of works composed in the years since he
has lived in the United States—works which in my opinion represent
a separate phase and a new level in his music as a whole." Combining
both the original article and Sessions's 1972 revision,[1] one can list the
Schoenberg works Sessions considers important: the Fourth String
Quartet, the Violin Concerto, the Second Chamber Symphony, the
Piano Concerto, and a work written three years after the 1944 article
appeared, the String Trio. About the last Sessions writes, "The Trio
seems to me in some respects the most perfect embodiment of
Schoenberg's essential musical character." In the earlier version he
writes, "I believe that in these works written since 1936 Schoenberg
has achieved a freedom and resourcefulness which carries them in this
respect far beyond his earlier works. . . . They differ first of all in their
longer and broader lines." He writes, too, of "a still wider range of
harmonic effect . . . a much vaster harmonic line."

Sessions also stresses the importance of Schoenberg's teaching: "Musical experience, and development through experience, is Schoenberg's watchword as a teacher." At least two of Sessions's students, Dika Newlin and Leon Kirchner,[2] had studied with Schoenberg and very likely reported their experience to Sessions. "His pupils speak of his boundless love for music—the energy of his enthusiasm for a classic work."

In 1972 Sessions recalled, "Partly as a result of this article (which, somewhat to my surprise, pleased him) I acquired a very satisfying and quite unforgettable personal relationship with Schoenberg, never as a 'disciple' but rather as a loyal friend."[3] This friendship was evidenced on Schoenberg's part by his gift to Sessions of the first page of "Die Jakobsleiter" and two Birthday Canons for Carl Engel. Possibly Sessions was overwhelmed by the generosity of these gifts, because, incredibly, he did not write Schoenberg a thank-you letter, and in fact did not write to him again for three years. All thirteen letters of the correspondence are published in my "The Correspondence between Arnold Schoenberg and Roger Sessions," *Journal of the Arnold Schoenberg Institute* 13, no. 1 (June 1990): 47–62.

1. The 1972 version, published in *Tempo* 103 (December 1972): 8–17, is reprinted in *Roger Sessions on Music: Collected Essays,* ed. Edward T. Cone (Princeton: Princeton University Press, 1979), 353–69. A translation of the 1944 article was published in German as "Schönberg in den U.S.A.," *Stimmen* 16 (1949): 440–43.

2. Dika Newlin (b. 1923) wrote about her studies with Schoenberg in *Schoenberg Remembered: Diaries and Recollections* (New York: Pendragon Press, 1980). Kirchner (b. 1919) studied composition with Bloch, Sessions, and Schoenberg; he taught at Harvard University 1961–89 and received a Pulitzer Prize in 1967 for his String Quartet No. 3.

3. Cone, ed., *Roger Sessions on Music: Collected Essays,* "Author's Note," 353.

▼

Roger Sessions to John Duke
als US-Nsmith

Sunday, July 30, 1944
Dear John,—   Princeton

This is primarily to thank you— + Dorothy + Oliver Larkin[1] too—for a delightful + interesting time in Northampton. It was so good to see you all again, + I look back on it with very special pleasure. It seemed hard to realize that it was so long since I had really been "in Northampton."

My only chagrin was that I felt I had not done nearly so well by you + Oliver + the girls as I would have liked. It would have certainly been better if I had tried to cover less ground but concentrated on the effort to make two or three points really clear.

I felt also that, if we seemed to disagree on certain points it was partly at least because you were thinking in terms of general objectives while I was at the moment preoccupied with certain aspects of the concrete situation as I have to face them, particularly with some of my pupils. The better [ones] find themselves bucking a very ruthless competitive system which is constantly attacking them at their most vulnerable + also most vital spot—their artistic integrity + self-confidence; + if I consider my most important role that of teaching them that their musical instincts (i.e. their real love + their real artistic conscience as opposed to what fashion or expediency seems to dictate at the moment) are infallible, for them at least, it is because I believe that is the only basis on which any conceivable measure of recovery from the manifest spiritual ills of the time can take place.

The result is of course that ten years ago I found myself most often encouraging them not to be little artificial + half-baked Schönbergs, Varèses, etc. (I still have that problem on occasion) while today what they have to struggle against is most often the criterion of immediate success + box-office appeal + mere *facility* dressed up in all kinds of tempting packages.

I think we have to accept, for the time being, a tremendous diversity in our artistic life, as there is in every other phase of contemporary life, + recognize that while what I have often called "individual isolation*ism*" is a disease, it is very often what is best + strongest in an individual that isolates him against his will, + that the duty, for the artist, of thinking + feeling things through to the limit, on every level, is not to be shirked in favor of any easy solution or apparent gain. I have always in that respect valued Schnabel's *mot* of some years ago in which he spoke of "the Alexandrianism of profundity + the Alexandrianism of superficiality"—both of them deadly dangers, not only to music but to everything else;— + dangers which can be avoided only by genuine artistic independence, + above all by strong + positive creative force.

The most serious danger today is that we offer the people "panem et circenses" [bread and circuses] + encourage them to demand no more than that. Should this demand become general + really compelling—if people demand no more of art and of culture in general than what is immediately acceptable to the majority, with a minimum of effort, then Fascism is around the corner whether we like it or not. And it is that, not the extreme introversion + narcissism and paranoia and self-pity of Romanticism's death-struggle, which is the prevailing tendency + therefore the most immediate danger of today.

Of course composers should write for whatever "occasions" are possible—though, as I think [of] our discussion throughout, Hollywood + the radio business are under the control of the same forces as are the concert hall + the opera house today—possibly under an even more ruthless control, since they involve far greater sums of money, and far more complicated economic forces. But the important thing is always *music,* in the fullest + most real sense of the world, + the clearing away of all barriers to vital musical experience on the part of all those who wish to participate.

I don't know whether these observations of mine are useful to you or not—if not, excuse me for having got started writing them to you. But I believe they may help clarify where I stand, in case I did not succeed in making that clear the other evening. I shall be in Hadley from the 13th to the 20th, though I have duties at Mt. Holyoke, as you know. But I would love to see you again, + in any case my Mt. Holyoke duties only take up my mornings, unless I am much mistaken.

Greetings to everyone
Roger

1. Oliver Larkin (1896–1970) taught on the art faculty at Smith College 1924–64. Dorothy (Macon) Duke was John Duke's wife.

▼

Roger Sessions to Arnold Schoenberg
als US-DLC

October 30, 1944
108 Dickinson Hall
Princeton, New Jersey

Dear Prof. Schönberg,—

I hope you will accept the enclosed article,—which will shortly appear in *Tempo,* the London publication of Boosey and Hawkes,— as a sincere if somewhat delayed expression of my very warm and affectionate birthday wishes. I tried to express in it something of the gratitude and admiration which every living musician owes to you and I only hope I succeeded in making this clear. It is always a source of great confidence and inspiration that you are here; and though I wish you were nearer, I always feel close to you especially through our mutual friends Steuermann and Kolisch and Jalowetz,[1] with whom I am often in touch.

I look forward with the greatest possible anticipation to the performances of "Napoleon"[2] and to your visit to New York; and I hope I may have an opportunity of seeing you on some occasion other than the official ones. I value so much the memory of the evening I spent with you at Miss Fisher's[3] in Hollywood, three years ago.

With every possible good wish for the future and hearty congratulations on a wonderful seventy years of rich and vital achievement.

Yours in deep and affectionate admiration,
Roger Sessions

1. Edward Steuermann (1892–1964) studied with Schoenberg 1912–14 and in February 1944 gave the first performance of Schoenberg's Piano Concerto. The violinist Rudolf Kolisch (1896–1978) formed the Kolisch Quartet in 1922 and in 1942 became the leader of the Pro Arte Quartet; he also studied composition with Schoenberg. Heinrich Jalowetz (1882–1946) studied with Schoenberg 1904–8; after emigrating to the U.S. he taught for many years at Black Mountain College in North Carolina.

2. Schoenberg's *Ode to Napoleon*, op. 41, for narrator, piano, and string quartet or string orchestra, was written between March and June 1942.

3. Dr. Caroline Fisher (1889–1985) was a professor of philosophy at the University of California at Los Angeles during the 1940s and 1950s.

▼

Arnold Schoenberg to Roger Sessions[1]
cc US-DLC

December 3[–8], 1944

Dear Mr. Sessions: [Los Angeles]

You would not believe how fast time passes when you are old. In a week—at the utmost—a month might have passed, and you cannot catch up with it anymore. As long as you were young, you could, and did. But now you even do not try anymore.

I see your article, which I have read at once and with the greatest pleasure, was sent to me—yesterday I would say—but I see it was October the 30th—

And today it is December 8 (eight), because I interrupted this letter for two reasons: First, I wanted to reread the article, second, I suddenly started with the long postponed plan of scoring and finishing "Jakobsleiter" which I had begun in 1917, 27 years ago.[2]

Now I am afraid I would never finish this letter if I insisted on writing all I wanted to tell you. But I see I would have to write almost the whole article, if I wanted to quote everything which pleases me.

Therefore I will restrict myself to two things: I send you a little "cadeau," [present] (a)* the first page of the score of "Die Jakobsleiter," (b) the two Birthday Canons for Carl Engel.[3] And finally I want to mention what I consider the greatest value for a possible appreciation of my music: that you say, one must listen to it in the same manner as to every other kind of music, forget the theories, the twelve tone method, the dissonances etc., and, I would add, if possible the author.

There are of course more and more profound ideas in this article, but I think this one is of the greatest assistance for a future understanding of my music. In a lecture "Veraltete und Neue Musik, oder Stil und Gedanke" [Outmoded and New Music, or Style and Idea], I expressed a similar idea, by saying "A Chinese poet speaks Chinese, but what is it what he *says*?" And I used to say: "That I write in this or that style or method is my private affair and is no concern to any listener—but I want my message to be understood and accepted."

I am most cordially, yours
[Arnold Schoenberg]

*this one under separate cover

1. Originally published in Arnold Schoenberg, *Letters*, ed. Erwin Stein (London: Faber & Faber, 1964), no. 196, pp. 222–23. First published in German, 1958.

2. Schoenberg had begun his revision of his oratorio *Die Jakobsleiter* (1917–22) in October 1944, but abandoned it.

3. "Jedem geht es so" and "Mir auch ist es so ergangen," both puzzle canons in three voices with text. Carl Engel had died May 6, 1944.

▼

Roger Sessions to Ernst Krenek
als US-SD

May 23, 1945
Princeton

Dear Ernst,—

I don't know whether Mark told you that I have just accepted a Professorship at the University of California. I am leaving Princeton with somewhat mixed feelings; but I felt finally that I needed a change, for several reasons; the chief one is that I am sure that, with my life as involved as it has become here + in N.Y. I will have a better chance to get quite a large number of notes on paper—they are waiting to be written down, so to speak.

I am writing you now because I have spoken of you in connection with two possible positions, one being of course the one which I am leaving, here in Princeton. Should this one be offered you, you would of course be in a very strategic position near N.Y. + at an institution with a great deal of prestige. But you know the advantages very well; I must tell you that, partly as a result of the crisis in the Department caused by my leaving, the handicaps under which the Department has suffered seem very largely to have been, or to be about to be, removed. If I did not want to go to California for reasons which have in very large part nothing to do with Princeton, I would have been very much tempted to stay on the terms which I was finally offered here.

Regarding the situation here there are a number of factors which might prove an obstacle to your being offered the job. I have of course nothing more to do with that, + you can perhaps guess what those obstacles might be; I have no way of knowing how strong they would be.

What I really want to say is in regard to the other one; the Department at Carnegie Institute of Technology in Pittsburgh. As far as I can judge there is an excellent chance of their approaching you, + since I spent some hours there recently, + had also a long talk in N.Y. with the President,[1] I believe I know something of the situation. I am writing you really in order to tell you that should you be considering a move, or willing to consider one, I think you might find Carnegie Institute very much worth considering. There is of course Frederick Dorian,[2] whom you know, + the other members of the faculty whom I met impressed me favorably—they were friendly + seemed very receptive to the various ideas that came up in the conversation, wh. was a general one apropos of some of the routine problems of musical education.

The President made an extremely favorable impression on me, both in Pittsburgh + N.Y., + I have some experience with college presidents! He is an engineer by profession, with a flair for painting, at which he spends his vacations. (The paintings are conventional, of course; but, as far as I can judge, they are not at all stupid.) He seems to have a genuine desire to build up a really good School of Music, + what I liked best of all was that he seemed concerned mainly with finding someone who would build the school into something really good, + then giving that man the fullest support, not only as a member of his staff, but as an individual artist. It did not get to the point of my being offered the job, especially as I had to let them know I had already decided to go to California; but I did know that I had been seriously considered. But I feel very definitely that it is something you might find really worthwhile, + that is why I am writing to you. Pittsburgh I daresay you know—it is dirty but very spectacular; + above all it seems—from all accounts—to be a really ambitious musical community. I was in Cleveland on the same trip + got a quite strikingly different impression there—so the Pittsburgh impression was all the more striking.

Well—I don't at all know what the outcome of the talk I had with Pres. Doherty will be: but when I spoke of you he seemed genuinely interested + even excited.[3]

I hope this letter will at least be a beginning toward making up for some of my failings as a correspondent. I meant to write you in Feb. after my lecture on your quartet[4] + the performance of the work wh. impressed me really deeply, + which, considering Princeton, was received very well indeed. I think my lecture helped though I was not entirely satisfied, principally because I felt more difficulty than in most cases to give a really good idea of your music on the piano. But the music I found very sympathetic indeed, + had a first-rate impression.

I look forward very much to our association in Gambier this summer.[5]

Cordial greetings from us both. As always
Roger

1. Robert E. Doherty (1885–1950), who had taught electrical engineering at Yale University (1931–36), was president of Carnegie Institute of Technology 1936–50. There he instituted the Carnegie curriculum, parts of which are still used today at the renamed Carnegie Mellon University.
2. Frederick Dorian (b. 1902), an Austrian American musicologist closely associated with the Schoenberg circle, directed the opera program at the Carnegie Institute of Technology 1936–54.
3. Neither the job at the Carnegie Institute of Technology nor the one at Princeton University went to Krenek, who since 1942 had been teaching at Hamline University, in Saint Paul, Minn.
4. Krenek's String Quartet No. 7, op. 96 (1943–44).
5. They both taught at Kenyon College.

B Y T H E S P R I N G O F 1 9 4 5 Sessions was ready to leave Princeton University and move to the West. Lisl Sessions disliked Princeton, and her husband had the idea that something artistically new was happening in California. "I went out there partly because I felt that other parts of the country were *too* dependent on New York. I had had the feeling that something indigenous was getting started out there." Decisive to him was the University of California's attitude toward his work as a composer. "One of the things that made me make the decision to move was that they said that my creative work was really important to them, and they wanted to plan my schedule so that it would favor that as much as possible. And they did. It was a quite different attitude from the attitude at Princeton."[1] Sessions's former teacher Ernest Bloch also taught at the University of California, 1940–52.

On September 27, 1945, shortly after arriving in California, Sessions wrote to Clara Steuermann:[2] "We are beginning to feel at home here + no doubt will soon begin to feel entirely as we ought to feel in California. It is a bit strange at first to realize that one is, presumably for good, permanently fixed at a point which has always thus far seemed somewhat remote, + thus far I have not seen anyone out here with whom I feel 100% at home. But, I have been working very well + to good purpose + that after all is the essential" (US-DLC). Sessions worked to good purpose indeed; in 1946 he finished his Second Symphony and Second Piano Sonata.

Sessions had not been able to complete a symphony for almost twenty years: the First Symphony was completed January 31, 1927, and the Second was premiered January 9, 1947. The First is dedicated to Sessions's father, who had died shortly before its completion. The Second, although dedicated to the deceased Franklin D. Roosevelt, had associations for Sessions with his mother, who had died December 2, 1946. The connection between death and symphonic music, which had begun with the unfinished symphony written for George Bartlett in 1917, lingered: the Third Symphony was commissioned in memory of Serge and Natalie Koussevitzky, and the Fourth Symphony's Elegy was written with the death of Sessions's brother, John, on September 19, 1948, very much in mind. (The work is dedicated "to my wife.")

The Symphony No. 2 was commissioned by the Alice M. Ditson Fund of Columbia University, which was controlled by Sessions's old friend Douglas Moore. Getting the work performed, however, proved to be difficult for the Ditson committee. Moore wrote to Sessions (December 10, 1945) that the committee wanted Leon Barzin (b. 1900), the music director of the National Orchestral Association, to conduct the work with the NBC Symphony Orchestra in May 1946.

After Barzin received the score—late—he decided he could not perform the work without adequate preparation. Moore wrote to Sessions (June 4, 1946) that they would transfer the rights to the premiere to Pierre Monteux, at that time the conductor of the San Francisco Symphony Orchestra, but stipulated that the first performance take place in New York. That, too, did not come to pass. A New York performance lead by Alfred Wallenstein, conductor of the Los Angeles Philharmonic, also fell through; on February 7, 1947, Moore wrote Sessions: "We seem to be beset by ill fortune about your symphony. Wallenstein tells me that he does not feel that he can undertake it with only three rehearsals" (US-NYpease). The Ditson Fund released themselves from their rights to the first New York performance and urged Sessions to accept any invitation he might receive. By Sessions's own arrangement the premiere had already taken place a month earlier in San Francisco with Pierre Monteux conducting the San Francisco Symphony.

Reviews were mixed. *Musical America* wrote, "It seemed to express the epitome of all that is worst in the life and thinking of today."[3] Three years later, David Diamond published a scathing attack on the piece, largely mouthing Boulanger's criticisms—a fact he used later by way of explanation to Roger and Lisl Sessions. The objections were that the first and third movements were too long; the second was too short and banal; the orchestration lacked variety; and the last movement "fail[ed] mainly for its inferior material."[4] But the San Francisco *Chronicle* review, by Alfred Frankenstein, as paraphrased in an article in *Time* magazine, called it "challenging . . . important . . . austere . . . fiendishly difficult . . . a complex of forceful and fruitful ideas which can be studied for a long time before they yield all their secrets."[5]

The anonymous *Time* writer offered a description of the composer, some antiquated gossip, and an unlikely association: "A musician's musician, Roger Sessions look like a swarthy, extremely precocious baby; he is probably the most difficult of U.S. composers. His twelve-year-old violin concerto bogged down all but one of the many violinists who tackled it. . . . Sessions believes that he is closer to Hungary's late, great Béla Bartók. . . . He has half-finished a third symphony [later abandoned] and has begun a four-act opera called *Montezuma*."[6]

This last piece of news did not escape the attention of Antonio Borgese, still living in Chicago and wondering what had become of his opera libretto.

1. Andrea Olmstead, *Conversations with Roger Sessions* (Boston: Northeastern University Press, 1987), 168–70.

2. Clara Steuermann (1922–82) was a teaching assistant to Schoenberg and a music librarian. She married Edward Steuermann in 1949, becoming his second wife.

3. Marjory M. Fisher, "Sessions Symphony Has Premiere," *Musical America,* January 25, 1947.

4. David Diamond, "Roger Sessions: Symphony No. 2," *Notes* 7 (June 1950): 438–39.

5. "Music: For F.D.R.," *Time,* January 20, 1947, 72.

6. Ibid.

▼

Antonio Borgese to Roger Sessions
cc I-Fborgese

February 27, 1947
Dear Roger: [Chicago]

It was a surprise, and a very pleasant one, to receive your and Elizabeth's Christmas wishes, with good news, as unexpected as long desired, of your family. Mine is all right. The rumor, a truthful one, perhaps has reached you that a second child whose name is Dominica (alias Nica) has squared three years ago my home.

Of my delay, of our delay, in reciprocating greetings and wishes, you and certainly Elizabeth will excuse Elisabeth and me; for probably another rumor, truthful too, has reached you: to the effect that both of us, husband and wife, are engulfed in this craziest and yet indispensablest of all enterprises, namely the drafting—in cooperation with a Committee of Solons and an outfit, Borgese-directed, or ardent associates—a draft of a world constitution[1] either to help prevent World War III, if such a purpose is sensibly conceivable, or to suggest a shape of things to come to the survivors of said war, if Einstein and other sages are right when assuming that anyhow there will be survivors (Toynbee, whom I met and heard last week in your Princeton, ventured half-jestingly the prophecy that the legacy of our ancient civilizations might be handed over by the atomic bomb, maybe to the Eskimos, maybe to the Pygmies of central Africa).

This year, 1947, seems to promise a certain number of surprises. Your reappearance on the Borgese horizon was one. Together with it came, even more startingly, the news forwarded by Elizabeth—that you were working on *Montezuma.* The news was confirmed a few days later in *Time* Magazine, January 20, where, however, the title

Montezuma was not accompanied by the name of its poet—as, you certainly grant, it should have been. Was it, is it, I wondered, my *Montezuma*? I think it was, it is.

It will be easy for you to believe that all through these years I had thought that you had altogether dropped my poem and the idea of writing music for it. This indeed was my interpretation of your silence—which lasted from December, '43 to the end of '46—as this was the reason for my not interfering for your silence. I remembered, of course, that you had had the text at various intervals from the beginning in the late 30's to the end in 1941, and that your idea— may I say your promise—since the poetic work was completed, was that your score would be ready not later than two years thereafter.

I know, needless to say, that an artist's time is not chronometric. Yours is not so; neither is mine, even though the margin of difference between objective and subjective time may be different with you and me. You will find it natural at any rate that I am desirous at this moment of more precise information than the generic one given by Elizabeth and the anonymous hint provided by *Time* (with no pun on time). You will find it also natural, and wise, that if you really are working and plan to work on that poem, an exchange of letters between us would be advisable, stating mutual consents and pledges and limits thereof. Friendship, a long and dear one like ours, ought not to be an impediment to clear understandings in practical matters. On the contrary, it ought to be an encouragement to the clarification of all issues. So please dispel your epistolographic inhibitions and write to me at your early convenience about your purposes and desires.

I have never left this desk, except for quick jaunts East, through a whole year. Elisabeth was in her paternal home in California[2] for a few days last fall; and there a photographer of the inner circle took pictures of mother and children, which I found quite lovable. We have not yet copies; but we are expecting them any day; and one in the small supply is earmarked for you. Please requite, if necessary in advance, the tiny gift. We should like to feel close again to you and your wife and your children.[3]

Affectionately yours,
G. A. Borgese

1. Borgese's *Foundation of the World Republic* (Chicago: University of Chicago Press, 1953), an incomplete draft of a world constitution, was the first volume of a three-volume set called *Syntax*.

2. Thomas Mann had moved to southern California in 1941.

3. Borgese's files contain no reply to this letter.

LIKE *Montezuma,* the ill-fated Violin Concerto reappeared, phoe-nixlike, on the scene. Violinist Louis Krasner had not forgotten the work. He wrote Sessions (March 26, 1947) that, having played both the Berg and the Schoenberg concertos with the Minneapolis Symphony and its conductor, Dimitri Mitropoulos (1896–1960), he wanted to interest the conductor in a performance of the Sessions concerto. (Mitropoulos had earlier wanted to present the concerto in New York, but Arthur Judson, with an eye toward the box office, had forbidden the work on grounds of its length.) Krasner wrote again on April 12 reiterating his request for a score, but did not hear from Sessions until June 30.

Sessions had been occupied that spring more strenuously than ever before, composing, at the suggestion of Henry Schnitzler, the son of the Austrian novelist Arthur Schnitzler and the dedicatee, his one-act opera *The Trial of Lucullus.* The hectic atmosphere that preceded its first performance, at Berkeley, April 18, 1947, was largely a result of the rehearsals' having begun before the score was completed.[1]

Sessions was still burning about the Koussevitzky episode, owing to some gossip by an unidentified "friend," and immediately wrote to Koussevitzky (July 18, 1947) informing him of the November date for the Minneapolis performance. Krasner wanted to ascertain whether Robert Gross and Stokowski had performed only the concerto's first movement on tour. Sessions wrote back (October 25, 1947; US-CAhoughton), "I saw Gross last spring (for the first time since 1941) + he said the last movement (plus Romanza) were omitted for lack of rehearsal time." Thus, the first two movements had been played before.

1. That atmosphere is captured in S. Earl Saxton's cartoon " 'The Trial of Lucullus' or a Sessions with Sessions," reproduced in Andrea Olmstead, *Roger Sessions and His Music* (Ann Arbor: UMI Research Press, 1985), 86–87. The cartoon figures are identified in S. Earl Saxton, "In Memoriam Roger Sessions," *Perspectives of New Music* (Spring–Summer 1985): 160–61.

▼

Roger Sessions to Louis Krasner
tls US-CAhoughton

June 30, 1947
Berkeley, California

Dear Mr. Krasner,

Thank you for your letter and please accept my apologies for my silence which is really shocking. I hope you will not interpret it as meaning any lack of interest on my part—the opposite is in fact the case. I simply have a dreadful habit of putting things off from day to day, and I had begun to have a desperate feeling that you might even decide that I was not worth bothering about.

I did however talk with the American Music Center in New York when I was there during the first week in May and understood from them that the score and parts were being sent to you. I should be interested to know whether it was necessary for you to make strong efforts since that time in order to locate them, or whether they actually did come reasonably quickly.

You spoke in your letter of a revised piano arrangement, and I actually have a revised arrangement of the first three movements which I could send you if you like. I am not sure however, that it is any improvement over what you have; it is as you may imagine very difficult to make the orchestral part easy to play on the piano, and in playing a piano arrangement at the University of Oregon this spring I found myself leaving out half the notes as I had always done before. In the last movement in fact I used the arrangement which I believe you have, since I decided that I was wasting my time in trying to make a simpler one. Please let me know whether you would like me to send you what I have and I will do so immediately if you wish.

I shall make every effort to be in Minneapolis for the performance[1] and of course if it could be arranged for me to either partly or wholly make expenses by means of a lecture at the University or elsewhere, I should be delighted. I hate to think of the Concerto being played without being able to hear it myself, especially when you are the soloist.

I will get busy on program notes and try to let you have them as early as possible. As far as the Spalding episode is concerned I feel I should check up on anything I have written before allowing it to be published. If you would care to send me the letter I wrote you—I would of course return it!—I could better judge whether that is the form in which it should be put.[2]

If you see Koussevitzky and talk with him about the Concerto, I will be very much amused to hear what he says. A friend of mine who talked with him recently quoted him as saying that I had never finished the Concerto and gave that as the reason why he had lost interest in me after having believed me to be "the greatest American composer," fifteen years ago. My files tell a somewhat different story, but I am naturally curious to know what his reaction will be when confronted with this work so soon after being assured by my friends that the work has been both published and performed since some ten years back!

I too would like nothing better than to go over the work with you once more. Unfortunately I see no way of being in the east this summer or fall.[3] I do hope however, to hear the performance and will do everything in my power to be in Minneapolis at that time.

Please let me know if there is anything I can do; and I will promise to answer your letters, especially since I have someone to whom I can dictate. I am really thrilled that you are giving this performance. With every good wish to you and Mrs. Krasner,

Most sincerely,
Roger Sessions

1. The performance took place November 14.
2. See letter dated October 26, 1937.
3. Krasner was living in Nantasket, Mass.

▼

Roger Sessions to Serge Koussevitzky
tls US-DLC

July 18, 1947
Dear Dr. Koussevitzky,   Berkeley, California

I was quite distressed to learn recently from a friend that you had never received a copy of my Violin Concerto, and that you were in fact unaware that I had ever completed it as I did twelve years ago. The work was published in 1937 and has been performed several times. Louis Krasner will perform it in November with the Minneapolis Symphony Orchestra.

I am sending you a copy of the score and will also see that you receive a copy of my Second Symphony which will be published by Schirmer in the near future.

It was very pleasant to have a glimpse of you in Cambridge at the Symposium and I am only sorry that the fact I was on a fleeting visit from the West made it impossible for me to see more of you.

With all good wishes,

Most sincerely yours,
Roger Sessions[1]

1. This letter, coming after a ten-year hiatus (on November 21, 1937, Sessions had written to suggest Koussevitzky program Bartók's *Music for Strings, Percussion, and Celesta*), marks the end of the two musicians' correspondence.

▼

Roger Sessions to Darius Milhaud[1]
als F-Pmilhaud

October 29, 1947
Dear friend,—   [Berkeley, California]

For some time I've intended to write to you, in order to say that you are missed very much here,[2] that I think of you very often, and that I always share in some sense and with very lively feelings of sympathy, of anxiety, and even with a little of hope, the events that you are going through.

Now I hear that you are not well. I hope above all that I am badly informed, or that it is not worse than just something inconvenient and temporary, and that your return to France will prove to be for you all that you wish for—without—listen well—your forgetting that we await you here with much impatience. I am very happy to hear that you conducted your Third Symphony.[3] For my part, I work assiduously on mine.[4]

Let me know, please, if there is something that I could do here for you, and if you have the opportunity to write a word to me, that would make me very happy. As for the situation in general, we have "meatless Tuesdays" and "eggless Thursdays" but we—Lisl and I— are not entirely satisfied, and if you have suggestions as to those things that we could do to aid more directly, please make them known. We would well like to send packages, but of what and to whom?[5]

In any case, mon cher, greet [your wife] Madeleine and Daniel affectionately for my part and know that we think and speak always of you here,

Always your,
Roger Sessions

1. Translated from the French by Andrea Olmstead.

2. Milhaud had in August returned to Paris to teach at the Paris Conservatoire.

3. Milhaud's Symphony No. 3, "Hymnus ambrosianus," received its premiere in Paris the next day, October 30. Around this time Milhaud, suffering from arthritis, began to conduct sitting down.

4. This symphony, also mentioned in the letter to Edward Cone reproduced later in this chapter, is not in Sessions's catalog of completed works.

5. A reference to the Marshall Plan, which Secretary of State George C. Marshall had proposed less than five months earlier.

▼

Roger Sessions to Arnold Schoenberg
als US-DLC

October 30, 1947
107 Tamalpais Road
Berkeley 8, California

Dear Prof. Schönberg,—

It is now nearly three years since I had from you a very beautiful letter, and the gift of the first page of your "Jakobsleiter" and your two birthday canons for Carl Engel. Both letter and gifts I should have acknowledged very long ago; but any of our mutual friends could tell you that I have what amounts really to a kind of disease—that I am likely to put off writing letters, and most especially the ones I care about writing, and then get discouraged. In any case I wish you could know that both your letter and your gifts are among my most cherished possessions—perhaps above all the page from the "Jakobsleiter" which I am so proud to have on the wall of my study.

Today I am writing you because I must tell you that in the last two terms my students have been working, in an "analysis" course, on your Piano Concerto, and this term, in a course in contemporary music, on your Fourth Quartet. The class which is studying the quartet now has fifty students, + they have spent six weeks on the quartet, with seven hours a week of listening to the records, with as much analysis as I feel will be helpful to so large a class, and a great deal of discussion of the issues in contemporary music. Though the quartet is much the most exacting work we will study I felt it was natural + logical to begin the course with this. You know at least as well as I that the quartet + the concerto are far beyond either the musical or the human experience of all but a small minority of the students— + I have tried to do my best in making it clear to them that great music, like everything else that is great, requires something of us—that one can only approach it by giving oneself to it and that what one receives from the music is only proportionate to what one gives. Their response has moved me deeply and has made me quite proud of them, + has taught me once more how easily one can underestimate the capacities of young people who haven't had enough time to become spoiled and confused. I think that at least some of them have learned to deeply love your music; and this makes me very happy.

Even this, however, is not what I really started to write you. That is—what a deep joy it has been to *me* to study your work again; how it grows constantly greater for me as I know it better. It is truly a source of deep comfort and faith to know that such music can be written in one's own time, and it gives one immensely renewed faith in the relevance of one's own efforts, as well as renewed courage to go on making them.

So I have to thank you, with all my heart.

I always have hopes of visiting Los Angeles and it would be a truly great joy to see you again.

With affectionate greetings,

Most sincerely,
Roger Sessions

P.S. Since I wrote this I hear that one of my pupils, a Mr. Walter Nollner,[1] is to visit Los Angeles this week end. It would mean a very great deal to him to see you and I have asked him to bring you my greetings. I wish so much that it might be possible for you to see him—he is a very fine person and, I believe, gifted.

1. Walter Nollner (b. 1922) studied at the University of California at Berkeley 1942–49. He taught at Williams College 1950–58 and Princeton University from 1958.

▼

Roger Sessions to Ernst Krenek
als US-SD

Saturday, December 6, 1947
[Dear Ernst,—]   Berkeley, California
[. . .]¹
You have been much in my thoughts, of course, since my visit to Minneapolis,² where I went to hear my Violin Concerto (a wonderful

performance) + to give some lectures at the University. I was often with your friends—not only Krasner + Mitropoulos, but Mrs. Biggs, Erickson,[3] Carpenter, + other young people whose names I have forgotten. We stayed with the Coopers—you may remember meeting David Cooper,[4] an ex-Princeton pupil of mine— + though you do not, I think, know them very well, they too are to be counted among your friends + supporters, as are also the Elliotts whom I saw—he is the head of the Psychology Dept. at the University + an old friend whom I had not however seen since 1917. You will, I hope, take it for granted that we talked of you very much. I was also very much impressed at the activity for Contemporary music that goes on there— under the leadership of yourself + Krasner + Mitropoulos—I can't deny that I had somewhat mixed feelings; I was torn between wanting you in California + feeling that what you had done, + were doing, in Minneapolis is so valuable that your departure from there would be a really great blow to the people who are doing the most constructive work. I felt keenly aware of what has always been one of my major premises regarding music in the U.S.—the fact that whatever hope there is here lies in the development of small independent groups in various centers, outside of N.Y.—and quite frankly, this region + the "Twin Cities" seem to me the most hopeful places in that respect, at present. It was both [sic] somewhat disenchanting to realize afresh how much this depends on two or three individuals, but of course at the same time it is encouraging to see how much these two or three people can accomplish. In any case you may be sure that we talked of you a great deal + with everyone. I also of course spoke of you in my second lecture on contemporary music. The lectures are to be published + I am busy getting them in order. As soon as I can get a copy I shall send you my remarks, which I hope will please you.

I have been once more preoccupied with the question of a possible job for you in this region + have had various conversations on the subject with Jane Hohfeld[5]—exploring any possibilities there may be. I shall have more with her + I hope with others. And we both want to talk everything over with you when you come. I wish I could say that the outlook were more hopeful than it seems to be. As long as a man of your calibre has the difficulties you have had, my own good fortune seems to me somewhat suspect. By this I don't mean to imply that I am lacking in self-esteem, which I am not; but that one has to realize anew that it is not one's best qualities or one's real achievements that bring one recognition of that kind.

I am happy to hear from Jane that you will be here after Christmas— + I am also sorry to have missed you when you were here. I thoroughly enjoyed my trip to Minneapolis, above all of course the really wonderful performance my Violin Concerto had at the hands of Krasner + Mitropoulos—I felt as if I myself could not have done it differently, as a whole or in details. You will appreciate too my real joy in becoming acquainted with Mitropoulos, whom I had never met before.

This is already an over-long letter, + I will not write more. Thank you again for the Symphony,[6] + I look forward eagerly to your visit later in the month.

And—greetings to your wife.

Affectionately
Roger

1. The first pages are missing.
2. Krenek had moved to Hollywood earlier in 1947.
3. Robert Erickson (b. 1917) studied composition with Ernst Krenek at Hamline University; in 1950 he attended a seminar in composition under Sessions in Berkeley.
4. David S. Cooper (b. 1922) studied at Princeton with Sessions 1942–44. From 1965 to 1969 he was director of the Manhattan School of Music.
5. Jane Hohfeld (later Galante) (b. 1924) had been a student of Krenek's at Vassar College, from which she graduated in 1945.
6. Krenek's unpublished Symphony No. 4, op. 113 (1947).

▼

Roger Sessions to Edward T. Cone
als US-Pcone

June 9, 1948
Dear Eddie,— [Berkeley, California]

I was so glad to get your letter + above all to hear the good news. I am sure the decision[1] is the very best possible one. Naturally I am curious about the "big name" especially since there are not so many big names available + fewer still really big people behind the names.

As for your questions:[2] (1) [If counterpoint were taught in the first year, what did Sessions think should follow in subsequent years, and in what order?] My solution of the problem of the second year would be, I think, one term of counterpoint + one of harmony; the same again in the Junior year, with careful "tying up" of the two subjects, by keeping always before the students' minds just what each subject leads to, + also whatever in each subject can be carried over to the other while the study goes on. In the beginning this would be a matter of getting a good relationship between treble + bass, in harmony, + getting a good rich blend of intervals, in counterpoint. I think a good case may be made out for doing one or the other for a whole year; but I am quite sure the above wd. be my own choice, on the premise that music consists of the interaction of both principles.

(2) [What did Sessions think of the relative merits of teaching counterpoint based on Knud Jeppesen and based on J. J. Fux as modified by Schenker?] Some of my feeling about XVI century counterpoint is undoubtedly "partisan prejudice"; as I have often said, there are many roads to New York, + the main thing, if one wants to get there, is to go. But what I feel is very important is that the rightful goal of "theoretical" instruction is *technique* + not "style." (Query: if it is "style," why the XVI century, precisely at a moment when musicologists deny the concept of even momentary progress in music but insist on historical relativity?) I myself had XVI century counterpoint with Bloch, + it amused me very much; but my criticism is that it wasted too much time in figuring out what the rules were to the detriment of emphasizing practice, about five or ten times as much as the student usually gets in actually putting voices together. So my objections to the XVI century conception really boil down to (1) the emphasis on imitation of a style is not only in itself highly artificial, since no style is ever static + therefore only a kind of more or less colorless generalization can be achieved; but there is the danger of inculcating what I might call genteel misconceptions as to the legitimate goals of musical study + even the nature of music itself. (2) It introduces irrelevant elements into elementary musical study, such as the modes, etc. The latter are useful to composers in a post-tonal, not a pre-tonal sense, + I feel students of "XVI century counterpoint" often get confused by trying to *hear* the modes as if they were actually *keys*, + c. This objection however is the least serious of the three. (3) I feel that it is too easy to "learn a style" without acquiring any really basic resources. Fux, extended to a study of combined species, does provide the means to a systematic acquiring of resources, + the basis for a much more thoroughgoing mastery of XVI century style, if that is what the student eventually wants, as well as for the mastery of what the composer needs. The point is that if a teacher emphasizes the matter of style, he generally does not empha-size sufficiently the acquiring of technique. It is not that the two are incompatible but that they are, so to speak, incommensurable; + the difficulty is a confusion of *aims*.

This latter is, I think, the real point. All of my objections can be answered in practice by a good teacher. If he knows clearly what he is trying to teach, then one can settle the matter very easily, + the XVI century is not an issue. But adherents of the XVI cent. cpt. idea generally are a little confused as to the basic problems—they are mixed up as to *culture,* as to *music* + therefore as to pedagogy. If one can unmix them there is no issue whatever. Therefore I think my answer as to counterpoint teaching at Calif. I would start by clarifying (or, let's say, trying to clarify) these fundamental issues— + perhaps content myself with that, as I believe that a teacher can do his best work only if he is free to work things out for himself; + if he pursues the right ends he will find methods suited to them.

(3) [Randall Thompson, the previous theory teacher at Princeton, had favored a fourth year of eighteenth-century counterpoint, but Cone proposed instead a course in strict tonal composition and analysis. What did Sessions think?] I think I would incline to agree with you rather than Randall here, though I am sure you wd. agree a good case can be made out for both sides. But I do feel that the more specialized aspects of compositional technique could well be saved for graduate work, + in fact that that might well be the line of demarcation between undergraduate + graduate study. The aim of undergraduate study, aside from harmony + counterpoint, could be the introduction to the problems of form as such. As I think I have told you often enough, I feel that the study of fugue is valuable in three definite aspects—apart from the purely polyphonic discipline which it fosters. 1) coordination between melody (or line) + harmonic feeling, 2) the acquiring of flexibility in harmonic sequence through study of Bach's technique, 3) the general stimulation of a feeling for the bass line + its importance.

Of course, I am sure that I might be reproached in all of these connections with minimizing the importance to the composer of a knowledge of the past, as such. I think you know what my answer would be: that the past is pawed over by our music departments + even our conservatories so much that it is necessary to finally insist that composition is a living thing + that familiarity with the past is no excuse for dodging the main issue, which is the ability of the composer to deliver his message clearly + adequately in his own terms, + the acquisition of all available means to do this. That is why I leave "style" entirely out of my composition teaching apart from the effort to show by analysis + by detailed criticism, how consistency of musical thought (and that is all that "style" is, after all—or perhaps more exactly it is how style is achieved) is achieved, where it *isn't* present + where it *is*.

I hope this is clear, +, perhaps even more, that it is legible. My newest toy is this ball point pen; it makes writing easier but not necessarily clearer.[3] I also have just finished my biggest work (+ most difficult)—a chicken wire fence to keep the dog in—involving the getting of 61 poles, the construction of two gates, + the hammering of about 10 000 000 000 staples—my hands are tired + covered with scratches! The new dog is adorable—at least as much so as Juix was, a light red one—he is going to be a very big cocker I think judging both from the size of him at present + his growth so far.

I am of course most eager to see— + hear—the songs; if you can let me have them I would be delighted.[4]

My symphony is coming on fast now + I am fairly well pleased— it will be my biggest work so far.[5] No. II comes off in Amsterdam about ½ hour from now;[6] I had a cable from Andrew [Imbrie] saying all is going well; + I hope there will be recordings.

I'm not going to write more now as I must get this off. Please let me know if I can help in any other way— + let me hear any news of you—and do send the songs if you have a copy.

Love from all of us,

Affectionately,
Roger

1. To turn over the teaching of undergraduate music theory at Princeton University to Cone, who had joined the faculty the previous year, and to other younger members of the music department.

2. This letter is in response to Cone's letter asking Sessions's advice on specific pedagogical issues. Summaries of Cone's questions are here inserted before Sessions's replies.

3. Although ballpoint pens had been manufactured for a half century, their use became widespread only in the 1940s.

4. Cone's 1949 "Scarabs" for soprano and string quartet, on Blackmur texts.

5. This is the incomplete symphony mentioned in the earlier letter to Milhaud.

6. At the Twenty-second Festival of the ISCM in Amsterdam, June 5–12, 1948, Sessions's Second Symphony was performed June 9 on a program with Karl-Birger Blomdahl's Violin Concerto, Arthur Malawski's Symphonic Etudes for Piano and Orchestra, and Rudolf Escher's *Musique pour l'Esprit en Deuil*.

▼

Arnold Schoenberg to Roger Sessions
als US-NYpease

July 17, 1948

Dear Mr. Sessions,   [Los Angeles]

I feel I am much indebted to you for the good letters I received from you. Were it not that my eyes are an obstacle to my writing and thanking you, I should have written you, after Mr. Kirchner played your music for me.[1] I was very pleased that I could follow your thoughts almost throughout the whole piece and it is that, why I said: "This is a language." I mean, it conveys a message and in this respect it seems to me one of the greatest achievements a composer could arrive at.

Thank you again for your kind words. I am very pleased to be in contact with you not only by the music we both love, but also through pupils, who love, what we love.

Cordially yours,
Arnold Schoenberg

1. Leon Kirchner had taken a score and tape recording of Sessions's Piano Sonata No. 2 to Schoenberg, who responded, "Now I know how Schumann must have felt when he first heard the music of Brahms" (interview with the author).

▼

Roger Sessions to Ernst Krenek
als US-SD

December 9, 1948

Dear Ernst,—   Berkeley, California

Jane Hohfeld + two of the three members of the program committee of the Composers' Forum[1] (I haven't seen the third, so I can't speak for him) are all most enthusiastic at the idea of doing "What Price Confidence?"[2] hereabouts sometime during the next year + a half. Jane will get the score, if possible, from Popper,[3] + we will then consider practicalities. The idea is an exciting one + I am quite determined to put it through if possible. I think it *is* possible but do not want to give you positive assurance till we have gotten further. It also is quite likely that we would have to plan it for next season rather than this.

Once more I hope you realize what a real success you had here + what a real following you have among the younger people in this region. That is, to be sure, not helpful in any immediate material sense + I have always that aspect of things in mind, as well as the other, in thinking of you. On the other hand it is clear to me that the two are not unconnected + I feel that performances of your work, + the genuine response which results—even when it does not produce immediate public repercussions—perhaps work more strongly in your favor than is immediately apparent. You would be at least as pleased as I am, by the warmth + the real enthusiasm which shows itself whenever I mention your name here, among those who heard the Sonata[4]— + it will certainly bear eventual results especially if we can follow it up, as I believe we can, with other performances.

It was good to see you in L.A., as it always is. You know I hope things will take shape as you want them; I hope Henry Schnitzler[5] may be able to help you with your plans for the opera, +c. Please let me know if I can be of use in any way.

Affectionately to you + Bertha

As always,
Roger

1. A concert series devoted to contemporary music and founded in 1946 by some of Sessions's students—Leon Kirchner, Earl Kim, Spartaco Monello, Leonard Ralston, and Leonard Ratner—that was to last two decades and become affiliated with the ISCM.
2. Krenek's *What Price Confidence?*, op. 111, a one-act chamber opera with a libretto by the composer, was not to be performed at Berkeley, but did receive its world premiere fourteen years later in Saarbrücken, Germany, in 1962.
3. Jan Herbert Popper (1908–87), Czech-American opera conductor and coach.
4. Krenek's Piano Sonata No. 4, op. 114 (1948).
5. Schnitzler was head of the department of drama at Berkeley.

▼

Ernst Krenek to Roger Sessions
als US-NYpease

December 18, 1948
3366 Charleston Way
Dear Roger,   Los Angeles 28, California

I am very happy indeed to hear about the favorable response that my sonata has found among the sensitive and intelligent younger set. And I am particularly happy about the possibilities for my little opera.

Jane mentioned to me that you might write another one to go with it.[1] That would make it a really perfect project. Let us hope that it will materialize.

I am very appreciative of your comforting and encouraging words. Being well aware of the value of the intangible factors, I am—I hope understandably—anxious to see some of them transformed into tangible assets within a reasonable span of time.

So far not much change can be registered. After Copland, Roy Harris has had his show at UCLA. I was not there, but several survivors reported with dismay and dejection.

I have finished a sonata for viola and piano which Jane plans to do with Mr. Molnar.[2] I think I can use it here too. There is also some demand for a string trio which I am planning to write soon.[3] My Studies in Counterpoint[4] has been published in Italy, and a little autobiographical book in Switzerland.[5]

Thank you once more for your encouraging words which do me a great deal of good. All the best from both of us to you all.

As always

Ernst

1. Sessions did not write another one-act opera, and there is no sign that *The Trial of Lucullus* was ever performed on a bill with *What Price Confidence?*

2. Ferenc Molnar (b. 1896), the violist (not the playwright). Krenek's 1948 Viola Sonata, op. 117, was commissioned, premiered, and recorded by Jane Hohfeld and Ferenc Molnar.

3. *Parvula corona musicalis ad honorem Johannes Sebastiani Bach*, string trio, op. 122.

4. *Studies in Counterpoint, Based on the Twelve-tone Technique* (New York, 1940; German translation, 1952).

5. *Selbstdarstellung* (Zurich, 1948), revised and enlarged as "Self Analysis," *New Mexico Quarterly* 23 (1953): 5–57.

A FRIEND OF SESSIONS'S in Berkeley was Thomas Mann's son, Michael, a violinist with the San Francisco Symphony who had performed in the premiere of Sessions's Symphony No. 2. Shortly after that performance, Michael Mann had written Sessions an admiring letter (January 12, 1947). Found in Sessions's estate was a draft copy, reproduced here, of a letter to Thomas Mann, whose novel *Doctor Faustus: The Life of the German Composer Adrian Leverkühn as Told by a Friend* was published in English in 1948.[1] As is well known, Schoenberg was upset by the novel; he felt that the parallel between Mann's protagonist and himself was too close, and the implication that the twelve-tone system was a product of the devil was too dreadful. His legal action resulted in Mann's appending an author's note to subsequent printings, which states that the twelve-tone system is "the intellectual property of a contemporary composer and theoretician, Arnold Schönberg. I have transferred this technique in a certain ideational context to the fictitious figure of a musician, the tragic hero of my novel. In fact, the passages of this book that deal with musical theory are indebted in numerous details to Schönberg's *Harmonielehre*."

In a sense Sessions was caught in the middle of this debate. "I was friends with both Thomas Mann and with Schoenberg. I was the best man at the wedding between Mann's daughter and Borgese, the librettist for *Montezuma*. One Thanksgiving dinner with Schoenberg the topic of Thomas Mann came up. Schoenberg remarked that he was afraid that history would credit the invention of the twelve-tone method to a little-known German composer named Adrian Leverkühn. I tried to reassure him tactfully; however, what was really going on in my mind was, 'What do you care? You will be remembered for your *music*, not for inventing the twelve-tone system.' "[2]

1. Translated by H. T. Lowe-Porter (New York: Knopf, 1948), the German original had been published by Bermann-Fischer Verlag in 1947.

2. Quoted in Andrea Olmstead, *Conversations with Roger Sessions* (Boston: Northeastern University Press, 1987), 171–72.

▼

Roger Sessions to Thomas Mann
als (draft) US-NYpease

Dear Dr. Mann,—

[December 1948]
[Berkeley, California]

I finished some days ago my first reading of "Doktor Faustus"—I read it in English, and shall now read it in German—and cannot resist sending you some expression of my deep gratitude.

Anything that I can say about the book is quite inadequate not only because of my own limitations, or even because one reading, in translation or even, I am sure, in German, is insufficient, but because the book in any case is so vast in its contacts and its implications, I feel quite simply that I shall be thinking of it and returning to it for years—and in fact how can one really come to the end of something that strikes so deeply to the heart, not only of the world in which one lives, but in a far deeper and more intimate sense, at the roots of one's own person, as a product +, one hopes, a not too irrelevant part of that world. I hope you will not find it indiscreet if I write you that I have been profoundly moved, and have felt, in reading it, a fresh urgency, a quickened insight, and the sense of vitality which comes from seeing more clearly than before into the nature of the ills from which one suffers, and feeling therefore just a little more hopeful, that at least those particular ills (you will realize I am sure that I do not speak at all as an individual) may one day be surmounted. For it is so clear that, though your story deals with Germany and is in the more literal sense the story of her agony, it is in its largest sense the story of the agony of our whole world—the macrocosmos as well as the microcosmos. In trying to clarify my thoughts I find that for me perhaps the most wonderful achievement of your books is your revelation of the former in terms of the latter. While I realize that often writers have tried to do this (I feel that as far as I am concerned for the first time in *Dr. Faustus* this has been done, not on a, so-to-speak, psychiatric level which is in the last analysis insufficient and which, however profound and however necessary [it] is eventually), my impression has been that they have never reached, at best, beyond the purely psychiatric level, or in other cases, a purely sociological one. What *Doktor Faustus* seems to make so vivid is that all of its facets are brought together on the deepest level of all, the ethical, and in the less obvious sense, the theological level. I do not say this very well but I cannot believe you will not know exactly what I am trying to say.

May I also say how keenly + how deeply I appreciated the specifically musical parts of the book? I am not referring only to the many pages in which you write of Beethoven and of other aspects of our musical heritage with such brilliance + such insight, but of your insight into the very nature of music itself. Perhaps above all—for it strikes most closely home—your insight into the artistic crisis of today—the problems or even the dilemma to which each of us has to find his own solutions, and to which no purely personal solution can be really adequate. It is so seldom that one sees this recognized, except on the quite false journalistic level or on the level of special pleading, for the spiritual crisis that it is—either because its implications are so frightening, or possibly because it is in the last analysis so personal a matter. Perhaps I could express what I mean most simply by saying that while I began by not being sure that Leverkühn was a convincing musical figure, I ended by recognizing something of Leverkühn not only in myself, but in every serious musician that I know—and vice versa. And if I firmly believe that despair is not the final word which contemporary music need, or indeed, *may,* utter, I believe none the less that until the implications of despair have been fully faced and its depths been fully experienced (till musicians have become "per du" [on a first-name basis] with it) any other last word is certain to sound a little hollow.

I am certainly not the one to confidently judge *Dr. Faustus* as a "work of literature" and in fact I have never been able to believe too strongly in such categories, though I am quite ready to admit that this could be a blind spot, especially since in my own work I have to recognize strivings which should make them at least intelligible to me. But I once read a statement somewhere regarding Ibsen's "Ghosts," that it was perhaps not his greatest work, though it was certainly his greatest deed. And it is above all as a very great deed—something possibly even greater than a "great book"—and as a very great experience that *Dr. Faustus* has touched me; and it is for this that I am writing to thank you, deeply.

Please forgive an all too long letter. But I did want to express to you what your book means to me, and to do this adequately would require many more pages.

And please accept our warmest greetings, to all of you, for Christmas + the New Year.

Most sincerely
Roger Sessions

▼

Thomas Mann to Roger Sessions[1]
als US-NYpease

December 31, 1948
1550 San Remo Drive,
Dear and very honored Mr. Sessions,   Pacific Palisades, California

It is not easy to find words to express the joy and emotion with which I received your letter. Your immersion in this book, which is very special to me and from which I have not yet completely detached

-361-

myself, has deeply touched me, and if an artist and someone who has so much understanding of the times as you do recognized the situation that I tried to present in it from his own experience, his own struggle and suffering as true and correct, then this has to be of the highest importance to me. *Dr. Faustus* is after all a musical novel and, indeed, almost a novel of music; and still the music in it is only foreground and stands for everything else: for the state of art in general, of culture as a whole, of humanity even.

It is the novel of the end of a period, and, as I well know, also as a novel an ending—since throughout the book tried to *be* that of which it speaks: above all also constructive music [*konstruktive Musik*]. It is a book for musicians, and if its story and basic idea cause the music in the story to seem a gift of the Devil, no sensitive person will fail to sense the profound involvement with music underlying this demonization [*Dämonisierung*], and to what extent the author considers himself a musician. You, the great composer, have not failed to sense this, otherwise you would not have written to me as you did. I thank you from the bottom of my heart.

How I wish that we could see each other again soon! I am to speak in Berkeley in the fall of 1949, but that is too long a time from now. If your travels would bring you to this area and to us long before this time—the whole family would be happy.

A happy fruitful New Year!

Your devoted,
Thomas Mann

1. Translated from the German by Gerhard and Annette Koeppel and Juliane Brand.

CHAPTER

1949-1954

N I N E

Duration THE YEARS 1949–54 Sessions was to make two
moves—back to Italy, for the first time in almost twenty years, and
back to Princeton University. Both moves were motivated by the same
incident: the retiring chairman of the University of California music
department, Albert Elkus,[1] was replaced in 1950 by Joaquín Nin-
Culmell.[2] With this change the department, in Sessions's words,
"exploded." Sessions's sabbatical, on a Fulbright grant to Italy, 1951–
52, was granted only with the understanding that he would return to
California to teach for at least one year, 1952–53.

Sessions tried, without success, to obtain jobs at the university for
at least three people: for Krenek and Milhaud, to replace him, and
for Krasner, to teach violin. Molnar got the violin position Krasner
was seeking; neither did Krasner receive a job at Stanford. The
university turned down Krenek, but was rejected by Milhaud. In the
end, the University of California decided not to hire anyone.

In his letter of November 7, 1949, Schoenberg wondered whether
Sessions had heard of Heinrich Schenker.[3] In fact, Sessions had published three articles on the theorist shortly after Schenker's death in
1935.[4] Despite his essentially negative view of Schenker's theories,
Sessions is credited by Milton Babbitt as having introduced Schenker's
term "tonicization" into English use, as opposed to the more literal
translation, "tonicalization." By the time Sessions published *Harmonic Practice*,[5] his views on Schenker had softened somewhat,
perhaps partly as a result of his contact with Schoenberg.

Sessions's association with The Juilliard School of Music (as it was then called) began during Christmas in 1948 when he was asked to give a set of lectures there in the summer of 1949.[6] The school's orchestra, conducted by Jean Morel, performed Sessions's First Symphony in the fall of 1949, and it is the recordings of that performance to which Sessions referred in his letter of November 28, 1949.

1. Composer Albert Elkus (1884–1962) studied in Vienna, taught at Mills College from 1929 to 1944, and, after leaving Berkeley, became the director of the San Francisco Conservatory 1951–57.

2. Joaquín Nin-Culmell, Cuban-Spanish pianist and composer (b. 1908), was chairman of the music department of Williams College in Williamstown, Mass., 1940–49. In 1950 he was appointed to Berkeley; he became professor emeritus in 1974.

3. Austrian music theorist Heinrich Schenker (1868–1935) endeavored to show that every tonal work could be reduced via an *Urlinie* (fundamental melody) and a *Grundbrechung* (bass) to an *Ursatz* (background). His major writings include *Harmonielehre* (1906), *Kontrapunkt* (1910), and *Der freie Satz* (1935), as well as monographs on Beethoven's Ninth Symphony (1912) and Fifth Symphony (1925).

4. "Heinrich Schenker's Contribution," *Modern Music* 12, no. 4 (1935): 170–78; "Escape by Theory," *Modern Music* 15, no. 3 (1938): 192–97 (in which Sessions refers to Schenker's *Der freie Satz* as "difficult and unfortunately, in large part, repulsive and sterile reading"); and "The Function of Theory," *Modern Music* 15, no. 7 (1938): 257–62. All three are republished in Edward T. Cone, ed., *Roger Sessions on Music: Collected Essays,* (Princeton: Princeton University Press, 1979).

5. Roger Sessions, *Harmonic Practice* (New York: Harcourt, Brace & World, 1951).

6. These lectures were published the next year under the title *The Musical Experience of Composer, Performer, Listener* (Princeton: Princeton University Press, 1950).

▼

Roger Sessions to Ernst Krenek
als US-SD

February 13, 1949
Berkeley, California

Dear Ernst,—

I am just back from three weeks in the East, + I found your book[1] waiting for me here. I had already seen it + leafed it over at Louis Krasner's at Minneapolis, as I have done here. I look forward to reading it with the greatest interest and *Teilnahme* [sympathy] but have not had time to sit down with it as yet—too many loose ends to catch up with. But I have it on my desk + as soon as I can feel that my time is really my own again I promise myself the really great pleasure + stimulus of reading it carefully. You know, I trust, that of my contemporaries you are the one to whom I feel closest, and whatever you write about yourself is of the greatest possible interest to me.

I stopped for a day in Minneapolis + saw Mitropoulos + also Louis Krasner, both at some length; I also had a long talk with R. Erickson on the 'phone. Needless to say we all spoke of you.

My trip was primarily a family visit, + I had only 3 days in N.Y. and two and a half in Princeton. In N.Y. I saw Fritz Cohen,[2] also Leon Kirchner + Milton Babbitt—they all sent you greetings—also Felix Greissle[3] with whom I had two very good talks. Unfortunately I missed Eduard Steuermann + also Mark Brunswick. I spoke with Frau Schnabel twice over the phone—A[rtur] S[chnabel] didn't feel up to a visit; he is still having to take drugs for his asthma, in order to keep from straining his heart. He still however expects to be in San Francisco to play two Mozart concerti, in May, with Mitropoulos.

I have just accepted an engagement to teach at The Juilliard School this summer, + look forward to being in the East for a little while again. My visit was a very full + very stimulating one + though I don't think I am ready to leave Calif. (I don't mean to imply that I ever will be!) it was good to be there in many respects.

Thank you again for the book, + do let me hear from you again. I will write you again shortly, + will let you know how things go about the opera project here.

Affectionately to you both
Roger

1. Krenek's *Selbstdarstellung* (Zurich, 1948).
2. Frederic Cohen (1905–1967), an opera director at Tanglewood and Juilliard.
3. Greissle (1899–1982) studied composition privately with his father-in-law, Schoenberg, and with Berg. In 1946 he had become an editor with the music publisher E. B. Marks, where he served as Sessions's editor from 1948 until his retirement in 1971.

▼

Roger Sessions to Louis Krasner
als US-CAhoughton

May 7, 1949
Berkeley, California

Dear Louis—(I hope you don't mind my using your first name—in any case I would be much pleased if you would use mine)

Just a word to tell you there is much activity here regarding your

interests. I 'phoned Crosten[1] at Stanford—he is an ex-pupil of mine—
+ found that he is definitely interested, though it is too soon for him
to know what kind of a position he will have available. I also have
spoken to Mitropoulos, + may have the opportunity to take Crosten
to meet him after the concert tonight, at which Szigeti plays the Berg
Concerto. Crosten knows of your connection with the Berg Concerto
(what a marvelous piece!)— + if he can make the concert we are to
meet afterwards + go in, to D.M. that is. Szigeti will also speak for
you, I am sure, if the opportunity arises, as it well may.

Also, as luck would have it, Walter Hendl[2] was here, + I had some
conversation with him regarding the Dallas situation. He is obviously
eager to have you there. Mitropoulos feels, as I do, that you would be
happier here in this region if it could be worked, + I know I would
be, if you could be at Stanford. I shall see if the situation can be
fostered in such a way as to turn the whole thing to your advantage.
The difficulty as I see it—aside from the necessity of getting Crosten
really *very excited* about having you here; is that Stanford University
is pulling itself gradually out of a very bad financial situation + may
not be willing to provide the necessary funds. That is between
ourselves, of course. As for Crosten he was favorably inclined +
grateful to me for 'phoning him. I was pleased particularly because I
tried hard to persuade him to get Ernst Krenek a couple of years ago
+ he turned thumbs down in an almost disagreeable way, even though
K—— had been offered to him on a silver platter; + his reactions
discouraged me at that time, though EK's situation is a very difficult
thing to deal with because of the antagonisms which several people
in the academic world feel for him—"key" people, unfortunately,
whose power is out of all proportion to their deserts.

In any case I am hopeful.

Greetings to you both + all. We will be passing through Minneapolis in June, when I shall be en route to the Juilliard School where I
am to teach this summer. Will you be there, around June 20–25?

As always,
Roger Sessions

1. William Loran Crosten (b. 1909) was head of the music department at Stanford
University 1946–72.

2. Hendl (b. 1917), who had just begun conducting the Dallas Symphony Orchestra,
studied conducting with Fritz Reiner at the Curtis Institute of Music and was associate
conductor of the New York Philharmonic 1945–49; he became the director of the
Eastman School of Music 1964–1972 and later conducted at The Juilliard School.

▼

Arnold Schoenberg to Roger Sessions
cc US-DLC

November 7, 1949
116 North Rockingham Avenue,
Dear Friend: Los Angeles 49, California

You would do me a great favor if you would give Mr. Moritz Violin,[1] a very old friend of mine with whom I have friendship connection for at least fifty years. I mean, if you could give him a chance to talk to you about the manner in which he would like to give classes in piano playing at the University of California.

I wonder whether you know the Viennese theorist, Dr. Heinrich Schenker, who has published quite a number of books on harmony and counterpoint and especially on this theory of his—the *Urlinie* [fundamental line]—if you have heard of it. Frankly, I was opposed against most of his conclusions, but on the other hand I have to admit that he has also made some very valuable analyses (of the Beethoven Ninth for example) and had some new ideas in respect to understand the thoughts of composers.

Mr. Moritz Violin was a friend and pupil of Dr. Schenker, and he believes in his theories and he has shown and explained me some of the things which he does with his pupils. I don't know whether you will believe in these theories more than I do. To me they seem a little exaggerated at least, but I would not say they are untrue. There are things which it might be of advantage to know. I think I know everything about music without knowing this. But, if you see the effect which it makes when he has explained what he does, first playing how it is usually performed and how it can be played according to his theories, then you will perhaps admit, as I have had to admit, that this is very impressive. Mr. Violin is, of course, an excellent piano player. I must say, the difference is striking.

I would like now, if you could give him a chance to show you these things, and if it would really be possible[,] to give him the chance to teach. I am certain something would come out of this, and certainly some who would take the thing serious enough and learn something from Mr. Violin, will have profited very much of this. I am sure of this, because Mr. Violin is a very serious man and a man of deep thinking and profound knowledge.

He calls this system, Applied Theory for Piano Playing. By this he means something which I would rather call in this manner: recognition of some aesthetic features of a composition makes you see the piece in a different light; not only in many details but also as a total. I think this is what he will show you.

I would like if you would inform me, whether you can do this, and afterwards what was the result of your interview with Mr. Violin. I would be very glad if this very valuable man could get a position for which he fights for many years, and you would do something good to a very serious man.

How is everything with you? When will you come again to Los Angeles? We will be glad to see you again.

With cordial greetings,

I am yours sincerely,
[Arnold Schoenberg]

P.S. Mr. Violin's address is: 44 Potomac Street, San Francisco 17, California.

1. Moritz Violin (1879–1956), a child prodigy pianist who met Schenker in 1896 and knew Brahms, had resigned from his position teaching piano at the Akademie in Vienna in 1912 in disgust with its politics. During this time he met and supported Schoenberg. After emigrating to the U.S. in 1939 and settling in San Francisco, he was never again to resume a full-time career as a musician. He was a ticket collector on a Bay Area ferry for a while, tried unsuccessfully to get a job with the San Francisco Symphony, and ended up with occasional jobs, including organizing a class at the YMCA in San Francisco.

▼

Roger Sessions to Ernst Krenek
als US-SD

November 7, 1949
Berkeley, California

Dear Ernst,—

I can't write you at this moment the letter you deserve but I don't want to delay in thanking you for the book on American music which came a couple of days ago.[1] The book seems to me,—I have had time only to "durchblättern" [page through] it rather extensively—of the greatest interest + importance, + you also may be sure I was pleased by the references to R.S., and most especially by the references to *Montezuma* on which I am working very hard now. I look forward to a thorough reading in the near future + will write you more extensively then.

For the moment I am up to the neck in a situation which would amuse you as an illustration of some of the conditions with which your book deals! Unfortunately it has nothing to do with my music, but with educational activities—specifically a harmony text book which I wrote last spring, at the behest of a publisher who now has asked me to make it more "accessible." Consequently it is both boring and urgent, since I am quite unwilling to let it interfere with important matters for very long.[2]

Mitropoulos is playing my Second Symphony on Jan. 12 + I am going to be in the east from just after Christmas till that time.[3] Is there any chance of your being in N.Y. around then?

When you have time, do send me news of yourself. You can take it for granted that I think + speak of you very often + am anxious to know how things go with you.

Greetings to you both—
Roger

1. Ernst Krenek, *Musik in goldenen Westen; das Tonschaffen der U.S.A.* (Vienna: Brüder Hollinek, 1949). The book mentions his integrity, his slow pace of composition, and his study with Boulanger (Bloch is not mentioned), and it connects him with the Schoenberg school. It discusses the Duo for Violin and Piano and *Montezuma*, and identifies a "Sessions school": Cone, Babbitt, and Imbrie.

2. Sessions's *Harmonic Practice*. The lengthy revisions required in bringing the book to press would cause Sessions to refer to it in a letter to Leon Kirchner (November 28, 1950, US-CAkirchner) as "that God damned fucking shitty harmony book." The book's acknowledgments mention Sessions's indebtedness to Hindemith, Schenker (toward whom he had warmed considerably since his chilly articles of the 1930s), and Schoenberg.

3. Mitropoulos conducted the work with the New York Philharmonic on January 12, 13, 14, and 15, 1950, on concerts broadcast from Carnegie Hall.

▼

Roger Sessions to Jean Morel[1]
cc US-NYpease

November 28, 1949
Berkeley, California

Dear M. Morel,—

I received the other day the recordings of your performance of my First Symphony and it is high time that I let you know how pleased I am. The recordings are first class—quite the best recordings of the kind which I have, and I am able to appreciate every detail. I have played them over and over again.

I am amazed by what you accomplished with what is, after all, a first class student orchestra. I have lived through enough performances—and rehearsals!—of that piece to know how difficult it is, and what pitfalls it contains. The results you obtained are the best possible evidence of your understanding of the work, of the care which you gave to its preparation, and of the technical maturity and the musical alertness of the players.

I think you will be pleased to know that this performance has brought me again close to this early work of mine, which I had half forgotten, and which in fact I had come to regard as very far away from the music which I write nowadays. I have discovered that it has far more of myself in it than I had thought—and with the distance of twenty-three years, I find myself thinking of it in a quite different light. That is partly because in your performance you solved problems, and brought out aspects of the work, which I had forgotten—and I can say too that quite a few things sounded for the first time just as I had remembered conceiving them.

So you see I am tremendously grateful to you and the orchestra. I hope you will give the players my thanks and my congratulations on a really splendid achievement, and accept the same, of course, for yourself!

I shall be in New York from Dec. 29 till Jan. 15, and would be very happy if we might meet.

Most sincerely
[Roger Sessions]

1. Morel (1903–75) taught at the Conservatoire Américain with Boulanger 1921–36 and from 1949 to 1971 conducted the Juilliard Orchestra, with which he performed Sessions's Symphony No. 1 on November 4, 1949. This was the first performance in New York for the twenty-two-year-old work. The program included Dukas's "La Péri" and Brahms's Concerto for Piano in D minor.

▼

Roger Sessions to Arnold Schoenberg
tls US-DLC

December 14, 1949
Dear Prof. Schoenberg,—   Berkeley, California

I received your letter nearly a month ago and I hope you will accept my sincerest apologies that I have not answered it before this. I asked Henry Schnitzler to call you and explain that I have been terribly harrassed and busy—I have to meet "deadlines" and have made no outside appointments at all.

Let me tell you that I have finally written Mr. Violin a note and asked him if we might make an appointment for early next week. I shall then no longer be teaching and will be able to see him at some leisure, and with a freer mind than would have been possible till now; and there will also be time to discuss the question with my colleagues before I leave for New York on Dec. 26.

Indeed I have since 23 years been acquainted with the work of Heinrich Schenker and I have read all of his books. I am so happy that my impressions have been much the same as yours. I liked very much his earlier work but found it more and more difficult to agree with his later theories, and even once wrote a very unfavorable review of his "Freie Satz," which I found extremely exaggerated and oversimplified and in fact "Procrustean" to an impossible degree. On the other hand I liked the "Harmonielehre" and the analysis of the Ninth Symphony, and some of his ideas have considerably influenced my own thinking about technical matters.

I shall look forward to meeting Mr. Violin and especially to listening with the greatest interest and *Teilnahme* [sympathy] to what he has to show me, and will be glad to do anything I can do for him. I hope you know that the fact that you ask me to do this means everything, quite aside from the pleasure I anticipate from Mr. Violin himself. The only reason I have not done so yet is that, as you well understand, I have two activities to pursue—that of composer and that of professor, and in the last few months I have been so foolish as to add a third, that of a writer of books—and I have been having my troubles.

I am always so happy when one of my pupils goes to Los Angeles and has a chance to see you; I know how tremendously much it means to him and I am so glad to have direct news of you on my own account.

I hope to be in Los Angeles in April for a few days, and look forward, as I hope I may, to seeing you at that time. Meanwhile we all send you our warmest greetings, for the holidays, the New Year, and thereafter.

Most sincerely,
Roger Sessions

▼

Roger Sessions to Dimitri Mitropoulos
cc US-NYpease

February 1, 1950

Dear Mitropoulos: Berkeley, California

[. . .]

I cannot possibly express to you my gratitude for the wonderful performance of my Symphony, or for the care and devotion you gave to it—and it was mostly the feeling that I could not possibly put it adequately into words, that delayed my writing. I don't know what more a composer could possibly wish for—and feel myself a thousand times fortunate. The whole experience was of the greatest possible importance for me—it gave me something which I needed very much and which I know is going to be very decisive in all the work which I have yet to do in the future. Thank you from the bottom of my heart.

Perhaps, if sometime—as I hope—I have the chance to see you at a time when you have more leisure, I can tell you this more fully.

I want you to know too that I have had many letters and other messages, both from friends and strangers, about the Symphony and nearly all have spoken quite specially about the marvelously eloquent performance.[1] You don't need to be told that the performance was a good one since you know all that you gave to it—but I am sure you will be happy to know that the eloquence that you put into it really met with a warm response.

I never expect nor even want, at this point, to have my music meet with unanimous approval, or anything like that. But what is of real help and encouragement to a composer like myself is to see that it arouses strong feelings—that it really communicates, even to those who dislike it. I have never had this feeling so clearly or so widely expressed as I have had it in these last weeks—and this too I owe in large measure to you.

I am working very hard and later in the spring I shall be sending you some new scores. Meanwhile my wife and my children join me in sending you our very warmest greetings.

Devotedly

[Roger Sessions]

[P.S.] Please forgive the typewriter—people tell me they can't read my handwriting!

1. Krenek wrote from the Chicago Musical College on January 16, "how much I like to hear your symphony (it was nice to hear your voice too!). My favorite places are the opening section and the slow movement. The 'scherzo' is charming, I wished it were longer. The whole work impressed me deeply, and I was happy to hear it in what seemed to me an excellent rendition" (US-NYpease). In answer to a letter from a Mrs. David Morton of Amherst regarding the symphony, Sessions wrote in part, "I need hardly tell you that I assume no responsibility whatever for the adjective 'cerebral' as applied to my music!" (January 25, 1950, US-NYpease).

▼

Antonio Borgese to Roger Sessions
cc I-Fborgese

February 23, 1950

Dear Roger: [Chicago]

The pleasant memory of our January reunion [in New York] has not faded. Elisabeth and I hope for repeats, not so far between as they have been through these years.

I trust I am correct in stating as follows the agreements so uncontroversially reached during that hour.

It is agreed that you have the exclusive uses of *Montezuma,* as a text for opera, with the proviso that the score, with orchestration and everything ready for actual performance, will be ready not later than September 1952. Should it not be so, I would be free to offer the text to some other composer.

I deeply hope and strongly trust that the deadline will be met. I am glad that it was you who proposed the date, September, 1952, and that you found it fair that a terminal date should be set for your use of a text which has been at your disposal scene for scene since its inception in 1939[1] and in its entirety since 1941. We agreed in thinking that a set date may well contribute to the sharpening of your genius and will toward the completion of the work.

It was also agreed that whatever royalties or revenues may accrue to any musical use you make of that text shall be evenly divided, 50-50, between you and me, and, likewise, that publicity and presentation will be evenly fair, 50-50, to poet and composer; so that, e.g., owing to the alphabetic precedence of the poet for which he pleads not guilty, the combined product will be announced as "By G. A. Borgese and Roger Sessions."

It was finally agreed, particularly under the benevolent inspiration of your wife, that while I, obviously, shall do all that is in my power to have your music preferred by any producer, I should be now and remain free to avail myself of any motion picture or television or such like opportunity that might appear for the use of my text. I add, as I added, that I am unaware of any chance for any such opportunity to materialize in the near future, before the opera is finished.

I know that as a rule you are not a prolific writer of letters of this kind. This is the reason why I am enclosing carbon of this letter. If you think that my statements are correct, all you have to do is to countersign the carbon and send it back to me while keeping the original for your file. If even this is too much of a nuisance for you I trust the benevolent Liesl will take care of everything (except, of course, the signature).

You have not answered my query whether, as far as you know, there are records of the Death of Seneca.[2] Krenek—all absorbed, I read, in the preparation of a television opera[3]—has vanished from my sight and hearing.

Of hydrogen[4] and One World we shall talk again at our next reunion, here or over there. When? In the meantime you know what we obdurately think; for you see, I guess and hope, *Common Cause*.[5]

Affectionate greetings from both of us to both of you; they are extensible to the progeny.

G. A. Borgese

1. Borgese must mean 1937.

2. Borgese may be referring to Seneca's farewell to his followers in Monteverdi's *L'Incoronazione di Poppea* (1642), act 2, scene 3.

3. Krenek's opera *Dark Waters* (1951).

4. In January 1950, as a response to the Soviet Union's first successful atomic bomb test in September 1949, President Harry Truman had approved a U.S. project to develop a hydrogen bomb. The first successful H-bomb test came in November 1952.

5. A reference to Borgese's book *Common Cause* (New York: Duell, Sloane, and Pearce, 1943).

Roger Sessions to Arnold Schoenberg
als US-DLC

Tuesday night [June 1951]
The Figueroa Hotel
[Los Angeles]

Dear Prof. Schönberg,—

I found your book,[1] forwarded from Berkeley, waiting for me at the Music office of U.S.C. this morning, and hasten to thank you most warmly for sending it to me. I had, of course, planned to get it and read it in any case; but I shall treasure this copy in a very special sense as coming from you.

I have been distressed to hear that you are not feeling well this summer,[2] and sorry to have not been able to see you, on that account. I do hope that this may still be possible; but your health and well-being are so very important, to everyone, that that is my real concern.

With every possible good wish.

Most cordially,
Roger Sessions

1. *Style and Idea*, ed. and trans. Dika Newlin (New York: Philosophical Library, 1950). This book of fifteen essays was reprinted and expanded as *Style and Idea: Selected Writings of Arnold Schoenberg*, ed. Leonard Stein, trans. Leo Black (New York: St. Martin's Press, 1975).
2. Sessions's concern was well founded: Schoenberg died Friday, July 13, 1951.

SESSIONS'S MOVE to Florence in the fall of 1951 placed him in contact with old friends, such as David Diamond, Antonio Borgese, and Dimitri Mitropoulos, all of whom were also in Italy during his sojourn. The move also led almost immediately to a meeting with the Italian composer Luigi Dallapiccola (1904–75). Years later, Sessions reminisced:

In 1951 I returned to Europe after an absence of eighteen years. I spent the winter in Florence, the city that I most love, and which I had, before and during the war, despaired of ever seeing again. The evening of our arrival my wife and I met our friend Leonardo Olschki, who knew I hoped to meet Dallapiccola; he immediately proposed to call him by telephone, in order to arrange a meeting between us. The result was an invitation to spend an evening which I shall always remember, and the beginning of a friendship that has meant at least as much to me as any other, in a life that has been rich in precious relationships. I felt an instant and lively sympathy which, as the autumn, winter, and spring passed, developed into a deep affection, and an ever-growing admiration for a personality that was vivid, profoundly cultivated, and gifted, all in the highest degree.[1]

Sessions mentions Dallapiccola in his earliest preserved letter from Italy, that to a former composition student at Berkeley (1948–51), Harold Schiffman. Schiffman (b. 1928) was to attend Princeton as a student of Sessions four years later, after an army stint at Fort Devens, Massachusetts, a location that conjured memories of Sessions's World War I–era experiences. He taught at Florida State University from 1959 to 1985.

Sessions traveled to Paris in April, to Switzerland, to Milan (where he reunited with Borgese in the spring and renewed their collaboration on *Montezuma*), to Rome (where he saw David Diamond), and to numerous other Italian cities to give lectures in Italian on American music. These lectures were later collected, translated, and published in English in 1956 under the title *Reflections on the Music Life in the United States*.[2] However, because Sessions disliked the translation (he had not seen any proofs before publication), he renounced this book as not his own work.

Sessions wrote to Diamond in Rome on April 21, 1952, "P.S. You may be interested to know that I have accepted the Princeton job—a very handsome one I must say— + am very happy to have done so." Letters to Diamond were, however, much terser than the ones in the thirties.

Sessions and Lisl wrote three long letters (June 9, 12, and 14, I-Fborgese) to Borgese concerning the arrangements for Borgese to rent a house in Fiesole for the 1952–53 academic year. The Sessionses described in detail the house and everything a renter would need to know. Borgese did rent the house, where, quite unexpectedly, he died of cerebral thrombosis on December 4, 1952, three months after the proposed deadline for the completion of *Montezuma*.

1. Roger Sessions, *In ricordo di Luigi Dallapiccola* (Milan: Suvini Zerboni, 1975), 44.
2. New York: Merlin Press, 1956.

Lisl and Roger Sessions in Florence in 1952. Courtesy of David Diamond.

▼

Roger Sessions to Harold Schiffman
als US-Tschiffman

December 8, 1951
Dear Harold,—   35 Viale Milton, Florence[1]

I am furiously busy these days, what with giving one lecture a week, in Italian, on "The present state of music in the U.S.," writing a couple of articles[2] (I had no business to do this but the subjects of both made them almost obligatory) and at the same time keeping the vital thread of *Montezuma;* but I must send you a word, before the decisive moment, in answer to your very nice letter. I wrote an all too hasty note to [your fiancée] Manon[3] whose letter arrived a few days before yours. The news was, of course, not unexpected + I am of course very happy for you both.

Why is it that when one's friends marry, one [is] inevitably prompted to Olympian reflections and pieces of advice, which certainly no one ever really wants, + which, like all advice, is never taken except by those who would take it in any case! The answer—so simple, after all—just occurs to me this minute, + I, also, speak from a more varied experience that I should have had, + I am afraid it too has an all too Olympian sound. It is that one knows that no matter what has preceded the marriage, the latter inevitably turns out always to be something at least a little different from what one has expected, and that, exactly like any work of art, one has to work at it very hard in order to achieve the result one wants! As I write, I become more + more pleased with my simile, for in marriage as in art the ultimate enemy is pedantry, and the ultimate danger that of expecting one's collaborator to do what one is really obliged to do oneself. But I am letting myself be carried away by my own ideas—please don't suspect me of impertinence, which is not intended at all. The main thing is that I am really devoted to both of you, + wish you everything good.

It amuses me that you are at Ft. Devens, which is in a sense an old stamping ground; since my personal experience of World War I took place there, in the summer of 1918. I was rejected for enlistment, + went there to work in a "Soldiers Club" in Ayer; + it was while I was there that I was rejected also for the draft. My brother-in-law [Paul Andrews] was a captain on the staff of a brigadier general + I sometimes went in + had lunch with him at the camp itself, which was an affair of temporary shacks with tar-paper roofs and as I remember, a lot of mud! I remember the tar-paper roofs especially— + remember also distributing invitations to dances etc. + sometimes finding that those invited were forbidden to come because they had syphilis or something of the kind. I daresay the place is a good deal changed from those days. Again, excuse my garrulousness; I'm really more sympathetic than this all sounds. I myself would have liked to hear the *Erwartung* performance; I had a rather glowing account of it from Martha Long,[4] who heard it over the radio + raved about the soprano, as about other aspects of it.[5]

It was very intriguing to read that you may be "in a position to see us all" before too long. I suppose that means the possibility of your being transferred overseas. It would be amusing if we should all meet in Florence—there are several other possibilities too. We don't have fondue in Italy but these other things of that nature which have their own special charm.

Florence is a relatively quiet place but there are some very congenial people here—among them Luigi Dallapiccola whom I see very often. He lives very near us, + I have found him most congenial—many of our trains of thought, + even our relations with certain individuals, have been quite uncannily parallel. He is the only musician whom I have found with whom I feel I have very much in common; but there are others—not professional musicians but people of high general culture + understanding—who make life much more than bearable. As for the Italian people, I have always loved them. They have been a civilized people long enough + their civilization—or culture, if you like—goes so very deep that it has, more than with any other people I have ever known, become identified completely with the earth, + makes of them the most natural + fundamentally decent people on earth. Naturally there are exceptions; but I could illustrate what I mean by a dozen instances that have happened to one or the other of the various members of my family.—[. . .] Unfortunately the U.S. has not done a too good job in public relations here, + a lot of people are wondering at what we will do next, + whether we really give a hoot about Italy or Europe except as, at best, a buffer against Russia. Luckily, they like us—Americans, I mean—as people, and are inclined to be on our side for that reason; + I think perhaps we are beginning to realize that if one wants people to understand one, one has to begin by understanding them + their problems. That is the root of the matter. In any case European civilization is far more of a going concern than a great many Americans like to think—+ I have many impressions which tend to convince me that Italy at least is in a far healthier state, even economically, than she was eighteen years ago. One's impressions come + go, of course; + there is immense poverty here—most of all, certainly, in the South which I have never seen. If we could only get rid of the threat of war, an infinite amount could be done + the European future could be very bright. It isn't that people fear war here so much; no one here, as far as I can see, thinks there is going to be one, unless, they say, the U.S. really wants it; + one sees clearly how much the influence of mass thinking has to do with all this, in the United States even more than here. But everyone except the Communists (who are, I am told, not so strong as they appear) realizes that we have to re-arm, the only question is how a nation like the Italians, who have so little to live on, who are overpopulated, + who have no raw materials to speak of, are going to manage it. They do have immense energy, + a terrific will to work—I could tell you stories about this, too!—so I don't doubt they will do their part. But coming back to Europe again I am struck even more than before by how different it is from what the information we get at home tells us; and I think that is dangerous. I suppose one thing is that I read two or three Italian newspapers a day—two Florence ones and a Milan one— + talk about these things also with a variety of people, + not only Italians and Americans, who know Europe + Italy well. And I have the feeling that the American papers printed over here—the *Herald Tribune* in Paris, + "The American" in Rome—do a fair job. But diplomatically + propagandistically— + I don't mean necessarily on the highest level we pull a lot of news.

I apologize for all this; I didn't mean to get started on it—it only is on my mind a good deal + I wish I could do something about it. I do as well as I can both privately and in my lectures, which I give in Italian. That is quite fun; the difficult part is giving a real picture of what the U.S. is like to a non-American audience. The interesting thing is that as my lecture on each subject proceeds, the main process of assembling facts adds up to a much more positive and really hopeful picture than I had imagined.

The main thing however is my very, very best wishes to you + Manon, in which of course we all join.

Affectionately,
Roger

1. The envelope is addressed: "Pvt. Harold A. Schiffman, RA 19416429, ASATR, 86622 AAU, Fort Devens, Massachusetts, Stati Uniti." The back of the envelope reads: "Your army address above looks utterly formidable, + should strike terror into the hearts of all our enemies!"

2. Sessions's only articles published between the 1951 *Harmonic Practice* and the 1956 *Reflections on the Music Life in the United States* were "Some Notes on Schönberg and the 'Method of Composing with Twelve Tones,' " *Score* 6 (May 1952): 7–10, and "Music and the Crisis of the Arts," *Frontiers of Knowledge* (1954): 32–39.

3. Sessions's and Bloch's Swiss friend Manon Berthoud (1914–69).

4. Soprano Martha Long (b. ca. 1925) had sung in the Berkeley production of *The Trial of Lucullus*. Sessions wrote his *Idyll of Theocritus* with her voice in mind.

5. Mitropoulos conducting the New York Philharmonic, November 15, 16, and 18, 1951, with soprano Dorothy Dow.

▼

Antonio Borgese to Roger Sessions
cc I–Fborgese

January 17, 1952
5124 Hyde Park Boulevard
Chicago 15, Illinois

Dear Roger:

Your letter was read with deep enjoyment. I am glad you and your family are over there and, it seems, happy to be there. Of course I am eager to know your Italian impressions and appraisals, and I am counting on a stop-over of yours in Chicago when you are back. Or do you think that there will be a chance of meeting in Italy? I shall be there (Università degli Studi, Milan) from mid-April to very early in June.

Needless to say how thrilled I am by the good news on *Montezuma*. As to the cuts, or as you call them, the "processing" of the text, I never sincerely thought that you could put to music and song *ca.* 17,000 words without asking of our audience an endurance much bigger than Wagner ever asked. As a matter of fact, I have always expected, all through these years, proposals and suggestions from you as to surgical interventions and the thereby needed sutures. They would have come no doubt if we had been so close in space during your work as we were at the time of the genesis. Destiny has willed otherwise, and co-respondence, when one of the co-respondents is Roger, Roger must admit it, is a poor substitute for con-versation. Such as things appear at this moment, the poet is, how should I say?, "blank" about what the composer-surgeon has been doing to the poet's child. Not that I question your literary competence; I do not know anyone among the living musicians—and I know very few in the past—whose poetic taste and background were as eminent as yours. You will find, however, legitimate—even more than legitimate, natural—that I should like very much to know, as early as possible, your planned operations in all details, with such precise references to the passages involved as to make them easily (and legibly! I mean, if you don't mind, typescript) conspicuous to me. I hardly doubt that I will approve them. I do not doubt at all that, were there any dissent, the dissent would be easily and promptly overcome.

As to the practical side, I wonder whether you received a letter of mine (with clipping) about the Stravinsky premiere in Venice.[1] You may have seen now that *Wozzeck* is scheduled for La Scala next April. It seems that Italy is openminded and open-earred [*sic*] to modern music in all its aspects. The world resonance from a world premiere in Venice is as vast and deep as desirable, and acceptance of an opera like *Montezuma* at the Venice festival might be more likely and less wearisome to materialize than at the Met. Your present sojourn—an element of fact which was unknown to me when I wrote about Stravinsky—and your prestige in Italy should help. If you initiate action in this direction, I may perhaps contribute some lateral aid next spring.

Please inform me. Please answer as promptly as your enjoyable and enjoyed letter preannounces.

All our greetings and wishes to Lisl and kids.

Affectionately yours,
G. A. Borgese

1. Stravinsky's opera *The Rake's Progress* was first performed at Teatro La Fenice in Venice, September 11, 1951. Stravinsky conducted the La Scala chorus and orchestra.

Sᴇssɪᴏɴs's ᴘᴏsᴛᴄᴀʀᴅ ᴀɴᴅ ʟᴇᴛᴛᴇʀ to Luigi Dallapiccola from the ship S.S. *Excambion* en route back to the United States (September 5, 1952, I-Fb) mark the beginning of their long correspondence, which was conducted entirely in Italian. Dallapiccola had taught at Tanglewood that summer; commenting on that, Sessions observed, "I continually ask myself (as you can easily imagine) what teaching composition is, and very often it seems to me that I do nothing but to be a little kind, give some encouragement, etc.,—and it is enormously satisfying to me that what I do doesn't differ much from what a colleague and friend like you does." He also demonstrated his inability truly to estimate how long the completion of *Montezuma*, on which he had worked during the summer in Austria, and whose deadline of September 1952 was at hand, would take him—another decade: "My *Montezuma* grew wonderfully in Austria during the summer; I have reached a point where I am working rapidly and confidently. Right now I am impatient to get back to my own desk and to my own room where I finally plan to finish it all in the next three or four months, and then to the orchestration!" (I-Fb).

Dallapiccola, traveling in Mexico, responded (September 21, 1952, I-Fb) that he had been offered a lecture at Berkeley in October "and I (in spite of the ridiculous financial compensation) will accept, because of my great wish to see once more my friends Sessions and Milhaud,[1] and to take a look at San Francisco, about whose beauty I have heard tales for decades."

Sessions's response, both to Dallapiccola and to the Schiffmans, outlined his situation on the faculty of Berkeley as a "lame duck." What had also dismayed him about the University of California was that he, and all faculty members, had had to take loyalty oaths as part of the anti-Communist hysteria that led to the House Un-American

Activities hearings during the McCarthy era. Schiffman remembers Sessions being asked if he believed in "private enterprise." Sessions responded, "Of course—composing is the most private enterprise there is."

Sessions continued his correspondences with violinists Rudolf Kolisch and Louis Krasner, even writing Krasner a letter of recommendation (January 5, 1953) to the Fulbright Commission. Krasner's performance of Schoenberg's Violin Concerto may have pulled Sessions further in the direction of twelve-tone writing, to which he refers in his letter to pianist Beveridge Webster.[2] Sessions wrote to Krasner (January 20, 1953, US-CAhoughton):

> I also want to tell you how tremendously happy I was to hear the Schoenberg Concerto over the air.[3] I took it down on tape, and have listened to it, of course, repeatedly since then. It was a dazzling performance, and a revelation even though I knew the work and loved it very much before I heard it. I have always felt, as I have heard that Schoenberg himself felt, that this Concerto was his greatest work, and I could not have imagined a finer performance—it seemed the kind of performance that one dreams of having when a work is, say, twenty-five years old, and has been mastered in every particular, so that the performer seems completely at home with it. It seemed so sad that Schoenberg could not have heard it himself; it would have been such a joy for him!

1. Though Milhaud was teaching at the Paris Conservatoire, he continued to make annual visits to Mills College, where he retained his position.
2. Webster (b. 1908) taught piano at The Juilliard School 1946–90.
3. Krasner played the Schoenberg Violin Concerto, op. 36, with the New York Philharmonic, Dimitri Mitropoulos conducting, at Carnegie Hall November 29 and 30, 1952.

▼

Roger Sessions to Luigi Dallapiccola[1]
als I-Fb

September 26 [1952]
Dearest Luigi,—   [Berkeley, California]

I was very happy to receive your letter and above all, to know that we will be seeing each other again so soon here at Berkeley. I am also a little worried because you don't mention the other letter that I wrote almost three weeks ago c/o Jose Limantour (L[ukas] Foss,[2] whom I saw in Austria, gave me this address.) I'm wondering if you've received it. In the letter I said that we're expecting you here, that there's always a room for you in our home, + that I'm impatiently waiting for you.

I'm embarrassed and very disturbed that the financial conditions offered you by the department are so threadbare. There's no need to add that I didn't know anything about it and that unfortunately because of the bureaucracy here at the University, which is particularly formidable, there's very little I could have done in any case. I will investigate this matter carefully, but more out of curiosity than the hope of changing the present situation. I am sorry.

Regarding the situation here in the department, it appears to me to be very obscure. I have no doubt that most of my colleagues here at the University are fond of me and would have proposed that I remain here. At the same time, I'm forced to notice, not without amazement, that they really don't care, that—except for Imbrie—they don't care in a visible fashion about all that I've tried to build here, or for what I've done for teaching music composition, or for what could be done after I've gone. Since the majority of the more talented, and also more successful, students were my students, I can't help but be satisfied! Naturally I spoke a lot about you + I keep hoping that your presence here will serve to wake them up a little. But it seems to me entirely possible that with regard to the type of music and musical tendencies that both of us represent—and I'm not referring to dodecaphony— the prevailing mood is decidedly "vorrei e non vorrei" ["I want to and I don't want to"], without the youthful vivacity of Zerlina! We shall see.

[. . .]

I spoke over the phone to Mrs. Connors, who told me about what you wrote regarding the way to present the conference. Mrs. C. is a slightly confused young woman, and it appears to me that your proposal was at least a little complicated if not a bit excessive in asking for an English translation, especially, after you were offered so little as an honorarium. I must confess that I am afraid that you'll find all of this to be impossible, and I hasten to tell you that we can—you and I—combine forces to solve the problem as you wish, and that I will very willingly be at your disposal as a translator or as an interpreter. It matters very much to me that you come, in any case, and I also don't want to overlook anything that could help this conference to be as successful as possible.[3]

I mentioned your visit to Darius [Milhaud] and I gave him your address; we will speak again. He is exceptionally well now and it did me good to see him again.

I was very happy to receive the program of your concert and I hope it went as well as possible. I will enjoy listening to all the things you have to tell about your American and Mexican trip.

Consequently, please drop me a line to let me know when you will arrive, and also if I can assist you in any way with the conference. Many affectionate greetings from all of us—also, when you write, to Laura and Anna Libera.[4]

I shake your hand very affectionately,
Roger

1. Translated from the Italian by Pina Pasquantonio.
2. Composer, conductor, pianist Lukas Foss (b. 1922) had been a Fellow of the American Academy in Rome 1950–51.
3. In a letter to Dallapiccola of October 6 (I-Fb) Sessions wrote, "I was amused that your suggestion—you read in French while I summarize every once in a while—corresponded exactly to what I had thought of doing, as the best and most natural way of solving the problem." The conference went well, and Dallapiccola wrote a thank-you letter to Sessions October 30.
4. Laura Dallapiccola was Luigi Dallapiccola's wife. Annalibera Dallapiccola, their daughter, was a pianist; her father dedicated to her his *Quaderno musicale di Annalibera* (1952; rev. 1953).

▼

Roger Sessions to Harold and Manon Schiffman
als US-Tschiffman

Dear Manon,— + Harold,—

October 6, 1952
Berkeley, California

[. . .]

I am very much tempted to say you are lucky not to be in Berkeley. Unfortunately the place has changed very much this year; of the old crowd only Bill Carlin (+ Gay, of course, who has developed a great deal) + Jack Swackhammer are here.[1] Andrew [Imbrie] of course is still on the Faculty + there is also a very nice young couple—Seymour + Miriam Schiffren [*sic*][2]—S.S. is a young + very gifted composer from New York who has come out as Instructor, + who is a real asset. But ever since a half year before I left—I don't know whether you were aware of it or not—the change in spirit had begun to take place; + the dispersion of the old crowd is only a kind of "outward + visible sign" of this change. Around the Music Department now everything is a little stiff + efficient, + I feel a little noisy + vulgar + slightly obscure—not only R.S. personally but everything he represents. The first week I was here it bothered me very much, + I felt angry + at bottom heart-sick; but I've gotten quite used to it by this time—it is my last year, + to Hell with it.

Of course part of this is because it *is* my last year; but I'm afraid that is only a rather small part of it—part of it dates at least as far back as the "year of the oath," + even a little before; part of it comes from the fact that the GI bill has run out; part of it comes certainly from the fact that the vitality of the war years has spent itself in frustration + that the country as a whole has settled partly into a sort of resigned mediocrity. (If we succeed in electing [Adlai] Stevenson I'll take a little of this back.) The Nin-Culmell regime has simply taken on a character which I fear is all too general. The most depressing aspect of it all from my personal point of view is that while there is plenty of loud lamentation that R.S. is leaving, there seems to be less than no concern (except from Andrew) to preserve what he tried rather hard to build up, + in some measure succeeded in building up; + no one except Andrew seems willing to move to get someone really good to take my place. A couple of people have told me that I am "irreplaceable," which would be flattering if it were not patently a half-way excuse for not really facing the situation; + it is of course a convenient cover for people who don't want another strong personality in the Department, + a convenient screen for a situation in which there are covertly opposing camps, + some people who would fight bitterly against one or the other of the most obvious candidates. But this is the one issue that really interests me, + though I don't anticipate a very satisfactory outcome I intend to fight as well as I can for the appointment of someone who will really attract good pupils— other than that it doesn't matter so much who it is. Unfortunately it has been pointed out to R.S. that as a "lame duck" he doesn't really have much influence around here any more.

I didn't really mean to get started on all this, + I fear it gives a somewhat distorted picture of my state of mind, though not an exaggerated one of the changes around here. As for me I am of course only half here in any case; I have a wonderful job in Princeton + am looking forward more eagerly than I can tell you to getting back, not only to Princeton, but to the East where after all I really belong, + to New York where the decisive battles are fought. I have every hope of being able to build on more solid ground what I wanted to build here—it will in some ways not be so pleasant, but it will be exciting + real + ultimately more demanding.

Meanwhile, the year in Europe was really wonderful. It was marvelous to be back in Florence, which is always an intoxication. It was of course strange + exhilarating to see Italy without Mussolini, to see something of old friends + to make some new ones—primarily Luigi Dallapiccola with whom I got along extremely well, + of whom I saw a great deal, + also some other musicians—Pietro Scarpini, an absolutely first-class pianist, the violinist Materassi, the cellist Pietro Grossi who also lives in Florence.[3] I found Italy temporarily at least in wonderful shape, though there are terrific economic problems + the possibility always of dangerous political upheaval. France on the contrary I found depressing in the extreme; + Germany,—in which we spent four days, but from which we gained many further impressions later in Austria—also in splendid shape, but, in view of the world situation, on the whole rather terrifying. I'm afraid we are going to wake up some day to find we have another first-class German problem on our hands, mainly because of our own ineptitude. Austria is of course more hopeless than before, even; Switzerland essentially quite unchanged except for more + bigger cars, + faster driving— oh well, you know all this. But returning to Europe was like a home-coming, even though to a somewhat shattered + impoverished home. That of course is another reason for returning East; one is so much nearer.

I mustn't write more, + in fact I'm afraid I have let off a certain amount of steam in this letter! Forgive me if it is a bore. But I am sure you must have heard similar stories from others, + I know too that you are not entirely unconcerned about Berkeley—less unconcerned, perhaps, than I.

The best to you both, from all of us.

Affectionately,
Roger

(P.S.) *Montezuma* has progressed splendidly + I have great hopes of finishing it before the year is out. Also other things—but of that more another time.

1. William Carlin (b. 1927) was a student in Sessions's Berkeley seminar 1947–52 and also studied with him at Princeton. His first wife, Gay, was another Sessions pupil. Jack Swackhammer (b. 1928) was a student of Krenek and Sessions; he taught at the University of California at Berkeley.

2. Seymour Shifrin (1926–1979), composer and teacher at Brandeis University.

3. Scarpini (b. 1911), a pianist, taught at the Conservatory of Florence. Sandro Materassi (b. 1904) studied violin in Florence and Budapest. He performed with Dallapiccola, who dedicated his *Tartiniana II* for violin and orchestra to Materassi. Pietro Grossi (b. 1917), cellist and twelve-tone composer, writes and works with electronic music.

▼

Luigi Dallapiccola to Roger Sessions[1]
als I-Fb

October 10, 1952
My dear Roger,   Los Angeles, California

Thanks so much for your kind letter of October 6.

I am delighted that everything is all right concerning my lecture (we'll agree on its total length when I arrive) and I am also delighted that, once again, our points of view coincide on how to give it.

I will arrive on Monday the 13th in the evening, and I am planning to let you know via telegram the exact time and place of my arrival. I am very sorry to have to put off this piece of news until the last moment, but the Italian Consul in Los Angeles, being busy here for Columbus Day, has asked me to go to Pasadena (where I had also been invited) to represent my country for the opening ceremony of the International Olympic Games.

Now, since I am in America (luckily) as Luigi Dallapiccola and not in an official position, and since the Italian government would have probably sent some zero from the Roman-government-neoclassic-counterreformation-baroque sphere, I find my doing a favor for such a government very "witty." We enjoy ourselves the way we can.

Thanks for having taken a "preparatory" look at my *Prigioniero*.[2] When I see you, I'll tell you about my interesting meeting with Stravinsky, whom I had not seen since 1937. He was extremely cordial; he does not seem to dislike Wagner, and he has added a twelve-tone part to his recent "Cantata."[3] In Italy we used to say:

As long as man has a tooth in his mouth
he doesn't know what the future holds for him . . .
[*fin che l'uomo ha un dente in bocca
non sa mai quel che gli tocca . . .*]

And for my part, once more, I find what happens in this world very interesting and instructive . . .

All my best wishes to your wife and children. Please believe me to be your friend.

Yours affectionately,
Ld

1. Translated from the Italian by Valeria Secchi Short.
2. *Il prigioniero* (opera in one act, libretto by Luigi Dallapiccola, after Villiers de l'Isle-Adam, Comte de Coster), 1944–48; first performed by the RAI (Radiotelevisione Italiana), December 1, 1949, and staged in Florence, Communale, May 20, 1950.

3. Stravinsky's Cantata, a setting of late medieval English verse for soprano, tenor, women's voices, and five instruments published in 1952 by Boosey & Hawkes.

▼

Roger Sessions to Beveridge Webster
tls US-NHwebster

November 28, 1952
Dear Beveridge: [Berkeley, California]

Thank you for your letter. I had already heard of the performance at Brooklyn and the projected performance in Pittsburgh but didn't realize that you were tackling the First Sonata too. Needless to say I am delighted and wish I could hear you. I will do what I can in the way of notes. I am dictating this off the cuff and only hope that I can say something that will be really helpful. As a matter of fact I think there are some interesting things to be said about the First Sonata at least.

A few days ago I heard the new records of my Black Maskers Suite,[1] which I hadn't heard for quite a number of years. What struck me above all was its essential relationship to my more recent music. Certainly it is technically very much less mature, and psychologically, if I may put it that way, much less developed. I believe that my music has gained a flexibility of movement and a depth of texture which it did not have at that time, and which I didn't possess the means to give it—I started to write, perhaps not even the impulse; but on second thought, the impulse must have been there in view of what I have to say about my First Sonata.

The First Sonata was begun in 1928 [1927] and occupies an important place in the line of development which started somewhat after the Black Maskers. Looking back to that time I remember that I was impelled to that development by a very searching self-criticism which I put myself through after The Black Maskers. I was acutely aware of what, during the composition, I had felt as my own technical limitations, and I was also aware that I had relied rather heavily on the psychological and associative elements of the "subject" to carry me through, especially at moments where my technical resources had seemed to me insufficient. It is true that I feel today that I may well have exaggerated in this respect; if so the exaggeration was at least a fruitful and useful one.

You will remember of course that this was the period in which

Stravinsky was entering on his "neo-classic" phase; and that seemed to me to offer a direction from which I could gain the resources which I needed. Naturally I could write pages about this, and give you many details for which there is no time at this point. Looking backward I can realize that my approach was a quite different one from Stravinsky's and that a part of the experience consisted in fighting stubbornly against the reservations which I always felt regarding the final validity of such an approach as his. Naturally every work has its own value and I do not mean to deny in any degree whatever the validity of these works themselves, when I say that my First Symphony, my First Sonata, and even to some extent my Violin Concerto were all stages in the process of finding my way back to the music of which I was dreaming when I wrote The Black Maskers in 1923. It was not, of course, really a "way back," but an extremely important phase of my development. In any case I am sure you will know how to take such statements as I have just made.

I believe also, at this late date, the First Sonata is not likely to be played in the completely frigid manner in which many of its earliest performers tried to play it. The relative paucity of expression marks in the text was due, believe me, not to any dogma regarding "objectivity" but to an all too naive belief that the character of the music would naturally suggest its own mode of performance—a "singing" tone, a long breath requiring a real dynamic curve, and a ringing tone quality. The greatest mistake from this point of view lay in the fact that (I am afraid out of sheer helplessness) I indicated only a very few pedalings. Actually I assumed that the pedal would be used rather freely throughout, as it certainly should be. Please take all this as a grant of carte blanche rather than as an attempt to tell you how to play the Sonata! Essentially it is by way of explaining how I feel about the work itself, and where I place it in regard to my total production to date.

In my little book entitled The Musical Experience (pages 50–53) are a couple of paragraphs which describe the way the work started in my mind: first with the chord of measures 234–235 which became a kind of obsession as I was walking one day in Pisa. Next, the phrase of measures 27–39 with which I planned to start a regular, detached first movement. When I discovered, however—after a surprising length of time—that the vague but all too strong dissatisfaction I felt with this beginning was due to the syncopated rhythm before any regular beat was established, I immediately thought of the music of the andante Introduction in B minor, and realized that I wanted to bring it back later as the real slow movement of the piece. It was one day somewhat later that, following a semi-conscious train of thought from the chord of measure 234, I found myself back, exactly as in the final text of the Sonata, at the B minor of the Introduction, and realized that this key relationship had been subconsciously in my ear all the time.

When I composed the section beginning measure 252 I felt that it was something quite new and possibly the beginning of a quite new phase in my music, and in a way which I would find it very difficult to define I still feel that it is very close to my later music, perhaps closer than anything else in the Sonata except perhaps certain passages in the Finale.

The last movement gave me a lot of trouble particularly in the choice of a key. I originally had planned to write it one tone lower, i.e., in what I thought of as the key of B major, starting on C sharp instead of D sharp. This however seemed to me to fall flat. I realized that my ear was pulling me towards the D sharp, and then only much later, when I was well along in the actual work on the movement I realized that the D sharp was the real tonic of the piece, and the note on which it had to end.

I can't think of much else to say about the First Sonata, except that for me in this, as also in the Second Sonata, the tone quality which results from the piano writing has always seemed to me a very important part of the character of the piece. I might say also that while the introductory melody has often been likened to Chopin, I conceive it as something rather different—the nearest thing in the music of the past would be a Bach "aria" (Italian Concerto) or perhaps still better, such a Mozart slow movement as that of the little C major Sonata [K. 545]—in other words the long phrases and not the detail are the real key to the expression. I imagine however that you know this without my telling you, especially as it really applies to the Sonata as a whole.

It is harder to write of the Second Sonata, partly because I wrote it much more recently and thus don't see it from such a distance; partly because I wrote it very quickly, in about five weeks; and partly because I felt technically completely free and without preoccupation when I wrote it. I started it as the result of a suggestion by Andor Foldes,[2] for whom I intended to write a short piece. The principal ideas of the various movements, including that which begins at measure 34, all occurred to me at the same time, and I hoped to make out of them a piece that would be not only short but easy to play— the latter is a constant ambition of mine which I have never yet succeeded in fulfilling! As the work progressed I started at one point referring to it as a sonatina; and only later and with some surprise and genuine reluctance did I realize that it would have to be a real sonata. Naturally, in a piece of this kind one can not speak of keys or of tonal structure in the usual sense of the word. It was the first of my works however in which I used no key signature. I believe however that it embodies a structural element which can be compared to contrasts between keys in a piece based on strictly tonal principles. Unfortunately I don't know of any terms in which this element can be defined. As far as I am concerned I feel it in all contemporary music including that based on the 12-tone system, but I doubt if the terms in which it can be convincingly defined will be discovered for many years. The Sonata itself is not based on the 12-tone system, though adepts of the system have remarked, and pointed out to me, that it is really very close to it. The work that I have written since then, especially my Second Quartet, is still closer. I have now arrived at the point where I feel that in all likelihood I shall some time go the whole way; but I am very glad that this evolution has been gradual and genuinely subconscious and absolutely undogmatic.

Regarding the analogy with tonal contrast I would suggest a comparison of the effect produced by, first the opening measures and the section beginning at measure 34; second, between measures 34–66 and measures 131–164. Perhaps an easier comparison would be between measures 78–79, measures 86–87, and measures 92–93. The difficulty is that I myself could not elucidate further than this; the passages in question simply represent stages in the structure of the work which obviously correspond with each other. Similar places can of course be found in the other two movements. I find for instance in the last movement that a low F in the bass always accompanies a real recapitulation of the main theme of the last movement, and that at the beginning of the middle section the motif itself begins with an F. This however is a discovery that I have made just now while turning over the pages of the Sonata in the attempt to find something to say about it; I never was aware of it before. I also see that at the very end of the Sonata the F persists from measure 394 and that the final progression is based on the gradual progression of this F down to the final C.

I have the feeling that I have really been furnishing you mostly with a few titbits which of course I hope will be helpful. Actually I am of course realizing that you know these pieces well enough to play them—better that is than I know them myself—and therefore you know where the themes recur, where the climaxes come, and what the various themes consist in. I am sure you realize also that I made a truly horrible mistake in the metronomic indication of the last movement of the Second Sonata, which should be 58 to 63 and not 88 to 92.

Forgive me for writing you such a long letter which however I hope will be helpful.

With every good wish and sincerest thanks for the real seriousness which you have brought to my work—it makes me look forward the more to seeing something of you next year when I am in the East again and to perhaps hearing you play these works some time—

Most cordially,

Roger (excuse this bad pen)

1. Walter Hendl conducting the American Recording Society Orchestra, Desto D404.

2. Hungarian pianist Andor Foldes (b. 1913) is the dedicatee of Copland's Piano Blues No. 2 (1934); he also played the Piano Fantasy and Sonata (in 1948). Sessions initially dedicated his Second Sonata to Foldes; his name appears on the holograph but not on the published score.

SESSIONS'S RELATIONSHIP with the performing rights organizations, the American Society of Composers, Authors, and Publishers (ASCAP) and the younger Broadcast Music, Inc. (BMI), can be gleaned from his letters to and from Krenek and to Copland. The dispute involved the American Composers Alliance (ACA). Copland described the situation:

> In the early forties we [the ACA] ran into problems stemming from the necessity to choose between affiliation with ASCAP or BMI. (Until 1938 ASCAP had been the principal collector of performance fees. BMI was founded when radio broadcasting grew, with the function of licensing radio rights and with the idea of breaking the ASCAP monopoly.) As members of ASCAP, Virgil [Thomson] and I of course preferred that ACA connect with them; others, Roger Sessions included, sided with BMI. ASCAP was reluctant to settle an agreement to control the collection of fees for ACA. After three years of discussions between the ACA and ASCAP (not always friendly), a decision was made when BMI offered a contract of $10,000 for ACA radio rights in 1944. We needed the money. Those who held dual membership in ASCAP and ACA were forced to choose one or the other. I resigned as president of ACA.[1]

Copland had chosen to stay with ASCAP and asked Sessions to do the same. William Schuman had gone to BMI in 1952, but Piston, Harris, Carter, and others did not do so until later. Evidently, Sessions was persuaded by Robert Burton.[2] Before Sessions replied to Copland, he had already encouraged Krenek to join BMI in a letter of May 13, 1953.

1. Copland and Perlis, *Copland: 1900 through 1942* (New York: St. Martin's Press, 1984): 277–78.
2. Robert J. Burton (1915–65), always called "Judge Burton," had championed country music from BMI's birth in 1940. He became president of BMI, a position he held until his untimely death in 1965.

▼

Roger Sessions to Aaron Copland
tls US-DLC

July 24, 1953
Dear Aaron: [Berkeley, California]

Thank you for your long letter which arrived about a month ago. I appreciate tremendously the trouble you took, and you have certainly put the issues very clearly. Since I am afraid I shall very possibly prove a disappointment to you in this matter, I want to make my position as clear as I can. Let me assure you I have not only given the question a great deal of thought, but made various inquiries which have always, however, led to a similar result as far as I am concerned.

In the first place it won't be possible for me to wait till I get to New York before making a decision, since resignations from ASCAP have to be in before September 1st, and it is quite unlikely that I can be in New York before that time. For that reason I feel I must come to a decision at least before we leave Berkeley, as we shall be doing on August 8th. I realize that there are disadvantages in this, the main one being that I have only the friendliest feelings towards ASCAP, and that you and Douglas [Moore] have both appealed to me in the connection. But unless some very definite development should change the picture quite radically, I shall have to make up my mind within the next two weeks.

The crux of the matter for me at the present moment rests on two very factual considerations. First of all, what I have been offered by BMI goes far beyond anything that has been proposed or even intimated by ASCAP—so far beyond it that I don't see the slightest possibility that ASCAP could meet it, nor do I see any valid reason, from ASCAP's point of view, why it should try to do so; I would in fact consider it quite out of order, in fact, even to suggest the possibility.

The BMI agreement includes not only a performing rights contract but other provisions which have to do with publication—not entirely unlike what ASCAP proposes. But while ASCAP has selected a publisher for me, the BMI agreement leaves me free to choose my own; and the suggestions that have been made have all very real advantages from my point of view. Chappell and Co., on the other hand, has none whatever that I have been able—after inquiry from several sources—to discover. I have no assurance whatever, in other words, that I would fare as well with Chappell as I do with my present publisher, Marks, and considerable reason to believe that I would fare less well.

Secondly—and almost more important to me—my connection with BMI is sponsored by men who not only believe in my music and in its future but who have already in quite other connections given me tangible proof of this. The proposal regarding publication, to which I have already referred, is one clear way in which this shows in the contract which I have been offered. With all loyalty towards the colleagues whom you mention, and sincere friendship for the four of you that I know, you would hardly claim that the group as a whole looks conspicuously friendly either to my music itself or to what I have always stood for! nor, once again, would I dream of suggesting that it is under any obligation to be so. But the hard fact is that the contract that has been offered me is couched in terms which present a real incentive and even a challenge to me to go on producing the kind of music which I have to produce. On the other hand, the suggestion of Chappell as publishers of my music seems to me an indication of where I stand as far as ASCAP and its Advisory Board is concerned.

The whole point is that a decision in favor of ASCAP looks, under the circumstances, like a real sacrifice: a greater one, in fact, than I would feel justified in making, from the standpoint of my family if from none other.

These are perhaps the two major considerations which still incline me towards BMI. As you can easily see, they imply a number of intangibles, about which I speak very reluctantly, since one can so easily be misinterpreted in such matters. Certainly I have no wish to compromise the efforts of composers to make the most favorable terms possible as far as performing rights are concerned. I think I also understand quite well the business factors involved; since years I have tried to understand these things, and have written and spoken enough on the subject to convince anyone that I am not precisely naive on the subject. But I feel that there has also to be some place for those of us who, because the music makes heavy demands on the performer and/ or the listener, or because they have chosen to swim against prevailing currents, have to rely on those who believe strongly in them in terms of the future. I also find it very hard to believe that my acceptance of very favorable terms from BMI can seriously hamper composers in getting more favorable attention from ASCAP. If anything—and both you and Douglas [Moore] confirm this—it would seem to me to tend to have rather the opposite effect. The plain fact of the matter is that in both organizations the element of sheer prestige would seem to be overwhelming as far as "serious" composers are concerned; and it is therefore natural for a composer like myself to lean toward the organization where his prestige value seems the greatest, especially since prestige, being intangible, is not a commodity with which one can bargain very effectively.

I don't know whether I have made myself clear or not. I am deferring my decision regarding ASCAP for a little while longer, because I feel that I owe you at least the time to reply. I hope in any case that you will realize that I am giving the matter very earnest thought.

I too am happy—more happy than I can say—to be moving east again, and am beginning to be very excited that it will be so soon. You may be sure that I look forward to seeing you again and, as you say, talking of many things!

As always,
Roger

▼

Ernst Krenek to Roger Sessions
als US-NYpease

December 17, 1953
2177 Argyle Avenue
Los Angeles 28, California

Dear Roger,

I should have written to you long ago, and I thought of it many times. Finally a very nice conversation I had last Sunday with Mr. Burton made me decide not to postpone it any longer. You probably know that I made a contract with BMI, and I am very grateful to you for having made this contact for me. These gentlemen were very nice indeed, let me come last summer to New York for a day when I was teaching in Toronto, and treated me with respect and sympathy, which I appreciated very much. What they are going to pay me, is not a fortune (which I did not expect), but it is considerably more (very much so) than what I was used to receive from ASCAP, and this a great help indeed. I hope that this association will eventually produce other good results. It is certainly very nice to be affiliated with an organization whose top people seem to take a certain personal interest in the "serious" composers with whom they have contracts.

I was glad to hear from Burton, that you are nicely and satisfactorily established in Princeton, and I wish you would tell me more about it. I am sure that there you have formed after all the congenial atmosphere you were missing, and I hope that the vicinity of New York gives you sufficient opportunity to live up to the responsibilities which you always have felt having in regard to musical activities and standards on a larger scale.

I have been frightfully busy ever since I returned from my very enjoyable summer trip, which took me to Toronto, Ann Arbor, Chicago, Albuquerque, Aspen, Washington State, Berkeley (KPFA), the High Sierra, and other beautiful places. I am orchestrating my new opera which I hope to produce in Europe in 1955,[1] and there were quite a few other projects to be taken care of on the side, among them a Violin Concerto[2] commissioned by the Northwest German Radio. I plan to go to Europe next August, for about three months, and then again in 1955, when the opera will be ready, as I hope.

Next March I hope to come to New York for a short visit and I certainly hope to see you then. Please drop me a few lines, if you can, and let me know briefly how everything is with you.

Thanks again for the BMI contact, and all good wishes for Christmas and New Year—I still remember your fabulous eggnogg, and I wish I could partake of another of the kind!

As ever,

Your friend
Ernst

1. *Pallas Athene weint* received its premiere in Hamburg October 17, 1955.
2. Krenek's Violin Concerto no. 2, op. 140 (1954).

▼

Luigi Dallapiccola to Roger Sessions[1]
tls I-Fb

December 27, 1954

My dear friend Roger,   34 via Romana, Florence

it is especially during these days at the end of the year (always days of spiritual "stocktaking") that I realize with great shame that it is quite a while since I have given you news about me. Thanks, first of all, for news of you and also for the news you sent me through our dear Scarpini . . . and please forgive me.

Our trip to Spain has without a doubt stirred great emotions in us; and, like all emotions, it has somewhat distracted us. In twelve days I gave nine concerts with Cassadó[2] and with a German clarinet player (program: Bach, Suite in C major for cello solo; Beethoven: Sonata, Op. 102, No. 1 and No. 2; Brahms: Trio, op. 114), I also gave a concert of my music in Madrid (Piccolo Concerto; Music for Three Pianos; Ciaccona, Intermezzo, and Adagio for cello; Canti di Prigionia),[3] while performing we traveled eight thousand kilometers. Also before and after this concert tour I gave two lectures in Barcelona. Though all of this was not the real reason for our emotions. This, my first trip to Spain, has given me my definitive understanding of Goya, and just this was worth the trip. I was (or I thought I was) sufficiently prepared to understand this great painter. Still it had always escaped me that of all the artists of our Western civilization he is the only one who, like Beethoven, started his production with his roots in the 18th century, continued it by dominating his century and by going beyond it, and eventually put down new roots in the 20th century. "The Dairy-Woman from Bordeaux," his penultimate picture, would be enough to show us how all of Picasso (even the most "advanced") is already all there in a "nut-shell." And what about "The House of the Deaf-man?"[4] Frankly I don't know anyone who ever had such evident and terrifying conversations with the Devil . . .

We got back about twenty days ago and on the 30th we'll be going to Piedmont to visit my old mother for New Year's Day. We had planned everything so that we could go to La Scala for the [Italian] premiere of David[5] by Milhaud. Instead, since the performance has been postponed to January second, I alone will be able to go. I feel strongly about it, for various reasons: not least the memory of the evening spent with you at Mills College, when Darius talked to us about the "Commendatore" and of the symbolisms he discovered in the name David.

Then I will return home right away, in order possibly to finish the sketch of the much-tormented last piece of the *Canti di Liberazione*[6] (which is coming along fine): then I'll leave for Hamburg. Those good people of the Stadttheater have invited me for the third time and I cannot (nor do I want to) refuse. I will see the tenth performance of *Volo di Notte* [*Night Flight*][7] (that will be performed together with *Erwartung* on the same evening). I must add that after so many years I look forward to seeing my first opera. The most recent reviewers in Düsseldorf, while praising its performance, pointed out that they were expecting more, after comparing it with its "model" performance of Hamburg . . . It is so rare to hear talk of "model" performances in the mud of the Italian theatrical life, that I want to see exactly what it is all about. I will not fail to write to you about it since I presume that your opera must be almost completed and I do not doubt that as an "interested party" (or eventually "interested") this may be of some concern to you, too. During my short stay in Hamburg I will also perform some of my pieces at the Radio.

This is all, or almost all. Italian theaters are not looking for me, nor am I looking for them. And such theaters, perhaps, try harder and make an effort for foreign composers (I know that Milhaud is happy about how his rehearsals are going); but for me they'll never do so. Fortunately the situation is now clearly defined: I say "fortunately" because this way misunderstandings are not possible any more.

Scarpini has returned from New York absolutely ecstatic. And I know that he has already received their invitation for November 1955, as a real proof of the great success and of the great positive impression he made. I do not know if I wrote to you that I was very happy with the Louisville performance.[8] And I do not doubt that you too will be very pleased when Maestro Whitney[9] will start on your *Idyll of Theocritus*.[10]

After some bureaucratic difficulties, smoothed over at the last moment, the Martiranos[11] (whom you met at our house: he is very dark like a Calabrese, she is very blond) have left for America and they have happily arrived there. I believe that Mr. Martirano will get in touch with you, sooner or later. Even at the moment of his departure I told him to contact you for any possible problem of an artistic nature about music, certain that you'll be able to solve it, also certain that you'll find Mr. Martirano quite an interesting young man.

We are pretty well and we hope that all of you are perfectly fine and that your work goes satisfactorily. I'll tell you once more that your Second Quartet has been a real joy for me.[12] Thank you.

Every good wish to all of you for the New Year and, hoping to have your news soon. I shake your hand with great affection and send you all our truest friendship.

Your always affectionate
Ld

1. Translated from the Italian by Valeria Secchi Short.
2. Gaspar Cassadó (1897–1966), a distinguished Spanish cellist who had studied with Casals.
3. Piccolo concerto per Muriel Couveux, piano, and chamber orchestra (1939–41); Musica per tre pianoforti (1935); Ciaccona, intermezzo e adagio for cello (1945); Canti di prigionia (Queen Mary Stuart, Boethius, Savonarola), for chorus, two pianos, two harps, and percussion (1938–41).
4. The Quinta del Sordo, Goya's country house 1820–23, which he decorated with the "black paintings," works that anticipate twentieth-century expressionism and that now are housed in the Prado Museum, Madrid.
5. Milhaud's five-act opera, op. 320 (1952), had received its premiere in Jerusalem June 1, 1954.
6. Canti di liberazione (1951–55), first performed in Cologne October 28, 1955.
7. The one-act opera Volo di notte (1937–39, after Antoine de Saint-Exupéry's novel Vol de nuit), in which Dallapiccola first juxtaposed diatonic and twelve-tone passages.
8. The October 2d performance of Dallapiccola's Variazione per orchestra, a version of his Quaderno musicale di Annalibera.
9. Robert Whitney (1904–86), conductor of the Louisville Orchestra 1937–67. He obtained money from the Rockefeller Foundation to commission and record composers such as Dallapiccola and Sessions.
10. Commissioned by the Louisville Orchestra and dedicated to Luigi Dallapiccola, the Idyll was sung by Audrey Nossaman, soprano, and conducted by Robert Whitney at its premiere, January 14, 1956.
11. Salvatore Martirano (b. 1927) had studied at Oberlin and Eastman, and with Dallapiccola 1952–54. In 1956–59 he held the Rome Prize fellowship. This was one of many instances when Dallapiccola and Sessions would discuss and often exchange students, the exchanges sometimes being facilitated by Fulbright grants.
12. Sessions's Quartet No. 2 was published in 1954 by E. B. Marks.

1955-1963

T E N

THE ENTIRE DECADE of the 1950s was Sessions's most successful in terms of completing new works, performances of new and old works, and public recognition. In addition, Sessions continued to work on his "magnum opus," *Montezuma,* whose piano-vocal score he finished July 1, 1962. The intensity of these activities may explain why there are so few letters for some of these years.

Sessions had begun writing in the twelve-tone system with his solo Violin Sonata (1953), after having been immersed in Schoenberg's music and in a friendship with the older composer. Felix Greissle, Schoenberg's son-in-law, became Sessions's editor at E. B. Marks and his friend. His relationship with the Italian dodecaphonist, Luigi Dallapiccola, flourished in the 1950s and 1960s. Friendships with Ernst Krenek, Louis Krasner, Aaron Copland, and David Diamond continued through the mails, as did his relationships with former students Leon Kirchner and Harold Schiffman.

By the time of the Princeton Seminar in Advanced Musical Studies (August 17–September 5, 1959), which Sessions organized, his reputation as a twelve-tone composer and that of the Princeton University music department as a center for this type of music had—whether Sessions wished it or not—solidified in many people's minds.

Sessions's letters to the Schiffmans continued to discuss more personal matters, such as marriage and, in a letter of February 20, 1955 (US-Tschiffman), children: "Finally, your latest news is very exciting! and we are so happy for you both. It is very good news indeed, + I believe you will always think it so. Children certainly don't make life easier, but they add incalculably to the sum of one's existence, + life would be quite incomplete without them."

▼

Roger Sessions to Leon Kirchner
als US-CAkirchner

July 17, 1955
Lenox, Massachusetts

Dear Leon,—

It was wonderful to hear from you—not only on personal principles but because it gives me the occasion (not the *opportunity* which alas I always have but do not use properly) to write to you, which I have intended to do for a long time, but have simply, with my usual procrastination, put off. It has been so good to think of you on the scene of ancient loves and wars[1]—not after all so ancient as all that but still so definitely of the past as far as I am concerned—and to have news of you from time to time against that background. I hear that you are a success as a teacher + a real + important force in the musical community there, + though this is what I expected, it is good to hear [it] from so many sources. I hope life is reasonably satisfying for you there + also have been very happy to hear that you are producing + that we will hear your Concerto[2] at last in New York this coming winter.

I too have been busy since I left California + have by this time all the "success" I need for easy + not too preoccupied functioning—perhaps a good deal more varied responsibilities (the I.S.C.M., the Schnabel committee, +c.) than I would prefer, but it seems to be a matter of real responsibilities which I must meet, + which I have not yet learned to meet more than indifferently well.

As far as music is concerned, you have probably heard rumors of my "Idyll of Theocritus" which is a setting for soprano + orchestra of the most flaming + passionate love poem (and a good deal more than that—it contains nearly everything, in fact) in the whole of Western literature. It hasn't been performed yet, so I am a little chary of proclaiming too loudly that I consider it my most important work thus far. You may also have heard that I recently finished an Anglican Mass[3] for the 50th anniversary of Kent School, where I went to school in 1908–11. It is not a big piece but it is music definitely by me. Both Theocritus + the Mass will be published about the same time + will make a strange combination. Also that I am writing a Piano Concerto + a Symphony for Juilliard + the Boston Symphony respectively.[4]

So much for news. One by-product of this changed situation is of course my presence here, which I am enjoying immensely. I won't go into this subject very far as it wd. take long, + besides, I have been here [at Tanglewood] only two weeks + my reactions are still in a fluid state. They are however clear enough for me to be touched very deeply by this really very impressive monument that Tanglewood is— the realization of a dream of a man[5] with whom I neither agreed nor, in the last years, "got along" (it was his doing, not mine) but who after all was a human being who loved music + who did probably more than anyone else to make life more tolerable for American musicians, including very definitely myself. I like the atmosphere here + this in spite of, I am quite sure, seeing it without undue illusions.

What you say in your letter regarding Beethoven vs. the fossils + mollusks touches, as I needn't tell you, a thoroughly responsive chord, + we could talk for hours on the subject, + undoubtedly would if we were together. It is of course a real problem nowadays, though I suspect it always has been, in one form or another. Basically— + " 'musique' concrète" is neither the only or the most dangerous of its manifestations, as I'm sure you'll agree—its most dangerous effect is that on young composers who see in it an easy solution to all problems—this of course includes the absurd Webern cult, which is fundamentally the same thing, + which would annoy Webern heartily if he were here to see it. But to the slogan of that group, "Schoenberg est mort" ["Schoenberg is dead"] one should simply answer "Webern aussi, et cinq ans plus tôt" ["Webern too, and five years earlier"].[6]

These are perennial problems, + not really so characteristic of our time as we like to think—one must simply remember Debussy's admonition to the young E. Bloch—"on est peu" ["one is little"]— + incidentally take enough time out to wish the latter had succeeded in adjusting himself better to that fact + taken it more completely to heart. But I have learned that the more "success" one has, the more lonely one feels.[7]

Meanwhile I have your "Sonata Concertante"[8] which I brought here to study at more leisure. I do not yet feel I know it well, so won't try to write about it beyond the mere observation that I am pleased + convinced that all is still well with you musically—which means of course development as well as the original very great gifts.

[. . .]

Much love to everyone, + write me again soon—above all tell me more about yourself + your work. I'll really try to be a better correspondent.

I miss you, too.

Roger

1. The previous year Kirchner had left the University of Southern California, where he had taught since 1948, to return to the Bay Area, taking a position at Mills College.

2. Kirchner's Piano Concerto No. 1 (1953) received its premiere in New York February 23, 1956, conducted by Dimitri Mitropoulos.

3. For unison voices and organ. Both the Mass and the *Idyll of Theocritus* were published by E. B. Marks in 1957. The Mass was premiered in April 1956 at New York's St. John the Divine, Sessions conducting.

4. The concerto, commissioned by The Juilliard School of Music for its fiftieth anniversary and dedicated to the memory of Artur Schnabel, received its first performance February 10, 1956, with Beveridge Webster as the soloist and Jean Morel conducting. The Symphony No. 3, dedicated to the memory of Serge and Natalie Koussevitzky, received its premiere December 6, 1957, by the Boston Symphony Orchestra, Charles Munch conducting.

5. Serge Koussevitzky.

6. A reference to Pierre Boulez's article "Schoenberg Is Dead," *The Score* 6 (May 1952): 18–22, in which Boulez posited Webern as the true exponent of the avant-garde.

7. Possibly a reference to Schoenberg's 1937 article "How One Becomes Lonely," reprinted in *Style and Idea,* ed. Leonard Stein, trans. Leo Black (New York: St. Martin's Press, 1975), 30–53.

8. For violin and piano (1952), premiered in New York, November 30, 1952.

▼

Roger Sessions to Aaron Copland
tls US-DLC

August 22, 1955

Dear Aaron: Princeton

I started a letter to you at the end of my second week in Tanglewood, telling you how much I was enjoying it and thanking you for giving me the opportunity to go there. But unfortunately my laziness got the better of me and so the letter was never sent. Now I am writing you to tell you the same thing, but with even more reason and conviction since I have it all to look back upon. It was a very rich time for me, and I enjoyed every minute of it. It was above all gratifying to me to come once more in touch with Koussevitzky, even though it had to be posthumously. But I appreciated more than ever what he was and what he intended to do, and I found the experience an extremely moving one.

Aside from that I enjoyed immensely all the people whom I saw there, above all perhaps those whom I already knew and got to know better. Perhaps even more than anything else I enjoyed seeing something of Lenny Bernstein,[1] whom I had known only slightly before, but whom I feel I got to know quite well this summer. I was more than ever impressed with his gifts, and found him about as congenial as anyone could ask both as a musician and as a human being. I don't mean that there may not be points on which we differ; but I feel we agree completely on all real essentials. I also enjoyed Ingolf Dahl, Hugh Ross, Ralph Berkowitz,[2] and a number of the members of the opera department, of whom I saw a great deal. Of course I must not forget to mention Mrs. Koussevitzky,[3] who is a lovely person and with whom I had some very fine talks. The main point is that it was a really wonderful summer.

I found Boris Blacher[4] extremely congenial and we spent a great deal of time together and had many fruitful discussions, mostly over drinks in the garden behind the Curtis Hotel—we had a sort of "Stammtisch" [family table] there where we met regularly late in the evening and were often joined by others, including students and out-of-town visitors. We found ourselves in agreement on a surprising number of points, including our approach to the problem of teaching, and also on the individual students. It was a very nice relationship and I feel that some of the students profited and got a good deal out of the fact that Blacher and I became such close friends, so that they were able to consult whomever they chose as the occasion demanded; it also was good for them to see that we generally told them substantially the same things. On the whole the students were a very satisfactory bunch. I perhaps overdid things a little in assigning 11 to each of us, and in addition to that I had the Finnish boy, whom I found awfully lacking in certain very elementary things, but who is intelligent and responsive and serious, and who pleased me enormously at the end by telling me he thought I had really helped him. I had one really first class talent—Salvatore Martirano; and we both felt that Blacher's pupil, E. J. Miller,[5] was a close runner-up.

Richard Maxfield,[6] whom I brought up, according to your suggestion, to run the student concerts did an excellent job and several people told me that they thought the results compared very favorably with those of former years. We got Berkowitz to schedule a number of the more important rehearsals, and on the whole they worked out fairly well. You know what the problems are, and we ran up against them too. I can see very well why they are bound to arise. We had splendid cooperation from singers, pianists, and to a large extent from wind players; also, a couple of the student conductors were extremely helpful. On the other hand, some of the string players were difficult. I gather that string players have become a major Tanglewood problem; there was some discussion in faculty meetings as to what can be done about it.

I came to be very aware of certain basic problems, and in fact one of the main purposes of this letter is to give you my thoughts on the subject—for what they are worth and to be used as you see fit. First of all, I came to feel that six weeks is too short a time. One gets to know one's students during the first two weeks, and by the beginning of the fifth week everyone begins to realize that it is almost over, and to scramble to get the loose ends and to bring the summer to a satisfactory conclusion. I came to feel that the third and fourth weeks were the time when most was accomplished, and it seemed to me that two weeks more in this middle period would work wonders. I therefore feel that it would be a wonderful thing if the school could run for eight weeks, and if the greater part of the student performances and opera productions could be put together in a sort of supplementary festival during the last two weeks after the close of the regular Boston Symphony festival.

Secondly, I have the impression that the death of Koussevitzky left the school to all intents and purposes without any real head. I talked very frankly with quite a number of people about this—including Mrs. Koussevitzky—and I am sure you will not be surprised to hear that feeling is quite general on this point. I also learned that the question is a far more complicated one than it seems to be from the outside. I therefore feel a good deal less like suggesting solutions than I did when I first discussed the subject. But I did see a number of situations which seemed to call for decisive action from the very top, and where the lack of a person both competent and willing to make such decisions was keenly felt. If my experience in other institutions is valid in this connection, such situations are likely to recur more and more frequently as time goes on.

I write you all of this, of course, in the spirit of a disinterested observer and at the urgency of several of the people with whom I spoke there. I therefore hope you will not feel that I am being indiscreet.

Blacher and I were somewhat concerned by the fact that we got, on the whole, much less work out of our students than did anyone else on the campus from theirs. We discussed the matter a great deal and

I talked it over with quite a number of other people on the campus. I think we all understood what the reasons were, Tanglewood offers so many opportunities for a young composer aside from the study of composition, that he is thoroughly apt to feel that it is most important for him to take advantage of them as long as he is there. Furthermore, as I myself learned, Tanglewood is not the easiest place in the world in which to concentrate.

On the other hand, it seemed to me that it was not the best thing in the world to have a group of students in a school who were relatively unoccupied, and whose contribution was less tangible than that of the other students. It seemed to me that it tended a little to make them a kind of a race apart from the others, effects which, while not very spectacular, were certainly not desirable either from their own special point of view or from that of the school as a whole.

This also is a tough problem, but I wonder if it might not be solved in something like the following manner (I will admit that some of my ideas are the result of a talk I had with Goldowsky[7] about the way he organized the opera department). Why couldn't composers be selected, say, about the middle of February and assigned specific compositions, to be finished two weeks before the end of the term? The assignments would be like commissions, the [payment associated with the] commission being of course the privilege of studying at Tanglewood. The nature of the works thus assigned would of course depend on the number and type of performers which could be allocated that early (and of course on the basis of advance planning by several people concerned) for the job of performing the works in question, at one or more concerts during the last week of the school. The composition teachers, instead of having regular appointments with each individual student, would keep office hours—say, three hours each morning—and each individual student would be expected to report weekly for consultation with the teachers assigned to him.

Naturally there is much more behind these ideas of mine than I can possibly put into a letter, and I am sure that most of what has led me to these conclusions will have often occurred to you too. However, I became so thoroughly enthusiastic about the whole Tanglewood idea that I would gladly make any contribution I can to its continued success and prosperity; hence the above reflections, for what they are worth. If you ever feel like talking these things over more thoroughly, I would of course be glad to do so. I hope at least that you will gather from all of the above what a really wonderful time I had there.

I hope your summer has been a successful and a productive one. I am still in the throes of my piece for the Boston Symphony and also the one for the Juilliard School, but I hope and expect to have them ready on time. You may be sure we spoke of you very often at Tanglewood, and missed you very much. If you ever feel like being absent again, do keep me in mind as your substitute! Or, better still, it would be very nice if we could sometime be there together.

With best of luck for the rest of the summer and for your trip back, and I will look forward to seeing you this Fall.

As always,
Roger

1. Leonard Bernstein (1918–90) taught classes 1951–55 at Tanglewood, where he had studied with Koussevitzky 1940–41. Already Bernstein had gained much respect as the assistant conductor of the New York Philharmonic; he would become that orchestra's principal conductor in 1958.

2. The German composer Ingolf Dahl (1912–70) had come to the U.S. in 1935 and had taught at the University of Southern California since 1945; he taught at Tanglewood 1952–55. Hugh Ross (1898–1990) was an organist and conductor of the Winnipeg Male Choir, Winnipeg Symphony Orchestra, and the Schola Cantorum in New York. Pianist Ralph Berkowitz (b. 1910) was dean of the Berkshire Music Center 1947–65.

3. Koussevitzky had married Olga Naoumoff (1901–78), a niece of his first wife, Natalie (d. 1942), on August 15, 1947.

4. Blacher (1903–75), a prolific German composer, was director of the Hochschule für Musik in West Berlin 1953–70.

5. Edward J. Miller (b. 1930) studied at Hartt College of Music and at the Berkshire Music Center with Chávez and Blacher 1955–58. He taught at Hartt 1959–71, then at Oberlin Conservatory.

6. Maxfield (1927–69) had studied at Berkeley with Sessions and at Princeton with Babbitt, and later taught at the New School for Social Research and San Francisco State College. Much of his music after 1959 employed electronics.

7. Boris Goldowsky (b. 1908), perhaps most familiar as a moderator for the New York Metropolitan Opera's radio broadcasts, directed the opera workshop at Tanglewood 1942–64 and founded the New England Opera Company in 1946.

ON NOVEMBER 1, 1955, Luigi Dallapiccola wrote Sessions a long letter (I-Fb) detailing the events surrounding the previous spring's meeting of ISCM members, which until now he had had to keep secret. A movement had begun to expel the society's honorary president for life, the English Schoenberg pupil Edward Clark (1888–1962).[1] The composer Benjamin Frankel[2] (1906–73), an apparently somewhat strident member of the British Communist party, had accused Clark at the meeting of mismanaging the society's funds. Clark had slapped Frankel's face and sued him. Frankel announced in June that he had won the suit, but in July another ISCM member, Don Banks,[3] sent Dallapiccola newspaper clippings contradicting this. Dallapiccola and Malipiero, with Clark's permission, then appealed on Clark's behalf to Goffredo Petrassi, the president of the ISCM, who appeared hostile until Dallapiccola and Malipiero threatened to resign, at which point Petrassi softened his tone and agreed to inform the other members about the affair. Dallapiccola now asked Sessions to explain all of this to Copland, the vice president of the society.

1. Clark was elected president of the ISCM in 1947. He was married to the composer Elizabeth Lutyens.
2. His name appears in the correspondence variously as Fränkel and Fraenkel, just as Clark's name sometimes gains a final *e*.
3. Banks (b. 1923), an Australian composer, studied with Dallapiccola for a year in Florence in the early fifties.

▼

Roger Sessions to Luigi Dallapiccola[1]
als I-Fb

November 24, 1955
57 College Road
Princeton, New Jersey

My dearest friend Luigi,

I am afraid that you must consider me a most ungrateful man for having not only so long delayed answering your lovely letters, but above all for not having thanked you for sending me the *Canti di Liberazione*, which I studied with particular attention, and which I took profound pleasure in reading, but which moved me in a way that few pieces of music can. They seem to be among your most important works, and in that respect there is much to say, from many points of view! There is such a tremendous strength in the musical language, an intensity of expression and conviction, and a preoccupation with "last or ultimate" things both in music and in human spirit, which are almost rare qualities in music today. It is music to be studied in depth and with love, and I promise not to be delinquent in either instance.

Many thanks for the great letter on the Clarke-Fraenkel-Petrassi issue (the letters reveal him to be a mediocre and limited man). I will concern myself with it and in fact, am almost decided on going to

Stockholm[2] because of it. Unfortunately, and for reasons which I will subsequently explain, internal politics of the American section are involved, and because of this I have decided to gather information confidentially on the legal proceedings and events preceding them in such a way that neither you nor Malipiero will be involved. In your letter you mentioned Glock,[3] but only (it seems to me) to confirm what you had written to me—a precaution not really necessary for me! What I would need ideally is a person not connected with the English section nor with the politics of the I.S.C.M., but who would be well informed about all of those events and who could write to me confidentially and without any inhibitions. Don Banks, for example, or else someone older. What do you think and have you any suggestions? And where could I write to D.B.? Sorry but I have to act sub rosa for the moment; it is important right now that no one here be aware that I am taking an interest in this.

There is so much to write—P. Scarpini must have written you about the "reading" of my *Idyll of Theocritus* with two pianos[4] which was very well received; the premiere is about to take place in Louisville on January 15. P.S. had bad luck in New York because of a terrible accompaniment by Mitropoulos and by the Philharmonic;[5] but his own performance was very beautiful. It was triumphantly acclaimed all over the country outside of New York—we hope to see him again before his departure for Italy.

I have some enthusiastic letters from the students Sturm[6] and Maxfield—and some indirect news about Martino[7]—I am very happy they are working with you. I was delighted to meet S[alvatore] Martirano, who seems to be a very valid young man of great promise. Naturally I am *very happy* that you will be at Queens College next year and that we will see each other every once in a while in New York and hopefully in Princeton. There is so much more to write; but I am writing at least the most urgent things and I am very busy in finishing without too much delay my Piano Concerto (for the Juilliard School) and my Third Symphony (for Boston).

Affectionate greetings to Laura and Anna Libera.
Roger S——

1. Translated from the Italian by Pina Pasquantonio.
2. The ISCM festival in Stockholm, May–June 1956.
3. Sir William Glock (b. 1908), publisher of *The Score* and later controller of music at the BBC.
4. At Juilliard, with the soprano Martha Long.
5. Scarpini played Mozart's Concerto for Piano and Orchestra, No. 22 in E-flat

major, K. 482, on three Philharmonic concerts, November 3, 4, and 6, 1955, with Dimitri Mitropoulos conducting.

6. George Sturm (b. 1930) studied with Dallapiccola in Florence 1955–57 on a Fulbright grant. From 1958 to 1977 he headed the performance department at G. Schirmer/Associated Music Publishers in New York.

7. Donald Martino (b. 1931), a twelve-tone composer who had studied with Sessions and Babbitt until 1954, had gone to Florence to study with Dallapiccola on a Fulbright scholarship 1954–56. He later taught at the New England Conservatory, Brandeis University, and Harvard University. His *Notturno* won a Pulitzer Prize in 1974.

▼

Roger Sessions to Luigi Dallapiccola[1]
tls I-Fb

January 24, 1956
Princeton

My dearest friend Luigi,

Today your welcome letter arrived; I was about to write to you not only about the happy events in Louisville, but of many other things. Naturally I am very happy to write a letter to Rome on your behalf, and I assure you that the letter that I will write immediately will be a masterpiece that should be very useful. I must confess that it seems grotesque that you should need such a letter for the Commission for Cultural Exchange between Italy and the U.S. . . . . . !!!!!! The "masterpiece" is on its way to Rome with this same mailing (26/I/56).

You must certainly have received our postcard [January 14, 1956] from Louisville written before the premiere of *Theocritus*. As you predicted, I was extremely pleased with Maestro Whitney—he is a man of true worth, an excellent musician, a tried and efficient conductor, so conscientious both as an artist and as a man that I find it moving. Great satisfaction also with Miss Nossaman, who sang admirably, even though until then she had never had anything to do with "that type of music." She was fired up with enthusiasm and, even though she didn't feel quite at home, presented the text and the music in an almost impeccable fashion. Later on, without a doubt, she will feel more free and will add strength and intensity—qualities that she already has begun to obtain but which in this piece are never quite enough. Martha Long, who sang it at the Juilliard when Scarpini heard it (with two pianos), has an exceptional ear, an extraordinary comprehension, and although she lacks the variety and purely vocal refinement that Miss Nossaman has, sang it even better, and the tapes of her performance, which I sent to Louisville, helped us a great deal. The orchestra will play better in the next performances: they are missing the last touches (maybe even the second to last!), a real pianissimo is missing, there are some rough spots, and some weak points; the English horn is weak (he will be substituted), the clarinetist is a little shy, and the first horn was injured and is in the hospital; his substitute was not refined. But in the long run they played with warmth and above all Maestro Whitney understands the music. The result was that the work was presented, even at the premiere, in its essential parts, and no need to tell you that's what counts. The public was alive with warmth and enthusiasm, and the press was magnificent. So, everyone is happy.

Now, as you know, I am waiting for the premiere of my Piano Concerto, which will take place on February 10 at the Juilliard School.[2] I finished it just before leaving for Louisville, and given the interruption for the premiere of *Theocritus*, which still seems to be my most important work, I have the impression that I still don't know the Concerto nor my impressions of it. It is for that reason that I still haven't sent it to Scarpini, as I had promised to do. As soon as I'll have heard it and gotten a sense of it, which I have momentarily lost, of the whole thing, I plan to send it to Florence . . . I am also very busy with my Third Symphony, which will be played in Boston in March.[3]

Meanwhile I met Petrassi and I conversed almost officially with him for an hour and a half. He was very friendly and it always pleases me to speak Italian even when much isn't being said. I was at a cocktail party where I saw Rieti and Rolf Liebermann,[4] who are also very friendly. With certain types of people I can converse in a civilized fashion even though there is little I want to say or hear.

Needless to say, all your comments about my Sonata for Violin gave me great pleasure. Regarding the instructions "attacca" at the end of the second and third movements you are of course completely right: it is impossible to execute and I realized it from the first time it was played. Maybe I should have deleted these indications from the edition, but I believe you will understand why I left them. Regarding the other difficulties, there is nothing to reply: certainly we will eventually listen to the *Canti di Liberazione* and also I hope, my Sonata (it was well-played in San Francisco and New York)[5] but meanwhile your score always gives me immense joy.

I still don't have the information I want from London [ISCM] but I must confess it's my fault. I assure you though that I haven't forgotten and I'll immediately write to Mr. Dent, whom I know, and also to Maestro Bliss,[6] whom I've known for many years. It is uncertain whether I will be able to come to Stockholm; they still don't know the program nor the dates in New York and if it is before June 9, it would depend on my leaving Princeton a little earlier than planned and even more so on being able to secure a reservation before June 1. If it will in any way be possible, I will be there.[7] Meanwhile, I am waiting for the rest of the information you wrote to me about.

I haven't received [George] Sturm's letter, so I know nothing about the translation you mention. If he could drop me a line about it, I'll give it my immediate attention. I apologize for the inefficiency of the mail at Princeton.

I saw Greissle yesterday who spoke to me about a singer who will come to perform your Cantata[8]—something I am truly looking forward to although the definite date is still unknown. Fortunately for me, it didn't take place at the same time as Louisville. Rest assured that I will be there; meanwhile Greissle will send me your letter and I will do all I can for that young lady whose name Greissle had momentarily forgotten.

A thousand pardons for this long letter too full of R.S. and his concerns. All best wishes from the three of us—[. . .]—to all of you.

Very affectionately,
R—— S——

1. Translated from the Italian by Pina Pasquantonio.
2. Two letters to the pianist Beveridge Webster containing scraps of the Piano Concerto, reminiscent of Sessions's brinksmanship with the first Piano Sonata and John Duke twenty-eight years earlier, are quoted in Andrea Olmstead, *Roger Sessions and His Music* (Ann Arbor: UMI Research Press, 1985), 111.
3. Sessions did not finish the Third Symphony until September 25, 1957.
4. Liebermann (b. 1910) is a twelve-tone composer active in opera and radio, who was head of the Hamburg Opera.
5. Sessions's Sonata for Violin, premiered in San Francisco in 1953 by Robert Gross.
6. Sir Arthur Bliss (1891–1975) taught at the University of California at Berkeley 1939–41 and became director of music at the BBC 1942–44.
7. Sessions wrote Dallapiccola January 15, 1956, the day after the Piano Concerto's premiere, to tell him that the *Idyll of Theocritus* was to be performed in Stockholm on June 5.
8. *An Mathilde* for female voice and orchestra (1955), performed in New York on May 7, 1956. Based on poems of Heinrich Heine and reduced for piano by Pietro Scarpini, the piece was published by Suvini Zerboni in 1957. The singer was soprano Magda Laszow, who performed with the Juilliard String Quartet and conductor Jacques Monod.

Roger Sessions to Luigi Dallapiccola[1]
als I-Fb

June 3, 1956
Stockholm

My dearest friend Luigi,

[. . .]

As you can see, we have been in Stockholm for five days. Everything is going well with *Theocritus*—Martha Long is magnificent and the conductor, S[ixten] Ehrling,[2] is excellent, as is the orchestra. I heard the rehearsals and they are already better than Louisville, which wasn't that bad after all (I will let you hear a recording that I brought with me.)

In London I had a chance to refine my impressions of the Clark-Fränkel affair. I am convinced that my sympathies are similar to yours. Here, Mr. Bromer tried—without any initiative on my part—to convince me otherwise, but naturally he did not succeed. I will try to discuss it with Glock, who will arrive in a few days; but with regard to the final results of the meetings, the prospects are not very good. It seems that the present sympathies of the English section lie naturally with Clark. I find it could become very serious if they try to veto the performance of Fränkel's *Concerto*,[3] which good or bad was selected by the jury. The ill will against Clarke seems to be caused by his alleged alliance with Capdevielle[4] more than from this affair with Fränkel. They accuse him of wanting to destroy the ISCM, and would like his election to the honorary presidency to be declared illegal—in accordance with the rules set up by the ISCM. You can well understand that I can express my personal feelings informally but that I must act carefully with respect to the American section, where I have found the tendency either to come to terms with the Society in general or to detach itself from an issue that seems far-removed. I am delighted that I stepped down as head of the American Section. It is something that doesn't suit me and I don't feel up to accepting all that responsibility.

I still haven't told you how happy I was to receive—the day before our departure—your "An Mathilde." I immediately put it in my suitcase and I study it with devotion and pleasure. It consoled me for that stroke of bad luck (nothing serious, but decisive) that prevented me from going to New York for the performance on May 8, which went extremely well, and was received with great enthusiasm, as you must certainly have heard.

-414-

We expect to arrive in Florence and stay for a few days around the end of this month; Materassi, who I am delighted is here, also leads me to hope that you will be there. Otherwise, let me know where I can find you. We will be here until July 11—afterward (for good or bad!) care of the American Express Co. in Copenhagen until the 17th. From then on, I'll let you know later. I absolutely don't want to miss seeing you before New York in the autumn.

Meanwhile, many cordial thoughts from Lisl and me to all three of you.

Affectionately,
Roger

1. Translated from the Italian by Pina Pasquantonio.
2. Swedish conductor Ehrling (b. 1918) was the chief conductor at the Royal Opera in Stockholm 1953–60. He later conducted at Juilliard, Denver, and San Antonio.
3. Fränkel's Violin Concerto, dedicated "to the memory of the six million."
4. Pierre Capdevielle (1906–69), French composer and pianist.

▼

Roger Sessions to Luigi Dallapiccola[1]
als I-Fb

June 12, 1956
Vadstena, Switzerland

My dear friend Luigi,

We are still traveling, and there is no time or concentration to write about all I'd like to tell you regarding the Stockholm affair. You must already know that we succeeded in having Clarke elected Honorary Member. It is less than what you wanted and less than what I wanted; but there is no doubt that nothing more could have been done, and more than what I would have thought possible. I am very happy to have been the President of the Commission that recommended it. There are many details that will be food for discussion; I spoke at length with Glock and in a certain sense we worked together. Even Fränkel helped promote our cause through a venomous speech that brought into the open all the most scandalous aspects of the affair and had exactly the opposite effect from the one he had intended!

Theocritus went rather well, and in general had much success.[2] Martha Long sang very well, with intelligence, with musical finesse, and with spirit and tenderness, but her voice, I must admit, is not big enough; the orchestra could have played more delicately, and the hall does not favor any soloists, as I was able to observe with all of the other soloists and as, I believe, Materassi will tell you. At any rate, *Theocritus* seems to have made a very good impression and I am reasonably happy with the importance this may have. There are some developments that will have (or, rather, could have) great importance for me and for the progress of my music in Europe.[3]

We saw a lot of the Materassis, and enjoyed ourselves together. We hope to see them in Florence.

I apologize for these few inadequate paragraphs—but at any rate we will see each other again, in all probability in two weeks—that is, on the 26th.

An affectionate hug—and greetings to all of you.

Roger

(P.S.) I received your letter just at the right psychological moment!

1. Translated from the Italian by Pina Pasquantonio.
2. Performed June 5, 1956, at the ISCM Festival on a concert with music by Barry Moss, Toshiro Mayuzumi, Mario Peragallo, and Guillaume Landré, conducted by Sixten Ehrling.
3. Possibly Sessions refers to talks with Glock that resulted in the publishing firm of Boosey & Hawkes representing his music in Europe.

ONLY TWO OF SESSIONS'S LETTERS from 1957 survive; both are to Harold Schiffman, who had resumed his study with Sessions at Princeton during 1955–56. Sessions wrote to Schiffman from Zurich January 10, 1957. On November 23, 1957, he wrote again to tell Schiffman that the Boston Symphony would present the first performances of his Third Symphony on December 6, 7, and 10 in Boston, on December 11 in New York, and on December 12 in Washington. In the same letter Sessions advised Schiffman, who had moved to Florida, "Quite apart from the Ph.D. business, I feel that if young composers in the U.S. would think more often of taking N.Y. gradually from the rear or by flank attack rather than by direct assault, the result would be more productive in very many ways. I trust I make myself clear (N.Y. is only a symbol, after all)" (US-Tschiffman).

In the latter part of 1958 Sessions scrambled to complete his Fourth Symphony, commissioned by the Minneapolis Symphony in celebration of the Minnesota centennial, in time for its deadline of December

31, 1958.[1] Lending urgency to the deadline was his contract's stipulation that this payment depended on the work's being completed on time. Nonetheless, Sessions found time in the autumn for a month-long trip with Peter Mennin, Ulysses Kay,[2] and Roy Harris to the Soviet Union, where his *Black Maskers Suite* was played. He wrote Krenek (November 7, 1958, US-SD):

> By the time I see you my whole Russian experience, which in retrospect seems an incredibly full one, will be thoroughly digested, and I hope I'll be able to talk about it with a coherence that really satisfies me; at the moment, I am preoccupied with questions of cultural exchange which in that particular area seem both hellishly complicated and extremely important. I, too, didn't get much out of Shostakovich, though if my Russian were more fluent I might have gotten a little bit more. He impressed me chiefly as one of the most nervous men I ever met, which may or may not have something to do with the basic questions involved.

Most of the few letters surviving from 1958 concern the Princeton Seminar in Advanced Musical Studies, set for August 17 to September 5, 1959.

Sessions drafted a proposal about the establishment of a seminar for the president of Princeton University, Robert F. Goheen. The following quotation is taken from the proposal, which was also sent to Krenek.

> Mr. Paul Fromm[3] of the Fromm Foundation in Chicago has proposed the establishment with the Foundation's support of an institute of postgraduate study in Music which he would like to establish at Princeton University during the late summer of 1959. The aim of the institute would be to study, on the highest level, the dominant trends in contemporary musical thought.
>
> It is felt that such a project would respond to a genuine need in the musical life of both the United States and the world in general. There is no institution devoted, that is, to studies at this advanced level on this side of the Atlantic; and the comparable institutions which exist at this time in Europe have tended to orient themselves in the direction of not only study but also doctrinaire propaganda. It would be the aim of the proposed institute not only to examine all contemporary doctrines freely, but to assert the primacy of musical experience and imagination, insisting on the categorical distinction between artistic production on the one hand and systematic thought on the other. By "contemporary musical thought," as expressed above, is meant, therefore, not primarily theory and aesthetics, but the experiences and techniques which go into the formation of the

musical sensibility of today. Mr. Fromm asked me to assume the direction and the leadership in planning this enterprise. Discussions have been held between Mr. Fromm and myself, with the additional participation of Messrs. Babbitt, Cone, and [Arthur] Mendel.

Having written Copland (January 7, 1959) to ask him to recommend students for the seminar, Sessions wrote two weeks later asking whether Copland himself would serve as a guest lecturer. Sessions sent Krenek a list of the participants so far: Ginastera, Copland, Varèse, Greissle, Steuermann, and Allen Forte. Numerous letters to Copland and to Krenek concern the business of getting pieces and parts for the seminar's workshops, and letters after the September close of the seminar deal with getting the guests' papers collected for an issue of the *Musical Quarterly*.[4]

No sooner had the Princeton Seminar ended than plans began for another the following summer. Sessions wrote to Dallapiccola (October 29, 1959) asking him to participate during the summer of 1960.

1. The Symphony No. 4 was first performed January 2, 1960, in Minneapolis, with Antal Dorati conducting.

2. In 1958 Mennin (1923–83), who had studied at the Eastman School of Music with Howard Hanson and Bernard Rogers, left his teaching post at The Juilliard School to direct the Peabody Conservatory, in Baltimore; in 1962 he would return, as president, to Juilliard. Ulysses Kay (b. 1917), also a student of Hanson and Rodgers at Eastman and of Hindemith at Yale, had been a Fellow at the American Academy in Rome 1949–52.

3. Fromm (1906–87), a German-born wine importer and music patron, founded the Fromm Music Foundation in 1952.

4. *Musical Quarterly* 46, no. 2 (April 1960), ed. Paul Henry Lang, a special issue entitled "Problems of Modern Music: The Princeton Seminar in Advanced Musical Studies." The contributors were Lang, "Editorial"; Paul Fromm, "The Princeton Seminar: Its Purpose and Promise"; Sessions, "Problems and Issues Facing the Composer Today" (reprinted in *Roger Sessions on Music: Collected Essays,* ed. Edward T. Cone [Princeton: Princeton University Press, 1979], 71–87); Edward T. Cone, "Analysis Today"; Elliott Carter, "Shop Talk by an American Composer"; Vladimir Ussachevsky, "Notes on a Piece for Tape Recorder"; Ernst Krenek, "Extents and Limits of Serial Techniques"; Allen Forte, "Bartók's 'Serial' Composition"; and Milton Babbitt, "Twelve-Tone Invariants as Compositional Determinants." This issue was reprinted as *Problems of Modern Music,* ed. Paul Henry Lang (New York: W. W. Norton, 1960). Others present at the seminar were Robert Craft, Copland, Felix Greissle, John Tukey, Edgard Varèse, and Stravinsky. The Lenox Quartet was in residence.

▼

Roger Sessions to Ernst Krenek
tls US-SD

January 6, 1958 [i.e., 1959]

Dear Ernst: Princeton

Thank you for your letter of December 14, which I would have answered some time ago had I not been working furiously on my Fourth Symphony, which I finished on December 31. I am delighted to hear of all of your activities, and am sure it must be very satisfying to you, even though it sounds somewhat strenuous. I wish you many more such weeks!

As far as the titles of courses are concerned, we have simply put out a very general statement, and may well end up by not giving the courses any particular titles. I do like very much all that is suggested by the titles you propose, and look forward to many talks with you on the subject. I don't know whether you happened to see the series of articles to which I contributed in the British magazine, *The Score*,[1] apropos of what seemed to me some rather asinine remarks by Mr. Peter Stadlen[2]—including a "reply" by P.S., in which he missed the point of some of my remarks through apparently not bothering to look up the specific references which I made to certain works of Bach and Beethoven.

I think perhaps I have not made myself completely clear as far as the question of "sectarianism" is concerned. I know, of course, that we will be called "sectarian" regardless of whatever we do, and to tell the truth, this particular aspect of the question doesn't bother me at all—in fact, one could almost say that the louder such talk, the clearer sign it will be that we have done a good job. In stressing the question of non-sectarianism, I simply wanted to underline a serious rather than, let us say, a journalistic approach to the whole matter, and an essentially independent one; also, a willingness to meet serious challenges, provided any are forthcoming, which I very much doubt. I trust that the names of the people involved will convey a sufficient amount of healthy "sectarian" spirit of the kind that you want—I hope you know me well enough to realize that I am (even at the age of 62) unalterably opposed to castration in any form—or to its female equivalent, whatever that is called.

I am spending the morning to-morrow with Paul Fromm, and later Bob Craft will join us. Paul's concert in honor or Stravinsky on

Sunday was a tremendous success in spite of, I suppose—and strictly between ourselves—fewer rehearsals than would have been completely comfortable. It was a very distinguished affair, however, and it was heartening to see that Schoenberg and Berg were very nearly as vociferously applauded as Stravinsky himself, who, after all, was present.[3]

I am sending this to Vienna, and believe it should reach you before the 20th. If you pass through New York on the way back to California, please do give me a ring.

The very best to you both for the New Year.

Affectionately, as always,

Roger

1. Roger Sessions, "To the Editor," *The Score* 23 (July 1958): 58–64.

2. Peter Stadlen (b. 1910), English pianist and writer. After having given important performances of music by the Second Viennese School, Stadlen became disillusioned with serialism. Stadlen had written "Serialism Reconsidered," *The Score* 22 (February 1958): 12–27, to which Sessions's piece cited in note 1, along with articles by Roberto Gerhard and Walter Piston, was a reply. Stadlen then answered all three composers in " 'No Real Casualties'?" *The Score* 24 (November 1958): 65–68.

3. The Fromm Music Foundation sponsored a concert at New York's Town Hall, January 4, 1959, at which Robert Craft (b. 1923) conducted the American premieres of Stravinsky's *Threni: Lamentations of the Prophet Jeremiah,* Schoenberg's *Drei kleine Orchesterstücke,* and Alban Berg's *Altenberg Lieder,* along with Stravinsky's *Symphonies of Wind Instruments* and Schoenberg's Five Pieces for Orchestra. Stravinsky participated in the rehearsals and subsequently conducted *Threni* for Columbia Records.

▼

Roger Sessions to Ernst Krenek
tls US-SD

February 24, 1959

Dear Ernst: Princeton

I wonder if you ever received the enclosed. The reason I ask is because Rosamond Sayre[1] had a letter yesterday from Paul Fromm's office, asking that 6 copies of the brochure be sent to you. She did this yesterday.

The main purpose of this letter is to ask you if you have tapes of your works which you would be willing to let us use this summer, or preferably if you would be willing to let us have them copied so that we can have them permanently in our library. We have, I believe, everything that has been commercially recorded, but we are anxious to acquire everything else we can get our hands on.

As for news: our lecturers are all signed up, except Ginastera and Milton's philosophical and scientific people. Also, we have had replies from 33 people all over the country, and already from several prospective students. We have had enthusiastic letters from some of the latter, and it looks as if we would have no trouble in getting the number we want. Also, we are going to have a string quartet here,[2] so that we will have some music as well as talk—I don't know what, as yet.

I myself have been very busy lately. I finished my Minneapolis commission—Symphony No. 4—on December 31st, and am now working on what I shall probably call a Sinfonietta, for the State of Oregon, as well as on my Rhapsody[3] for Paul Fromm. My Violin Concerto, finished in 1935, was just played for the first time in New York by Spivakovsky and Bernstein,[4] and had a tremendous success— better late than never! It was actually a stunning performance, and, as I have a special fondness for this piece, I am, of course, very happy about it.

The very best to you both,

Affectionately, as always,
Roger

1. Sessions's former sister-in-law, and the dedicatee of the first Piano Sonata, became the secretary for the music department at Princeton 1945–60, where her husband, Daniel Sayre, had founded the School of Aeronautical Engineering. She typed Sessions's letters, occasionally wrote some of them, and took care of the finances for the Seminar in Advanced Musical Studies.

2. The Lenox Quartet: Peter Marsh, Theodora Mantz, violins; R. Scott Nickrenz, viola; Donald McCall, cello.

3. The Sinfonietta, renamed Divertimento, received its premiere on January 9, 1965, by the Honolulu Symphony, George Barati conducting. The work was performed incomplete by its commissioner, the Portland Symphony, in commemoration of the one-hundredth anniversary of the state of Oregon. It is dedicated to Carl Haverlin, then president of BMI. The Rhapsody, commissioned by the Baltimore Symphony Orchestra and dedicated to its conductor, Sergiu Comissiona, was performed in March 1970. Sessions did not write a Rhapsody for Fromm.

4. The Violin Concerto was played on February 15, 1959, by the New York Philharmonic, with Tossy Spivakovsky, violin, and Leonard Bernstein conducting.

▼

Roger Sessions to Ernst Krenek
tls US-SD

March 26, 1959
Dear Ernst: Princeton

Thank you for your good letter. I must not forget to tell you that we have learned that the "Fromm Quartet" is not to be called the "Fromm Quartet" any longer. They are the players sponsored by Fromm at Tanglewood, and the name is being changed [to the Lenox Quartet] simply in order that nobody shall be tied down by it. I might add that they gave a fairly acceptable performance of my First Quartet, which I think you know, in Tanglewood last summer,[1] after having had the music for only five days, an all-too-typical Tanglewood *Angelegenheit!* [affair] But this was not their fault, and I was extremely impressed by what they accomplished in so short a time.

I think what we will do will be to send them both your 6th and 7th Quartets, with a strong recommendation that they do the 6th, if possible. I know one of these works, and, in fact, gave a lecture on it here 15 years ago, or so. I am not quite clear which it was, but I am very fond of it, in any case.[2] We read in some dictionary before I wrote to you that the 7th was written in 1952, but, on the other hand, the Quartet about which I spoke was played here by the Budapest Quartet. In any case, I hope the above procedure is satisfactory to you. I think that they will play anything we ask. I am asking them to do my Quintet,[3] which I wrote a year ago.

We are now in the process of choosing students, and there seem to be some very good ones.

The very best to you both,

Always affectionately,
Roger Sessions

1. July 11, 1958, by the "Fromm Fellowship Players."
2. Probably Krenek's String Quartet no. 7, op. 96 (1943–44). He wrote his String Quartet no. 6 in 1937, and no. 8 in 1952; he renumbered them.
3. The Lenox Quartet, with J. Fawcet, viola, gave the New York premiere of Sessions's 1958 Quintet, November 23, 1959.

▼

Roger Sessions to Igor Stravinsky[1]
als CH-Bsacher

September 20, 1959
70 Alexander Street
Dear Igor Fedorovich—   Princeton, New Jersey

Many thanks for your kind letter and I'm sorry not to have answered you earlier. I have to admit that no one has ever invited me to play the piano! And I had to ask myself whether it was possible to accept the invitation without a danger of compromising the performance. But I like "Les Noces" very much and I didn't want to deny myself either the pleasure or the honor of taking part in this happy and important event.[2]

Hence I looked through the music thoroughly and convinced myself that I could play it. I sincerely thank you for the invitation and promise you that I'll play it as well as possible.

Please convey my regards to Madame—and also to Bob Craft.

Sincerely yours,
Roger Sessions

1. Translated from the Russian by Theodore Levin.
2. Stravinsky had invited Sessions, Copland, Samuel Barber, and Lukas Foss to play the four piano parts in a performance of *Les Noces* on December 21, 1959, and in a recording for Columbia Records (MS 6372). The other performers were soprano Mildred Allen, mezzo Regina Sarfaty, tenor Loren Driscoll, bass Robert Oliver, and the American Concert Choir, Margaret Hillis, director.

▼

Roger Sessions to Leon Kirchner
als US-CAkirchner

November 29, 1959
My dear Leon,—   Princeton

I had a long talk with Felix G[reissle] as I promised to do. He showed me the carbon of his last letter to you, to which he has had no answer. I am even more certain than I was before that you have misunderstood him + that he is well disposed and ready to do anything he can in your behalf. I told him that I had urged you to write him at length, putting the whole situation on paper; + it is quite possible—though I am not sure—that he will write to you. I did

– 423 –

Roger Sessions (far right) with (from left to right) Samuel Barber, Igor Stravinsky, Lukas Foss, and Aaron Copland during a rehearsal for Les Noces *recorded on December 21, 1959. Photograph by Don Hunstein.*

not suggest that he should, since after all it is not my affair. But I also told him that I would like to keep in touch with the situation, + I shall certainly do so—as a favor, I hope, to both of you.

Naturally, I don't mean to push this thing any further than you want it pushed. But the whole publishing situation is at best rather grim these days—virtually no one buys music any more, not even "popular" music; publishers live by the school trade + scores like yours + mine (+ those of every "serious" composer I know except perhaps Stravinsky) are a luxury or, if you like, a "prestige" item from which only the most far-sighted members of the publishing business expect ever to make real money, even in the future. Felix is not only one of the far-sighted ones; but in my own case he has been invaluable to me, both as a friend, and also as a musician with whom I can really talk—there are not so many of these—and on whose judgment I can rely. For these reasons I value the association very much indeed, and I think you, too, would in the last analysis find it a godsend. Do remember, however, that he can do only as much as his firm, backed by BMI, can pay for.

Needless to say, I will understand any decision you make. But it seems to me stupid to let a palpable misunderstanding continue when the underlying disposition is so obviously good. Unless you find something definitely better I would strongly urge you to see what you can arrange with Felix.

As far as BMI and ASCAP are concerned I am not going to put myself in the position of Douglas Moore (i.e. a proselytizer for BMI [as Moore was for ASCAP]), + I feel that you— + everyone else, for that matter—should affiliate yourself as you feel best suits your interests. I myself have never felt any nostalgia changing over, + these have more than been borne out by events. The fact that Marks is affiliated with BMI was only a very slight factor in my decision. Felix had already been my publisher for six years, + put no pressure on me further than to point out that it might make his job as my publisher easier in certain respects. When I did join BMI I was in fact offered other publishers in case I wished to change, but I preferred to stay with Felix. That too I have never regretted.

I am still puzzled and quite surprised by your statement that I am always "too busy" to see you + can only reiterate that there is nothing in it at all. This too I don't think we should discuss by letter— one can so easily drift into misunderstandings. And I don't intend to let that happen if I can help it. There is no earthly reason why it need happen if we both really take pains to guard against it. But if we are to do that you must realize that I, like yourself, have a great deal in my life, and give me the benefit of the doubt, as I give the same to you.

It was good to hear your quartet[1] + above all to hear it a second time the other night. The performance was far better than it was, here, in August. I must confess to that on that earlier occasion it seemed to me a little bland, + I much preferred your Trio[2] which was also played at our Seminar, as you doubtless know. The other night, however, I had a different impression; I felt that the quartet might well be a real + important development in your work, especially in the direction of integration + continuity. Such a development is precisely the one I should have most wished for you; and even though (of this I am not entirely sure) such a development is very apt to mean a temporary sacrifice of certain qualities, that sacrifice is more than balanced by one's real gain in the development itself— + in any case the quality which one has sacrificed will almost certainly return in strengthened form. In any case I am happy about the quartet particularly the first two + above all the second movement.

It is late + I won't write more. Let me hear from you when you can + give my best to [your wife] Gertrude + the family.

As always,
Roger

1. Kirchner's 1958 String Quartet no. 2. (His Third Quartet [1966] won the Pulitzer Prize.)
2. Kirchner's Trio for Violin, Cello, and Piano was premiered November 30, 1954, in Pasadena, Calif.

▼

Roger Sessions to Paul Fromm
tls US-CAmus

September 23, 1960
Princeton

Dear Paul:

A letter from me to you has been in the works for at least ten days. You are certainly one of the most understanding men I know, and I only hope that you realize that I am, these days, driven not only from without—that is, the necessity of finishing Montezuma in good time and being sure that it comes out unscathed in the process—but what is even greater, the pressure of the ideas themselves to get themselves out and down on paper! I wish you could also understand, which you probably cannot quite, that writing to you always seems to me more of a joy and a luxury than an obligation.

Thank you for sending me the correspondence with Mr. Raven[1] (as I write this Rosamond remarks, "Quoth the Raven, 'Nevermore.' ", which, after all, sums the matter up.) No need to comment on Mr. Raven's manners; I was intrigued, however, by his somewhat less than tacet insistence that it was for him rather than for musicians themselves to determine the artistic policy of the Chicago Orchestra. I thought this was a point on which orchestra managers were rather sensitive, as far as public relations are concerned; I certainly think they should be.

Of course, I will be very glad to conduct the Black Maskers, and I am very pleased that Thor Johnson[2] feels like conducting the Fourth Symphony himself. As far as rehearsals and preparation are concerned, I shall still be in Chicago for nearly two weeks, and want to help in any way I can at that time. Incidentally, I have hopes that Lisl may come with me, as she wants very much to do. These involve both my daughter's plans and those of the people who are going to rent our house, and we are trying to clarify the situation.

Rosamond has written you already a little regarding the balance sheet of the Seminar. It will be several weeks still before we know in precise figures where we stand, but it is clear that there will be a substantial balance.

From every indication the Seminar was again a real success. The Seminarians were not only interested, but have especially stressed the value of the rehearsal sessions. We ourselves feel that we could manage this side of things better on a future occasion and could foresee the problems in advance, as it were, better than we were able to do this time, but the net result was excellent. I can only say thank you for everything, and please forgive me again if I seem a little distracted in these days!

With warmest greetings to you and Erika,

Devotedly
Roger

1. Seymour Raven, orchestra manager of the Chicago Symphony from 1960 until he was dismissed in 1964.
2. Conductor Thor Johnson (1913–75) studied with Koussevitzky 1940–41 and served as music director of the Cincinnati Symphony Orchestra (1947–58) and the Nashville Symphony Orchestra (1967–75).

▼

Roger Sessions to Luigi Dallapiccola[1]
als I-Fb

October 6, 1960

My dearest friend Luigi,   [Princeton]

What can I say about *Il Prigioniero* than that we heard it at the City Center last night?[2] It is the first time I heard it at the theater and I was more captivated than ever; I still am—today I read the score twice—I can't forget it. There is no doubt that it is one of the principal works of our time, and we were profoundly moved by it. I must add that the audience seemed greatly impressed; every indication points to a great success.

I was prepared to be let down by the performance, since Stokowski was going to conduct. Instead I was pleasantly surprised; the orchestra played with precision, great flexibility, and passion. The singers were very good, the intonation was much better than I expected (forgive me if this doesn't sound completely enthusiastic—it was in fact delightful); and they were visibly moved and devoted. Vittorio Rieti told me that the performance at the Juilliard School was even better,[3] but naturally, I can't judge. The only defect at the City Center is the weakness—from a dynamic and numeric point of view—of the chorus; a defect which I must admit, is very important, especially in the last scene, in which a sense of the vast forces is missing which tends to reduce it—here I am exaggerating a little—to an almost private affair between the Inquisitor and the Prisoner. One more thing: if you permit it, I would like perhaps when I am in Florence next spring to go over the English translation with you, which seemed very good on the whole but which in some particulars could be improved. But I should be sure . . .

I had intended to write to you about Rzewski,[4] whom you must already have seen. I haven't forgotten having told you a year ago that I considered him—and still do—an exceptional talent. During the past year, however, I was at times discouraged by his pretentious and deep-down not-serious tendencies; when I spoke to him about it, he always admitted it and apologized by saying that he is going through a period of transition and that above all he must get away from the University's influence—something I can fully understand but which, of course, offers no solution to Rzewski's problems. Above all I hope I haven't caused you any inconvenience and that you don't feel obliged to do anything for him on my account. I am sure that if he would try to take matters into his own hands and become more serious than he was last year, he still has a chance to develop well. He is certainly a talented, intelligent boy and deep down very honest.

I am still working on *Montezuma* and can in fact think of almost nothing else. There is still a long way to go but I am working better than ever in my life and hope to do and to have done well. The public horror of our era makes more imperative than ever the obligation to create something and to put into it all that one can. I often think of *Ulisse*[5] and hope that your work is going well. I am waiting for the results with high hopes.

I never thanked you for the postcard you sent from Cologne about my symphony, which moved me and for which I am grateful.[6] [. . .]

At any rate, I thank you from the bottom of my heart for *Il Prigioniero* and for many other lovely compositions. I will be over-joyed to see you in Florence next February.[7]

Affectionate greetings to Laura and Annalibera. Fondly your
Roger

(P.S.) I had a tape of *Theocritus,* which I conducted, sent to you.[8] I hope you received it.

1. Translated from the Italian by Pina Pasquantonio.
2. The New York City Opera produced *Il Prigioniero* twice that season; the second time was on a double bill with *Orfeo* October 5. The singers included McKnight, Treigle, Cassily, Stern, and Macurdy; Leopold Stokowski conducted.
3. The Juilliard Opera Theater, under the musical direction of Frederic Waldman and stage design of Frederic Cohen, produced a newly commissioned English translation of Dallapiccola's *Il prigioniero* (*The Prisoner*) March 15–19, 1951.
4. Frederic Rzewski (b. 1938) had studied at Princeton 1958–60 and, on a Fulbright scholarship, in Rome 1960–62, where he founded the performance ensemble Musica Elettronica Viva.
5. Dallapiccola's *Ulisse* (*Ulysses*), a two-act opera (1959–68).
6. Dallapiccola's card (June 16, 1960, I-Fb) called the symphony "an emotional crescendo obtained with the minimal amount of sounds" (translated from the Italian by Valeria Secchi Short).
7. Sessions would travel to Germany, England, Scotland, France, Italy, Greece, and Switzerland from February 1961 through the summer.
8. Sessions conducted the Princeton Symphony Orchestra in a performance of his *Idyll of Theocritus* on April 11, 1960.

▼

Roger Sessions to Luigi Dallapiccola[1]
tls I-Fb

My dear friend Luigi,   December 1, 1960

[. . .]

You will notice that the postponement of *Montezuma* has not altered our plans to come to Europe; first of all I had already gotten leave for the second semester and it was too late to change it and I am experienced enough to know that to stay in Princeton on leave amounts to never having been on leave at all! Anyway, I'll be in Florence around February 20, after spending some time [. . .] near Cologne. Then Lisl will abandon me for a few weeks, traveling in Spain (—"son già mille e tre"—)[2] whereas I will be in Florence for at least two months. In April I have been invited to spend a week, all expenses paid, in Tokyo by the Committee for Intellectual Liberty (N. Nabokov). I suppose you have been invited as well and I dream of the chance to have you as a companion to travel with, leaving from Rome or Milan—is there any chance of this happening? I haven't accepted yet, but I think it wouldn't interrupt my work much, and frankly it represents an opportunity to see the Far East, which most probably I will never have again.

Montezuma's postponement was a disappointment for me, but I think it's for the best. First of all, I was working feverishly and the preoccupation and tension not only to finish in time but to have everything in perfect order became almost unbearable. Since the main principals had to be found here in America, there were innumerable details I had to take care of, besides the score itself; all of this can now be accomplished with more tranquillity. In fact, beginning ten days ago I am once again working with joy not contaminated by anxiety, and have allowed myself all of the summer to finish the orchestral score (the first act has already been copied in piano-vocal score and the last pages of the last act will be copied by the time we leave for Europe, in the first days of February.) I must also pursue my career as a conductor (!). I will conduct my Third Symphony on January 14 in Oberlin, and *The Black Maskers* on the 29th in Evanston, Illinois, where three concerts of my music will be held—including a production of *The Trial of Lucullus*. My Fourth Symphony and my Piano Concerto will be played, as well as a program of chamber music.[3]

All that you write about the *Prigioniero*—and about *Volo di Notte*—of course pleased and interests me. If it will be performed in Genoa in March I will certainly make the trip to hear it. I understand only too well that you want to place "conditions"; a few years ago my experiences with *Lucullus* convinced me once and for all about what extraordinary things a director who neither understands nor wishes to understand the intentions of the author or composer can do.[4] But I am truly overjoyed that the nineteen years of quarantine are about to end—an inevitable but nonetheless satisfying thing . . . and *Ulisse*? Have no doubt that I think about it continuously and wait for it with great expectations.

[. . .]

You of course must have followed the news of the elections here—the result was extremely satisfying for us and we ardently hope that Kennedy will not betray the trust that his most ardent supporters have placed in him.[5] Personally I would have preferred [Adlai] Stevenson, but K. is young and undoubtedly very intelligent, and it seems to me that things have already taken a turn for the better in the country. His political opponents do everything possible to make trouble—few of my compatriots are aware of what a dangerous game this is to play;

but until now he gives an impression of strength and authentic courage, and I think we can allow ourselves a little hope . . .

Thank you again for your dear letter. I am very happy that I will see you again rather soon. Remember me to Laura and Annalibera with great affection.

Your devoted
Roger

1. Translated from the Italian bt Pina Pasquantonio.

2. "There are one thousand and three," from Leporello's catalogue aria in *Don Giovanni*.

3. Paul Fromm sponsored a "retrospective one-man exhibition" of eight of Sessions's works, January 26–29, 1961, at Northwestern University. The works were Symphony No. 4, Piano Concerto (played by Gui Mombaerts), "The Black Maskers Suite," *The Trial of Lucullus*, String Quartet no. 2, String Quintet, Four Chorale Preludes for Organ, and the Mass for Unison Choir and organ.

4. Sessions refers to a 1955 production at Princeton University.

5. Sessions received an invitation to John F. Kennedy's inauguration and left Evanston during the festival's rehearsals to attend.

▼

Roger Sessions to Paul Fromm
als US-CAmus

December 5, 1960

Dear Paul,—   [Princeton]

At last we are near the end of the accounting for this year's Seminar, and Rosamond will shortly be sending you the full accounts for both of these two years. Under separate cover, I understand, the Controller's office will be sending you a check for the balance. This has been much on my mind, and I hoped that it would be forthcoming much before this. It has been on Rosamond's, too, and when I last spoke of it to her, before these last two days, she had just been in touch with the Controller's office regarding it. They move in a slow and majestic fashion over there, but it is a relief that they are at last getting it in shape.

After some hesitation I have decided to write you about a matter that has disturbed me since I heard of it two or three weeks ago. I learned that the Fromm Foundation had, among others, been approached for funds in connection with the projected performance of *Montezuma*, in spite of the fact that I had made it clear that I hoped this would not be done. Of course I had kept myself aloof from the whole business of raising money for this purpose, and since this was the case, and also for other reasons, I felt that it would be indiscreet to explain the strong reasons, personal and otherwise, why I did not wish the Fromm Foundation to be approached. I am very sorry that it was done, and only hope that it was made clear, at least, that I in no way authorized it. But I would also hate it if it had caused you any trouble or embarrassment—I sincerely hope it didn't.

[. . .]

Montezuma, actually, has been postponed till the spring of 1962[1]—the decision was made ten days ago and I must admit is a good deal of a relief to me. I told Lisl it would probably add ten years to my life! The pressure was pretty grim at times—not only that of finishing in time but it was complicated by details of organization, and worry about rehearsals, too. The pressure is not gone yet. I still have to accomplish in two years what took Wagner three or more—instead of having to do it in a year and a half! But this simply means that I can take a little better care of myself, especially in the matter of rest; + above all it will insure a much better performance. The postponement was decided upon, in fact, for that reason, coupled (according to a letter from Dallapiccola) with the possibility that the big theatre in Florence, which is being remodelled, may not be ready in time; and *Montezuma* cannot be done in a smaller theatre. This was a disappointment at first, but I had to realize that it is for the better.

On Jan. 14 I conduct my Third Symphony in Oberlin. I suppose there is only the slightest of possibilities that you might be in the neighborhood at that time—but it would be wonderful, nevertheless, if you could be there.

With affectionate greetings to Erika as well as to yourself,

As always,
Roger

1. The premiere of *Montezuma* was delayed, because of Sessions's failure to complete the orchestration, two more years. It was not produced in Florence.

AFTER THE SESSIONS FESTIVAL at Northwestern several newspapers, including ones in London, published reviews of the concerts.[1] Donald Janson's "Sessions on Campus" in the *New York Times* ended with the following: "The degree of success was a matter of opinion. The composer himself pronounced the performances 'excellent.' Mrs. Sessions, who flew here with their daughter, Elizabeth, a ballet student at Barnard, just in time for the week-end of music, said that many of the nuances were missing. Most of the music lovers in the audiences that turned out in the frigid weather went along with the composer's plea to hear the contemporary scores with 'a willing and gracious ear'—and were pleased."

Sessions was furious with this quotation of his wife's comment and wrote to Ross Parmenter of the *Times* about it. With Sessions in Europe, Felix Greissle interceded to sort out the misunderstanding between composer and critic.

1. Donal Henahan, " 'A Willing Ear' for Sessions," New York *Herald Tribune*, February 5, 1961; "A Composer for Titans," *Time*, February 3, 1961; Donald Janson, "Sessions on Campus," *New York Times*, February 5, 1961.

▼

Roger Sessions to Felix Greissle
als US-NYkalban

February 18, 1961
Dear Felix,— Cologne

I got your letter today + suppose you are right. I wonder if you would think I had made a mistake in saying in my letter to Parmenter that the quotation from Lisl was "without foundation." It had the foundation simply that she said it about one piece only (the Mass); that means that it was quoted wholly out of context, as well as having been said, expressly, "off the record." I thought the only way to deal with this was to phrase matters exactly as I did. I suppose you pointed all this out to Parmenter; it still seems to me a breach of ethics to print statements that are specified as "off the record"—also to print them out of context. I shall of course never make a statement "off the record" again. I forbear further comment, on paper at least.

But—I would be grateful if you could send a note to Paul Fromm, telling him of your conversation with Parmenter, + if you have time, enclosing a carbon of the letter I wrote. I shall write him too,[1] but don't want to send him your letter to me—I have already written to Howerton—before I saw the *Times* article. Lisl wrote him afterwards; but I shall probably write him again later.

Anyway, the press seems to have the upper hand + you are undoubtedly right that we should drop the matter as far as they are concerned.

I suppose you saw the *Tribune* article, which Betsy[2] sent me; also

Frankenstein's, which was really quite perceptive in certain respects. I suppose you have seen [it] also. A cousin, who lives in London, sent me a copy of an article that he saw in the London *Times*[3]—quite nice. If you haven't seen these, let me know + I will send them on.

I have about decided *not* to go to Japan in April. First of all, + *decisive, Montezuma* really must take first place; + after the whole Northwestern business the interruption would be, I feel, too much. Secondly (+ this put me off) I have just seen the programs for the Festival, + though there are works by Virgil Thomson, Carter, Harris (!), Piston, Cowell, Copland. R.S. is conspicuous by his absence; + Ives, though this is undoubtedly due to the fact that Bernstein + the Juilliard Quartet are mainly those involved, + not, probably, malice aforethought on the part of Messrs. Nabokoff + Thomson. Also I don't see much point in taking a 5000 odd mile air trip just to give a lecture lasting fifteen minutes on "Extending the Classical Syntax"— whatever that may mean. So—unless you think it of real importance for me to go, I think I shall *absagen* [decline]. If you think this is a false move, please wire me, *preferably* by Feb. 23rd (Thursday) at the Hotel de Suède, 15, Quai Saint-Michel, Paris. Later on that day (7.25 PM) I leave for Florence, where I can be reached c/o American Express Co., Lungarno Corsini (wire *Amexco* Florence).

We leave here Monday morning (Feb. 20). *[. . .]* I will not write more in detail now; but everything seems fantastically difficult, + better, than before. I am really thrilled.

Montezuma progresses splendidly + I shall send you a good installment, as I promised, from Paris.

All the very best, from us both + to both you + Jackie.[4]

Always devotedly
Roger

1. The next day Sessions sent Fromm a postcard (February 19, 1961, US-CAmus): "I shall write you very shortly + tell you (as I think Felix Greissle will also have done) about the thing with the NY Times + why both Felix + I—and Lisl—thought better *not* to pursue the matter." However, Sessions did not write the promised letter.
2. Sessions's daughter, Elizabeth.
3. The London *Times* published an article and a photograph with the headline "Sessions Opera on Montezuma—Work Begun in 1935 May Be Finished This Year." The article, written by an anonymous correspondent, described Sessions: "A sprightly man of 64, Mr. Sessions smiles and carries himself somewhat like a lovable character from one of Dickens's novels." It quotes Sessions as saying, "This festival [at Northwestern] is of course of very great importance to me, but I hope it is also the start of more and better recognition for American composers."
4. Greissle's second wife.

▼

Roger Sessions to Felix Greissle
als US-LA

April 17, 1961

Dear Felix,— Athens

Many thanks for your letter. Let me speak first of the I.S.C.M. Of course you have my proxy. The story is the same old one, of course + unfortunately not confined to the I.S.C.M. But I give you my proxy, naturally, not on the grounds of personal friendship + trust (for wh. no proxy is needed!) but because the I.S.C.M. needs that you keep a free hand. We have *got* to establish + maintain the principle that only those who are willing to really help carry them out are the ones wh. should make the decisions. I'm delighted that the concert went well, + was looking forward to hearing about it.

I guess you have my news in the note I sent Tuesday night with the music. In reply to the first part of your letter, I see no reason at all why I need to check the last pages of the Third Symphony unless, as you say, you run into difficulties.[1] As to *Lucullus,* I wonder whether— if it is not too late—I ought to add some stage directions, which simply don't exist in the score. The other point of view wd. be of course that it can be staged in several different ways, + that the text gives the basic indications. What do you think?

I am of course having a wonderful time here + though I don't go so fast as I would in a settled condition I manage to get a little done on *Montezuma* each day. The main thing is to keep "in" it all the time, so that I will not find, as I did after Northwestern, that it takes weeks to get back "into" it again!

Greece is of course marvelous. But of this more later. We leave tonight for a long day tour of the islands—Crete, Rhodes, Cos (the scene of "Theocritus") Halicarnassus, Patmos, Delos, Mykonos. Back here Saturday, + back in Florence a week from Friday (i.e. the 28th). Address there: Pensione Quisiana e Ponte Vecchio, 4 Lungarno Archibusieri

Much love to the whole family—

Affectionately
Roger

P.S. Very happy to hear of Raimondi's performance.[2] If you see him, please thank him for me + give him my congratulations.

Will write soon again—lots to tell you.

1. The Third Symphony was published by E. B. Marks in 1962. The publication of *Lucullus* was never released for sale, owing to permission problems with the Brecht estate.

2. Matthew Raimondi, the first violinist of the Composers String Quartet, has played Sessions's Solo Sonata, as well as his two quartets.

▼

Roger Sessions to Helen Carter[1]
als CH-Bsacher

July 12, 1961

Dear Helen,— Nyon, Switzerland

Thank you for your note. I have already written Felicia Geffen consenting to second Andrew Imbrie—the only one she mentioned—for the nomination to the [National] Institute [of Arts and Letters]. Also I will gladly be the 2d for Stefan Wolpe.[2] Please use my name. Of course Leon Kirchner should be a member—if he isn't one already. I would gladly nominate him, but am not sure on this point. We will be home Aug. 15—would that be time enough?

Nyon is on the Lake of Geneva between Geneva + Lausanne. We are here mainly because some old + very dear friends, Jean + Denise Binet, lived just above here for years. J.B.—a composer of whom perhaps Elliott knows—died last year + we are here seeing something of his widow. It is a lovely place, too, of course, though like all this region getting terribly overcrowded.

Congratulations to Elliott on the Double Concerto.[3] The opera [*Montezuma*] isn't finished yet—about 6 months more. But it has made good + very satisfying progress.

I look forward to seeing you both. Tell Elliott I shall have much to tell him + discuss with him when we meet again. On the whole my impressions have been on the good side, with qualifications of course. *Die Jakobsleiter* was wonderful, + also *Moses + Aron*, which I heard at La Scala. Both had an amazing success. It is strange how nothing is "difficult to listen to" any more—perhaps Schönberg is more so than most other things because one is forced to listen for something besides sound.

Roger Sessions with pianist Leonard Mastrogiacomo and composer Harold Schiffman in Tallahassee, 1963. Photograph by Ken Richards, courtesy of Harold Schiffman.

Elliott Carter and Roger Sessions in Aspen in 1963. Courtesy of the Harvard Music Library, Fromm Collection.

But I won't try to write more now. Give Elliott "Godspeed" from me, in every respect, + the very best to you both.

As always
Roger

P.S. We leave for points north (perhaps as far as Inverness) in a couple of days + should you or Elliott wish to reach us perhaps the best wd. be c/o H. [Hartog], Schott + Co. 48 Gt. Marlborough St. London W.1.

1. Helen Frost-Jones married Elliott Carter in 1939.
2. Wolpe (1902–72) studied in Vienna with Webern and emigrated in 1938 to the U.S., where he became an influential composer and teacher at Long Island University 1957–68.
3. Carter's Double Concerto for Harpsichord and Piano with Two Chamber Orchestras, commissioned by the Fromm Music Foundation and first performed on September 6, 1961, in New York with Ralph Kirkpatrick, harpsichord; Charles Rosen, piano; and Gustav Meier, conductor.

ON FEBRUARY 25, 1962, Sessions wrote Paul Fromm about his impressions of Leon Kirchner, who had recently been appointed to the Harvard University faculty. Kirchner seemed to him "more relaxed, simpler, and less aggressive than I have seen him for quite a number of years." Sessions had been in Boston to conduct his Fourth Symphony at the New England Conservatory,[1] where another former student, Robert Cogan (b. 1930), was teaching. Cogan and his wife, Pozzi Escot, received a letter from Sessions (March 22, 1962, US-CAcogan) thanking them for writing a highly complementary article about Sessions, which despite his efforts was never published. Sessions found the article "the best introduction to my music that I know; in fact the only one that seems to me at all in a class with it is the article of Elliott Carter on my Violin Concerto."[2]

1. The concert, February 21, 1962, included music by Weber, Mendelssohn, and Mahler, conducted by Frederik Prausnitz, the Conservatory Symphony Orchestra's regular conductor 1961–69.
2. A reference to Elliott Carter, "Current Chronicle: New York," *Musical Quarterly* 45 (July 1959): 375–81.

▼

Roger Sessions to Paul Fromm
als US-CAmus

August 31, 1962

My dear Paul,   Princeton

Thank you so much for your postcard. I hope you had a good rest
in Wisconsin.

I am writing to tell you that Lisl's mother[1] died peacefully yesterday
noon. We were with her when she died, but she had been in a coma
for five days, and in fact had not been really aware of anything since
her second operation. She just took too much of a beating—but it
couldn't be avoided as long as there was any chance of saving her. We
had wonderful doctors and nothing was spared to get the very best
care for her. We all loved her devotedly—she was an extraordinary
person who was a source of vitality to everyone who knew her. Lisl
will miss her very sorely.

I will not try to write more; I look forward keenly to seeing you at
the Gotham on the 24th, at one o'clock, and meanwhile am not
mentioning the matter of the magazine [*Perspectives of New Music*]
to anyone. I am confident that you understand my point of view, and
if at any point you think I am unreasonable I count on your telling
me so. Our affectionate good wishes to you all.

Faithfully,

Roger

1. Ruby Marble Franck (1879–1962) lived in Palo Alto, Calif.

▼

Luigi Dallapiccola to Roger Sessions[1]
als I-Fb

September 16, 1963

My dear friend Roger,   Florence

I do not mean to start with the usual sad stories in order to justify
my prolonged silence . . . first of all thanks and thanks again for those
delightful music notebooks [quaderni di carte da musica] and please
forgive me if I write you six months late.

If I think about our last meeting in New York, I suppose that the opera's score is [now] really finished. You had talked to me about six months' work or a little more: taking into consideration the fact that your [projections] were a little tight, I hope that now you have breathed that big sigh of relief that usually follows great events (and I believe that in your case it is indeed a great event). I have worked quite a bit myself but I will not now go into details. In a couple of weeks the "Prayers"[2] I wrote for Berkeley—and that I had "reworked" quite a bit—should be published by Suvini Zerboni; the rest is proceeding slowly, but it is proceeding.

This summer we traveled to Greece for twelve days, on our way to Israel. Now, though I had heard people say wonderful things about Greece, no words are powerful enough to say "what Greece *still* is." (For how long? Here is the problem. Think: a lucky country, without television. But what is happening now? It seems that the Italians are going to build it for them, as war reparations. One avenges oneself, as one can . . .) My most *violent* impressions were Mycena and Tirinto, which impressed me most deeply. There I understood how little "beauty" means, or at least what we are used to define as "beautiful." It seems very appropriate here to mention that famous intuition about "beauty" in music given by Schoenberg half a century ago.[3]

At La Scala I heard Stravinsky's "The Flood."[4] What do you think of it? To me it is something "impossible," something so out of balance between what we see and what we hear as to make us wonder if it is *all* wrong. Perhaps if it were performed and sung by children (with all the necessary changes), it would become "possible." But I am not sure.

Please write me, when you can. Please tell Betsy that we often think of her. And you should know that the three of us love the four of you very dearly.

With much friendship.
Luigi

1. Translated from the Italian by Valeria Secchi Short.
2. *Preghiere* for baritone and chamber orchestra, first performed in Berkeley, Calif., November 10, 1962. The text is by Murilo Mendes, translated by Ruggero Jacobbi; the music was published in Milan by Suvini Zerboni in 1963.
3. Schoenberg writes in his *Harmonielehre:* "Beauty exists only from that moment in which the unproductive begin to miss it. Before that it does not exist, for the artist does not need it. To him integrity is enough. . . . With the latter [beauty] the formula ultimately fails; sensations of beauty must be explained by the sense of beauty"

(*Theory of Harmony*, trans. Roy E. Carter [Berkeley and Los Angeles: University of California Press, 1978], 325–26).

4. Stravinsky's *The Flood*, written in 1961–62 for television, was broadcast on CBS June 14, 1962, and staged in Hamburg at the Staatsoper April 30, 1963.

CHAPTER

1964-1972

E L E V E N

$\int$ ESSIONS AND HIS WIFE spent the spring and summer of 1964 in Europe. They were being supported by a Ford Foundation grant that placed them in Berlin during the rehearsals for the premiere of *Montezuma*, April 19. Former students of Sessions assembled in Berlin for rehearsals and the performances of *Montezuma;* Mark DeVoto, Peter Maxwell Davies, John Harbison, and Richard Trythall all planned to be in attendance. But it was to Dallapiccola that Sessions wrote his most intimate feelings about the production; after all, Dallapiccola was to have his *Ulisse* performed by the same company. In his letter of September 6, 1964, to Dallapiccola Sessions referred to the booklet that BMI had assembled about him, for which Dallapiccola had written at some length:

My first meeting with Roger Sessions goes back to the fall of 1951. . . . Roger knows how much I love his Fourth Symphony and how ever since its first reading I was struck by its so very singular "divergent" process: as the emotion increases, the sonorous means which are used become less. He knows that I consider his Violin Concerto a unique piece and that there are very, very few other works which I should so much like at least to be able to hear, in an adequate performance. It will tell him nothing new when I write of how much I was moved on receiving the very poetic and so inspired *Idyll of Theocritus,* by the dedication of which he chose to do me honor. . . . Roger should know that in that dedication [of the *Cinque Canti* to Sessions], besides admiration for the inspired artist and the conscientious craftsman, is embodied admiration for his character and personality as a human being.

To Sessions's delight Dallapiccola was to be in the U.S. during the fall of 1964. His arrival coincided with the election of Lyndon Johnson and inspired Sessions to write about the political situation. On October 27, 1964, Sessions wrote to Dallapiccola (in Italian, as always), "I'll see you in New York the evening of November 4 (let's hope that in the same day we will all find out that Johnson was definitely elected, and that we will be freed from any worry as far as that is concerned!), and I am delighted."

During the summer of 1965 Sessions visited South America. He taught at Juilliard during the 1965–1966 year, where his *The Trial of Lucullus* was produced on May 19 and 21.

Over the summer of 1966 Sessions again spent time at Tanglewood. On September 17, 1966, he moved to California to become Ernest Bloch Visiting Professor there for a year, living at 1411 Hawthorne Terrace in Berkeley.

A month after celebrating his thirtieth wedding anniversary, Sessions celebrated his seventieth birthday. He wrote Felix Greissle (January 1, 1967), "Once more, it was wonderful to hear from you on my birthday. It is a little strange to actually be 70 years old, but as long as I don't feel that old, it is not catastrophic!"

▼

Roger Sessions to Paul Fromm
als US-CAmus

February 7, 1964
Dear Paul,—   Kastanienallee 34, 1 Berlin 19[1]

I was glad to have your letter, especially since I had hoped I had not expressed myself in mine in a way that would seem tactless to you.[2] Obviously it didn't and I am only glad—because I honestly think it will spare you quite a bit of trouble—that the basic issue has come out into the open so clearly + so soon. I am surprised however that it should have come out such a clear issue. I am certainly no fan of Hindemith, either musically or personally. But even though—frankly—I detest his music and dislike his personality, he certainly is one of the leading musical figures of the last half-century, whether any individual musician or music lover likes it or not—and this whole business of Ben's past seems to me so arrogant as to amount to childishness. The business with Xenakis is clearly somewhat of the same kind, though it isn't quite so easy for me to see from your enclosures exactly what happened in that case. I am sure you are taking the right tone with B[en] B[oretz].³ I feel however that some way should be found to bring such matters as these before the whole group before they come to the point of any action whatever. As I told you before, I don't think Ben is really acting entirely on his own; to what extent and in what precise manner this is true I don't of course know. If there were a fairly representative and not too large group, people would at least have a chance to take a stand on these issues. Whether they would actually do so I cannot be quite sure; I was not too happy about the *Haltung* [behavior] of two or three of the people at that luncheon meeting—possibly because they are not really sufficiently interested, or possibly because they can't bear to become unpopular with anyone whatever. It may be, too, that the people I have in mind were not sufficiently *au courant* to be quite aware of the underlying issues.

In any case, my dear Paul, I am entirely on your side. I do think, however, that it is going to be very difficult to change the magazine very much as long as people who are actively determined not to change it have the power to make the decisions—not only the big ones but, what is even more important in a situation of this sort, also the many little ones on which the actual contents of the magazine finally depends.

We are really very nicely settled here—Charlottenberg, West End—after some initial problems. It is very nice to have Elliott Carter here too + we see of course a great deal of him.⁴ Next week at the opera we get going on *Montezuma* (my contribution to the preparations I mean). It had to wait on the premiere of [Strauss's] *Die Frau ohne Schatten* which comes tomorrow night. I am pleased with the cast they have chosen for *Montezuma*, and I guess the singers have been working hard and steadily. The warmest of greetings to you all, from Lisl too.

With warmest affection

As always
Roger

P.S. The Hinteengeist will be most warmly appreciated, both inwardly(!) and outwardly!⁵

1. Sessions was in Berlin for the rehearsals and premiere of *Montezuma*, thereby missing the premiere of his Fifth Symphony on this date; it was performed by the Philadelphia Orchestra conducted by the work's dedicatee, Eugene Ormandy (1899–1985).

2. On January 26 Sessions had written to Fromm while en route to Germany about his concern for the direction the journal *Perspectives of New Music* was taking.

3. Composer and theorist Ben Boretz (b. 1934) was a student of Sessions and Babbitt at Princeton. Boretz was the music critic for *The Nation* 1962–69 and, with his former teacher Arthur Berger, founded and co-edited *Perspectives of New Music* (1962–82).

4. Like Roger and Lisl Sessions, Elliott and Helen Carter were in Berlin on a Ford Foundation grant.

5. Fromm was a wine importer, and several of Sessions's letters in these years acknowledge gifts of wine and brandy.

▼

Roger Sessions to Luigi Dallapiccola[1]
als I-Fb

March 25, 1964
My dear friend Luigi, Hotel Cipriano, Venezia

We are in Venice for a few days' rest before returning to Berlin next Monday for the last three weeks of preparations for *Montezuma*, which will be premiered (God willing) on April 19. The last weeks have been extremely arduous primarily because the orchestral parts contained many errors—mostly in the second act—which I had to check very carefully, and secondly because the score is very difficult and to feel completely at ease we would need to have ten or rather fifteen more rehearsals. But they say this is normal for a premiere; certainly the main singers seem to me to be very good and to have a solid musical background; and everyone's goodwill—that includes the orchestra, which is magnificent—is impressive, [illegible]. But I arrived here exhausted, and we are truly enjoying these days of rest in a quiet (albeit expensive) hotel. I can be away from Berlin because in this week the Opera Theatre is busy with *Parsifal*—but from next Tuesday on I have some busy weeks ahead of me!

The last months have been very busy. After having completed, in the month of October, the score for *Montezuma*, I finished my Fifth Symphony in January, which was played (very well, judging from the tapes) in Philadelphia; last June I had already finished a *CXL Psalm* for soprano and organ, commissioned by the Princeton Theological Seminary for a commemoration.[2] You will see that I have worked—maybe even a little too much. I also hope I have worked well.

Needless to say I was thrilled to hear that next year *Ulisse* will be performed in Berlin. I suppose this means that if you haven't yet completed it, you are in the process of doing so. I send you my warmest congratulations and am very anxious to hear your great opera. I am also a little saddened at the thought that it will be extremely difficult for me to come to Europe next year and see the performance, which will indubitably be one of the most important musical events of our time. You are certainly aware of how I feel about you and about your music and you will understand that *Ulisse* is very dear to me.

I am also sad that I will no longer be here in Venice in ten days when Scherchen[3] conducts your *Canti di Liberazione*. It was a pleasure to read the announcement but a disappointment when I saw "April 5."

I hope that all of you are well. Betsy is corresponding with Annalibera, as you know; she is doing very well, and is studying at Princeton with great profit. *[. . .]*

I suppose it is highly improbable that you will be in Berlin on April 19, but it is superfluous for me to say how delighted I would be if you could be there.

Fond embraces from your affectionate and faithful

Roger

1. Translated from the Italian by Pina Pasquantonio.
2. Published in 1964 by E. B. Marks in its organ version, and premiered by soprano Janice Harsanyi in 1966.
3. Hermann Scherchen (1891–1966), who had toured with Arnold Schoenberg 1911–12, was a distinguished conductor of modern music, notably in festivals at Donaueschingen and elsewhere.

▼

Roger Sessions to Mark DeVoto[1]
als US-MdeVoto

April 1, 1964
Berlin

Dear Mark,—

Many thanks for your long letter, which I would answer more fully if I had time; or if it had reached us last week in Venice, where we took a little visit, thanks to Richard Wagner for taking up Holy Week with *Parsifal*.

Having an opera produced is strenuous business. I had a lot of trouble, had to spend days + nights checking—there were bad mistakes in the parts, and *Montezuma*, they tell me is the most difficult work they ever had (the orchestra, not the singers except for Monte-zuma himself). But—they are all very cooperative, the orchestra is excellent + the chorus unbelievable, + the singers musically first-class. So, let's hope.

Anyway, I am writing to wish you Godspeed for the coming event[2]—and naturally our thoughts, with much affection. I wish I could make some sage and helpful remarks on the subject of birth, +c. but on the whole it is no doubt better not to attempt this. The main thing is that we both wish you both well!

Thank you for being so nice to Betsy. We are delighted that you enjoy her; we thought you would—she enjoys you very much!

The premiere of *Montezuma* comes on the 19th, not the 17th as formerly planned. Max Davies, + the Harbisons[3] can of course come to the Hauptprobe [dress rehearsal], I suppose on the 17th or 18th, if they are here. If you have time to think of such things you might give them our telephone number here, 94-28-75; probably around 8.45 to 9.15 A.M. is the best time to phone us. But don't have this on your mind! There is plenty else for you to think about.

Once more, all the very best, from us both.

Affectionately,
Roger Sessions

P.S. Dick Trythall[4] was in Greece for the holidays, but should be back shortly.

1. DeVoto (b. 1940) has edited Piston's *Harmony*. He studied with Sessions at Princeton 1961–64 and copied out *Montezuma*'s solo voice and choral parts.
2. The birth of DeVoto's first child.
3. The British composer Peter Maxwell Davies (b. 1934), who studied with Sessions at Princeton on a Harkness fellowship in 1962, wrote two articles on the opera for the *New York Times*: "Montezuma," April 21, 1964, 43:1, and "Montezuma Creates a Stir in Berlin," May 3, 1964, 2, 11:3. John Harbison (b. 1938), who studied with Sessions and Earl Kim at Princeton, was then teaching at Harvard, and later taught at the Massachusetts Institute of Technology; his cantata *The Flight into Egypt* won a Pulitzer Prize in 1987.
4. Richard Trythall (b. 1939) studied with Sessions at Princeton 1958–61. Later he became music liaison for the American Academy in Rome.

Roger Sessions to Luigi Dallapiccola[1]
als I-Fb

Thursday, April 23 [1964]

My dearest friend Luigi,   [Berlin]

First of all, thank you for your dear and lovely letter, and also for the telegram that I received at the opera just when I was about to give the "Hals und Beinbruch" ["Break a leg!"] to the singers and which gave me a true impression of both you and your dear family. Both the letter and the telegram gave me a clear sense of your friendship, which is one of the most precious things in my life and which, of course, I will never forget.

What to say about *Montezuma?* The performance was very good (a very dangerous moment in the second act prodigiously overcome by Hollreiser[2]—[tenor Helmut] Melchert (Montezuma) was temporarily lost, no one or almost no one took notice, and I realized that I was more curious and interested to see the result that frightened!). But the opera is extremely difficult and nobody felt totally confident—the execution is still a little rigid, or rather I should say very rigid—but it is no one's fault; the opera is very difficult, with many changes in time signatures—these seem to be the most serious—above all I would say, in Germany. I must emphatically state that everyone worked with the utmost devotion and that this was, and remains, perhaps the nicest experience of this sort that I've ever had in my life—and what I say goes for everyone in the opera. The singers were very good, so much so that it seems a little ungenerous of me to tell you alone that they are all not of the same caliber.

So—with regard to the audience, I still don't know exactly what to say. The press—with the exception of Stuckenschmidt[2] and Joachim, who spoke well of it albeit with a certain amount of caution—was downright evil and at times openly malicious; there was a demonstration at the end (I was on stage) from the gallery that mixed in with the applause, which was enthusiastic and continued for a while; later as they told me there were some fistfights. This went on at the end of the third act; after the first and above all after the second act, there was only applause. The opposition began with occasional laughter here and there at certain words in the German text (which we had anticipated might happen; they will be modified for the rest of the performances). There was also enthusiasm (confirmed by telephone calls the following day and even by a mailman who approached me today in the street, to express his personal enthusiasm and that of the people sitting near him in the audience). So, we shall see. I feel as if I'm in "No man's land"; right now I don't know what to think. For tonight's performance, with my permission we will make some *"Kurzungen"* [cuts] in the third act; I don't know whether they will be useful or not—at any rate, it will all remain in the score.

This last remark leads me to the next—it is for you alone, since I would *never* want to divulge this criticism of people who worked so long and well for me—however, it could be useful to you when you are preparing *Ulisse* here. I think that in the direction and in the conception of the scenes two rather serious errors were committed. First of all, [the director Gustav Rudolf] Sellner is not a musician, although he is an expert of the theater and a man of goodwill. In other words he didn't always understand what was going on in the music; even Scherchen, whom I saw in Venice, warned me about this, but I was so busy with the musical aspect that I didn't see what was going on with the scenes until the last week, when it was already too late to make fundamental changes. Thus, the effect was not always in harmony with the intentions of the music. I have no reason to believe that this ruined the overall effect, or that at this point it has any more meaning for me than a minor delusion; however, they [the sets] are not right, only because Sellner, who totally respected the importance of the music, lacks a sense of the immediate, or better still, of the practical that no expert musician would lack. Every suggestion I made (unfortunately only in the last days) was listened to with respect and attention. He worked on the end of the opera (the Chorus of Clouds) until the last moment; it is a very complex problem, about which we had many conversations and telephone calls, and which had a very *beautiful* result (N.B. above all in the second but also in the first performance).

The second observation I'd like to make is that the fundamental conception of the scenery—or let's say the scenic conception—seems perhaps to be formulated in a little too grandiose a manner with respect to the real musical necessities. That is—they made some enormous sets, very beautiful per se, but difficult to move around; it resulted, first of all, that in the second act, at a certain point we had to fill a pause with an improvisation on the timbali, short enough not to disturb but which destroys or at best alters the continuity and the immediate and loud contrast that I had desired at this point. Even more serious is the fact that in the third act, almost at the last moment, we had to decide to use only one set for the entire act; otherwise (1) the singers in the first scene would have been too far back to be heard well or to hear the orchestra well, (2) it was too dangerous to try to move those two enormous things in time for the final scene, and furthermore they made a very disturbing noise. Consequently it was not possible in the first scene of the act to give an *auto-da-fé* that cannot be seen but is heard in the music, and which one must be conscious of at least to the point that one realizes something horrible is happening. With the one set the *auto-da-fé* would take place toward the middle of the stage, where you can't even light a cigarette, and so Montezuma and Cortez and Alvarado are looking at and talking to the darkness, and I as well would imagine that no one can understand anything. The end result was that with my approval, all of this scene was cut along with two other things in the same act which in any case is the most difficult both musically and scenically (as well as musically) for the public. I suppose that for the purposes of the performance these cuts were for the best, there is no doubt, however, that with simpler scenery, many things would have been clearer.

Saturday [April 26, 1964]

I am writing now after the second performance, which in certain aspects was encouraging both for the more assured and less tense execution (I forgot to say that the "premiere" was the *first* time the entire opera was performed from beginning to end without technical interruptions) and for the way it was received by the public—calmly, courteously, and in part appreciative and enthusiastic. Sellner and Hollreiser seemed "erleichtet" [relieved] and even satisfied, and everyone is convinced that the demonstration at the premiere was plotted in advance—at any rate, nobody is without a certain dose of scandals. There were even some enthusiastic articles from abroad, even from West Germany. So, we shall see; [in English:] "So far, so good."

[In Italian:] At any rate Berlin—quite aside from *Montezuma*—is in a condition that worries many people of goodwill. Much is said about a growing conservatism and xenophobism, especially among youth, and about a complacency owed to a general feeling that Berlin is no longer a crisis point in world affairs (at least since the "Cuba crisis" in October 1962) and also to the fact that it is a place where young West Germans can escape to avoid doing their military service, etc., etc. These remarks reached me from responsible and certainly well-informed sources; naturally, I accept them with a certain amount of reserve since I cannot judge completely for myself. I know, however, that the project that was formed in 1961, to attract foreign artists and intellectuals to Berlin, has not worked out for the best, at least until now; many of them (or should I say many of us) are more or less uncomfortable and unhappy here. There is *very* little—or rather almost no—modern music to listen to here, besides Henze,[3] who is the current hero and who I find to be a friendly and pleasant young man, but in no way a great figure, at least until now. Besides *Montezuma*, which is in no way a part of this project of the Berlin Senate and the Ford Foundation, there seems to be no reason why Elliott Carter, Xenakis, Gilbert Amy,[4] to name a few of the project's composers whom I see now and then, live here—no performances, few contacts, and even a certain amount of hostility toward the project itself, from people who are busy with their own *routine* and who resent (even openly) what they call America's effort to "bring culture to Berlin." One mustn't say that this reaction is based on a complete misunderstanding, albeit more or less voluntary, of the idea. The preoccupation I mentioned earlier goes beyond the fate of contemporary music, and if what they say is true, it is not such an unfortunate phenomenon from the standpoint of the world situation, even though it is a little sad for Berlin itself.

I apologize for this enormous letter; I will briefly write what I still have to say. First of all, I am very happy, as always, to hear about your progress with *Ulisse*. The words of Valéry that you quoted[5] are beautiful and varied; I can't remember ever having heard them. I delight with you in the joy that comes from long and patient work, or at least so it seems to me from all that you've ever told me. Thus, besides the great interest and complete faith, not to mention the conviction that it will be a great opera, it's not up to me certainly to be impatient—nor to anyone else, for that matter!

Secondly, we hope to be able to go to Siracusa—from May 9 on, for at least a week; we asked for reservations beginning May 9. We would like to stop in Florence for a couple of days if you will be there, otherwise we will probably return here since I must go to America in the second week of June and to London for another week; at any rate I would like to see you if at all possible—it would seem strange, to say the least, to spend six months in Europe without even saying hello—or speaking with you.

I'd like to say one more thing that has been on my mind for some time now. Since I am not Italian, I don't exactly know the proper use of "tu." I would be very happy if we could use it but I fully understand that this is not only a national custom but also a personal one, and I have realized that being the older of the two, it is up to me to suggest it first. So, if you in your response should like to call me "tu" I would be very happy, but if you should prefer "Lei" as always, please do so without embarrassment. I have lived too long and understand too well to be in any way vulnerable in this sort of thing!

At any rate, please let me know if we'll have a chance to see one another, let's say from May 16 on.

Affectionate greetings from both of us to all three of you.

Yours faithfully,
Roger

1. Translated from the Italian by Pina Pasquantonio.
2. Heinrich Hollreiser (b. 1913) conducted the Vienna State Opera 1952–61 and was chief conductor at the Deutsche Oper in West Berlin 1961–64.
3. Hans H. Stuckenschmidt, "Der weisse Gott Cortez in Montezumas Azteken-reich," *Melos* 31 (June 1964): 192–94. Stuckenschmidt (1901–88), a professor of music history at the Technical University in Berlin, was an influential critic and writer on modern music.
4. Hans Werner Henze (b. 1926) had moved to Italy in 1953.
5. French composer and conductor Gilbert Amy (b. 1936) and Greek composer Yannis Xenakis (b. 1922) had studied with Milhaud and Messiaen.
6. "A work of art is never finished, only abandoned."

▼

Roger Sessions to Felix Greissle
als US-LA

May 13, 1964
Siracusa [Sicily]

Dear Felix—

Thank you so much for your good letter. You know perfectly well, I am sure, that our friendship means to me exactly what, as you say, it does to you; please don't ever doubt that for a minute.

I am happy and relieved that things have cleared up regarding the sale of the firm,[1] + above all that, as I gather, they have turned out favorably for you.

I hope by this time you have received the pictures I sent; + I may have written you that I have many more to show you when I come. Several gratifying developments have happened since I wrote; the public at the fourth performance was a large one, + was noticably warmer, + the singers smiled and bowed at their curtain calls (five in all, I guess) for the first time. A lot of them came to my apt. to drink wine on Thursday night + they told me that things were going with

Roger Sessions with Luigi Dallapiccola. Photograph by Hy Reiter.

*Roger Sessions with Felix Greissle in the early 1960s. Courtesy of Broadcast
Music, Inc.*

Montezuma exactly as they had with *Moses + Aaron*. You are of course right about the critics; but remember (I am talking of Stuckenschmidt + Joachim, who are the only ones who count) (1) they don't really know my other music at all as it hasn't been played in Berlin (2) The premiere took place, + had to, before the work had been fully rehearsed—Hollreiser told me they should have had two weeks more to adequately prepare it. Also, as you say, I was partly the victim of an anti–Deutsche Oper, anti-Sellner faction in Berlin which resents contemporary music at the opera. But as time has gone on I have realized that all of that is of no importance at all—so once more I guess it has been a triumph (I missed the fifth + last performance of the season, last night—but *Montezuma* is already announced for the Festwoche in September).[2]

We are having a lovely time here. Saturday we go to Palermo, thence to Florence, where, May 20 to 25th we will be at Hotel Principe, Lungarno Vespucci.

Love to you both
Roger

1. The publishing company of E. B. Marks was founded in 1894, renamed in 1920, and became Edward B. Marks Music Corp. in 1932. A sale to the Music Corporation of America in 1964 fell through. In 1967 it purchased the catalog of George M. Cohan Music Publishers and in 1971 Belwin-Mills took over distribution of its publications. In 1983 the firm was purchased by a group headed by Freddy Bienstock Enterprises.

2. This performance of *Montezuma,* like many such scheduled performances, did not take place.

▼

Roger Sessions to Luigi Dallapiccola[1]
als I-Fb

September 6, 1964
My dearest friend Luigi,   Princeton

I was just writing to you to thank you for your lovely letter regarding *Montezuma,* when the doorman brought me a large envelope from Oliver Daniel,[2] with a copy of the words you wrote for the booklet they are preparing about me. He already told me that he had written to you about this, and I must confess that I was a little embarrassed that you had to be interrupted this way.

It would be impossible for me to express, my dear friend, how deeply your words moved me, both those in the letter and those in the booklet. I am even more moved at the thought that these words spring from a deep and faithful friendship, which is even more precious than your words of praise, given that they not only provide moral support and recognition, but also a sharp sense of one's own insufficiencies. Thank you, my dearest friend, from the bottom of my heart; your generosity and affection are more dear and precious to me than words could ever express.

I am happy that the score for *Montezuma* reached you, and your first impressions overjoy me, and allow me to hope that I fulfilled at least the most necessary part of all I had set out to do. Since the score was sent to you, I made a few changes in the role of Cortez (mainly in the second and third acts) and I unburdened the orchestra a little in a few spots in both Act I and Act III. With Montezuma's very difficult role I could do little—I ended up inserting possible alternative notes in the third act. It's true that Melchert (very good but over fifty, who sings with such physical intensity that in certain moments one is almost afraid for him) felt obliged to make some cuts (above all in the extremely important pages 465–467—measures 823–36). From my standpoint those pages are of capital importance; so I can only hope that one day I will find a tenor who can sing them, finally without the "ossia."

I even wrote a few introductory remarks, for the edition that will come out in two or three months, on the way of singing (bel canto, etc.)—and up to a certain point on the way of producing it.[3] It goes without saying that I will send you a final copy when I have one.

I don't know exactly where to send this letter—to Europe, to Argentina? I hope it eventually reaches you. I am more than happy of course that in a while you will be here with us.[4] Unfortunately the current political situation here is both critical and dangerous.[5] There is no doubt that Goldwater represents a very ugly part, unfortunately not altogether new, of our country. One mustn't speak of Fascism or even of war but rather of politics that are not geared toward very probable or immediate *consequences,* and of a blind and idiotic simplicity. I don't think he will win, but he has fanatical and dedicated supporters, so there is always a possibility, and his defeat, in order to be completely satisfying, should be strong and crushing. The next eight or nine weeks will be awful and worrisome. Fortunately Johnson and [Hubert] Humphrey seem to be very capable men and there's no denying that their supporters include some of the best elements in the country with the exception of some politicians—like Rockefeller[6]—

who are trapped by their party's abnormal situation, but whose best interests and political future depend on a decided defeat of the candidate they supposedly support. A strange, abnormal and very preoccupying situation—but let's hope.

I hope all of you had a happy summer and in your case, also a productive one. As for me, I orchestrated my *Psalm 140,* and I am working on my Sonata (no. 3) for piano.[7]

Very affectionately,

Your faithful

Roger

1. Translated from the Italian by Pina Pasquantonio. Probably in response to Dallapiccola's use of "tu," here he also uses the familiar "tu."
2. Daniel (1911–90) had been director of concert music administration for BMI since 1954.
3. A page of instructions for interpretation appears in the score of *Montezuma* and in subsequent Sessions scores.
4. Dallapiccola would be in the U.S. in the autumn of 1964.
5. A reference to the approaching presidential election on November 3, 1964. The candidates were Senator Barry Goldwater and President Lyndon Johnson.
6. Nelson Rockefeller, then the governor of New York and the leader of the Republican party's liberal-moderate wing, had lost the nomination to the archconservative Goldwater.
7. The *Psalm 140,* for orchestra and soprano, was completed June 2, 1963, and performed by the Boston Symphony Orchestra February 11, 1966, Erich Leinsdorf conducting, Anne Elgar, soprano.

▼

Luigi Dallapiccola to Roger Sessions[1]
tls I-Fb

June 18, 1965

My dearest friend Roger,   Florence

at last I am able to thank you for your letter of February 10![2] Young Harbison brought (or sent, I am not sure) your letter while I was in Germany; [my wife] Laura told him to call after March 26, the day of my return from Rome, where I had to conduct a concert of my music. No news of him. Only last week, when I had to begin rehearsing for a rather original concert (half music by Janáček, half mine), did the above-mentioned young man pop up to ask me if he could come to one of the rehearsals. And so at last we met and could talk. From him I had your latest news and the "official" confirmation that you will be at Juilliard next year.[3]

−456−

We did not meet again, among other things because I am leaving soon. I am going [to the sea] earlier this year for the simple reason that Annalibera has college final exams and since Laura knows that I get nervous and that in such circumstances I become an "element of disorder" ["*elemento di disordine*"], she clearly told me to go to the beach, where the rest of the family will follow me after the exams . . .

I have received a very sweet letter from Greissle, in which he told me that he had sent me the [piano] score of *Montezuma:* I am sure that it will arrive while I am away, since he sent it by regular mail, and, since now it is in its last and definite version, I am very curious to observe the slight changes you already talked to me about. To observe, and, of course, to learn something.

I am going to shut myself up in Vittoria Apuana in order to work eight hours a day and perhaps more (provided my eyes and nerves will allow it), so that I'll be able to prepare, in the meantime, the score of the whole first act of *Ulisse.* I just need to compose a few pages for its completion, at this point. Its performance is set for September 1967. I have two years and I am convinced that I can do an "honorable" ["*pulito*"] job. Thank you for keeping me up to date with your new works (Third Sonata and Sixth Symphony),[4] for which I wish a happy christening and long and happy life.

We remember you all with great affection and warmest friendship: thanks for the score and "hugs."

Best wishes from the three of us.

Your affectionate,
Luigi

1. Translated from the Italian by Valeria Secchi Short.
2. On February 10, 1965, Sessions had written asking Dallapiccola to meet his former student John Harbison, whose "parents have been friends of ours for almost thirty years (his father, who passed away a few months ago, was a very esteemed historian of the Renaissance and a professor at Princeton). I consider him an exceptional young man not only for his attributes as a composer but for his personality, his intelligence, and for his general culture, and, more particularly, his musical culture" (I-Fb).
3. Sessions taught at The Juilliard School of Music 1965–66; the school produced his *Trial of Lucullus* on May 19 and 21, 1966, as part of a double bill with Hugo Weisgall's *Purgatory,* to excellent reviews: Raymond Ericson, "Operatic Ghosts and Shades," *New York Times,* May 20, 1966; Michael Steinberg, "Sessions' 'Lucullas' Impresses at Juilliard," *Boston Globe,* May 26, 1966; Irving Kolodin, "Murder, to Music, at the Juilliard," *Saturday Review* 49 (June 4, 1966); and David Drew, "Out of Limbo," *New Statesman,* June 24, 1966.
4. The Piano Sonata No. 3, commissioned by Eugene Istomin and completed in 1965, did not receive its premiere until the Cuban pianist Jacob Lateiner (b. 1928)

performed it in Los Angeles March 3, 1969. The Symphony No. 6 received its premiere November 19, 1966, in Newark, N.J., by the New Jersey Symphony.

▼

Roger Sessions to Mark DeVoto
als US-MdeVoto

July 3, 1965

Dear Mark,—   63 Stanworth Lane, Princeton

Thanks for your nice long letter, which I am answering the day of its arrival. (I'm trying to turn over a new leaf—+ who knows what may come of it?) Your information is correct (even though it did come through Milton [Babbitt] who is not always the most accurate of informants!) but in 1967 after Berkeley we will return here, + I to the Juilliard.[1] Also this summer, specifically two weeks from this coming Wednesday, we fly to Buenos Aires, stopping at Rio, + returning via Santiago de Chile, Lima, and Mexico City; we'll be back about September 14th.[2]

It is my Sixth Symphony that I am working on, though I still have to finish the last movement of Piano Sonata No. 3. After that comes the Cello Concerto,[3] + then three more commissioned works, which will probably include Symphony No. 7. I won't go into more details at this point. All of them are large, but there are smaller things, too, secretly in the works. Give my best to Jack Avshalomoff[4] (also to the beautiful lady bassoon player who is married to the trumpeter,—etc. etc. They did nobly by my Divertimento.). *Lucullus* is not yet published—*Montezuma* took too much work + cost too much money, + my Duo[5] and my Violin Concerto are being reissued + decently printed. But *Lucullus* will come along, soon, I hope.[6]

Your life sounds idyllic + I am delighted to hear of [DeVoto's daughter] Emily. You also seem to be enjoying Oregon which certainly has its points. We are all well. Betsy takes her generals in October + is already petrified at the prospect (quite without cause barring always the quirks of circumstance). As you see, we have moved,[7] but having dreaded it for months we find we quite enjoy living in a smaller place—it is also a much quieter one, and in many ways hellishly convenient. Of course we have only been here for four days; but even the cat seems to like it! I am of course Emeritus now, and also got an L.L.D. (?!?) from Brandeis this spring—so I feel venerable and at the same time tickled to be out of the University, with all due respect to all concerned—and affection, too, of course.

Thanks again for your letter, and love to you all.

Always,
Roger Sessions

[P.S.] Address in August: Instituto Torcuato Tella Florida 936, Buenos Aires, Republica Argentina

1. In the autumn of 1966, after spending the summer at Tanglewood, Sessions returned to Berkeley to serve as the Ernest Bloch Visiting Professor at the University of California 1966–67. Seventy years old, he was retired from Princeton University but continued to teach—at Juilliard—for sixteen more years.
2. This trip had been arranged in part by Alberto Ginastera.
3. Sessions never completed a cello concerto; possibly this was an earlier version of his Concerto for Violin, Violoncello, and Orchestra, finished in 1971.
4. Jacob Avshalomov (b. 1919) was the conductor of the Portland Junior Symphony.
5. For violin and piano (1942), dedicated to Irene and Frederick Jacobi.
6. Sessions's opera *The Trial of Lucullus* remains to this day unpublished.
7. From 70 Alexander St. to 63 Stanworth Lane, in Princeton. Both houses were own by Princeton University; Sessions never owned a home.

▼

Roger Sessions to Paul Fromm
als US-CAmus

August 14, 1965
Buenos Aires

My dear Paul,—

I am thoroughly appalled that I have not written you to thank you for the wonderful package of wine that arrived over three weeks ago (no, unfortunately *four*!), just before (well, a few days before) we left for South America. I hope you will understand that, aside from my own very bad habit of procrastination, we're still up to our ears getting settled in our new apartment, and then immediately setting off for what was to us an entirely new landscape and milieu. Our new apartment is small, but to our surprise we are not sure we don't like it even better than 70 Alexander St. It is cozy and clean; my study is quite small, but it is nice to have those of my books which I like within arm's length, even though I don't often reach out for them! The wine is there waiting for us when we get back, and I can assure you we are looking forward to it—we will be there Sept. 14th.

South America has been a wonderful experience for us so far—we spent three days in Rio, which is a very sympathetic place, and, God knows, a spectacular one. B.A. is not so spectacular, but thoroughly sympathetic. I like Ginastera[1] very much, and am happy to see he has real influence here. We have also heard a good deal of music—one of the best performances of *Falstaff* I have ever heard, and I have heard some good ones. The public here is very warm, and as far as I can see, very well-informed and even very sympathetic to contemporary music of all kinds. I am really enjoying it; my students, from all over Latin America—from Puerto Rico to Argentina, with some from Costa Rica, Bolivia, + those from Chile (even perhaps the best two are Chilean, though I am not sure)—are alert, intelligent, and aware of all that goes on in the world.

You know young Davidoffsky?[2] He is an Argentinian, but really lives in N.Y. It has been a great pleasure to get to know him here + to see something of him. His music is certainly some of the best I have heard from the "avant garde." He is in some ways a little like Martirano—the type of personality that I instinctively believe in even if I don't always agree with everything he does. In saying this I am not thinking of Davidovsky as of Martirano and the somewhat deplorable piece we heard in N.Y. last spring.[3]

In any case, please forgive me for having been so slow in writing, if you can. And much love to you and Erika and the Fromm family.

Affectionately from us both

As always
Roger

1. Argentinian composer Alberto Ginastera (1916–83) taught at the National Conservatory in Buenos Aires 1948–58.
2. Mario Davidovsky (b. 1934) had come to the U.S. in 1958. His *Synchronisms No. 6* for piano and electronic tape won a Pulitzer Prize in 1971.
3. Possibly Martirano's *Underworld* (1965).

▼

Roger Sessions to David Diamond
als US-Rdiamond

Saturday, November 26 [1966]
Dear David,   1411 Hawthorne Terrace, Berkeley

Both Lisl and I were surprised and touched that you should have remembered our [thirtieth] wedding anniversary! Thank you so much—+ it was good to have a few lines from you.

Our trip East was a hectic one—+ I didn't have time to look around! I had to spend a day + a half getting to Poughkeepsie + back, for a lecture + a concert at Vassar—+ I didn't let anyone know about the performance in Newark,[1] mainly because I always feel on such occasions that if I do so it half implies that I would be offended if they didn't come. Actually I didn't try to get in touch with anyone as we found ourselves virtually all booked up by the time we got there! + had hardly any time even to phone my friends, much less see them. [. . .]

Anyway I hope we will see each other before too long—and warmest thanks for your message!

As always
Roger

1. The premiere of the complete Symphony No. 6. (A January 1966 performance by the New Jersey Symphony gave only the first two movements.)

▼

Roger Sessions to Luigi Dallapiccola[1]
als I-Fb

September 26, 1967
Princeton[2]

My dearest friend Luigi,

I have been delinquent far too long; I didn't even write to you when that terrible disaster struck our beloved Florence,[3] although I thought of all of you continually; and I didn't even thank you for your very dear and very touching letter for my 70th birthday [December 28, 1966]. I can only say that my silence dates back to the beginning of the bombings in Vietnam, and to my shame, my profound embarrassment, and to the struggle against the desperation that assails me over what happened and what continues to happen there. Many times I began to write; but there was too much to say, and it would be impossible for me to write to you without saying things one hardly dares to put on paper—hence my procrastination.

But I don't want to bother you with explanations; I only want to repeat once again that I am always your faithful and devoted friend—both yours and your family's—and the thought that we shall see each other again in a few days at Ann Arbor[4] fills me with immense joy. I only hope you can find a way to forgive me.

I was delighted to learn that *Ulisse* is now ready and it will be performed in Berlin next spring. One week ago, I heard a rehearsal of your Variations in Chicago. As always, your music does wonders for me—it remains one of the sources of courage in these troubled times.

As ever your faithful and affectionate
Roger

1. This letter, here translated by Pina Pasquantonio, is published in Italian in *Luigi Dallapiccola: saggi, testimonianze, carteggio, biografia e bibliografia,* ed. Fiamma Nicolodi (Milan: Suvini Zerboni, 1975), 103.
2. Sessions returned to Princeton in the autumn of 1967 and resumed teaching at The Juilliard School.
3. In 1966 the flooded Arno, whose waters rose as high as twenty feet, had destroyed many priceless cultural artifacts.
4. Where Sessions's Symphony No. 7 would receive its premiere October 1, 1967, with Jean Martinon, the symphony's dedicatee, conducting the Chicago Symphony Orchestra.

▼

Luigi Dallapiccola to Roger Sessions[1]
cc I-Fb

December 14, 1967
Florence

My dear friend Roger,

I wish I could talk about music with you, but . . . what can you do in a moment like this? I am writing you because I do not know if you have heard about the "Isang Yun case" (for us musicians), about the case of the Korean intellectuals living in Europe, kidnapped by the Seoul counterespionage, brought back to South Korea, and two sentenced to death, others to a life sentence. Among this latter group is the very gifted composer Isang Yun.[2] In Europe we wrote a petition that in a few days got 161 signatures (published in *Zeit* in Hamburg); in Italy we have taken special steps at the Foreign Ministry. In spite of all this, this morning I read that the sentences have been given. After asking Laura for her advice, I sent two telegrams. [in English:] AMERICAN ACADEMY OF ARTS AND LETTERS: PLEASE URGE PRESIDENT JOHNSON TO INTERVENE IN BEHALF OF KOREAN INTELLECTUALS KIDNAPPED IN EUROPE AND CONDEMNED ACCORDING TO INHUMAN LAWS THANK YOU SINCERELY—L.D. (The second:) IGOR STRAWINSKY: I TELEGRAPHED AMERICAN ACADEMY OF ARTS AND LETTERS ASKING TO URGE PRESIDENT JOHNSON TO INTERVENE IN BEHALF OF INTELLECTUALS CONDEMNED IN SEOUL. YOUR SUPPORT AS THE MOST IMPOR-

TANT OF ALL WHO SIGNED PETITION FOR ISANG YUN WOULD BE
EXTREMELY WELCOME THANK YOU YOURS L.D.

[In Italian:] If you need some more facts, please call our old pupil
George Sturm. And, if you could press my request at the Academy,
you will do a great work for a good and right cause. *Our most
affectionate wishes, also from Laura.*

Affectionately yours

[Luigi]

1. Translated from the Italian by Valeria Secchi Short.
2. Isang Yun (b. 1917) had gone to Berlin from Korea in 1956 to study with Boris
Blacher and Josef Rufer at the Berlin Hochschule für Musik. On June 17, 1967, he
and his wife were abducted from West Berlin by the South Korean secret police, taken
to Seoul, and tried for sedition. Yun was sentenced to life imprisonment, his wife to
three years' imprisonment. Twenty-three celebrated musicians wrote a letter of
protest, which, combined with West Germany's threat to cut off aid to South Korea,
resulted in the release of Yun and his wife after two years' detention. They returned to
Germany.

▼

Roger Sessions to Luigi Dallapiccola[1]
als I-Fb

March 31–April 1, 1968

My dearest friend Luigi, Princeton

I must have seriously deluded you—and once again I must ask your
forgiveness. You clearly told me that the business of the translation[2]
was urgent, and now I an forced to admit that in all probability, it is
too late. What I can't even explain to myself is that not only did I
think about it, I asked the opinion of others, and I even searched
within the score thinking that maybe I could find other things besides
the ones we had already spoken of, with the hope of offering some
useful suggestions—this search was naturally without result since I
am not familiar with the English translation that has already been
done. Unfortunately, the heart of the matter is that I didn't write to
you. It is true that in the last two months I worked incessantly night
and day on my Eighth Symphony, which had to be ready for the
premiere at the Philharmonic on April 18 (but will now take place on
May 2)[3] and that I was distracted to such a fault. I write all this not
to justify myself in any way, but only in the hope that you can
maintain a trace of trust in our friendship.

-463-

Concerning the most important thing: I still believe that for "il rogo" the best translation would be, as I already told you, "the stake";—believe me, no one could mistake that topic in the context of the drama. "The pyre" is not as good because it leads one to associate it with a funeral ceremony and not an execution.

For "s'è fatta luce"—"I see the light now" seems good to me and it goes along with the meaning you intend it to have. I still find that "I see" would be preferable (at [rehearsal no.] 910) to "now I see" because of the inflection; "now I see" would require a longer note on "now." But if you say, "I see" the accent falls on the word "see" and I don't know if you'd like this or not. I myself would find the falling minor third and the long note (m. 910 C, m. 911 B♭) enough to compensate for placing the accent from "vedo" to "I see."

Once again, I reproach myself more than I can ever say for being so late.

I must also tell you that as soon as I got your letter about the composer Yun, I immediately tried to contact George Kennan, the President of the Academy.[4] Unfortunately he was away, but I spoke to his secretary, to whom I explained the problem, and who spoke with him. They explained that it would be most difficult to get a declaration from the Academy, because for a declaration of this sort they need the consensus of all the members, and for "political" issues of this nature, that consensus is lacking in the Academy, especially given the current situation (Vietnam, etc.). But I spoke with Elliott Carter, since he lives in New York and finds it easier to communicate than I myself do, and I can assure you that many people have taken the matter to heart and that everything possible is being done. Naturally the "Pueblo" affair[5] has made these efforts even more difficult, but now E.C. tells me that they are trying the possibility of appealing directly to the South Korean President[6] and naturally I will participate as well if they decide on this "démarche" [approach].

Regarding the overall situation, we were shocked at yesterday's announcement that Johnson will not be a candidate for the Presidency but feel somewhat encouraged by [Eugene] McCarthy's and [Robert] Kennedy's candidacies. All these events seem to have changed the perspective—we still don't know in what way, but instead of torpor and almost desperation there are evident signs of vitality, energy, and purpose. However, it seems to me that the situation will remain uncertain for some time, and although undoubtedly a *crescendo* has begun, some surprises await us before the trombones come in. Johnson's retirement appears genuine; the efforts at negotiation seem insufficient, and we are so accustomed to disappointments and to being cheated that we are always watchful and suspicious. In all of this situation, the young people are truly extraordinary—they have found a reason for living, they work, they travel and [illegible]: and they have really produced some unexpected results—so, who knows? At least for the moment, the overall aspect of our political situation has been transformed, and the air has become fresher and one can almost see cause for hope. At any rate, it is very impressive and very moving even if one is aware of the immense obstacles that remain and which must be overcome. It is already a miracle, which requires our faith as well as our awareness.

Moreover, it is a pleasure to write to you, and for the moment, to forget that I have certainly disappointed you—believe me, I beg of you, that it is always a comfort for me to know that you are there, and that there is your music—an enormous comfort.

As ever, your faithful,
Roger

1. Translated from the Italian by Pina Pasquantonio.
2. Of Dallapiccola's *Il prigioniero.*
3. The Symphony No. 8, commissioned by the New York Philharmonic Orchestra for its one hundred twenty-fifth anniversary and dedicated "To my daughter, Elizabeth," received its premiere May 2, 1968, with William Steinberg conducting.
4. Kennan (b. 1904), the diplomat and authority on Soviet relations who formulated the U.S.'s "containment" policy toward the Soviet Union, was a professor at Princeton's Institute for Advanced Study and president of the American Academy of Arts and Letters.
5. The capture on January 23, 1968, of the U.S. Navy intelligence ship, the USS *Pueblo,* by North Korean patrol boats off the coast of North Korea. After U.S. military threats and lengthy negotiations, the ship's crew were released December 23, 1968.
6. Park Chung Hee had come to power in the military coup of 1961.

▼

Ernst Krenek to Roger Sessions
als US-NYpease

May 11, 1968
623 Chino Canyon Road
[Palm Springs, California]

Dear Roger,

in *Time Magazine*[1] I read about your "uncompromising" Eighth Symphony, and I wish to congratulate you upon its being just that. I only wish to have an opportunity of hearing not only it, but also a number of other works you have created since we met the last time—I believe, it was in Aspen, and I am afraid it's quite some time ago.

Two years ago we have moved to Palm Springs, because we love the desert and the dry, hot air, and the big, bare mountains. We are going to Europe more or less every year. Only two weeks ago we have returned from there. I have conducted concerts, broadcasts, opera (a revival of "Jonny spielt auf" in—of all places—Regensburg; it also was done in Salzburg a little later), TV and such. I had a very pleasant time in Prague—the first time since 1935. We must hope that they can keep up what they are trying to do.[2]

How is everything with you? Where are you now located? Is there any possibility of seeing you again? We'll be at Ravinia in July, then at Tanglewood, early August at Dartmouth, and in September briefly in New York. It would be wonderful to have some personal contact again after so many years.

With good wishes and love "von Haus zu Haus" ["from our house to your house"]

as always affectionately
Ernst

1. The anonymous reviewer for *Time* (May 10, 1968, 85) wrote: "At Manhattan's Philharmonic Hall last week, his new *Eighth Symphony*—masterful in its lyric use of twelve-tone principles, fearless in its glacial austerity—laid one of the big eggs of the season. . . . Stubborn New England descendant of *Mayflower* pilgrims that he is, he refuses to bid for easy success with the latest fashions. For that reason, he has had to settle for the high esteem of colleagues and critics, and the reputation of a Zeus on a cloud-cloaked Olympus doing his own thing, virtually daring the multitudes to like it. . . . 'What can one do about audience psychology?' he asks. 'Immediate response is not what one is preoccupied with. The job of the composer is to write the music he loves best. I think that's true of anything anyone does seriously.'"

2. Years of liberalization had led to the installation of a reformist Czechoslovak government in the Prague Spring of 1968. The brief period of remarkable civil liberties ended with the Soviet military occupation on August 20.

▼

Roger Sessions to David Diamond
als US-Rdiamond

August 10, 1968
My dear David,—   Princeton

The quartet[1] arrived two days ago, having been mis-forwarded from Ipswich, which delayed it I suppose a little longer. I should have written you immediately, but put it off because I wanted to get to know it a little, and especially because I felt a little sheepish till I had discovered the "R.S." quotation of which you speak. That it escaped me until I really read the work through for the third time is a tribute to the fact that the piece is *really* yours, and that the fragment in question is thoroughly integrated into the whole—as one would, after all, expect. But I am very much touched, nevertheless, by the quotation, and delighted and honored by the piece itself. It is beautifully written for quartet—very transparent in texture, and, it seems to me, very clear in the general design. Excuse me—I hope this sounds as it is intended to sound, and I assure it is not meant as an ex-teacher putting an ex-pupil on the block! As you know very well, the qualities I have spoken of are neither very common, or are they at all easy to achieve!—Naturally it is the music itself which is really important, but the hardest to put into words. From the start I found very beautiful things in it, and each time I have read it I have found more, as one reads more fluently and takes in more of the detail. The very end— which really includes the whole last section, leading of course up to the *very* beautiful final page, seems to me especially beautiful—but it of course is the result of something that has gone before, and I am not implying any less appreciation of the earlier parts in singling [out] the last part (Doppio Canone) especially. What I want you very much to realize is my love for the piece and my deep appreciation of the dedication. Thank you, David.

Lisl sends her love along with mine.—+ I hope we will meet sometime, somewhere this winter.

As always, affectionately,
Roger

1. Diamond's String Quartet No. 9 (1966–68), with hidden quotations from Sessions's Piano Concerto and Violin Concerto.

▼

Luigi Dallapiccola to Roger Sessions[1]
als I-Fb

October 3, 1968
Berlin

My dearest friend Roger,

I will not waste time with a person like you, who knows what a world premiere means, in order to apologize for not having thanked you until now for a very precious letter[2] from you nor to apologize if

I have waited five days before telling you how much your telegram, so full of friendship, has consoled us. I greeted Sellner and our mutual friends of the Deutsche Oper for you; they appreciated your greetings very much and they reciprocate them with great friendship.

What can I tell you about the performance?[3] I can't imagine wishing for a better *Uraufführung* [first performance], that is to say, something that must be created *ex novo* [from scratch], piece by piece, since there is yet no tradition of how to perform it. They were saying around here that such a difficult opera had never been performed (difficult especially metrically); and I have always answered that it was a matter of time and of patience, and that already in a few years it would become a little less difficult. One knows that our profession is the school of patience.[4]

On the 10th we'll resume our journey south. I'll stop in Milan, since I'll have to see my publishers and I'll have a score for voice and piano of *Ulisse*. I leave a day before the premiere.

I feel very tired, but this time it was well worth it, I think.

Every good wish to you and your dear ones also from Laura. (Anna Libera was here for the dress rehearsal and the premiere performance and seemed very moved.)

With all my love believe me

your old admirer and friend,
Ld

1. Translated from the Italian by Valeria Secchi Short.
2. Sessions had written to Dallapiccola September 22, 1968 (I-Fb): "At such an important moment I must jot down a few words to let you know that I am constantly thinking of you and of the final preparations for *Ulisse,* and hoping that everything is proceeding with satisfaction. I don't have to say that it is an event of primary importance, first of all for music and for musical drama, that is to say for all of us. For this reason and for many other more personal ones, I would, more than I can say, like to be present in Berlin next Sunday. . . . But I will be present with all my thoughts and all my hopes, for you, for your work, and for those that I always consider to be my friends at the Deutsche Oper." (Translated by Pina Pasquantonio.)
3. The first performance of *Ulisse* took place (in German) September 29, 1968, by the Deutsche Oper in Berlin, conducted by Lorin Maazel.
4. Sessions would frequently quote this aphorism in Italian.

▼

Roger Sessions to Luigi Dallapiccola[1]
als I-Fb

October 19, 1968
My dearest friend Luigi, Cambridge, Massachusetts

Yesterday afternoon we received the score for *Ulisse,* and you can't imagine what joy it gave me to receive it and see it for the first time. Thank you—and thank you for the lovely inscription, which I value more than I can say.

It goes without saying that from the minute I received it, I read it avidly ("lost to the world" was Lisl's comment). Naturally this only means the beginning, and after three and a half hours of reading (I read only the text, but I found myself continually captivated not only with the vocal melody but also with the orchestra). I had a very real impression of the prologue and of Act I; the second act still awaits me, even though I read a few parts of the last pages. But even so far, I was struck by the ardor and depth of your creativity, be it musical, dramatic, or poetic, and by the formidable beauty of every moment. I can only say, yet again, thank you from the bottom of my heart.

Naturally I was overjoyed to get your letter with the welcome news that you were very pleased with the "premiere." Later I heard good things about it from other sources. It was delightful to read the names of many people who sang in *Montezuma*—Miss Bernard + Melchert, Krukowski, Mercker, Driscoll[2]—I am very happy for you that it went well. I can understand that they found it "difficult," but we know, as you say, that both patience and time are required—and that your music (I hope mine as well) was not in any way written for the lazy or for the arrogant.

You will notice from the address that for this winter we will be living—at least until the end of May 1969—at Harvard, where I hold the position of "Charles Eliot Norton Professor of Poetry"—which means I must give six lectures which I have entitled "Questions about Music."[3] There are many things to say, I believe, that are not without importance in the current situation.

And—more importantly for me—in the month of May, a second performance of *Montezuma* will take place in Boston.[4] Every effort is being made to produce it along my ideas; we have chosen some really excellent singers, among whom Bernard, who sang Malinche in Berlin, has accepted in theory, but it is subject to the approval by the Deutsche

Oper, which must allow her to take a leave of absence for an adequate amount of time. It [the Opera Company of Boston] is an ambitious company that has performed for the first time in America both *Lulu* and *Moses and Aron,* for which they were praised by everyone. The orchestra is the Boston Symphony and the conductor for *Montezuma* will be Gunther Schuller,[5] who is very good and very devoted. So, let's hope for the best. They show great desire to perform it in a way that corresponds to my ideas (and those of Borgese). She is an extraordinary woman who will be directing and who was the first to notice, at last, all the defects of the performance in Berlin.[6]

Tomorrow I will send you my two latest publications—my Fourth Symphony which you already know, and five [*sic*] pieces for violoncello.[7][. . .] It's awfully little compared with the score of *Ulisse,* but I hope you will enjoy them, and at any rate they come will all my thanks, admiration, and affection.

Meanwhile I anticipate the pleasure of seeing *Ulisse* performed at the City Center, and I hope to see you then. I still don't know when it will be; but rest assured that I will be there—if not at the premiere, though I would hope to make it, at least at one of the other performances. This depends, of course, on my obligations here.

I won't write about political events, which, as you can well understand, worry us a great deal.[8] We must vote, albeit without enthusiasm, for Humphrey—the alternatives are far from good, and in the case of Wallace, very dangerous.[9] Do you remember Churchill's words "God protects the stupid, and the United States of America"—and one fervently hopes that this continues to be true.

So, my dear friend, warmest thanks for the score and above all for the opera *Ulisse,* and affectionate greetings from

your devoted Roger

P.S. I found a few misprints in the edition of *Ulisse* that you must have already seen (𝄢 instead of 𝄞 in the last line of the last page, for example, and "Die Mäghe" instead of Mägde p. 21 measure 141). If it would be useful to you, I could make note, very carefully, of those that strike me.

1. Translated from the Italian by Pina Pasquantonio.
2. Annabelle Bernard sang Malinche, Helmut Melchert sang Montezuma, Ernst Krukowski Bernal Diaz the Old, Karl Ernst Mercker Bernal Diaz the Young, and Loren Driscoll sang Alvarado.
3. *Questions About Music* (New York: Norton, 1971).
4. This planned production of *Montezuma* in the spring of 1969 by Sarah Caldwell

and the Opera Company of Boston would be delayed seven years, until the spring of 1976.

5. The composer and conductor Gunther Schuller (b. 1925) at that time was president of the New England Conservatory and chairman of the composition department at Tanglewood. He conducted the recording of Sessions's Violin Concerto (CRI220) with Paul Zukofsky.

6. American conductor Sarah Caldwell (b. 1924) studied with Richard Burgin and in 1958 formed her own opera company in Boston, with which she staged the first American performances of Schoenberg's *Moses und Aron,* Berg's *Lulu,* and Zimmermann's *Die Soldaten.*

7. The Six Pieces for Violoncello (1966).

8. Earlier that year gunmen had assassinated Dr. Martin Luther King, Jr. (on April 4), and Senator Robert Kennedy (on June 5).

9. In November the Republican presidential candidate, Richard Nixon, narrowly defeated the Democratic candidate, Hubert Humphrey. George Wallace, an Independent, carried the Deep South.

▼

Luigi Dallapiccola to Roger Sessions[1]
als I-Fb

November 13, 1968
My dearest friend Roger,   [Milan]

I am in Milan for the reading rehearsals of *Ulisse* and I know that I will not be able to write you a letter that would properly answer yours, which has moved me so much for the warmth of friendship that fills it. Thank you for writing me the way you did. More I can't say, for the moment.

Indeed no present could have been dearer to me than receiving your *Fourth Symphony* (you know what I think of such a work and you know why: I will not, then, repeat it) and those *extraordinary* pieces for 'cello alone, which I wish to be able to hear one of these days (and I hope soon).

Your letter has brought me a piece of news of the greatest importance for our Art, precisely that Boston will have the privilege of the first American performance of your *Montezuma.* This is really a big piece of news! And I will not stop to discuss [it] if in your country they have waited a bit too long to have the public know such a great work. To have an opera performed a few years late is not fatal for those operas destined to stay: it is fatal only for "transitory" art.

I won't tell you how anxiously our family has been following the American elections; we were constantly listening to the radio.

I know, I am sure, that the results have been disappointing for you.

Though let us accept willingly the new president, if he'll be able (as it seems) to definitely end the tragedy of Vietnam. This problem is extremely serious and urgent: I am convinced that without such a problem the brutal and unjustified Russian oppression in Czechoslovakia would not have happened. We admire the great heroic effort of the Czech people and we anxiously wonder how long it will last.

Thanks for having pointed out to me a few misprints in the edition of *Ulisse*. Unfortunately there are many more, which will be corrected when the first edition has been sold out.

I think, we think, about you all with the greatest friendship and affection.

Thanks again and hugs.

Very affectionately yours
Ld

1. Translated from the Italian by Valeria Secchi Short.

▼

Elizabeth Sessions to Paul Fromm
tls US-CAmus

March 4, 1969
Dear Paul: [Princeton]

It is the same old story as usual. Today I opened the letter that you sent to Roger as he is in Los Angeles until Thursday night [March 6]. Naturally we received the wine, and naturally Roger insisted that he be the one to write to you, and alas, naturally, he never did. Mea culpa consists in my not learning my lesson from the past and writing anyway. I am really quite disgusted with this, as it seems to me when one receives a wonderful present the obvious thing to do is to acknowledge it promptly. We did open one bottle of the Mosel, as we were in Princeton for Christmas, and it was delicious, in fact, so outstandingly good that when we return in June I am going to try to order a case from you if this is at all possible.

As you probably know by now we are living in Cambridge this year where Roger is the Norton Professor. We are certainly enjoying it very much, and I am going to hate to go back to Princeton, as this is a much livelier community with many more resources. The advent of Gunther Schuller, and Earl Kim,[1] have all contributed to suddenly making this a real musical center. I do not mention Leon [Kirchner] as he stood alone, virtually, until these other people came.

Last night Roger supposedly heard for the first time his third piano sonata in L.A., the one commissioned by Istomin, which Lateiner finally played for the first time. If I weren't so mad at him (Roger) I would say I hoped he had a good performance and still liked the piece.

I can imagine how much you are enjoying your grandchild, and envy you having your daughter and her family so near. Do give my best to Erika, and I assure you, when Roger returns he will get *hell* from me.

Sincerely,
Lisl

1. Composer Earl Kim (b. 1920) studied with Schoenberg, Bloch, and Sessions and taught at Princeton University (1952–67) and at Harvard University (1967–89).

N O LETTERS TO OR FROM Sessions appear to survive from the year 1969. In 1970 Sessions drafted the following letter to Aaron Copland, which, however, is not preserved in the Copland archives, implying perhaps that Sessions never sent it.

Sessions did not write as many letters in the 1970s as he had in the 1960s. But he did write to soprano Janice Harsanyi (b. 1929), who taught at Westminster Choir College in Princeton 1951–65, on February 7, 1971. "Of course, I have always felt, and often said, that you sing my music better than anyone else. But the fact that, after having known it and sung it so often for the last sixteen years, you can still feel this way about it, and take the trouble to tell me so, means a very great deal indeed."

Two letters (May 15 and May 21, 1971) to Paul Fromm arrange once again for Sessions to visit Fromm in Chicago following the premiere on May 23 in California of Sessions's cantata *When Lilacs Last in the Dooryard Bloom'd,* commissioned by the University of California to commemorate its centenary (in 1964) and dedicated "To the memory of Martin Luther King, Jr., and Robert F. Kennedy." Meanwhile, Fromm had commissioned Sessions to write a Concertino for Chamber Orchestra, premiered April 14, 1972, by the Contemporary Chamber Players of the University of Chicago, conducted by Ralph Shapey (b. 1921). Sessions attended this performance and referred to his stay with Fromm and his wife in his letter of July 1, 1972.

▼

Roger Sessions to Aaron Copland
als(draft) US-NYpease

Dear Aaron,—   [November 1970]

Welcome to the seventies![1] You will find, I am sure, that they are both pleasant and productive, and—if your experience is at all like mine—not at all like what one imagined they would be some years earlier! Of course you know this already. I wish you very many and very "happy returns."

My wishes are of course, first of all, personal wishes for an old and deeply beloved friend—as I look back to our first meeting, in Paris,[2] it doesn't seem that long ago, in spite of all that has taken place—and is still taking place in the world. One reason why the time seems so short is that you have kept your vitality so magnificently, not only becoming a very important figure in our musical life but doing so in such a manner as to make the number of years seem quite irrelevant. This is a very happy state of affairs for all of us, and thus we must add our gratitude to our congratulations and our good wishes.

All power to you, my dear Aaron, and the very best in the coming years.

In old and affectionate friendship, as always
Roger

1. Copland turned seventy November 14, 1970.
2. In June 1924. See chapter 1, p. 46, note 1.

▼

Roger Sessions to Ernst Krenek
als US-SD

                                                              January 8–9, 1972
Dear Ernst,—   [Princeton]

You can't imagine what a real joy it was to hear from you. An anniversary[1] (not that seventy five is such a magic number, though it is, of course, three quarters of a century) has the very great advantage that one hears from some of one's old friends, and perhaps a moral advantage (less pleasant, but no doubt salutary) that somehow one is led to contemplate one's sins. Certainly one of mine is the one which I understand least—that of negligence—gross negligence—in keeping in touch with my friends. To be quite specific, the friendship and affection which you so kindly + so beautifully express is equalled, I am sure, by my own; I think of you very often, + speak of you—but I find it very hard to write precisely the letters that are most important to me, and put them off—sometimes until I fear my friends will not want to hear from me. That has never yet happened, as far as I know—and I must ruefully admit that this particular failing of mine takes quite a toll of my self-esteem. Anyway, thank you—von Herzen [from the heart].

You give me much more credit than I deserve, but if I have helped you, I assure you that I have been amply rewarded in so far as what I tried to do was successful.

God knows I understand what you say about the state of this country in the last twenty odd years. Not necessary, of course, to go into particulars—you know what I would say just as I know what you would. As for the musical world—spending two days a week around Lincoln Center, as I do, offers unparalleled opportunities for observing it in its least encouraging aspects. I can't imagine a more efficient observation point in that respect. I am not of course referring to the Juilliard School[2] itself so much as the "cultural" and social + economic premises which are behind it, and the pressures of which one is aware constantly. Not that these pressures touch me very much personally—the fact that a "Composition" department is very much a matter of window dressing as far as the school as a whole is concerned, gives one the privilege—at least at my age—of a certain aloofness + indifference; and the money they pay me makes it possible for us to live in a little more than simple comfort. (The fact that both our children are settled, +, Thank God, happily married, helps too!) The big problem as far as I am concerned is having to deal with students who, with some exceptions, have totally inadequate basic musical training, know a minimum of musical literature, and that not well. I was about to add "in the sense that you + I would use the term"—but that would be so much of an understatement that it would make no real sense. They don't really, very often, seem to have any idea of what knowing a piece of music really well means, and, it seems, are too impatient to try. Furthermore, the school does not offer any remotely adequate training in the elementary processes of putting notes together—"Composers" are mixed with "performers" in the preparatory courses + the result is that nobody learns much of anything.

Regarding "our spiritual grandchildren" I certainly have been aware of the attitude of which you speak; though I have felt, especially in the last two years, some signs of change—first of all in the younger ones, but later, curiously enough, in some of their immediate elders. I have attributed some of this, in my own case, to the fact that, in the first place, I have had the opportunity to show them that I am fundamentally "on their side," and like them even though I don't really feel obliged to court them or to concern myself with their attitude toward me. Secondly, they know of course, that I am in the position of recommending them for grants and that sort of thing, + even (thank God, not too often!) serving on the committees which do the actual awarding. However, I have come to believe that there is more to it than that. It seems to me that a lot of pseudo-"revolution-ary" euphoria has become a great deal thinner than it was, say, seven or eight years ago, and that some of the more gifted + intelligent people have begun to get fed up with the slogans and the clichés and to realize that their "revolution" has not produced results that were as new or even as decisive as they expected. Also they have seen some of their most spectacular colleagues pursuing not very consistent means of keeping in the limelight, even sometimes trying "this" or "that" gimmick—and the result has been a good deal of cynicism.

You will see from this that I, too, am not very impressed by most of what goes on. One thing that has surprised me is that (apart from the very early process of getting used to certain devices that have long since become so common as to be virtually outmoded by this time) I have found everything much "easier to listen to" than I would have expected, and essentially quite unchallenging, even when I rather like it, as I certainly sometimes do. The only trouble is that virtually none of it—even in the case of composers who are obviously both very gifted and thoroughly competent—seems to me to add up to anything very outstanding. Or perhaps I should say rather that simply, the music seems to me often static, essentially monotonous, and in the largest sense shapeless. This is of course a general statement + subject to some qualification—+ I still make honest efforts. Sometimes I am told that these characteristics are intentional, + I of course have heard various "aesthetic" pronouncements which tend to show that that may well have some truth in it; but as far as I am concerned the effect is all too often that of an essentially short piece which keeps on going for a long time without ever achieving the design of a large one. I too wish we could see each other more often, as I would much value your observations on these and other matters.

It's high time that I (speaking of "keeping on going!") bring this long letter to an end. Of course I would hate to have you leave this country, though I can understand very well why you are tempted to do so. I have not been entirely free from such thoughts myself, though obviously my situation in that respect is different from yours since you have roots in Europe, and mine are here. Anyway, I hope you will decide to stay here; I can only say, we need you still.

The very best to you both, and *very many* thanks for your letter.

Affectionately as always
Roger

1. Sessions's seventy-fifth birthday, December 28, 1971.
2. The Juilliard School had moved from 122d Street to Lincoln Center in 1969.

▼

Roger Sessions to Paul Fromm
als US-CAmus

July 1 [1972]
Princeton

Dear Paul,—

First of all, thank you for sending me the Powers article,[1] which I had not yet seen. Needless to say it pleased me very much indeed. It was also very kind and thoughtful of you—very characteristically so, in fact if I may say so—to send it to Mr. Edwards and ask him to send it on to "Sir George."[2]

All this adds another point to the immense debt of gratitude I owe you—the kind of debt which, instead of a burden, is a joy and a privilege and a luxury—the interest which it accumulates has the extraordinary property of increasing one's riches instead of diminishing them!

I also read, with great interest, the Harvard announcement—needless to say, I wish you + the [Fromm] Foundation, all success with the new set-up.

I should have written you before this, to thank you + Erika [for all you] did for us, to make our time in Chicago pleasant + in every way worth-while. Actually, we have been through quite a tough time since we got back; especially Lisl who bore decidedly the main brunt of it.

She had quite a bad attack of dysentery, starting the day after we got back. The doctor was not perturbed by this and it passed; but he found that she was "fibrillating" and that the drugs she was taking were not doing their proper job of "converting" her. After days of waiting he decided to put her on a stronger drug; and to determine the proper dosage he sent her to the coronary unit at the hospital for detailed observation of her heart action. To make a long story short, the quinidine did convert her, and as the doctor said, he learned a lot about her condition in the process; but her pulse and her blood pressure went down so low that I gather it scared the doctor—it gave me one sleepless night after I observed, on the illuminated dial over her head that her heart beat, though regular, was below 40! The next day he told us that he had previously planned to send her to N.Y. to get a "pace-maker," but that she had improved so much that he had changed his mind, and instead took her off all but one of the drugs she had been taking for several years. She was obviously recovered, but apparently her whole system had quite a shaking up—incidentally she has given up smoking, too—+ she is just beginning to get used to some of the changes in familiar reactions that all this has brought about.

I finished my Three Choruses on Biblical Texts,[3] for the Amherst College anniversary, a week ago, and am now concentrating on a book—an "Introduction to Music," believe it or not—that I promised to write all too many years ago; and I shall write no more music till I have finished it.[4] Luckily it is about a third written + I have real hopes of finishing it in Aspen this summer. I undertook it partly from a bad habit of finding it difficult to say "No" but also with the feeling that so many bad books have been written along those lines that perhaps one should be written by someone who knows more about it than most of the writers on the subject do—in other words, it seemed a challenge, and I guess it is one. I am trying to do my best, in any case, + find I have some things to say which seem to me important.

We leave for Aspen (Aspen Institute for Humanistic Studies, Box 219, Aspen, Colo. 81611) on Wednesday, + expect to be there till the end of August. They will give the Double Concerto[5] [. . .] July 10, + the Concertino, I think on the 24th.

Love from us both to you + Erika,

Roger

1. Harold S. Powers, "Current Chronicle," *Musical Quarterly* 58 (April 1972): 297–307, a review of *When Lilacs Last in the Dooryard Bloom'd.*

2. Sir Georg Solti (b. 1912) had been appointed conductor of the Chicago Symphony Orchestra in 1969 and was knighted in 1972. Fromm's attention may have worked; three and a half years later Solti conducted *Lilacs* with the Chicago Symphony.

3. First performed February 8, 1975, at Amherst College, with Lewis Spratlan conducting.

4. Sessions would not complete this book. He continued to compose, though no longer at the rapid pace of the 1950s and 1960s.

5. The Concerto for Violin, Cello, and Orchestra, commissioned by The Juilliard School for its sixty-fifth anniversary, had premiered November 5, 1971, in New York, with Leon Barzin conducting and violinist Paul Zukofsky.

▼

Roger Sessions to David Diamond
als US-Rdiamond

December 9, 1972
Princeton

Dear David,—

Please forgive me for not answering your letter sooner. It is my bad habit of putting things off, + then not realizing how the days have passed. It *is* a wretched habit, and I am disgracefully afflicted by it.

Actually I have not been idle; though I did misunderstand your letter, apparently, and I have to apologize for that, too. What happened was that I found it waiting for me on a Wednesday night after returning from a quite tiring day in N.Y. + read it, I'm afraid, too hastily. I got the impression that what was wanted was works by young composers; I did make some inquiries about these, and went through a pile of them that I have here in my study—but found nothing that would fit the occasion you have in mind. It was not till the last few days that I realized that what was wanted was music by members of the [National] Institute [of Arts and Letters].

Naturally, I would be highly in favor of having your Quartet (either the one dedicated to me [the ninth] or any other you might choose) played on this occasion—whether you would feel embarrassed about this, as the Chairman of the Committee, I wouldn't know. I don't really see why you should. I feel that my own music need not be considered—I have been played before on these occasions, and I would say that this should be for somewhat younger people. I would say the same, presumably, about Aaron + other members of our generation, though I would make no objection if you felt otherwise; it's just a *feeling* on my part, + of no importance.

How about Arthur Berger, Elliott Carter, *Ross Lee Finney, Andrew*

Imbrie, Leon Kirchner, *Nicholas Nabokoff,* or Vincent Persichetti?[1] The three I have underlined have not been performed very much around N.Y. and if they have music that would be suitable it might be nice to have something by them.

I should have written you all this two weeks ago + feel very badly that I didn't do so. I *have* had a number of things that came up, rather suddenly, + had to be attended to—but I'm tired of making excuses for things that I could and should have done, but simply put off, because of bad habits that have become far too ingrained.

Anyway, my dear David, it is always good to hear from you, and I'm afraid I don't always make this very clear!

We are leaving in ten days (Dec. 21) for Amsterdam, + then for four days in London. If there is anything I can do before the 21st (actually, before Tuesday the 19th, since I am on Tuesdays + Wednesday in N.Y. at the Juilliard) let me know. I could write some letters, of course.

Affectionately as always,
Roger

1. Finney (b. 1906) taught at the University of Michigan 1949–73. Persichetti (1915–87) headed the composition department at The Juilliard School 1946–87.

WHETHER FROM old age or from a lack of commissions in the mid-seventies, Sessions slowed down after having finished his Three Choruses on Biblical Texts. Lisl was slowing down as well, as the letter to Paul Fromm indicated. Sessions did not finish his *Introduction to Music,* nor did he seriously begin a planned autobiography. After many years of exertion composing—as if to make up for the lost time he had spent in his twenties and thirties—he began a new phase of stocktaking.

Sessions's December 9th letter was his last to David Diamond. Afterward, letters would be unnecessary: Diamond join the Juilliard composition faculty in 1973 and saw Sessions weekly for the next decade. The letter touched on the kinds of personal problems that had plagued their relationship. The word "misunderstand" arises between them one last time; this relationship was destined always to be difficult. Diamond looks back on their relationship: "When, a half century later, we would find ourselves together at Juilliard, the far past came into its proper perspective, and we were finally the colleagues we were meant to be, free of rancour and anxiety, and yes, he would even own up that, as I had been hotheaded and impulsive in my youth, so had he been egotistical and shortsighted."[1]

1. David Diamond, "Roger Sessions Remembered," *Perspectives of New Music* (Spring–Summer 1985): 139.

1973-1985

THE PERIOD OF PROLIFIC CREATION had come to a close in 1972. From then until his death in 1985 Sessions would complete only two large commissions—the Ninth Symphony (1978) and the Concerto for Orchestra (1981). Sessions wrote few letters in the last twelve years of his life. Among these is a final letter to his old friend Aaron Copland, who had attended an all-Sessions concert presented February 7, 1973, by the Performer's Committee for Twentieth-Century Music at Columbia University. Copland later wrote in his autobiography: "Roger and I had not seen each other much in recent years. Since the early years when we had put on the Copland-Sessions Concerts, I had never been sure how Roger felt about me. I was pleasantly surprised to receive a warm and friendly letter from him the day following his concert."[1]

It was while Sessions was teaching two days a week at The Juilliard School, where I taught music history, that I first approached him with the intention of writing about his music. Our weekly interviews, conducted in his office at the school, began in October 1974 and continued for six and a half years, broken only in the summers by Sessions's retreats to Franconia, New Hampshire, and my trips to Aspen, Colorado.[2]

Sessions's letter (July 4, 1974) to Paul Fromm mentioned the arrival of his second grandchild, Roger, who was born May 4, 1974. Almost simultaneously he was cited by the Pulitzer Prize committee for his lifetime achievement in music. Nevertheless, Sessions referred in this letter to the past season as "somewhat grim as far as my music was concerned—six postponements of performances, all for plausible reasons."

Sessions's friend Darius Milhaud had died during the summer, on June 22, 1974, and another blow was to come with the unexpected death of Luigi Dallapiccola on February 19, 1975. Only two months before his death Sessions had renewed their correspondence, which had lapsed for five years. In his letter of response (January 5, 1975) Dallapiccola was preoccupied with death. Lisl responded first to news of Dallapiccola's death by writing to Laura Dallapiccola (February 24, 1975, I-Fb): "Roger and I are desolate to hear the sad news of Luigi. We think and speak of you constantly and it is terrible to think of the suffering and loneliness you must be going through now. Roger was devoted to Luigi and now he says, 'I no longer have anyone to talk to.' " Sessions decided to dedicate his Five Pieces for Piano, which he was then working on and which was originally intended for his granddaughter, Teresa, to the memory of Luigi Dallapiccola.[3] During 1975 Sessions wrote a memorial to his friend: "One's sense of personal loss is overwhelming, and the loss suffered by the whole musical world is immeasurable. His music remains and will always remain a living consolation and a source of deep enrichment for all who truly love music on its highest level."[4]

Sessions's Whitman Cantata was given its east coast premiere at Harvard University, March 24, 1975. In January 1976 the Chicago Symphony Orchestra performed the cantata as part of a bicentennial celebration.[5] Again Sessions saw his friends the Fromms in Chicago and wrote them on February 14, 1976.

On March 30, 1976, Sarah Caldwell's Opera Company of Boston was finally successful in staging *Montezuma*. All Sessions's students mentioned in his letter to me and I traveled to Boston for the performance, as we had done the previous spring for the Cantata. Sessions's excitement about the performance of *Montezuma* is evident in his letter to Harold Schiffman.

During the spring of 1977 Sessions's students and I were responsible for two eightieth-birthday concerts at Juilliard devoted to his music. These turned out to be the only two New York observations of that event. One was the New York premiere of the Sixth Symphony.[6] The other was a chamber music concert (March 22, 1977) that included songs, the Second Sonata (played by Beveridge Webster), Pages from a Diary, the Second String Quartet, and the *Canon* to the memory of Stravinsky.

Sessions wrote to me eight times during the summer of 1977,

during which I traveled to Tanglewood to hear the Boston Symphony's performance of *When Lilacs Last in the Dooryard Bloom'd* in August. My interest in seeing Forty Acres must surely have given rise to many childhood memories for Sessions. He wrote, "It moves me very much to think of you as going to Hadley; and I wish I could be there to show you around, in person." He wrote with plans for me to meet his sister-in-law, who lived until 1988 at the brown house across from Forty Acres. However, we did not meet.

1. Aaron Copland and Vivian Perlis, *Copland: Since 1943* (New York: St. Martin's Press, 1989), 379. A photograph of the two composers at the premiere of Sessions's Eighth Symphony in 1968 appears on page 348 of that book. The concert included Sessions's Third Piano Sonata and Romualdo's song from *The Black Maskers*.

2. See the Introduction to Andrea Olmstead, *Conversations with Roger Sessions* (Boston: Northeastern University Press, 1987).

3. Premiered in California and New York in 1977 by Robert Miller.

4. Roger Sessions, *In ricordo di Luigi Dallapiccola* (Milan: Suvini Zerboni, 1975), 45.

5. The Harvard performance, conducted by Michael Senturia and sung by Diana Hoagland, D'Anna Fortunato, and Alan Baker, was presented by the Fromm Foundation. The Chicago Symphony Orchestra, conducted by Sir Georg Solti, played the cantata three times, January 29, 30, and 31, on a program with Stravinsky's *Oedipus Rex*. Sarah Beatty, Josephine Veasy, and Dominic Cossa sang the solo parts.

6. March 4, 1977, The Juilliard Orchestra with Jose Serebrier conducting.

▼

Roger Sessions to Aaron Copland[1]
als US-DLC

Thursday, February 8, 1973

My dear Aaron,—   Princeton

I don't flatter myself unduly that my delinquencies as a letter writer are as notorious as I, alas, deserve! but I can't refrain from writing to tell you how tremendously touched I was to see you last evening. I felt afterwards that, simply because I have never quite learned how to behave on such occasions, I might not have made my feelings as clear to you as I would have liked to do.

Believe me that you took the trouble to come meant more to me than I can possibly say. Although I don't feel in the least as if my life were drawing to a close or anything like that, I have gotten to the point where I have quite a long past to look back at, and take a great deal of pleasure and satisfaction in remembering things which have made a very rich life for me, combined with a good deal of somewhat rueful amusement as I remember my own antics at times. The main thing here is how much I value your friendship, and what a delight it is—on levels ranging from Washington Ave., Brooklyn upwards, so to speak—whenever we have a glimpse of each other; all too rarely since, *gratias Dei*, we are both of us still very busy!

In any case, it was a great joy to see you. Quite apart from the fact that I had a big surprise in the excellent way in which my music was performed, your presence "made" the evening as far as I was concerned. Thank you, my very dear friend—always, more power to you.

Always yours, in old affection, in which Lisl joins me.

Roger

1. This letter is reproduced in Copland and Perlis, *Copland: Since 1943*, 378.

▼

Roger Sessions to Madeleine Milhaud
als F-Pmilhaud

October 21, 1974

My dear Madeleine,—   Princeton

This is a belated letter to tell you of our warm sympathy and our deep personal sorrow when we learned of Darius's death. He was not only one of the musicians whom I valued and admired most, but a wonderful human being for whom I always felt a deep affection and for whose friendship I was proud, and profoundly grateful.

When we learned the news we were in the country in New Hampshire, quite by ourselves, and had no means of knowing how to reach you.

Please don't feel obliged to take the trouble of answering this; but Lisl and I want you to know that we think of you always with warm affection.

Devotedly,

Roger

Roger Sessions to Luigi Dallapiccola[1]
als I-Fb

December 8, 1974

My dearest friend Luigi,   Princeton

I grabbed the chance to overcome the vagaries of the American and Italian postal systems, by sending, through my good friend Henry Weinberg,[2] my last three scores that have recently been published, hoping that you will enjoy them and that they demonstrate how often I think of you and that despite my long silence, my affection, not to mention my love and admiration for your music, remain as vivid as ever. For too long a time I've given scarce evidence of this in spite of the numerous opportunities—Annalibera's wedding, your illness, which I was not informed of until you had recovered, and, finally, your seventieth birthday, which took place many months ago.[3]

The pieces I am sending you include my cantata on Walt Whitman's elegy written after President Lincoln's assassination, during the last days of our Civil War. I hold it to be my most important work of these last years and certainly a work in which I put a good part of myself. You will notice that I changed publishers; Presser worked very satisfactorily for me—this score (the cover is horrible, but I believe the contents are much better!) was prepared in a hurry for a performance which was subsequently postponed until this season. I am also sending the score of my Eighth Symphony as well as the score of a more modest piece—my "Concertino" for Chamber Orchestra.

Since I last saw you, much has happened. The happiest event was [Sessions's daughter] Betsy's marriage to a physics professor, and above all the birth of her son (Roger!), seven months ago,[4] a charming baby who is vigorous and strong. Lisl wants me to tell you that she would have written to Laura had we not heard that letters, more often than not, don't reach Italy. At any rate, Betsy seems miraculously transformed. Lisl is in not so excellent condition, she fractured a pelvic bone a year and a half ago, and she also has a heart condition which on a day-to-day basis is not serious but it is preoccupying because we don't know how it will develop. As for me, I am in very good health—I had a few troubles, above all last year, when I had an unpleasant and uncomfortable skin ailment, but it was no way serious. Most of all I still have a lot of music to write.

Naturally you know about what went on in our country. We

replaced an inconsistent, very dangerous, lying, and irresponsible president [Nixon] with one who according to provincial criteria is certainly honest but, alas, is stupid [Ford].

At any rate, my dearest friend, writing to you does me more good than I can say. I wish you and Laura the best of luck and much happiness for the coming year, and rest assured that we think of you and speak of you always with the same vivid affection.

As ever your faithful and devoted,
Roger

1. Translated from the Italian by Pina Pasquantonio.
2. Weinberg (b. 1931) studied with Milton Babbitt and Roger Sessions at Princeton and with Luigi Dallapiccola in Florence.
3. February 3, 1974.
4. May 5, 1974.

▼

Luigi Dallapiccola to Roger Sessions[1]
tls I-Fb

January 5, 1975
My dear Roger,   [Florence]

our friend Weinberg was brought me your letter and your music. Needless to say how glad I was to see your handwriting again after five years and to see some of your music.

You know how it is during holidays: you just don't have any peace. I say that only to tell you that, so far, I have only been able to read your *Eighth Symphony* and that I heard the record of it, conducted by Prausnitz.[2] In my opinion it is an extremely poetical work, essential, where nothing is lacking and where nothing is too much: I don't doubt that your daughter Betsy must be proud of the fact that you dedicated it to her. Congratulations to Betsy for becoming a mother, and to both you grandparents! I imagine it must be quite a feeling!

I hope to be able to read your other works, and especially the cantata on the Whitman text, during the next month. For the moment I just leafed through the pages (with the pleasure Schumann once wrote about), waiting to have more of my own time.[3]

We were very sorry to hear about Lisl, especially since we did not know anything about it. We can only wish her the quickest possible recovery.

I feel pretty down today. In the paper I read the news of Carlo Levi's death, painter and writer.[4] I wonder if you ever met him. I think you probably read that wonderful book of his "Cristo s'è fermato a Eboli," translated in every language. He wrote it while he was in Lucania during his political exile.

Of course Levi was a famous antifascist, one of those of the Turin school. During the war we saw quite a bit of each other, and we used to talk about our future plans. (Alas! such plans were so far from reality. But we did not know it then.)

[. . .]

Every good wish to all of you.

With great cordiality,

Your friend,
Luigi

1. Translated from the Italian by Valeria Secchi Short. Along with this letter Dallapiccola sent Sessions the score of his a cappella choral work *Tempus destruendi/tempus aediticandi* (1971).

2. Frederik Prausmitz (b. 1920) conducted at The Juilliard School 1947–61. The Eighth Symphony is recorded, along with Sessions's Rhapsody for Orchestra, on *Argo* ZRG 702, with the New Philharmonia Orchestra.

3. In 1831 Robert Schumann wrote in the *Allgemeine musikalische Zeitung* of Chopin's Opus 2: "I leafed about absentmindedly among the pages; this veiled, silent enjoyment of music has something magical about it." Oliver Strunk, *Source Readings in Music History* (New York: W. W. Norton, 1950), 830.

4. Carlo Levi (1902–75) had founded an antifascist movement, the Italian Action party, in 1930, and had been arrested twice on political charges. A painter, sculptor, journalist, writer, and politician, he had served 1963–72 in the Italian Senate, elected on the Communist ticket. His memoirs of the year 1935 in the small Italian town of Gagliano, *Cristo s'è fermato a Eboli* (Turin: Einaudi, 1945), were translated by Frances Frenaye as *Christ Stopped at Eboli: The Story of a Year* (New York: Farrar, Straus, 1947).

▼

Roger Sessions to Laura Dallapiccola[1]
als I-Fb

Dear Laura,—

March 14, 1975
Princeton

You have been constantly in our thoughts these last weeks, and, since you had our telegram and Lisl's note, I felt I could express myself better if I didn't hurry.

Both Lisl and I feel the loss more keenly and more deeply than I can possibly say. Among all my contemporaries Luigi was the one composer with whom I always felt I could speak freely and without reserve; he was the one whose music and whose thoughts I valued above all others, and the one living composer who represented for me my awareness that the continuity of music at its highest point is still unbroken and that truly great achievement still existed and may be possible. Perhaps above all a human being to whom I was devoted, whose friendship I treasured very deeply, and for whom my admiration was completely unsullied.

I won't try to say more now. Please understand my writing you in English—I can express myself more confidently in my own native language, much as I love yours. I hope we will see you before too long—for I must come again to Florence.[2]

But meanwhile please be assured that we always think of you with deep sympathy and devotion.

As always faithfully,
Roger

1. The second paragraph of this letter is published in *In ricordo di Luigi Dallapiccola* (Milan: Suvini Zerboni, 1975), 54.
2. Sessions returned to Florence in the summer of 1979.

▼

Roger Sessions to Andrea Olmstead
als US-Bolmstead

Friday, March 19, 1976
[Boston]
Dear Andrea,—

Could I ask a great favor of you? Miss Caldwell has urged me strongly to be present in Boston for the remaining rehearsals of *Montezuma* beginning tomorrow (Saturday) and I feel that I must do so, under the circumstances. This means that I will miss my students and classes this next week, as well as the following two weeks, and I wonder if you would be so good as to tell my students—if you see them—that I shall miss them and am not neglecting them lightly, and will arrange to give them all extra time when I get back.

I am writing the Secretary of the Faculty as well as Mr. Mennin—but above all I would like them to know—Joel [Feigen] and Dan [Brewbaker] and George [Tsontakis] and Matthew (Harris) and Ken [Frazelle], and of course Tod [Machover] and Joe Tamosaitis[1] if you should see them—that I am not running out on them, and have them on my mind and apologize.

Things are going splendidly in Boston—singers, orchestra, chorus, and everything that has to do with the stage. As is always the case in theatrical performances, all will be exciting but to all appearances totally chaotic from now on until the last moment before the first performance.

Forgive me for asking you to be my emissary to my students—and many thanks.

And—good luck to all of you—and apologies for my absence! And above all thanks!

As always,
Roger Sessions

1. All seven composers were born in the early fifties. Feigen taught at Cornell University and currently teaches at the Manhattan School of Music. Brewbaker taught at Westminster Choir College and The Juilliard School Pre-College. Tsontakis is on the faculty of the Aspen Music School and Harris lives in New York. These four composers received doctorates from The Juilliard School. Frazelle is on the faculty of the North Carolina School for the Arts, and Machover, after having worked at IRCAM in Paris, teaches electronic music at MIT. Tamosaitis is an active double bassist.

▼

Roger Sessions to Harold Schiffman
als US-Tschiffman

May 20, 1976
Princeton

My dear Harold,—

It is high time that I thanked you for your beautiful letter, which not only touched me deeply, but also pleased me at least as much as anything that has been said or written to me about *Montezuma* and the Boston production; and that says very much. From my point of view the production was presumably the highest point in my musical career, and of course that it was so really wonderfully "received" was a great gratification, and *much* more than I expected at this point.[1]

The performance you heard was really the best of all, and the "second cast" of Montezuma and Malinche detracted nothing from this; they were both first rate, as the first two were, and I tried to show them that on the stage afterward.[2] The whole cast, in fact, was absolutely formidable, without any exception. Of course I knew that from the beginning (I had been listening to rehearsals, off and on, since mid-December, and when, that first time, I told Sarah C[aldwell] that everyone was on the right track, + that I supposed that was her doing, she said "Oh no; I just know how to pick the right people").

Of course that theatre,[3] with no orchestra pit and with a stage twelve-feet deep, causes problems, always; and with a larger stage much more could be done, as also with an orchestra pit the singers would never have been covered by the orchestra. But these seemed very minor details to me—the whole work was really *there,* and I am so happy that you could see it and realize what a tremendous achievement the production was.

It was good to see you again—and Betsy was so disappointed to miss you. I wish you could have met her husband and [my], as of now, not of then, two-year-old grandson, who is enchanting.

Once more, many thanks for your letter, and warmest greetings from us both.

Affectionately as always,
Roger

1. The reviews included William Bender, "Three for the Opera," *Time* (April 12, 1976): 84; Richard Dyer, "Momentous 'Montezuma' Impressive Yet Baffling," *Boston Globe* (April 11, 1976); Thor Eckert, "'Montezuma'—Sarah Caldwell's Personal Triumph," *The Christian Science Monitor* (April 5, 1976); Leighton Kerner, "An American Opera Comes Home," *The Village Voice* (April 1976); Irving Kolodin, "Opera and the Power that Corrupts," *Saturday Review* (May 15, 1976); Andrew Porter, "The Matter of Mexico," *The New Yorker* (April 19, 1976): 115; and John Rockwell, "Sessions's 'Montezuma' Comes to the U.S.," *New York Times* (April 2, 1976).

2. The first cast was Phyllis Bryn-Julson (Malinche) and Richard Lewis (Montezuma); the second cast was Pamela Kucenic and John Moulson.

3. The Orpheum Theatre, a renovated vaudeville and movie theater.

▼

Roger Sessions to Andrea Olmstead
als US-Bolmstead

August 3, 1976
Dear Andrea,—   Franconia, New Hampshire

Here is the article I told you about.[1] I thought you might like to have a rest from R.S. and his concerns this summer, otherwise I would have sent it before! You certainly have enough to do—and I think you *should* have a raise!

I think the article is quite good—it is by a former pupil of mine who has distinguished himself very much in the ensuing fifteen years. It contains some quite remarkable things as far as insight is concerned to the real nature of my music—what the latter is "all about," so to speak; and in spite of some very minor inaccuracies in chronology (due perhaps to the fact that he is not familiar with certain works) it is an excellent account of my development as a composer. All this quite aside from the fact that I was—naturally—deeply touched by what he says about me.

We have been thoroughly shocked and distressed by the disaster in Colorado these last few days, + have been relieved to realize that it was some hundred and fifty miles from Aspen!

We too were impressed by the Democratic Convention, and I am glad you are going to vote for Carter. The Republicans are acting in true Hollywood style—at its shabbiest.

All the very best to you, and enjoy yourself. Lisl sends her greetings.

Affectionately,
Roger Sessions

1. John Harbison, "Roger Sessions and *Montezuma*," *New Boston Review,* June 1976; reprinted in *Tempo* 121 (June 1977): 2–5.

▼

Roger Sessions to Paul Fromm
als US-CA mus

Dear Paul,—

October 18, 1976
Princeton

I can't forgive myself for the mistake I made about the date of your [seventieth] birthday. This was due partly to the fact that we heard in September that a movement was being planned to send you a message or a gift in which I would be asked to participate, and that I would be notified about the particulars later. I never heard any more about this, and planned to write you myself. The real mistake was that I had the date of October 28 in mind; and when Lisl told me that it was September 28, + I was sure she had written the wrong date by mistake. To my horror I have now discovered that I was wrong—I did remember the 28th—that is after all the number of my own birthday, but I got the month wrong.

I still hope, however, that you will accept my warmest and most affectionate good wishes, belatedly though they reach you. Every composer in the country owes you a great debt, and I one of the most, and please don't believe that I am not constantly aware of it, and aware of the energy and the warmth and the good will that has gone into it, and the problems you have so often had to face in doing all of this. And many of us realize that any help you are giving to individual composers is a help to us all.

However, our wishes for you rest on not only gratitude but warm affection. I hope you are fully recovered from the illness you had last spring and wish you both a splendid year.

With sincerest affection,
Roger

Peter Mennin, the author, and Roger Sessions in 1977. Vincent Persichetti is in the background. Photograph by Whitestone Photo.

Roger Sessions to Andrea Olmstead
als US-Bolmstead

July 15, 1977
Dear Andrea,— Franconia, New Hampshire

I meant to write before this to thank you for your 'phone call—over two weeks ago! It was refreshing to hear from you—all the more so as it came at a somewhat dramatic moment. I had just come up from a trip down to the basement—unfortunately it was really a "trip" on my part, two steps from the bottom (perhaps a "slide" on wet steps), landing on concrete, on my left knee and somewhat twisting my ankle. Your call took my mind for a few minutes off the problems of getting off the next morning, with my leg cramping my style, as it still does, somewhat. As you see, we made it; driving was for days the most comfortable thing I could do, since it didn't involve my left leg, which I could keep in a comfortable position. The main thing, however, is that it was very nice to hear from you.

I was very sorry to hear of the upset of your plans for the summer, and am not sure I fully understood what you said about the causes for it, and didn't want to pry. But I am very sorry that you should have had this disappointment [of not going to Italy], and a hot summer—not to mention the [July 13] blackout, a scandalous and in any case a distressing and in so many cases a dangerous affair!—is not a very good substitute for several weeks in Tuscany, especially on one's first visit.

At Betsy's, where we stayed five days on the way up here, we played the tapes of *Montezuma,* which are *excellent.* In the fall when I get back to the school I shall try to have them copied.

Mr. Greissle phoned me here shortly after we arrived, + told me you had an appointment. I hope you will have a good time. Not everyone likes him—including the other members of my family—but he is a first-class musician + has been an *invaluable* friend of mine, although there are many rather important aspects of my background that he knows nothing about and never showed much interest in—because he is a Viennese, I suppose, dyed in the wool.

All the very best for the summer, and no more black-outs! Take care of yourself, too.

With much affection, always,
Roger Sessions

▼

Roger Sessions to Andrea Olmstead
als US-Bolmstead

July 26, 1977

Dear Andrea,—   Franconia, New Hampshire

I was happy to get your letter, which seems to have crossed mine to you. Your account of the blackout was the first (+ so far the only) one we have had from a bodily witness. I was in N.Y.—just coming down the steps from the Claremont Ave. Juilliard—at the time of the '65 one, + luckily got a cab; it was interesting and of course *far* easier on everyone than this nightmare. I am glad it was not worse for you.

I enjoyed the rest of your letter too; but I want mainly to write about your projected trip to Tanglewood [to hear the cantata],[1] + possibly also Hadley. Judging from my road map I would say it is about thirty-five miles from Rowe (closer in fact than Lenox) to Northampton, and from Northampton to Hadley is three. From the traffic light in Hadley to our houses would be not quite two miles (north on Route 47). It would be nice to think of your going there, and seeing my old haunts.

To get to Hadley from Rowe I suppose you would take Route 2 to the Greenfield exit on Route 91, though your friend at Rowe might be able to suggest a shorter way via Route 9, which leads through Northampton.

The old house is not, I think, known as "Forty Acres" except in the family,[2] but as the "Porter-Phelps-Huntington House," and as I have told you it is run by an association under the auspices of the Mass. Historical Association. In the old brown house where I lived (about 150 yards south of the other side of the road) my sister-in-law lives, and if you should want to speak to her, her phone number is (413) 584-1854. [...]

In Tanglewood, at Gunther Schuller's concert on August 15, he is conducting my Second Symphony[3]—which should be a good performance. G.S. is one of the younger musicians I think most of—as you know, he is the one who conducted the recording of my Violin Concerto.[4]

I was interested to hear of your progress with your work, and needless to say wish you the best with it! I also was interested to hear of your meeting with Mr. Seeger.[5] I haven't seen him for some forty years at least, but I always found him a very nice man.

My [Ninth] Symphony is going well, I think; I have nearly finished the first movement, and am already well into the second. I'm afraid it will not [be] very easy to play, but it has to be what it has to be!

I had a phone call today from Mr. Greissle who just got back from his vacation in the Adirondacks. I shall be curious to hear how you get along with him.

Also—naturally—I shall be very much interested to see whatever you feel like showing me of your work—at the Juilliard in the fall, perhaps. But I don't want you to feel obliged to show me anything until you really want to.

Meanwhile all the very best to you.

With sincerest affection, always,
Roger Sessions

1. The Boston Symphony Orchestra performed Sessions's *When Lilacs Last in the Dooryard Bloom'd* on August 13, 1977, Seiji Ozawa conducting.

2. The house is known publicly by the name "Forty Acres."

3. Gunther Schuller conducted the Berkshire Music Center Orchestra August 16 in a concert that included, in addition to the Sessions, music by William McKinley, Armin Loos, Betsy Jolas, and George Antheil.

4. Paul Zukofsky with the French Radio and Television Philharmonic Orchestra with Gunther Schuller conducting on Composers Recordings Inc. (CRI 220 USD).

5. Charles Seeger (1886–1979) was an eminent ethnomusicologist, composer, and teacher. His second wife was the composer Ruth Crawford.

▼

Roger Sessions to Andrea Olmstead
als US-Bolmstead

August 7, 1977

My dear Andrea,— Franconia [New Hampshire]

You certainly write good letters, and I feel very delinquent in my answers. I have, each time I have received one of them, thought,—after my answer—of things I should have added in my answers to them. This time I would like to do better. But my only excuse is that work on my 9th Symphony has been musically taxing.[1] I hope this is because it is a big work with unusual problems and not because of the inexorable problems of old age! Actually I am quite convinced it is not the latter; I have plenty of musical ideas, but I set myself a rather special task in this work and it involves both agony and joy in the making of it. That is a fairly (nonsense; *thoroughly*) familiar experience for a composer, but it seems more acute than usual this time. I find it comforting to read the score of my 7th Symphony[2] and to discover that it did, from my point of view, come out right that time!

As you will have gathered, we will not be going to Tanglewood; but will listen over the media to the performance, with a friend up here, who gets Tanglewood (the BSO, that is) over the radio or television. I am sending messages to Seiji Ozawa and to the three soloists.[3] I [hoped] to be there, but it would be a day's journey to get there and another one to get back, and I cannot afford the time; it would be exhausting for Lisl, too. But I shall be there in spirit—as I shall be also on Monday night when Gunther S[chuller] conducts my Second Symphony. He is a fine conductor and a first-class musician and one of the younger musicians whom I both admire most and am most personally fond of. Also it is a long time—ten years, I guess—since I heard my Second Symphony, which I still like and which brings back precious memories—of Monteux and of Mitropoulos and also of Schnabel and of Fritz Stiedry,[4] who came to all the rehearsals in New York.

It moves me very much to think of you as going to Hadley; and I wish I could be there to show you around, in person. I am writing my sister-in-law (Mrs. John A. Sessions) to tell her you may call her. I hope you'll get a view of the river from the old house on the "back stoop," as it was called always. Of course much is changed since my childhood days—it is, also, in the brown house where I spent most of my time.

You are quite [right] in assuming that you will need a car to get there, or in fact much of anywhere in Western Mass.

[. . .]

Take care of yourself. Massachusetts drivers are the worst in the world, or at least in the U.S. God knows why—but they are. Even automobile insurance is much higher there than anywhere else.

I was interested in your account of your meeting with F[elix] G[reissle]. His wife Jackie is not Schönberg's daughter; the latter died I think in 1950, and was Felix's first wife.[5] The suggestion that you write to David Drew[6] is an *excellent* one—D.D. as you know is a really dear friend of mine and I know he will be interested. I was also interested in F.G.'s comments on my music. He is right about my use of the chorus—his comments on my use of the row also are discerning though there is more to be said.[7]

There—I have at least done better than previously, and enjoyed it!

My leg is much better, but still a little swollen—it takes a long time to get over these things. Your remarks about old age amused me. As a lady whom I knew most of my life once said, "Old age is not for sissies" and it is just as well for us patriarchs to keep that in mind—also—which many people don't know—to face the fact that we are old. It really isn't bad at all, and I certainly am lucky to have a good constitution—a "good machine" as my doctor once told me. But one never knows what may happen next, and it is well to keep that at the back of one's mind.

So—I do hope you have a good time, both in Tanglewood and in Hadley and Northampton. Godspeed!

Always with much affection,
Roger Sessions

1. The Symphony No. 9, commissioned by the Syracuse Symphony Orchestra and dedicated to Frederik Prausnitz, would be completed in 1978 and first performed by that orchestra, conducted by Christopher Keene, on January 17, 1980.

2. Symphony No. 7 was published by Theodore Presser in 1977.

3. Ozawa (b. 1935) has been music director of the Boston Symphony Orchestra since 1973 and artistic director of the Berkshire Music Center since 1970. The soloists in the August 13, 1977, performance of *When Lilacs Last in the Dooryard Bloom'd* were Esther Hinds, soprano; Florence Quivar, mezzo-soprano; and Dominic Cossa, baritone. John Oliver directed the Tanglewood Festival Chorus. The same forces had recorded the cantata the previous spring for New World Records (NW 296).

4. The Viennese conductor Fritz Stiedry (1883–1968), a close associate of Schoenberg's, whose works he championed, had conducted the Berlin Municipal Opera in the years Sessions had been there.

5. Schoenberg's daughter Gertrud (1902–47) married Felix Greissle in 1921.

6. Drew (b. 1930), English writer and editor of *Tempo*, became director of publications at Boosey & Hawkes in 1975.

7. Greissle spoke of Sessions's attention to the harmonic—as opposed to linear—uses of the row.

▼

Roger Sessions to Andrea Olmstead
als US-Bolmstead

August 21, 1977
My dear Andrea,—   Franconia

[. . .]

I am so pleased, too, that you and Judy C[lurman][1] had such a good time in Hadley. I am sorry you missed my sister-in-law; but she wrote me, after I wrote her about you, that she might be out when you called first, since she spends a lot of time in one of the Northampton suburbs with a cousin who lives alone and who has had a serious breakdown + whom she herself, finding her in dreadful shape, took to a nursing home there. She had gotten some papers and my mother's book[2] out to show you, but I don't think you needed them! I had asked her to see that you saw most of them any way—the stoop, for instance, and the view across the river, with the church and its bell—not to mention, of course, the river itself.

Incidentally—I remember the picture with the "life like" instruments—but it is my aunt, not my mother, playing. I'd love to see the pictures you took, some time!

I heard the Cantata, and we all agreed that the performance was a wonderful one—perhaps, in my feeling and also in Lisl's, the best of all. L. remarked that they played and sang as if it were Handel's *Messiah* or some other very familiar work in the repertory. I was so happy that you were there.

Now I am going to ask a big favor of you, and I hope you won't mind—I seem to be ask[ing] you favors all the time. But I hope that this one will not be an arduous one at all. My daughter Betsy phoned me last night and told us that she and her husband had finally suceeded in selling their house, which they have been trying to do for a long time, since they are miserable both with the specific place where they live, and *must* go back to New York. Betsy has already done a lot [of] house hunting, as her husband has, also; and they are thinking of your general region—upper west side. Would you mind if they 'phoned you, and asked you questions about it? Where they could get information, etc. My son-in-law's name is Robert Pease, and they live in New Paltz, N.Y. in case you find them hard to identify if they call. Both Lisl + I would be enormously grateful.

I must stop for now. We are leaving here on Sept. 6 (the day after Betsy's + your birthday) + will be back in Princeton no later than the 14th.

One more scrap of information—I had a very nice card from Dan Brewbaker, in Florence, also Mrs. Dallapiccola spoke of having seen him, in a letter to Lisl. He seems to be having a wonderful time.

Once more—all the *very* best—+ I look forward to seeing you—+ have a lot to talk about.

Most affectionately,
Roger Sessions

1. Clurman was then the music history teaching assistant at The Juilliard School and now conducts the New York Concert Singers.

2. Ruth Huntington Sessions, *Sixty-odd: A Personal History* (Brattleboro, Vt.: Stephen Daye Press, 1936).

▼

Roger Sessions to Andrea Olmstead
als US-Bolmstead

September 2, 1977

My dear Andrea,—

Franconia

We are in the throes of getting ready to leave here next Tuesday but I do want to send you a line or so to send you belated birthday greetings! I started to write a couple of days ago, and then came your letter, and an almost ecstatic account by Betsy over the phone of the time she spent with you. She said you helped her a great deal and she had a wonderful time talking to you! You can't imagine how much it means to her to find someone with whom she really enjoys talking. In telling me about it over the phone she really laid it on thick!

Don't be at all worried about boring me in telling me about your happiness! What would be extremely boring—for you—would be if I or any one else should indulge in "wise" comments or proferred advice. When one is really fond of one or the other of two people involved one always loves to hear of their happiness when it is as real as yours.

I'm happy you saw Joe T[omasaitis]; he is one of the nicest of my students. As for the clippings he showed you, I saw them all (including the Cantata) and was completely mystified by all of them, whether the remarks were "favorable" or "unfavorable"! I don't mind in the least people saying they don't like my music, but when they miss every point while trying to be specific—either pro or con—I am bewildered—as Bob Miller, who sent me the one about the Cantata, also observed.[1]

I have been thinking about your book,[2] and have thought, a little rueful in the thought that I could have not [*sic*] been more of a help. When we see each other I will tell you about some ideas I have about how I could do better, if you would like me to.

In any case, I look forward very much to seeing you again next

−500−

month! Forgive this very hasty note and thank you for all you have written me, + remember that my heart is with you. [. . .]

Most affectionately as always,
Roger S—

[On back of envelope:] I forgot to tell you I finished the first movement [of the Ninth Symphony] on Tuesday—the second is already under way.

1. The review both Robert Miller and I were referring to was Donal Henahan, "A Soothing Sessions Leads Off Contemporaries at Tanglewood," *New York Times*, August 15, 1977. Robert Miller (1930–81), a pianist, attended Princeton (B.A. 1952) and became associated with the Group for Contemporary Music.
2. Andrea Olmstead, *Roger Sessions and his Music* (Ann Arbor: UMI Research Press, 1985).

▼

Roger Sessions to Andrea Olmstead
acs US-Bolmstead

September 8, 1978
Dear Andrea,—   Princeton

Thanks a thousand times for your warm communications + apologies for my failure to answer them before. I am madly at work on the last movement [of the Ninth Symphony] which I expect to have finished before school begins—thus had to turn down the invitation to present awards at the [First Annual Rockefeller-Kennedy Awards for Excellence in the Performance of American Music] piano competition. There is much to answer + talk about in your letters—including Mr. D[iamond]—at whom I am—strictly between ourselves—annoyed. I enjoyed the program of [Aspen's production of Peter Maxwell Davies's] *The Martyrdom of St. Magnus*.[1] Please get in touch with me at School on Tuesday A.M. or P.M. October 3rd.

Love to you both,
R. Sessions

1. Davies's chamber opera *The Martyrdom of St. Magnus*, to a libretto by Davies after G. Mackay Brown, was first performed, Davies conducting, in St. Magnus Cathedral, Kirkwall, Orkney, June 18, 1977.

However LITTLE SESSIONS might have felt like an octogenarian, he must surely have felt the pull of the past from several directions.

One, of course, was my work on his music, which by 1978 had covered virtually all of his pieces in detailed interviews. This must have brought about a retrospection on his part as I delved into the stories of his ancestors, brought in photographs, asked questions about all of his music, and had him read everything I had written about him and his music. Other musicologists, too, sought Sessions's cooperation for their work on his old friends. One such was Peter Heyworth, working on a biography of Otto Klemperer;[1] he asked Sessions about him.

There were further disappointments and postponements. One was the continually delayed Juilliard performance of *Montezuma*; another was the San Francisco Symphony's postponement of the planned performance of the Sixth Symphony. However, the premiere of the Ninth Symphony took place on January 17, 1980. During the summer of 1980 Sessions took a short trip to Liechtenstein, from which he sent me a postcard (July 22, 1980).

Sessions was reunited with his old friends Aaron Copland and Virgil Thomson one last time for a "Composers Showcase" of Stravinsky's *L'histoire du soldat* at the Whitney Museum in New York on September 30, 1981. Robert Craft conducted Speculum Musicae in a performance in which Thomson read the role of the Devil, Copland the Narrator, and Sessions the Soldier. The *New Yorker* commented, "Mr. Copland was the most coherent speaker and Mr. Thomson the most perky, but Mr. Sessions' soft, bewildered protestations won the heart."[2] Sessions had already contributed a memorial to Stravinsky in 1971, when *Tempo* asked sixteen composers to write a canon in his memory. Sessions's one-minute muted string quartet appeared in *Tempo* in 1972.

1. *Otto Klemperer: His Life and Times* (New York: Cambridge University Press, 1983). Heyworth (1924–91), an American writer living in England, also brought out *Conversations with Klemperer* (London: Faber & Faber, 1985).
2. Andrew Porter, "Musical Events," *The New Yorker* (October 19, 1981).

▼

Roger Sessions to Peter Heyworth
als UK-L

March 26, 1979

Dear Mr. Heyworth,—   Princeton

This is just to tell you that your documents arrived yesterday + I have already done my part. Unfortunately the Post Offices are closed (because of the holiday on Monday) till Tuesday; but I can assure you they will go off on Tuesday morning.

I have heard from a rather surprising source that you have been trying to get information on Klemperer's stay in Vienna, 1933–34, I believe. If you still need this information may I suggest that you write to Mr. Felix Greissle, 65 East Gate, Manhasset, Long Island, N.Y. 11030. Mr. Greissle is Schönberg's son-in-law and lived in Vienna till he left just after the Anschluss in 1938. He was very close to Webern + saw him constantly, and of course was in touch by correspondence with Schönberg. He has told me he knew + saw Klemperer during the time he was there. Mr. Greissle is a close friend of mine and in fact has edited my music since 1948 with three different publishers. When I saw him last Tuesday I asked him if he would mind my suggesting to you that you write to him about this matter.

Please forgive this brief note. These are very busy days before we leave next week.

Sincerely— + with best wishes!

Roger Sessions

▼

Roger Sessions to Peter Heyworth
als UK-L

April 29, 1979

Dear Mr. Heyworth,—   Princeton

Your letter arrived yesterday; and I shall be very happy to give you whatever support I can furnish! My time is limited also, as we leave here on June 5 for some weeks in Florence. You do not say what your exact deadline is, but as soon as I receive the necessary form I will fill it out at once and return it to you or send it as otherwise stipulated.

I believe very much in your project, as I trust you know already.

Klemperer was certainly not only a first-rate musician—*and* conductor—but he grew steadily during his whole lifetime despite several appalling personal crises (really a kind of Phoenix!) and was all in all an absolutely unique personality.

Thank you for your inquiries about my wife. She is in very good shape in spite of her chronic "heart condition" which does make problems for her in getting about. But she takes good care of herself, and I try to help her as much [as] I can. Incidentally, we subscribe to the *Observer,* which we consider on the whole the best newspaper at least in the English speaking world (it arrives sometimes somewhat irregularly!) and we enjoy encountering you in some of its pages from time to time.

With warm greetings,

Most cordially,
Roger Sessions

P.S. Should your researches bring you back again to the U.S. please don't hesitate to let me know if I can be of help.

We are watching the political news from England these days with close attention and suspense![1]

1. Chaotic labor strikes in the winter of 1978–79 led to the dismissal of Prime Minister James Callaghan on March 28, 1979. On May 3 the election of Margaret Thatcher would bring the Conservative party to power.

▼

Roger Sessions to George Tsontakis[1]
als US-NYtsontakis

March 8, 1981[2]
Princeton

Dear George,—

Thank you for your letters. The last one, which arrived five days ago (or rather, six!) surprised me. Italy is a funny place as well as a wonderful one—funny because of certain types of Italian people. The kind of pseudo "Avant garde" reaction to your music which you describe[3] is some thirty years out of date in other parts of the world, and many of its original representatives have abandoned it! I'm sorry you had that experience—as you tell it it also looks like a rather cheap way to treat visitors to any country. All that I can say is that the Santa Cecilia [Conservatory] was always (in my time, any way) a reactionary

Tue, Mar. 3

ROGER SESSIONS
63 STANWORTH LANE
PRINCETON, NEW JERSEY 08540

Dear Felix, —

At last, here is the check I should have

sent you days ago. I am very sorry, but this

damned virus infection has taken a lot out

of me.

I have had the first two pages of my

Concerto for Orchestra Xeroxed and shall send

them on to you as soon as I can find a way

to wrap them properly, which ought not to take

long at all. You will get them certainly a day

or two after you get this.

In any case, all the very best to you &

to Jackie.

Affectionately,

Roger

Letter from Roger Sessions to Felix Greissle, March 3, 1981.

institution! I really am surprised that it should be so in that particular way!

If you should go to Florence, why don't you call Signora Dallapiccola, and give her my (and my wife's) greetings. She would love to hear from you + might ask you to come to see her. She would like you, I know. She is somewhat lonely (really very much so, I think) and is a very nice human being (see on the other side of this for her address).

All is well here at the Juilliard. I am working very hard on my Concerto for Orchestra[4] (deadline around June 1) + have a *fairly* light schedule in N.Y. Are you still in touch with Dan [Brewbaker]? I have heard he has left Cologne *[. . .]* and would appreciate it very much if you would let me know where he is. I owe him a letter since a couple of months at least.

Mr. Greissle seems well. I had an infected sinus which kept me in for ten days, but am very well now.

All the best + let me hear from you again. And the very best of luck.

Affectionately,
Roger Sessions

[P.S.] (Signora Laura Dallapiccola, 34 Via Romana, Firenze)

1. Tsontakis (b. 1951), who had studied with Sessions at The Juilliard School 1974–80, was in Rome at the time of this letter. He was also a friend of Felix Greissle's.
2. In a letter to the author (January 20, 1989) Tsontakis remarks, "Isn't it funny how he first wrote 1971, then changed the 7 to 8? Why, what's a decade or two among friends?"
3. Tsontakis had written Sessions that his "expressionistic" style "was taboo, at least for my class at St. Cecilia."
4. The Boston Symphony Orchestra, conducted by Seiji Ozawa, gave the first performance of the Concerto for Orchestra on October 23, 1981. In 1982 the work received a Pulitzer Prize, the second time that honor was be bestowed on the now eighty-five-year-old composer.

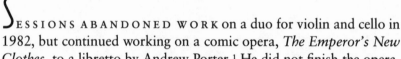

SESSIONS ABANDONED WORK on a duo for violin and cello in 1982, but continued working on a comic opera, *The Emperor's New Clothes,* to a libretto by Andrew Porter.[1] He did not finish the opera, however, or any other music after the completion of the Concerto for Orchestra in the summer of 1981.

New York finally heard *Montezuma* February 19, 21, and 23, 1982, when the Juilliard American Opera Center presented three performances of the opera.[2] The press was nearly unanimous in its dislike of the work.[3]

In old age loss is inevitable. Barbara Sessions died July 4, 1980, and Lisl Sessions, who had been confined to a wheelchair, died July 9, 1982. Felix Greissle had died a few months before, on April 26, 1982, only a week after Sessions had sent him his greetings (April 19, 1982). Sessions stopped teaching at Juilliard in 1983, at the age of eighty-six, and lived by himself at 63 Stanworth Lane in Princeton.

Because my husband, Larry Bell,[4] won the Rome Prize for the year 1982–83, we lived at the American Academy, from which I wrote Sessions. On his eighty-sixth birthday (December 28, 1982) I called him from Rome and learned that, not surprisingly, he missed his wife, but was writing music.

On December 8, 1984, I wrote, "I thought you'd like to know that your *Black Maskers Suite* was performed beautifully last Saturday night [December 1] in Rome. Larry was there for a performance of a piece of his on the same concert and brought back [this] program for you. The Orchestra played quite well and the entire concert will be broadcast on the RAI radio in Italy. (The Italian program notes call the play a 'Commedia!')"

On January 21, 1985, I wrote Sessions for what was to be the last time: "I hope you are doing well and had a Happy Birthday and New Year! Work on *Roger Sessions and His Music* is finally coming to a close: I'm finishing the Index and proofreading the galleys now. I've been working on the book every day, and it is due at the printers 8 February. It should be published during the third week in March." Fate was not kind in the timing of the publication. As predicted, the book was shipped from the printers on March 15. On Saturday, March 16, 1985, Roger Sessions died in Princeton Hospital.

He had suffered a stroke in February and had been admitted to the hospital with pneumonia on Tuesday, March 12. His body was cremated in a private ceremony and buried in the Old Hadley Cemetery, along with both his parents, his brother, and a sister, Mary, who had died as an infant, but neither wife. The *New York Times* obituary stated, "Mr. Sessions enjoyed such esteem among his fellow composers and other musicians that it was once remarked by one of his colleagues that 'everybody loves Roger Sessions except the public.' "[5]

Perspectives of New Music published a collection of memorial essays that summer, including prose by Elliott Carter, David Diamond, and Harold Schiffman. Vincent Persichetti submitted a drawing of the composer.[6]

1. South African music critic Andrew Porter (b. 1923) championed Sessions's music in *The New Yorker*.

2. Frederik Prausnitz conducted; James Dietsch sang Cortez, Robert Grayson, Montezuma, and Hei-Kyung Hong, Malinche.

3. Reviews included Peter G. Davis, "Montezuma's Revenge," *New York Magazine* (March 8, 1982): 89–90; M. Hoelterhoff, "Four Odd Operas Get a Hearing," *Wall Street Journal* 62 (March 5, 1982): 10; Kurt Oppens, *Opernwelt* 23, no. 6 (1982): 54; J. W. Freeman, *Opera News* 46 (April 17, 1982): 38ff.; and Andrew Porter, "A Magnificent Epic," *The New Yorker* (March 15, 1982): 128–37 (a favorable view).

4. Bell (b. 1952) studied composition at The Juilliard School with Vincent Persichetti and, at the suggestion of Persichetti, with Sessions 1979–80.

5. Donal Henahan, "Roger Sessions, a Composer and Professor, Is Dead at 88," *New York Times,* March 18, 1985, 1.

6. "In Memoriam Roger Sessions," *Perspectives of New Music* (Spring–Summer 1985): 111–65.

▼

Andrea Olmstead to Roger Sessions
als(draft) US-Bolmstead

Dear Mr. Sessions,

November 5, 1982
American Academy in Rome

It was very comforting to me to talk with you on the phone in September. I don't know if I made *you* feel any better, but you made me feel that you had adjusted to your loss and your natural strength will pull you through what must be a difficult time. I wish I had something very profound or helpful to say, but I know that you understand how sorry I am. Your wedding anniversary is coming up soon and many memories are surely still in your mind. All I can say is that I think of you every day and hope that all is going well with your composition, the opera, and teaching at Juilliard.

[. . .]

Although I really love it here, I miss you and Juilliard a lot. I often think of what you're doing, up there on the fifth floor. Seven years of seeing you every week is a hard habit to break and I miss it. I do hope you're feeling well and that, if you have the time, you'll write. You'll get an answer because you know I'm a good correspondent.

Take care.

Much love,
Andrea

Roger Sessions in 1982. Courtesy of Broadcast Music, Inc.

▼

Andrea Olmstead to Elizabeth Sessions Pease
cc(handwritten) US-Bolmstead

March 19, 1985

Dearest Betsy and Bob + Roger, [Boston]

I was deeply saddened to learn of the loss of your father. He was loved by everyone who knew him well. Fortunately for all of us, we have his spectacular music as his great legacy.

If there is anything that you need that I could help with, please do not hesitate to ask. Larry and I extend to you our sincerest condolences.

With much love,
Andrea

▼

Elizabeth Sessions Pease to Andrea Olmstead
als US-Bolmstead

[April 17, 1985]
[New York]

Dear Andrea,

Many thanks for your lovely note, which I just got last Friday (due to the Post Office's goofs). My father's death, despite his age, has been a terrible shock and frankly, very hard on me.

I know you were disappointed that he did not live to see your book published. However, I want you to know that he was very happy and excited last winter when he received word from you that it was about to be published. I would like very much to see it.

I am grateful that Dad was able to live independently until February, and that he didn't suffer much. He had two wonderful women, Mary and Betty, working for him, and many friends (among the musicians the Babbitts and Ed Cone) visited him constantly.

Many thanks again.

Love,
Betsy

SOURCES

SESSIONS'S LETTERS are scattered through numerous private collections and libraries in the United States and Europe. Although some correspondents, such as Serge Koussevitzky, Elizabeth S. Coolidge, and Arnold Schoenberg, kept their own copies of letters sent to him, the bulk of surviving letters sent to Sessions are kept now by his daughter, Elizabeth Sessions Pease, in New York City. This collection occupies several boxes of hundreds of letters, in which are found some files of letters (for instance, those letters from Louis Krasner and Ernst Krenek), but in which most letters are haphazardly stored without the letters' envelopes and their valuable addresses and postmarks. Numerous family letters are also found here, including letters from Barbara Sessions and to Ruth Huntington Sessions. These letters will someday be housed in a library archive.

Another collection of letters to Sessions was packed away by Barbara Sessions before the couple's departure for Europe in 1925; these were stored by Sessions's brother, John, at the family home in Hadley, Massachusetts. This collection of some eight hundred letters covering the period 1915–25 includes letters to Barbara Sessions and those from Harvard friends John Burke, George Bartlett, and Frederick van den Arend, as well as from the Reverend Frederick Sill, Theodore Chanler, and Jean Binet. About four hundred of these letters are by Roger Sessions, three-fourths of them to Barbara Sessions and the remaining to George Bartlett. (Sessions's letters to Bartlett, spanning six years, were returned after Bartlett's death in 1921.) Letters from Sessions's brother, John, are included, but none from Roger to John Sessions. This collection came into the possession of John Sessions's daughter, Sarah Chapin, who has ordered, typed, and annotated them. It is currently housed in Concord, Massachusetts, and is discussed in the second and third issues of the *Roger Sessions Society, Inc., Newsletter.*

Learning that letters did not exist was as valuable as finding out that they did. The following is a list of persons who kindly informed me that they did *not* have any letters from Sessions: Milton Babbitt; the Berenson estate at villa I Tatti, Florence; Mark Brunswick's widow, Natascha; Robert Brustein; Sarah Caldwell; Vivian Fine; Earl Kim; Otto Klemperer's daughter, Lotte; Minna Lederman Daniel; David Lewin; Roy Harris's archive; Donald Martino; Andrew Porter; Jerome Rosen; Gunther Schuller; Barbara Sessions's sister Rosamond; and Virgil Thomson. (The following did not respond to my inquiries and may or may not have letters: David Drew; John Eaton; Sir William Glock; John Harbison; Dika Newlin; Richard Trythall; Frederic Rzewski; Artur Schnabel's son, Karl Ulrich; and Ellen Zwilich.)

Those persons (or their estates) who kept Sessions's letters and cooperated in my obtaining letters are discussed here alphabetically according to correspondent. Several of the libraries required written authorization from the Sessions family to obtain photocopies of their letters. For this authorization I am grateful to Elizabeth Pease. Others required permission from the recipient's estate, as was the case with letters to Bloch. For this permission I am grateful to Suzanne Bloch. Permission to publish was a separate issue, and it was necessary to obtain permission from all of the letters' authors or from their estates.

Arthur Berger has one letter from Sessions, dated December 1942. Part of this letter is published in *Perspectives of New Music* (1985): 118. It is in his collection in Cambridge, Massachusetts.

Jean Binet's collection of fourteen letters and postcards from Roger Sessions and one from Barbara Sessions are housed at the Paul Sacher Stiftung in Basel, Switzerland. Binet's letters to Roger Sessions are in Sarah Chapin's collection. Although one can study the Sacher materials in Basel, the foundation does not allow photocopies to be made of any items in their collection. An exception was made for me in the case of the two letters to Stravinsky; at its annual meeting the board of trustees voted to allow me to receive copies of those two letters. Thanks to the personal intervention of Elliott Carter, I was able to receive from the Paul Sacher Stiftung copies of the three letters from Sessions to him. Because of Paul Suits's visits to the Sacher Stiftung, I also have copies of all Sessions's letters to Binet.

The Library of Congress has six letters from Sessions to Ernest Bloch. This collection was donated by Bloch in 1925, sealed for twenty-five years after his death, and opened in 1984. Permission from Bloch's daughter, Suzanne, as well as from the Sessions family, was required to obtain these.

Antonio Borgese's letters from Sessions are divided between the archives at the University of Florence's department of literature and Borgese's family collection in Florence. Together there are twenty-four letters from Sessions and copies of three from Borgese to him.

Nadia Boulanger's personal archives are kept at the Bibliothèque Nationale in Paris. In order to obtain these letters one must contact the Fondation Lili et Nadia Boulanger and obtain permission from Annette Dieudonné. There are fifteen letters from Sessions to Boulanger and nine from Barbara to her in the collection. Evidently none from Boulanger to Sessions survives.

The letters to Elliott Carter are discussed under Jean Binet.

Robert Cogan, who lives in Cambridge, Massachusetts, possesses one letter from Sessions dated March 22, 1962.

In Princeton, New Jersey, Edward T. Cone has five letters from Sessions. Aside from the one published here, the others date from the years 1948–58.

Letters from and to Elizabeth Sprague Coolidge are kept at the Library of Congress Coolidge Collection. There are eleven letters from Sessions to Mrs. Coolidge and carbons of hers to him.

Copland's eighteen preserved letters to Sessions are in the Sessions family's possession. I gave photocopies to Copland. The total number of letters in their correspondence is 107. Copland saved and dated (occasionally incorrectly) almost every letter he received from Sessions. I obtained these letters from Copland's home in Peekskill, New York; they are now in the Library of Congress.

Luigi Dallapiccola's letters to Sessions were returned to Laura Dallapiccola by the family after Sessions's death in 1985. Signora Dallapiccola donated them to the Archivio Contemporaneo "A. Bonsanti" in Florence and helped me with the letters' annotations and translations. There are found fifteen letters from Dallapiccola to Sessions and twenty-six from Sessions to Dallapiccola.

Mark DeVoto kept two letters from Sessions, dated April 1, 1964, and July 3, 1965, in Medford, Massachusetts.

Sessions kept eight of David Diamond's letters to him; Diamond filed and preserved over fifty from Sessions in Rochester, New York.

Some were damaged by fire, and one needed the expertise of a conservator to open. Many of their envelopes are also preserved.

John Duke's materials are held by Smith College, where his five letters from Sessions are found in the college's archives in Northampton, Massachusetts.

Alfred Einstein's extensive correspondence with Sessions is "all lost," according to Eva Einstein's comment on the index to Einstein's papers at the library of the University of California at Berkeley. The only items in that collection are a postcard dated August 22, 1946, and a typed letter giving Sessions's résumé, dated June 21, 1928.

Ken Frazelle preserved four cards from Sessions, which he keeps in Winston-Salem, North Carolina.

Paul Fromm's collection was given to Harvard University's Loeb Music Library. In it are found twenty-two letters from Sessions to Fromm, three from Lisl Sessions, and three copies of letters from Fromm to the two of them.

Miriam Gideon's two letters from Sessions are in her New York apartment.

Felix Greissle's collection of letters is housed at the Arnold Schoenberg Institute in Los Angeles. Permission from Jacqueline Greissle was needed. The collection contains fourteen letters from Sessions to Greissle dated from 1961 to 1982. Bernard Kalban, of E. B. Marks, has kept seven of Sessions's letters to Greissle and one to himself.

Two letters to Peter Heyworth, both dated 1979, are in his London home.

Andrew Imbrie, in Berkeley, California, wrote that he has "quite a number of letters"; but he declined to show them to me.

Leon Kirchner has two letters from Sessions in his Cambridge home, and a copy of another one to him is in the Sessions family collection.

The copyright to Otto Klemperer's letters belongs to his daughter, Lotte Klemperer, and is acknowledged here. Four letters from Klemperer to Sessions were found in the Sessions family collection, and four of Sessions's letters to him are likewise found there.

Sessions's eleven letters to Serge Koussevitzky—in French, Russian, and English—are preserved in the Koussevitzky Collection at the Library of Congress. There too are carbons of Koussevitzky's four letters to Sessions (of which the originals are found in the family collection).

Sessions also filed eighteen letters from Louis Krasner. Krasner's own collection of letters, including nine from Sessions, has been given to the Houghton Library at Harvard University.

As mentioned above, Sessions filed the thirty-eight letters he received from Krenek. Krenek saved his twenty-one letters from Sessions, which are now housed in the library of the University of California at San Diego, along with photocopies of Krenek's letters, which I gave the library.

Both the draft copy of Sessions's letter to Thomas Mann and Mann's response are found in the Sessions family collection, as is a letter from Mann's son, Michael. Permission to publish was necessary from Elisabeth Mann Borgese and from Mann's publishers, S. Fischer Verlag.

Madeleine Milhaud provided four letters to her and her husband, Darius Milhaud, which she keeps at her home in Paris. Apparently none from Milhaud to Sessions exists.

Sessions's sixteen letters to me are in my personal collection in Boston. I also have copies of some of my letters to him.

Harold Schiffman kept seven letters from Sessions in Tallahassee, Florida.

Permission to obtain copies of letters from the Arnold Schoenberg Institute in Los Angeles was given by Lawrence Schoenberg and the Library of Congress. The originals of two of the letters from Schoenberg to Sessions are in the Sessions family collection, with copies both at the Library of Congress and the Institute. One letter not at the Institute, dated July 17, 1948, is owned by the Sessions family; I gave them a photocopy. Sessions's ten letters to Schoenberg are preserved at the Library of Congress, again with copies at the Institute.

Thirty letters were exchanged between Sessions, then in his teens, and his headmaster, the Reverend Frederick Sill. Both sides of the correspondence are found in the archives of the Kent School, Kent, Connecticut, and Sill's are also in the Chapin collection.

Twelve letters from Sessions to Nicolas Slonimsky (eight in Russian) are deposited in Slonimsky's collection at the Library of Congress. There appears to be none preserved from Slonimsky to Sessions.

Sessions's four letters to Albert Spalding are found in the Spalding Collection at the Boston University Library.

As mentioned under the Jean Binet entry above, Sessions's two letters to Stravinsky—one in French and one in Russian—are housed at the Paul Sacher Stiftung, Basel, Switzerland.

George Tsontakis has at least one letter, dated March 8, 1981, from Sessions in his personal collection in New York.

Paul Turok has two letters and two postcards (all dated 1951) in his New York home.

Beveridge Webster possesses one long letter (November 28, 1952) and numerous slips of paper from Sessions that do not rightfully qualify as letters, but are better described as hurried notes accompanying extra bars of the Piano Concerto, which Webster premiered. All are in Hanover, New Hampshire.

INDEX

148, 150, 436, 511, 512; letters to, 64–65, 82–83, 162–66, 194–98
Birth of a Nation, The, 12, 13
Birthday Canons for Carl Engel (Schoenberg), 334, 338, 349
Bizet, Georges, 144
Blacher, Boris, 405, 406, 408, 463
Black, Leo, 375, 404
Black Maskers Suite, The (Sessions), 33, 34, 39, 46, 47, 53, 74, 75, 77, 126, 127, 133, 142, 147, 153, 157, 158, 159, 174, 186, 190, 198, 200, 217, 218, 221, 222, 223, 224, 229, 237, 389, 417, 426, 430, 431, 507; Romualdo's Song, 246, 484
Black Mountain College, 117, 296, 337
Blackmur, R. P., 355
Blackout, New York City, 494, 495
Blaiklock, Mary, 16
Bliss, Sir Arthur, 292, 413
Blitzstein, Marc, 45, 133, 139, 153, 216
Bloch, Ernest, xviii, xix, xx, 6, 32–33, 34, 35, 37–38, 44 (photo), 46, 47, 59, 60, 63–64, 74, 77, 124, 125, 129, 152, 160, 232, 238, 334, 341, 353, 369, 380, 403, 473, 512, 513; letters from, 63–64, 80–81, 109–12; letters to, 39–41, 41–43
Bloch, Ivan, 32
Bloch, Lucienne, 32, 59, 70, 110, 111
Bloch, Margareth Schneider, 32, 63, 81, 110
Bloch, Suzanne, 32, 111, 512, 513
Bloch, Ernest, Visiting Professorship, 459
Blomdahl, Karl-Birger, 355
Blondel, Urrita, 269
Blum, Léon, 251
Bodenhorn, Aaron (photo), 44
Boepple, Paul, 210, 238
Böhm, Adolph, 119, 121
Bolshevik, Sessions as, 40
Bonime, Gertrude, 93, 94
Boosey & Hawkes, 135, 336, 389, 416, 498
Boretz, Ben, 443–44, 445
Borgese, G. Antonio, xvi, 261, 294, 297 (photo), 342, 359, 375, 376, 470, 513; letters from, 343–44, 380–82; letters to, 296–98, 299–300, 301–2, 303, 304–8, 311, 316, 321–22

Borgese, Elisabeth Mann, 343, 373, 515. *See also* Mann, Elisabeth
Borgese, Nica, 343
Boris Godunoff (Moussorgsky), 37
Boston Conservatory of Music, 201, 210, 237
Boston *Evening Transcript*, 16, 75, 77, 84, 85
Boston *Globe*, 77, 457, 491
Boston Herald, 75, 81
Boston Post, 16
Boston Symphony Orchestra, 5, 14, 61, 68, 71, 75, 80, 87, 89, 103, 150, 152, 158, 160, 162, 231, 234, 243, 266, 403, 404, 407, 410, 416, 456, 470, 484, 496, 497, 498, 506
Boston University College of Music, 237
Boston University Library, 515
Botticelli, Sandro, 49
Boulanger, Lili, 45
Boulanger, Nadia, xv, xvi, xx, 34, 45, 46, 61, 62, 65–66, 67, 69, 71, 74, 77, 78, 80, 91, 100, 105, 106, 114, 116, 118, 119, 120, 122, 123, 124, 125, 126, 127, 129, 134, 141, 146, 148, 154, 157, 158, 164, 168, 169, 170, 174, 186, 208, 213, 235, 240–41, 242, 263, 343, 369, 370, 513; description of, 317; and Diamond, 255, 263, 265–66, 270, 274, 276, 279, 280, 282, 285, 312; and ISCM, 182; letters to, 68, 87–88, 137–38, 170–72, 186–88, 201–2, 202–3, 249; mother (Princess Mychetsky), 61, 68, 148, 155, 172, 188, 202, 203, 249
Boulez, Pierre, 404
Bourne, Randolph, 39
Bowles, Paul, 168, 170, 212
Boyden, David, 202
Boys' High School, 45
Brahms, Johannes, xviii, 15, 18, 24, 31, 155, 209, 226, 262, 267, 356, 368, 370
Brand, Juliane, 361
Brandeis University, 387, 411, 458
Brant, Henry, 152
Brecht, Bertolt, 219, 436
Breitkopf & Härtel, 165
Brewbaker, Daniel, 489, 490, 499, 506
Bridge, Frank, 34

52, 74, 75, 87, 136, 222, 224, 245, 431
Chotzinoff, Samuel, 109
Christian Science Monitor, 86, 491
Churchill, Mary, 92, 94, 95, 97, 99, 101, 105, 107, 108, 127, 128, 133, 140, 141, 145
Churchill, Winston, 470
Ciaccona, Intermezzo, and Adagio (Dallapiccola), 398, 400
Cincinnati Symphony Orchestra, 127, 158, 427
Cinque Canti (Dallapiccola), 442
Citkowitz, Israel, 78, 79, 87, 120, 121, 124, 129, 132, 145, 147, 148, 152, 156, 223
City Center (New York), 427, 470
City University of New York, 319
Ciuscolo, 299
Civil War, 496
Clark, Edward, 408, 409, 414, 415
Cleveland Institute of Music, 33, 34, 35, 43, 48, 59, 94
Cleveland Orchestra, 34
Cleveland *Plain Dealer*, 34
Cloyne School, 8
Clurman, Harold, 71, 75, 185
Clurman, Judith, 498, 499
Cocteau, Jean, 158
Cogan, Robert, 438, 513
Cohan, George M., Music Publishers, 454
Cohen, Frederic, 365, 429
Cohen, Sabina Diamond, 265, 266, 277
Cohn, Arthur, 293
Cohu, Merry, 31
Collier, Russell, 111
Cologne Opera, 160
Colorado College, 317
Columbia Concert Corporation, 221
Columbia Records, 233, 420, 423
Columbia University, 16, 210, 341, 482
Combarieu, Jules, 14, 15
Comissiona, Sergiu, 421
Committee for Intellectual Liberty, 429
Common Cause (Borgese), 349
Common Story, 1
Communism, 382, 488
Communist Party, British, 409
Communists, 194, 379

Composers Forum, 356, 357
Composers Recordings, Inc., 317
Composers String Quartet, 436
Concertino (Binet), 82–83
Concertino (Stravinsky), 133
Concertino for Chamber Orchestra (Sessions), 473, 478, 479, 486
Concerto for Chamber Orchestra (Diamond), 329
Concerto for Left Hand (Ravel), 231
Concerto for Orchestra (Sessions), 482, 506, 507
Concerto for String Quartet, Clarinet, and Piano (Harris), 145
Concerto for Violin, Violoncello, and Orchestra (Sessions), 459
Concerto in F (Gershwin), 121
Concord Sonata (Ives), 106
Concord Summer School of Music, 116, 117
Cone, Edward T., xv, xvi, 211, 234, 235, 317, 334, 349, 369, 418, 510, 513; letter to, 352–55
Connors, Mrs., 384
Conservatoire Américain, 45, 370
Conservatory of Florence, 387
Contemporary Chamber Players, 473
Continuum for Orchestra (Bell), 507
Contraception, 12
Coolidge, Albert Sprague, 268, 269
Coolidge, Elizabeth Sprague, xx, 97, 98, 213, 214, 241, 242, 261, 270, 511, 513; letters to, 248, 251–52, 252–54, 266–69, 309–10
Coolidge, Margaret Coit, 268, 269
Coolidge Festival, 214
Coolidge Prize, 41
Coolidge Quartet, 162, 259, 262, 266–67
Cooper, David, 351, 352
Copland, Aaron, xv, xviii, xix, xx, 45, 46, 61, 113, 146, 168, 186, 202, 213, 237, 241, 243, 245, 251, 264, 265, 269, 293, 310, 326, 328, 358, 393, 401, 409, 418, 423, 434, 473, 479, 482, 513; on Diamond, 274, 282; on jazz, 75, 76; as lecturer, 86, 87, 95, 96, 98; letters from, 76, 78, 79–80, 86–87, 91–92, 97–98, 99–100, 100–101, 103–4, 104–5, 106–7, 293; let-

Fischer, Edwin, 196, 198
Fischer, Marjory M., 343
Fischer, S., Verlag, 515
Fitelberg, Gregor, 181, 182
Fitelberg, Jerzy, 147, 149, 150, 152, 165, 173, 174–75, 182, 205, 262, 265, 266
Five Phrases (Thomson), 99, 100
Five Pieces for Orchestra (Schoenberg), 420
Five Pieces for Piano (Sessions), 483, 484
Five Songs (Citkowitz), 168
Flagler, Anne Lamont, 282, 283
Flagler, Henry Harkness, 283
Flaming Angel, The (Prokofiev), 117, 120
Fleg, Edmond, 36
Flight into Egypt, The (Harbison), 447
Flood, The (Stravinsky), 440, 441
Florida State University, 376
Foldes, Andor, 391, 393
Fondation Lili et Nadia Boulanger, 513
Fontainebleau, 262, 265, 276, 317
Ford, Gerald, 487
Ford Foundation, 445
Foreign Press Association, 249
Fort Devens (Mass.), 376, 378
Forte, Allen, 418
Fortunato, D'Anna, 484
Forty Acres, 70, 484, 495, 496
Foss, Lukas, 383, 385, 423
Foster, Barbara. *See* Sessions, Barbara
Foster, Eleanor, 21, 30
Foster, Frank, 21
Foster, Inez, 21
Foster (Sayre), Rosamond, xviii, 21, 61, 77, 90, 116, 134, 199, 207, 420, 421, 426, 431, 512
Foundation of the World Republic (Borgese), 344
Françaix, Jean, 202, 203, 204, 310
Franck, César, 14, 231, 308
Franck, Elizabeth, 240, 241; letter from, 250–51. *See also* Sessions, Elizabeth
Franck, Ruby Marble, 439
Frank, Anita, 44 (photo)
Fränkel, Benjamin, 408, 409, 414, 415
Frankenstein, Alfred, 329, 432, 434
Frau ohne Schattan, Die (Strauss), 444
Frazelle, Kenneth, 489, 490, 514
Freischütz, Der (Weber), 305

Frenaye, Frances, 488
Freud, Sigmund, 329
Frobenius, Theodore, 189
Fromm, Erika, 427, 432, 460, 473, 477
Fromm, Paul, xix, 417, 418, 419, 420, 421, 431, 433, 438, 445, 473, 480, 483, 514; letters to, 426–27, 431–32, 439, 443–44, 459–60, 472–73, 477–78, 482, 492–93
Fromm Foundation, 417, 418, 420, 431, 438, 477, 484
Fromm Quartet, 422
Frontiers of Knowledge, 380
Fulbright grant, 383, 429, 400, 411
Fuller, Alvin T., 82, 84, 85
Furtwängler, Wilhelm, 209, 211
Fux, J. J., 353

Galante, Jane. *See* Hohfeld, Jane
Galloc, 269
Ganthier, Msgr. 42
Ganz, Rudolph, 124
Gassmann, Remi, 178, 182
Gebhard, Heinrich, 30, 31
Geffen, Felicia, 436
Gerhard, Roberto, 204, 420
Germany, 194
Gershwin, George, 98, 108, 119, 211
Gerstlé, Henry, 328
GI bill, 386
Gianneo, Luis, 269
Gideon, Miriam, xv, 319, 320, 329, 514; letters to, 317–19, 330–32
Gieseking, Walter, 80, 121, 128, 130, 135, 137, 159, 160, 165
Gilman, Lawrence, 15, 16
Ginastera, Alberto, 418, 421, 459, 460
Giotto, 49
Glinski, Mateusz, 181, 182
Glock, Sir William, 410, 414, 415, 416, 512
Goebbels, Joseph, 209, 211
Goethe, Johann Wolfgang von, 18, 111, 162
Goheen, Robert F., 417
Goldberg, Albert, 80
Goldmark, Rubin, 124
Goldowsky, Boris, 407, 408
Goldwater, Barry, 455, 456
Goliath (Borgese), 296, 298
Golschmann, Vladimir, 119, 121
Gonzalez, Victor, 189

Marsh, Peter, 421
Marshall, George C., 349
Marshall Plan, 349
Martin, Frank, 62, 134, 149
Martino, Donald, xv, 410, 411, 512
Martinon, Jean, 462
Martirano, Salvatore, 399, 400, 405, 410, 460
Martyrdom of St. Magnus, The (Davies), 501
Marx, Joseph, 160
Mason, Daniel Gregory, 15, 16, 41
Mason, Lowell, 16
Mass (Sessions), 402, 404, 431, 433
Mass in C (Beethoven), 10
Massachusetts Institute of Technology, 447, 490
Masses, The, 25, 27
Massine, Léonide, 251
Mastrogiacomo, Leonard, 437 (photo)
Materassi, Sandro, 387, 415, 416
Mavra (Stravinsky), 219
Maxfield, Richard, 405, 408, 410
Mayuzumi, Toshiro, 416
McCall, Donald, 421
McCarthy, Eugene, 464
McCarthy, Joseph, 383
McKinley, Carl, 162
McKinley, William, 496
McPhee, Colin, 133, 153
Meier, Gustav, 438
Meiklejohn, Alexander, 28, 29, 31
Meiklejohn, Mrs., 31
Meistersinger, Die (Wagner), 10
Melchert, Helmut, 448, 455, 469, 470
Melody, Sessions on, 54
Mendel, Arthur, 134, 418
Mendelssohn, Felix, 209, 226, 438
Mendes, Murilo, 440
Mendoza, 269
Mennin, Peter, 417, 418, 489, 493 (photo)
Merchant of Venice, The (Shakespeare), 34
Mercker, Karl Ernst, 469, 470
Meredith, George, 13
Messiaen, Olivier, 452
Metropolitan Opera, 157, 381, 408
Mexico, 190, 205, 261, 269, 270, 294, 297, 300, 316, 382

Meyer, Alfred H., 169, 170, 177
Michelangelo, 49
Milhaud, Daniel, 348
Milhaud, Darius, xvi, 48, 114, 117, 143, 145, 153, 164, 329, 355, 363, 382, 383, 384, 399, 400, 452, 483, 485, 515; letter to, 348–49
Milhaud, Madeleine, 348, 515; letter to, 485
Miller, Edward J., 405, 408
Miller, Robert, 484, 500, 501
Mills College, 364, 383, 398, 404
Minneapolis Symphony Orchestra, 247, 288, 347, 416, 418, 421
Missa Solemnis (Beethoven), 10, 20
Mitropoulos, Dimitri, 345, 351, 352, 365, 366, 369, 375, 380, 383, 404, 410, 411, 497; letter to, 372
Modern Masters, 209
Modern Music, 60, 62, 71, 73, 75, 78, 81, 91, 92, 96, 98, 101, 121, 128, 130, 134, 139, 143, 145, 169, 211, 246, 262, 295, 296, 310, 364
Modern music, Sessions on, 143, 179
Modernism, Sessions on, 38, 50
Moe, Henry, 71, 91, 94, 288, 290
Moldavan, Nicolas, 262
Molnar, Ferenc, 358, 363
Mombaerts, Gui, 431
Monello, Spartaco, 357
Monod, Jacques, 413
Monteux, Pierre, 115, 117, 342, 497
Monteverdi, Claudio, xvi, 136, 182
Montezuma (Sessions), 262, 294, 297, 300, 301–2, 303, 304, 311, 316, 321, 342, 343, 345, 359, 368, 369, 373, 376, 377, 381, 382, 401, 426, 428, 429, 431–32, 434, 435, 436, 440, 442, 444, 445, 447, 448–52, 454, 455, 456, 457, 458, 469, 471, 483, 489, 490, 492, 494, 502, 507
Moog, Dr., 95
Moore, Betty, 59
Moore, Douglas, 34, 35, 52, 59, 101, 210, 293, 324, 341, 394, 425; letter to, 234–35
Moore, Emily, 59
Morel, Jean, 364, 370, 404; letter to, 369–70
Morton, Mrs. David, 373

Sala, Oscar, 182
Salle Chopin, 145
Salle Playel, 114
Salome (Strauss), 16, 77
Salón Mexico, El (Copland), 269
Salzedo, Carlos, 106, 224
Samaroff, Olga, 124
Saminsky, Lazare, 158, 246, 319
San Antonio Symphony Orchestra, 415
San Francisco *Chronicle*, 329, 342
San Francisco Conservatory, 60, 364
San Francisco State College, 408
San Francisco Symphony Orchestra, 342,
  358, 368, 502
Sandberg, Carl, 204
Sanders, Mrs. Franklin, 41, 43
Sanders, Robert L., 181, 182
Sandi, 269
Sanromá, Jesús, 118, 121, 176, 267
Santa Cecilia Conservatory, 504, 506
Sarfaty, Regina, 423
Sás, Andrés, 269
Satie, Erik, 48, 124
Saturday Review, 457, 491
Sauguet, Henri, 123, 124
Saxton, S. Earl, 345
Sayre, Daniel, 199, 201, 421
Sayre, Rosamond Foster. *See* Foster, Ros-
  amond
Scarabs (Cone), 355
Scarpini, Pietro, 387, 398, 399, 410–11,
  412, 413
Schelomo (Bloch), 133
Schenker, Heinrich, 78, 353, 363, 364,
  367, 368, 369, 371
Scherchen, Hermann, 446, 449
Schiffer, M., 219
Schiffman, Harold, 376, 382, 401, 416,
  437 (photo), 483, 508, 515; letters to,
  377–80, 385–87, 401–2, 416, 490–
  91
Schiller, Heinrich, 152
Schirmer, G., 36, 347, 411
Schloezer, Boris de, 96, 97, 201
Schmitt, Florent, 121, 164
Schnabel, Artur, 91, 165, 174, 184, 196,
  206, 209, 213, 217, 220, 335, 365,
  404, 497, 512
Schnabel, Karl Ulrich, 512
Schnabel, Mrs. Artur, 365

Schnabel Committee, 402
Schnitzler, Arthur, 345
Schnitzler, Henry, 345, 357, 370
Schoenberg, Arnold, xv, xviii, xix, 105,
  106, 109, 149, 151, 165, 166, 196,
  197, 209, 210, 213, 218, 269, 309,
  317, 333, 334, 335, 343, 359, 363,
  365, 369, 375, 380, 383, 401, 403,
  404, 408, 420, 436, 440, 446, 473,
  498, 503, 511; letters from, 337–38,
  356, 367–68; letters to, 336–37,
  349–50, 370–71, 375. *See also* Sec-
  ond Viennese School
Schoenberg, Gertrud, 497, 498
Schoenberg Institute, 514, 515
Schola Cantorum, 408
Schott & Co., 161, 165, 438
Schuller, Gunther, 470, 471, 472, 495,
  496, 497, 512
Schuman, William, 293, 394
Schumann, Robert, 160, 356, 487, 488
Schuster, Alice, 213–14, 215
Score, The, 380, 404, 410, 419, 420
Scriabin, Alexander, 97
Seaman, Julian, 152–53
Second Chamber Symphony (Schoen-
  berg), 333
Second Viennese School, xvi, 130, 181,
  182, 197, 340, 369, 420. *See also*
  Berg, Alban; Schoenberg, Arnold; We-
  bern, Anton von
Seeger, Charles, 106, 495, 496
Selbstdarstellung (Krenek), 358, 364,
  365
Sellner, Gustav Rudolf, 449, 450, 454,
  468
Sentimental Melody (Copland), 79, 80
Senturia, Michael, 484
Serebrier, José, 484
Serialism. *See* Twelve-tone method
Sessions, Adeline (aunt), 102, 242
Sessions, Archibald (father), 1, 2, 4
  (photo), 5, 19, 21, 75, 341, 507; letter
  from, 17–18
Sessions, Barbara Foster (wife), xix, xx,
  12, 21, 22 (photo), 27–28, 30–31, 33,
  36, 42, 44 (photo), 46, 60, 61, 64–65,
  67, 68, 69, 70, 73, 75, 77, 78, 79–80,
  83, 87, 88, 90, 92, 97, 101, 108, 113,
  116, 118, 124, 126, 128, 129, 133,

Page 534

Truman, Harry S, 374
Trythall, Richard, 442, 447, 512
Tsontakis, George, 489, 490, 506, 515;
letter to, 504–6
Tukey, John, 418
Turandot (Gozzi), 34
Turok, Paul, 516
Twelve-tone method, xix, 384, 392, 400,
401, 411, 413, 420
Two Pieces for String Quartet (Cop-
land), 79, 80, 97, 145
Two Pieces for Violin and Piano (Noc-
turne and Serenade) (Copland), 66,
68, 71
Two Preludes (Crawford), 98

Über neue Musik (Krenek), 295, 296
Übung in drei Stucken (Hindemith), 96,
97
Ukrainian Suite (Porter), 100
Ulisse (Dallapiccola), 428, 429, 430,
442, 445, 449, 451, 457, 461, 468,
469, 470, 471
Ullman, Viktor, 149, 157
Unaufhörliche, Das (Hindemith), 182,
196
Università degli Studi, 381
University of California at Berkeley, xv,
202, 240, 261, 263, 338–39, 341,
350, 352, 361, 364, 367, 382, 384,
408, 413, 443, 458, 459, 473, 514
University of California at Los Angeles,
337, 358
University of California at San Diego,
515
University of Chicago, 473
University of Denver, 174
University of Florence, 513
University of Miami Symphony Orches-
tra, 229
University of Michigan, 480
University of Minnesota, 351
University of Oregon, 346
University of Rome, 261
University of Southern California, 375,
404, 408
Ussachevsky, Vladimir, 418

Valentino, Rudolf, 81
Valéry, Paul, 451
Van den Arend, Frederick, 5, 6, 11, 14,
19, 21, 25, 31, 511

Vanzetti, Bartolomeo, 81–82
Varèse, Edgard, 86, 106, 175, 201, 335,
418
Variations (Copland), 160, 181, 190
Variations (Krenek), 295
Variazione per orchestra (Dallapiccola),
400, 462
Vassar College, 295, 312, 352, 461
Vatel (chef), 106
Veasy, Josephine, 484
Veblen, Thorstein, 25, 27
Verdi, Giuseppe, xviii
Vienna State Opera, 452
Vietnam war, 461, 464, 472
Villa-Lobos, Heitor, 269
Village Voice, 491
Viola Concerto (Hindemith), 117, 120
Viola Sonata (Krenek), 358
Violin, Moritz, 367, 368, 370
Violin, 24, 314, 319–20, 371
Violin Concerto (Berg), 286, 288, 345,
366
Violin Concerto (Carpenter), 284
Violin Concerto (Diamond), 242, 263,
264, 266
Violin Concerto (Fränkel), 415
Violin Concerto (Hindemith), 317
Violin Concerto (Krenek), 397
Violin Concerto (Schoenberg), 288, 333,
345, 383
Violin Concerto (Sessions), 80, 85, 89,
120, 123, 134, 136, 149, 151, 166,
168, 169, 173, 184, 189, 190, 202,
213, 220, 226, 230, 231, 232, 236,
240, 243, 246, 258, 259, 262, 283,
286, 316, 318–19, 322, 342, 345,
346, 347, 350, 352, 390, 421, 442,
458, 467, 471, 495
Violin Concerto (Stravinsky), 198
Violin Sonata (Bloch), 37–38, 39, 40–
41
Violin Sonata (Chanler), 71
Violin Sonata (Delaney), 97
Violin Sonata (Elwell), 97
Violin Sonata (Sessions), 401, 412, 413,
436
Violoncello, 26
Virgil, 170
Vitebsk (Copland), 79, 80, 143, 145,
152